The Oxford Centre for Staff and Learning Development

Proceedings of the 1999 7th International Symposium

Improving Student Learning

Improving Student Learning Through the Disciplines

Edited by Chris Rust

Published by
THE OXFORD CENTRE FOR STAFF & LEARNING DEVELOPMENT
Helena Kennedy Building
Oxford Brookes University
Headington Hill Hall Campus
Headington
Oxford
OX3 OBP

Improving Student Learning
7 Improving Student Learning Through the Disciplines

ISBN 1 87357664 1

British Library Cataloguing-in-Publication Data.
A catalogue record for this book is available from the British Library.

Printed 2000

Typeset in Palatino by Nina Woods

Many thanks to Chris Hands and Meg Richardson for the Tables and Figures

Printed in Great Britain by
Oxonian Rewley Press Ltd
Oxford

Printed on paper produced from sustainable forests.

This publication is dedicated to Alistair Morgan who died in 1999. He had been an active member of the ISL planning committee and contributor to the symposia since they started in 1993. He will be sadly missed.

Contents

Preface vii

Part I
Keynotes

1 Re-writing texts, re-presenting courses
Rob Pope 9

2 Disciplinary styles in the scholarship of teaching: reflections on the Carnegie Academy for the Scholarship of Teaching and Learning
Mary Taylor Huber 20

3 'We are many and the forms are few':the relation of form and content in subjects and in the 7th ISL Symposium
Colin Evans 32

4 'Are the pedagogies of the discipline really different?'
Graham Gibbs 41

Part II
Background to the territories

5 Human cognition and student learning
Roger Lindsay 52

6 Phenomenography: discernment and variation
Keith Trigwell 75

7 Conceptual issues in Higher Education
David Gosling 86

Part III
Subject plenaries

8 Issues and challenges in the teaching of modern languages
Lore Arthur and John Klapper 96

9 Teaching and learning practices commonly used in art and design education
Jackie Cobb 106

10 Uncovering problematics in art and design teaching and assessment
Allan Davies 112

11 Communications, technology and teamworking
R. G. Harris and T.J. Mulroy 117

12 Small worlds on an interconnected planet: teaching and learning geography in Higher Education
Mick Healey, Alan Jenkins and Pauline Kneale 125

13 Teaching mathematics as a way of life
Ken Houston, Pat Rogers and Adrian Simpson 135

14 The pedagogy of chemistry teaching in Higher Education
Richard Moyes 146

15 Pedagogy in physics
Ashley Clarke 150

16 Disciplinary differences and commonalities across the humanities, arts and social sciences
Ellie Chambers and Andy Northedge 157

17 Musicians' experience of the musical world: relations with teaching and learning
Anna Reid 168

18 Teaching how to learn, learning how to teach: educating musicians for the twenty-first century
Janet Ritterman 185

19 Phenomenography and the disciplinary basis of motivation to learn
Rosanna Breen, Roger Lindsay and Alan Jenkins 197

20 What do professional skills mean for different disciplines in a business school? Lessons learnt from integrating professional skills across the curriculum
Barbara de la Harpe, Alex Radloff and John Wyber 208

21 Traditional teaching of music and dance as a generic model for education
Mo Dodson 224

22 Do development interventions shape conceptions of teaching in art and design?
Linda Drew 230

23 Modelling the student experience of studying mathematics
Malcolm G. Eley and Jan H. F. Meyer 245

24 Developing a epistemological pluralism through a web-based post-graduate science and mathematics education course
Robert Fox, Allan Herrmann and Peter Taylor 258

25 Reconciling pedagogies in interprofessional shared learning - exploration of the value of interprofessional learning strategies from the educator's perspective
Peter Funnell and Melanie Jasper 265

26 Researching the role of group work in learning, teaching and assessment: a comparative case study of two degree programmes
Malcolm G. Eley and Jan H. F. Meyer 274

27 Information skills: do we help our students enough?
Lin Norton and Bill Norton 283

28 Disciplining interdisciplinarity: the design studio and the scholarship of integration
Dave O'Reilly, Nick Weaver and Mary Caddick 294

29 Qualitative aspects of teaching and assessing in the chemical engineering curriculum: applications of the SOLO taxonomy
Thomas Olsson 304

30 Does what students experience in their first class depend on the subject they are studying? Exploring the goals lecturers set and the instructional activities they use in the first class in different discipline areas
Barbara de la Harpe and Alex Radloff 325

31 Protocols for pedagogy transfer?
Roy Seden and Jenny Rice 336

32 Learning strategies in social science students as measured by the Learning and Study Strategies Inventory (LASSI)
Chris Slade and Vivienne Brunsden 351

33 Challenges to professional education: learning in work-place settings
Jenny Spouse 364

34 Discipline based research into student learning in English, Law, Social Work, Computer skills for linguists, Women's studies, Creative writing: how can it inform our teaching?
Gina Wisker, Jillinda Tiley, Mary Watkins, Sharon Waller, Janice MacLaughlin, Julian Thomas and Alistair Wisker 377

35 The rear-view mirror tells a story: subject area differences in undergraduate non-completion and their implications for the improvement of learning in higher education
Chris Slade and Vivienne Brunsden 398

36 An experiment in teaching computer science by borrowing teaching techniques from other disciplines
Moya Adams and Richard Buckland 410

37 Engineering - learning to create
Caroline Baillie and Simon Dewulf 420

38 Improving written and spoken communication: innovative practices in undergraduate English studies
Simon Avery and Cordelia Bryan 432

39 Communicating across the interdisciplinary divide: how teaching methods affect the transfer of knowledge from one discipline to the other
Linda Byles and Ruth Soetendorp 442

40 The impact of discipline dependent pedagogies on the acquisition of IT skills: lessons for the improvement of student learning
Jane Core, Katherine Wiles and Petra Leimich 452

41 Instructional consultation among disciplines
Michael A. Kerwin 465

42 Learning by developing interactive multimedia resources
Monica McLean and Tim Denning 472

43 Biological essays: how do students use feedback?
Stephen Merry, Paul Orsmond and Kevin Reiling 483

44 The use of computer-based open learning to support student practical laboratory work
Ian M. Symonds 490

45 Discipline differences in relations between learning, teaching and ways of leading teaching departments
Keith Trigwell, Michael Prosser, Elaine Martin and Paul Ramsden 502

46 Engineers are different: the application of alternative pedagogic strategies in an engineering context
S. Wareing and F.J. van der Linde 510

47 In-service education of science and mathematics teachers: which factors generate best practice?
Paul Webb 518

48 Using teamwork as a learning and assessment strategy to increase understanding of the biological sciences and their relevance to nursing practice
Ann White 528

49 Linked teaching: an innovative approach to teaching nursing students physiology
Stuart Brand, Roy Smith and Nigel Wynne 538

Preface

There seems to be a general acceptance that academic staff are more likely to show allegiance to their School or Department, and their disciplinary community or 'tribe' (Becher, 1989, 1994, and others) than to their institution. More recently, Jenkins (1996) and others have built on this argument to question the traditional role of staff and educational (academic) developers and the value of their usually generic attempts to develop the academic faculty in issues of teaching and learning, compared with development that is specifically discipline based and focused. And linked with this question has been the assertion that there are different disciplinary pedagogies. In the UK, this argument seems to have been so persuasive that for some years now we have had nationally funded projects to develop aspects of good practice in individual disciplines (Fund for the Development of Teaching and Learning), and most recently we have had the decision to establish the Teaching and Learning Subject Network (TLSN) based around 24 different Subject Centres, each one catering for either a single discipline or a cluster of aligned disciplines (see http://www.ltsn.ac.uk). In Australia, the National Teaching Development Grants provided as part of the CAUT (Committee for the Advancement of Teaching) initiative funding were also largely discipline based.

In the USA, the CASTL (Carnegie Academy for the Scholarship of Teaching and Learning) programme managed by the Carnegie foundation has not only been working with academics from different disciplines to develop their practice but has also made some attempt to identify the disciplinary differences in their pedagogy (and this was discussed in one of the three key-note presentations, all of which are included in these proceedings). Elsewhere, however, there seems to have been little attempt so far to seriously examine this assertion about different disciplinary pedagogies. Are they really different or simply perceived to be different? If they are different do they have to be because of the nature of the discipline or are these differences simply historical and/or cultural? If the former, how can we explain the fact that the same disciplines may be taught in very different ways in different countries? What exactly are these different pedagogies? Are some more successful than others? Could some disciplines benefit from borrowing and adapting methods used in others?

It was at least to start a discussion around some of these questions that the theme for the 7th annual Improving Student Learning Symposium was chosen as Improving Student Learning Through the Disciplines. Held in York, England, the Symposium again attracted over 200 participants from over 15 different countries. The major aim of the Symposium is to provide a forum which brings together those who are primarily researchers into learning in higher education and those who are primarily practitioners concerned more pragmatically with improving their practice, but from whichever starting point, papers are only accepted if they take a sufficiently scholarly research-based approach.

This time, in addition to research papers, academics from different disciplines were invited to lead special plenary sessions to explore the facets of the pedagogy of their discipline and these have been written up and are included in these proceedings.

I would again like to publicly acknowledge the invaluable contribution made by Felix Lam, who left the Oxford Centre this year, to both the organisation of this symposium and the production of these proceedings, as well as for all the preceding six symposia. She certainly must take much of the credit for their success. I would also like to thank Nina Woods who has taken over from Felix and ensured the final production of these proceedings.

Chris Rust
Oxford Centre for Staff and Learning Development, Oxford Brookes University, July 2000

Bibliography

Becher, T (1989) *Academic tribes and territories*. Milton Keynes: Open University Press
Becher, T (1994) The significance of disciplinary difference, *Studies in Higher Education*, **19**(2), 151—161
Jenkins, A (1996) Discipline-based educational development, *International Journal for Academic Development*, **1**(1), 50—62

1 Re-writing texts, re-presenting courses

Rob Pope

School of Humanities, Oxford Brookes University

Keywords critical-creative; critique, editing; intervention; publishing; rewriting

1.1 Overview

The aim of this chapter is to present some textual activities and learning strategies current in contemporary English Studies and to offer them for adaptation by colleagues in other areas. All of these activities involve the radical critiquing and critical-creative rewriting of texts. By extension they entail the exploring and often the crossing and re-configuring of current disciplinary boundaries. Most of the learning strategies featured require a great deal of negotiation and collaboration, and therefore entail not a little potential for misunderstanding and conflict. There are risks as well as opportunities. In education broadly conceived — as opposed to training narrowly conceived — you can't have the one without the other.

The conference session to which this chapter relates (the first key-note) was designed likewise. It was practical and participatory as well as creative and critical in emphasis. As a result, much that *in context and in the event* was found to be either appealing or appalling, stimulating or threatening (responses were extreme and spanned the whole range) cannot really be reproduced here. What will be offered, therefore, is an overview of the main principles at issue and the main methods in play. These culminate in an account of a collective student project which modelled a number of these activities and strategies with other students in mind. The latter is also an instance of one course being used to re-present (gather, edit and publish) materials from another. Further reading is signalled at the close.

1.2 Pedagogic principles (to be debated and disputed)

First, however, I shall re-affirm some general principles to do with pedagogy and textuality. These informed the practice of the session as they do the theory of the present chapter. The fact that these principles take the form of propositions which may themselves be challenged and changed — not simply read and assented to — is itself part of the matter at issue. (Notice that, paradoxically, if you absolutely agree with all of these propositions, then in effect you don't! Conversely, if you don't agree with them, in effect you may!)

1. In serious teaching and learning, play and enjoyment are among our greatest assets.
2. Knowledges (plural) are various, shifting and interrelated: *know-how* (practice, technique) and *know-why* (theory, value) as well as *know-what* (facts, data).

3. Academic subjects are what lecturers and students dis/agree they are. As 'disciplines', they entail rewards and penalties for (not) playing the game; also penalties and rewards for evolving new games.
4. Ultimately all knowledge is interdisciplinary. We are all playing the same game - differently.
5. Everyone involved in education is in some sense a learner-teacher; everyone is also a participant-observer. But each one takes on various roles at various moments.
6. People are like texts are like disciplines in that we/they are both products and processes: apparently fixed, finished and closed — but also fluid, fractured and open.
7. All communication — and therefore all teaching and learning — involves exchange and change. Textual ex/changes cannot be divorced from social ex/changes.

1.3 Textual principles (to be read and re-written)

1. In reading texts we re-write them.
2. Interpretation *of* texts always entails interaction *with* texts.
3. Interaction *with* texts always entails intervention *in* texts.
4. One text leads to another and another and another — so we had better grasp texts intertextually, through comparison and contrast.
5. One speech leads to another and another and another — so we had better grasp texts interpersonally, through dialogue and exchange.

1.4 Types of critical-creative rewriting and textual intervention

All the following strategies are used in English Studies as ways of exploring texts in terms of what they do *not* say or might say *otherwise* — in other times and terms, for instance. Conversely, these strategies allow us to see much more clearly what the initial text *does* say and *how*, in its own times and terms. The method is basically dialectical (to do with challenge and change) and dialogic (to do with translation and transformation). It may be applied to any kind of text, fictional or factual. Readers may thus readily imagine for themselves ways in which such rewriting strategies could be adopted and adapted — or perhaps are already used in some way — when handling texts or other artefacts in their own discipline. Section 1.5 below outlines a method that can be applied to textbooks, monographs and articles of all kinds. (For examples of these present strategies in action, see Pope, 1995: 196—202; 1998a: Part 4 and 1998b.)

A. ALTERNATIVE SUMMARIES AND THE ARTS OF PARAPHRASE
Summarize the text in a variety of ways so as to draw attention to different aspects of its preoccupations or construction — and to your own methods of paraphrase. For instance, a series of summaries varying between a phrase, a sentence, 50 words, and 100 words can be very revealing in establishing what you consider progressively more or less central in terms of themes, events, figures, strategies, etc. Each of these can then be compared with those of colleagues so as to identify areas of overlap and difference. Devising posters, adverts, songs, trailers and reviews based on the text in hand is another, critical-creative way of exploring summaries. Alternatively, you might 'paraphrase' the text drawing on one of a range of critical-theoretical discourses: Marxist; Feminist; Psychoanalytical; Post-/Structuralist; Post-/Colonialist; Post-/Modernist; etc. In all these ways you would in effect 'translate' and thereby transform the base text. You would also learn to treat your own apparently 'merely descriptive' summaries as forms of discourse — and your own

apparently 'natural' and 'neutral' discourses as specifically value-laden ways of categorizing, labelling and explaining.

B. CHANGED TITLES, INTRODUCTORY APPARATUSES AND OPENINGS

Intervene in these areas of the text so as to disturb and reorient them. Aim to cue the reader for a slightly (or very) different reading experience — one with slightly (or very) different expectations as to genre, centre of interest, discourse, outlet, market, communicative relations, etc.

C. ALTERNATIVE ENDINGS

Alter the ending of the initial text so as to draw attention to some option not explored or in some way foreclosed. Go on to explore the reasons why such an ending was not desirable, advisable or possible in the base text at its initial moment of production. Then consider why you, in your own moment of reproduction, opted for it. Notice that, like all the exercises, this is an opportunity to explore historical differences and not simply express personal preferences. Arguing vigorously both 'for' and 'against' all these endings, each in its own historical moment, is a good way of interrogating assumptions about 'progress' or 'regress', absolute 'preferences' and 'eternal values'.

D. PRELUDES, INTERLUDES AND POSTLUDES

Extend the text 'before', 'during' or 'after' the events it represents so as to explore alternative points of departure, processes of development, or points of arrival. What overall premises, procedures and aims are highlighted by this strategy? And how far are you seeking to complement or supplement the base text? Really 'ludicrous' preludes, interludes and postludes often sport with a variety of historical moments as well as a variety of genres and discourses, and narrative and dramatic strategies.

E. NARRATIVE INTERVENTION

Change some 'turning point' in the narrative so as to explore alternative premises or consequences. Also consider ways of framing or 're-focalizing' the narrative so that the very process of narration is reoriented, and perhaps made more (or less) obvious. This method of exploring continuities and discontinuities, kinds of textual cohesion and perceptual coherence, can be applied to 'histories' as well as 'stories'. It can also be applied to single sentences and propositions, as well as to lengthy novels, films and treatises. It all depends how — and how far — you distinguish narrative from other modes of representation and exposition.

F. DRAMATIC INTERVENTION

Change the direction of a scripted drama or transcribed conversation by intervening in a single 'move' or 'exchange'. Also consider figures you might reorient or insert so as to alter the emphasis or choice of topic and the course of the action. This can be done in conjunction with E and G.

G. NARRATIVE INTO DRAMA — DRAMA INTO NARRATIVE

Explore 'showing' through 're-telling', and 'telling' through 're-showing'. And thereby examine the peculiar configuration of re/presentation in your base text.

H. 'IMITATION'

Re-cast the initial text in the manner — and matter — of another author (director, theatre or film company, etc.). This is no mere matter of slavish imitation, even if such a thing were practically or theoretically possible (which strictly it isn't). Rather, it entails transformations of fundamental issues and discourses, along with settings and contexts, etc. For it soon becomes obvious that re-writing, say, some Shakespeare 'in the manner' of Ibsen, Brecht or Churchill (or Austen, or Dickens, or Joyce, etc.) is no mere question of 'style'. It also entails transformations of 'matter' as well. Another's 'word' always implies a whole 'world'. Negotiating the different ways in which different authors or directors might work up ostensibly the same figures, situations and issues is an excellent way of seeing that they are not quite — or at all — 'the same'. A variation on this activity is to select some contemporary item (a news story, anecdote or joke) and work it up in the manner and matter of the base text under consideration.

I. PARODY

Exaggerate some features of the initial text, or introduce incongruous (perhaps anachronistic) frames of reference so as to throw its characterstic style or preoccupations into relief. Crude parody is burlesque. Subtle parody can be so implicit and ironic that its parodic intent may be all but invisible. Both can be critically and creatively valid — and great fun. Either way, parody can be an act of affectionate celebration of an author's work. It is not necessarily either negative or destructive. In fact, the most searching and revealing parodies are usually those grounded in a mixture of fascination and frustration with the initial text.

J. COLLAGE

Gather a diverse and perhaps disparate range of materials directly or indirectly relevant to the initial text: sources; parallels; contrasts; bits of critical commentary; relatable words, images, pieces of music, etc — often from other periods and discourses. Then select from and arrange these materials so as to make a number of implicit statements about the base text. There is a fascination in both the finding and making of physical and perceptual patterns; and a skill — as well as serendipity — in inviting your reader or viewer to perceive meaningful differences and discern implicit preferences. 'Collage' is neither more nor less than the art of 'sticking together' — with your base text, your material and any prospective readers, viewers and audiences. It's as simple — and complex — as that. As always, the commentary should seek to make explicit what was implicit, and to lay bare the process of composition.

K HYBRIDS AND 'FACTION'

Re-cast two or more related texts in a new textual mould so as to produce a compound — not merely a mixture. Compounding conventionally 'fictional' and 'factual' texts usually produces 'faction' — in every sense. (Alternative metaphors for this process include grafting a new plant from two 'parent' plants so as to generate a hybrid; or the biological process of cross-fertilization between species.) In any event, experiment with ways of making texts coalesce as well as collide. In this respect the generation of 'hybrids' is distinct from the sticking together of 'collages'. There is more obviously the making of a 'new and organic whole' than a 'mechanical assemblage of old fragments'.

WORD TO IMAGE, WORD TO MUSIC, WORD TO MOVEMENT, WORD TO ...?

This is a catch-all reminder that verbal texts can be very revealingly understood in the attempt to transform them into another medium, sign-system or mode of communication and expression. Film, video, photography, painting and sculpture; all kinds of music; dance, mime and numerous kinds of performance art; even clothes, architecture, smells, touches and tastes ... These all offer alternative ways of 're-realizing' and 're-cognizing' the actual and potential meanings, effects and values of a particular string of words — long or short, epic or epigram, novel or one-liner, single sound or letter. A *transference* always entails a *transformation*. So these are all ways of intervening in the text's play of differences and sorting out your own frames of reference in your own preferred modes and materials.

YOUR OWN PERMUTATIONS, EXTENSIONS AND ADDITIONS

Meaning precisely that...

1.5 Challenging and changing text-books, monographs and articles

The following suggestions relate specifically to the creative critiquing of standard textbooks. But they can readily be adapted for set texts and recommended reading of all kinds, including monographs and articles.

Take the preface, introduction and contents pages from the latest edition of a standard text-book. Look out for:

- all the main ways in which the text — and by extension the subject — has changed since the previous edition(s);
- what the writer explicitly says s/he is talking about (emphasizing, centring). Identify *present* key terms;
- what the writer implicitly reveals s/he is not talking about (marginalizing, ignoring). Identify *absent* key terms;
- other subjects/disciplines, knowledges, technologies and skills that are being drawn upon so as to construct the present subject/discipline as in some measure an *interdisciplinary field;*
- the nature and status of the author(s), publisher and readers — its communicative context.

Put another way, use the text-book in hand to draw attention to:

1. the continuously changing nature of the subject; i.e. continuous *and* changing;
2. what it does — and does not — claim to cover; i.e. its presences and absences;
3. shifting relations to technological and social changes and to 'other' disciplines;
4. who the book is — and is not — by and for;

Go on to build up projects based on Rewriting, Research and Reflection (the three Rs). Most immediately, these may explore in detail the organization and emphases of the book in hand relative to other text-books (both actual and potential). By implication and extension, projects will thereby explore aspects of the actual past and present of the subject, also its current and future potentialities.

1.6 Representing courses, modelling activities

(Using one course to edit and publish work from another)

The impetus for this particular project came from the need to support first-year students who were encountering a substantially new and unusual textual activity (in this case the critical-creative rewriting of literary texts through imitation, parody, regenreing, intervention, etc.; see above). The aim was to provide examples of previous student work in an effective, enjoyable and hopefully inspiring manner. And the basic method was to use another, relatively open and flexible advanced course (an Independent Study module) to gather, edit and eventually 'publish' work from the course in question and present it to students the following year.

Projects in which students gather, edit and internally publish their own and other students' course-work are still curiously rare — though not unheard of — in English Studies in Higher Education. Naturally such projects are more common in courses where Publishing, Media Studies and Communications figure with English as components. Partial parallels can also be found in the practice of editing and publishing texts generated in Creative Writing workshops combinations (see Hunter and Pope, 2000). None the less, in English Studies at large, as in many subjects, the massive resources of students' own work and their considerable potential reserves in energy, commitment and enthusiasm often remain largely untapped. Such resources and reserves are especially valuable — and often all the more necessary — when students are being encouraged to work with texts in relatively new and potentially intimidating ways. Indeed, they are peculiarly appropriate when, as here, the chief materials and methods in play have to do with the rewriting of texts. Specific textual activities are thus fully realized as learning strategies and both can feed into the redesign of individual courses and, by extension, the recreation of the subject as a whole.

This project took place in the context of a well-established modular degree programme and spanned the first and second years of courses in English Studies. The course from which materials were gathered is a first-year course called *Texts, Problems and Approaches*. This course occurs in the second and third terms of a three-term first year and is compulsory for all students of English. Of the 150 or so students taking this course each year, approximately 80 take English with another subject (the most common combinations are English with History, History of Art, Social Sciences, Education, Languages or Publishing); 20 take only English; and the other 50 take English 'on the side', with subjects other than English as their named degree.

Texts, Problems and Approaches is the backbone of the first-year work in English Studies and has, as two of its informing principles, the analysis and theory of intertextuality and the practice of 'rewriting'. Many texts are therefore presented in pairs: *Hamlet* with *Rosencrantz and Guildenstern*; *Jane Eyre* with *Wide Sargasso Sea*; *The Clerk's Tale* (which features Patient Griselda) with Caryl Churchill's *Top Girls* (which features another version of her). At the same time, students are strongly encouraged — though not quite compelled — to get in on the act of rewriting themselves: shifting points of view; switching genres; changing endings; recasting one author's text in the manner of another; and so on. All these rewrites must be supported by a commentary which explains the processes of decision-making involved and explores the critical-historical relations between the text as the student found it and the text as s/he subsequently re-made it. It is these last, student-generated rewrites with commentaries which were the object of the present project, both as actual materials to be gathered from the past and as potential materials to be stimulated in the future. Here are the list of Contents and parts of the Preface.

Re-writings. A Book of First-year Course-work,
edited by Elaine Hunter, Phil Higgins *et al.*

Preface		iii
One:	Types of Textual Intervention	1
Two:	Impure Imitation and Parody	6
Three:	Adapting and (Down-)Dating	21
Four:	Re-Genreing	27
Five:	(Non-) Parallel Texts	40
Six:	Drawing on Other Formats and Discourses	49
Seven:	The Commentary	57
Conclusion		59
Acknowledgments		60
Bibliography		61
Appendices:	*A. Suggested Work-pattern*	63
	B. Students' Tips	64

from the PREFACE

This book is written in response to the dilemmas facing first year English course-work, in particular the dilemmas generated by the course-work set in Module 2306: *Texts Problems and Approaches*. As an alternative to an essay question we were invited to produce a piece of adaptation or rewriting. Up until this point there had been little opportunity for any of us to adapt texts, so we felt ill-equipped to tackle the task or even know where to begin. For anyone attempting adaptation or rewriting for the first time we aim to show you how exciting it is and hopefully take some of the mystery away. [...]

A discussion on the possibility of compiling some of the years' rewrites into a book for everyone to read, enjoy and maybe gain some inspiration from turned an idea into this project. We aimed to produce something that will aid future students and complement the work of the English Studies Department. This book is written from the perspective of English Studies' students for those fellow students who may be struggling to understand or those who merely want to consider other approaches. [...]

The various examples of re-writing have been gathered from fellow students. We are not holding them up as models but as examples of method and production. Each relates to specific texts and the level of understanding will vary as to the knowledge of the original texts. However, this should not deter you from seeing how any text can be adapted into any form. The same basic principles will apply.

To get a feel for the texture of the actual editing (which was deliberately minimal and advisory rather than evaluative) as well as a sense of the kinds of rewriting featured, below are some extracts from the last sample. Seven others of very different kinds and qualities were featured elsewhere. In the latter respect two further principles of selection are worth stressing: (i) examples were chosen so as to represent a wide range of effort and ability (not simply 'the best'); (ii) there was no indication of grades achieved (simply a reminder of course guidelines if a major component such as the commentary had been omitted). Here, then, is the opening of 'Chapter Six: Drawing on Other Formats and Discourses'.

This last piece of work is a conversation between a student and Griselda from 'The Clerk's Tale'. A dialogue. It is in answer to the instructions:

Engage in an imaginary dialogue between yourself and one of Chaucer's female or male characters, or between yourself and Chaucer, Use this dialogue to explore the problems of 'The Clerk's Tale'. Append a commentary explaining rationale, problems, possibilities, etc.

Phil's commentary is attached and gives a detailed account of his work. It is worth reading for tips on how to write the commentary. He considers the problems of a modern reader reading a fourteenth century text. By 'talking' to Griselda it is possible to bridge the gap between Chaucer's time and our own. The course-work is hinged around two critics' opposing arguments. This framework can be used for any text.

Conversation with Griselda in the West Wing of Little Walter's Palace. (Philip Higgins)

from The Rewriting

PHILIP: Hallo Griselda.

GRISELDA: Oh you must be the student. Twentieth century, am I right? Do I dismount and come into the palace. The groom will take your er...

PHILIP: Honda. It's a Honda 250.

GRISELDA: Yes, well, anyway. Do come along. I'm so glad to have someone to talk to off the record. Glad to have someone to talk to at all these days, come to think of it. Since Walter died, and little Walter took over, I've been shunted off into the west wing (that's where we're going now, its right along this corridor I'm afraid). And I used to talk to my daughter, although there was always a distance once the initial enthusiasm of the reunion and all the hoo-hah had died down. I've come to the conclusion that the children couldn't quite place me. There was a lot of pain beneath the surface. (It's up these stairs, all the way to the top). Well, now she's gone. Married off. taken away from me again, I suppose [laughs]. So life is very quiet. [...]

PHILIP: Well, I've read your story in 'The Canterbury Tales', which is why I'm here, and I am finding it quite difficult to pin you down. Chaucer lets us into your mind and that seems to increase the sense of pathos. Your suffering seems greater because you are human and yet at the same time you are depicted as a Christian ideal of the virtuous woman. An example: 'Of virtuous beautee ... the faireste under the sonne'. So there is a paradox. The more human you are the greater the power of the tale as an example of 'constance' in the face of adversity, but because you are depicted in this way, it is harder to see you as an ideal. Your function cannot be reduced to the allegorical. And from that perspective your passivity is hard to account for. So how would you regard yourself?

GRISELDA: Obviously I am human. I have always been human, the Tale will show you that. Remember the context. I was the daughter of the poorest man on Walter's estate. I see things differently now, of course. But then I knew nothing but humility. The bible was the word of God. This was true for everyone. That a woman should obey her husband, that a vassal should obey his lord, this was not questioned. That I would marry Walter when he asked was a given. And that once married I should obey him was without question. [...]

PHILIP: Okay, but you said you see things differently now.

GRISELDA: Of course, I'm also a literary character, you know (which is a mixed blessing). As long as Chaucer's around, I'll be around, and probably I'll outlast him in some form or other. Times have changed. The bible is no longer the word of God. There is, perhaps, no longer any God. As that biblical God fades, so do the biblical ideals and the paradox dissolves. And as the times change, my memories change. At first I had no memories. I still had faith; and faith, it seemed had been rewarded; the wound made whole. I lived with Walter, as the Clerk said, 'in concord and in reste'. People may have questioned Walter's motives in testing me so cruelly, they may have questioned my humanity as I let my children be taken away, but they left the happy ending alone. Now, there are questions about that ending [...]

from The Commentary

[...] It is the 'changeableness' which I found fascinating in 'The Clerk's Tale' and wished to explore both from the perceptiveness of Chaucer's 'half-unconscious' process (that appearance of tensions within the tale) and from the perspective of a modern reading of the tale. One aspect of changeableness' in 'The Clerk's Tale', and in most of Chaucer's writing, is the tension between the tale as a literary construct, of whatever genre, and the human realization of the characters within it. [...]

I decided to present Griselda as seeing herself as human throughout the dialogue so that she would have to justify her actions. But, at the same time, I wanted her to appear to present her justification from a perspective corresponding to the idealistic function of her character. I, therefore, had her defending her actions in terms similar to those of Griselda in Caryl Churchill's 'Top Girls'. The context of Griselda's appearance in 'Top Girls' draws attention to the relationship between her idealistic function and historical social expectations placed upon women. [...]

Temporarily at least, then, there is a discrepancy in elements of the tale that would have been accepted unquestioningly by a fourteenth century audience but which are unacceptable to a modern one. I note that I have portrayed Griselda as a character who can look back on her actions and see possible failings but is not quite sure enough to want to redress them, or capable of doing so. This is perhaps a reflection of that temporality involved in any reading of the text: she, after all, will outlive us readers and be read again in new contexts.[...]

1.7 In place of a summary

Rather than simply repeating what has been said in reduced form, the present writer asks the present reader to do two simple yet crucial things in light of the above:

1) To return to the *pedagogic and textual principles* in 1.2 and 1.3 and ask how far s/he agrees with them;

2) To consider in what ways the *types of critical-creative re-writing* described in 1.4 might be adapted for use in her or his own discipline.

1.8 References and further reading

The following books and articles support textual practices and learning strategies similar to those featured in this paper. Some (marked*) relate to critical-creative activity in general. Most of the rest relate to critical-creative rewriting and English in particular, but offer much of more general pedagogic interest, too.

*Bakhtin, M. (1990) *Speech Genres and Other Essays (Aesthetics of Creative Discourse).* Austin:University of Texas Press.

Bassnett, S. and Grundy, P. (1993) *Language through Literature: Creative Language Teaching through Literature.* London: Longman.

Brown, J. and Gifford, T. (1989) *Teaching 'A' Level English Literature: a Student-centred Approach.* London: Routledge.

Burton, D. (1982) Through a glass darkly — through dark glasses, in R.A. Carter (ed.), *Language and Literature: An Introductory Reader in Stylistics.* London: Unwin, pp. 195—216.

Carter, R. and McRae, J. (eds) (1996) *Language, Literature and the Learner: Creative Classroom Practice.* London: Longman.

Corcoran, B., Hayhoe, M. and Pradl, G. (eds) (1994) *Knowledge in the Making: Challenging the Text in the Classroom.* Heinemann and Boynton/Cook: London.

*Donahue, P. and Quandahl, E. (1992) (eds) *Reclaiming Pedagogy: The Rhetoric of the Classroom.* Carbondale ILL: Southern California University Press.

*Eco, U. (1978) *The Role of the Reader: Explorations in the Semiotics of Texts.*
Bloomington, Indiana: Indiana University Press.

*Elbow, P. (1987) *Embracing Contraries. Explorations in Learning and Teaching.* New York: Oxford University Press.

Evans, C. (ed.) (1995) *Developing University English Teaching.* Lampeter: Edwin Mellen Press.

Fetterley, J. (1991) *The Resisting Reader: A Feminist Approach to American Fiction.* Bloomington, IN: Indiana University Press.

*Hooks, B. (1994) *Teaching to Transgress.* London and New York: Routledge.

Hunter, E. and Pope, R. (2000) Recreating texts, editing courses, in S. Avery, C. Bryan *et al.* (eds), *Innovations in Literary and Textual Studies.* SEDA.

*Hutcheon, L. (1985) *A Theory of Parody: The Teaching of Twentieth-century Art Forms.* London: Methuen.

Knights, B. (1993) *From Reader to Reader.* Brighton: Harvester Wheatsheaf.

Kress, G. (1995) *Writing the Future: English and the Making of a Culture of Innovation.* Sheffield: National Association for the Teaching of English.

Laszlo, E. (1993) *The Creative Cosmos: A Unified Science of Matter, Life and Mind.* Edinburgh: Floris.

Maybin, J. and Mercer, N. (eds) (1996) *Using English: From Conversation to Canon*. London: Routledge and Open University.

Morgan, W. (1992) *A Poststructuralist English Classroom: The Example of Ned Kelly*. Melbourne: Victoria Association for the Teaching of English

Nash, W. and Stacey, D. (1997) *Creating Texts*. London and New York: Longman.

Pope, R. (1995) *Textual Intervention: Critical and Creative Strategies for Literary Studies*. London and New York: Routledge.

*Pope, R. (1997) Critical-creative writing strategies: reading as re-writing, in C. Rowland and E. Chambers (eds), *Quality and Creativity: Teaching and Learning in Arts and Humanities Higher Education*. The Open University.

Pope, R. (1998a) *The English Studies Book*. London: Routledge, esp. Part Four, 'Textual activities and learning strategies'.

Pope, R. (1998b) Rewrite Chaucer! critical and creative strategies in the teaching and learning of medieval literature, in G. Waite, J. Harris *et al.* (eds), *World and Stage: Essays presented to Colin Gibson*. University of Otago Press, 1998.

Pope, R. (1999) Critical-creative rewriting: a briefing, *European Society for the Study of English: European Messenger* **8**(2).

* Pope, R. (in preparation for publication 2001) *Creativity*. Routledge New Critical Idiom Series.

Schilb, J. (1996) *Writing Between the Lines: Relations between Composition Theory and Literary Theory*. Portsmouth NH: Boynton/Cook and Heinemann.

Scholes, R., Comley, N. and Ulmer, G. (1995) *Text Book: An Introduction to Literary Language*. New York: St Martin's Press, 2nd edn.

Scholes, R. (1998) *The Rise and Fall of English*. Newhaven: YaleUniversity Press.

*Spivak, G. (1994) *Outside in the Teaching Machine*, London and New York: Routledge.

Thompson, J. (ed.) (1992) *Reconstructing Literature Teaching*. Norwood, S.A.: Australian Association for the Teaching of English.

Tweddle, S. *et al.* (eds) (1997) *English for Tomorrow*. Buckingham: Open University Press.

*Ulmer, G. (1985) *Applied Grammatology: Post(e)-Pedagogy from Jacques Derrida to Joseph Beuys*. Baltimore Md: Johns Hopkins University Press.

2 Disciplinary styles in the scholarship of teaching: reflections on The Carnegie Academy for the Scholarship of Teaching and Learning

Mary Taylor Huber

The Carnegie Foundation for the Advancement of Teaching

2.1 Introduction

The emergence of a scholarship of teaching and learning is testimony to changes that are taking place across higher education in the United States and, as we've seen here at York, in other countries as well. We know that there have always been a few hardy souls who have made teaching and learning in higher education a central focus of scholarly concern. We also know that there are small groups of scholars who identify themselves professionally as educators in their particular fields. For most faculty members in higher education, however, discussions about teaching and learning tend to be fugitive affairs. Our colleagues may care deeply about their courses, their students, and their department's curriculum, but do not usually see their own teaching and learning as a matter for scholarly enquiry and communication. As a recent recipient of a prestigious teaching award told us: 'I may be an award-winning teacher, but when it comes to the *scholarship* of teaching, I get a zero.'

Now, with heightened expectations for social and financial accountability, more formalized criteria for evaluating teaching performance, the explosion of information technologies, the popularization of new pedagogies, and a commitment to educate a more diverse set of students, faculty members across the board are being encouraged to take a more professionalized, systematic interest in curriculum, classroom teaching, and the assessment of student learning. And this is just part of the change that's taking place. Growing numbers of college and university instructors are indeed trying to improve their practice, but some are also beginning to ask questions and seek answers that may be of wider interest, and to share what they are doing with campus colleagues and disciplinary peers. What this all adds up to, we at The Carnegie Foundation believe, is the beginning of a scholarship of teaching and learning across higher education and of an academic culture more open to the investigation, documentation, and discussion of significant issues in the teaching of one's field.

Today, I want to consider the look and feel of what's beginning to come out under this new flag. Reflecting on the experience of participants in a new Carnegie Foundation programme aimed at fostering a scholarship of teaching and learning in higher education, I will take up three related issues concerning the role of the disciplines in shaping the work at this early date. The first concerns the evolution of discourse about teaching and learning within the disciplines; the second asks how disciplinary styles influence the design of projects on teaching and learning; and the third concerns the nature and role of interdisciplinary exchange. These issues are important to examine, I suggest, because they will affect the future positioning of this work.

2.2 Conversations about teaching and learning

First, a word about the Carnegie Academy for the Scholarship of Teaching and Learning, which we call CASTL. Funded by The Pew Charitable Trusts and The Carnegie Foundation for the Advancement of Teaching, CASTL's higher education programme is a $6-million, five-year effort to foster a scholarship of teaching that aims to improve the quality of student learning and raise the level of conversation about teaching in colleges and universities of all kinds. Now in its second year, the programme is approaching this task in three ways: first, through national fellowships for individual scholars in selected disciplines who wish to investigate and document significant issues and challenges in teaching and learning in their field; secondly through a companion programme for colleges and universities prepared to make a public commitment of their own to fostering teaching as scholarly work; and finally, through work with scholarly societies who are interested in supporting teaching and learning in the disciplines. The idea is not just to encourage individuals who want to explore ways to improve practice, but also to help foster communities of scholars who share, critique, and build upon each other's accomplishments.

Yet what kinds of communities should these be? CASTL's programme is built on the premise that these should be disciplinary communities, in part because of the importance of the disciplines to a scholar's academic identity, and also because teaching is not a generic technique, but a process that comes out of one's view of one's field and what it means to know it deeply (see Shulman, 1987; Grossman *et al.*, 1989). But CASTL is also committed to the value of conversation and exchange among the disciplines, as a way of building and strengthening the cadre of instructors in and around the academy who are committed to exploring teaching and learning as part of their teaching practice. As Shulman notes, every faculty member in higher education belongs to both a 'visible' and an 'invisible' college, and one must work with both to 'expand the focus of journals, academic conferences, and hiring processes to give a higher profile to the scholarship of teaching on campus and beyond' (1999, p. 17).

CASTL was inspired by many streams of thought and practice, including work that deepens our understanding of teaching knowledge (Shulman, 1987), sharpens our focus on student learning (Cross, 1990), broadens our definitions of academic scholarship (Boyer, 1990; Glassick, Huber and Maeroff, 1997), and widens our view of the audience for teaching, to include peers as well as students (Hutchings, 1996, 1998; Shulman 1997).[1] Most of this work shares a concern with the level of conversation about teaching and learning among college and university instructors. Unlike the rich discourse most scholars enjoy in their own fields, talk about teaching has been impoverished by a familiar litany of complaints. For starters, most faculty members have had no training as teachers, a problem that graduate programmes are only beginning to address. Secondly, teaching has not counted for much in the reward system, especially on the research university campuses that tend to shape the ambitions of higher education more generally. And finally, teaching has been the most difficult to evaluate, in part because it has been so hard to 'make public'. Most disciplines work with a traditional set of pedagogical practices, but are only now developing a critical discourse about them.

We can turn to the field of literary studies for an example of the prevailing pattern and how it is beginning to change. You may be familiar with the work of Wayne Booth, a distinguished literary theorist at the University of Chicago, who is also a passionate advocate for undergraduate teaching. In *The Vocation of a Teacher*, his collection of speeches and essays, Booth offers a charming footnote on the sources of his knowledge about teaching, which is diagnostic, I think, for the field as a whole. He first lists several books 'that teach about teaching by force of example' — Ashton-Warner's *Teacher* (1963), Barzun's *Teacher in America* (1945), Erskine's *My Life as a Teacher* (1948), Highet's *The Art of Teaching* (1950), Narayan's *The English Teacher* (1945), and Passmore's *The Philosophy of Teaching* (1980).[2] On the more technical side, he lists (and I quote) 'Joe Axelrod's obscure little pamphlet on "The Discussion Technique in the College Classroom" (or some such title), published sometime in the late forties and now, so far as my own shelves can tell me, lost to the world.' But, Booth admits, 'More important than any of these have been thousands of staff meetings and conversations with colleagues in America and England ...' And, he adds, 'I am ... not even beginning to list the many works that have influenced my thinking about [my subject] or about what I ought to teach' (Booth, 1988, pp. 209—10, n. 1).

I take this account as fairly typical for most faculty members, and not just in literary studies. There's a willingness to separate questions about content about which one claims expert knowledge, from questions about teaching, about which one does not. There's the heightened importance of meetings and personal conversations where the 'wisdom of practice' is exchanged. And, finally, there's literature: not scholarly bibliographies that include up-to-date developments, but works that one has found more or less by chance at critical moments in one's career. Most of the books Booth cites are classics of their genre. Collectively, however, they testify to the short reach of specialist research on teaching and especially on learning.[3]

This 'expert' research on teaching and learning remains foreign territory to many academics in the US, despite the best efforts of teaching and learning centres, national curriculum initiatives, conference and workshop organizers, and popularizing publications. In part this is because academics are not in the habit of reading about teaching and learning: thus when a problem turns up, they are more likely to ask advice from an old friend or colleague than to go to the library for help. I think, too, that academics are turned off by popularizations that don't give readers a hold on the research and arguments of the original work (Shulman, 1997; Cross, 1998). Indeed, as Pat Cross has argued, expert research on teaching and learning will likely be discovered by scholars only when they start asking questions that such literature may help them formulate and resolve (1998).

In fact, this is beginning to happen in literary studies right now, spurred in part by the changes in the culture of higher education that I mentioned before. For example, recent issues of both *The Chronicle of Higher Education* in the US and *The Times Higher Education Supplement* in the UK include an account of a 'teaching seminar'initiated by Elaine Showalter, past president of the Modern Languages Association and professor of English at Princeton University. In this seminar, Showalter and her graduate student teaching assistants compiled teaching portfolios, kept journals, and explored the literature on teaching and learning in higher education in order to help them learn how 'to convey content, information, and critical sophistication to their jaded, recalcitrant, or aesthetically resistant students' (1999, B6). Showalter confesses her initial fears in presenting herself as a 'pedagogical expert', but concludes that 'now, two teaching seminars and several hundred dollars later, having gained much more in intellectual excitement and new ideas than I risked in putting my ego on the line, I'm eager to share my bibliography with other instructors in the liberal arts' (1999, B5).

The readings Showalter recommends share with Booth's a marked bias towards the styles of writing and argument familiar to people in humanities' fields, but result from a systematic sampling of literature that is up to date. They include book-length guides to teaching, which summarize recent research on learning (Schoenfeld and Magnan's *Mentor in a Manual*, McKeachie's *Teaching Tips*, Lowman's *Mastering the Techniques of Teaching*, and Eble's *The Craft of Teaching*), essays and case studies on classroom discussion (*Teaching and the Case Method*, by Barnes, Christensen and Hansen and *Education for Judgment*, edited by Christensen, Garvin and Sweet), one book on research findings (Ramsden's *Learning to Teach in Higher Education*), memoirs of teaching careers (Tompkins's *A Life in School* and Kernan's *In Plato's Cave*), and inspirational works like Palmer's *The Courage to Teach* and Brookfield's *Becoming a Critically Reflective Teacher*.

What Showalter has done so publically helps give legitimacy to a process that science studies scholars call 'reconstruction' (Hess, 1997, p. 139) — the effort to reinterpret and remake knowledge as it moves out of its own expert producer group and into other groups elsewhere. Making public the results of her efforts to engage expert literature on teaching, and learning (and pronouncing it intellectually exciting to do so), is an important contribution to the scholarship of teaching and learning in literary studies and neighboring fields. It will help broaden the range of reference that practitioners in these fields can draw on as they identify and examine issues relevant to work with students and classroom practice.

2.3 Disciplinary styles

And this brings me to the question of disciplinary styles, because one of the main challenges to developing a scholarship of teaching and learning in higher education is that in most disciplines this process of 'reconstruction' has just begun. There are a few exceptions and promising developments, but there remains a great deal more to be done before it is commonplace for scholars to examine their teaching practice in light of what is known or imagined possible in one's own or other fields. It is true that vigorous curricular movements, like the 'new calculus' or 'multiculturalism' have raised pedagogical consciousness in many academic departments,[4] but there is still a long way to go before work on teaching and learning is brought more centrally into the world of disciplinary scholarship (Shulman, 1993).

What does this mean? As my Carnegie Foundation colleagues, Pat Hutchings and Lee Shulman, argue, this means taking an attitude of enquiry towards the subject, and it means making one's work public so that colleagues can review it according to accepted standards, so they can critique it, and so that they can then build upon it in their own work (1999). This kind of work is being undertaken by a small but increasing number of scholars these days, including those associated with the national fellowship and campus programmes of CASTL (the Carnegie Academy for the Scholarship of Teaching Learning). They are asking how to improve student learning in a course they teach; they are looking at what kinds of learning might be desirable to aim for; they are experimenting with ways to document what happens in a course; they are seeking ways to make it available for colleagues to comment upon and review (see Shulman, 1998). And, one of the things we are finding out is that scholars usually begin by following disciplinary models developed for other purposes when faced with the new task of exploring teaching and learning in their field.

A recent course portfolio project coordinated by the American Association for Higher Education is a case in point (Hutchings, 1996, pp. 49—60; Hutchings, 1998; Huber, 1998). Indeed, Bill Cerbin, a Carnegie scholar, and course portfolio pioneer, describes the very origin of the idea of documenting the unfolding of a single course from conception to results through an analogy to the investigative traditions of his discipline, psychology.

> I began to think of each course ... as a kind of laboratory — not as a truly controlled experiment, of course, but as a setting in which you start out with goals for student learning, then you adopt teaching practices that you think will accomplish these, and along the way you can watch and see if your practices are helping to accomplish your goals, collecting evidence about effects and impact ... the course portfolio is really like a scholarly manuscript ... a draft, of ongoing inquiry' (1996, p. 53).

To people in other fields, the look and feel of a course portfolio is somewhat different. For example, Steve Dunbar, a mathematician, thinks of analogies to modes of presentation in his own field:

> When I get done I'm going to have something fewer than 50 pages — maybe closer to 30 — that I can give to colleagues to assess ... for mathematical content and validity of data: Were my goals good goals? Did I actually meet these goals? ... [R]eviewers can analyze the portfolio as they would a piece of research. [It will be] comprehensive and data-based in a way that people haven't often seen (1996, pp. 57—58).

And consider Carnegie scholar Bill Cutler's course portfolio for an Introductory Survey in American History (see Cutler, 1998, pp. 19—24). He approached this task as though he were creating both a narrative record of what happened in the classroom and an archive to back it up, including artefacts like the syllabus and reading list, student papers and alternative perspectives from the graduate students who served as teaching assistants.

Clearly, disciplinary styles empower the scholarship of teaching not only by giving scholars a ready-made way to imagine and present their work, but also by giving shape to the problems they choose and the methods they use. Here we may find helpful Joseph Schwab's elegant distinction between the substantive and syntactic structures of the disciplines, by which he means, first, the conceptions that guide enquiry in a discipline (1964, p. 25), and secondly, the 'pathways of enquiry [a discipline or small group of disciplines] use, what they mean by verified knowledge and how they go about this verification' (1964, p. 21).[5] In other words, when we look at scholarly projects on teaching and learning, we can ask how they have been informed by substantive and syntactic structures from the authors' own fields.

Let's look at the substantive area first. Randy Bass, a Carnegie scholar who teaches American Studies in an English department, suggests that the scholarship of teaching and learning involves transforming a 'problem' one has encountered in the classroom into a 'problem' for study, meaning a problem that has some body of thought and literature behind it (1999). Bass himself realized he had a classroom problem when his students evaluated him poorly after he introduced Internet activities into his course. Transformed into a problem for study, this became an enquiry into his goals for student learning, an issue with deep roots in the humanities, where the tension between general education and close reading has engaged humanists in debate since at least the sixteenth century.[6] Bass concluded that his primary goal was not for students to cover a large number of books, but for them to leave his course reading more like experts who can interpret a text in light of other texts and events of its times.

Consider, by contrast, another English professor, Beverly Guy-Sheftall, who teaches women's studies at a historically black college for women in the US south. Guy-Sheftall's classroom problem concerned students' resistance to material on gender, sexuality, and race which is mostly at odds with their strongly held beliefs. To make this a problem for study, Guy-Sheftall engaged ideas from a new wave of feminist pedagogy, which acknowledges the necessity for some emotional discomfort if learning is to take place. She interviewed students about their changing attitudes towards the subject-matter throughout the course, looking closely at their answers for insight into which materials were helping them to move more effectively around the highly charged gender issues discussed in class.

Like Bass and Guy-Sheftall, most Carnegie scholars choose topics about teaching and learning that have resonance within the conceptual structure of their discipline, thus giving their problem for study intellectual authenticity and weight. The same can be said of methods: most people inquiring into teaching and learning try to make use of the normal procedures in their discipline. For example, quite a number of our applicants from the sciences and mathematics have been involved in curricular reforms that advocate some use of cooperative learning in the classroom and want to prove its worth. But proof means something quite rigorous in science fields. As one applicant wrote,

> In order to convince the teachers of organic chemistry (as well as other science disciplines) that there truly is a place for active and cooperative learning in the chemistry classroom, they will need to see good data that support this theory. Scientists are scientists and they know that the data do not lie.

In certain social science fields, a similar spirit prevails. Carnegie scholar Dan Bernstein, a psychologist, is using the experimental methods of his field to help him decide which teaching techniques are helping his students gain a better understanding of psychological measurement. He started down this path when he realized that his students did not seem to be getting some of the key concepts from his well-polished lectures alone. Hypothesizing that students might do better with more opportunities to interact with the material, Bernstein gave one group of students a live lecture on the topic, gave a videotape of his lecture to a second group of students, and gave an interactive author-ware program on the topic to the rest. When reviewers of the study suggested he needed better control conditions, Bernstein then compared performance among groups reading irrelevant material, groups reading relevant material, groups hearing a live lecture, and groups working on the Web. 'This is what you get when you enter into that community,' Bernstein jokes, 'additions of more conditions.' He continues to test and retest new innovations: 'Statistics are fine,' he says, 'but replication is the most important thing you can do.'

For many instructors, however, pedagogy is still a new topic for mainstream scholarship in their field, and even in psychology, as Bernstein would be the first to agree, classroom research does not present ideal conditions for following most methodological protocols. If you are working in a field where quantitative methods predominate, it is often hard to observe the normal scruples about sample sizes and representativeness, along with the other niceties that normally warrant confidence in research results. Of course, scholars may find this work very helpful in focusing attention on student learning and in thinking about what works best in their courses. But, some worry that methodological issues may limit their work's reach beyond their own classroom, and that it may not find a receptive audience among their disciplinary peers.[7] Indeed, even when your field emphasizes interpretation over explanation, and welcomes ethnography, contextually rich case studies, or close readings, it can be a challenge to develop an approach to the study of teaching and learning that both you and your colleagues find interesting and sound.

2.4 Interdisciplinary concerns

Such discontents are to be expected when scholars venture outside the usual bounds of discourse in their intellectual community. For parallels, we can look at what happens in other newly developed areas of enquiry before shifts in disciplinary practice are normalized. In my own field, anthropology, traditional ethnographic practices have been changing over the past 15—20 years. Yet, as George Marcus notes, it is still the case that exploratory projects into new interdisciplinary areas, like science studies, can seem 'personal and relatively undisciplined, as not quite anthropology' (Marcus, 1998, p. 242). This new work can be exciting, but until its anthropological readership picks up, a 'certain accountability' is missing. Without 'a sustained discussion among anthropologists ... the close assessment of arguments and ethnographic claims has been curtailed'. In the meantime, however, something is gained because anthropologists engaged in exploratory ethnographic work with new kinds of subjects are finding audiences among colleagues in other disciplines who are viewing that same territory from different points of view.

Interdisciplinary communities are equally important for the scholarship of teaching and learning. Indeed, they are so important that the Carnegie Foundation has been trying to encourage the formation of such groups and networks of scholars both nationally and on individual campuses. For one thing, these communities can be sanctuaries, where people can find friendly critics for their work, and with whom they can engage in 'corridor talk' about who's doing what, conference opportunities, getting published, finding money, career strategies and all the other information that is typically passed on informally about the conduct of scholarly work (see Downey, Dumit and Traweek 1997.) For our national fellows, this includes a listserv for ongoing informal communication, and opportunities to meet face to face during the two-week sessions that mark the beginning and end of their fellowship and for a couple of days mid-way through the academic year.

These scholars often express relief at finally having a group of colleagues with whom they can talk without going back to square one, and with whom they get collectively smarter about general pedagogical issues that appear to go beyond subject matter.[8] For example, in presenting her work on teaching women's studies, Beverly Guy-Sheftall noted that she had become more reflective about student learning due to the Carnegie programme, and more willing to take risks, including risks to her own values and beliefs. However, it is important not to confuse collegiality and support with interdisciplinarity per se. By some criteria, you only have real interdisciplinarity when you have 'the explicit formulation of a uniform discipline-transcending terminology or a common methodology' (Gibbons *et al.*, 1994, p. 29). Guy-Sheftall, however, is convinced that differences between the disciplines in regard to the scholarship of teaching are profound and deep.

And she may be right. One's own disciplinary style may give direction to one's own work in this new area, but it can also limit one's appreciation of other people's work. Women's studies, for example, is more sensitive than most to the moral and political dimensions of pedagogy. And there are also problems arising from the different ways in which new knowledge is produced. One Carnegie scholar, a psychologist, explained the problem this way:

> Being at a relatively small school, I am aware of the different approaches to traditional research among disciplines, and how research in a discipline is sometimes belittled by other disciplines. For example ... I've heard psychology types dismiss English lit. research as purely speculative and lit. types dismiss psychology as inhumanely mechanistic. While I don't think such criticism inevitable, research does differ among disciplines and it seems logical to me to anticipate the same kind of tensions [in the scholarship of teaching and learning] that exist in traditional research.

It must be said, too, that the problem is exacerbated by the dominance of social science methods in traditional education research and in evaluation studies — a fact that presents a significant challenge to new recruits from specialties where that approach is not much appreciated or used. One university participating in our campus programme has actually set aside money for colleagues who do have statistical expertise to serve as consultants to those who do not. Now, this is a wonderful idea: there's nothing wrong with this set of methods, and no doubt they open doors for those who master them. But it must be recognized that they can also be very discouraging to scholars with little interest or experience in this research tradition. At one session last June, the new class of Carnegie scholars were debating whether they would accept as the scholarship of teaching a project that examined a single student's key moments of engagement with the material for a course. Most of the humanists said 'yes,' but the past editor of the journal *Teaching Sociology*, said that a report on research with a sample of one would simply not be acceptable in his field. To which an historian cried: 'But do we *all* have to be social scientists?'

Clearly, the answer is 'no'. If scholarly attention to teaching and learning in higher education is to gain through multi- or interdisciplinary exchange, then a variety of questions need to be asked and a variety of approaches should flourish. Our Carnegie scholars include psychologists like Bernstein, who are comfortable with statistical methods, but also humanists like Guy-Sheftall, who prefer 'close reading' as a way to analyse student interviews and essays. The challenge here is to reconceptualize relationships between the disciplines, so that the lessons flow in all directions rather than demanding the diffusion of one privileged way of knowing.[8] Our first class of Carnegie scholars used a carpentry metaphor to express the same point: 'If you only have a hammer then everything looks like a nail.' As one of our business scholars concluded, the most intellectually exhilarating lesson of working with people from different disciplines was to learn about the many different tools they collectively had at hand.

2.5 Conclusion

The placement of the scholarship of teaching and learning in the larger world of knowledge production is very much up for grabs right now. Its genres, topics and methods are being invented as we speak; its role in academic careers is being written case by case; new practitioners announce themselves every day; and they are just beginning to seek each other out. We can see that disciplinary styles are rightly influencing the way scholars approach teaching and student learning, but disciplinary 'boundaries' in this area are not that well-established, facilitating border-crossing and collaboration across fields. One of the big questions now is whether scholars of teaching and learning can fascinate their disciplinary colleagues as much as they fascinate those from other disciplines working in the same vein (see Marcus 1998, p.244). Can the discourse that is beginning to take on life in multi- or interdisciplinary discussions be registered and legitimated within the heart of the disciplines themselves?

I think it is an open question whether this work will end up looking like 'normal' academic science or not. Will the scholarship of teaching and learning find its home with other pedagogical discussions — on the margins of most disciplines? Will it gain ground in disciplinary forums and/or emerge as an interdisciplinary field of its own? And here's another possibility. Might the scholarship of teaching and learning live a more punctuated life, like those transdisciplinary, problem-solving, task forces that Michael Gibbons and his colleagues (1994) describe as a new mode of knowledge production? One thing we've learned from trying to encourage the growth of a scholarship of teaching and learning so far is that here there are no either/or's. The correct answer almost surely will be: 'all of the above'.

It's ambitious to try and foster the broad development of a scholarship of teaching and learning, but it's not starting from scratch. As we at this conference well know, there is a strong foundation on which to build. There are many forums in which the exchange of information and ideas about teaching and learning in higher education already take place. And there are many people investing a great deal of intellectual interest and energy in them. Many of these discussions are already squarely within the scope of what we are calling the 'scholarship of teaching and learning,' and many others are open to the ideas behind it. The aim is to enrich these conversations, expand their scope, and ultimately help make them so attractive and intriguing that scholars will *want* to turn to the literature, or to a pioneer colleague at another institution or even down the hall, for ideas and feedback as they try to make their own classrooms better places for all students to learn. As intellectually compelling work in the scholarship of teaching and learning becomes better known, teachers will not have to reinvent the wheel, but can build on — and contribute to — what their colleagues have already achieved.

Notes

1. I am indebted to Pat Hutchings's account of the history of the notion of the scholarship of teaching, as used in the Carnegie Academy for the Scholarship of Teaching and Learning (1999, pp. 3—5).

2. I have included full references to the books cited by Booth and by Showalter in a separate list at the end of the reference section.

3. This particular 'expert' literature (like many others) still struggles to reach scholars and teachers in other fields, and bridge what some experts themselves misleadingly call the theory/practice divide. This is misleading, in part because it implies that practitioners who do not work with theory developed in 'my' field are working with no theory at all (see Shulman, 1987; Cross, 1998).

4. See, for example, the National Research Council's recent report (1999) on undergraduate education in the SMET disciplines — science, mathematics, engineering and technology.

5. Shulman and his colleagues later used these categories to help understand the several ways in which subject-matter knowledge affects teaching (see Shulman, 1987; Grossman, Wilson and Shulman, 1989), but precisely because they shape both research *and* teaching, they are helpful in understanding their intersection in the scholarship of teaching and learning as well.

6. Bushnell (1994) links 'our own struggle to expand the canon while reading the text responsibly' to the discussion that took place among sixteenth-century humanists. By the end of that century, she says, 'when concern for argument and structure, or the "body" of the text, came to dominate humanist rhetoric and grammar, conflict had begun to arise between the admiration of general education and a demand for the kind of close reading that construes a whole text'.

7. One Carnegie scholar, citing a recent article about the second-class status that education researchers accord 'classroom research' by teachers in primary and secondary schools, worried that scholars of teaching and learning in higher education might also have to ask whether there are other kinds of validity they could claim for their work (see also Anderson and Herr, 1999, on the status of practitioner research in schools and universities).

8. Shulman (1987, p. 8) lists seven different categories of 'teacher knowledge,' of which 'general pedagogical knowledge' is just one.

9. I am paraphrasing here from Gary Lee Downey's discussion of 'partner-theorizing' as an appropriate stance for anthropologists working in science and technology fields. Partner-theorizing, according to Downey 'reconceptualizes relationships within and between academic disciplines, as well as between modes of academic and popular theorizing, as flows of metaphors in all directions rather than the necessary diffusion of truthful knowledge and power from the inside out' (1997, p. 120).

2.6 References

Anderson, G.L. and Herr, K. (1999) The new paradigm wars: is there room for rigorous practitioner knowledge in schools and universities?, *Educational Research* **28**(5): 12—21, 40.

Bass, R. (1999) The scholarship of teaching: what's the problem?, *Inventio: Creative Thinking About Learning and Teaching* **1**(1). (http://www.doiit.gmu.edu/inventio/randybass.htm)

Booth, W.C. (1988) *The Vocation of a Teacher: Rhetorical Occasions: 1967—1988*. Chicago: The University of Chicago Press.

Boyer, E.L. (1990) *Scholarship Reconsidered: Priorities of the Professoriate*. Princeton, NJ: The Carnegie Foundation for the Advancement of Teaching.

Bushnell, R. (1994) From books to languages. *Common Knowledge* **3**(1): 16—38.

Cross, P. (1990) Teachers as scholars, *AAHE Bulletin* **43**(4): 3—5.

Cross, P. (1998) What do we know about student learning and how do we know it? Keynote address, American Association for Higher Education. Annual Meeting, Washington, DC.

Cutler, W.W. (1998) Writing a course portfolio for an introductory survey course in American history, in P. Hutchings (ed.), *The Course Portfolio,* Washington, DC. American Association for Higher Education, 19—24.

Downey, G.L., Dumit, J. and Traweek, S. (1997) Corridor talk, in G.L. Downey and J. Dumit (eds), *Cyborgs and Citadels: Anthropological Interventions in Emerging Sciences and Technologies*. Santa Fe, NM: School of American Research Press, pp. 245—63.

Downey, G.L. and Lucena, J.C. (1997) Hiring in to a contested field of education. In G.L. Downey and J. Dumit (eds), *Cyborgs and Citadels: Anthropological Interventions in Emerging Sciences and Technologies*, Santa Fe, NM: School of American Research Press, pp. 117—141.

Gibbons, M., Limoges, C., Nowotny, H., Schwartzman, S., Scott, P. and Trow, M. (1994) *The*

New Production of Knowledge: The Dynamics of Science and Research in Contemporary Societies. London: Sage.

Glassick, C.E., Huber, M.T. and Maeroff, G.I. (1997) *Scholarship Assessed: Evaluation of the Professoriate*. San Francisco: Jossey-Bass.

Grossman, P.L., Wilson, S.M. and Shulman, L.S. (1989) Teachers of substance: subject matter knowledge for teaching, in M.C. Reynolds (ed.), *Knowledge Base for the Beginning Teacher*. New York: Pergamon Press, 23—36.

Hess, D.J. (1997) *Science Studies: An Advanced Introduction*. New York: New York University Press.

Hutchings, P. (1996) *Making Teaching Community Property: A Menu for Peer Collaboration and Peer Review*. Washington, DC: American Association for Higher Education.

Hutchings, P. (1999) Preface. In P. Hutchings and C. Bjork, 'The Scholarship of Teaching and Learning in Higher Education: An Annotated Bibliography'. Mimeo. Menlo Park, CA: The Carnegie Foundation for the Advancement of Teaching.

Hutchings, P. (ed.) (1998) *The Course Portfolio: How Faculty Can Examine Their Teaching to Advance Practice and Improve Student Learning*. Washington, DC: American Association for Higher Education.

Hutchings, P. and Shulman, L. (1999) The scholarship of teaching: new elaborations, new developments, *Change* **31**(5): 11—15.

http://www.carnegiefoundation.org/OurWork/OurWork.htm

Marcus, G.E. (1998) *Ethnography through Thick and Thin*. Princeton: Princeton University Press.

National Research Council (1999) *Transforming Undergraduate Education in Science, Mathematics, Engineering, and Technology*. Washington, DC: National Academy Press.

Schwab, J. (1964) Structure of the disciplines: meanings and significances. In G.W. Ford and L. Pugno (eds), *The Structure of Knowledge and the Curriculum*, Chicago: Rand McNally & Company, pp. 6—30.

Showalter, E. (1999) The risks of good teaching: how 1 professor and 9 TA's plunged into pedagogy, *The Chronicle of Higher Education*, 9 July 1999, B4—B6 (see also Making a mark in the classroom, *The Times Higher Education Supplement*, 3 Sept. 1999, 16—17).

Shulman, L. (1987) Knowledge and teaching: foundations of the new reform, *Harvard Educational Review* **57**(1): 1—22.

Shulman, L. (1993) Teaching as community property: putting an end to pedagogical solitude. *Change*, Nov./Dec.: 6—7.

Shulman, L. (1997) Disciplines of inquiry in education: a new overview. In R.M. Jaeger (ed.), *Complementary Methods for Research in Education*, 2nd edn, Washington, DC: American Educational Research Association, pp. 3—30.

Shulman, L. (1998) Course anatomy: the dissection and analysis of knowledge through teaching, in *The Course Portfolio: How Faculty Can Examine their Teaching to Advance Practice and Improve Student Learning*. Washington, DC: American Association of Higher Education.

Shulman, L. (1999) Taking learning seriously, *Change*, July/August, 11—17.

Reading lists cited

Ashton-Warner, S. (1963) *Teacher*. New York: Simon & Schuster.

Axelrod, J. *The Discussion Technique in the College Classroom*. (publication details not available)

Barnes, L.B., Christensen, C.R. and Hansen, A.J. (1994) *Teaching and the Case Method: Text, Cases, and Readings*. Harvard Business School Press.

Barzun, J. (1945) *Teacher in America*. Boston: Little Brown (reprinted in 1986, Lanham, MA: University Press of America).

Brookfield, S.D. (1995) *Becoming a Critically Reflective Teacher*. San Francisco: Jossey-Bass.

Christensen, C.R., Garvin, D.A. and Sweet, A. (eds) (1991) *Education for Judgment: The Artistry of Discussion Leadership*. Harvard Business School Press.

Eble, K.E. (1988) *The Craft of Teaching: A Guide to Mastering the Professor's Art*. San Francisco: Jossey-Bass.

Erskine, J. (1948) *My Life as a Teacher*. Philadelphia: J B Lippincott Co.

Highet, G. (1950) *The Art of Teaching*. New York: Knopf.

Kernan, A.B. (1999) *In Plato's Cave*. Yale University Press.

Lowman, J. (1995) *Mastering the Techniques of Teaching*. San Francisco: Jossey-Bass.

McKeachie, W.J. (1999) *McKeachie's Teaching Tips: Strategies, Research, and Theory for College and University Teachers*. Houghton Mifflin.

Narayan, R.K. (1945) *The English Teacher*. London: Eyre & Spottiswoode.

Palmer, P.J. (1998) *The Courage to Teach: Exploring the Inner Landscape of a Teacher's Life*. San Francisco: Jossey-Bass.

Passmore, J.A. (1980) *The Philosophy of Teaching*. London: Duckworth.

Ramsden, P. (1992) *Learning to Teach in Higher Education*. Routledge.

Schoenfeld, A.C. and Magnan, R. (1994) *Mentor in a Manual: Climbing the Academic Ladder to Tenure*. Magna Publications.

Tompkins, J.P. (1996) *A Life in School: What the Teacher Learned*. Addison Wesley Longman.

3 'We are many and the forms are few': the relation of form and content in subjects and in the 7th ISL Symposium

Colin Evans

Birkbeck College, London

> There are three conditions which often look alike
> Yet differ completely, flourish in the same hedgerow:
> Attachment to self and to things and to persons, detachment
> From self and from things and from persons; and, growing between them, indifference
> Which resembles the others as death resembles life...
>
> T.S. Eliot, *Four Quartets*, Little Gidding, III

3.1 Keynotes as form

I was asked to deliver the third 'keynote' which would close the symposium. This meant responding to what I had experienced — including the other keynotes — and helping my fellow participants to make meaning from their experiences which, inevitably, were very different from mine. But the (doubtful) privilege of speaking solely on the basis of my experience and responses over the three days was not available since I had been asked in advance to provide a title and 500 words for the programme and I had agreed since this was the form I was offered and it seemed considerably less threatening to have a title, 500 words and a few transparencies than to start with a blank sheet and my own sensibilities. In reality I am sure that if I had pointed out to the organizers that there was a contradiction they would have readily left a blank in the programme under my name. It didn't occur to me at the time. There is a message there.

I started my talk by referring to the two other keynotes — present examples of the form I was working with. Mary Huber had also started the second keynote by referring to the first: 'If Rob Pope's keynote was Keynote Future', she said, 'mine is Keynote Past.' I said mine would be 'Keynote Here and Now'. And, in spite of the prior preparation, I did attempt to focus on the here and now — the tiered seats of the lecture room, the location away from the rest of the conference, the artificial light and the window whose blind could be opened, the empty seats of those who had left early or left after lunch, the presence in everyone's consciousness of images, memories, all different, all adding up to fundamentally disparate narratives and mine being in no way special or privileged although I was the monologist.

Now that I am writing this, after the event, the situation and the form are quite different. I could simulate it by writing now, in the present tense, the text I never wrote down and pretending that there was a text — or a tape which has been transcribed. I prefer to espouse another form — the academic article — and to write in the past tense a reflective and reflexive account of what I said and did there and then. Both the keynote and this article are examples of what I have called elsewhere (after Bateson) the metalogue[1] — occasions where the communication itself is illustrative of the content being explored.

The conference was about student learning through the disciplines. I see disciplines as being (among other things) collections of forms which particular groups traditionally and conventionally work with. So the issue of how students learn through the disciplines is the question of how students learn or fail to learn through the forms they are offered and how they might learn with and through people whose attachment is to forms different from theirs. In this symposium we were all learners and what applied to us applies to our students. So the question of our relation to the forms of the symposium is a good starting point.

My relation (and Rob Pope's and Mary Huber's) to the form of the keynote and participants' response to our use of the form is an example among many but it has the advantage of immediate presence since the audience, the organizers and I lived with its reality and its consequences. The comments in the (unusually full and helpful) evaluations are very illuminating in this regard. Some participants liked especially 'the unusual things' and singled out Rob Pope's opening keynote.'Seeing Rob Pope in action' was a plus for one participant; his unusual keynote was, said another 'refreshing'. But others said that one of the *worst* things about the conference for them was hearing 'hard negative comments about Rob's keynote' and others were indeed negative — 'a bore' (!) 'self indulgent'. I spent some time over lunch that day persuading one young participant that his disappointment (Rob had not checked the hard work that he, the participant, had done during the keynote) was a sign of the participant's attachment to a particular kind of learning and relation to authority.

The responses to mine were mostly positive. I wonder why. Had some potentially hostile people left by then? Mine was less radical and challenging than Rob's but people still spent time at my request in silence with their eyes closed conjuring up images and metaphors from the conference — their own personal versions of my own which included elephants, matches and batteries from Rob's opening, the beautifully built ancient steam locomotive which was no longer functional because the tracks had changed (= the university), the jokes like free-form crocheting and the things I'd learned such as there being in England an institution with a 'Director of Corporate Excellence' — in other words I asked for and engaged in daydreaming — an activity which has always been strongly discouraged in education). Had the acceptable form of the keynote changed by then so that mine was a sort of Hegelian synthesis of Rob's innovation and Mary Huber's traditionalism (it is striking that Mary's paper seems to have produced no responses from participants at all, though one did prefer it, by implication, saying that the first and the last 'were too self-conscious of form').

I have taken this particular close-to-home example as a starting point for a reflection about our attitudes to the forms. I base this reflection on the lines from Eliot quoted above: *attachment*, *detachment* and *indifference* are three positions we can hold with regard to a particular form. Indifference is the feeling which makes us replicate forms unconsciously. It is, as Eliot sees, a kind of death. Attachment is the feeling which makes us defend the forms we cherish and give them continued life. Detachment is the ability to select appropriate forms for learning from a repertoire, to know when forms have outlived their usefulness, to bid them farewell and to bear the loss. It is hard to achieve.

The questions for us are, it seems to me:

- What are the forms for learning?
- What is the nature of our attachment to familiar, traditional forms?

- How do we avoid indifference?
- How do we achieve detachment?

I am not promising to answer these questions in this piece but I hope to clarify them for myself and others. I start with the first. What are the forms?

3.2 Forms

3.2.1 In space

We do our learning work in spaces. The conference used the space provided by York University. We all moved from space to space in complex and often baroque ways. Some were distant one from another. Sometimes we were required to be in one space at one time and instantly transport ourselves to be in another space at exactly the same time. In some of the spaces we were crowded; in others we were scattered; sometimes we sat in rows, at others around or on or under tables. Our learning experience was determined by this use of physical space in ways we may not have been fully aware of, although the rich evidence of the evaluations shows how salient this physical reality was for people.

I once took part as a staff member in a Group Relations conference organized by the Grubb institute in London.[3] The characteristic of these conferences is that the tasks are underspecified so that it is possible to focus on the aspects which are normally invisible. One of the 'events' was the 'large group' event — five 90-minute sessions interspersed with other events; 35 people in one room with the task of working at what was happening in the large group in the here and now and by extension what happens in large groups generally. The three staff members who were part of the group met before the first session to decide how the furniture should be arranged. Of the various forms (rows, a big circle, concentric circles, an X, chairs stacked by the door ...) we chose a spiral (or rather one of us chose and the others acquiesced). This seating arrangement was a dominant theme throughout the five sessions as we worked on the significance of the original choice and the symbolic meaning of particular points on the spiral.

Another 'event' — called the 'praxis event' — required all conference members to work to their own chosen task. I spent the time writing, and produced this poem, based on my experience of the spiral seating arrangement.[4]

HELIX

We are many and the forms are few.
And still they hold their own against us.
The moves of chess outlive the walrus tusk,
The onyx and the carved yew.

Within an abstract, bounded space
Imagine now a conjoint line
Of vertebrae, a snaking spine,
Curving with the ancient grace

Of nebulae or fossil ammonite,
The potent force of maypole, compacted spring

> Or of the humble gut, digesting
> In its patient coils by day and night.
>
> This is the containing form. As, every time,
> Words, discrete and proud, must take
> Position for the meaning's sake,
> For the tender rhythm and the rhyme,
>
> So within the form's obscure constraint,
> Iron maiden, love's embrace,
> We take our own allotted place,
> To play our role, invent our fate.
>
> We are many and the forms are few.
> And still they hold their own against us.
> The moves of chess outlive the walrus tusk,
> The onyx and the carved yew.

This poem does what poems do: it expresses ambivalence — feelings which can't be translated into non-contradictory propositional statements. (My distinction, via Eliot, between detachment and indifference is a bit more propositional). In the poem the form's constraints are 'obscure' — they can be a torture device or a condition of procreation and new life. It looks as if we are in conflict with them: they are 'against' us; they hold their own but we strive to break them. But they represent the natural world of life and also the symbolic order — language and the possibility of structured, rule-based dialogue as in chess. The poem is a metalogue — an enactment of its own theme since it uses the voluntary formal constraint of a tight rhyme-scheme to say that constraint is a condition of creativity. It could be argued that the repetition of the first stanza is a mistake since it sides with the conservative closedness of the form rather than the openness of the desire to mutiny and break — with all desire's potential for both growth and destruction.[5]

You may feel that these thoughts are a long way from how we choose to set out the chairs in a room. But furniture arrangement is not a trivial matter and it can stand very well as an exemplar of how we use attachment, detachment and indifference with regard to forms in space. Visit any organization and you will quickly see the preferred form. The recently designed Humanities building in the University of Cardiff has rooms of varying shapes and sizes (the 125 railway carriage shape seems a popular one) but most are equipped with fixed tiered seating — you can go to almost any university in the world and find this form; where there are seminar rooms in a university there will be tables arranged in a hollow square; the Tavistock is likely to have circles of ten or so chairs without tables; the courses put on by the Centre for Higher Education Studies in the Institute of Education in London are characterized by a number of clusters of chairs around tables ... These arrangements are powerful and everyone in the institution knows what is normal although it is rarely written down. Change the arrangement without putting it back and you may be asked to 'leave the furniture in the prescribed place'.[6]

I once took part in a conference in the USA. The topic, as it happens, was the pedagogical nature of the disciplines. The form chosen by the organizers and used in previous conferences was the dialogue: each session had two speakers on a stage in front of a large audience seated in rows with a third person as moderator. Our threesome's topic was to be

'Whose class-room is it?' There were a few sessions before the one I was involved in and the 'dialogues' were in fact back-to-back monologues. I thought that for the classroom session it would be fruitful to change the standard seating arrangement and have all the seats in the large room (about 200) in threes so that everyone could dialogue (and metalogue) about whose classroom this one was, or, more specifically, where the power and the authority lay.[7] I got assent for this from my two colleagues[8] (but not from the conference organizers) and, early in the morning, the porters rearranged the chairs into threes, ignoring the stage and the sound system.

The three of us 'speakers' sat in our chairs and started on time. When participants turned up, there was turmoil. Some were angry, some walked out ('Sixties stuff' was one comment I recall), some piled around the three of us and became an audience, some (mainly I think the young and the less powerful) formed groups of three or more and asked themselves 'Whose class room is it?' It was a very high-energy almost explosive session and the following break was also quite controversial as the conference organizers challenged me to justify what I had done to their conference (classroom).

As always when there is a 'happening' of this kind the analysis is complex and I certainly question now the appropriateness of an outsider, an invited guest, disturbing someone else's cherished form, however well I could justify it in terms of it being 'my' classroom and my choosing to put that into question.

For our purpose the story demonstrates the power of the furniture (the chairs were back in rows for the next session but they carried the aura of their transgression for the rest of the conference) and enables us to ask our questions about attachment, detachment and indifference. I believe that although some may have been indifferent, many people in the conference were attached to that form: they had invested in it. For it to be broken up was shocking. I would like to claim I was detached (as outsiders often are[9]) and wanted to use the furniture to make for more powerful learning — but I may well have had then my own attachments, if not to a seating arrangement then to transgression and mischief. A's attachment confronting B's attachment is frequent.

Last year I ran a session about this with my teaching creative writing MA students in Cardiff. We started with tables and chairs, then got rid of the tables, then made a circle of chairs, brought the circle closer in, took the circle further out. Each individual felt more or less discomfort in each position. When we'd finished experimenting, the question arose about how we should sit for the rest of the session. I said people should sit where they liked and the result was students scattered all over the room.[10] There are practical 'detached' reasons for seating arrangements — for example, the need to see an OHP or each another (pictures of high-level conferences or the British cabinet room show people lined up along one side of a table and unable to talk to one another easily as they would in a circle) but there are other reasons which are to do with our attachment to a certain *distance:* 'the hollow square is not about economizing on tables but about making artificial distance between participants'.

In terms of keynotes, the tiered lecture room speaks eloquently of power relations and the answer to the question 'Whose classroom is it?' is 'It is mine since I speak and you are silent.' One participant's feedback was that the keynotes were the worst part because 'I can't bear sitting in a lecture theatre whatever the style of the speaker'; many others deplored 'monologues', 'papers being delivered', 'being lectured at'. The question for organizers of a future conference is whether they will reproduce the dominant form of this one or go for the emergent form, represented by the process groups. Or, in my present terms, whether going for the monologic/didactic is a matter of indifference (this form is the dominant, taken for granted form everywhere), attachment (this form is cherished and familiar and attractive — to break it is to create anxiety, diminish learning and attract fewer people) or detachment — a cool assessment of task and resource. We shall see.

3.2.2 Forms in time

We live in time and, if only because of our bodily needs, learning sessions need to be divided into units. These smaller units may be the standard hour of the lecture (derived from the intervals between bells in mediaeval monasteries) or the standard 90 minutes of the Group Relations conference. Larger units may be sequences of these arranged as modules, and modules arranged as curricula. In our institutions there is a lot of randomness (indifference) since no-one can control the sequence of classes followed by any student. But in conferences and workshops it is possible to design things to produce synergy through juxtaposition. A DUET[11] workshop for example is a weave whereby three or four separate strands run throughout and produce a 'text'.

The same questions of attachment arise with time as with space. I am going to be taking part in February in the Grubb Institute's Teaching and Learning workshop which is in the Tavistock tradition.[12] The workshop director phoned me up to ask what I thought about having one-hour sessions rather than the traditional 90-minute ones (in order to solve a design problem concerning the number of sessions overall). My first reaction was shock-horror and a ready-prepared rationale for the 90-minutes form; fortunately I was able to summon up some detachment and we'll try it out. But my attachment to the overall design, the weave, sub-groups with the same task and not parallel different ones — this would take some shifting.

In the same way I would take some convincing that a form where sessions are of unequal length and whose duration was determined by external events is satisfactory. To try to draw the form of the York conference in time was quite difficult and this difficulty is one of the reasons for the anxiety many participants seem to have felt (and which I felt myself as I strove to be in the right room at the right time for the right length of time). Learning needs a secure container (another word for form) and one which can be easily internalized. The less we have to think about the container the more energy we can give to the content. But we (participants) can be indifferent to the container only because others (the organizers) have attachment for it.

Another problem is the nature of the different elements whose weave made up the conference (the 'four kinds of session' listed on p. 7 of the programme were hard to distinguish on the ground — some of them were two back-to-back sessions and the keynote was another kind of session).

As with my thoughts on furniture you may think that this is carping: but all over the world conferences are designed without these things being taken into account. Conference design, like course design, is made subordinate to content and this is to reduce the learning impact of the enormous amount of work that organizers do.

3.2.3 Communicative forms

When I was a student of French in the late 1950s my week centred around one exercise: we would be given a piece of English prose, always from a novel, often about trains or violent storms, and have to translate it into French. We would hand the translation in and the following week get it back with corrections written on it. The lecturer would then go through the text giving the correct version and explaining where we had got it wrong. This was 'Prose Composition' and was one of three basic exercises which structured the timetable (the others were translation out of French and essay-writing in the French style). 'Prose' derived directly from the teaching of classics: when modern languages started, teachers simply took over the exercises of ancient languages (omitting 'verse composition'). When I got a job as a lecturer in French I was required to teach prose and, initially at least, the passages I had translated and my teachers' 'fair copies' served me in good stead. I then proceeded to spend a whole career vainly trying to get linguists to abandon what is a singularly ineffective, even counter-productive way of teaching.[13] It is surface learning at its most typical and encourages dependency long after students should be autonomously using language to express their own ideas and take moral responsibility for them. It is also too far removed from what people actually do in work situations.

The other day I was running a staff development workshop on course design and one of the young participants, not knowing of my background in French, introduced herself by saying that her problem was that she had decided that prose translation as practised in her department was not effective but didn't know how to design an alternative or how to overcome her colleagues' resistance. *Plus ça change*!

Other disciplines have similar inherited exercises and ways of working: mathematicians write on the board and and students copy it down — sometimes what the teacher writes is what he or she copied down as a student; even a new 'subject' like creative writing has developed a standard workshop format, each group member providing a piece of writing and critiquing others' writing ...

These traditional forms structure classes, provide secure containers for work and are sometimes functional: but, when indifference sets in, their routine predictability is inimical to creative learning and precludes adaptation to a changing world (in my modern languages example — the change from a dead language to a living one and from a literary world to a commercial one). But university teachers have been socialized very strongly into a discipline which includes these practices and to detach from them is to allow this identity to be threatened.

So, not only do we meet at a particular time for a particular period of time in a particular space — a conjuncture which is a part of a whole design, a particular form, but what we do in that time and space is also determined by sequences of communicative activity we call exercises or methods of delivery. To use a flip-chart or indeed any visual support in a university committee (or a group relations study group) is to be transgressive: in an IBM meeting *not* to use visuals is transgressive. OHPs are becoming the dominant form in university lectures but it was interesting to see how two forms can happily co-exist unsynthesized as Mary Huber read her paper (old form) and had an assistant show the OHP slides (new form). In terms of how a large group of learners can be managed we had a wide range: the parallel sessions are a way of dividing up the large conference group; within those groups there were occasions when the large sub-groups were divided into smaller syndicates and others when the monologic dominated. The process sub-groups ('space to process thoughts and ideas' — p. 11 of the programme) were an interesting case — clearly designed as an interactive communicative form at the opposite end of the spectrum from the keynote but much too large to do the reflective and exploratory cross-discipline work required. The process group I was in worked well once we had divided into two groups but the low level of authority given to the chair 'Each group will have a nominated chair but ultimately it is the responsibility of the group ... p. 11) was indicative of a lack of conviction about this innovative form.

In general one of the most interesting things about the conference was the sense of its being poised between a dominant form which is monologic and didactic and an emergent form which is dialogic, exploratory and interactive. That the monologic is dominant is evidenced by this book which records in a high-status way the monologues but not the dialogues as if the former were the *real* 'proceedings'. But this is to simplify: Rob Pope took a traditional monologic form — the keynote address — and transgressively made it dialogic (referring to Bakhtin who invented the term). The simple buzz-group which I used is also dialogic and there must be many university teachers who have seen that done in conferences or elsewhere but who have never done it themselves.

3.3 Conclusion: cultures

We have been reflecting about cultures. There are institutional cultures and there are disciplinary cultures; there are conference cultures. The institutional culture of Higher Education is still in a way pre-Gutenberg. Throughout the world people are still reading papers aloud to each other as if they were precious single-copy manuscripts and the scribes were on strike for longer prayer-breaks. The disciplinary and subject cultures are at last being studied (and this conference was a valuable contribution to that work). Tony Becher's book[14] is an important source although he deals only with the research elites and not the day to day activities of the footsoldiers which is what I attempted in the two areas I am familiar with.[15]

Cultures do change. They have to change in order to survive and some are now saying that the university has to change if it is to survive as a creator of knowledge.[16] But change — individual or institutional — is not easy. My story about prose translation is the story of an attachment fight. The story of attempts to produce change in institutional forms over the last ten years is one where enthusiasts have produced materials which they have sent out into the world[17] in the hope that they would be used. So innovations in one discipline might be incorporated into the forms of another. But often the people who saw the material were other enthusiasts, and the hard, risky work of persuading an individual or a group to move from indifference ('We've always done it this way and it's working') to attachment ('I can defend this way') to detachment ('I'll give it a go') is presumed already done once the materials have been produced and dispatched. But there is a link between culture and identity and we cling to the identities we have patiently built up. I lived through a merger in which autonomous language departments and a department of Politics were merged into a School of European Studies. The School has never achieved the sense of identity which the departments had and the departments have never been prepared to abandon their original identity or move easily between different identities. This is largely because it was assumed that people would change their identity and bear the loss — that institutional management of this loss was an unnecessary expense.

This conference was an attempt to facilitate learning for a large group of people. To this end the organizers designed it creating a form in time and space. In one sense it was a disciplinary conference — and the question was about improving student (i.e. participant) learning *through the discipline of staff development or higher education studies;* the suggestion that other disciplines should modify their cultures or be open to different cultures only has credibility if those making it are prepared to do the same. There is a necessary attachment to the forms of previous conferences — without this attachment the organizers would not have the necessary energy and passion to do the work. But my argument has been that detachment is needed as well. We have to ask at the end of an endeavour such as this questions about what works for learners and furthers the learning task? What provides for the variety of learner needs — security, challenge, stimulus ... Publishing the whole of the evaluation comments is an excellent step. This piece of writing is designed to facilitate the work of the designers of the next conference as they select their forms from their collective repertoire and to enable those who were at the conference to reflect on whether the forms of the '99 conference helped or hindered their learning through the discipline of higher education studies.

Notes

1. C. Evans (1990) Teaching the humanities: seminars as metalogues, *Studies in Higher Education* **15**(3): 287—97.
2. See Coleridge's poem 'Frost at Midnight' — 'I brooded all the following morn, / Awed by the stern preceptor's face, mine eye / Fixed with mock study on my swimming book ...' and Jon Cook's account (Cook (1995) An end to boredom in education, *Developing University English Teaching*. Mellen).
3. Working and being in systems, Grubb Institute, London, October 1995.
4. Clue: I own three chess sets.
5. This commentary owes a lot to written comments made to me by the late Barry Palmer.
6. A participant sent me after the conference an eloquent photograph from a sign in a room in his institution — a diagram of the seats (in rows) and the injunction to 'ensure the furniture in this room is positioned as shown at the end of each lecture'.
7. I discuss these issues of power and authority in Chapter 4 of the DUET book cited in note 2 above.
8. The nature of this assent would however be worth exploring.
9. Only an outsider could have saved Welsh rugby.
10. An account of an experiential group with MA students and involving furniture is C. Evans (1995) Group process and writing process, *Studies in the Education of Adults* **27**(2): 157—72.
11. DUET is the Developing University English Teaching project. See the book cited above and the website http://www.uwe.ac.uk/duet
12. Grubb Institute Annual workshops on Teaching and Learning: in London: 4—6 February 2000: tel: 0171-278 8061.
13. For what it's worth I published my first diatribe against prose in *Les Langues modernes* in 1976!
14. T. Becher (1989) *Academic tribes and Territories*. Open University Press.
15. C. Evans (1988) *Language People* and (1993) *English People*, both Open University Press.
16. R. Barnett and A. Griffin (eds) (1999) *The End of Knowledge in Higher Education*, Institute of Education.
17. I recently received in the post a very expensive and high-quality pack of materials — CD roms, work-books — about science teaching produced from a funded teaching grant and I asked myself what thought had been given to implementation and persuasion.
18. See Peter Marris (1994) *Loss and Change*, RKP.

4 Are the pedagogies of the disciplines really different?

Graham Gibbs[1]
Centre for Higher Education Practice, Open University

4.1 Overview

The 1999 Improving Student Learning Symposium was concerned with the pedagogy of the disciplines — about how learning and teaching are different as a consequence of the inherent nature of different disciplines. But what is it that actually differs and to what extent are these fundamental differences, and what is really generic? This chapter is based on a workshop undertaken at the start of the Symposium and on discussion which took place in 'Process Seminars' throughout the Symposium. It explores a range of perspectives on disciplinary differences and generic commonalities. It is clear that many disciplines have unique characteristics and that the forms knowledge take, and the forms of discourse involved, are often unique. The conclusion of the workshop, the 'Process Seminars' and this chapter, however, is that there is a great deal more in common than many teachers normally perceive or acknowledge. Many teaching methods described as discipline-specific are used widely across disciplines and take much the same form regardless of context. Furthermore most generic principles of learning apply to a considerable extent to most contexts, though with different balances of emphasis in different disciplines. While only a sociologist can apply generic principles and methods appropriately to the teaching of sociology, it is largely generic principles and methods, and not sociological principles and methods, which need to be applied.

4.2 Introduction

It is clearly difficult to spread teaching and learning practices between disciplines. The organization of the Fund for the Development of Teaching and Learning in England along discipline-specific lines, and the creation of discipline specific networks (the 'Subject Centres') for the UK, has acknowledged this difficulty. Teachers identify themselves by their disciplinary affiliations and the 'community of practice' in higher education is largely a number of communities of disciplinary and research practices, rather than a single generic community of teaching practice. However, while the cultural and organizational imperatives of educational development strategy are hard to argue with, it is less clear that these cultural, even tribal, differences, are justified in terms of the teaching and learning practices and principles involved. This chapter considers these differences in relation to eight issues:

- knowledge of disciplinary content;
- characteristics of the discipline and the nature of disciplinary knowledge and discourse;

- characteristics of disciplinary cultures;
- characteristics of disciplinary learning styles;
- characteristics of disciplinary, institutional and national conventions in curriculum design and teaching methods;
- generic teaching and learning methods;
- generic principles of learning;
- methodologies for researching disciplinary pedagogy.

4.3 Knowledge of disciplinary content

At one extreme it might be argued that it is not possible to teach anything without having a full grasp of the subject matter oneself, and that this knowledge is the one essential of teaching. If you want to explain anything to a student you need to understand it yourself first. When responding to students' questions it can clearly be effective to respond with questions, rather than answers, but subject matter knowledge can clearly help you to formulate much more useful questions. When correcting students' answers it is clearly helpful to know whether they are correct or embody misunderstandings.

However there are arguments which might modify the strength of this position. First, the lack of a relationship between various measures of research productivity and scholarship, on the one hand, and teaching effectiveness, on the other (see Hattie and Marsh, 1996, for a review of this literature) raises questions about how developed the subject expertise needs to be before it is sufficient to enable the teacher to teach effectively. Teaching competence does not flow automatically, or even easily, from subject knowledge.

Second, as Carl Rogers would argue (Rogers, 1969), what supports learning can be more to do with humanistic principles and practices and can start from learners' interests and knowledge and experience as well as from teachers' knowledge. Constructivism assumes that learners have to construct their own understanding, whatever their teachers already know. Some subjects lend themselves to starting from experience, common sense and first principles, more than others. For example most mathematics differs from most social science in the extent to which it is possible to support learning without oneself having a solid subject knowledge. Some subjects contradict everyday experience. Educational processes involving self-directed learning and learning contracts, such as those involved in the School for Independent Study at the Polytechnic of East London (Percy and Ramsden, 1980), have characteristically operated within some subject areas but not others. It was considered possible to support students in their learning almost regardless of what they wanted to learn, whether or not there was a subject expert in the School, but only within certain boundaries, and only because disciplinary knowledge existed in the library or in other academics outside the School. This phenomenon is also evident in supervision of undergraduate projects and dissertations. Some History teachers, for example, are perfectly prepared to supervise a student regardless of their choice of dissertation topic, because what is perceived to matter is the methodology and discourse of being a historian, rather than the supervisor's knowledge of the specific topic the student wants to study. These supervisors would not believe themselves to be competent to supervise an Engineering student. Teachers differ in their belief in the primacy of content or process in their supervisory role, and again this emphasis is clearly different in different disciplines. In science, undergraduate final year projects may be specified for students to choose from, to make sure that adequate supervisory expertise is available (as well as for practical reasons).

This disciplinary difference in the relative importance placed on content and process changes to some extent when the curriculum is organized in interdisciplinary ways. For example in Problem Based Learning in Medicine it is common for tutors to be allocated to tutor groups tackling problems about which they are not an expert, in order that they can concentrate on the tutoring processes involved and not intervene inappropriately with their subject knowledge. Experienced tutors may be allowed to tutor in areas they are knowledgeable in once they have learnt not to use this knowledge inappropriately!

Another aspect of disciplinary knowledge is teachers' 'craft knowledge' about how to explain difficult concepts. Experienced teachers have anecdotes, exercises, forms of explanation, examples, modelling, and all kinds of pedagogic devices which they have found to work in the past to explain particular content. Lee Schulman of the Carnegie Institute uses the term 'pedagogic content knowledge' to refer to this kind of knowledge. Whatever the generic characteristics of such pedagogic devices such as 'using examples', 'structuring explanations' or 'modelling', the actual form and effectiveness of these depends crucially on discipline-specific experience of teaching that particular concept or method. At this level the use of subject expertise is integrated with use of generic pedagogic devices and modified by experience of having undertaken this integration before. The relative roles of subject expertise, generic pedagogic devises and craft experience can be difficult for a teacher to untangle.

A final aspect of disciplinary knowledge considered here is the knowledge experienced teachers have of the ways in which students understand and misunderstand key concepts. Phenomenographic studies of students' understanding of key concepts (e.g. of the economics concept of 'price', Dahlgren, 1978) have highlighted the importance of such teacher knowledge. If students regularly make the same kinds of mistakes and pass through the same kinds of stages of sophistication of understanding of particular concepts, this is invaluable for teachers to know. Generic pedagogic devices can be used (such as getting students to articulate their common-sense conceptions before starting to grapple with scholarly alternatives) which link content and process. Generic methodologies can also be used to acquire an understanding of students' conceptions and forms of learning (Angelo and Cross, 1993) but what is learnt by using these generic methodologies can only be interpreted and used appropriately by discipline experts.

4.4 Characteristics of the discipline and the nature of disciplinary knowledge and discourse

How a discipline is taught is linked inextricably to the way knowledge is generated within the discipline and to how the discourse of the discipline functions. A student going straight from a lecture in physical geography to a lecture in human geography would probably be struck by the sudden apparent lack of 'right answers' and the confusing variety of alternative theories. There might be less quantitative data, less controlled experiments, and more scope for debate, and even opinion. Theory would be presented as an interpretive account involving disputed meanings, rather than as a 'law of nature' or involving agreed definitions. It would still be a lecture, but the nature of the knowledge presented, and what the student is supposed to do with that knowledge, would be completely different. Mary Lea (Lea and Street, 1998) has reported in previous ISL Symposia how students have difficulty understanding the different demands of even closely related disciplines. While they might be writing essay in two disciplines the nature of the discourse involved may be so different as to lead to success on one and failure in the other, wrongly diagnosed as a lack of study skill or effort.

At the Symposium, it was argued by Andy Northedge that in the social sciences what is difficult for students to grasp is not the facts, or even particular concepts or theories, but how to become a participant in social science discourse, or to become familiar with the discursive context within which those facts are significant. To be able to 'think like a sociologist' or to be familiar with the kinds of debates which sociologists engage in, may be considered to be much more important than to be able to explain about any particular sociological theorist. In History, being able to recognize that alternative interpretations of historical evidence may reflect different implicit theories of social change may be seen as much more important than to be able to remember dates or even to be able to explain the theories. In terms of Perry's scheme of intellectual and ethical development (Perry, 1970), students could probably get away with staying at Stage 1—4 for much of their science education but this would cause them difficulties even in Year 1 if they were studying Sociology or History.

These different epistemologies and discourses are reflected most obviously in the balance of teaching methods used. Science students often experience a proportionately large number of lectures presenting propositional knowledge, and attend a large number of experimental laboratory sessions in order to demonstrate laws of nature in action. Social science students experience fewer lectures but a comparatively greater volume of discussion, to debate alternative explanatory frameworks. Engineering, with its predominance of procedural knowledge, involves much practice in solving specified types of problems using standard techniques. Teacher education, with the knowledge base of professional competence less well defined, involves much work-based practice to acquire craft skills.

The extent to which these pedagogical patterns are fully justified, however, can be questioned. It is unclear why some social sciences and humanities place so little emphasis on practice in using standard methodologies (in or outside labs) and unclear why some sciences use so little discussion and present theory in so unquestioned a way. It is also obviously possible to teach disciplines in ways which do not follow so directly from their epistemology. For example some engineering is taught at Coventry University through group-based and problem-based discussion, without undertaking experimental work in labs or using conventional timetabled lectures at all (Griffiths, 1992). As we shall see below, conventions about pedagogic processes within disciplines differ more widely than one might imagine, given the supposed centrality of their epistemology and form of discourse. In other words the form of teaching is not an inevitable consequence of the form of knowledge in the discipline. So where do these forms of teaching come from?

4.5 Characteristics of disciplinary cultures

Try linking each of the discipline areas in the left-hand column of Table 4.1 with one of the associated cultural descriptions in the right hand column. My guess is that despite the unfair caricatures involved, most academics would readily agree which description linked with which discipline.

Discipline area	Cultural description
Art	Hierarchical and status-driven, formal social relations
Engineering	Adversarial, tough minded.
Business studies	Supportive but disorganized, informal social relations
Social workers	Unsociable loners but very bright
Mathematics	Principled, democratic, indecisive
History	Bohemian and individualistic
Law	Aversion to use of IT, or any 'modern' methods
Medicine	Predictable, conservative, and dressed in tweed jackets
Sociology	Pragmatic, opportunistic, and dressed in suits

Table 4.1 Characteristics of disciplinary courses

Whether or not these descriptions are fair, what is probably not in doubt is that departments have distinctive cultures and these are somewhat predictable according to their disciplines, and you can sometimes pick up aspects of these cultures within a few minutes in a department. These cultural characteristics can sometimes be related to the culture of the profession to which they are associated, for example in Law and Medicine. They are also likely to have implications for features of the teaching and learning culture, such as the level of formality and social distance involved in social relationships, the degree of negotiation and democracy involved in decision-making about the curriculum, methods and assessment, the level of organization and efficiency, and so on. It is easy to imagine a teacher mistaking a feature of disciplinary culture for an inevitable characteristic of disciplinary pedagogy. A teacher saying 'There is no place for student centred learning in my subject' might simply be reflecting the lack of democracy and student interaction which characterizes the culture of her department.

It is not just teachers who can be wrapped up in disciplinary cultures: students also have pedagogic preferences which may have nothing to do with inherent features of the discipline. It is common, for example, for engineering students to dislike having to discuss problems in groups, for design students to treat design briefs somewhat flexibly while science students do the task exactly as set and dislike open-ended projects. Student preferences may shape the forms of pedagogy commonly used in a discipline and what forms of pedagogy it may be possible to implement successfully may be constrained, at least in the short term, by disciplinary cultures.

4.6 Characteristics of disciplinary learning styles

Kolb (1984) has reported that experiential learning styles differ widely between professions and between academic disciplines. Physics is, predictably, high on abstract conceptualization and low on concrete experience. Engineering is high on active experimentation and low on reflective observation. Nursing is highly convergent while arts are highly divergent. Sociology is wholist while statistics is serialist, and so on. There might be individual cognitive differences or personal preferences which shaped the choices teachers originally made as students when initially entering disciplines. The demands of the work involved in the discipline might also be influential. For example if much of physics involves theory and mathematics rather than application, while much of engineering involves design and application based on principles developed by others in the sciences, then it is not surprising that physicists and engineers display the different learning styles that they do.

Whatever the source of these learning styles they are bound to have an impact on the choices of teaching methods that the teachers in these disciplines make. Mathematicians characteristically expect students to spend much time, on their own, thinking their way through abstract problems. Engineers expect students to spend much time in workshops applying what they have been taught in lectures in practical demonstrations. It is unclear whether this is an inevitable feature of the pedagogy of the discipline or a by-product of the learning style of the teachers in the discipline. It is also likely that students choose disciplines which involve learning processes which match their learning styles, and this can reinforce teachers' preferences for teaching methods: for example progressively emphasizing convergence rather than divergence.

However learning styles are flexible and context dependent, not fixed or 'hard-wired'. Flexible, effective learners can use all styles with equal facility. Effective teachers can accommodate a range of styles in the demands they make of students and this requires the use of a range of pedagogies. Nurse education in the UK has undergone a revolution that has drawn on the ability of nursing students to go round the complete experiential learning cycle using all learning styles in a balanced way, and this has involved new teaching and assessment methods that are more varied and balanced in their demands. It is not yet clear whether nurses educated in these new ways develop more balanced learning styles than the previous generation — the demands of their working environment may outweigh the impact of the pedagogical process that trained them. What is clear, however, is that what was perceived as the pedagogy of nursing, linked as it was to an extreme learning style, has been transformed. It was not a characteristic of the inherent pedagogy of nursing but only of the way nursing had traditionally been taught and organized in the workplace.

What some teachers may take to be an inherent characteristic of the pedagogy of their discipline may be no more than a disciplinary habit born of the learning style preferences of its members, reinforced by generations of choices. I suspect that many disciplines would benefit from pedagogies that made more balanced demands on the learning styles of their students.

4.7 Characteristics of disciplinary, institutional and national conventions in curriculum design and teaching methods

Most teachers I meet, and most papers about teaching within disciplines I read, seem to take the basic pattern of teaching, learning and assessment in their discipline for granted. When I have suggested that, for example, they might not need as many lectures, or as much class contact, or that more practice and feedback might be appropriate, I am told that I obviously do not understand the inherent demands of their discipline. But I do not have a 'taken for granted' perspective. I have had the privilege to visit, as an educational consultant, over 150 institutions in over 20 countries, and have worked in virtually every discipline area. What has struck me more than anything else is just how differently subjects are taught in different places.

Teaching engineering at the University of Lulea in northern Sweden involves perhaps five times as much laboratory work as at the University Politecnica de Catalunya in Barcelona, and at the University of Roskilde perhaps twenty times as much group project work as 100km away in Copenhagen. Engineering at the Open University in the UK is taught at a distance and yet scored a maximum 24 out of 24 in the national Teaching Quality

Assessment of its course while involving no conventional teaching at all. Engineering at the University of Southern Queensland in Australia succeeds in achieving almost all its laboratory-based educational aims through work-based learning, outside of laboratories. The assumptions of engineering lecturers about 'how engineering has to be taught' look somewhat unfounded in the light of these variations.

Class contact time for studying medicine varies from about eight hours a week to about 40 hours a week and involves methods as varied as wall-to-wall lectures and no lectures at all. Clinical experience may not start until year four or may start in week one. Assessment may involve almost exclusively single-discipline multiple-choice questions or almost exclusively interdisciplinary analysis of complex medical cases. Medical faculties have changed from one pedagogic extreme the other without the sky falling in. So what does the pedagogy of medicine really consist of?

Music is taught exclusively on a one-to-one basis in many conservatoires and exclusively with ensemble playing at others. Language teaching involves almost exclusively lectures and individual study in some universities and almost exclusively interactive, experiential and group learning in others. Some teaching of English at Oxford Brookes University shares few features in common with teaching of English at Oxford University, two miles away, other than that students read literature and write essays. Even the nature of the essays can differ almost beyond recognition. These English teachers do have crucial features in common: they both analyse cultural artefacts and they use a somewhat similar range of analytical tools in doing so. But the way they teach students how to do these things varies enormously.

Almost every taken-for-granted perspective on the 'inherent demands of the discipline' I have encountered has been totally contradicted by others in the same discipline at another institution doing things completely differently. This has perhaps made me overly sceptical about claims of the inherent nature of disciplinary pedagogy, but it has also made me feel that the onus is on disciplines to prove their case rather than for me to prove mine.

Some pedagogies are nothing to do with disciplines at all, but are institutional conventions or even national conventions, and have been adopted by disciplines without realizing that this is the case. It is not an inevitable characteristic of studying literature that it has to be supported by one-to-one tuition on an occasional basis with almost no other teaching, and yet that is how Oxford does it. Most American universities would do it with large lectures followed by smaller (though still often large) 'sections' taught by Teaching Assistants. The Oxford system would assume that much learning comes from writing and formative assessment and would expect students to write at least an essay a week. American courses might require a 'term paper'. What is obvious here is that key features of the pedagogy are to do with institutional conventions rather than with the discipline. There are often more similarities between the ways different disciplines are taught within an institution, than there are within disciplines across different institutions.

4.8 Generic teaching and learning methods

Language teaching may be characterized by the giving of immediate feedback to learners on their live performance in speaking the language (unlike, for example, teacher training, where feedback is characteristically sporadic and delayed). Medical teaching may be characterized by live 'modelling' of the diagnosis of a case, where the focus is less on the content of the specific case than on the form of analysis (unlike, for example, Law, where the analysis of cases is usually seen only after it is complete, hiding the process of analysis from sight). Design education may be characterized by the extent to which the act of design itself makes up a large component of student learning and starts at the beginning of studies (unlike, for example, science, where students actually designing their own experiments may be rare and may not begin until the third year). Engineering and computing may be characterized by the extent to which students gain weekly practice in applying concepts and using techniques learnt that week, through tackling problem sheets (unlike in social science, where concepts, methodologies and techniques are seldom applied and practised to any great extent). Many disciplines use characteristic pedagogic manoeuvres or tactics. But as in these examples there is no reason why these tactics could not be employed in other disciplines — and indeed these tactics may be used in these disciplines from time to time — they are simply less commonly used. Is it the case that teaching methods only differ between disciplines in the balance of emphasis and use?

There are a number of teaching methods about which there is a considerable body of empirical evidence concerning effectiveness, and relative effectiveness compared with other methods. For example Donald Bligh's revision of 'What's the Use of Lectures' summarises over 700 studies (Bligh, 1998). The lecture, while varying in form and function between disciplines, is a generic method and the evidence is generic evidence, usually spanning many disciplines. It may be that methods such as lectures have unique forms of effectiveness (or ineffectiveness) in specific disciplines, which the generic evidence could not predict — but the disciplines do not yet have much evidence that this is the case. Arguments for the use of lectures on disciplinary grounds, as with a paper at the Symposium arguing for the use of lectures in mathematics, seem particularly weak in the absence of evidence that Bligh's meta-analysis does not apply to them.

4.9 Generic principles of learning

The previous section focused on empirical evidence of effectiveness of specific teaching methods. This section is concerned with underlying principles of learning. There is a very substantial literature, drawn mainly from cognitive psychology, about how human learning of concepts works, how memory works, how attention works and so on. Psychology normally assumes that such human functions are universal: that if they can be observed and explained in one context then they must operate in all contexts. However these theories are based on experiments which, in the main, do not involve naturalized studies of student learning in higher education, and this sometimes limits their applicability. In the last twenty years there has been very much more work which has studied learning not in the laboratory, but in the classroom and the library, and not the learning of lists of information, but the learning of complex academic disciplines, in real courses. This has produced the insights upon which the Improving Student Learning Symposium was built. Colossal volumes of American empirical research have been summarized in meta-analyses such as Astin's comprehensive review of what makes a difference to student learning in college (Astin, 1993) and the 'Seven Principles of Good Practice in Undergraduate Education' (Chickering and Gamson, 1987). These provide the most generic principles that are available to us to guide our pedagogy. Sociologists and social psychologists have studied group functioning and how learning takes place in 'communities of practice' and have developed their own list of principles of learning in social settings. There is no shortage of such generic principles for disciplines to learn from. But are all disciplines equally subject to these generic principles?

At the Symposium there was a fascinating presentation about the pedagogy of languages. In it a videotape was shown of an *ab initio* Russian language class, using a 'total immersion' method. The audience was asked to identify the pedagogic methods and principles involved. These included:

- much repetition by the instructor;
- much oral practice by the students — doing, not just listening passively, and involving all students;
- careful structuring of each stage in the presentation and practice so that each rule was introduced one at a time and added to the next rule until quite a complex set of grammar rules had been built up;
- practice at combining and using the rules in familiar and in new ways;
- providing an enjoyable and socially safe environment in which to practice and perform.

The particular application of these principles was unique to language teaching and looked nothing like any teaching I have ever seen in engineering, for example. The degree of repetition used would be unlikely to be required anywhere in engineering. However all the above principles still apply to all other disciplines. Repetition is a feature of practice in tackling problems or using equipment in engineering too. Careful structuring of explanations and building from the simple to the complex, active learning, socially supportive environments, these are all generic pedagogic principles, though they may have particular forms of applicability to language learning and different forms of applicability to engineering learning. I have seldom seen so many sound principles packed into such a short period of teaching, and the instructor had to be experienced as a language teacher and to know her Russian fluently to apply these principles effectively. But at the level of pedagogic principles there was nothing new here.

It seems distinctly possible that there are in fact no non-generic learning principles. There isn't an addendum to the 'Seven Principles of Undergraduate Education' which says 'these principles apply to everything except Egyptology and Inorganic Chemistry'. They are generic principles which it would be reasonable to assume applied to everything until it had been demonstrated otherwise.

One exception may be in languages. It has been argued that there is a unique human ability to learn language involving a 'language acquisition device' that enables children to learn both grammar and vocabulary, at an astonishing rate and with great accuracy, simply by engaging in meaningful communication, without any formal instruction. This theory has had much influence on forms of language teaching, though this language acquisition device may have an upper limit on the age at which it operates effectively and requires more massive practice and more meaningful communication than can be provided easily in classrooms. The 'total immersion' class seen on the video described above did not in fact simulate the confused and drawn-out nature of everyday language acquisition in children, but was highly structured and condensed, using generic principles of learning. To my knowledge there has been no suggestion that humans have a 'sociology acquisition device' with unique characteristics, or any other such discipline-specific learning capabilities.

Another exception may be Mathematics. Mathematicians have developed their own language and way of describing what is going on in mathematics education (see for example

Mason, 1999). What is distinctive about much of this literature is the way mathematics itself is woven into the explanations and examples of principles. It is difficult or impossible to disentangle the pedagogy from the mathematics, and that is perhaps what is distinctive about it. It is clear that there are generic principles that apply to mathematics education. For example the cognitive psychology information processing capacity principle of 'the magic number seven plus or minus two' can be used to 'chunk' long mathematical proofs so that each chunk is of no more than five lines, and has a label identifying the heuristic involved. This greatly helps students to understand and remember proofs. Many of Mason's pedagogic suggestions can be understood as developing mathematically specific forms of 'metacognitive strategies' in students. To what extent the mathematics literature can largely be interpreted in terms of general psychological principles of cognition, concept formation, learning and memory, is still open to debate. Mathematicians seem keen to assert the uniqueness of their pedagogy and psychologists seem keen to assert the generality of theirs, but have trouble with the maths. Like languages, mathematics has its own language, and that may be its primary distinctiveness.

4.10 Methodologies for researching disciplinary pedagogy

At the Symposium Mary Huber from the Carnegie Institute argued that teachers from the disciplines should not have to become social scientists in order to develop the scholarship of teaching of their discipline. Instead she encourages teachers to exploit the methodology and discourse of their own discipline. For example a literature teacher might exploit stories and analogies from literature itself in illuminating teaching situations, or use the methodology of discourse analysis to understand an interaction with a student. A technologist might use systems theory to analyse nested levels of systems within which student learning takes place. A medic might design and undertake experimental studies involving quantitative measurements and a control group, and use familiar statistical methods to analyse the data. In this sense the methodology for studying and improving teaching might also be seen as discipline-specific.

It would be difficult to argue against the potential for richer and more varied methodologies that this approach might offer. It might also be harsh to deny teachers from within disciplines the comfort they might feel working within familiar paradigms. However it is not surprising that the social sciences have made most progress in making sense of student learning. These, after all, are the disciplines which have developed methodologies and theories specifically to study and explain human behaviour and performance. It would be odd, indeed, and an indictment of the social sciences, if methodologies from other disciplines proved more powerful or useful to make sense of pedagogy, whatever discipline it took place in. The psychology of learning does not exclude the learning of geology and the social psychology of groups does not exclude insights into the behaviour of groups of geology students. Often the theories and methodologies developed by social scientists need adapting to make them even more appropriate to specific contexts, but that does not invalidate their applicability. The theory and methodology of sedimentology, in contrast, is unlikely to have much to offer to the understanding of the pedagogy of geology, however much it was adapted. My own view is that to study and improve teaching, teachers from all disciplines *do* have to become social scientists, to some extent, because it is an aspect of human behaviour that they are engaged in and are studying, not an aspect of, for example, sediments.

4.11 Conclusion

This chapter was written, quite deliberately, as an antidote to the claims made by most of the papers at the Symposium, that their discipline has a unique pedagogy. It probably overstates the degree of generality of pedagogies, and under-estimates the importance of those elements of pedagogy which are discipline-specific. It is perhaps best seen as providing a series of tests against which any claim of discipline specificity of pedagogy could be checked.

Note

1. Graham Gibbs is Professor and Director of Research at the Centre for Higher Education Practice at the Open University. He has recently been writing (generic) distance learning materials for courses on teaching and course design for teachers in higher education. These materials contain discipline-specific examples of the application of generic principles. The courses have discipline-specific tutors and tutor-groups. The courses have recently added discipline-specific materials on the teaching of Maths and Languages.

4.12 References

Angelo, T.A. and Cross, K.P. (1993) *Classroom Assessment Techniques: A Handbook for College Faculty*, 2nd edn. San Francisco: Jossey-Bass.

Astin, A.W. (1993) *What Matters in College? Four critical years revisited*. San Francisco: Jossey Bass.

Bligh, D. (1998) *What's the Use of Lectures?*, 5th edn. Exeter: Intellect.

Chickering, A.W. and Gamson, Z.F. (1987) Seven principles for good practice in undergraduate education, *American Association for Higher Education Bulletin* **39**, 3—7.

Dahlgren, L.O. (1978) Qualitative differences in conceptions of basic principles in economics: A contribution to the discussion of the validity of examination results. *4th International Conference on Higher Education*. University of Lancaster.

Griffiths, P. (1992) Problem-based learning in Automotive Engineering Design. In Gibbs, G. (ed.), *Improving the Quality of Student Learning*. Bristol: Technical and Educational Services.

Hattie, J. and Marsh, H.W. (1996) The relationship between research and teaching: a meta-analysis, *Review of Educational Research* **66**(4), 507—42.

Kolb, D. (1984) *Experiential Learning*. N.J.: Prentice-Hall.

Lea, M. and Street, B (1998) Student writing in higher education: an academic literacies approach, *Studies in Higher Education* **23**(2).

Mason, J. (1999) *Teaching Mathematics in Higher Education*. Milton Keynes: Open University.

Percy, K. and Ramsden, P. (1980) *Independent Study*. Research into Higher Education Monographs. Guildford: Society for Research into Higher Education.

Perry, W.G. (1970) *Forms of Intellectual and Ethical Development in the College Years: A Scheme*. New York: Holt, Rinehart & Winston

Rogers, C. (1969) *Freedom to Learn*. Columbus, Ohio: Merrill.

5 Background to the territory — human cognition and student learning

Roger Lindsay
Psychology Department, Oxford Brookes University

5.1 Overview

This chapter aims to develop a model that is useful in understanding the main features of student learning. The form taken by the model is grounded in an account of evolving views of explanation in Psychology. The content of the model is justified by considering landmark studies and key issues. Some examples of implications and applications of the model are discussed.

5.2 In the beginning — associationism begat structuralism and behaviourism

The oldest and most spectacular fissure cutting through theories of the nature and origin of human knowledge is that which divides rationalism from empiricism. Rationalism, already to be found more or less fully worked out in the writings of Plato tends not so much to explain learning, as to explain it away. Knowledge comes not from the senses but from reason, and is not of the apparent world but of some more ideal version. Empiricists generally took the world to be more as it seems, and focused their enquiries on how we come to know it as we do. Empiricism is the historical progenitor of psychological learning theories, though many compromises needed to be forged with rationalist critics before empiricist dogmas began to resemble scientific theory.

Empiricism developed from a philosophical tradition going back at least to Aristotle, who provided empiricist philosophy with the beginnings of a theoretical approach, as well as an epistemology. The epistemology was the doctrine that human knowledge comes from the senses, and its source and object is the familiar external physical world of everyday experience. If our knowledge of the world comes from learning, what is learning and how is knowledge produced by it? This is at bottom, not a philosophical question but a psychological question, and the answer however crude, was at least a first approximation to a psychological theory. The theoretical approach which Aristotle proposed was called *associationism*.

Associationism was to be reformulated, refined and elaborated over the next 2000 years. Anderson and Bower (1973) suggest that associationism is more a theoretical framework than a theory, as endless variations around the same core set of assumptions can be formulated. These assumptions themselves Anderson and Bower call *metafeatures of associationism* and characterize as four in number:

1. the *atomist* assumption;
2. the *reductionist* assumption;
3. the *sensationalist* assumption;
4. the *mechanist* assumption.

An archetypal associationist theory would thus presuppose that human knowledge arises from a learning process. It would then assert that knowledge is built up from elementary components (atomism) which are connected together by the mental processes of association. Psychological explanation of knowledge thus takes the form of analysing knowledge into the components of which it is formed (reductionism) and specifying the associative processes which operate to combine them together. In an empiricist theory the basic elements of knowledge are most commonly identified with simple sensations (sensationalism), and the rules by which sensations are combined together are invariably assumed to be simple, serial and linear (mechanism).

For most of the 2000 year period during which associationism went virtually unquestioned as the theoretical framework within which human learning was to be explained, it went hand in hand with a method of enquiry which seemed similarly to be without rival or alternative. This universally accepted methodology was *introspection*. Introspection, the use of a supposed faculty of 'inner vision' to investigate mind was not *a*, but *the* method of investigating psychological states and processes. The point could be illustrated by quoting from any one of hundreds of thinkers during the period between Classical Greek thought and the nineteenth century. A typical example is the British Empiricist philosopher Thomas Hobbes: 'Whosover looketh into himself, and considereth what he doth, when he does *think, opine, reason, hope, fear* &c. and upon what grounds, he shall thereby read and know what are the thoughts and passions of all other men upon the like occasion.' Hobbes recommends readers to inspect his writings and views of the mind and: 'to consider if he also find not the same in himself. For this kind of doctrine admitteth no other demonstration' (Hobbes, 1651).

In the light of this history, it is hardly surprising that when psychology finally began to establish itself as an independent area of enquiry, to be pursued along scientific lines, associationist theory and the methodology of introspection were the two most prominent features of the infant discipline. The person generally credited with explicitly pushing to make psychology a science was Wilhelm Wundt, and the symbolic event which demonstrated his intention was the establishment of the first psychological laboratory at Leipzig in 1879. Wundt's belief was that the failure to make any discernible progress in psychology for two thousand years was not because associationist theory and introspective methods didn't work, but because they had not been pursued with sufficient rigour. He sought to remedy this by carefully training observers to use the method of introspection, by teaching them a specialized vocabulary, and by systematically controlling the conditions under which introspective reports were collected. The label which historians of psychology give to Wundt and those who shared his approach is *structuralism*: the systematic use of introspection to analyse conscious events into their elementary components, and to isolate the laws and principles which operate to combine simple elements of consciousness into more complex experiences.

Ironically, taking introspection into the laboratory did not amplify its strengths and so impel psychology into a new period of scientific progress. Instead it led to progress in psychology by exposing the impossibility of basing an empirical science on introspective methods. The chief problem was that even under the most carefully controlled conditions, and when trained in technique and terminology, observers still produced conflicting introspective reports. When conflicts occurred, they could not be rationally settled because introspective reports of conscious experience cannot be checked by third parties. It also became clear that many well-practised psychological processes, for example adding two digits together, were not accompanied by relevant conscious experiences at all. Introspection it appeared, could not be applied to much of human mental experience and when it could be applied, it does not yield findings which are consistent, replicable and cumulative: the basic requirements of any methodology which can support scientific progress.

While the failure of structuralism might seem like a disappointment, it actually triggered psychology's first great leap forward — the abandonment of introspection as a primary methodology. The reaction to structuralism's failure came with the publication of John Watson's paper 'Psychology as the behaviorist views it' (Watson, 1913), and had two key components: replacement of introspection with objective methods, and rejection of consciousness as part of the subject matter of psychology. Watson had carried out his doctoral research into the behaviour of dogs, and this experience had made him very aware of the limitations of introspection. Instead he advocated that psychology should investigate publicly observable behaviour, not privately experienced consciousness. Only in this way could the findings of the new science be exposed to the quality controls that are fundamental to scientific enquiry, and connect ontologically with the investigations of publicly accessible reality carried out by other sciences.

If the shift to an objectivist methodology was essential to the development of a scientific psychology, the rejection of consciousness as a legitimate part of its domain was an irrelevance and a mistake. Its effect was to put whole tracts of psychological phenomena outside the pale: perception, memory, creative thinking, intentional behaviour, language, and aesthetics to mention but a few examples. Much of the next half century was to be taken up by the need to demonstrate that mental phenomena which are not directly accessible to public inspection are central features of the psychological landscape. Watson's mistake was to conflate together the two concepts of *basic data* and *legitimate phenomena*. He was right to argue that because they can't be checked or replicated, introspective reports cannot be included among basic data in psychology. He was wrong to conclude that this means that mental constructs must be excluded from psychology altogether.

Behaviourism also had a second major weakness: its failure to challenge associationist theory. Superficially, behaviourism seems to differ dramatically from structuralism. Its fundamental units are not sensations and experiences, but Stimulus—Response (S—R) bonds. Its mechanisms of learning are not the laws of association, but the principles of conditioning. How different this seems. If we return to Anderson and Bower's (1973) metafeatures of associationism however, it becomes clear that in truth nothing much has changed. The atoms are S—R bonds rather than elements of conscious experience, but the atoms are still there. Complex behaviour is explained in terms of the simpler conditioning processes which underlie it, rather than in terms of association between ideas but explanation is still reductionist. Sensations take the form of physical stimuli rather perceptual events, but the system is still driven by sensory events. And the principles of conditioning are certainly no less mechanistic than the laws of association. While behaviourism brought about a revolutionary change in how psychological knowledge is established, it did little to change how that knowledge is organized and understood beyond relabelling terminology and proscribing any theoretical terms with mental referents.

Before psychology was fully ready to begin the establishment of a scientific knowledge-base, it was necessary to remove the restrictive assumptions which behaviourism imposed upon both the domain and the content of psychological theory. Early challenges came from Gestalt psychology, and even from within learning theory. By the late 1950s, they arose on every side. Mentalism was triumphantly reintroduced and the limitations of associationism finally became understood.

5.3 The cognitive underground and technological change

The central problems addressed by academic psychology when it began to establish itself as an independent discipline were largely inherited from philosophy, and focused on how knowledge is acquired through perception and learning. Oddly, thinking and reasoning remained largely outside the domain of psychology, mainly because these faculties were generally considered to be unproblematic. At least from Aristotle onwards philosophy had made great strides in formalizing reasoning through the study of logic. This area of enquiry saw further rapid developments during the second half of the nineteenth century. Thinking and reasoning were considered unproblematic because it seemed obvious that thought was nothing more than the application of the rules of logic. Teaching problem-solving involved no more than teaching logic, and the only job remaining for psychology was explaining why people sometimes made errors in reasoning (Woodworth and Sells, 1925). This independence of the study of rational thought from the rest of psychology was partly responsible for the development of the technology of IQ testing, with its assumptions that knowledge is not relevant to reasoning ability, and that intellectual power can be measured by assessing performance on content-free logic problems. A second consequence of the idea that rational thought and the ability to do logic were identical was the fostering of an unduly optimistic attitude to artificial intelligence. After all, if the equation worked, then machines which can do logic are capable of rational thought. The progressive demonstration that there is more to thinking than logic, but that machines might be able to help illuminate these other processes as well has been a unique consequence of twentieth-century technology.

An influential demonstration that humans don't simply solve problems by applying logic was developed by P. C. Wason (Wason, 1966). Figure 5.1 presents two versions of a task which requires participants to evaluate an inference of the form '*if p then q*'. Version 1 uses abstract symbols, Version 2 substitutes meaningful objects in a real world version of the task. A large majority of people who try to solve Version 1 get it wrong (the answer is 'E' and '7'). An equally large majority get Version 2 right. (the answer is '£100' and unsigned reverse). Logically these two problem variants are identical, yet *psychologically* they are very different. So people can't just be doing logic.

The conceptual developments necessary to analyse and explain mental phenomena could not entirely arise from inside the discipline of psychology. The core of explanation is the demonstration of a fruitful analogy between phenomena in a problem domain, and phenomena in a second domain which is better understood. A major problem for psychologists has been identifying plausible models for explaining mind — mind just didn't seem to resemble anything else in the world. During the twentieth century a series of technological innovations have occurred which have led to the development of mind-like artifacts. This process actually began in the nineteenth century when Charles Babbage devised his celebrated 'Difference-Engine', a physical device of cogs and pulleys which in principle was capable of doing arithmetic. A much more important development was the realization by Claude Shannon that any set of well-formed formulae in truth functional logic could be modelled using electrical circuits consisting of switches and relays. Logic is not a unique capability of brains, but a consequence of the way physical systems are organized.

The version at the top is the 'classical' version and very few people get it right. The version at the bottom uses familiar instead of abstract materials and very few people get it wrong. (Note: cards are used in actual demonstrations and there is then no need for the italicized indication of 'front' and 'reverse'.

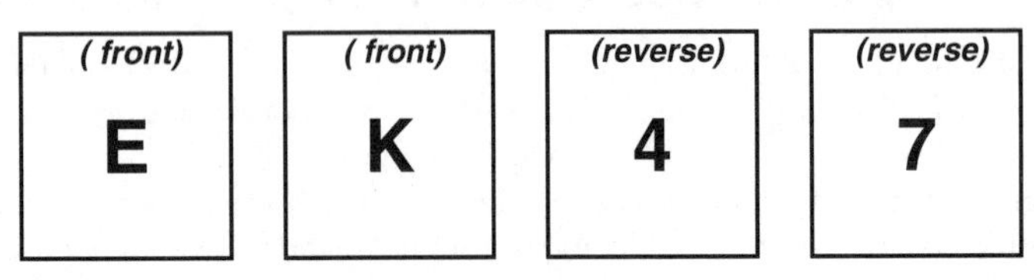

Version 1

The four cards above are drawn from a pack, all of which have a letter on one side and a number on the other.

Consider this rule:
'If a card has a vowel one side, then it has an even number on the other.'

Which cards is it essential to turn over in order to establish whether the rule is false?

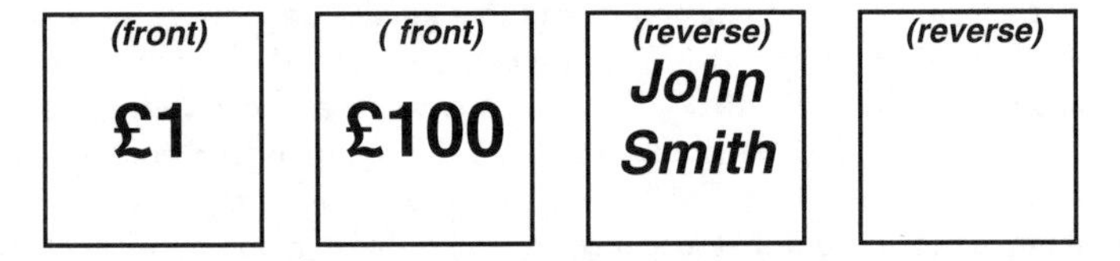

Version 2

The four cheques above have been accepted by a shop which asks its till assistants to observe the following rule:

'If a cheque is for £5.00 or more then the customer is required to sign the reverse.'

Which cheques is it essential to turn over to establish whether the rule has been obeyed?

Figure 5.1 Two versions of Wason's Selection Task (Wason, 1966)

In 1949 Shannon and Weaver carried this insight a good deal further with the development of the mathematical theory of information (Shannon and Weaver, 1949). The conceptual significance of this development is hard to overstate. Descartes had made one immense step forward when he had suggested that physical behaviour had a naturalistic explanation. He believed that nerves worked the muscles like the wires and rods which controlled the puppets and marionettes in vogue at the time he wrote. Despite the demonstration by Volta and Fritz and Hitzig during the nineteenth century that both peripheral nerves and the brain itself were not mechanical, but electrical in nature, the model of psychological causality underlying behaviourism remained a mechanical one. Stimuli were thought to cause responses as a result of physical links, just as pressing a key causes an organ to emit a musical note. Part of the reason for this was the absence of any model of physical events which allows them to be independent of the structures through which they are realized. Information Theory provided such a model. Information requires physical events for its expression, but it is not identical with the events themselves, but with the relations between them. The same information can be freely translated from one set of physical inter-relationships to another: for example from a distribution of magnetized particles on a tape or disk, to an array of switch settings and from that to a set of voltages controlling the movement of a speaker cone or the luminance of phosphor elements in a CRT.

If information theory freed psychology from the search for mechanical causes, the development of stored programme digital computers provided it with an example of physically realizable systems that are controlled by symbol sequences. The theoretical work of Turing (1951) and then the physical development of Von Neumann computers gave psychologists models of systems which didn't fit the behaviourist world view. To explain the behaviour of a Von Neumann computer it was necessary to refer to the program controlling it; yet that program was not a part of the computer's observable behaviour. The idea of an unobservable sequence of symbols controlling a physical system was not only not philosophically absurd, it was readily demonstrable. Much the same conclusion followed from Wiener's work on cybernetics (Wiener, 1948). If anything violates behaviourist assumptions about the control of behaviour, it is the idea that people might behave as they do because of intentions and purposes they have formed. What could be more thoroughly mental? Yet Wiener's work showed that prosaic physical systems such as boiler/radiator/thermostat loops, or ballistic missiles could easily be controlled by the discrepancy between a symbolically represented state and the present state of the system.

5.4 Psychology comes of age — the 'Cognitive Revolution'

By the late 1950s all of the ingredients for psychology's next big step forward were in place. The Gestalt psychologists had demonstrated that perceptual interpretation requires processes that are both mental and not susceptible to reductionist explanation, and that human problem-solving also seems to depend upon conscious structuring of the task environment (Koffka, 1935; Kohler, 1925; Duncker, 1945). Tolman had produced convincing demonstrations that even the laboratory rat establishes abstract cognitive maps of the environment, as well as learning particular responses (Tolman, Ritchie and Kalish, 1946). Krechevsky (1932) and others had shown that even to explain maze-learning behaviour in rats it was necessary to suppose that they tested abstract hypotheses. Blodgett (1929) provided convincing evidence that animals would learn without reward, while Butler (1954) argued compellingly that monkeys are motivated by cognitive drives such as curiosity. In a direct challenge to behaviourist assumptions Bruner, Goodnow and Austin (1956) published a book called *A Study of Thinking* which investigated mental strategies in hypothesis testing among college students. Broadbent's (1958) *Perception and Communication* argued that mental processes underlie selective attention, and proposed a whole decision-making apparatus involving memory systems and communication channels to explain the data he reported.

The combined effect of all of these studies made it impossible to resist the idea that mental constructs which are not directly observable are nevertheless an indispensable part of psychological explanation. But in acknowledging the need for mental constructs, psychology was not just flipping back to structuralism. For one thing, the methodological lessons of behaviourism had been well-learned: psychological theory must be tested against publicly observable data. But this doesn't rule out theoretical constructs which can't be observed — even physicists allow themselves to postulate unobservable processes, for example occurring deep inside the sun, providing the theory which includes them is objectively testable. For another, the development of mechanical information processing devices meant that generic physical models of unobservable mental processes were already in existence, and specific models of the processes underlying particular behaviours had become a practical possibility.

By the second half of the 1950s it was beginning to look as if progress in developing of a satisfactory framework for the development of a scientific psychology could be summarized through the following formulae:

(1) Structuralism = mentalist associationist theory + introspectionist methodology
(2) Behaviourism = non-mentalist associationist theory + objectivist methodology
(3) Cognitive Psychology = mentalist associationist theory + objectivist methodology

At the end of the 1950s associationist theory itself finally came under critical attack. The precipitating cause was the publication of B. F. Skinner's *Verbal Behaviour*, a bold if not hubristic attempt to account for human language within the framework of behaviourist assumptions (Skinner, 1957). The precipitated consequence was Noam Chomsky's devastating review of Skinner's book (Chomsky, 1959), which not only held up for inspection the shortcomings of behaviourism's account of language, but also displayed its general deficiencies as an account of complex behaviour. Here are some of the central points of the critique. Behaviourism supposes that verbal behaviour is elicited as an associative response to the stimulus environment, yet language behaviour is striking because it is so evidently context free. People can speak of mountains while deep in mines. Behaviourism supposes that sequences of verbal items are learned, yet most of the sentences that people produce are original, and people can produce sentences which are indefinitely long. Bever, Fodor and Garrett (1968) formalized the implicit argument against associationism by describing the grammar of an artificial language whose sentences are symmetrical reflections about their mid- point. This language is easily learned; but its grammar requires an abstract term (that doesn't feature in any of the sentences. Using this device, the grammar of Mirror Language is captured in rules 1—3 in Table 5.1. Associationism requires rules 1a—4a to generate the sentences of mirror language, but these rules also generate non-sentences such as aabb.

Sentences	*Non-sentences*	*Rules*			*Non-rules*
aa	ab	1.	X →[1] aXa	1a.	a→ a
abba	aabb	2.	X → bXb	2a.	a → b
aabbaa	aabaab	3.	X→ ϕ [2]	3a.	b→ b
ababbaba	abababab			4a.	b → a

1 The → symbol is commonly used in linguistics as an element of "rewrite" rules. "X→Y" is to be read as "Rewrite the expression 'X' as the expression 'Y'".
2 The ϕ symbol is used in linguistics to mean the "null" symbol. X→ϕ is to be read as "Rewrite the expression 'X' as a null symbol" It is equivalent to deleting X from an expression.

Table 5.1 Rules of a Mirror-image Language

The implications of these arguments are clear. Language behaviour cannot be explained by lists specifying what can be followed by what, it also requires rules which refer to the abstract structure of behaviour. This is a complicated way of saying that cognitive psychology needed to abandon associationism to embrace something like (4) below:

(4) Cognitive Psychology = mentalist theory + objectivist methodology

With this final liberating move, the 'cognitive revolution' was complete.

5.5 Converging on consensus — modelling the cognitive system

During the first half of the 1960s the paradigm shift to cognitive psychology swept through academic departments in UK and US universities. By the second half of the decade it had become the new standard theory. Learning theory began to disappear from syllabuses and attention, memory and language began to take its place. Equally telling, the university student began to replace the laboratory rat as the standard participant in psychological experiments. The conceptual progress implicit in the shift to the cognitive paradigm was immense. It centred on the shift to methodological objectivism, the abandonment of associationism in favour of a methodologically disciplined mentalism, and the recognition of information and symbolic control as the appropriate conceptual framework for psychology. But much more than this seemed to have become clear. The stored-program computer provided a valuable model for the mind-brain relationship, but it also seemed to make clear and explicit the explanatory goals of psychology as a discipline. If human behaviour is controlled by an underlying program which is symbolic and abstract (in the sense that not all of its referring expressions directly denote elements of observable behaviour), then the central goal of psychology is to investigate and describe this program. Psychology's goal will be accomplished when the description is sufficiently complete to allow the program to be compiled and run on computer. That is, when human behaviour can be successfully simulated.

During its associationist phase psychology had obviously been theoretically deficient in some pretty fundamental respects. Less obviously, it had also been *meta*theoretically deficient. It had not been at all clear what form a psychological theory should take, how theories should be tested, nor what a successful theory should accomplish. There was now for the first time, a recognition of these metatheoretical questions, and a theoretical approach which offered an answer. Unfortunately, it was soon to become clear that the proposed answer wasn't entirely successful.

5.6 Acknowledging diversity — the problem of individual differences

One immediate problem with the program-reconstruction/behaviour-simulation strategy is fixing the scope of the behaviour to be explained. One answer is to seek to explain the whole of cognition in one go, but this has a vanishingly small chance of success, and a putative explanation of the whole cognitive system would have so many parameters that failure would be unilluminating. How would an investigator know what to modify? On the other hand 'divide and conquer' approaches produce the 'decoupling' problem — how can a simulation of language behaviour work without making assumptions about perception, memory, problem-solving etc. And if the simulation fails, is this because of intrinsic faults or assumption-failure? Finding a principled solution to this problem remains a serious challenge.

From the viewpoint of a psychologist interested in student learning, there is a second and equally fundamental problem. If the goal of psychology is to specify the cognitive program underlying human behaviour, doesn't this imply that everybody has the same program? If the program is reconstructed and run, whose behaviour will it resemble? The explanatory strategy rapidly begins to look unsatisfactory when individual differences between learners is brought into the picture. This concern was given substance by a study reported by Hunt, Marin and Stone (1966). Hunt *et al.* were trying to write a computer program which modelled human performance in a concept formation task. In tasks of this kind, the investigator defines a universe of objects (e.g. every card that bears **one** or **two**, **large** or **small**, **triangles** or **circles** upon it). The experimenter then defines one attribute combination (e.g. any card bearing a **small triangle**) as the concept to be identified. Participants are told whether or not a number of objects from the object universe are exemplars of the concept. They must then try to specify the attributes defining the experimental concept.

Hunt *et al.* discovered that no single program could model the behaviour of their participants as a group. However, a series of computer programs giving a good approximation to the decision performance of participants could be written when the group was subdivided into Psychology students, History students, Mathematics students and students from the Stanford University Gifted Students Program. Much the same methodological moral emerges from evidence of cross-cultural differences in cognition (Cole, Gay, Glick and Sharp, 1971), or most dramatically by extreme individual performance which is sometimes not readily compatible with theoretical models of normal memory (Klatzky, 1975).

The implication of individual differences in cognition is that the human cognitive system must be seen more as more like a programming environment, or 'cognitive architecture' (Newell 1990) than as a specific program or suite of programmes. This insight provides a welcome increase in theoretical flexibility, while simultaneously making the business of generating precise and testable predictions very much harder.

5.7 Defrosting cognition — introducing motivation and emotion

It is a basic fact about cognition that logic can never supply a reason for action. Cognitive processing can elaborate *means* but cannot establish *ends*. Cognitive Psychology has ignored this fact for most of the time for which it has been the dominant paradigm. The explanation is probably that the 'springs of action' lie in motivation and emotion, and these processes are easily put aside as affective rather than cognitive. In addition to the general problem of why anyone does *anything* in student learning there are also more specific problems such as why students choose to go to university? Why they study particular disciplines? Why they do, or don't drop out and why and under what conditions they change their beliefs and activate or modify their knowledge bases? This treatment of cognition as independent of affect is sometimes referred to as 'cold cognition', by contrast with 'hot cognition' (Abelson, 1963) which incorporates such factors as motivation, mood, emotion and even psychopathology. During the 1970s, the absence of any satisfactory general treatment of the affective domain began to be seen as a scandal, much as behaviourism lost credibility in the 1950s for ignoring language. In the 1980s however, the deficiency began to be remedied and cognitive explanations of emotion in particular began to emerge as a major research area (Frijda, 1986; Strongman 1996).

Cognitive Psychology is well equipped to handle motivation. We saw earlier that one of its precursors was a rejection of a mechanistic framework within which human behaviour was the product of extrinsic causes. Cybernetics had rehabilitated purposive explanation by showing that a goal representation can be internal and symbolic, and yet suffice to physically control behaviour. This emphasis on internal control was an explicit part of Cognitive Psychology from its inception, featuring for example as a central theme of one of the formative manifestos of the new theoretical approach (Miller, Galanter and Pribram 1960). Despite this theoretical capability, in practice Cognitive Psychology has been slow to provide detailed or practically applicable accounts of the role of motivation in cognition and learning.

5.8 Student learning

The development of the information processing approach to mind did a huge amount to construct a theoretical framework within which, for the first time, an account of student learning became possible. The construction of this framework required the preliminary demolition of numerous obstacles to progress: the utility of introspection as a methodology, the sufficiency of logic as an explanation of rational thought, the adequacy of associationist theory and the restrictive assumption that causes of behaviour must be physical and extrinsic to the organism being some of the most important. But the information processing approach did not immediately lead to a theoretical account of student learning, instead it became preoccupied with seeking to develop models of human performance in restricted task environments (called 'experimental paradigms') such as selective attention and free recall. In part this was undoubtedly a reaction to the failure of grand theoretical schemes of the past, in part a response to the decoupling problem. Over twenty years or so, theoretical understanding from these limited-scope modelling exercises began to pool and accumulate in four major domains: analysis of perceptual input; cognitive control processes; memory, particularly for verbal information, and motor skills. While a great number of well-grounded and empirically reliable statements can now be made in these areas, this is a long way from constituting a theory of student learning. Student learning as the process underlying assessed performance in Higher Education is quintessentially a product of the whole cognitive/affective system. The explanatory strategy of divide and conquer does not yet enable knowledge in separate investigative domains to be synthesized into a coherent model. As a starting point for the development of student-learning-oriented model of cognition it might be helpful to briefly review current understanding in the four areas where coherent theoretical progress has been made.

5.8.1 Perceptual analysis

Information is captured via sensory receptors and held in a modality-specific Sensory Memory (SM) for a second or two. Some proportion of this incident information activates related information in a long-term memory (LTM) store. If activated information is relevant to current goals or triggers an automatic interrupt (as for example a pain signal might), then some version of it, often in a verbal format, becomes available to awareness and to a

Working Memory (WM). Information in WM remains available for 10—15 seconds but may be held for longer periods via rehearsal. WM is the component of the cognitive system which assembles information relevant to current goals into plans which allow these goals to be attempted or achieved. WM also takes over control if a plan being 'automatically' implemented (i.e. without WM involvement), for example as a program of motor commands subserving locomotion, is interrupted. In the case of a student listening to a lecture, this process will consist of spoken words being auditorily perceived and triggering related information in LTM. If the student is currently trying to understand what is being said, the verbal material that becomes available to WM can now be used to formulate plans for writing notes, or for creating new LTM entries or cross connections via rehearsal processes.

5.8.2 Attention and control

WM takes decisions slowly, and only makes one or two of them at a time, consequently it has a restricted capacity to process information rapidly. As WM monitors goal selection and pursuit, sensory inputs, motor programme execution (e.g. actions or speech), some memory input/output processes and emotional state, as well as the construction and implemention of plans, there is a constant need to apply priorities justifying allocation of WM space. Allocation of WM space corresponds to 'paying attention'. Presence in WM is closely associated with conscious awareness, though it is doubtful if the relationship is one of identity. WM control of action is not necessary when plans are sufficiently developed and explicit to cope with every contingency in their implementation environment. So WM seeks to develop plans to this point and remove itself from the control loop. The distinction between control processes which require WM involvement and those which do not is often made by distinguishing between 'controlled' and 'automatic' processes. A lecturer trying to maximize the quantity of student learning must do so by maximizing the quantity of lecture-relevant information which captures WM space. This might involve for example, using language which triggers LTM activity (instead of unfamiliar jargon), ensuring that students identify and accept current goals to which lecture information is relevant, helping students to relate information to goals as it becomes cognitively available, suppressing speech and action sequences which are not lecture-relevant, and making an effort to produce lecture-relevant emotions which cognitively displace lecture-irrelevant emotions.

5.8.3 Memory

The pre-cognitive concept of *learning* is closely tied to the idea of forming associations between sensory impressions or stimuli and responses. It has been largely replaced by the idea of forming and elaborating representations within memory. Most models of memory assume that memory is organized around the representation of objects (e.g. 'book'; 'amoeba'; 'electron'). Events are then constructed out of linked collections of objects. Learning can thus take two basic forms: making a new entry in memory, or constructing a new relationship between existing entries. Making a new entry in memory can in turn be decomposed into three sub-processes: concept formation (development of the abstract representation itself); stimulus learning (acquiring the perceptual 'call-sign' for the concept) and response learning (developing the articulatory programme required to name the concept. New conceptual relationships may be very simple (e.g. learning that a known object has an unsuspected property) or very complex (e.g. constructing a model of the relationships between people and places described in a novel). It has become common to follow Tulving (1972) in distinguishing between *episodic* and *semantic* memory. Episodic memory is supposed to record episodes, often biographical, which occurred at particular times and places. Semantic memory records timeless generic information such as 'cats have fur'. Particular acts of memory (for example, a student memorizing facts from a lecture) are generally believed to require the deliberate construction of new connections between the information currently in WM and other material in WM. There is substantial evidence that people may choose between 'shallow processing' leading to storage of the particular perceptual representation within which information is presented and 'deep processing' that involves transforming, recoding and elaborating information (obviously, this is a continuum, not a simple dichotomy). Deep processing appears to produce more durable memory traces. Cognitive Psychologists have also identified a kind of future-oriented memory called 'prospective memory'. Prospective memory enables people to remember to take medication in three hours' time, or to go to a lecture on Tuesday. Student learning often involves something rather like prospective memory in the sense that students may seek, not just to remember some collection of concepts and facts, but to organize that collection of concepts and facts so that it (and as little else as possible) becomes available in a specific assessment context.

5.8.4 Skill acquisition

Motor skills are usually assumed by cøgnitive psychologists to be different in kind from propositional knowledge and it is common to signal this difference by distinguishing procedural knowledge ('knowing how') from declarative knowledge ('knowing that'). Most of the basic muscular routines which make up speech and action are acquired in early life. Skill acquisition for adults therefore consists of learning to produce particular sequences of already-learned elements efficiently, in particular contexts, without the intervention of WM. It is a familiar paradox in the skills literature that whereas expert performance can only occur once WM has been removed from the control loop, conscious awareness of the control process requires WM involvement. It follows that, while experts are unaware of the processes underlying their performance, anyone who is aware is not an expert performer. This clearly has implications for the methodological limitations upon phenemenological analysis and introspective reporting. These generalizations apply to language production as well as physical action. It is evident that people are generally unaware of the cognitive processes underlying speech — for example phoneme articulation or grammatical sequencing — even quite complex cliché sentences may be articulated without conscious attention. It is doubtful whether this capability embraces novel sentences which might be expected to involve WM precisely because of the novel element involved. The principles involved in skill learning are unsurprising given the processes involved. The chief objective is to create an efficient (i.e. containing few or no redundant elements) motor program that is under environmental control and so requires no WM intervention. This objective is only satisfied when the program incorporates definitions of the perceptual conditions associated with every possible error condition and the corrective action to be taken. Elimination of redundancy, identification of the perceptual diagnostics for error conditions and the generation of correction routines will primarily require practice and feedback. Investing the required practice time will require incentive. Ensuring optimal memory storage of the developing control programme will require an appropriate balance between practice sessions and rest.

5.9 Missing pieces

In terms of providing a theoretical account of the human information processing system which is sufficient to accommodate the phenomena associated with student learning, there are three areas where cognitive psychologists have signally failed to join up the dots: characterizing beliefs, explaining belief-change, and accounting for motivation to learn. Below an attempt will be made to remedy these deficiencies, but first attention should be drawn to the work of investigators who have already spotted some of the gaps and made suggestions as to how they might be plugged.

The gaps that have been noticed are conceptual change (Strike and Posner, 1992) and motivation to learn (Pintrich, Marx and Boyle, 1993). The starting point of the conceptual change model is the observation that psychological models of cognition can describe how knowledge is represented, and even how change in knowledge can occur. They do not explain when and why knowledge change takes place. Conceptual change models such as those of Strike and Posner assume that change within an individual's conceptual framework is analogous to change in scientific paradigms. Concepts are claimed to exist within an interrelated network that is described as a 'conceptual ecology'. The core ideas are that ideas compete for inclusion within the network, and that changes to one part of the network have knock-on effects elsewhere. The conditions for change are that new ideas must resolve *dissatisfaction* with existing conceptions, while being at least as *intelligible, fruitful* and *plausible* as the ideas with which they are in competition. The two central analogies in this conceptual change model both fail in key respects. The analogy with scientific change fails because what makes a theory paradigmatic is its acceptance by the majority of a scientific community. No satisfactory account is given of how this phenomenon can be reproduced within an individual. The 'conceptual ecology' analogy fails in several respects, but a particularly difficult problem is that whereas inclusion within an individual's conceptual network is apparently all-or-none, the mechanism of evolutionary selection depends upon quantitative variation in reproductive success. Both of these difficulties are caused by the assumption that what a learner cognitively represents is knowledge, and if an idea of something is represented within the network it is represented only once

Pintrich *at al.* register the familiar complaint that the conceptual change model is 'cold' and rational. On this model, if certain intellectual conditions are met, a network change is bound to occur. They argue that in the real world, students have *goals, values* and beliefs about *self-efficacy* and *control* that interact with the formal, abstract characteristics of knowledge. More specifically, Pintrich *et al.* claim that there are two motivational factors, one (incorporating goal-orientation, interest and importance) that concerns their reasons for choosing to do a task, and a second that concerns their ability to succeed (incorporating expectancy components that include self-efficacy, attributions and control beliefs). Finally, Pintrich *et al.* assume that a social-cognitive perspective on motivation implies context specificity, and thus that local features of task and classroom organization will create, shape and constrain motivation.

While there is little doubt that Pintrich *et al.* have located a genuine weakness in information processing analyses of student learning, their attempts to remedy the problem are disappointingly vague.

> Goals are cognitive representations of the different purposes students may adopt in different achievement situations ... There are a variety of different conceptualizations of academic achievement goals, but the main distinction is between an intrinsic, mastery, and task involved orientation and an extrinsic performance and ego-involved orientation
>
> (Pintrich *et al.* 1993, p. 176.).

Pintrich *et al.* consider that a mastery orientation is more likely to produce the conditions under which conceptual change is likely to occur than an ego orientation, and argue that in turn, such features of the learning situation as task authenticity, classroom authority structure and evaluation procedures influence the orientation taken by students. Finally, the effect task characteristics is supposed to be mediated by the *interest, value* and *importance* of the task, the beliefs students hold about their self efficacy, or ability to perform the task, and the beliefs they hold about the extent of their control of the learning situation. (Pintrich *et al.*, pp. 186—8).

Though a persuasive *a priori* case is made for supposing that the factors reviewed are indeed influential in determining whether conceptual change occurs, little is said to illuminate what exactly conceptual change is at the level of specific cognitive representations, nor is any explanation offered of when or why specific cognitive changes occur. As a result, Pintrich *et al.* find themselves mystified by paradoxes such as the fact that prior knowledge can sometimes facilitate and sometimes impede conceptual change, and the fact that an absence of prior knowledge should present least barriers to learning, but learning is usually best when prior knowledge is present.

The present chapter takes the view that a satisfactory account of student learning must come to much closer grips with the microstructure of knowledge representation and a sketch of how this might be achieved is offered below.

5.10.1 Propositional information

Information in propositional form has three fundamental properties. First it is represented as a string of symbols, and as this requires rules for symbol use, a given string may be in conformity with these rules or not, and so be *well-formed* or *anomalous*. Secondly it is associated with a *truth value*, that is, it may be true or false. Thirdly it is either *intentional* or *extensional*. The truth value of an *intentional* proposition derives from internal concordances within the symbol system itself, but the truth value of an extensional proposition can be established only by comparing the symbolic expression which expresses that proposition with the state of the external world under specified conditions. These different features of propositional information define five distinct categories of proposition which are illustrated in Table 5.2.

In cognitive science it is a common assumption that human knowledge and belief is either represented in a propositional form, or exists in some form which maps directly on to propositional representations.

5.10.2 Propositional attitude

Inspection of the examples above shows that nothing intrinsic to the propositions themselves reveals which category they fall into. The ill-formedness of 'water is cats' is a judgement on which English speakers will generally agree, but only as a result of their knowledge of how English sentences are formed. Similarly, there is nothing about 'cats are

Type of proposition	Example
Ill-formed	Water is cats
Well-formed true intentional	Water is wet
Well-formed false intentional	Water is dry
Well-formed true extensional	Cats are furry
Well-formed FALSE Extensional	Cats are green

Table 5.2 Five categories of proposition

green' and 'water is dry' which signals that one is only contingently false while the other is false of necessity.

It follows that to use propositional representations as vehicles for knowledge and belief, agents need a characterization of the cognitive status of a symbolically represented proposition, as well as an description of its content. Linguists and philosophers have used the term 'attitude' to refer to this extra ingredient (Barwise and Perry, 1983; Fodor 1978). Using this terminology, one might say for example that the declarative sentence 'aliens exist' has the same propositional content for all speakers of English, but it is associated with one propositional attitude for a fanatical believer in extra-terrestrial life who 'knows' it to be true, and a different one for a sceptic. Again, the propositional attitude would be interrogative in 'do aliens exist?', imperative in 'let aliens exist' and optative in 'would that aliens existed'. We shall try to accomplish the same objective using a different device. It is helpful to begin by distinguishing belief from knowledge, or **B information** from **K information**.

5.10.3 Belief

A belief is a conceptual relationship that is expressed in propositional form and which is relevant to action planning in at least one identifiable action context. When information in propositional form is classified as **B information**, it is associated with an index of strength. This will be referred to as the **Epistemic Credibility Index** (**ECI**) and is a number between zero and one that is proportional to an agent's subjective confidence that the proposition is true. The **ECI** for **B information** is context sensitive, so that the **ECI** associated with a particular proposition will vary from one action-planning context to another. Whether an agent acts as if a proposition is true in a particular action-planning context depends upon both the magnitude of the **ECI** and the outcome structure of the action context. For example, an agent may chose not to act upon a near certain belief if the result of its failure is something sufficiently catastrophic, such as an evening without alcohol. Assignment of an **ECI** of 1.0 to a propositional representation in some of the action contexts in which it applies is not in itself sufficient to convert it into knowledge.

5.10.4 Knowledge

Information in propositional form which is classified as **K information** has an **ECI** of 1.0 in all action contexts which are considered real. Thus if an agent knows that snow is white, then actions which incorporate the assumption that snow is white can safely be planned with respect to all real action contexts. This is not to say that propositions known to be true have an **ECI** of 1.0 in all conceivable action contexts. An imaginary action context can be defined as an action context in which at least one item of **K information** is counterfactually assigned an ECI of less than 1.0. An agent who knows that snow is white may readily be able to imagine that it is not, but the proposition can nevertheless be employed in any real world action-planning context, regardless of outcome structure. Evidence regarded as sufficient to justify classification as **K information** may have one or more of a variety of provenances such as source credibility (for example: parent, teacher, textbook); experimental test, experienced validity, revelation etc. When the source of **K information** credibility is an inference justified by the rules of the symbol system within which propositions are expressed, the truth which results is intentional and the **K information** which results holds in all possible as well as all actual worlds. For example, squares are not circular, and not-white is not identical with white, in any possible world.

Reasoning outside the context of cognitive science, philosophers have expended much effort on attempting to discover the circumstances under which the claim that a proposition expresses an item of **K information** is justified. No completely satisfactory criteria have ever been identified, leading some philosophers to express serious misgivings about the foundations of human epistemology. Within the context of cognitive science matters can be viewed with more sanguinity. It seems unlikely that human cognitive processes have evolved at the species level and developed at the level of the individual to provide indubitable certainty to reassure doubters, or to allow sceptical philosophers to be confounded. Rather, cognitive processes have evolved to assist organisms to produce actions which increase their probability of survival. Knowledge is the means, action the end. Furthermore the transfer of a proposition from the category of **B information** to the category of **K information** is not triggered by arrival at some threshold level of certitude, nor by the satisfaction of some fixed set of criteria.

Preoccupation with the conditions under which knowledge claims are justified has led to neglect of the consequences of deciding that a proposition is known to be true. And where the consequences have been explored, it is the social or dialogic consequences that have attracted attention. This has produced the following oddly bathotic chain of reasoning:

(a) Certainty beyond the possibility of sceptical doubt justifies the claim that proposition *p* is known.
(b) If *p* is known then *p* can be asserted as true.
(c) The assertion that '*p* is true' means the same as '*p*'.

Actually, the social and dialogic consequences of knowing *p*, don't seem to be very different from the equivalent consequences of being extremely confident that *p*. The kinds of consequences which do, however, seem to be dramatically affected by the transfer of a proposition from the category of **B information** to the category of **K information**, are the *cognitive* consequences.

The background to this claim has already been partially established. The effect of evolution is to improve the efficiency with which species optimize some parameter such as survival duration or reproduction frequency. Phenotypic organisms contribute to this process by seeking to achieve goals that are represented within their cognitive structures. The means by which goals are achieved is by generating effective actions, and the effectiveness of action is enhanced by adaptive learning, particularly by using environmental information stored in the form of propositional representations. In this context, what difference is produced when belief is re-designated as knowledge?

Perhaps the most important difference is that because the **ECI** associated with **B information** is related to the value of the evidence which supports them, and evidence-value is liable to change with time, **B information** propositions must be rechecked every time they are used in an action context which has a significantly valued outcome structure. By contrast **K information** propositions never need rechecking. One consequence of this is that powerful inference procedures (such as the first order predicate calculus) can be used on collocations of propositions which exclusively contain knowledge, but not on sets which incorporate beliefs. The destructive effect of belief statements on formal reasoning is known in AI as the 'circumscription problem' (McCarthy, 1980).

A second consequence is that memory structures can be established which use devices such as embedding and recursion. This enables considerable economies in storage space and processing time to be achieved Collins and Quillian 1969; Collins and Loftus 1975; Anderson 1983), but also increases vulnerability to corruption. If the propositions 'all animals have skin', 'all animals ingest food', 'all animals move', and 'all animals reproduce' is **K information**, then representing the single fact that an *Okapi is an animal* in memory provides access to a host of other facts through inference, without any need to store them separately. But knowledge must really be secure to be used in this way: the cost of one incorrect entry is potentially immense if that entry becomes recursively embedded, possibly many layers deep, as a part of later entries.

Finally, because **K information** does not need checking, it can be incorporated into cognitive programs which run automatically, without conscious supervision. The great benefit of this kind of automaticity is that it frees up the limited capacity central executive. In large part the development of expertise in a cognitive domain consists in the process of learning to act automatically, and this usually means that actions are not under conscious control. Unlike novices, expert performers are rarely aware of the cognitive decision processes underlying their behaviour. Once performance becomes automatic, cognitive programs can be run in parallel, so an agent can for example, perceptually interpret the local environment, type on a word-processor, and hold a conversation simultaneously. This kind of automatic processing is critically dependent upon **K information**. Physical skill learning often employs propositional information in the early stages of skill acquisition: 'beat the egg whites until stiff, free-standing peaks appear', 'change gear when the rev counter reaches 12,000'. Performance would be seriously disrupted if it became necessary to revise the propositional information used to establish automatic motor programmes of this kind.

Text and dialogue comprehension is even more dependent upon previously stored **K information**. Schank and Abelson (1977) point out that all text comprehension involves knowledge-dependent inferences of which the agent is largely unconscious. They illustrate their point with text fragments like this one:

> *Terence got on a bus to go to work. He sat down. When the conductor came, he realized that he had left his money at home, so he had to walk to work.*

Interpretation of such text is only possible if background knowledge such as *bus travel requires tickets, conductors sell tickets, purchases require money* etc. is supplied by the reader. Competent speaker/readers of English use information from their own memory to fill in the gaps and allow the comprehension process to flow. It is important to realize that this interplay between text and memory is part of the standard process of interpretation. No spoken or written language segment can 'internally' supply all of the information required for its own interpretation. But if the 'knowledge' supplied is uncertain or incorrect, then comprehension will either be hugely slowed as assumptions need to be checked, or become corrupted into miscomprehension.

5.10.5 Action

Action plans may be computed in real time, or preserved in memory as 'stored programs'. Action plans which contain no propositional information which is not **K information** are effectively context free as the validity of their propositional content is not sensitive to variation in contextual features. Action plans of this kind can be activated without any need for conscious monitoring. Action plans containing **B information** must be reviewed in each action context before implementation.

5.10.6 Action contexts

Actions result from the implementation of plans and plans are associated with sets of implementation criteria. An action context is the set of situations in which the implementation criteria for a given plan is satisfied. Action plans may incorporate propositional knowledge, particularly when the actions resulting from the plan take the form of dialogue or text production. A given item of propositional knowledge may feature in more than one action plan and so may be associated with many action contexts..

5.10.7 Propositional learning

There are four main types of propositional learning.

5.10.7.1 Belief acquisition

1. discovery of previously unknown conceptual relationships which can be expressed in propositional form (potential belief);
2. discovery that information in propositional form can be applied to support action planning in at least one context (belief);
3. assignment of strength indexical to information in propositional form which can be applied to support action planning in at least one context;

5.10.7.2 Knowledge acquisition

1. Discovery of previously unknown conceptual relationships which can be expressed in propositional form and establishment that they can be designated as **K information** propositions.
2. Establishment that one or more propositions containing **B information** can be redesignated as **K information** propositions

5.10.7.3 Belief revision

Belief revision consists in changes to the conceptual content of an item of **K information**, changes to the context identifiers associated with it or change to its strength indexical.

5.10.7.4 Knowledge revision

Knowledge revision consists in changing the epistemic designation of an item of propositional information from K to B. Knowledge revision has three effects: it changes action choices in contexts to which the changed item is relevant, it changes the set of action plans which can be preserved as stored programmes and implemented without monitoring, and it invalidates a set of action plans which has been stored already.

5.10.8 What student's learn

5.10.8.1 Learning and action planning

Though student learning is often treated in Psychology and Education as if it were predominantly or exclusively an abstract cognitive process, in fact it is almost invariably a form of action planning. This is more or less guaranteed by the association between learning and assessment. In effect the local imperative driving the student is something like:

> *'establish conceptual structures and bodies of information in propositional form which are sufficient to support generation of appropriate action in the assessment context which I will encounter later'.*

There may of course, be more generalized and deferred imperatives provided by the student's own motivational system such as:

> *'establish conceptual structures and bodies of information in propositional form which are sufficient to support generation of appropriate action in future real-world-contexts in which it is important for me to act effectively'.*

Or more instrumentally:

> *'establish conceptual structures and bodies of information in propositional form which are sufficient to support generation of appropriate action in future contexts in which financial rewards depend upon the effectiveness with which I act'.*

Perhaps the most important implication of this analysis is that student motivation can be explicated with reasonable clarity as a function of the number of action contexts to which an item of propositional information is considered to be relevant and the importance associated with each context:

$$M = \sum_{k=1}^{n} I_k \times f n_A$$

where **M** is motivation to learn, $\mathbf{n}_A$ is an action context and **I** is the subjective importance associated with that context.

5.10.8.2 Action planning and memory organization

When students encounter propositional information in a scholastic context which differs from the propositional information already represented within their own internal cognitive structures, they need to make two interdependent decisions.

1. **Do I wish to learn this information?**

The answer to this question will depend upon a trade-off between motivation (**M**) which can be treated as a proxy for expected payoff, and the cost of any learning which occurs. Learning cost will be lowest for the acquisition of new information, and greatest when modification is required to knowledge already embedded in stored action programmes.

2. **What form should any learning take?**

- *Propositional information with a epistemic credibility index of 1.0* — integrate into knowledge networks; incorporate into new action programs and store for automatic implementation when appropriate; substitute for pragmatically equivalent **B Knowledge** and for inferior **K Knowledge**.
- *Propositional information with a epistemic credibility index of less than 1.0* — incorporate into new action programs, substitute for **B knowledge** with lower generality or epistemic credibility index; do not store programs for automatic implementation.

3. **When will learning occur?**

Previous investigators have noted that mere exposure to information is not sufficient to produce learning. The present theoretical analysis allows more a detailed account to be given of the conditions under which learning is likely to occur. The main determinants can be listed as follows:

1. The learner must believe that the learnable information is relevant to at least one context within which the subjective importance of appropriate action exceeds zero.
2. The learner must believe that the epistemic credibility index associated with the learnable information exceeds zero.
3. In the case of novel information, the learner must believe that the cognitive cost of incorporating the learnable information into their cognitive structures is justified by the expected payoff.
4. In the case of corrective information, the learner must believe that the cognitive cost of revising existing programs is justified by the expected payoff.

Strike and Posner (1985) have sought to conceptualize the process of belief modification which underlies student learning by analogy with Kuhn's notion of paradigm shift in science at large. This process accurately captures the fact that conceptual change is not monotonically related to information capture, and the fact that current conceptual states may resist modification by new and corrective information. The analogy fails, however, because the basis mechanism underlying Kuhnian change is the set of decision processes occurring within a community of scientists. Students do not appear to have anything resembling a community of scientists within their cognitive systems. They do however have good reason to resist conceptual change if the information to be modified is already embedded within a large number of pre-stored programs.

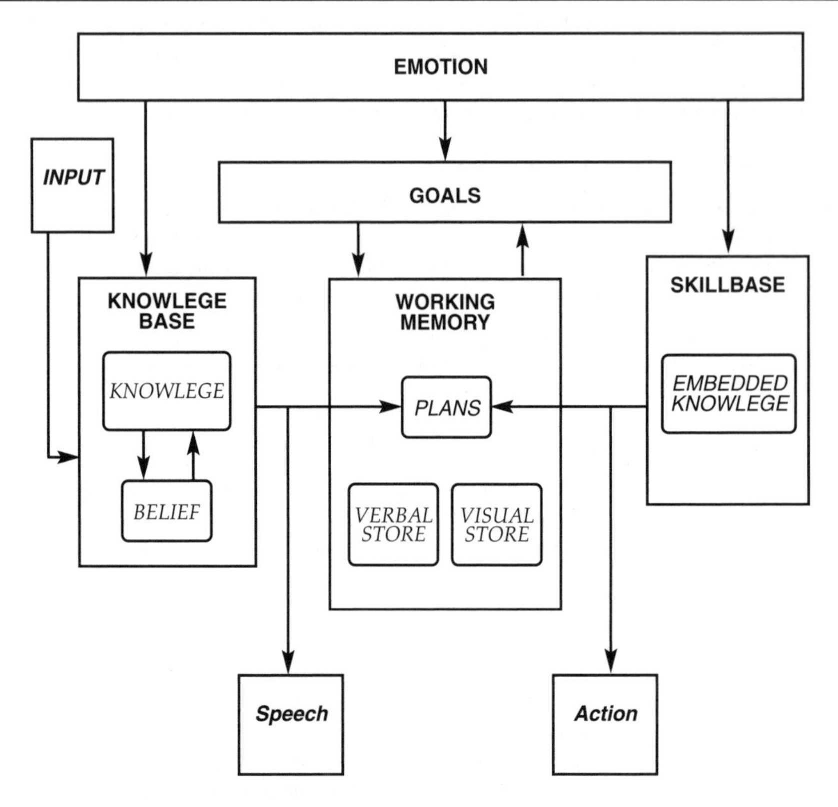

Figure 5.2 Representation of some of the main components and flow-of-control relationships required in an information-processing model of student learning

5.11 Towards a cognitive model of student learning

Figure 5.2 offers a preliminary sketch of a model capable of accommodating some of the most conspicuous features of student learning discussed above. Foremost among these is the incorporation of *belief, emotion, goals* and *plans*. A further important feature is the recognition that knowledge (and belief) is incorporated into action plans, as well as being organized within semantic and episodic memory systems. In interpreting the model it should be noted that to reduce its visual complexity, only a proportion of information flow routes are illustrated by arrows.

Psychology has come a long way towards being able to explain complex conceptual learning in the twentieth century. But as discussion above demonstrates, there are still some crucial steps to be taken before the trick can be done. Figure 2.1 indicates what some of them are.

5.12 Implications for the facilitation of learning in practice

5.12.1 Preconditions for learning

1. Students must be aware of what they are intended to learn.
2. Students must be aware of goals which new material can be used to achieve.
3. Students must attach importance to achievable goals.
4. Thoughts, emotions and motor activity should reinforce, not compete with learning.
5. Students must be aware of their own pre-existing beliefs.

5.12.2 Conditions for learning

1. Existing beliefs are deficient.
2. New material remedies deficiencies.
3. New material is intelligible.
4. New material is accepted.
5. New knowledge allows achievement of significant goals.
6. Students are aware of what actions allow goal achievement.
7. Students are aware of how new knowledge is relevant to potential action.
8. Students can identify action contexts in which new knowledge is relevant.
9. Learner can deploy new knowledge in action contexts.

5.13 References

Abelson, R. P. (1963) Computer simulation of 'hot' cognition. In S. S. Tomkins and S. Messik, *Computer Simulation of Personality*. New York: Wiley.

Anderson, J. R. and Bower, G. (1973) *Human Associative Memory*. Washington DC: V. H. Winston & Sons.

Anderson, J. R. (1983) *The Architecture of Cognition*. Cambridge MA: Harvard University Press.

Barwise J. and Perry J. (1983) *Situations and Attitudes*. Cambridge MA: Harvard University Press.

Bever, T.G. Fodor, J. A. and Garrett, M. (1968) A formal limitation of associationism, in T. R. Dixon and D. L. Horton (eds) *Verbal Behavior and General Behavior Theory*. Englewood Cliffs: Prentice-Hall.

Blodgett, H. C. (1929) The effect of introducing reward upon the maze performance of rats. *Univ. Calif. Publ. Psychol.* **4**, 113—34.

Broadbent, D. E. (1958) *Perception and Communication*. London: Pergamon Press.

Bruner, J. S., Goodnow, J. J. and Austin, G. A. (1956) *A Study of Thinking*. New York: Wiley.

Butler, R. A. (1954) Curiosity in monkeys. *Scientific American*, February, 70—5.

Chomsky, N. (1959) Review of *Verbal Behavior* by B. F. Skinner, *Language* **35,** 26—38.

Cole, M., Gay, J., Glick, J. and Sharp, D. W. (1971) *The Cultural Context of Learning and Thinking. New York: Basic Books.*

Collins, A. M. and Loftus, E. F. (1975) *A spreading activation theory of semantic processing,* Psychological Review **82,** 407—28.

Collins, A. M and Quillian, M. R. (1969) *Retrieval time from semantic memory,* Journal of Verbal Learning and Verbal Behavior **8,** 240—7.

Duncker, K. (1945) On human problem-solving, *Psychological Monographs* **58**(270).

Fodor, J. (1978) *Propositional attitudes,* Monist.

Frijda, N. H. (1986) *The Emotions.* Cambridge: Cambridge University Press.

Hobbes, T. (1651) *Leviathan.* London: A. Crooke.

Hunt, E. B. Marin, J. and Stone, M. (1966) *Experiments in Induction.* Cambridge MA: MIT Press.

Klatzky, R. (1975) *Human Memory: Structures and Processes.* San Francisco: W. H. Freeman.

Krechevsky, I. (1932) *'Hypotheses' in rats,* Psychological Review **39,** 516—32.

Kohler, W. (1925) *Experiments with Apes.* New York: Harcourt Brace Jovanovich.

McCarthy, J. (1980) *Circumscription — a form of non-monotonic reasoning,* Artificial Intelligence **13,** 27—39.

Miller, G. A., Galanter, E. and Pribram, K. H. (1960) *Plans and the Structure of Behavior.* New York: Holt, Rinehart & Winston.

Newell, A. (1990) *Unified Theories of Cognition.* Cambridge, MA: Harvard University Press.

Pintrich, P. R., Marx, R. W. and Boyle, R. A. (1993) Beyond cold conceptual change: the role of motivational beliefs and classroom contextual factors in the process of conceptual change, *Review of Educational Research.* Summer **63**(2), 167—99.

Schank, R. C. and Abelson, R. P. (1977) *Scripts, Plans, Goals and Understanding: An Inquiry into Human Understanding.* Hillsdale NJ: Lawrence Erlbaum.

Shannon, C. and Weaver, W. (1949) *The Mathematical Theory of Communication.* Urbana Ill: University of Illinois press.

Skinner, B. F. (1957) *Verbal Behaviour.* New York: Appleton-Century. Crofts.

Strike, K.A and Posner, G. J. (1985) A conceptual change view of learning and understanding. In L. West and L. Pines (eds), *Cognitive Structure and Conceptual Change.* New York: Academic Press, pp. 211—31.

Strike, K. A. and Posner, G. J. (1992) A revisionist theory of conceptual change. In R. Duschl and R. Hamilton (eds), *Philosophy of Science, Cognitive Psychology, and Educational Theory and Practice.* Albany NY: SUNY, pp. 147—76.

Strongman, K. T. (1996) *The Psychology of Emotion,* 4th edn. Chichester: Wiley.

Tolman, E. C., Ritchie, B. F. and Kalish D. (1946) Studies in spatial learning. I. Orientation and the short-cut, *Journal of Experimental Psychology* **36,** 13—24.

Turing, A. M. (1951) Computing machinery and intelligence, *Mind* **59,** 433—60.

Wason, P. C. (1966) Reasoning. In B. M. Foss (ed.), *New Horizons in Psychology,* Vol. 1. Harmondsworth: Penguin, pp. 135—51.

Watson, J. B. (1913) Psychology as the behaviorist views it, *Psychological Review* **20,** 158—77.

Wiener, N (1948) *Cybernetics.* New York: Technological Press of M.I.T and John Wiley & Sons.

Woodworth, R. S and Sells, S. B. (1935) An atmosphere effect in formal syllogistic reasoning, *Journal of Experimental Psychology* **18,** 451—60.

6 Phenomenography: discernment and variation

Keith Trigwell

University of Oxford

6.1 Overview

This chapter contains the essence of the notes that were used in the seminar on Phenomenography in the Background to the Territory series. Conclusions of the group in the exercises used in the seminar are included in the descriptions that follow.

The seminar began with a description of the contribution phenomenographic research has made to learning and teaching in higher education. Phenomenography was positioned within a range of other research perspectives such as first order and quantitative approaches. It emphasized that like these other perspectives phenomenography helps address some, but not all, questions about learning. The fundamentals of the phenomenographic research approach (that it is a *relational second-order* perspective, that it aims to describe the *key aspects of the variation* of experience of a phenomenon rather than the richness of individual experiences, and that it yields a *limited number of internally related,* hierarchical categories of description of the variation) were discussed. This chapter follows the same format.

6.2 Discernment and variation

Experiencing variation is an essential aspect of being able to distinguish between things, and it can be argued that both variation and discernment are therefore vital in the process of learning. The importance of the role of variation in learning is described by Bowden and Marton:

> To discern an aspect is to differentiate among the various aspects and focus on the one most relevant to the situation. Without variation there is no discernment. We do not think in a conscious way about breathing until we get a virus or walk into a smoke-filled room. Learning in terms of changes in or widening in our ways of seeing the world can be understood in terms of discernment, simultaneity and variation. Thanks to the variation, we experience and discern critical aspects of the situations or phenomena we have to handle and, to the extent that these critical aspects are focused on simultaneously, a pattern emerges. Thanks to having experienced a varying past we become capable of handling a varying future.
>
> (Bowden and Marton, 1998, p. 7)

So, an awareness of the variation in the understanding of a phenomenon to be learned is a valuable asset for the teacher of that phenomenon. Phenomenography is an approach to research, the outcome of which is a description of the qualitative variation in the ways a group of people experience a phenomenon. In effect it 'lists' experienced variations of the phenomenon. The contribution that it has made to higher education comes in lists (or outcome space) in two different areas. The first contribution made by phenomenography was concerned with student learning and included descriptions of the variation in ways of experiencing the processes of higher education (Marton, Hounsell and Entwistle, 1997). More recently attention has been turned to teaching (Kember, 1997; Prosser and Trigwell, 1999) and leadership (Trigwell *et al.*, forthcoming).

The second contribution is in descriptions of the qualitative variation in the way students' object of study is understood. These studies show that there are a limited number of variants on the qualitatively different ways of conceiving of the object of study and that an awareness of this variation may be a valuable teaching aid. An indication of some of the higher education fields studied using phenomenographic methods in shown in Table 6.1. An example of how the information collected from such an analysis can be used in teaching is given in Millar, Prosser and Sefton (1989).

Field		Reference
biology	photosynthesis	Hazel, Prosser and Trigwell, 1996
chemistry	states of matter	Renström, Andersson and Marton, 1990
	mole concept	Lybeck et al., 1988
	atomic structure	Keogh, 1991
computing	programming	Booth, 1992
economics		Dahlgren, 1997
geology	mapping	McCracken and Laurillard, 1994
health science	physiotherapy	Abrandt, 1997
	aseptic technique	Davey, 1995
mathematics		Crawford et al., 1994
music	instrumental	Reid, 1997
politics	political power	Theman, 1983
physics	electricity and magnetism	Prosser, 1994; Millar, Prosser and Sefton, 1989
	sound	Linder and Erickson, 1989
	mechanics	Johansson, Marton and Svensson, 1985; Prosser and Millar, 1989; Bowden et al., 1992

Table 6.1 Some studies of variation in understanding by higher education field

One set of results (outcome space) from the study on learning instrumental music (Reid, 1997) contains three ways of conceiving of the music object (an outcome of the learning of a musical instrument). The three ways are qualitatively different in meaning, with the focus being on the instrument; on the music; or on the musician.

> [Music] as technique relates to the physical aspects of playing the *instrument* as well as notational elements such as phrasing, accents or articulation.

> [Music as] sound and communication [is] related to the belief that each piece of music has an inherent meaning that is constituted by such things as style, period, harmony and composers' intent. It is the [inherent meaning of the *music*] that is communicated to an audience.
>
> Music as personal meaning ... involve[s] aspects of [technique and sound and communication], but these aspects were reinterpreted by the participants through the notion that music is a way of expressing personal meaning and understanding of the world through music performance. It is the *musicians* ideas that are expressed through the music's inherent meaning.
>
> (Reid, 1997, p. 204, my emphasis)

There is, however, also a structural differentiation present here in the form of logically related hierarchies. (An outcome space is far more than a 'list'.) Seeing the playing of music as a way of expressing personal meaning (a focus on the musician) is still seen to be achieved through the development of technique and the communication of sound. And, communicating the meaning of the music (a focus on the music) is still accomplished through the playing technique and an awareness of phrasing, accents and articulation. The category which focuses on the musician is structurally related to the other two and would therefore appear to be the most inclusive and complete. In other words, there are internal relations in the outcome space.

If we now look at the nature of these conceptions, or what has been learned or understood, differences to traditional ways of thinking become apparent. This perspective on learning outcomes is in contrast to views that a successful learning outcome is one in which a student can accurately reproduce 50 per cent or more of what they are being taught. It is also in contrast to related views that the product of learning is *more* knowledge: adding an extra amount to what is there. A teacher with a focus on the product of learning as experiencing something in a qualitatively different way is more likely to engage in teaching that explores variation in ways of understanding, that illustrates variation in ways of understanding and encourages deep approaches to learning. To be able to see the learning outcomes in terms of qualitative differences is an important part of good teaching.

These are examples of the contributions that phenomenography can and is making to higher education. But what is phenomenography and, as we will see below, what is it not?

6.3 Phenomenography: a definition

Phenomenography is the empirical study of the limited number of qualitatively different ways in which we experience, conceptualize, understand, perceive, apprehend etc., various phenomena in and aspects of the world around us. These differing experiences, understandings etc. are characterized in terms of categories of description, logically related to each other, and forming hierarchies in relation to given criteria. Such an ordered set of categories of description is called the outcome space of the phenomenon, concepts in question. Although different kinds of data can be used, the dominating method for collecting data is the individual interview which is carried out in a dialogical manner. The interviewee is encouraged to reflect on previously unthematized aspects of the phenomenon in question. The interviews are transcribed verbatim and the analysis is carried out in an iterative manner on those transcripts. Distinctly different ways of experiencing the phenomenon discussed in the interview are the units of analysis and not the single individuals. The categories of description corresponding to those differing understandings and the logical relations that can be established between them constitute the main results of a phenomenographic study (Marton, 1992).

This research approach has been articulated more fully by Marton and Booth (1992) and has also been the subject of several critiques which help give some insight into some of the philosophical and theoretical foundations of phenomenography (Ashworth and Lucas, 1998; Richardson, 1999). The principles and practice of phenomenography are also addressed in Bowden and Walsh, 1994; Prosser, 1993; Trigwell, 1997 and on the Land of Phenomenography website.

The key aspects of a phenomenographic research approach (some of which are not acknowledged in the two critiques of the approach mentioned above) are that it takes a

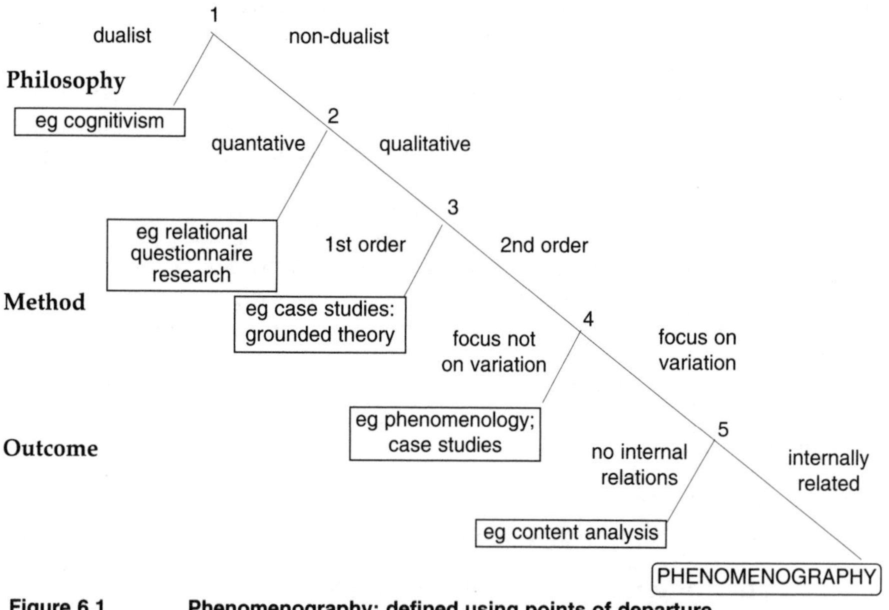

Figure 6.1 Phenomenography: defined using points of departure

relational (or non-dualist) qualitative, second-order perspective, that it aims to describe the *key aspects of the variation* of the experience of a phenomenon rather than the richness of individual experiences, and that it yields a *limited number of internally related,* hierarchical categories of description of the variation. These five aspects are illustrated in Figure 6.1 as five points of departure. Each of the points of departure (1—5) are described more fully in the text following the figure.

6.4 Points of departure (refer to numbers 1—5 in Figure 6.1)

1. *Phenomenography is non-dualist rather than dualist*: Unlike philosophies underpinning cognitivism and individual constructivism, which are dualist in considering the individual or subject to be a separate entity from the phenomenon or object, the phenomenographic philosophy is non-dualist. Reality is not seen as being 'out there'. It is seen as being constituted as the relation between the individual and the phenomenon.
2. *Qualitative rather than quantitative*: Phenomenography can be seen as being philosophically or methodologically qualitative.
3. *Second order rather than first order*: In a first order approach, the researcher describes the phenomenon as perceived by him or her, whereas in a second order approach, it is the experience of the phenomenon as described by others that forms the basis of the researcher's description.
4. *Focus on the variation*: The phenomenographic approach focuses on the key aspects of the variation in the ways a phenomenon is experienced. This is fundamentally different to most other research approaches, and has consequences which must be taken into account. First, because the focus is on the differences, aspects or ways of experiencing a phenomenon which are common across the whole sample are not incorporated. This results in an outcome space which is a partial description of the experience of the phenomenon, rather than a full rich description as might be expected using a phenomenological approach. Secondly, because the focus is on variation in ways people experience a phenomenon, the study must include a range of individual's experiences, and the sample is selected to maximize the possible variation.
5. *Articulation of the internal relations between the different ways of experiencing a phenomenon*: It is this element that distinguishes phenomenography from outcomes with lists of essentially unrelated categories, such as in a content analysis.

6.5 An illustrative exercise

In an exercise used to illustrates these five points of departure, seminar participants are asked to read the two extracts from interviews with Lecturer A and Lecturer E which follow, and to describe the variation in what the teachers are focusing on, and the variation in how those teachers described how they carried out what it was they were trying to do.

These extracts clearly show that these two university teachers approached their teaching in fundamentally different ways, with fundamentally different conceptions of what constituted teaching and learning within the context in which they are teaching.

Lecturer A seems to have adopted an approach to teaching based upon what he does. The focus is on himself — the lecturer, and then what students do in relation to the lecturer. Lecturer E, on the other hand, seems to have a focus on what the students do and think and then what he should do in relation to that. This lecturer's focus seems to be on the students. Here we are not talking about how well each of the lecturers did what they set out to do, but on the qualitative variation in what they are trying to do and how they are trying to do it. From another perspective, it seems that Lecturer A is trying to transfer his knowledge to the students. The intention seems to be to transfer knowledge and information. On the other hand, Lecturer E seems to be trying to develop and change the way the students think about and understand the concepts and ideas constituting the subject matter. His intention seems to be to engage students in the process of conceptual change and development.

The full interviews, of which these extracts are a part, and those of 22 other teachers, formed the data set for a phenomenographic study of conceptions of teaching and approaches to teaching (Trigwell, Prosser and Taylor, 1994; Prosser Trigwell and Taylor, 1994). The outcome space of the conceptions of teaching study is given in Figure 6.2, and the internal relations of this outcome space in Figure 6.3.

Teaching is seen as:

A: transmitting concepts of the syllabus
B: transmitting the teachers' knowledge
C: helping students acquire concepts of the syllabus
D: helping students acquire teacher' knowledge
E: helping students develop conceptions
F: helping students change conceptions

Figure 6.2 Outcome space for conceptions of teaching study

Lecturer A

Q: *Just as a general lead in question, what do you think, generally that the course is about?*

A: What are the objectives of it? Well I, many years ago prepared a list of specific objectives for the course and they were very useful for helping me in planning the course. Planning the assessment, planning the lectures and so on, and in the past I have given that list to the students, but now I make them aware of them in the way I lecture rather than giving them a whole list. I find preparing a list of specific objectives relating to the chemistry content. For example, one specific objective might be that a student should be able to develop the ability to classify molecules as polar or non polar. And a whole list of very specific objectives like that. As I say, I find that very helpful planning my own lectures and just planning the whole course. At the start of each lecture, or during the lecture or at times which I think appropriate I make the student aware just exactly the sort of skill I hope they are going to develop as a result of the learning experience that we're currently involved in and it's very very important.

...

Q. *How do you go about, what do you do in preparing for lectures?*

A: I think it's very important to have it clear in your own mind and let the students be very clear too about what you expect them to do as a result of any learning experience, what you expect them to be able to achieve. So in preparing for an hour lecture I decide what I want the students to get out of this lecture, specifically what I want them to be able to do as a result of this lecture. So that is one of the first parts of planning my list if you like, planning my lecture. I also plan them in a way so that I know the notes that I want the students to get. I'll write my notes in such a way so that the students don't have to decide when to take notes, I tell them to. I'll dictate to them, I have handouts prepared, I have gaps in them that they fill in and I take that decision away from the students about when and how to take notes because I feel it's very important that the lecture, tutorial or whatever the session, is a learning experience at least and not just a note taking exercise. And indeed in the very first lecture of any class I have, not just first year students, I explain to the students about my lecturing style, so they know where they stand. I explain to them the sort of things I'm just telling you, that is, they don't have to worry about when to take down lecture notes, I'll tell them, now it's time to take down some notes. And normally what I like to do is to get them thinking with me, for say five or ten minutes or so about various concepts, skills, and then we'll take some notes.

...

Q: *Can I ask about your decision when to suggest they take notes and when they should just listen. For each of those could I ask why, when you decide it's a good time for them to take notes, why do you do that?*

A: Why do I do it, rather than let them decide?

Q: *No, why do you think it's, in the periods that you think it's a good time for them to take notes, why do you do so?*

A: Well as I say the lecture, tutorial whatever is tightly structured before I go in there. In other words I like things carefully planned, so that you know, I've made the judgement about when it's time to take down some notes. I make that judgement. I think it's important the students do get a good set of lecture notes, particularly when we're talking specifically now about first year, I think it's very very important. At all undergraduate levels, I think it's important they come away with a good set of notes. After all there are exams we expect these students to pass, and you know, we could debate the merits and demerits of examinations but the point is they have to pass formal examinations. There are certain skills which they are expected to be able to achieve so they can pass these examinations, and I think having a good set of notes can help them.

Lecturer E

A: What do I do in lectures? Well, talk mostly. But — taken up, eh, I do some ... things ... use a reasonable number of what we call buzz sessions. We ask the students some questions, to get them to discuss it, take answers back. I've been doing that for the last few years, um.

And... we discuss the answers.

Q: *So you've already told me some other things that you're doing, so we might go through the list and ask what you hope to achieve by doing those things. So, lets just, the buzz session. What do you hope to achieve by doing them?*

A: Well, getting the students to eh, to think, to be actively involved in what's going on, to think about it themselves. And I think the buzz-session technique eh, is, is easier than asking individual people to respond to direct questions people come back and say ... things without necessarily having to represent only their own point of view I use it just to get people involved eh, getting them to think about...

Q: *Why do you want them to do that?*

A: 'Cause I think that's how learning happens. And I think the tradition of lectures is a pretty passive sort of thing, just spraying out information. What I read about research on the subject indicates it's not a terribly good method of transmitting information ... (pause). I think, more explicitly what I want to achieve with, eh, buzz-sessions and the questions, and stuff is confronting students with their pre-conceived ideas about the subject which quite often conflict with what we're talking about, the official dogmas as it were. Um, so you've got to bring out that conflict and make the people aware that what they already know may not be what is the official line, as it were.

Q: *Mm.*

A: And I think the buzz sessions and quizzes attempt to do that. I mean, I select questions for those things, which are designed to bring up those conflicts.

Q: *Right. Demonstrations? What do you hope to achieve by giving demonstrations?*

A: Same sort of thing quite often, create a bit of interest, break it up, eh, ... put a bit of variety into the thing first up. But I think that demonstrations are fairly memorable, if they're good ones, you can remember seeing something, they provide some pegs to hang things on quite often, even if they're quite silly demonstrations. I do some silly things sometimes, like throw lumps of jelly around, which is, um, nothing in itself, but I guess it's just a bit of showmanship.

Q: *So ...*

A: You, you hang the ideas on something. That gives people something to remember.

Q: *Right, so memory, and interest and any ... any other specific reasons or ...?*

A: Well, there's the traditional one, that this is, you know, we showing you what really happens, and this is ... what ... the principles of the subject, in operation...um, and I guess if they're short ones, so that's not ... eh, I tend to keep away from demonstrations that are fairly long taking lots of readings and writing them down, saying look at all those total numbers and that proves this thing or not that works. Yeah, it's illustrating, illustrating examples, applications ... principles that we're talking about. But also sometimes the puzzle, the quiz ... here you get a demonstration, do something, and quite often something unexpected, and get people to say 'look I'm gonna do this, what's gonna happen?' And do it, and what happens is different from what most people are going to guess, and then you get them thinking about that. And quite often they would answer the question wrong , then, say 'hey that's homework, go and think about that for next time'.

Q: *Great. All right ... and one final topic is the questions that you prepare to ask the students. What do you, when you prepare questions ... hope to achieve?*

A: Same sorts of things, getting 'em involved, confronting their conceptions with ... eh, well, confronting them with the conflict between conceptions they already have ... and eh ... the new knowledge we want them to acquire ... and in general, keep encouraging people to think about it and get involved.

The extract from Lecturer A contains a description which is similar to conceptions A or B, while Lecturer E's descriptions are consistent with conceptions E or F.

The relations between this study and the five points of departure in Figure 6.1 are outlined below.

STRUCTURAL	REFERENTIAL		
	Syllabus/text concepts	*Teachers' conceptions*	*Students' conceptions*
Teacher:			
1 transmitting information	A	B	
2 helping students acquire concepts	C	D	
3 helping students develop conceptions			E
4 helping students change conceptions			F

Figure 6.3 Internal relations of conceptions of teaching

1. The study was conducted from a *relational* perspective in which the conceptions of teaching were seen as being constituted as the relation between the teachers and the teaching environment. In this case, the environment was the teaching of first-year students studying physical sciences (chemistry and physics) in two Australian universities.
2. The study was *qualitative,* being based entirely on the transcripts of interviews with the teacher.
3. A *second-order* perspective, in which the experience of the teacher, as expressed in the

interview, was used as the basis of the analysis. In this case, as in other studies, the researcher may not agree with the described experience of the phenomenon (teaching) but they are recorded as a valid experience.

4. The outcome space concentrates on those aspects of the experience which *vary*. It does not constitute a full and rich description of the experience of teaching and a category of description is not a rich description of a conception. Some elements, such as a love of the subject they were teaching, were expressed by many teachers who, on other dimensions differed considerably and together they expressed views which covered all the six categories. Because these elements (such as love of the subject) are not key aspects of the variation, they have not been included in the description of the variation (the outcome space).
5. The internal relations of the categories of description and between the categories of description are illustrated in Table 6.1. We have previously described the hierarchy of the structural component as follows:

> The purposes of teaching are to increase knowledge through the transmission of information (1) to help students acquire the concepts of the discipline (2), develop their conceptions (3) and change their conceptions (4).
>
> (Trigwell and Prosser, 1996)

Lecturers who experience teaching as in conception F see teaching as being inclusive of structural elements 1—4, while a teacher with a view consistent with conceptions A or B is unlikely to be able to see teaching as being more than transmission.

The seminar concluded with a brief discussion of the methods of phenomenographic interviewing and analysis and was summarized through reference to the works of Bowden, 1996; Trigwell, 1997; and Francis, 1996.

6.6 References

Abrandt, M. (1997) *Learning Physiotherapy: The impact of formal education and professional experience*. Linköping University, Studies in Education and Psychology, No. 50.

Ashworth, P. and Lucas, A. (1998) What is the 'world' of phenomenography?, *Scandinavian Journal of Educational Research* **42**, 415—31.

Booth, S. A. (1992) *Learning to Program: A Phenomenographic Perspective*. Göteborg, Acta Universitatis Gothoburgensis.

Bowden, J. (1996) Phenomenographic Research — some methodological issues. In G. Dall'Alba and B.Hasselgren (eds), *Reflections on Phenomenography: Towards a Methodology?* Göteborg Studies in Educational Sciences, 109, 49—66.

Bowden, J., Dall'Alba, G., Martin, E., Masters, G., Laurillard, D., Marton, F., Ramsden, P. and Stephanou, A. (1992) Displacement, velocity and frames of reference: phenomenographic studies of students' understanding and some implications for teaching and assessment, *American Journal of Physics* **60**, 262—8.

Bowden, J. and Marton, F. (1998) *The University of Learning*. London: Kogan Page.

Bowden, J. A. and Walsh, E. (eds) (1994) *Phenomenographic Research: Variations in Method*. Melbourne, Royal Melbourne Institute of Technology.

Crawford, K., Gordon, S., Nicholas, J. and Prosser, M. (1994) Conceptions of mathematics and how it is learned: the perspectives of students entering university, *Learning and*

Instruction **4**, 331—45.

Dahlgren, L. O. (1997) Learning conceptions and outcomes. In F. Marton, D. Hounsell and N. J. Entwistle (eds), *The Experience of Learning: Implications for Teaching and Studying in Higher Education*, 2nd edn. Edinburgh, Scottish Academic Press, 23—38.

Davey, J. (1995) Aseptic Technique: What and how students of nursing learn. Unpublished Master of Nursing Thesis. University of Sydney.

Francis, H. (1996) Advancing phenomenography — questions of method. In G. Dall'Alba and B.Hasselgren (eds), *Reflections on Phenomenography: Towards a methodology?* Göteborg Studies in Educational Sciences, 109, 35—48.

Hazel, E., Prosser, M. and Trigwell, K. (1996) Student learning of biology concepts in different university contexts, *Research and Development in Higher Education* **19**, 323—6.

Johansson, B., Marton, F. and Svensson, L. (1985) An approach to describing learning as change between qualitatively different conceptions. In L. H. T. West and A. L. Pines (eds), *Cognitive Structure and Conceptual Change*. New York, Academic Press.

Kember, D. (1997) A reconceptualisation of the research into university academics' conceptions of teaching, *Learning and Instruction* **7**, 255—75.

Keogh, L. (1991) Student conceptions of atomic structure: a phenomenographic study. Unpublished BSc(Hons) dissertation. University of Western Australia.

Land of phenomenography, http://www.ped.gu.se/biorn/phgraph/welcome.html

Linder, C. J. and Erickson, G. L. (1989) A study of tertiary physics students' conceptualization of sound *International Journal of Science Education* **11**, 491—501.

Lybeck, L., Marton, F., Strömdahl, H. and Tullberg, A. (1988) The phenomenography of the 'Mole Concept' in chemistry. In P. Ramsden (ed.), *Improving Learning: New Perspectives*. London, Kogan Page, pp. 81—108.

McCracken, J. and Laurillard, D. (1994) A study of conceptions in visual representations: a phenomenographic investigation of learning about geological maps. Paper presented at the Ed-Media World Conference in Educational Multimedia and Hypermedia, Vancouver, Canada.

Marton, F. (1992) Phenomenography and 'the art of teaching all things to all men', *Qualitative Studies in Education* **5**, 253—67.

Marton, F. and Booth, S. (1997) *Learning and Awareness*. New Jersey, Lawrence Erlbaum Associates.

Marton, F., Hounsell, D. and Entwistle, N. (1997) *The Experience of Learning: Implications for Teaching and Studying in Higher Education* 2nd edn, Edinburgh, Scottish Academic Press.

Millar, R., Prosser, M. and Sefton, I. (1989) Relationship between approach and development in student learning, *Research and Development in Higher Education* **11**, 49—53.

Prosser, M. (1993) Phenomenography and principles and practices of learning, *Higher Education Research and Development* **12**, 21—31.

Prosser, M. (1994) A phenomenographic study of students' intuitive and conceptual understanding of certain electrical phenomena, *Instructional Science* **22**, 189—205.

Prosser, M., Trigwell, K. and Taylor, P. (1994) A phenomenographic study of academics' conceptions of science learning and teaching, *Learning and Instruction* **4**, 217—31.

Prosser, M., Walker, P. and Millar, R. (1995) Different student perceptions of learning physics, *Physics Education* **31**, 43—8.

Prosser, M. and Millar, R. (1989) The 'how' and 'what' of learning physics, *The European Journal of Psychology of Education* **4**, 513—28.

Prosser, M. and Trigwell, K. (1999) *Understanding Learning and Teaching: The Experience in Higher Education*. Buckingham: Open University Press.

Reid, A. (1997) The meaning of music and the understanding of teaching and learning in the instrumental lesson. In A. Gabrielsson (ed.), *Proceedings of the Third Triennial European Society for the Cognitive Sciences of Music Conference*. Uppsala, Uppsala University.

Renström, L., Andersson, B. and Marton, F. (1990) Students' conceptions of matter, *Journal of Educational Psychology* **82**, 555—69.

Richardson, J. T. E. (1999) The concepts and methods of phenomenographic research, *Review of Educational Research* **69**, 53—82.

Theman, J. (1983) *Uppfattningar av polititisk makt* (Conceptions of political power). Göteborg, Acta Universitatis Gothoburgensis.

Trigwell, K. (1997) Phenomenography: an approach to research. In J. Higgs (ed.), *Qualitative Research: Discourse on Methodologies*, Sydney, Hampton Press, 39—47.

Trigwell, K. and Prosser, M. (1996) Changing approaches to teaching: a relational perspective, *Studies in Higher Education* **21**, 275—84.

Trigwell, K., Martin, E., Prosser, M. and Ramsden, P. (forthcoming) Variation in the experience of leadership of teaching in higher education, *British Journal of Educational Psychology*.

Trigwell, K., Prosser, M. and Taylor, P. (1994) Qualitative differences in approaches to teaching first year university science, *Higher Education* **27**, 75—84.

7 Background to the territory: conceptual issues in higher education

David Gosling

Head of Educational Development Services, University of East London

7.1 Introduction

In this chapter I shall be examining some of the assumptions which underpin research into improving student learning. I will argue that the currently dominant research discourse in higher education fails to address some key questions. These questions are ones which may be broadly characterized as 'philosophical' — that is questions about the aims of learning, values in education, the nature of knowledge and rationality and political and ethical questions about the educational enterprise. The failure to address these questions has two consequences. First, there is a tendency towards an excessive reliance on technocratic conceptions of learning and secondly, there is insufficient discussion about important matters which should be the subject of debate by both teachers in higher education, and educational developers who have the role of assisting teaching staff to be more effective.

7.2 The dominant discourse in learning, teaching and educational development

Most of the literature concerned with 'improving student learning' is about how students can be better encouraged, or facilitated, to learn the skills and subject matter of a course. The language of this discourse is often technocratic and instrumental and uses terms such as 'effective learning', 'efficiency', and 'productivity' (e.g. Akerlind and Trevitt, 1999). Within this discourse, findings report on how different factors influence the 'effectiveness' of student learning. For example,

> Studies of teaching effectiveness have found that course organisation and instructor practices are more important than class size in producing positive student outcomes
>
> (Gilbert: 1995 p3).

Such statements may then be the subject of further research (Lucas and Gibbs *et al.*, 1997), but the assumption behind such further studies is that the purpose of the research is to confirm or disconfirm an hypothesis within the limits of the research methodology. The further assumption is that recommendations can then be made to teachers in higher education about what teaching methods and class organisation they should use to achieve 'effective learning' based on the conclusion of the research.

Researchers using a phenomenographic methodology adopt a rather different approach. Here the critical question becomes 'how do people experience learning?'. The declared purpose is not to test hypotheses, but rather to allow the subjects to describe their awareness of learning and to produce a descriptive account of their experience. For example, in one of the more important recent studies, learning is described as 'proceeding from an undifferentiated and poorly integrated understanding of the whole to an increased differentiation and integration of the whole and its parts' (Marton and Booth, 1997). However, categorization of the experiences into different 'approaches to learning' have led to some conclusions being drawn about which approach is likely to be effective in higher education and how such approaches can be encouraged. For example, a recent study, using this methodology, concludes that

> A major task of teaching is to ascertain the perceptions students have of their learning situation, and work towards developing learning and teaching contexts which students experience in similar ways to that which the teacher designs.
>
> (Prosser and Trigwell, 1999, p. 25)

Thus we find that teachers are being recommended to adopt particular practices on the basis of the research findings and much of Prosser and Trigwell's research is to examine what happens when they do so. In this way they hope that their analysis 'bridges the gap between educational research and teaching practice in higher education' (ibid., p. 7)

The phenomenographic method has been criticized for the way in which its exponents have shifted from a supposedly descriptive methodology to a set of prescriptions about teaching practice and for the way in which the assumptions of the researchers may influence the categorization of the students' experience (Ashworth and Lucas, 1998). My concern is a different one. I accept the importance of the research into students' experience of learning and that this research may have significant implications for teaching methods. My contention is that both the psychological methodologies alluded to above do not address issues that require more attention and discussion than the recent literature in this field has given to them. These are questions such as 'What does it mean to learn something?', 'What is the relationship between learning and coming to know?', 'How is improving learning related to conceptions of reason and rationality?', 'What is worth knowing?'

This is not to say that these philosophical questions are more significant than those which other disciplines enquire into. Philosophers such as Rorty (1980) have challenged the idea that philosophy is necessarily a 'foundational' discipline which can issue in universal truths. Rather it is argued that in the area of research into student learning we must not lose sight of other kinds of enquiry in order to prevent the illusion taking hold that

> There will be objectively true or false answers to every question we ask, so that human worth will consist in knowing truths, and human virtue will be merely justified true belief.
>
> (Rorty, 1980, p. 388)

In order to provide a 'background to the territory' I shall be considering some of the philosophical issues which arise for improving student learning in relation to views about the nature of knowledge and reason, conceptions of 'the learner' and finally some questions of ethics and value.

7.3 Learning and 'coming to know'

Learning implies that an individual comes to know something or knows how to do something. Although knowledge is not the only end-state towards which learning is directed — for example one might learn how to be happy or achieve spiritual enlightenment — it is probably fair to say that most learning in higher education is aimed at widening or deepening students' knowledge in some way or another. If as Hirst (1973, p. 168) has argued, 'the intention of all teaching activities is that of bringing about learning' then it follows that teaching too is fundamentally about students' acquisition of knowledge. Marton and Booth (1999, p. 1) argue that 'How do we gain knowledge about the world?' is the epistemological form of the question 'What does it take to learn?' The importance of establishing this link between learning and knowledge is that without it we have no basis for determining whether or not a student has learned successfully and without such a basis the teacher cannot assess students, assign marks or award degrees.

Clearly then it is important that we have a view about what it means to come to know something, to have knowledge, or to know how to do something, but much of the history of science and philosophy calls into question the extent to which we can be confident in what we claim to know. It has been argued that, in some sense, knowledge is always and necessarily provisional and open to challenge, yet we cannot survive without making some assumptions about what it is reasonable to claim to know. Many have debated how much certainty is necessary for someone to claim to know something and here we are not referring to psychological certainty (i.e. a feeling of confidence in one's own beliefs) which is no guarantee of knowledge, but rather the basis upon which the knowledge claim is founded. This brings into focus issues the nature of evidence, the relationship between evidence and conclusions we draw from it, when it is right to think that the evidence provides us with sufficient grounds for believing a proposition to be true and when it is not. The development of knowledge over time has led to increasing recognition of differentiation between so-called 'disciplines' in the way in which knowledge claims are expressed and verified, or, indeed, the extent to which it is believed that claims can be verified. Thus what counts as evidence and how much confidence can be assigned to it varies from one discipline to another.

The implications of these epistemological questions for student learning, and therefore for teaching, are profound. As students move through the hierarchy of 'levels' of higher education (SEEC, 1996), the distinction between the transmission of knowledge and its generation becomes increasingly blurred. It is therefore one of the characteristics of *higher* education that students are taught to question and analyse critically what is presented to them as knowledge in order that they might participate in the debate about what can reasonable be said to be known. This may seem far-fetched when a teacher is presenting some basic science to first year undergraduates. Yet even here the possibility that science, at some time in the future, will reformulate what is taken to be a fact, should be drawn to the attention of all students in order to encourage a questioning frame of mind. Too often students are assessed on their ability to reproduce information without regard to its epistemological status. Improving student learning should include a critical analysis of the grounds upon which beliefs are held and the provisional nature of all knowledge claims.

This is not to say that 'anything goes' and that any answer might be right. On a Popperian view it is always easier to determine what has been shown to be wrong than it is to say what is right, although a post-modernist approach would challenge this verificationist distinction. Teachers in higher education are introducing students to a discipline-based discourse which will include rules about what may or may not be said at a given time. Much of what students learn is the language of the subject and the internal rules for substantiating claims with the subject discourse and how to challenge those claims.

It follows then, that what will count as 'improving student learning' will be open to change over time, both within and between disciplines. Equally what constitutes 'educational development' will reflect different conceptions knowing and ways of coming to know which are inherent in the range of disciplines found in universities and colleges (Jenkins, 1996). But perhaps the most important consequence is that the traditional relationship between the learner and the teacher must also be reviewed. For if it is the case that knowledge cannot be taken as a given, then both the student and tutor are engaged equally in the task of defining truth. The normal power relationship, in which control is exercised by the knower over those coming to know, comes under challenge. Habermas (e.g. 1981, 1987) is one modern philosopher who has argued that the end of the Enlightenment project, which assumed that civilization was moving towards a more and more perfect characterization of truth, means that all parties must strive towards what he calls 'communicatively achieved agreement'. To have a rational basis

> agreement cannot be imposed by either party, whether instrumentally through intervention in the situation directly or strategically through influencing the decisions of opponents
>
> (Habermas, 1984, p. 287) .

Higher education, on this view, is not simply about producing 'effective learners', nor can learning be measured by its 'efficiency', because there is no clear way of determining that learning has been achieved. If Habermas is right, we would need to look for other ways of evaluating the effectiveness of the higher education enterprise — such as the extent to which students are able to participate in the process of defining knowledge on an equal basis, the extent to which they have undergone a transformation of their thinking through negotiation, and their ability to be self-critical of their own formulations. My point here is that the goals of 'improving student learning' may be radically different depending on the epistemological standpoint adopted.

7.4 Learning and rationality

If our epistemological stance is important, then so too is our view of rationality. Within the Kantian tradition of Western philosophy, reason is characterized by necessity and universality. If an argument is logically valid then it forces a conclusion which applies to all who recognize the 'force of the argument'. Validity is determined *a priori*, in contrast to empirical or inductive conclusions, which are always inferior because less certain. Universal reason is unconditioned by time or place or circumstances and is 'self-evident'. The language of rationality gives authority to those who claim to 'see' self-evident truths which are 'proved' by logical argument.

Feminist and post-modernist writers have challenged this tradition as being masculine and 'logocentric' (e.g. Gilligan, 1982). Under the influence of philosophers such as Wittgenstein, Derrida, Foucault and Rorty much of modern discourse emphasizes the contingency and conventionality of many of the rules which operate within the disciplines. Indeed the notion of a 'discipline' itself comes under fire, suggesting as it does the force of regulation and rule-bound behaviour. In the place of universality we are asked to acknowledge the irreducible plurality of incommensurable 'language games' and 'forms of life' (to use Wittgenstein's preferred terms). Truth, instead of being total and timeless becomes irremediably 'local', subject to historical and cultural variability. Systems of thought, or 'meta-narratives' such as Marxism, are rejected as totalizing and are replaced by more fragmentary and conditioned theory. The central role of 'signs', notably language, which condition our thinking is central to this so-called 'post-modernist' leading to conclusions about the incommensurability of translation between languages and between systems of thought.

What are the implications of this collection of ideas for student learning? This is a large subject to tackle in a short space (see Barnett and Griffin, 1997), but let me suggest two broad implications. On the one hand it suggests that 'improving student learning is as much to do with enabling students to see alternative ways of thinking, of being tolerant of the diversity of forms of thought, to move away from dogmatism and intolerance as it to do with simply learning 'efficiently'. What students' learn and how it affects the transformation of their personal outlook is at least as important the effectiveness of the learning. There are also implications for the teacher, who must, equally, be willing to listen to different voices, to make space for students to construct their own understandings and not to pre-determine what might be right answers or correct reasoning. Even in the sciences the dogmatism of the expert is under challenge. Many received ideas about medicine, health, diet, climate, the environment, agriculture have come under fire. The wild, 'illogical' and disregarded theories of yesterday can become the accepted opinion of today.

Feminists have argued that the distinctive voice of women should be heard (Gilligan, 1982) and that greater legitimacy should be given to 'animating learning from experience' through autobiography and 'experiential learning' as opposed to knowledge constructed by others for the purposes of others (Boud and Miller, 1996, Boud, Cohen & Walker, 1993). There are also claims for alternative world views from cultures and ethnic groups outside the dominant Western philosophy to be given greater credence and serious treatment. As knowledge become globalized and the student body becomes more culturally varied these arguments are likely to assume greater importance in the UK as they already have done so in the USA. In universities such as East London, South Bank and North London, where there are substantial numbers of non-white students, the importance of revising the curriculum to give space for alternative voices, and to recognize that certain views associated with disempowered minorities have been suppressed, is a significant issue (Jiwani &Gosling, 1997, Cohen, 1965).

The second implication, which I can only touch on, follows from what was said about the absence of 'legitimizing grand narratives' and the emphasis on the particular and the local rather than the universal. This has led, on some views, to an increasing concentration on consumption, the market, and the individual student as consumer of knowledge and skills — 'competences' — which he or she can sell. Lyotard (1984, p. 5) has argued that knowledge has become commodified — 'an informational commodity indispensable to productive power'. This view of education as a kind of consumerism has been linked to the advocacy of 'student-centredness'.

> The valuing of knowledge in terms of its performity suggests that the learner is a co-implication of contemporary discourses of individualistic learner-centredness and current trends towards the marketisation of learning opportunities.
>
> (Usher, Bryant and Johnston, 1997, p. 14)

Educational developers have to decide what ideological assumptions under-pin student-centred learning which they have typically advocated. Although the justification given is normally supported by psychological research, there may be underlying trends towards individualization driven by cultural norms that the psychological research is merely reflecting. The emphasis on skills, competences and capability has been challenged by Barnett (1994), including the academic competences associated with specific disciplines. In its place, following Rorty's idea of the edifying conversation (Rorty, 1980, p. 365) he has argued for greater attention to be given to the processes of dialogue, conversation and critique (Barnett, 1994, p. 185).

7.5 Conceptions of 'the learner'

This brings us to some issues about the nature of 'the learner'. In the literature on deep and surface learning there is an attribution of intention to the learner. For example, in this discussion of the 'surface' approach, Biggs comments as follows:

> Do not think that Robert is irredeemably cursed with a surface approach. What we know is that under current conditions of teaching he chooses to use a surface approach ... The conclusion that in Robert we have an incurably surface student on our hands might in the end prove to be correct, but that conclusion is way down the track yet.
>
> (Biggs, 1999, pp. 14—15)

Whereas he describes students using a 'deep approach' as follows:

> When students feel this need-to-know, they try to focus on underlying meaning ... When using the deep approach in handling a task, students have positive feelings: interest, a sense of importance, challenge, even exhilaration. Learning is a pleasure. Students come with questions they want answered, and when the answers are unexpected, that is even better.
>
> (Biggs, 1999, p. 16)

What assumptions are being made about the 'learner' in these extracts? The first thing we might notice is the way students are being referred to as examples of types about whom generalizations can be made. Secondly, there is an attribution of individual agency — that is, students are assumed to be making their own autonomous choices about the approach to learning adopted. Thirdly, judgements are being made about the students' experience in a strongly value-loaded way. There is a threat that the surface approach may be 'irredeemable' or 'incurable' whereas the deep approach is associated with a vocabulary of 'importance', 'exhilaration', 'pleasure' (see Webb, 1996). Students as 'learners' are described in ways which separate them from their personal or social characteristics and focus on just one aspect of their behaviour — 'Robert takes notes and selectively quotes them back'. Robert becomes a disembodied 'learner' whose actions are nevertheless thought to be transparent to the researcher who has analysed and 'diagnosed' the nature of his actions.

This way of viewing the psychological subject has a long history in Western thought. Descartes provides the key text of the 'self' as the idealized 'thinking being' in the Meditations, when having doubted everything he arrives at his conclusion 'I think, therefore I am' (Descartes, 1966). But in recent times this view of the self as 'the sovereign rational subject — atomistic and autonomous, disengaged and disembodied, and at least on some views, potentially and ideally self-transparent' (Baynes, Bohman and McCarthy, 1988, p. 4). But this view has been significantly challenged in recent times.

> Nor is it possible to ignore the intrinsically social character of 'structures of consciousness', the historical and cultural variability of categories of thought and principles of action, their interdependence with the changing forms of social and material reproduction.
>
> (ibid.)

In other words we cannot understand Robert without knowing something about his social and material position in the world, nor can his behaviour be interpreted without reference to social norms and context. We cannot assume that individuals act rationally or autonomously, nor can we make global judgements about what 'approaches' are to be positively, or negatively, valued.

We can summarise the two positions as shown in Table 7.1.

Sovereign rational subject	Irrational, decentred
Atomistic	holistic
Autonomous	social
Disengaged	engaged, partial, committed
Disembodied	embodied, gendered, situated
Ideally self-transparent	unconscious, subconscious

Table 7.1 Opposing views of the 'subject'

7.6 Learning and values

Finally I would like to move on to some issues in ethics and questions of values. We have been discussing 'what counts as knowledge?', 'what do we understand by reason and rationality?' and 'what is a learner?', but we may also ask 'what is worth knowing?', 'what do we value in learning' and 'what ethical issues are there in the relationship between the learner and the teacher in higher education?'.

We have noted earlier that a characteristic of post-modernism is the undermining of traditional systems of thought — or 'meta-narratives'. Nowhere is this more evident than in the area of ethics and values. Indeed it has been argued that questions of value have been reduced to a matter of individual choice of 'lifestyle practices'. We have noted that learning has become individualized. So too, it is argued, have decisions about ethics become merely expressions self-awareness, of self-referential taste, style, and preferences — marking out differences in identity (Usher *et al.*, 1997, p. 18). Student choice in what to study and what is of value becomes central to this conception of higher education. Students have 'rights' because, as individuals, they control their own meanings and values.

This reduction of ethical questions to consumerism is in tension with some other trends that we find in higher education. One of these is the central role played by utilitarian thinking, particularly in policy-making. Put simply, utilitarianism suggests that value is determined by what brings greatest benefit to the greatest number. Although there are many forms of utilitarianism, put simply, utilitarianism suggests that value is determined by what brings greatest benefit to the greatest number (Smart & Williams, 1973). Justification of this kind are commonly used to support decisions about who has access to higher education, how should HE be financed, what priority should be given to HE compared with other social/political goals. Conflicts typically arise when utilitarian arguments produce policies which deny rights claimed by particular groups. The current debate about student tuition fees is a case in point, when a political decision taken on the basis of maximizing benefit is thought to deny a group (in this case students) of what they claim to be a 'right' — namely to free higher education. In some ways there is nothing new about such conflicts — teleological justifications are always liable to be in contradiction to ontological justifications — but in the current state of confusion about ethics there appears to be no way of applying any higher level justification to resolve such tensions.

A second trend is towards various types of 'communitarian' ethics, which suggest that value is assigned from with the norms and traditions of social groups, whether these be family, religion, nationality, or ethnic group. Within this tradition the kind of value-conflict described above is less likely to occur — particularly in more collective and authoritarian value systems associated with some religious groups. But conflicts do occur between the values of particular groups and the requirements of higher education. For example, in the sections above, I referred to Habermas's demand for negotiation and open dialogue between teachers and students. Universities in the West place a high value on freedom of speech, and particularly on 'academic freedom' but when this freedom is used in a way which is offensive to particular groups there is a clash of value systems which cannot be resolved to everyone's satisfaction as the Salmon Rushdie affair demonstrated.

As lecturers and educational developers we are often faced with value choices, although these are not often made explicit or justified. The learning and teaching literature in the West endorses values of co-operation, tolerance, understanding of others, equality of opportunity, respect for individual's dignity and self-worth, self-fulfilment, autonomy, fairness. We place a high value on independence and autonomy, although we also value the ability to work in groups cooperatively with colleagues. In a survey undertaken at the University of East London with academics, students and external examiners, on the characteristics of graduateness, the ethical goal of learning tolerance of alternative views scored as highly as cognitive goals such as the ability to think critically (UEL, 1995). One example where the ethical goals of higher are made explicit is in the SEEC generic level descriptors, where 'ethical understanding' and 'responsibility' are categories of level indicators (SEEC, 1996). According to this schema, improving student learning is about students moving from 'limited awareness of ethical issues' (level 0) to 'awareness of personal responsibility and professional codes of conduct' (level 3).

What passes as 'effective teaching strategies' and what constitutes 'effective learning' will depend on what student behaviour is valued. A teaching method which is 'effective' in the sense that students successfully learn a given body of material, may still be criticized because individual student autonomy is denied and student choice is absent. The preference for 'deep learning' over 'surface learning' is not just about what is effective, it is also about what we value in our students. Objections to the 'conventional lecture' are not only about its limited success in achieving learning, the objection is also that 'it is more likely to underline an impression of the lecturer as an unapproachably remote authority' (Ramsden, 1992, p. 165). But in some cultures that would be a correct and approved impression. If we approve of approachability and informality it is because of some deeper value set which is not easily made available for scrutiny or challenge.

7.7 Conclusion

In this 'background to the territory', I have attempted to sketch out some of the philosophical issues which arise when we start to think about what we understand by 'improving student learning'. We have seen that there are many issues which relate to our conceptions of learning, knowledge, reason, the learner and values which are often not discussed in much of the research literature. We have also seen that we need to be wary of thinking that 'learning effectiveness' is a simple matter. It is important that we ensure that these questions are raised and discussed, because without them our discourse can be dominated by assumptions that have not been critically assessed. Our goal has been, as Rorty has suggested, to 'continue the conversation' rather than 'find the truth' (Rorty, 1980, p. 373). We need to remember this when we think about 'improving student learning' and resist attempts, whether by researchers or by policy makers, to close down the conversation by declaring that 'effective teaching occurs when ...' or 'students learn best when ...'. This chapter is an attempt to open discussions and to keep the conversations going.

References

Akerlind, G. and Trevitt, C. (1999), Enhanced Self-Directed Learning through Educational Technology, *Innovations in Education and Training International*, Vol 36, No 2, (May) pp96-105

Ashworth, P. and Lucas, L. (1998), What is the 'World' of Phenomenography, *Scandinavian Journal of Educational Research*, Vol 42, No 4, 415-421.

Barnett, R. (1994), *The Limits of Competence: Knowledge Higher Education and Society*, Buckingham, SRHE and Open University Press.

Barnett, R. and Griffin, A. (1997) (eds) *The End of Knowledge in Higher Education*, London, Cassell.

Baynes, K., Bohman, J. and McCarthy, T. (1988) *After Philosophy, End or Transformation?*, Cambridge, Massachusetts, MIT Press.

Biggs, J. (1999), *Teaching for Quality Learning at University*, Buckingham, SRHE and Open University Press.

Boud, D., Cohen, R. and Walker D. (1993) (eds) *Using Experience for Learning*, Buckingham, SRHE and Open University Press.

Boud, D. and Miller, N. (1996) *Working with Experience, Animating Learning*, London, Routledge.

Cohen, P. (1995) Crisis of the Western University, in *For a Multicultural University*, Working Paper No 3, Centre New Ethnicities Research, University of East London.
Descartes, R. (1966) *Philosophical Writings*, (trans Anscombe, E. & Geach, P.T) London, Nelson.
Gilbert, S. (1995), *Quantity education and does size matter?*, AUE Research1, No 1, 1-7.
Gilligan, C. (1982) *In a Different Voice: Psychological Theory and Women's Development*, Cambridge MA, Harvard University Press.
Gosling, D. (2000) (forthcoming) Using Habermas to evaluate two approaches to negotiated assessment, *Asessment and Evaluation in Higher Education*.
Habermas, J. (1981) *Modernity versus Postmodernity*, New German Critique, 22: 3-141
Habermas, J. (1984) *The Theory of Communicative Action*, Vol 1, (trans McCarthy T.) London, Heineman)
Habermas, J. (1987) *The Philosophical Discourse of Modernity*, Twelve Lectures, (trans Lawrence, F.) Cambridge, Polity Press.
Hirst, P. (1973) 'What is Teaching?' in Peters, R.S. (ed) *The Philosophy of Education*, Oxford, Oxford University Press, pp.163-177.
Jenkins, A. (1996) 'Discipline-based educational development', *International Journal for Academic Development*, Vol, No 1, May, pp.50-62.
Jiwani, A. and Gosling, D. (1997) 'Course Design for multi-ethnic student groups', *Improving Student Learning - Through Course Design*, OCSLD, 314-330.
Lucas, L., Gibbs, G., Hughes, S., Jones, O. and Wisker, G. (1997) 'A study of the effects of course design features on student learning in large classes at three institutions: a comparative study'. *Improving Student Learning - Through Course Design*, OCSLD, pp.10-24.
Lyotard, J. F. (1984) *The Post-modern Condition: A Report on Knowledge*, Manchester University Press.
MacIntrye, A. (1981) *After Virtue*, London, Duckworth.
Marton, F. and Booth, S. (1997) *Learning and Awareness*, New Jersey, Lawrence Erlbaum Maherah.
Prosser, M. and Trigwell, K. (1999) *Understanding Learning and Teaching: The Experience in Higher Education*, SRHE/OU Press, Buckingham.
Ramsden, P. (1992) *Learning to Teaching in Higher Education*, London, Routledge.
Rorty, R. (1980), *Philosophy and the Mirror of Nature*, Oxford, Blackwell.
Sandel, M. (1982) *Liberalism and the Limits of Justice*, Cambridge, University Press.
SEEC, (1996) *Protocols and Guidelines* (with Higher Education Credit Initiative in Wales), Southern England Consortium for Credit Accumulation and Transfer.
Scheffler, S. (ed) (1998) *Consequentialism and Its Critics*, Buckingham, Open University Press.
Smart, J.J.C. and Williams, B. (1973) *Utilitarianism: For and Against*, Cambridge, University Press.
Taylor, C. (1985) *Philosophy and the Human Sciences*, Cambridge, University Press.
University of East London, (1996) Graduate Standards Survey, undertaken on behalf of the Higher Education Quality Council of the UK.
Usher, R., Bryant, I. and Johnson, R. (1997) *Adult Education and the Post-modern Challenge*, London, Routledge.
Walzer, M. (1983) *Spheres of Justice*, Oxford, Blackwell.
Webb, G. (1996) *Understanding Staff Development*, Buckingham, SRHE and Open University Press.

8 Issues and challenges in the teaching of modern languages

Lore Arthur[1] **and John Klapper**[2]

1. The Open University; 2. University of Birmingham

8.1 Overview

Anyone who has ever attempted to study another language will know that it is by no means a straightforward matter. On the one hand, it can be exhilarating to have a meaningful conversation with a native speaker of that language. On the other, it can be a frustrating and difficult experience. There are, after all, thousands of different words to remember and complex rules to apply. Rather like those attempting to keep fit in group situations, language learners feel exposed when confronted with others who seem to be able to speak the language so much better than they can. Then there is an expectation among learners and at least some professionals that learners should aspire to the linguistic competence of native or near-native speakers, an almost impossible task.

But how does one learn another language? What skills and motor functions are involved? How does what research tells us about first and second language learning influence our understanding of what is good teaching practice? Theoretical approaches to first language acquisition, or the development of children learning their mother tongue (L1), and the teaching and learning of another, second language (L2), have led to the gradual acceptance in foreign or modern language pedagogy that languages are learnt both consciously and subconsciously, that is both formally and informally, in and outside educational institutions, with or without the help of the teacher. Insights gained from behaviourist, cognitivist and humanistic approaches to psychology, have hastened the move away from a teacher-led and teacher-controlled environment to one which seeks to understand and accommodate what is commonly termed learner-centred approaches, and to recognize individual learner differences in motivation, aptitude, learning styles and learner strategies (see Skehan 1989, Mitchell and Myles 1998). These relatively recent developments have led to a fundamental change in the way many think languages should be taught.

8.2 Methods and approaches

Language teaching in higher education is very disparate and shows the influence of a number of different methodologies, some dating back over a hundred years. In the nineteenth century languages were considered worth learning primarily for educational purposes, as a method of training the mind in rational thinking and analytical problem-solving. The emerging university discipline of 'modern languages' subordinated pragmatic thoughts of language as a means of communication to the need to gain academic respectability. The key approach was the grammar-translation method. This assumed that languages consisted of a collection of rules and words, which could be readily described and listed. It was the role of teaching to exemplify the rules, to present them deductively, to encourage memorization and to provide practice with a conscious focus on form. Typically, the deductive presentation of a point of grammar used sample sentences which had been artificially constructed for that purpose. '*La plume de ma tante*' characterized much traditional school-based teaching. It is surprising how influential and durable the grammar-translation method has proved to be. Until well into the 1960s it continued to be the standard method of teaching in most British secondary schools and to this day shapes the practice of some modern language departments in British higher education and a good many more in continental Europe (see Hawkins, 1981, pp. 117—33 for a readable historical survey). Other, more reform-minded teaching methods emerged in the course of the early twentieth century. Amidst a plethora of names, the 'direct method' was the one which eventually stuck. It indicated the necessity to form a direct association of objects and concepts with words in L2, sought to avoid reference to the mother tongue more or less completely and to accord grammar a more subordinate, accompanying role. The rise of the direct method went hand in hand with the spread of the relatively new discipline of phonetics, which provided the framework for the new emphasis on the spoken word. Although the direct method has long since fallen out of favour in many educational settings, it still provides success for some commercial language teaching companies.

The most significant post-war development in language learning was the rise of audio-lingualism, a methodology based on drilling, the formation of habit and the avoidance of error. Audio-lingualism was remarkable for bringing together a range of different disciplines and linking them to the development of technology (most notably the tape recorder and the language laboratory), with the aim of producing a scientific approach to language learning. It had its origins in the behaviourist view that language learning, like all other kinds of learning, was dependent on the formation of habits. According to work in psychology (e.g. Bloomfield, 1933; Skinner, 1957), all human behaviour is to be seen as a process of stimulus and response in which 'successful' responses are 'reinforced'. If such reinforcement is constantly repeated, the stimulus will eventually prompt the same response time after time. The audio-lingual method was still structured around grammar and one of the main reasons for the failure of both it and its closely related offshoot the audio-visual method (cf. Hawkins, 1981, pp. 172—5) was the belief that practice alone was sufficient for learning to take place, that there could be automatic transfer from the classroom to naturalistic language use. As Johnson (1994, p. 126) notes: 'The conditions of practice are so remote from what actually happens as to be useless; the expected transfer from practice to production does not occur because practice offered in the class is so unlike the production of real life.'

In the late 1950s and 1960s there was a significant shift in the world of linguistics from structural to generative approaches. The former focused on the description of the surface structure of language and had been used to support audio-lingualism, while the latter emphasized that language itself is governed by rules and the creative way we use language. Skinner's work was fiercely criticized by Chomsky whose *Syntactic Structures* (1957) heralded the dawn of the generative age. Chomsky argued that children do not learn and simply reproduce huge numbers of sentences and phrases, in the way behaviourism had suggested, but that they constantly create new language which they have never learnt before. They can do this because they have an innate language faculty, called the language acquisition device, which enables them to discover and internalize rules from language they are exposed to. The fact that children are not just copying language but trying to apply rules in these ways is seen in such common infant utterances as 'we sawed', 'she gived' and 'he goed'. Subsequent research in the emergent discipline of Second Language Acquisition (SLA) first showed considerable similarities between the stages of first language acquisition among children, and then broadly similar acquisition between young first and adult second language learners of English (see Ellis, 1985, pp. 54—68 for a review). At the same time SLA began to suggest that errors are both an inevitable and necessary element of the acquisition process, and that since many errors do not resemble either L2 or L1 forms, they must be part of an internal learner system. Thus such variants as 'he goed' or 'she bringed' are quite natural transitional stages which all foreign/second language learners pass through on the way to formulating the respective correct form. SLA research reveals that second language competence is developmental and variable, that it grows gradually as a function of both conscious and subconscious learning and that the errors learners make play a major part in the learning process.

8.3 Communicative language teaching

Apart from investigating acquisition orders and the role of error, the post-Chomskian world of language learning also developed in another important direction. Objecting to an exclusive focus on language learning as the acquisition of a system of grammar-based rules, Hymes (1971) introduced the concept of 'communicative competence'. The term denotes a learner's need to focus on appropriate language use, that is on using language for particular purposes and in particular situations and settings; grammar meanwhile is to be seen as just one aspect of communicative competence alongside these other rhetorical and socio-cultural aspects. The key features of Communicative Language Teaching (CLT) can be summarized as:

- an emphasis on learners' needs;
- a focus on meaning;
- the creative use of language;
- the use of authentic language and materials;
- the use of L2 in the classroom;
- cultural awareness;
- an inductive approach to grammar;
- learner interaction.

This refocusing involved a revolution in syllabus design and language teaching. Earlier grammar-based language teaching had adopted a rigid, graded approach to the language syllabus, teaching the present tense long before any past tenses or introducing nouns before pronouns, etc. By contrast, CLT, under the influence of insights from SLA research, embraced what was termed the functional-notional syllabus (Wilkins 1976). According to this, the first and most important stage in syllabus design was to consider what learners are likely to have to do in the language (e.g. thanking someone, apologizing, expressing opinions), on to which should be mapped the expressions, vocabulary and grammar required to articulate them. The functional-notional reorientation proved particularly influential in the work of the Council of Europe (van Ek, 1975) and has had a decisive effect over the past 25 years on the design of teaching materials.

SLA research has also established that those learning a second language display pretty much the same order in their acquisition of certain grammatical forms and that there are similarities with first language acquisition. This has led in some quarters to the extreme view that learning the mother tongue involves essentially the same process as learning a second language. Consequently, a number of pedagogical theorists have proposed a strong version of CLT in which the dominant factor is meaningful input and little room is left for error correction or a focus on language form. Krashen (1985), for example, argues that subconscious acquisition (i.e. learning through use) is essentially different from conscious learning (e.g. learning noun declensions, verb conjugation, etc.) The former is dependent on natural interaction with the second language and meaningful communication, while the latter depends on a focus on form and rules, usually but not necessarily based on classroom learning.

Undoubtedly there are some similarities between first and second language acquisition: both depend, to some extent, on learners interacting with speakers of the second language and engaging with increasing amounts of information which steadily build on a previous store of knowledge. For this reason target language use in the classroom and working with as wide a range of authentic texts as possible are now both generally recognized as crucial aspects of language learning, particularly at advanced levels. Authentic texts, that is texts originally aimed at native speakers of that language, and real-life tasks provide learners with an explicit learning purpose in which the focus is on the message and the achievement of the task, and this explicit focus encourages *implicit* learning of syntactical, morphological and lexical features of the target language.

However, this is far from being the whole story. Although L2 acquisition may resemble L1 acquisition in a number of important ways, most L2 learners approach the target language with a degree of proficiency and literacy in their first language. This means that they can use reading and writing to help promote their second language learning. They also bring to the language-learning process a capacity for exploring grammatical forms in a conscious and explicit manner, and are able to talk about language, for example by using metalanguage. These facts make second language learning in a formal educational setting a much more deliberate and intentional process. Furthermore, research into so-called form-focused learning (Long, 1983; Ellis, 1989; Spada, 1997) has shown that a conscious focus on grammar serves to speed up the language acquisition process and enables learners ultimately to attain higher levels of proficiency.

The difficulty, however, is that knowing formal rules does not by itself guarantee the ability to formulate language which obeys these rules. This is a real problem for many learners, especially those combining languages with other disciplines in HE: in language learning, inductive learning processes are just as important as the more cognitive, deductive approaches typical of many other academic disciplines, in which it very often *is* possible to learn things as a result of explicit rule teaching and error correction. Language learning, however, is not always a conscious activity dependent on the availability of explicit knowledge about the language and the way it functions, but rather the product of a complex process of both conscious learning and the gradual, subconscious development of an internal ability to use language naturally and spontaneously without reference to the conscious mind.

It is the challenge of the language classroom to develop learners' internalized linguistic competence, that is their implicit knowledge of and capacity for appropriate language use, *in tandem with* explicit knowledge of grammatical and phonological rules. This requires the development of a steadily expanding body of interlocking skills through imitation, repetition, drilling and frequent practice in extended contexts to the point where these skills become automatic and subconscious. The analogy with piano playing seems most appropriate in this context: 'Just as the novice pianist must consciously learn finger placements and pedalling, so the language learner must consciously learn bits of language — words and phrases, pronunciation and patterns of intonation — that become embedded in memory and can be accessed spontaneously' (Little and Ushioda, 1998, p. 15).

For this reason the strong version of CLT is now justifiably viewed with suspicion. It is criticized, in particular, for failing to build up free communicative activity through pre-communicative exercises which consciously focus on grammatical forms and which practise and internalise new language structures in a clear pedagogical sequence. Without this systematic rehearsal, learners are unable to handle language flexibly, to adapt and recombine elements of language in new communicative settings.

8.4 Individual differences: theoretical and practical perspectives

Communicative Language Teaching developed out of the realization that learners, particularly adults, have differing needs and motivation for learning another language. These differences are apparent in most teaching and learning situations. In addition, learners enter the learning situation with a variety of prior learning experiences, differences in aptitude, personality, intelligence and preferred learning styles. All these factors have led to a plethora of research, particularly over the last two or three decades. Not surprisingly, the question of 'nature' or 'nurture' has bedevilled the professional discourse here as much as in other areas of education. A number of persistent questions remain: Why are some learners simply better linguists then others? To what extent is excellence linked to having a good memory, intelligence and personality? What do learners actually do when learning a language? In this kind of discussion terms such as 'remembering', 'forgetting', 'skill', 'motivation', 'inhibition' and 'risk taking' are inevitably influenced by the theoretical approaches of cognitive psychology and psycholinguistics:

- *conceptual and verbal learning* which includes information, knowledge, ideas, concepts and systems of thought;
- *skills learning* which refers to the acquisition of sensory-motor processes, for example the articulation of a variety of sounds;
- *effective and social learning* which refers to emotional conduct and expression, social attitudes and values (see Stern, 1983).

Theories of language acquisition are broad-based. They emerge from studies of disparate groups of learners with very diverse cultural backgrounds in a variety of different countries and educational settings. Furthermore, in common with most other areas of academe, one can discern distinct trends and fashions. In general, however, studies tend to focus on the characteristics of learners, how a second language is learned and what kind of procedural factors influence its success. For example, research into personality traits lends support to the view that outgoing, extrovert students are more successful language learners than more inhibited, introverted ones, but such observations may confirm stereotypes and half-truths (Stern, 1983, p. 379). Other factors, such as positive task orientation or certain emotional and social predispositions may either help or hinder aspects of language learning. Theories of motivation distinguish between extrinsic or instrumental motives and intrinsic or integrative motives. Successful learners, it is argued, must be psychologically prepared to adopt various aspects of behaviour which characterize members of another linguistic-cultural group. The orientation is integrative if learners wish to learn more about other cultural communities because they are as interested in the other culture as they are in their own (Gardner and Lambert, 1969, p. 3).

The suggestion that learners possess an innate aptitude for language learning has not been free from controversy — though more conclusive answers may eventually emerge out of research into neurolinguistics. Most aptitude tests, if they are used at all, focus on those characteristics which are regarded as specific to language learning, that is the ability to:

- pay attention to and discriminate the sounds of a language, i.e. a learner's 'phonetic coding ability';
- relate speech sounds to some form of graphemic representation, in other words, to establish sound-symbol relationships;
- attend to the formal characteristics of a language, i.e. grammatical sensitivity (Stern, 1983, p. 370).

Critics of such tests maintain that success in any or all of these cannot be dissociated from social factors such as class, education, age and prior learning experiences. Some researchers seek links between first language learning and the aptitude to learn a second one, while others consider that factors such as attitudes, the readiness to learn, motivation, the maintenance of motivation or the degree of acculturation have greater significance (Skehan, 1989). Perhaps more noteworthy is the assumption that having a 'good' memory is linked to success in language learning. The ability speedily to recall words or chunks of language no doubt helps in all learning situations. To learn a second language, therefore, means to learn a skill, as was pointed out earlier on in this paper. Various aspects of the task must be practised and integrated into some kind of fluent performance. This requires automation and restructuring, as learners simplify, unify and gain increasing control over their internal representation. In other words, learners need to be able to activate their short-term memory so that utterances become automatic or internalised before they can be transferred to a different speech context. This ability may account for the learner variability that characterises all learner language (McLaughlin, 1987, pp. 133—4).

The view that the main characteristics of SLA consist of the acquisition of complex cognitive skills dominates current theoretical discourse. There is also a pedagogical view that learners will benefit from recognising their own preferred learning styles and being taught various learning strategies. Theories of learning styles are similar to those postulated in generic learning theories. They refer to a series of opposites such as field dependence and field independence, broad and narrow categorization, or to those taken from Kolb's model which distinguishes between divergent, assimilative, convergent and accommodative learning styles (Kolb, 1984, pp. 76—8). While theories of learning styles concentrate on how learners are different from one another, learning strategies emphasize the active involvement of learners in the learning process, in particular their ability to process information that enhances comprehension of the foreign language and to retain this information for future use. The various models of learning strategies are generally classified into three broad categories:

- metacognitive strategies focus on special aspects of language learning such as listening for key words or phrases, planning for the organization of either written or spoken discourse, monitoring the production of language or the comprehension of information that needs to be remembered, and checking comprehension after completion of, for example, a listening task;

- cognitive strategies involve repeating the names or items to be remembered, grouping and classifying words, using information texts to guess meaning, deducing or applying rules to the understanding of language, using visual images or linguistic information to link new ideas with known information;
- social and affective strategies focus on issues such as working with peers to solve problems, pooling information, checking notes, questioning for clarification and using mental redirection of thinking to ensure that a learning activity will be successful (see O'Malley and Chamot, 1990; Mitchell and Myles, 1998).

The influence of SLA research, combined with a determination to implement equal opportunities for all, has led, at least in some institutions, to a wider acceptance of differentiation in language pedagogy. In practical terms differentiation allows for mixed-level teaching by accommodating the needs of both stronger and weaker students at the same time. Various relatively simple techniques (the use of open and closed questions, for example) permit tension-increasing and tension-reducing strategies within the same group of learners. In addition, the recognition of individual learning strategies sensitises learners to more generic transferable skills, for example 'learning how to learn' and 'reflective practices' such as diary writing, and to appropriate study skills. However, these issues require the development of a cohesive, widely accepted framework for 'good' language teaching practice, one which is underpinned by clear theoretical generic and subject-specific principles, as promoted, for example, by the Institute of Teaching and Learning in Higher Education. It is one which, alas, has eluded scholars and practitioners alike over many years.

Little and Singleton (in Duda and Riley, 1990, p. 19) sum up many of these issues by stating that

> language teaching methodologies need to be based on sound principles, and much research remains to be done before we shall be in a position to make large claims and be wholly confident in our predictions. In the meantime, we may find that we can achieve a great deal by just consulting our learners and encouraging them to reflect critically on the learning process. For it seems to be a general rule that human beings perform best when they know what they are meant to be doing, why they are meant to be doing it, and by what means they are most likely to do it successfully.

8.5 Developments in higher education (HE)

The substantial changes which have occurred in language teaching in recent years have to be seen in the context of university modern language study and the issues currently facing higher education. Whereas 40 years ago almost all HE language courses were characterised by a predominantly post-A level intake, by translation into and out of the target language, academic essay writing, the study of phonetics and 'conversation classes', the picture is now a lot more complex. More languages are offered *ab initio*, that is at absolute beginner's level. In terms of pedagogy, there is now less emphasis on translation, especially in the early stages of the undergraduate degree. In several institutions there have also been moves towards increased use of the target language as the medium of instruction and towards broadening the range of functional, employment-related activities such as oral presentations, group discussions, debates, the writing of précis, summaries, letters, reviews and reports.

Paradoxically, in times of increased emphasis on quality assurance, the pressures on resources and research activity for full-time members of staff have led to greater use of part-time staff, postgraduate research students and 'colloquial assistants' — now usually called foreign language assistants — in the delivery of key course components to the expanded numbers pursuing language degrees.

Although the number of 'specialist' (i.e. single honours) language students is currently in decline, overall numbers increased dramatically in the early 1990s, with well over 60 per cent of the total falling into the category of 'non-specialist' language students (Thomas, 1993). This is largely attributable to the rapid growth of language courses on so-called IWLPs, or Institution-Wide Language Programmes, usually delivered by languages centres. These range from one-semester modules to full four-year degrees with a year abroad and account for anything between 10 and 25 per cent of course credits. One of the features of the provision for non-specialists, in contrast to much language teaching in academic departments, is the use of trained 'dedicated', full- or, more likely, part-time language teachers, often operating on non-academic contracts.

Another key feature in HE modern language study concerns the nature of the incoming student. Following the opening up of language learning to a far wider ability range with the introduction of the GCSE examination and the National Curriculum requirement for all pupils of compulsory school age to study a modern language, teaching methods and assessment procedures in schools are now no longer designed to prepare pupils for an academic career in linguistics and literature. Rather, language learning has become a common entitlement and schools are charged with making language learning seem both achievable and worthwhile to pupils with widely differing needs. 'A' and 'AS' levels in turn have changed in response to the skills and interests of potential learners and to current thinking on teaching and assessment, with the introduction of a modular structure and increased use of the target language as the medium of communication. These reforms are criticized in HE for shifting the balance too far from accuracy to fluency and for improving neither. In particular, HE linguists are highly critical of first-year students' lack of grammatical competence. Whatever justification there is for these criticisms, HE now faces the challenge of finding imaginative and effective ways to tackle these deficiencies while simultaneously building upon the different skills incoming students possess.

There remain other issues to address. These relate to the image language learning has within academia and the public at large. The fact that linguists themselves emphasize the need for a practical, skills-related approach, has, at least in some quarters, relegated a hitherto respectable academic pursuit to one which operates a service function within higher education, much to the detriment of those who seek higher academic status. This is not to argue for an 'ivory tower' approach striving for excellence among relatively few, but for a recognition that excellence combined with scholarship is achievable even in the context of mass education.

8.6 Conclusion

Learning another language to a high level of proficiency and a sophisticated level of cross-cultural understanding requires the same dedication, intelligence and analytical skills as all undergraduate study. However, the social recognition and standing of competent linguists in the labour market is less easily controlled. It remains an unacceptable fact that, in this country at least, linguists, be they translators, interpreters or language teachers, tend not to be well paid or to achieve high social status. There is an additional dilemma: English has, in the minds of many people, become a world language by virtue of the political and economic progress made by English-speaking nations over the past 200 years, and it is likely to remain so, gradually consolidating its position across the world. It is estimated that 300 million people have English as their mother tongue and a further 300 million use it as a second language in their own countries, while another 100 million use it fluently as a foreign language in countries where English has no official status. This represents an increase of 40 per cent since the 1950s (Crystal, 1987, p. 358). However, the current impact of the Internet and the world-wide information explosion make the use of English as a global language seem increasingly likely. In the British context, it is not surprising therefore that the ability to speak another language has rarely achieved its deserved educational and social status, despite the rhetoric of politicians and educationists in recent years. It is difficult to see how these developments will impact on HE modern language study in years to come. The recent decline in applications to modern language courses might turn out to be an early warning sign of an unstoppable decline.

8.7 References

Bloomfield, L. (1933) *Language*. New York: Holt, Rinehart & Winston.

Brown, R. (1973) *A First Language: The Early Stages*. Cambridge, MA: Harvard University Press.

Chomsky, N. (1957) *Syntactic Structures*. The Hague: Mouton.

Crystal, D. (1987) *The Cambridge Encyclopaedia of Language*. Cambridge: Cambridge University Press.

Duda, R. and Riley, P. (eds) (1990) *Learning Styles*. Nancy: Presses Universitaires de Nancy.

Ellis, R (1985) *Understanding Second Language Acquisition*. Oxford: Oxford University Press.

Ellis, R. (1989) Are classroom and naturalistic acquisition the same? A study of the classroom acquisition of German word order rules, *Studies in Second Language Acquisition* **11**: 305—28.

Gardner, R.C. and Lambert, W.E. (1969) *Attitudes and Motivation in Second Language Learning*. Massachusetts: Newbury House Publishers.

Hawkins, E. (1981) *Modern Languages in the Curriculum*. Cambridge: Cambridge University Press.

Hymes, D. (1971) *On Communicative Competence*. Philadelphia, PA: University of Pennsylvania Press.

Johnson, K. (1994) Teaching declarative and procedural knowledge. In M. Bygate, A. Tonkyn and E. Williams (eds), *Grammar and the Language Teacher* Hemel Hempstead: Prentice Hall.

Kolb, D. (1984) *Experiential Learning: Turning Experience into Learning*. New Jersey: Prentice Hall.

Krashen, S.D. (1985) *The Input Hypothesis: Issues and Implications*. London: Longman.

Little, D. and Ushioda, E. (1998) *Institution-wide Language Programmes*. CILT/Centre for Language and Communication Studies, Trinity College Dublin, London/Dublin.

Long, M. (1983) Does second language instruction make a difference? A review of the research, *TESOL Quarterly* **17**: 359—82.

McLaughlin, B. (1987) *Theories of Second Language Learning*. London: Edward Arnold.

Mitchell, R. and Myles, F. (1998) *Second Language Learning Theories*. London: Arnold.

O'Malley, J. and Chamot A. (1990) *Learning Strategies and Second Language Acquisition*.

Cambridge: Cambridge University Press.
Skehan, P. (1989) *Individual Differences in Second Language Learning*. London: Edward Arnold.
Skinner, B.F. (1957) *Verbal Behaviour*. New York: Appleton-Century-Crofts.
Spada, N. (1997) Form-focussed instruction and second language acquisition: a review of classroom and laboratory research, *Language Teaching* **30**: 73—87.
Stern, H.H. (1983) *Fundamental Concepts of Language Teaching*. Oxford: Oxford University Press.
Thomas, G. (1993) *A Survey of European Languages in the United Kingdom.* London: CNAA.
van Ek, J.A. (1975) Systems Development in Adult Language Learning: The Threshold Level. *Council of Europe.*
Wilkins, D.A. (1976) *Notional Syllabuses. A Taxonomy and its Relevance to Foreign Language Curriculum Development.* Oxford: Oxford University Press.

9 Teaching and learning practices commonly used in art and design education

Jackie Cobb
Kent Institute of Art & Design

9.1 Overview

This chapter addresses the patterns of teaching and assessment methods and associated learning activities which are characteristic of art and design higher education. It will address, by looking at the historical development of British art and design education, how the pedagogies associated with art and design have been determined by cultural traditions, economics and new developments within the discipline.

Traditionally, in Western art and design education, great importance is attached to individual creativity; arguably more so in fine art than in design. Thus, it has been common practice to encourage students to identify and develop their own creative strategies and artistic individuality from relatively early in their educational life. Art and, to perhaps a greater extent, design courses may also have specific aims and objectives, and the curriculum and course delivery is usually structured to allow room for individuality within a set course framework. However, the relationship of individual student aims to course requirements is not and has not traditionally been the same for all subjects within the discipline. In particular, historical attitudes as to the nature of art education have been quite different to attitudes to design education.

9.2 The historical development of art and design teaching in the West

The formal beginnings of art and design education in the West started with the medieval guilds. Until the Renaissance, art education was a primarily practical business, which was concerned with training tradesmen or workmen in the skills of their trade. It was not classed as one of the 'Liberal Arts', which were for the education of freemen or gentry. Unless he was a monk, the medieval artist-craftsman was a member of a guild, where apprenticeships were offered to potential craftsmen by a qualified master within a specific guild, to work and learn in his workshop. On production of a successful 'masterpiece', the journeyman would receive permission from the councillors of his guild to set himself up as master of his own shop. This was the beginning of what later became known as the '*Atelier*' (from the French for *workshop*) teaching system, and is the root from which studio-based teaching developed.

A change in attitude to the status of art education came about in the Renaissance, as the demand arose for educated artists capable of conceiving imaginative historical and religious compositions. In fact, Leonardo da Vinci was to describe art as a *scientific* subject, and thus a *liberal art* worthy of academic enquiry. Lorenzo de Medici set up a school of painting and sculpture in Florence in 1488, where apprentices could come and go irrespective of their guilds, and later, Cosimo de Medici established the first corporate art academy. Although neither Leonardo nor his contemporary Michelangelo ran a formal academy, their workshops showed evidence of a new type of art student, in that both artists had working with them groups of well-born and well-educated student/assistants. Following the Medici Academy, other Italian art academies were also established, and Italy became the main European focus for art education until the seventeenth century, when royal patronage in Paris saw the establishment of the French Royal Academy of Art.

In turn, Britain set up its own Royal Academy, modelled, like the French Academy, on Cosimo de Medici's original Art Academy in Florence. However, by the nineteenth century, the quality of teaching in the British Royal Academy was low, with a contemporary describing it as:

> One of the august Forty sitting with us the prescribed two hours, rarely drawing, oftener reading ... scarcely ever teaching.

The academicians showed very little enthusiasm even to deliver lectures, and the collapsed lecture system was only reinstated after the Academy came under political attack. The Academicians eventually delegated all their teaching duties, and teaching posts were opened up to non-Academy members. British art students, disenchanted and bored with the education on offer in their own country, eventually turned to Paris for their art education (MacDonald, 1973).

By the latter half of the nineteenth century, many Parisian artists were offering *atelier*, or workshop-based teaching, very much on the lines of the apprentice system. These developed into what became known as the *atelier routine*, which attracted young artists from all over Europe and the USA. The established routine was: *atelier*, or life-drawing studio in the morning, drawing and painting from works in the Louvre in the afternoon. Studies were supplemented by regular painting competitions, which usually took scenes from the classics as their subject matter. Students were also expected to make drawings from life in the streets and cafes. Work was regularly inspected by the *atelier* master who would decide whether the quality was sufficient to ensure a continued place at the *atelier*.

Potential atelier students had to arrive early on Monday mornings to secure a place for the week or fortnight in the over subscribed life-drawing studios. A teacher was not always present, and the model's pose was usually set and changed by a *monitor*. The studios were noisy and active (although all speech was required to be in French), and silence only reigned when the master or the visiting professor made his weekly round of the easels, spending a few minutes with each pupil. (In contrast, art schools in Britain at this time, although often providing a more thorough education than the schools of the Royal Academy, would typically have the students draw from antique casts, in silence, from 10 a.m. to 5 p.m. for five and a half days per week, under the constant supervision of a teacher.)

The popularity of the French atelier routine continued until the rise of the new Impressionist movement, which brought about a change in the way artists practised and, in turn, in their perceived academic needs. The grammar of formal 'life' classes, and drawing classes in perspective and anatomy etc. were beginning to lose their relevance for many art students, and the *atelier* routine began to wane in popularity, eventually to disappear.

Back in Britain, the nineteenth century economic rise of manufacturing, and the need to increase exports, saw, in 1836, the Select Committee on Arts and their Connection with Manufacturers recommending that a Normal School of Design (later to become the Royal College of Art) should be established in London, to train young artisans in design for industry. The Royal Academy made it clear that this new school should not encroach on the curriculum of the schools of the Academy. They stipulated that the new School of Design was a school of ornamental design only, and they obliged every student who entered the school of design to sign a declaration not to practise as a historical, portrait or landscape painter. They believed that 'artisans' should neither be shown 'High Art' nor be allowed to study the live figure, lest they were tempted to rise above their station by engaging in a more highly accredited and honoured occupation (Frayling, 1987).

The atmosphere at the design school was that of a strictly controlled classroom. On entry, the pupils (some of whom were as young as twelve years old) went straight to their places with their drawing boards and paper, and then sat in rows behind the stands upon which their boards rested, while the master handed out diagrams of patterns or ornament on cards, or in books, so that they could copy 'from the flat'. If a pupil was advanced enough to draw 'from the round', a cast of ornament or an actual ornament was placed on the stand in front of him. The pupils were not allowed to talk, or to move about, or to touch any casts, so that even their concept of the round was flat.

To the British fine art establishment, design for ornament was considered to be the lowest branch of art, even below that of handcrafts, and it was usually reserved for the lower social classes. But this strong distinction between high and low art was not common to all European countries. For example, the students at the Academie des Beaux Arts de Lyon, a school with a strong reputation for producing talented designers, considered themselves to be artists in the highest sense of the word, even though they were all the sons of factory workers selected by the mayor.

9.3 Modern educational developments

Design schools in Germany evolved as educators in manufacture with which art is concerned. In 1919 Walter Gropius, director of what has been called the most significant art school in the twentieth century, produced a manifesto for the Weimar Bauhaus which stated that it would bring together all the different arts and crafts. He maintained that a thorough training in all art and craft subjects was the fundamental basis of all creative activity. Gropius proclaimed a co-operative of artists, architects and craftsmen, similar to the medieval guild associations of church builders and artisans, and he demanded that all students be trained in workshops. By 1924, the Bauhaus had somewhat redefined its direction to put less emphasis on crafts, and more on design for production, in particular for mass-production. The Bauhaus workshops became laboratories for the production of models and prototypes for industrial mass-production.

The original Bauhaus courses consisted of three stages: the preliminary training, the workshop apprenticeship and, finally, architectural training, which involved practical work on a construction site. The titles and stages of the Weimar Bauhaus were: Apprentice, Fellow and Master.

The preliminary course was developed in 1921 by Johannes Itten. Itten, who had been strongly influenced by advanced ideas of educational reform during his studies to become a teacher, developed what was to become the model for the future British foundation courses in art and design. Itten's course, planned as an introduction to the Bauhaus design programme, was intended to liberate students from second-hand traditional information, by making them learn basic principles from direct analyses and direct experiences with materials. His students were able to playfully experiment with many different materials and objects, and he considered this course to be the basis of a comprehensive, integral education. In contrast, Gropius regarded this period as preparation for a potential employment as an architect or designer. This conflict eventually resulted in Itten's resignation. The preliminary course was then taken over by Laszlo Moholy-Nagy, who concentrated on conveying rationally comprehensible elementary theories consisting of systematic exercises. From 1924, the preliminary classes became increasingly school-like, and the course was renamed Basic Training 3 (Fohl et al, 1996).

Bauhaus scholars spread their methods to many other art and design schools in Germany and the USA. During the 1950s, ideas and methods from Itten's Preliminary Course and Moholy-Nagy's Basic Course were adopted by British art schools, including the now renamed Royal College of Art, eventually forming the basis for the new art and design foundation courses.

Teaching on British foundation courses, and also the first year of higher-level courses, continued to be quite course-led, with these early years often used to re-assess a student's potential and to make-good any deficiencies, but many advanced courses began to arrange their teaching to become gradually more student-led, until, by the final year student/tutor relationships became more like critical advice to a colleague. When the art and design courses were awarded degree status, there were many debates as to the nature and function of art and design education. The Summerton/Coldstream plea that art and design education should be considered not merely as a professional training towards a vocation but should be treated as an alternative form of higher education in its own right, the equivalent to reading the humanities at a university, is a reminder of Leonardo's description of art as a 'liberal art, worthy of academic enquiry' and of Itten's approach to his preliminary course.

Debate also arose as to the appropriate type of teaching for these new courses, with some people feeling, like Gropius, that students should have a thorough and methodical educational experience, and others believing that over-teaching could do damage to individual creativity. This argument reflected a fundamental difference of belief in the nature and value of particular art and design activities. If art and design was believed to be an instrument of liberal education it could be permitted to develop in untrammelled personal freedom of expression. If it was a utilitarian activity, it was invariably taught systematically and methodically (MacDonald, 1973).

9.4 Project-based learning

Projects or assignments have become the traditional learning vehicles in art and design, and the means by which students engage in experiential learning. The proposal is structured to mirror the practice of the professional artist or designer, and has been developed to broaden creative, intellectual and practical ability. It commonly consists of a subject or theme; research and cultural contexts; identified learning outcomes; physical creative requirements and criteria for assessment or evaluation.

There is considerable debate about the extent to which fine artists could reasonably be expected to be explicit about what they are doing or what they intend to do. Some people feel that to attempt to explain is always reductive, if not actually destructive (Painter, 1994).

It can also be argued that the shift in art teaching from 'academic realism' to creative self-expression (which has been particularly evident since the rise of the Impressionist movement) has not resulted in sufficient clarification of how a student 'discovers his own path in art' (Leepa, 1973).

However, it has been pointed out that a successful dialogue of student and coach need not necessarily end in the student's compliance with the coach's intentions, and when a student fails to understand through apparent incapacity or unwillingness to learn, the coach ought to consider the possibility that the 'failure' is attributable not to the student's shortcomings or even to the tutor's inadequate coaching but to the student's refusal to give up something he or she sees as valuable. (schon, 1987).

Written or verbal briefs have been used as a means of addressing the problem of individual choices of creative direction. They can be used to agree a set of objectives between the student and the tutor, and can enable tutors and students to jointly identify individual student direction.

9.5 Studio supervision

Tutors engaging in general studio supervision either interact with students as a whole class, using a more expositional form of teaching, or with individuals in a series of 'show and tell' type tutorials. In the latter, tutors will usually circulate in the studio where students are working on individual or group projects, and teach in an ad-hoc manner, responding to students' immediate needs. The advantages of this type of interaction is that the teaching is in the context of the student's own doing, and, as such, is focused on the individual learning needs of the student.

The interaction between teacher and student during the process of 'learning by doing' can raise problems that are inherent in the process. In the hands of a good teacher the method has been seen to work — though not without tensions, but when the teacher cannot rise to its demands it has been felt that what all too often takes place is a process of indoctrination (Field, 1970).

9.6 The 'Crit'

Critical reflection and evaluation in art and design has always been an integral part of the creative process. Art and design tutors have used critical feedback for formative and summative assessment in order to encourage reflection on and enhancement of students' own creative and critical faculties. The crit offers a unique opportunity for open discussion, in a public forum, of individual project work. Peer support and understanding is also enhanced by the public crit.

The critical evaluation of student's work has latterly been affected by the focus on achievement. That is, on an evaluation of what has been learned, rather than on the intrinsic value of the finished object. Thus, there can be confusion in both the student's and the tutor's mind as to what exactly is being discussed in the crit or assessment. It has also been argued that the quality of a work of *art* (as opposed to that of a piece of design) must be determined by the quality of its *creator*: by his intelligence, his level of personal and social sensitivity, his energy, his dedication, and his technical competence. 'He does what he is' (Copplestone, 1983).

Many tutors now believe that confusion as to the aims of a particular project, and what exactly is going to be assessed, can be substantially clarified be agreeing these before the project begins. For those who believe this to be a constricting process which prevents creative divergence, it has been suggested that changes of direction or objectives can also be agreed whilst the project is under development. It is generally recognized that the art and design instructor has a very firm function in an instruction or critique session. Most tutors agree that, when responding to a student's work the tutor can usefully engage in ideas relevant to the student's understanding, direction and experience, in order to evoke the student into dialogues, not only with tutors and peers, but also with him or herself (Leepa, 1973).

To conclude, the learning vehicles in art and design education which have stood the test of time remain: learning by doing (experiential learning); self-directed study (autonomous learning), and critical feedback (reflective practice). While there still remain important areas for discussion, such as the differences between fine-art practice and design practice, and instruction versus creative freedom, it can be seen that art and design education has retained and successfully developed its pedagogic practice, to maintain its own valuable characteristics and at the same time to embrace current educational philosophy.

9.7 References

Copplestone, T. (1983) *Art in Society*. Prentice Hall.

Field, D. (1970) *Change in Art Education*. London: Routledge & Kegan Paul.

Fohl, T., Siebenbrodt, M. *et al.* (1996) *The Bauhaus Museum*. Berlin: Deutscher Kunstverlag,.

Frayling, C. (1987) *The Royal College of Art*. London: Barrie & Jenkins.

Leepa, A. (1973) *Art and Self in New Ideas in Art Education*, ed. Battock. New York: Dutton.

Macdonald, S. (1973) *The History and Philosophy of Art Education*. London: University of London Press.

Painter C. (1994) In *Artists in the 1990s: Their Education and Values*. Wimbledon School of Art in association with the Tate Gallery.

Schön, D.A. (1987) Educating the Reflective Practitioner. California: Jossey-Bass Inc.

10 Uncovering problematics in art and design teaching and assessment

Allan Davies

Centre for Learning and Teaching in Art and Design: The London Institute, Royal College of Art and Wimbledon School of Art

In the original 'Improving Student Learning' project (Gibbs, 1992), nine strategies were identified as having the potential for improving the quality of student learning. Their success, however, was predicated on whether they embodied the four key elements: a motivational context; learner activity; interaction with others; and a well structured knowledge base, identified by John Biggs (Biggs, 1989) as the key features in promoting a deep approach to learning.

This chapter considers the common teaching practices of art and design higher education in this context. It explores to what extent the key practices — project based learning; the public critique; studio-based teaching; and the 'final show' — embody the four key elements identified by Biggs, and identifies some of the emerging problematics.

Project-based learning is one of the nine strategies identified by Biggs and to that extent conforms to the expectations, involving both learner activity and requiring a sound knowledge base and often involving working with others. However, we should be cautious about making assumptions here. Students whose conceptions of learning are teacher-centred could have difficulty in coping with the type of work which does not provide right or wrong answers or clear-cut guidelines for carrying out the tasks. Entwistle (Entwistle, 1998) pointed out that one of the fundamental challenges for teachers is that of enabling students to conceptualize learning as a dynamic, transformational activity which contributes to their overall perspective of the world rather than a dualistic conception whereby there are perceived to be only right or wrong answers to the tasks set and their duty is to find these answers. In interviews with art and design students (Davies, 1995), many of those taking a predominantly surface approach to a task reported that their focus was on finding the right answer or, more specifically, trying to identify what the teacher might regard as the right answer and, consequently, offering that as a solution. On the other hand, some projects can be so tightly formulated by the teacher pre-specifying behavioural objectives that there is, in fact, little room for novel learner activity or the enhancement of the knowledge base.

The establishing of 'learning outcomes' within project-based learning is becoming increasingly common within art and design, particularly with the emergence of modular programmes. The quite explicit expectation by Subject Quality Review in Art and Design for programmes to have learning outcomes reinforces this, yet their appropriate use in project-based learning has yet to be articulated. Learning outcomes which are offered to students as a list within a project, without there being any underlying challenges within the tasks set which might encourage active engagement in the outcomes, will be seen merely as hurdles to get over or even inconveniences within the milieu. Tightly constructed projects containing specified learning outcomes may well be necessary, particularly for the purposes of accountability, but they are not sufficient for promoting a deep approach to learning (Davies, 1999).

The public critique of student work might well aspire to a motivational context but there is little evidence in the literature that this is the case. The success of these occasions depends on how well structured they are and on what everyone, including the teacher, believes they are attempting to achieve. A teacher with a closed conception of teaching might organize a 'crit' which is based entirely on his or her opinions of the work on display — the 'connoisseur' approach — believing that this is what students want. For students who have not performed well there is the possibility of public shaming. Stephen Brookfield (Brookfield, 1998) offers a sobering account of how easy it is for the teacher to misperceive the real needs of the learner on such occasions and by so doing compound the problems or difficulties the learner had in the first place. What pressures are there here for students to conform rather than take a risk? Philippa Ashton observed that in these types of sessions

> each student would be asked to explain her work to date. The tutor would begin the discussion with the same introductory question and the subsequent discussion took very much the same form as one-to-one teaching. Many students when questioned said that they found these sessions boring, over long and not useful. (Ashton, 1997)

In such circumstances, and in order to avoid public shaming, students might well take an approach to learning which is counter to the intentions of the teacher. Using these sessions as learning opportunities needs careful thought and construction if we are to avoid embarrassment, anxiety, boredom, compliance, subservience and so on as being the most significant learning experiences of the event. Indeed, anxiety-provoking assessments were regarded in the original research project as contexts for promoting a surface approach to learning. The timing of the event and the size of the group are important features to be considered at the planning stage. Crits at the end of a project give little or no time for students to act on what can be very useful advice in the resolving of their understanding of the project. Uncertainty as to whether the crit is formative or summative can lead to frustrations on the part of students. Large group crits need careful management to maintain the interests of all students and to assume that an approach to small group activity can be easily taken to the larger group context can be mistaken.

Studio-based teaching, sometimes disparagingly referred to as 'studio cruising', could be considered as embracing all four key elements but it was the subject of a seminal work by Cal Swann (Swann, 1986), in which the effectiveness of the method was questioned. Much depends on the conceptions of learning and teaching held by both teacher and student and the appropriateness of the context is crucial. Philippa Ashton, in commenting about the studio method, observed that, in one-to-one encounters, the staff invariably spoke more than the students (Ashton, 1997). In many of these cases the teachers hold conceptions of themselves as a resource of knowledge and/or skills to be drawn on. Their role is perceived by them as being the experts who have the knowledge and the skill which at some appropriate point needs to be transferred to the student. The teacher-centredness of this approach is also often shared by the students, although, as students also perceive their teachers as the final arbiters of the quality of their work, their perception of the relationship is somewhat more complex.

This ambiguous role of the teacher as both mentor and judge is recognised as particularly problematic in institutions who are looking to realign their focus from a teaching to a learning paradigm (Barr and Tagg, 1997). In Transactional Analysis terms (Stewart and Joines, 1987), this relationship could be characterized as parent/child with little opportunity, because of the underlying perceptions of power and control, of the relationship moving to a more facilitative adult/adult relationship. Teachers rarely consider such encounters with students as anything other than helping them to learn yet these 'interventions' (Heron, 1976) play a significant part in the way in which students perceive the relationship between themselves and their tutors. In particular, the nature of the intervention can contribute to determining whether a student sees the tutor as someone playing an important facilitative role in a partnership intended to produce learning (both student and teacher) or as someone who is an 'expert' and holds special insights into the subject which the student can only acquire through regular timely encounters throughout the project. Nevertheless, the latter is what many teachers hold as good practice when they talk of promoting independence and autonomy. There are very serious questions to be asked here about whether one-to-one, 'sitting with Nellie', teaching is as effective as it is assumed to be.

The final show, or 'degree show', in art and design is something of a unique event in higher education in that the work prepared for the final assessments is put on public display. In the past the format was very much the same for every institution with a gallery-type display of graduating students' work. Nowadays, the format is determined by factors such as modularity and funding. Nevertheless, there are few who would disagree that this time-honoured ritual, however it is expressed, is considered as a fundamental feature of art and design education. One of the pressures on student learning, in the latter stages of their courses, has always been the presentation of the work for the show. Some modularized programmes, for differing reasons, have built into their scheme a module which is designed specifically for students to focus on the presentation. The emphasis on the material form and the making at the end of the course is interesting particularly in those cases where the quality of the learning is not part of the assessment criteria. Some programmes, modular or not, do not differentiate work submitted for the final assessment from the work presented for public scrutiny (and, indeed, there are instances of the final show being the only opportunity for external assessment — what you see is what you get!).

Graham Gibbs has commented, about assessment in general, that 'There is a considerable amount of evidence that assessment systems dominate what students are oriented towards in their learning' (Gibbs, 1992). Students take an increasingly strategic approach to their work as the assessments points get nearer. Up to now little research has been carried out on the approaches to learning that art and design students take as they prepare for graduation. As it is a final assessment, nevertheless, it is open for students to ask the question, 'What do I have to do to get the best marks?' With the added knowledge that their work will be available for 'public' scrutiny, they may take strategic approaches to learning that they would not normally take in a less public context.

Lin Norton (Norton, 1996) has worked closely with her psychology students in trying to uncover what they get up to and why in their attempts to improve their marks in essays and coursework. What was revealed was a whole range of activities which were highly strategic in nature and not entirely compatible with the pursuit of understanding. Getting to know the tutors, answering the easiest questions, avoiding controversy and so on were learner behaviours generated by the assessment circumstances. As working strategically is very much a human disposition, we might ask what art and design students get up to in similar circumstances. Would their approach to learning be any different if they did not have to display their assessed work to the public? It is a little more difficult nowadays to expect a consensus response to this question since, as noted earlier, the 'final show' will differ depending on the institution and whether its approach to modularity, if any, has affected the final presentation. Nevertheless, the issue remains the same.

In all of the cases above there is very little research work currently taking place which might throw light on the generally held assumption that the teaching and assessment strategies adopted in art and design are models of good practice. More research is clearly needed if we are even going to begin to respond to Entwistle's observation that

> In higher education, one of the main problems is that many staff still rely on a very limited discourse about teaching and learning. When they are asked about their teaching, lecturers typically reply in terms of their teaching procedures, and find it difficult to provide either explanations or justifications for their actions (Entwistle, 1998).

It may be the case that we have taken many of our procedures for granted but we will not know for sure what works and what doesn't work and under what conditions until we have carried out the research.

References

Ashton, P. (1997) Learning together: an exploration of how students use each other as a resource for learning. In Gibbs, G. (ed.), *Improving Student Learning Through Course Design*. Oxford: OCSLD.

Barr, R. and Tagg, J. (1997) From teaching to learning: a new paradigm for undergraduate education, *Change*, Nov./Dec.

Biggs, J.B. (1989) Does learning about learning help teachers with teaching? Psychology and the tertiary teacher, *Gazette (Supplement)* **26**(1), University of Hong Kong.

Brookfield, S. (1998) On the certainty of public shaming: working with students 'who just don't get it'. In *Improving Student Learning: Improving Students as Learners*. Oxford: OCSLD.

Davies, A. (1995) Evaluating a deep approach to assessment. In Gibbs, G. (ed.), *Improving Student Learning: Through Assessment and Evaluation*. Oxford: OCSLD.

Davies, A. (1996) Assessment and transferable skills, *Journal of Art and Design Education* **15**(3).

Davies, A. (1999) Using learning journals to identify critical incidents of understanding. In Rust, C. (ed.), *Improving Student Learning*. Oxford: OCSLD.

Entwistle, N. (1998) The contribution of conceptual research on learning and teaching: priorities in research into learning and teaching in higher education. CVCP/SRHE Research Seminar paper.

Gibbs, G. (1992) Improving the quality of student learning, *TES*.

Heron, J. (1976) Six category intervention analysis. *British Journal of Guidance and Counselling* **4**(2).

Norton, L.(1996) Coursework assessment: what are tutors really looking for? *Improving Student Learning: Using Research to Improve Student Learning*. Oxford: OCSD.

Prosser, M. and Trigwell, K. (1999) *Understanding Learning and Teaching*. Oxford: Oxford University Press.

Stewart, I. and Joines, V. (1987) TA today, *Lifespace*.

Swan, C. (1986) Nellie is dead, *Designer*.

Swan, C. *et al*. (1989) On not sitting with Nellie. CNAA/CHEAD seminar paper.

11 Communications, technology and teamworking

R.G. Harris and T.J. Mulroy
Sheffield Hallam University

The Engineering Education Research Group at Sheffield Hallam University has particular interest in ensuring the relevance of, and close links between, education and industry. Two particular areas of work have been the use of Geographically Remote Teams within project work, and Work Based Learning (WBL) and its assessment. The former uses communications technology to allow teams to work together even though they never meet, and via this approach it develops team working and communication skills. The latter uses a university approved framework to provide new routes towards qualifications, through the acceptance of experiential learning.

11.2 Introduction

Over a number of years the Universities of Glasgow Caledonian and Sheffield Hallam have co-operated to develop a project which develops the participants team working skills within a product development scenario.

The basis of the scenario is that a fictitious company needs to develop a new product (or range of products). The students work for a consultancy company that has been tasked with developing the new product. The consultancy company has half of its team based in Glasgow (the business elements) and half based in Sheffield (the engineering elements). The company for whom the product is to be developed has a fully documented history in terms of facilities, factory layout, employees and financial spreadsheets. These are available to the consultancy teams. The students work in groups with half of each group based in Glasgow, and half based in Sheffield. While they never meet in person, regular communication is achieved by such means as email, phone, fax, and most importantly video conferencing. The culmination of the work is a final presentation to the Members of the Board of the commissioning company with recommendations as to how they should proceed.

11.3 Methodology

The selection of the teams has been done in a number of ways during the period that the project has run between the two universities. Initially self-selection was used, however this led to an imbalance in the teams abilities. Selection based on prior knowledge of the individuals has also been used with some success. It did not necessarily make for an easy project as it challenged individuals to work with others who had a different set of values and work ethos. Most recently Belbin[1] analysis has been used. This allows a structured approach to the selection of team members with the possibility of selecting effective teams (at least in terms of final product, if not best learning). The team members also found it illuminating at a personal level.

A framework for the teams to work within was created. This has been designed to prepare the teams, allow them freedom to make decisions as appropriate, but provide feedback to staff on the progress of the work and allow for additional support where necessary.

Some elements of the framework are:

- team-working exercises prior to the selection of the team members;
- specialist lectures on elements such as sales, marketing and finance;
- set milestones for project;
- weekly presentation by one member of each team;
- virtual meetings between sites for each team, each week.

The progress of the work is monitored by the staff involved via informal discussion with the team members and by the presentations made.

11.4 Communications

The core of this work the effective use of communications; classically an area in which engineering based students are weak. The communications took place via:

- email
- mail
- World Wide Web
- fax
- phone
- video conferencing

The video conferencing is novel, in that it is used by the team members (i.e. students) merely as communications tool, in much the same way as a telephone is used. It is a low-cost system, based on ISDN[2,3,4] or IP. It provides for up to about four people at each end to conference, operating in a hands-free, full duplex mode. This allows a natural conversation to take place and a virtual meeting to operate, with all the normal flow of a meeting governed by interruptions, body language, and discussion.

11.4.1 Effectiveness

Research was done into the uses of the various communication media. The research was done by questionnaire after the completion of the work. The research reveals that if they are divided into their application, then clear differences of use appear. Clearly video conferencing is central to the decision-making process, in spite of it being a new technology with which none of the participants had any familiarity before the start of the project. No training was given on the use of the equipment; however, feedback suggests that it would be worth while to do so (see Figure 11.1).

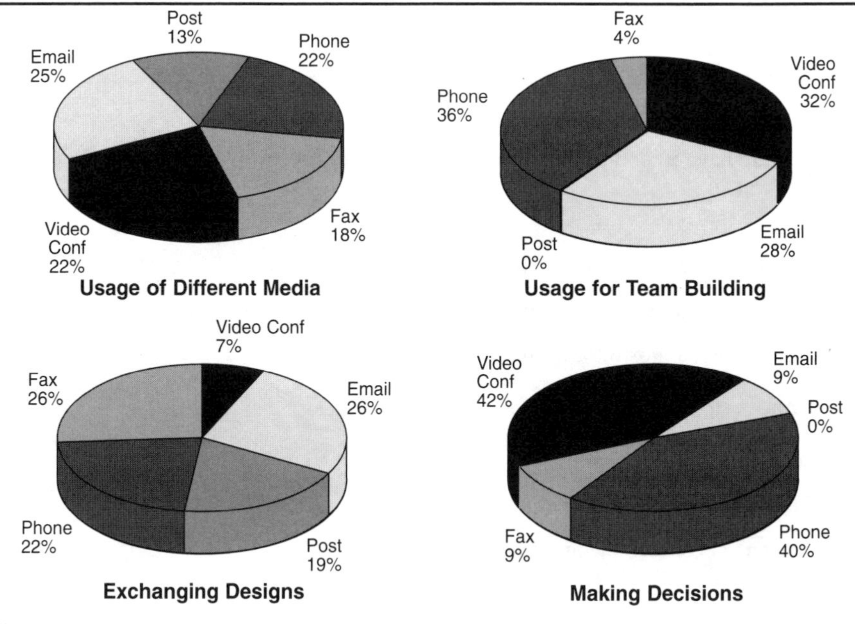

Figure 11.1

11.5 Skill development

One of the major aims of the project is to develop personal and professional skills. These are being demanded by the professional bodies via the Engineering Council and it's SARTOR[5] document. These include:

- ability to communicate effectively;
- teamworking;
- leadership;
- personal organization;
- ability to be self-critical and identify areas where CPD is needed;
- ability to research and present unfamiliar material.

The extent to which this has been achieved can best be illustrated by a selection of some of the comments made by the students on the questionnaires they completed:

Presentations

'my weakest area ... my confidence has grown ... verbal skills still need improvement'

'weekly presentation ... sessions I feared most ... I am getting better'

'made feel pretty good ... brought my confidence up ...'

Team work

'as time began to disappear the whole team really got motivated'

'real life situations are highlighted by the problems encountered'

'important to have a good degree of communication for successful completion of a project'

Conflicts

'conflicts were numerous ... sorted out with relative ease and speed'

'as the project progressed it was clear that a difference in attitude existed'

'the attitude was supportive and constructive'

Time management

'was not easy to say the least'

'a tool that I will try to develop as an engineer'

'project plan...never seen the importance of one until now'

Skills

'helped me understand a lot more about finance that I would have ever learned in any lecture'

'I had the chance to research ... something I have not had the chance to do before'

'the skills we have learnt, and problems overcome, have been of great benefit for the future'

Video conferencing

'unbelievable what body language signals were picked up ... seemed to shrink in their seats'

'it allowed a bond to be created that you cannot get on a phone or by email'

'facial expression, that tells you a lot'

'lets you be more frank'

11.6 Further work

The concept that has been developed within this project has been enlarged to become a SOCRATES project. This provides transnational working with the additional difficulties of cultural and language barriers. This work is still in its infancy and there has as yet not been an opportunity to evaluate it's efficacy. One difference between the two is that the SOCRATES[6] funded work makes use of a common work space to allow the video conferencing to provide a shared working environment in addition to a forum for discussion.[7,8]

11.7 Work-based learning

11.7.1 Introduction

Recent years have seen an increasing acceptance of vocational qualifications in the engineering profession. This trend has been largely instigated as a result of the introduction of the new National Vocational Qualifications (NVQs) along with Accreditation for Prior Learning (APL) schemes which aim to provide a route towards professionalism through acceptance of experiential learning.[9,10] This contrasts with the traditionally accepted route of full time academic study followed by post-graduate work experience.

For many years the new universities have encouraged students to acquire practical skills through the introduction of sandwich type courses. All too often, however, the students' experience on work placement has been mixed, and the learning thus acquired has been difficult to demonstrate and to accredit in the final award.

The introduction of NVQs has provided an ideal framework for work-based learning to be assessed and credit to be gained towards a higher qualification. NVQs are outcome-based qualifications, that is the outcomes are clearly specified at the outset in terms of a nationally agreed set of performance criteria. The award of the NVQ is then made on the basis of an assessment of evidence, provided in the form of a portfolio or by direct observation in the workplace, which demonstrates performance satisfying the specified outcomes.

This work-based learning route is of direct relevance to part time mature students whose normal work activities could be used as the basis for a vocational award contributing to the higher qualification being sought. This has an added advantage, of reducing the amount of time taken for such students to obtain a degree; currently around five years, by up to six months. For these reasons the initial studies at Sheffield Hallam have targeted second-year part-time students on engineering degree programmes.

Work-based learning can also be of use to the employer since it provides high quality and competent students who can contribute immediately to the work environment both at undergraduate and post-graduate levels. It is an implicit requirement that the employer contributes to the learning experience by providing the working environment and staff who contribute to the assessment process.

11.7.2 Methodology

Courses in many UK universities are unitized, and these are 'credit rated' within the Credit Accumulation and Transfer Scheme (CATS) framework. A single unit covering a particular subject in a particular year is taught and assessed by examination and a pass in the unit leads to the award of a number of CATS points. Typically, a full-time student would be required to accumulate 120 points per year, with a single unit representing 20 points. Units have an associated level (1, 2 or 3) depending upon the year of the course to which they relate (first, second or third).

For the award of a degree typically 360 points are required, 120 at each level. Students can thus opt to design their own degree curriculum (Combined Studies degrees) by choosing units on a university-wide basis and accumulating the required number of points over three or more years. These points are the property of the individual student and can be transferred between participating UK universities. Work-based learning fits neatly into the CATS structure since credit can be awarded in the form of CATS points replacing a taught unit at a given level.

The first stage in the assessment procedure is for the student to negotiate a contract with the university. This Learning Contract (also known as a Learning Action Plan or Learning Agreement) specifies a number of items:

- the level and quantity of credit which the unit will represent expressed in CATS points normally at degree levels 2 and 3 (second and third year degree) and the degree award title;
- the Learning Strategy, which outlines the tasks and activities which will give rise to the learning outcomes;
- the Learning Outcomes, identified as a list of phrases which specify unambiguously the changes which will have taken place in the individual as a result of the learning process;
- the sort of evidence which will be provided to demonstrate achievement of the outcomes and the assessment thereof;
- the duties and responsibilities of the learner, the university and the employing organisation.

This document is the key to the process and forms the basis for the work undertaken to fulfil the contract. The most difficult areas in drawing up contracts for engineering students have been found to be in writing the learning outcomes, and determining what evidence will demonstrate that the outcomes have been achieved. This evidence can be derived from many sources. In general documentary evidence may consist of written reports, computer printouts, project documentation and testimonials from managers. This could be supplemented by direct workplace observation or possibly audio visual evidence in the form of audio or video tapes or photographs.

The learning contract would normally be agreed after discussions between the student, the employer and the university. If the degree award is to be accredited by a professional body such as the Institute of Electrical Engineers (IEE) or the Institute of Mechanical Engineers (IMechE) then the contract should be moderated by, for example, the universities' external examiner. This would ensure that the necessary level of rigour is retained. In engineering, it is of some importance to maintain professional body accreditation and the institutions are currently advocating an evolutionary rather than revolutionary approach to these new teaching methods.[11]

On completion of the unit it is the responsibility of the university tutor, probably in collaboration with the supervisor from the employing organization, to assess whether the evidence provided demonstrates that the learning outcomes have been achieved. The assessor is required to determine if the learning outcomes have been met by examining all the evidence provided, some of which may be invalid or non-authentic.12 In particular the assessor must determine if the evidence matches the level of application specified in the learning outcomes. Additional evidence may be required which may be obtained by conducting a viva at which the workplace supervisor and assessor and possibly an external examiner are present, again introducing rigour to the process.

The skills that the assessor requires are therefore much broader than those required in the traditional method of assessment through formal examination. The issue of reliability between assessors also requires careful consideration.

11.7.3 Issues raised

In engineering, experience at Sheffield Hallam has shown that work-based learning is currently viewed very differently by the various participants in the exercise.

First, there are the learners themselves. The part-time students targeted in the initial exercise were generally positive about the notion of work-based learning. Their perceptions were however clouded by lack of understanding of the processes involved and experiences with, for example, distance learning. This new style of learning required a re-education process with the basic steps being explained in detail. Some students also failed to acknowledge the notion that the work place is a rich learning environment and a place where the theoretical framework provide during the taught elements of their course could be contextualized and put into practice.

For the employers it became clear that much confusion exists over the exact nature of work-based learning. There were employers who felt that this type of learning ran contrary to the role of the university, namely to provide academic teaching.

Employers play a pivotal role in work based learning. It is they who provide the environment in which the learning takes place and provide substantial input to the assessment procedure. It is vital that they wholeheartedly endorse these learning processes in higher education and participate in pilot studies such as the one forming the basis of this chapter. There is therefore a clear need for re-educating the employer base. Ways of achieving this are difficult to specify but in the current economic climate the onus will inevitably be on academia and professional bodies to prove the worth of these new initiatives in higher education and dispel the reservations of employers. This is not to say that many organizations are unwilling to pursue these ideas but that the pressures of the work place are such that there remains little time for the introduction of such new learning techniques. The development of Employer Workshops, as used in the current project, and the establishment of learning partnerships between universities and employers, an area currently being researched at Sheffield Hallam University, are ways of forging these important links.

For the academic community work based learning represents a radical change to the way in which learning is facilitated. The traditional route of teaching and assessment by formal examination is well established and accepted. The adoption of new assessment techniques and the need to examine the learning process will inevitably require substantial changes to the academic's working practices. This may not be an entirely unwelcome change but will require a cultural revision which many will find difficult.

There are also clearly issues surrounding staff development and resourcing. These new learning techniques will increasingly involve staff in one-to-one interviews with individual students both during the development of the contract and in the assessment. The traditional classroom environment will therefore be only one arena of operation for the academic tutor and the breadth of skills required will correspondingly be increased. This may be difficult at a time when the unit resource is being placed under ever increasing pressures and will require acceptance by senior management.

The administrative infrastructure required will also be different to that currently used in traditional taught awards.[13] It is vital to ensure that the results of assessments are reported both to the student and the appropriate university examination board. Since the assessment lies outside the normal mechanism of formal examination, mechanisms must be developed by which the results of the assessment of work-based learning can be fed into the system. None of these problems is of itself insurmountable. It will, however, take time and some effort to make vocational learning a nationally accepted and integrated part of engineering higher education award curricula.

11.8 Conclusion

The work that has been done on technology based teamworking can at this stage only lead to tentative conclusions. More robust research via, say, structured interviews on several more cohorts of students is needed to establish the validity of these preliminary conclusions. The concept of using remote teams and technology appears to be producing learning of a type that has proved difficult to deliver by more conventional means, and is seen to be beneficial by the participants.

In order to move forward with work-based learning it is important that the necessary cultural changes are made within institutions of higher education, the workplace and in the community at large. The workplace will have to be accepted by all stakeholders as a valuable and valid learning environment. There are, however, outstanding issues to be resolved with regard to the parallels and complementary aspects of the traditional classroom and work based teaching environments.

That work-place experiences can lead to learning is not in dispute. It is in the identification, quantification and assessment of these experiences and how they can be related to formally taught courses, that many challenges still exist which have yet to be debated and met.

11.9 Notes

1. R.M. Belbin (1981) *Management Teams: Why They Succeed or Fail*. Oxford: Butterworth - Heinemann.
2. http://www.intel.com/proshare
3. http://www.pictel.com/live200s.htm
4. http://www.man.ac.uk/MVC/SIMA/video3/one2.html#1.2.1
5. SARTOR, 3rd edn. London: The Engineering Council, 1997.
6. http://lower.gcal.ac.uk/research/socrates/index4.htm
7. http://bscw.gmd.de/
8. http://www.dgp.toronto.edu/people/BillBuxton/index.html
9. G. Jessup (1991) *Outcomes: NVQs and the Emerging Model of Education and Training*, London: The Falmer Press.
10. H. Black and A. Wolf (1990) *Knowledge and Competence: Current Issues in Training and Education*. Careers & Occupational Information Centre.
11. The Engineering Council (1994) *Review of Engineering Formation: Analysis of Responses*. The Engineering Council, May.
12. P. Critten (1993) *Learning Pack for Assessors*. Centre for Work Based Learning Partnerships, Middlesex University.
13. D. Portwood (1993) Work based learning: linking academic and vocational qualifications, *Journal of Further and Higher Education* **17**(3), Autumn.

12 Small worlds on an interconnected planet: teaching and learning geography in Higher Education

Mick Healey[1]; Alan Jenkins[2] and Pauline Kneale[3]

1. Cheltenham and Gloucester College of Higher Education: 2. Oxford Brookes University; 3. Leeds University

12.1 Introduction

> In another aspect and one that is of very practical concern to the beginner, science is a conversation. The conversation has been in progress for a long time — in the case of ocean waves, for a very long time. To make the analogy more exact, science resembles the babble at a very large reception...The participants in the conversation have sorted themselves into groups, and sub groups, each dominated by a few brilliant conversationalists who set the subject and tone. Some scientists wander from group to group, while others remain fixed. Some groups talk about similar things, and occasionally snaps of conversation pass from one group to another. You have arrived in the middle of a party... *My job is to catch you up on the conversation and show you how to find your way to the bar* [emphasis added]. (Kinsman, 1965, p.9).

Kinsman's extract introduces the key themes of our analysis of the pedagogy of geography, namely that:

- different disciplinary knowledges are ultimately interconnected, for their aim is to understand the complexity of our worlds;
- understanding this interconnectedness requires specialisation; and
- in the 'small worlds' of the specialists, they develop their understanding of particular elements of this complexity and use a variety of methodologies and languages of description and explanation.

When we first encounter the conversation of a discipline we are likely to feel like outsiders experiencing a babble of conflicting and distorting 'tongues'. Specialist language and concerns are vital to furthering understanding through research, but entering that world as a researcher from another discipline, or as a student, requires effective guidance. Kinsman's analogy, that his role as a physicist, writing to those scientists seeking to understand the world of waves, is 'to catch you up on the conversation and show you how to find your way to the bar' can also be used as an analogy for the role of a teacher of any discipline. We see it as particularly appropriate to geography as a research discipline and how that effects the pedagogy of the subject (see also Hay and Delaney, 1997).

Geography is not a tightly bounded discipline, such as physics or history, in terms of either subject matter or research methodologies (Biglan, 1973). 'Geography occupies a distinctive place in the world of learning, offering an integrated study of the complex reciprocal relationships between human societies and the non-human components of the world' (QAA, 1999, para 1.1). Geographers research aspects of the physical or human worlds, for example, the impact of climate change on vegetation type, or how changes in gender relations affect urban form and function. Or they may seek to analyse the interrelationships between physical and human worlds; for example, the interrelations between climate, city morphology and social behaviour during riots. In Kinsman's terms, while some geographers are fixed in the small world where they research and teach, that world is very different from that of their colleagues who teach on the same degree programme, while others 'wander from group to group'.

It is this variety of subject matter and methodologies of analysis that geographers often emphasize as its educational strength. It can offer a student a superb 'liberal education'. However, it can also offer a babble of contending, disconnected and even hostile voices. Scott Turow (1988, pp. 49, 58), described his first few weeks as a student at Harvard Law School as follows: 'The feeling aroused was something close to panic, a ferocious sense of uncertainty, and it held me, and I believe most of my classmates, often during that first week and for a long time after' Later, as one student answered a question, the instructor said, 'I'm glad you are talking that way. After all, you can't be a duck until you learn to quack.'

This article shows you what it is like to 'quack geography'; how as teachers we seek to take geography students into our small worlds and connect them into a coherent understanding of our worlds. In the conclusion we also suggest what of this is transferable to other disciplines.

The more specific themes are:

- What are the distinctive features of geography as a discipline for students and for staff as teachers?
- What do students and teachers do in university geography classes?
- In what ways do these features vary by department and internationally, for there is not one geography?
- What of this is transferable to other disciplines?

12.2 The nature of the geography undergraduate curriculum

The problem with attempting to reflect on degrees and curricula in geography is the diversity that exists at every scale. The common element in most programmes is economic, social and cultural geography for the Arts (BA) programme and weather, climate, soils and geomorphology for the Science (BSc) programmes. Most geography programmes though, whether arts or science, have both sets of modules. There are linking or cross-over elements that sit astride the human—physical divide, which may appear with words like resources, hazards or sustainability in the title. Modules based on regions may sit in this bridging area or may focus be on particular elements such as South African Politics (arts) or Sustainability of Tropical Landscapes (science or both).

There is a diversity of curricula that in quite unique ways address the social and physical worlds and their interconnections. With no professional body to dictate or shape the curriculum, and since 'Geography is what Geographers do', the scope is endless. Within any programme the detail, focus and spin is often the product of staff interests and may be highly idiosyncratic. Upper-level courses may be linked to staff research interests and here individual courses/modules may be strongly linked to 'outside' disciplines. For example, a course in political geography will take the student into the concerns and the language of political science. Some departments may choose to emphasize these connections into other disciplines in how they construct the overall geography curriculum; others may (also) seek to stress the connections between the geography programmes they offer.

What is clear from looking at programmes of study is that geography degrees often have a considerable number of embedded skills modules either with a direct skill focus or as part of a more general module. Generic and transferable skills may be embedded through 'Study Skills' or 'Tutorial' modules. Career development and business modules may appear with titles like 'Careers for Geographers' or 'Geographers and the Workplace'. More specific numeracy skills relate to IT through modules like 'Statistics for Geographers', 'Introduction to GIS', 'Quantitative Techniques for Geographical Data Analysis'. Specific techniques may be part of a module or its main focus as in 'Remote Sensing' or 'Air Photo Interpretation'. Science modules embed laboratory techniques and safety either in techniques modules or within modules like 'Soils', 'Weather', 'Water Quality' or, 'Geochemistry'. One of the most enjoyable modules is the 'Fieldclass', often residential, sometimes overseas. This is where academic geography is put into its real world context. These are increasingly supplemented by virtual field courses.

Appendix 12.1 presents extracts from the mission statements of contrasting geography departments. Looking across the range of statements one is struck by the upbeat selling nature of the messages, so essential to attract students in an increasingly competitive market. There are some strong links to local and regional issues and concerns as exemplified by the University of Melbourne extract. There are links to local problems and the links to meeting the needs of students from specific local areas, such as with Chester College which attracts students from a more local base than some universities. Almost every statement commits the department to covering human and physical issues and integrating them. Compared with the mission statements of previous eras they are more jolly, less academically dry. There are many references to the skills that will be acquired through the degree programme, IT, personal, transferable and practical skills are clearly the buzzwords of late 1990s promotions. Equipment also gets a mention, as in the University of Tokyo, the 'toys' available to students give an indication of the wealth and research focus of the department.

As the number of students taking geography degree courses in the UK increased during the 1980s and most of the 1990s the number of staff has increased, and the range and diversity of courses have expanded. Specialists from increasing numbers of sub-disciplines are brought on-board. Widening the curriculum and increasing the number of options in many departments has allowed students to select their own combinations of modules and follow their own interests to a greater extent than in the past.

The introduction of generic skill, career, workplace and specialist qualitative and quantitative techniques have followed to support personal project and research work in sub-disciplines. There is no specific skill set that a graduate geographer is defined by, although they should all be competent at word processing, analysing data, using statistical analytical techniques and applying geographical concepts to real-world problems. The increasing focus on key or 'transferable' skills (Chalkley and Harwood, 1998; Kneale, 1999) may reflect geography's wide-ranging concerns which enable a range of discipline and transferable skills to be integrated into the curriculum, and thus hopefully aid student employability and life long learning (Clark and Higgitt, 1997). It also reflects a harsher educational climate where disciplines compete for students. 'Non-vocational' disciplines such as geography have to reconstitute their curricula to develop student employability or geography staff find themselves and their courses reconstituted as tourism, business studies, and environmental management. Such has been the experience of a number of Australian geography departments (Rich *et al.*, 1997).

The staff in geography departments present varying and sometimes conflicting approaches and opinions to geographical topics. Most staff hope to stimulate their students to see that there is no one unique answer to any geographical problem. The aim is to encourage individuals to develop the skills to analyse and synthesise information and to apply their personal ideas to geographical problems. Hopefully students recognize the diversity that exists in all parts of the subject. Faced with a decision-making exercises about planning in a National Park, updating the processes and procedures at a chemical works, considering policy issues in transport for the next 5 and 10 year period or designing a water treatment works, there are no clear-cut right answers. There is a wide range of alternative strategies and approaches, decisions are nearly always compromises, subject to external influences; a babble of discussion from which an answer is drawn.

Is a geographer an employable graduate? Certainly any geography graduate should have had a good general education and more grounding than most in research techniques, IT, advanced communication skills, numeracy and literacy, analytical and problem-solving. The independence required in fieldwork, projects and dissertations should add self-confidence. Where students have taken part in employer partnerships, work placements, or year abroad activities, the added confidence and experience adds strength to their portfolio.

Diversity and interdisciplinarity are thus key elements of geography degrees. This may leave students confused at times as they hop between sub-disciplines, approaches and techniques. Those who choose to mix their arts and science content have to cope with the remarkably different discourses that formalize the cultural, social, economic and science elements of the courses, and within these discourses there is the babble of technical terms and nuances of technical language.

12.3 Methods of learning and teaching in geography

Methods of learning and teaching in geography in part reflect the nature of the subject that we explored in the last section. Geography, as we have seen, draws on the natural and social sciences and some aspects of the humanities. Not surprisingly many of the characteristic methods of learning, teaching and assessment associated with these groups of subjects are found within geography. Laboratories, practical classes and reports, associated with the natural sciences (Birnie and Mason O'Connor, 1998), and seminar discussions and essays, associated with the social sciences and humanities (Clark and Wareham, 1998), are all common methods of learning and teaching in geography. Thus variety and breadth of learning and teaching methods characterize the geography curriculum (Jenkins, 1998).

Lectures still dominate the student experience in most departments (Agnew and Lewis, 1998), although active involvement of students in the 'lecture' slots is increasingly common; many geography lectures are illustrated by slides. Some modes of learning and teaching are particularly emphasised in geography, though they are not unique to the discipline. Fieldwork, day and residential trips, is a characteristic feature of geography courses (Livingstone *et al.*, 1998). The trips may involve some 'look-see' activities, but most field courses are dominated by project work and the practising of field techniques for observing, measuring and collecting information (e.g. measuring water quality; interviewing residents; observing natural and human landscape). Role-play exercises are sometimes built into fieldwork (e.g. taking the roles of different groups in an environmental dispute). Fieldwork provides an important opportunity to develop skills in group work and individual initiative. Field courses frequently use less conventional methods of assessment (e.g. posters; consultancy reports; presentations; and field note books).

The UK Subject Benchmarking document for geography notes that 'Geography has been notable for its reflective concern with teaching methods, such that the discipline continues to lead in the creation and implementation of pedagogic innovation' (QAA, 1999, para 5.1). Many of these innovations have involved student-led approaches. Resource-based learning and Information and Communication Technologies (ICTs) have played a major part in these initiatives (Healey, 1998; Shepherd, 1998). For example, a suite of computer assisted learning packages (*GeographyCal*) was produced in the mid-1990s to support introductory courses in geography (Healey *et al.*, 1998), while the Virtual Field Course (VFC) project has produced a series of programmes to support and supplement learning in the field. The use of the Web is also growing rapidly, both to support student teaching directly and as a means of disseminating teaching materials and ideas. The development of the Virtual Geography Department (VGD) project in the United States and the resource database established by the Geography Discipline Network (GDN) are good examples of this trend.

Methods of learning and teaching vary between departments. This came out clearly in the UK Teaching Quality Assessment reports, which indicate that methods of learning, teaching and assessment vary between 'traditional' departments, which are more dependent on lectures and unseen examination essays, and more 'progressive' departments, which emphasize a greater variety of methods and have more student-centred learning approaches (Chalkley, 1996; HEFCE, 1995). However, even greater variety generally exists between individuals in the same department.

There are also important international differences in learning, teaching and assessment. For example, distance learning is more common in HEIs in Australia and North America than in the UK, and computer marked objective tests are more common in North American geography departments. However, an International Symposium on Learning and Teaching Geography in Higher Education showed that the differences within Anglo-American institutions are generally more a matter of emphasis than of major substance (Healey *et al.*, 2000).

Differences exist between disciplines in the combination of learning, teaching and assessment methods they utilise, and in the way they respond to pedagogic innovations. The nature of geography means that geographers are used to borrowing and adapting ideas from outside their discipline. Arguably geographers are also more open than many other disciplines to innovations in learning, teaching and assessment. There is evidence that geography is one of the leading disciplines in pedagogic innovation in the UK and the US. For example, in the UK Geography is the only discipline that received funding from the Teaching Learning and Technology Programme, the Fund for the Development of Teaching and Learning, Discipline Networks, and Key Skills programmes. Geography has its own international journal — *Journal of Geography in Higher Education* —dedicated to promoting learning and teaching of the subject. It also has several national networks, such at the GDN and the Subject Centre for Geography, Earth and Environmental Sciences (UK) and the VGD (US). The International Network for Learning and Teaching (INLT) Geography in Higher Education was founded in 1999.

12.4 Issues of generalization and transferability

We have now taken you around the babble of voices that is the contemporary geography curricula. We hope it now makes sense to you, and now we have all arrived at the bar, you can buy us a drink!

In conclusion we turn to the issue of what of this is transferable to other disciplines, for that was the brief to us as authors both for the conference workshop and this publication. The ideology of the conference organisers, one which is representative of many educational developers, seems to be that which is to be praised and valued is that which is generic or transferable. Often academics' concern for their discipline and research is seen an obstacle to improving student learning (Jenkins, 1996a; 1996b). So even in a conference on improving student learning through the disciplines, the pressure on discipline-based staff was to emphasize that which is generic and transferable. This can be counterproductive. If we are to persuade discipline specialists of the value of educational development, we need to start by valuing the disciplines themselves. Educational developers, we would argue (and one of us — Jenkins — would now describe himself in these terms), need to approach the small worlds of the disciplines, even one as friendly and open as geography, with interest, humility, curiosity and a recognition that at first there will be a babble of perhaps incomprehensible voices. As they start to understand the language of the discipline, they should join in, at first gently perhaps with questions, and then introduce some of their language and concerns in return. But first they have to listen and recognise the particular worlds of the discipline, and that each time they work with staff from different disciplines there will be a different language and culture to learn.

While arguing for respecting and valuing the peculiarity of these different disciplinary worlds we recognize the importance of reaching out and linking the geographic perspective to that of other disciplines, and suggesting what of our practice might be of more general import. In geography there are two seemingly conflicting ways of analysing (researching) and describing (teaching) the earth's surface. The ideographic tradition sees the world through a lens that identifies that which is unique; for example, how and why the landscapes of the Basin Range are distinct from say the Appalachians. By contrast the nomothetic tradition looks for broad similarities and generic explanations for patterns on the earth surface; for example, the hierarchical pattern of settlement sizes. At different times in its short history the discipline has emphasized these two different traditions, and at times there have been, and are, harsh and conflicting statements as to the value of the two approaches. While the curricula of the departments described above manifest different emphases of these two different perspectives, as a disciplinary community we have learned to value both these approaches.

Having read this far we recognize that you have valued our peculiar landscape, and thus we are now willing to suggest that which is perhaps transferable. What is most transferable, and which offers a realistic approach to improving student learning, is a perspective that values both that which is (seemingly) unique to each discipline and that which is (largely) generic, or perhaps particular, to that tribe of specialists on student learning in higher education.

The three of us have been involved in a variety of institutional, national and international initiatives to improve teaching in our discipline. In the small world of geography, at conferences and in publications we have sought to spread and shape the discussions about the teaching of the discipline. In part we have done that by trying to understand and then bring into our disciplinary conversation those pedagogic concerns of disciplines that are cognate to us. Thus in teaching the representations of landscapes we may well read the (pedagogic) literature and talk to colleagues in fine art, multi-media and cultural studies. But here we may have to translate and at first get students to use a simplified or 'pidgin' language in our introductory courses. We have spent much time talking and listening to colleagues in immediately cognate disciplines from art history to zoology that share our research and pedagogic concerns for fieldwork. Their pedagogic approaches and particular techniques may quickly transfer between disciplines (Jenkins, 1997). We have also come to see that other loosely bounded 'disciplines', such as environmental studies or women's studies, share similar pedagogic opportunities and problems; in opening up to students a variety of subject matter and research methodologies, and yet enabling them to bring it together in their own understanding and to quack in a way they understand. Here we are likely to see that it is in the ways these different disciplinary communities structure the whole curriculum, to enable students to specialize in particular interests, but link it back to some common core, that we can both most readily learn from their approaches and add our perspectives and innovations.

As we have sought to improve student learning in our discipline we have come across the small world of the specialist research literature on student learning, and attended conferences such as ISL. Here we have come across a set of contending languages and approaches. With time we have learned to quack terms such 'situated cognition', 'phenomenography', 'surface learning', and so on. With time we think we have begun to understand the language(s) of this strange tribe. We have then sought to introduce this specialist language into our discipline, even though that has at times attracted derision and anger from those who we thought were our disciplinary colleagues. In one major project, the Geography Discipline Network brought together a group of educational developers and geographers to write a series of books and linked department-based workshops to improve geography teaching. What we learned from that project is as follows.

- Educational developers / researchers have specialist (discipline) based understandings that enrich 'our' particular discipline-based worlds and can bring much wider understanding to our practices.
- Writing for discipline-based staff needs to be firmly grounded in particular examples and case studies drawn from their disciplines. Certainly when running workshops in geography departments, it became clear that these discipline-based case studies create an immediate connection with participants and provide a means of translating the more generic concerns into a language that made more immediate sense than the specialist discourse of student learning.
- There were frequent comments in the evaluations of these department-based workshops that showed that they were more positively received than the more generic workshops the staff had previously attended. Because we were speaking their language, shared their background and concerns our message was received more positively.
- Whether we had sufficiently incorporated into that message the specialist language and disciplinary concerns of educational developer colleagues on the project and the wider educational literature, is an issue that still concerns us, and is in part for you to judge. That is, if you will read our discipline-based pedagogy (see References).

So, in short, what is most transferable from our experience is this perspective — one that values both that which is (seemingly) unique to each discipline, and that which is (largely) generic or perhaps particular to that tribe of specialists on student learning. The next time you see one of us by a conference bar lets drink and quack about these issues.

12.5 References and further reading

Agnew, C. and Elton, L. (1998) *Lecturing in Geography*. Cheltenham: Geography Discipline Network, Cheltenham & Gloucester CHE.

Biglan, A. (1973) The Characteristics of Subject Matter in Different Academic Areas, *Journal of Applied Psychology* **57**(3): 195—203.

Birnie, J. and O'Connor, K.M. (1998) *Practicals and Laboratory Work in Geography*. Cheltenham: Geography Discipline Network, Cheltenham & Gloucester CHE.

Chalkley, B. (1996) Editorial I Geography and teaching quality assessment: how well did we do?, *Journal of Geography in Higher Education* **20**(2): 149—58.

Chalkley, B. and Harwood, J. (1998) *Transferable Skills and Work-based Learning in Geography*. Cheltenham: Geography Discipline Network, Cheltenham & Gloucester CHE.

Clark, G. and Higgitt, M. (1997) Geography and Lifelong Learning: a report on a survey of geography graduates, *Journal of Geography in Higher Education* **21**(2): 199—213.

Clark, G. and Wareham, T. (1998) *Small-group Teaching in Geography*. Cheltenham: Geography Discipline Network, Cheltenham & Gloucester CHE.

Hay, I. and Delaney, E. (1997) Worlds in our words: geography as a second language, International Research in Geographical and Environmental Education, **6**(2), 124—34 .

Healey, M. (1998) *Resource-based Learning in Geography*. Cheltenham: Geography Discipline Network, Cheltenham & Gloucester CHE.

Healey, M., Robinson, G. and Castleford, J. (1998) Developing good educational practice: integrating *GeographyCal* into university courses. In *Proceedings of the Institute of Australian Geographers and New Zealand Geographical Society Second Joint Conference*, Hobart, Australia, The University of Waikato, Department of Geography. Also available at http://www.chelt.ac.uk/gdn

Healey, M., Foote, K. and Hay, I. (eds) (2000) International perspectives on learning and teaching geography in higher education: a *JGHE* symposium, *Journal of Geography in Higher Education* **24**(2), forthcoming.

HEFCE (Higher Education Funding Council for England) (1995) *Quality Assessment of Geography, 1994—95*. Bristol, HEFCE.

Kinsman, B. (1965) *Wind Waves, their Generation and Propagation across the Ocean Surface*. New York, Prentice Hall.

Jenkins, A. (1996a) Discipline-based educational development. *The International Journal for Academic Development* **1**(1): 50—62.

Jenkins A. (1996b) The go-between: strategies for success and recipes for failure. In Leong, S and Fitzpatrick, D. (eds), *Different Approaches; Theory and Practice in Higher Education*. Perth, Higher Education and Research Development Association of Australasia, 3—7.

Jenkins A (1997) *Fieldwork with More Students*. Oxford: Oxford Centre for Staff Development.

Jenkins, A. (1998) *Curriculum Design in Geography*. Cheltenham: Geography Discipline Network, Cheltenham & Gloucester CHE.

Kneale, P. (1999) *Study Skills for Geography Students: A Practical Guide*. London: Arnold.

Livingstone, I., Matthews, H. and Castley, A. (1998) *Fieldwork and Dissertations in Geography*. Cheltenham: Geography Discipline Network, Cheltenham & Gloucester CHE.

QAA (Quality Assurance Agency) (1999) *Geography Draft Benchmarking Statement.* Gloucester: QAA.

Rich, D.C., Pitman, A.J., Gosper, M. and Jacobsen, C. (1997) Restructuring of Australian higher education: information technology technology in geography teaching and learning, *Australian Geographer* **28**(2): 135–57.

Shepherd, I. (1998) *Teaching and Learning Geography with Information and Communication Technologies.* Cheltenham: Geography Discipline Network, Cheltenham & Gloucester CHE.

Turow, S. (1988) *One L — What they really teach you at Harvard Law School.* London: Sceptre Books.

Web sites

GeographyCal: http://www.geog.le.ac.uk/cti/Tltp/index.htm
Geography Discipline Network: http://www.chelt.ac.uk/el/philg/gdn/
International Network for Learning and Teaching Geography in Higher Education: http://www.chelt.ac.uk/gdn/inlt/index.htm
Journal of Geography in Higher Education: an index, plus the abstracts from all the mainline papers, is available at http://www.chelt.ac.uk/el/philg/gdn/jghe/index.htm
Virtual Field Course: http://www.geog.le.ac.uk/vfc/
Virtual Geography Department: http://www.utexas.edu/depts/grg/virtdept/contents.html

Appendix 12.1 Selected extracts from Geography Department Mission Statements

The University of Newcastle, Australia — Geography and Environmental Science ... gives you an understanding of the environment (both physical and human) and the skills to communicate this understanding. The skills and techniques that you learn doing a Geography and Environmental Science degree are transferable to the employment sector.

The University of Melbourne, Australia — Welcome to the Department of Geography and Environmental Studies! Are you interested in social justice? Is migration your thing? How about economic restructuring in Asia? Perhaps you're concerned about Australian land degradation? Do you want to know about environmental policy overseas? Or biodiversity? Ever wondered about Mabo or fire ecology? ... Geography and Environmental Studies at the University of Melbourne is where it's at if you want to learn about society/environment relations.

Tel Aviv University, Israel — Department of Geography — Geography today is a multi-faceted, interdisciplinary subject that has expanded beyond the physical contours of the landscape to include the spatial dimensions of history, economics, anthropology and sociology as well as geology, climatology, computer sciences and the environment. The TAU Department of Geography is a full partner in the new geography, offering interdisciplinary undergraduate and graduate programs that draw from all these fields.

Tokyo Metropolitan University, Japan — Department of Geography ... covers major research areas in both physical and human geography as well as in both pure and applied geography: geomorphology, ... Main research facilities include a scanning electron microscope and microprobe analyzer (EDS), an infrared thermography, a meteorological satellite data receiving system, a refractive index measuring system, an analytical stereo-restitution, three sets of graphic work station and image data processing peripherals, and an experimental flume (8 m long and 1.2 m wide).

University College, Chester, UK — Department of Geography — The department offers a varied range of research-enriched modules in both physical and human geography, a variety of degree pathways, residential and local fieldwork a small and friendly departmental environment, excellent specialist equipment in remote sensing and Geographic Information Systems (GIS) work placements as an integral part of courses together with an emphasis on transferable skills development only 6 per cent of graduates unemployed (national figure for all graduates 9.7%) easily accessible from west Cheshire, Wirral and Deeside.

13 Teaching mathematics as a way of life

Ken Houston[1], Pat Rogers[2] and Adrian Simpson[3]

1. University of Ulster; 2. York University, Toronto; 3. Warwick University

13.1 Overview

This chapter considers how students can be introduced to the mathematical 'way of life' through the ways in which we teach them and how they can experience the creation and use of mathematics and, as a bonus, develop social and personal skills. The three voices of the chapter are those of an applied mathematician (who considers how the teaching and evaluation of a modelling course involve students in the authentic tasks of the applied mathematician), a pure mathematician (who explores how students can be moved on from their view of mathematics as the application of rules and formulae to developing their own mathematical voice) and a mathematics education researcher (who explores the issues of apprenticeship and communication in these courses).

13.2 Introduction

Some say that everyone should learn mathematics because it is useful; others say that mathematics is interesting in its own right because it is beautiful, thought-provoking and stimulating. On the one hand the pragmatic view, and on the other, the cultural. The courses described here, to some extent, represent these two extreme views. Most students, of course, will not desire to become fully fledged 'mathematicians', but our approaches reflect a belief that everyone is capable of thinking mathematically.

In this chapter, we describe the way in which professional mathematicians go about their business and discuss two curricula we have devised for students to introduce them to these ways of life. We also discuss how these courses are models for apprenticeship in mathematics.

13.3 The 'way of life' of an applied mathematician

An applied mathematician is someone who has a good knowledge of many aspects of mathematics, who has a good knowledge of some field of human endeavour like electrical engineering or economics, and who uses mathematics to solve problems. They will usually do this by creating a mathematical model of the situation and will have knowledge of a range of models that are used in the particular problem area and some models that are used elsewhere. Applied mathematicians may even be recognized in the world as engineers or as economists.

The mathematician will be part of a team. They will have to work with others who may be more knowledgeable than they are of the situation to be modelled or the problem to be solved. Using their knowledge of existing models, they may be able to 'tweak' one to match the present situation, or they may have to create something new. They may not be aware of a suitable model and will have to carry out research to see what has been done before. Once the mathematical model is created and the appropriate questions have been asked, then they have to use their mathematical knowledge to answer these questions. They will almost certainly have to use a computer to help with this task. Then they will discuss the answers they get from the model with the team to see if they have obtained sensible answers to the original questions that had been asked. The model may need to be revised. Finally the team will report to someone, perhaps in a written report, perhaps also in an oral presentation.

13.3 The 'way of life' of a pure mathematician

Another 'way of life' is that of the 'pure mathematician', the person who is interested in mathematics for its own sake but who also teaches many whose use for mathematics is more utilitarian.

The life of the pure mathematician is full of opposites. Fascinated by mathematics, its order, its beauty, its certainty, its uncertainty, its predictability, its unpredictability, its power to explain and its mystery, pure mathematicians can become obsessed when a theorem is in the proving, elated when the proof is in, and depressed in the intervening periods. It is an intensely emotional life, a creative life, and a life full of anticipation and doubt. It's a life of questions, and problems, and a few answers that generate more questions. Some of us care about the use that might be made of our results, most don't.

The way of life of the pure mathematician is very different from the same person's way of teaching. And therein lies a problem for many of the students we teach. The characteristic pattern of most mathematics teaching is: definition, examples, theorem, proof, and practice with basic skill-building exercises and contrived applications. It is a 'content'-driven, top-down, follow-my-example/rule/instruction pedagogy based on a dualist philosophy (Perry, 1970) which promotes surface learning (Marton and Säljö, 1984). Not unsurprisingly it leaves all but the mathematically gifted out in the cold. If it were not bad enough that this excludes many intelligent people from pursuing a discipline they may learn to love and excludes even more from jobs they will never be qualified to obtain, it plays havoc with the self-esteem and confidence of the many individuals it leaves by the way.

13.4 Innovative curricula in applied mathematics (Ken Houston)

Working on the principle that 'what you assess is what you get', it goes without saying that innovative teaching methods must involve innovative assessment methods, to determine if the intended learning has taken place, and to give feedback to students on their progress. Teaching, learning and assessment go hand in hand in hand. A number of innovative teaching and assessment methods for applied mathematics have been developed (Houston, 1994; Haines and Dunthorne, 1996).

In mathematical modelling, practitioners need to be familiar with other models and they need to be able to create their own. An introductory course in modelling at the University of Ulster covers these ideas. Students work in small groups of about four, (a) to study models and (b) to construct models.

For (a) they select a topic from a list, and, using the support material provided, they will use libraries and the internet to research the topic which starts in their sphere of competence and then extends it. Each group then prepares written notes of their investigation for the rest of the class, and delivers a 40-minute seminar to the class. In this way the whole class learns something about a number of topics and quite a lot about their own topic. These notes are read and assessed by the lecturer at least a week before the presentation and students have an opportunity to improve on their work.

While doing this, students learn to use a mathematical word processor and to prepare a presentation. They learn how to write informatively for an audience of their peers, and they learn to summarize and present the essence of a topic in a seminar.

The end of semester written examination, set by the lecturer, contains one 30-minute question on each of the seminar topics, and students have to answer four of these. They may answer the question on their own topic. (There are also some short questions lasting for one-hour on other topics in the course, namely the mathematical methods they have been taught to help them understand the mathematics behind the models they study for the seminars.)

An evaluation of this innovation suggested that students, not surprisingly, understood their own seminar topic very well, and that the most useful thing that helped them understand the other topics was the set of written notes. (Houston and Lazenbatt, 1999; Houston, 1998).

This is a form of peer tutoring which is of benefit to both tutors and tutees and which emulates several aspects of professional practice.

For (b), each group selects a topic from a list and carries out the suggested investigation, using the support material for guidance. The topics are varied and a little unusual for the students. The mathematics required is well within their competence, while the context of the investigation will usually be something they could encounter in everyday life. Before starting the investigation, students would have seen the lecturer carry out a similar investigation and reflect on the processes involved in modelling. The groups each prepare a written report as if to the 'client' who had commissioned the research. They also present a poster (Berry and Houston, 1995).

The timetable for the seminar presentations (a) is known in advance with the first group getting four weeks' notice and the others following as quickly as necessary to complete the programme within the semester. The modelling report is submitted on a date suggested by the group and agreed with the lecturer and is usually four weeks away from their seminar date. This encourages students to plan their work schedule well in advance.

Assessment criteria for all of the above activities are presented to students early in the semester and discussed with them. They see examples of previous students' work and are encouraged to criticize these. The students themselves assess the internal working of a group through a confidential peer assessment form.

To give further encouragement to the critical reading of published material, a *comprehension test* is set for the students. Comprehension tests are widely used in other subjects such as physics and English Literature. The aims of a comprehension test in mathematics, as proposed by Houston (1993a, b) are:

- to encourage students to read, with understanding, a mathematical article;
- to provide students with an opportunity to demonstrate their understanding of general mathematical processes, both pure and applied;
- to encourage students to develop their skills of communicating mathematics — reading, asking, answering and writing;

- to demonstrate to students that mathematics is a living subject and is used in contemporary situations.

The procedure is for the lecturer to select a suitable article and to construct a set of questions relating to the article. The following objectives are suggested.

Students should be able to:

- explain all statements like 'it can be shown that ...' or 'it follows from the above that ...' in the article;
- identify and explain all mathematical modelling assumptions made in the article;
- make constructive criticisms of assumptions made, mathematical analysis and calculations carried out, inferences and deductions made, processes carried out;
- locate and correct any mathematical or typographical errors in the article;
- have some wider background knowledge of the situation described in the article;
- generalize the ideas or apply the ideas to a different situation.

Students are given the following advice. While reading this article, and while preparing for the written examination, the following questions, which relate to the modelling process should be borne in mind:

- What modelling assumptions have the authors made?
- Have they stated these explicitly or are they implied by something the authors have written?
- Are they *reasonable* assumptions? Would you be happy to make these assumptions or would you make others?
- Do the authors justify the assumptions? If not can you give a justification of them?
- Can you follow the mathematics through from line to line? Have the authors made any mistakes?
- Are the numerical calculations right?
- Can you explain all statements like 'it can be shown that ...' or 'it follows that ...'?
- Have the authors attempted to validate the model by comparing with observations? If not can you suggest experiments that could be carried out?
- Do the authors draw valid inferences and conclusions from the work?
- Is sufficient background information to the problem given in the article or is it necessary to find out things from other sources?
- Can you relate the article to the Modelling Flowchart?

Experience using comprehension tests shows that students do indeed read the article carefully and are able, by setting their own test paper, to anticipate the examiner's questions. It usually proves to be a good discriminator between students.

The combined course work, which is very demanding, carries a 50 per cent weighting; the written examination contributes the other 50 per cent. Weekly scheduled time is devoted to group work and students also arrange other times when they work together.

13.5 Innovative curricula in pure mathematics (Pat Rogers)

A forceful impetus for changing my teaching has been reflecting on my own experiences in learning undergraduate mathematics and doing mathematical research. When I first started teaching, I adopted those practices I had observed as a student: I lectured. I believed that teaching at the post-secondary level involved the transmission of knowledge from me, the expert, to the students, the novices. I saw my job as exposing the students to the content of the course. The student's job was to master this material by listening attentively as I explained ideas, by watching carefully as I showed them how to solve problems, and by practising solving problems on their own at home (Rogers and Kaiser, 1995).

One important component of the expository method of teaching is the use of the distant authority to 'impart knowledge'. Practices such as lecturing subordinate students' knowledge and understanding to that of the professor and the even more distant authority, the textbook. Such an approach deprives students of the experience of the *process* by which ideas in mathematics come to be and perpetuates the view that right answers in mathematics are the exclusive and sole property of experts. Students permitted to see only the finished product may come to believe they can never create similar results for themselves. Solving problems *for* students does not teach them to solve problems for themselves. Instead, it disempowers students by rendering them passive, and conveys mistaken notions there is only one correct solution: the teacher's. It also gives students the impression that the teacher lacks confidence in their ability to solve problems for themselves. Such implicit judgements of students' abilities as well as the more explicit verbal and written judgements they receive can stifle students' emerging writing styles and diminish their confidence to engage in learning tasks. Indeed, while students do need to acknowledge that they will make mistakes, they also need to know that they are intrinsically capable.

My teaching now takes as its starting point a critical stance on the prior experience of the students. For example, in a course for primary school teacher candidates, early examination, validation and unmasking of the root of students' fears is a key feature of my pedagogy. In order for students to be able to engage fully in any course, it is essential that they be given the space to examine their feelings about mathematics, uncovering the systemic nature of the underlying causes of these feelings, and shifting the blame away from themselves. A series of exercises, journal writings, and discussion questions enable students reflect on their prior experiences, and come to respect their avoidance of mathematics as a sensible human reaction to an uncomfortable and sometimes abusive situation. Helping students to acknowledge what they know about themselves in relation to mathematics is an essential first step in releasing them from any resistance to learning mathematics.

After this key stage, we engage in 'authentic' mathematical activity coupled with reflection, in order to convince students that their experience with mathematics can be different. I use the term 'authentic' to describe mathematical activity that closely resembles the actual work of the pure mathematician rather than the artificial work students encounter in the classroom. The problems students usually encounter in school mathematics are contrived, often very simple or requiring only the straightforward application of a learned algorithm. They are solved fairly quickly, and even when they are 'real', the contexts chosen are so contrived as to render the problem uninteresting, or irrelevant to students' personal interests. Another serious problem with problem-solving in school mathematics is that it has been turned into a discrete, orderly topic, falsely conveying the notion that all mathematical problems submit to simple algorithmic techniques and methods of solution that can routinely be learned. None of this conforms to a notion of mathematics that those of us who love it would recognize.

The aim of the course then is to give students room to explore their relationship with mathematics precisely by engaging them in a deep way in the process of doing mathematics. In selecting problems for this stage of the course, it is not *what* they do that matters, but *how* they do it. My role is to create experiences that structure the domain of learning and guide the students' explorations. This requires open-ended problems which do not submit to quick and obvious solution, but whose solution might take several weeks of investigation (see, for example, Mason *et al.*, 1982). This stage proceeds with great caution, for it is fraught with difficulty. Students who have been made to feel insecure about their abilities and have negative associations with the subject, have learned their lessons well and are dualistic in their beliefs (Perry, 1970). They expect right answers, and they expect to learn them from the teacher by listening. Although learning by imitation has not worked for them in the past, it is nonetheless an approach with which they are comfortable. Indeed they often pressure me to treat them in the very ways that produced their alienation in the first place. School mathematics characteristically does not assist students in progressing beyond this very early stage of cognitive awareness; rather it seems to entrench it. So the need to provide safety and a climate of risk-taking, so essential in becoming a mathematician, goes hand in hand with the importance of providing a certain initial structure. This is a stage where providing challenge within a supportive environment is crucial to prevent students from becoming overly frustrated by not being provided with the learning they expect.

Another important focus at this stage is to teach students strategies for recording their thoughts while engaging in mathematics. These strategies help students develop consciousness of their internal monitor, a voice they have forgotten to listen to, which tells them to trust their intuition when they have an idea that might work and that warns them when it's time to quit. Through exploring an open-ended problem with no question, I model for the students strategies for getting started on investigating our own question, showing them how I react when I get stuck, making explicit for them the problem-solving processes we use as they arise in the course of our work together, and highlighting critical stages in the process when they occur. In this way, they meet problem-solving as an authentic part of doing mathematics, not as a topic among others such as fractions, arithmetic etc. In this way I put myself on the line as a learner, but I am doing so as an experienced mathematician who can also make explicit the nature of the processes of mathematical investigation.

After this the students work in small groups on investigations, initially chosen by me. During this period, students develop their abilities to listen to each other, to use the vocabulary of mathematics and to develop some experience in talking mathematically. Eventually, they also begin to pose their own questions. Throughout this period, I encourage risk-taking, putting students in situations they might experience as teachers, where, for example, they have to explain or convince, or where they are confronted with a student who has used an unexpected approach to solving a problem, one which they do not understand immediately. Another important role I play is to help students uncover the mathematics in the investigations we do (where's the mathematics?), as well as in everyday situations and materials, for example, card tricks, games, 3-dimensional constructions, paper-folding, knots, origami.

Once this way of working together has become comfortable for students they are able to start devising their own investigations (where's the curriculum?) that they can use in the classroom to teach curriculum topics. As they gain confidence they begin to approach their teaching of mathematics in a completely different way, with lots of questions and an openness to not knowing — something they used to find terrifying.

In this discussion of the way of life and teaching of the pure mathematician, two styles of reasoning are evident: (a) 'separate' reasoning, or the traditional style, characterized by objectivity, reason, logic, and an appeal to justice; and (b) 'connected' reasoning, also termed 'the different voice', characterized by subjectivity, intuition and a desire to maintain relationships (Gilligan, 1982). Shown examples of this classification, mathematicians will invariably agree that the 'connected' examples represented the way mathematicians do mathematics. '"[M]athematics is intuitive," they said. They stressed the creative side — they agreed that the "separate" list conveyed the way that mathematics is communicated in the classroom, in textbooks, and in their professional writing' (Buerk, 1985).

The fact is that mathematicians employ *both* forms of reasoning in their work. But the problem with mathematics teaching, particularly at the post-secondary level where the lecture mode of instruction is so predominant, is that the creative-intuitive form is largely eliminated. Students are not given the opportunity to be involved in the process of constructing mathematical ideas, a process in which the 'connected' thought is so important. There is an enormous cognitive gulf between the way mathematics is presented and the individual ways in which it is possible and natural to arrive at an understanding of it. Some students are able to bridge this gap for themselves, but many are not.

The development of students' listening, speaking, and questioning skills, and the encouragement of multiple perspectives and solutions are important aspects of mathematics teaching at all levels, but especially when working with future teachers. For if we wish them to employ 'connected' (Belenky *et al.*, 1986) teaching methods themselves, they must first experience them and have opportunities to practise them. It is therefore important to use a style of teaching that is true to the nature of mathematical enquiry, and this demands a radical departure from the traditional lecture methods normally employed in the university classroom (Rogers, 1992).

By providing opportunities for students to hear and to develop their own voices through engagement in authentic mathematical activity within the classroom, we may engage them in purposeful, meaningful academic discourse, allowing them to claim ownership of mathematics for themselves. By so doing, we will not only avoid discriminating against students who are currently denied access to mathematics (especially women), but also provide a more meaningful and equal mathematics education for *all* students (Rogers, 1990).

13.6 The apprenticeship metaphor (Adrian Simpson)

The courses described are implicitly models of the 'apprenticeship' metaphor. Both courses provide students with mathematical situations that encourage them to work in ways that are like the ways of the professional mathematician: whether an applied mathematician creating models to explain and predict a wide range of phenomena or a pure mathematician creating and exploring abstract structure.

Such apprenticeship models allow for many different interpretations. The image most commonly associated with the word 'apprentice' is of a young person brought into a position to work alongside an expert. The apprentice will be involved initially in menial tasks, perhaps with little relation to the skills they will ultimately acquire; they may then be asked to perform small subtasks which relieve the 'master' of some of the repetitive labour. As these subtasks grow in size and in the opportunity for decision-making, the boundary between the apprentice and expert begins to blur, until the apprentice is able to demonstrate the whole range of skills. Certain aspects of this metaphor are buried deep in traditional pedagogies, even at the university level: it is believed that larger cognitive capabilities are built out of smaller ones and learners should demonstrate abilities with the small sub-tasks before they move on to larger ones. This is part of the generally unexamined assumptions of our educational society which has it roots in behaviourism (Schoenfeld, 1987). Such a view is neatly parodied in (Brown, 1987) in which a mathematician is taught carpentry by being taught in great detail all the uses for a saw, then all the uses for a plane, then all the uses for a chisel etc., but is never involved in making a single piece of furniture.

However, the apprenticeship metaphor admits an alternative interpretation. The young apprentice, while focusing on the menial tasks and the smaller tasks, is becoming encultured: they are in the presence of someone who is a prototypical example of the artisan the apprentice aspires to be. In working alongside the expert, the apprentice is able to observe the skills as a whole, can ask questions at a wide variety of levels. The expert who is skilled at working with apprentices may provide them with tasks which are genuine examples of the work they aspire to and work with them on the task. This interpretation is close to Vygotsky's notion of the Zone of Proximal Development — the zone between what a learner can do with skilled support and what they can do alone. In *Mind in Society* (Vygotsky, 1978) he notes that all functions of cognition appear twice: first as an interaction with a (more skilled) other and then as an internalized function that does not require the external support. This clearly points to the importance of communication, which we will discuss below.

However, it is an aspect of this second interpretation of 'apprenticeship' which is seen in the two courses described above. Students are placed in the mathematical culture: a culture of problems to explore, whether they are problems from outside mathematics which can be modelled and which are understood through the study of mathematical constructs or whether they are problems within mathematics which require the learner to draw together disparate pieces of mathematics to build an understanding of the situation (Duffin and Simpson, 1999).

There are two main dangers in this interpretation which we must be aware of when we translate the ideas of these courses into other contexts: the assumption of continuity and the assumption of cold reasoning.

13.6.1 The assumption of continuity

Research in mathematics education has shown the existence of cognitive discontinuities at a wide variety of stages. Moving from naive counting strategies to the fluent use of known facts and more sophisticated strategies for addition is an early repeatedly observable cognitive discontinuity (Fuson, 1988). The move from arithmetic to algebra (Davis, 1975), the move from working with numerical systems to abstract systems (Dubinsky et al., 1994) and the move from general reasoning strategies to proof (Alcock and Simpson, 1999) are all cognitive discontinuities at different stages in the learning of mathematics. The assumption of many papers in the research of advanced mathematical thinking is that the move from school mathematics to university mathematics is the last such cognitive discontinuity. I suspect this assumption is flawed: recent interviews with students at various stages of their PhD studies has suggested to me that there are cognitive discontinuities at the postgraduate levels and beyond. Indeed, 'lesser' professional mathematicians, reading the personal description of a Field's prize winning mathematician's thinking (Thurston, 1995) can have as much trouble understanding how he is thinking about mathematics as a first-year student has in understanding their lecturers' thinking.

However, these cognitive discontinuities are at the level of engaging with particular skills and techniques in mathematics. The enculturation interpretation of the apprenticeship metaphor considers development at a different level. Above the level of understanding particular constructs (like a function or a topology), Novak and Gowin (1984) site principles, theories, philosophies and world views. The goal of becoming a mathematician relies on development at all of these levels, but it can be argued that developing the mathematical world view — mathematics as a 'way of life' — is the most important. However, the level of development of world views is just as littered with discontinuities as the level of development of particular constructs. Perry (1970) charts in great detail seven discontinuities in university students' world views, ultimately moving from seeing knowledge as right or wrong (with the teacher's role being to distinguish the two) to seeing knowledge as context dependent with the learner having to take a stance on which contexts and rules-of-context they will commit themselves to.

Both courses under discussion here aim to provide environments in which students move to a mathematician's view of mathematics. The pedagogy made explicit in both courses is designed to challenge the belief of students that mathematics has one and only one right answer which they should be able to get to within 10 minutes (Schoenfeld, 1987). These challenges may set students off onto a chain of changes in the way they view mathematics, such as those detailed in Table 13.1 (Simpson, 1994).

In encouraging students to reconceptualize mathematics in these different ways, we must be aware of the second assumption.

	View 1	View 2	View 3	View 4
What are proofs for?	Don't know	To test us	To ensure correctness	Convincing and explaining
Who proves things?	The teacher	The teacher (and us)	Mathmaticians	It should be everyone
How do they prove them?	Don't know	Recall	Logic	Exploring a problem

Table 13.1 **Alternative views of mathematics**

13.6.2 The assumption of cold reasoning

The assumption of many outside mathematics (and perhaps some inside) is that mathematics is cold and austere: mathematics is the antithesis of emotion (Buerk, 1982). However, in listening to mathematics students as they discuss concepts in the kinds of courses described in this article, one soon realizes that they are charged with emotion. Solving problems is an emotional business (Mason, Burton and Stacey, 1982).

Changing the way in which you think about mathematics is very difficult — previous deeply held, but unexamined, beliefs are brought into the open. While they are examined, deconstructed and reconstructed, the learner can be left feeling as if they are standing on quicksand. That all of this takes place as they move from school to the new, more heterogeneous society of university, only exacerbates the difficulty of this change. If the student is unsupported in rethinking their view of mathematics they may 'cool out', lose their enthusiasm for the subject matter and stop engaging with any mathematics (Cooper, 1990).

13.7 Communication

However, the other theme which is common in the two courses described is the important role played by communication. Going beyond a traditional form of communication in university mathematics teaching (almost exclusively from teacher to learner), the courses provide a level of support for the students to begin the emotional journey through the discontinuities. In both courses, there are opportunities for student—student, student—peer tutor and student—teacher communication at all kinds of levels: conversation, oral presentation and written reports. Active engagement in the communication process is at the heart of each course (Houston, 1998; Houston and Lazenbatt, 1999).

A sensitive teacher can listen to a student and hear the sounds of the struggle taking place as their view of mathematics is challenged. Such a teacher can tailor their language and assistance to the individual's needs. Indeed, it has been shown that students are able to choose for themselves the form of engagement they can and should be working with (Copes, 1974). The process of mathematics described above works in just this way: different groups of students can engage in the same problem in quite different ways: some might start from numerical calculations; some might draw on a particular sophisticated theoretical construct. Some might try a number of different models and concentrate on arguing which of those models best suits their 'client'. Each of these approaches challenges and supports a different mathematical world view.

13.8 References.

Alcock, L.J. and Simpson, A.P. (1999) The rigour prefix. In O. Zaslavsky (ed.), *Proceedings of the 23rd Conference of the International Group for the Psychology of Mathematics Education,* vol. 2, pp. 17—24.

Belenky, M.F., B.M. Clinchy, N.R. Goldberger and J.M. Tarule. (1986) *Women's Ways of Knowing: The Development of Self, Voice and Mind*. New York: Basic Books.

Berry, J.S. and Houston, S.K. (1995) Students using posters as a means of communication and assessment, *Educational Studies in Mathematics* **29**(1): 21—7

Brown, R. (1989) Carpentry: a fable, *Mathematical Intelligencer* **11**(4): 37.

Buerk, D. (1982) An experience with some able women who avoid mathematics. *For the Learning of Mathematics* **3**(2): 19—24.

Buerk, D. (1985) The voices of women making meaning in mathematics, *Journal of Education* **167**(3): 59—70.

Cooper, B. (1990) PGCE students and investigational approaches to secondary mathematics, *Research Papers in Education* **5**(2): 127—51.

Copes, L. (1974) *Teaching Models for College Mathematics*. Unpublished doctoral dissertation, Syracuse University.

Davis, R. (1975) Cognitive processes involved in solving simple algebraic equations, *Journal of Children's Mathematical Behavior* **1**(3): 7—35.

Dubinsky, E., Dautermann, J., Leron, U. and Zazkis, R. (1994) On learning fundamental concepts of group theory, *Educational Studies in Mathematics* **27**(3): 267—305.

Duffin, J.M. and Simpson, A.P. (1999) The search for understanding, *Journal of Mathematical Behavior*, in press.

Fuson, K. (1988) *Children's Counting and Concepts of Numbers*. New York: Springer-Verlag.

Gilligan, C. (1982) *In A Different Voice: Psychological Theory and Women's Development*. Cambridge, Mass.: Harvard University Press.

Haines, C.R. and Dunthorne, S. (eds) (1996) *Mathematics Teaching and Assessment — Sharing Innovative Practices*. London: Arnold.

Houston, S.K. (1993a) Comprehension tests in mathematics, *Teaching Mathematics and its Applications* **12**(2): 60—73.

Houston, S.K. (1993b) Comprehension tests in mathematics II Teaching Mathematics and its Applications **12**(3): 113—20.

Houston, S.K. (ed.) (1994) *Innovations in Mathematics Teaching.* Birmingham: SEDA.

Houston, S.K. (1998) Get students to do the teaching! In P. Galbraith, W. Blum, G. Booker and I. Huntley (eds), *Mathematical Modelling — Teaching and Assessing in a Technology Rich World.* Chichester: Horwood Publications, pp. 45—54.

Houston, S.K. and Lazenbatt, A. (1999) Peer tutoring in a modelling course, *Innovations in Education and Training International* **36**(1): 71—9.

Marton, F. and Säljö, R. (1984) Approaches to learning. In F. Marton, D. Hounsell and N.J. Entwistle (eds), *The Experience of Learning.* Edinburgh: Scottish Academic Press.

Mason, J., Burton, L and Stacey, K. (1982) *Thinking Mathematically,* Wokingham: Addison-Wesley.

Novak, J. and Gowin, D.B. (1984) *Learning How to Learn.* Cambridge: Cambridge University Press.

Perry, W.G. (1970) *Forms of Intellectual and Ethical Development in the College Years: A Scheme.* New York: Holt, Rinehart & Winston.

Rogers, P. (1990) Thoughts on power and pedagogy. In Burton, L. (ed.), *Gender and Mathematics: An International Perspective.* London: Cassell, pp. 38—46.

Rogers, P. (1992) Transforming mathematics pedagogy, *On Teaching and Learning* **4**: 78—98.

Rogers, P. and Gabriele Kasier (eds) (1995) *Equity in Mathematics Education: Influences of Feminism and Culture.* London: Falmer Press.

Schoenfeld, A. (1987) What's all the fuss about metacognition? In Schoenfeld, A. (ed.), *Cognitive Science and Mathematics Education.* Hillsdale: Lawrence Erlbaum Associates.

Simpson, A. (1994) Student attitudes to proof. In Tall, D. and Ervynck G. (eds), *Proceedings of the Advanced Mathematical Thinking Group of the 18th Annual Conference of the International Group for the Psychology of Mathematics Education.*

Thurston, W.P. (1995) On proof and progress in mathematics, *For the Learning of Mathematics* **15**(1): 29—37.

Vygotsky, L. (1978) *Mind in Society.* Cambridge, Mass.: Harvard University Press.

14 The pedagogy of chemistry teaching in higher education

Richard Moyes
University of Hull

14.1 Overview

This chapter sets out to respond to the questions set by the organizers of the conference.

1. What do the pedagogies of the disciplines consist of and why are they like that?
2. Is there evidence that the characteristic patterns of teaching and learning found within disciplines support student learning better than alternatives?
3. Can distinctive pedagogies be successfully transferred between disciplines?
4. When disciplines depart from traditional disciplinary patterns of teaching, learning and assessment, what are the consequences for student learning?
5. What are the generic features of disciplines' pedagogies and can they be applied to all disciplines?

14.2 What does the pedagogy of chemistry consist of and why is it like that?

The pattern of chemistry teaching in specialist chemistry courses has traditionally consisted of regular scheduled lectures supported by tutorials and laboratory classes. Expansion of provision has consisted of enlarging classes within the present specialist system, rather than looking to alternatives; joint or general courses are relatively uncommon. Lectures are strongly factual and often used to define the limits of the syllabus, with token statements being made about 'reading around the subject'. Tutorials usually take the form of dealing with sheets of problems. These problems are almost always solved convergently, leading to a 'right or wrong' approach; divergent problems, or problems with limited data are rare. The laboratory sessions mostly consist of developing skills through following instructions carefully with proper regard for safety (COSHH, Control of Substances Hazardous to Health), and preparing reports of a prescribed kind.

Less traditionally, courses are now provided for students without A-level mathematics, or physics or biology as there is a need to address the varied nature of current student entrant qualifications (Barker and Bennett, 1999). Many staff assume that their contact and success in science A-levels will be present in the students they teach, but average entrant A-level attainment is much less than that of successful academics, some of whom make little effort to follow changes in the schools. Academics hark back to the days when students of science specialized in science from an early age and took only sciences and mathematics at A-level. Students are now admitted with a range of A-level experience, which leads to the curious use of the term 'remedial', implying that many of the students are unfit for their courses on admission! Computing in various forms has been adopted to assist the teaching, partly as

CAL, but mostly as communication technology, word-processing, spreadsheets and database handling. Science students are usually well versed in basic C&IT on arrival. Key skills are given attention in undergraduate courses, so long as they are integrated with subject teaching. When key skills, such as team working, fall outside traditional teaching, they are, in general, neglected. Some insight on the pedagogy of chemistry teaching can be gleaned from the recently published benchmarks for the Honours B.Sc. degree (QAA, 1999).

Most chemistry teaching involves average class contact times of more than 20 hours a week, with much of this time spent in laboratories. Many universities have decided centrally that a reasonable learning week should consist of an average 40 hours of study. Thus for the chemist, little time is available for reflection and absorption of ideas when compared with the load of the arts student who may only have contact time of eight hours or less a week. It might be thought that the laboratory would provide supporting experience, but integrated practical and theoretical courses are rare. At their best, laboratory classes can be inspiring, knowledge- and confidence-building experiences, offering direct contact with staff and opportunities to discuss the subject. At their worst they can be boring repetitions of standard exercises which invite plagiarism of the worst kind. The use of standard forms of reports emphasizes uniformity and encourages the 'massaging' of results to obtain better marks. Some attitudes to assessment are strange, to say the least. Marks for laboratory work are often in the first-class range to distinguish those making the effort from those who do not attend. Similar standards apply to coursework. Again, plagiarism is a substantial and unrecognized problem and again , average marks are high. This gives students a false idea of the standards to expect in their assessments. Most staff rely strongly on the time constrained unseen examination which is given a heavy weighting in assessment. It is not unknown for unseen examinations to result in average marks below the pass mark; students pass the module by combination of high practical and coursework marks averaged with their unseen examination marks.

There is a strong view that all chemistry graduates should be capable professional chemists, although career opportunities in chemistry are declining through mergers and subsequent redundancies. The ethos of chemistry teaching in universities is controlled by professional accreditation and also by the baleful effect of the RAE. The primacy of research means that a major, if unstated, aim of most courses is to select the PhD-ready graduate. From this viewpoint courses are very successful judged by the 26 per cent of students who go on to higher degrees by thesis, with a further 10 per cent to taught Masters. Long-term careers in research are rare and it is said that more than 50 per cent of chemistry graduates will be working outside chemistry a few years after graduation.

14.3 Is there evidence that the characteristic patterns of teaching and learning found within disciplines support student learning better than alternatives?

Much of the teaching involves generic pedagogy adapted to the chemical area. The range of required abilities is great. Some facility with mathematical techniques is needed to express phenomena in algebraic terms. Successful students must be able to employ the chemical nomenclature and symbolism accurately, as molecular representations can vary from C_6H_{12}, a hexagon, or a three-dimensional representation on two-dimensional paper. Students must be capable of visualizing molecules in three dimensions and some aids are available. The careful and correct use of words is important and is said to involve students extending their vocabulary to as great an extent as those studying a language. Laboratories are used to develop manipulative skills as well as observation and deduction, but are mostly assessed by the quality of the written report. Traditionally, methods have been developed which address the specific learning problems of the subject — understanding molecular structure representations for example — but while a case can be made for these methods as a preparation for a research training, more general capabilities for employment are neglected. For example, very few opportunities exist in most traditional courses for team working, and students realize that to succeed they need to work individually in competition with their peers.

The Teaching Quality Assessment overview report for the subject (Hefce, 1994) found teaching to be satisfactory in all chemistry departments, but criticized a number of areas. These included the temptation to overwhelm students with too much curricular material and excessive class contact, a lack of assistance with study skills and time management, and the need for methods of assessment which allow candidates to demonstrate their strengths. The development of a wider range of approaches to teaching was considered disappointingly slow, and this included a lack of opportunities for independent learning for students. Although there have been useful developments, most of these criticisms are still valid. To deal with the excessive curricular content the three-year degree has been extended to a four-year 'undergraduate masters'. The M.Chem./M.Sci degree helps the research aspirations and provides a useful filter, as to progress to the final two years, students have to reach a minimum standard of performance . This has led to two related problems, the neglect of the three year BSc and temptation to increase further the curriculum overload.

Students, of course, rapidly learn to learn effectively in the circumstances in which they find themselves. Their environment is strongly research-oriented, and if they wish to progress to research, these methods are appropriate. How useful these methods are for general employment outside chemistry must be doubted. A recent report (Mason, 1997) shows that the chemical industry is reasonably satisfied with the output of graduates which come to them as 'professional chemists', so in this sense the pedagogy is appropriate.

14.4 Can distinctive pedagogies be successfully transferred between disciplines?

There are many pedagogical similarities between all of the sciences, mathematics and engineering. Similarities in the pedagogy of Chemistry and Physics teaching in universities include the following features.

Both subjects tend to teach through lecture courses, problem-solving and laboratory work. Both have high-class contact times which encourage student enquiry. Both have the aim of producing research scientists. Research success in RAE terms has a strong effect in both disciplines. They share mathematical approaches to describing phenomena, chemistry to a lesser extent than physics. Both need to enhance mathematical skills.

Problems in physics tend to have mathematical solutions, whereas in chemistry problems of synthesizing molecules also figure. Both subjects tend to look for a single solution from relevant data.

Chemistry laboratories are concerned with making compounds or analysing mixtures, with some attention to properties. Safe handling of hazardous materials has to be taught.

Chemistry is concerned with making molecules and understanding their properties. Teaching therefore concentrates on molecules, with consequences for understanding nomenclature and structure. The corresponding nature of Physics is discussed by Ashley Clarke in his contribution (see Chapter 15).

So distinctive pedagogies can and have been successfully transferred between disciplines, so long as the overall approach in these disciplines is similar.

14.5 When disciplines depart from traditional disciplinary patterns of teaching, learning and assessment, what are the consequences for student learning?

The traditional pattern of HE learning is through the search for evidence, the encouragement of independent thought and the nurture of good communication skills. So far as chemistry is concerned the departure from traditional patterns results in excessive memory work and reliance on recall of facts. Teachers excuse this with the oft-repeated statement that you need to know the essentials before you can think independently, but this apprenticeship never seems to end. There is a need for most sciences to teach the control of information in a more efficient and modern way, which takes appropriate account of present communication and information technology. Some substantial progress has been made in this direction, most good textbooks now include a CD-ROM and the use of the World Wide Web is increasing. Real progress will be made only by the extensive redesign of courses to make them stress good communication skills and independent learning. This is not to decry the extensive work by some university teachers who seek to improve their courses, but the majority of academics, with their eyes fixed firmly on career advancement by research, deplore the loss of time needed in order to tackle communication skills adequately. They much prefer to teach yet another specialist area of the subject!

14.6 What are the generic features of disciplines' pedagogies and can they be applied to all disciplines?

This question raises the inevitable doubt as to whether *any* subject has its own generic features. We need to remember Kuhn's description of science education as 'a dogmatic initiation in a pre-established tradition'. Most academics would maintain that their subject is 'different' and that teaching it requires a specialist approach. In many cases it can be shown that this 'difference' is not real, the view arises from the background and training of the academics concerned. The pedagogy of science teaching essentially presents the approach of the scientific method which involves the garnering of relevant evidence and the construction of a theory which explains the facts with demonstrable accuracy. This theory can then be used to predict further evidence. As such it is as relevant to the teaching of history as it is to chemistry, as has been pointed out in the past.

14.7 References

Barker, V. and Bennett, J. (1999) The post-16 university transition, *Education in Chemistry* **36**(4): 101.

HEFCE , Q.O. (1994) http://www.QAA.ac.uk/preface.htm (February).

QAA (1994) Benchmark papers, http://www.hefce.ac.uk/education/hefce/pub94/

Mason, G. (1998) *Change and Diversity: the Challenges Facing Chemistry Higher Education*. London: The Royal Society of Chemistry, March.

15 Pedagogy in physics

Ashley Clarke
Department of Physics & Astronomy, University of Leeds

15.1 What is pedagogy?

The Concise Oxford English Dictionary (5th edition) cites pedagogy as

> n the science of teaching

but physical scientists would rather agree with Professor Gibbs's definition in this conference abstract booklet as

> n the art and practice of teaching

The aim of the physical scientist is to devise repeatable, objective experiments to test his/her theoretical model of reality. There seems to be a reluctance for physical scientists to appreciate the research by educationalists into student learning — probably because the nature of pedagogical research does not display the same objectivity and mathematical underpinning as their own research speciality. For example, how can one devise repeatable experiments into student learning? The lecturer and the student cohort are in unique 'states of mind' for each lecture. The lecturer's effectiveness must depend upon how he/she feels on the day, his/her response to the students and the attentiveness of the student cohort. There are no unique solutions to improving student learning. A novel technique for teaching that works well for one academic may be inappropriate for the character of another (equally capable) academic. Pedagogy is an art, which hopefully improves with practice if the academic is open to trying new delivery techniques and continuously reassesses his/her performance.

15.2 What drives the physics discipline pedagogy?

There are a few identifiable drivers which are influencing physics academics' views on pedagogy at this point in time.

15.2.1 The changing abilities of the first-year undergraduates

Departments of physics have been encouraged to increase student numbers despite the fact that the number of students studying physics at A-level has been declining continuously for the past 15 years. Hence most departments must accept lower A-level grades to maintain a significant student population and they must also cope with non-traditional student entry.

15.2.2 Academics desire to produce research-ready graduates

As Dick Moyes argued in his presentation on pedagogy within the chemistry discipline (see Chapter 14), a major driver is the need to produce the research-ready graduate. Academics are still trying to produce student clones of themselves despite the fact that probably only 20 per cent will stay in R&D. Most departments of physics are now offering four-year MPhys (Master of Physics) degree schemes to better prepare students for research, in addition to the three-year BSc degree scheme.

15.2.3 Academics are under more pressure than ever before

The impact of the QAA Subject Review exercise has been to create more internal bureaucracy and paperwork. Departmental mission statements require an up-front commitment to individual teaching quality, active research output and a fair division of administration tasks between academics. Thinking time (for the academics) is now at a premium.

15.2.4 Evolution of HE Staff development

All academic staff whose ages exceed 40 years were literally 'thrown in the deep end' as far as teaching was concerned. The survival plan was simply to mimic one (or more) of your memorable teachers and ensure that you covered the given range of material. However, since the Enterprise in Higher Education development and the Dearing report, all new lecturers are being given guidance on teaching methodologies, pedagogy, course design and assessment via staff development courses. The arrival of the Institute for Learning and Teaching (ILT) will further encourage the more mature academics to review their teaching through portfolios.

15.2.5 Government's desire that HE produce employable graduates

The Royal Society of Arts 'Capability' movement and the significant funding by the DfEE of various initiatives associated with graduate employability over the past seven or eight years has certainly altered traditional academic values. The Enterprise in Higher Education scheme and the various DfEE sponsored Discipline Networks initiatives between 1994 and 1999 (including the Physics Discipline Network for which the author is co-ordinator) have funded significant developments within the Teaching and Learning agenda.

15.3 Falling numbers: the physics/maths synergy

One of the aims of the conference is to identify subject-specific differences in pedagogy and an obvious physics in specific issue is the level of mathematical knowledge and manipulation which is assumed vital by that subject's practitioners. In a typical physics degree scheme, the mathematics probably represents 35—40 per cent of the knowledge base.

Most departments of physics are concerned about the perceived lack of preparedness of first-year students in mathematics. A recent study has been undertaken by Tom Roper and Mike Savage at Leeds which draws upon similar studies over the past five years at

Newcastle, Herriot-Watt, Loughborough, Warwick, Coventry and Nottingham (Hunt and Lawson, 1996). Students in physics, mathematics and engineering (around 450 Leeds students) were given an hour-long diagnostic test which involved algebra, trigonometry, differentiation and integration questions. There were two unexpected results:

1. students with maths grades A and B at A-level cannot be assumed to be competent in basic mathematical skills;
2. most students have deficiencies in calculus and display a woeful lack of practice in solving calculus questions.

Clearly these issues have to be addressed by all departments of physics and solutions sought include the incorporation of 'Booster Maths' or 'Calculus Consolidation' courses running in parallel with first year lecture courses.

15.4 Assessment issues around traditional examinations

Prof. Paul Black has carried out a study into the final assessments for Honours degree physics around 1995. He was interested in the variation in the style of examination questions from one university to another and what student competencies were needed to answer them. He put forward his findings in an article for *Physics Education* in 1997 and also referred to the earlier work of Thompson (1979). Both studies came to similar conclusions — see Table 15.1 — which included the observation that the variability of question types between institutions appears to be staggering. However, a caveat to this work is that *no account was taken of project work* at these institutions — which might redress the apparent imbalance of the assessment of 'critical analysis and judgement'. This clearly raises the question of 'what does the assessment of a physics graduate's competence really mean?'

Categories of questions	Mean of nine universities (including A, B, C and D)	Univ A	Univ B	Univ C	Univ D
Recall, descriptions, derivations	48	76	61	41	10
Routine problems	24	16	12	27	32
Non-standard problems	17	5	4	9	47
Critical evaluation and judgement with emphasis also on presentation	11	3	2	23	11

Table 15.1 Profiles of marks assigned for various categories of question. Each figure is a percentage of the total marks for written examinations for the university specified.

15.5 Problematic areas for pure science pedagogy

My chemistry colleague for this session, Dick Moyes has identified the following problematic areas for the teaching of Chemistry in Higher Education:

- content overload;
- excessive specialization;
- little divergent problem-solving;
- little team working;
- poor preparation for employment.

These problematic areas could also be said to be relevant to the physics discipline and each one is addressed in turn below.

15.5.1 Content overload (or 'is traditional teaching all bad?')

15.5.1.1 Lectures

The physical sciences are built upon a vast knowledge base which is continually expanding and the perennial debate in the staff rooms has been 'What new information can we fit into this module?' Prof. Lewis Elton (1997) has recently pointed out

> **James's Law of Conservation of the Curriculum:**
> If you put something in, you must take something out

There has been a tendency for lecturers to try and cram still more content into their lecture module — which is admittedly crazy. Perhaps for this reason, one has the impression that the lecture is dismissed as useless by many educationalists. There is nothing wrong with the lecture *per se* but, in both the chemistry and physics disciplines, it is the amount of lecture and lab contact time per week which is truly staggering (typically 25+ hours). Clearly the variability of the lecture experience for the student will depend upon

(a) the competence of the lecturers
— in terms of confidence, preparation, enthusiasm and style;

(b) the motivation of the student cohort
— in terms of interest level, background, commitment and alertness.

Common sense would suggest that an effective lecturer should:

- define the scope/set the scene with the first lecture;
- ensure that each lecture has a 'beginning — middle — end';
- allow for the different states of preparedness of the students;
- make connections (i.e. counter the problem of 'modularization-itis');
- perform, i.e. lectures should be exciting and/or humorous, challenging and/or controversial, memorable (if possible for the content rather than the lecturer's idiosyncracies);
- ensure quality and breadth of coursework, notes and feedback.

If these precepts are followed, the lecture should be a worthwhile experience for the students and a cost-effective method for knowledge transfer.

15.5.1.2 Laboratory work: standard experiments versus projects

The first two years of physics degree schemes generally attempt to train students in as wide a range of experimental techniques as possible and usually the standard experiments will cover the same ground as the theoretical/mathematical underpinning in the lectures.

Most departments of physics have insisted on all final year students undertaking an open-ended investigation or project, either alone, in pairs or, in a few cases, in a small team.

Interestingly, if given the choice, most final year physics students prefer to work alone or with only one other friend (of their choosing) and often the reason given is that 'I do not want my assessment to be blighted by others!' In other words one must be prescriptive (or devious) in introducing team activities into physics project work, see for example Clarke (1995) for an idea on 'loosely-coupled teams'.

Current issues that are being discussed in connection with laboratory / project work are as follows.

(a) What is the true cost-effectiveness of projects in terms of academic manpower (and should it matter anyway)?

Projects have the capability of generating student enthusiasm and give the staff better evidence of the student's potential for research. Also project assessment allows us to stress the key skills elements (their attitude towards problem solving) as well as evaluating the quality of their final project report (data handling and critical analysis) through to the justification of their approach at the viva voce, the communication of their understanding of the project in a Final Report and also through their oral presentation skills. Another useful attribute of project work is that it allows the student to negotiate the scope of the project within fixed timescales and negotiate time-sharing of research equipment.

(b) Will virtual reality take over from real laboratory experiments?

It appears that more work has been undertaken by chemists into computer simulations of laboratory (and patently dangerous) experiments than physicists. This approach is attractive to university management because it is potentially cost-effective — removing the need for retention of valuable laboratory space, technical support and staff demonstration time.

15.5.2 Excessive specialism (or 'scholarship versus employability')

This issue is really the debate about discipline specific knowledge versus key skills. The author does *not* believe that scholarship and employability are mutually exclusive. A sound pedagogy should develop both — but how? It is not clear whether it is better to devise special bolt-on modules for key / transferable skills *or* to attempt to embed these skills within standard modules, i.e. to put the skills in a physics context.

However, do the students take either bolt-on or embedded skills development seriously anyway? Perhaps the only effective way to train students in the skills that industry require is for the students to spend time in industry. When *industry is paying* for a placement, or a project, the students know that they are accountable. The experience is real and the laid-back approach (which may be seen during some of our simulated academic activities) is no longer an option. If the *student is paying* to be entertained by the academics, there could be less motivation for them to take our pronouncements in this area seriously (especially when most students say they chose physics because of their excitement for the subject rather than thinking of their graduate career prospects). After conducting a survey of student attitudes towards graduate careers, it appears that over half of second year physics students still have no clear idea of their career path, (see Clarke, 2000).

15.5.3 Problem-solving (but what problem types are presented?)

Everyone in Higher Education is talking about 'problem-solving' in the disciplines, but the reality is that vastly different types of problem are being considered by different disciplines and the techniques for solving problems tend to be subject specific.

A typical problem in physics:

> Three point charges are located at the vertices of an isosceles right triangle, whose hypotenuse has length 2s. The charge at the right angle is +2q and the charges at the 45° angles are +q and -q. Find the magnitude and direction of the electric field at the midpoint of the hypotenuse.

The problem shown above does not use incomplete or fuzzy data, but is typical of first- and second-year physics undergraduate problems. Occasionally students will be asked to 'estimate' an answer (when they have to give reasonable values of physical parameters) but only for a small percentage of questions. This harks back to the work of Black (1997) on the assessment of question types. Recently, Garratt *et al.* (1999) have been working with problem styles which help develop the facility for 'critical thinking' among chemistry undergraduates and there are clear lessons here for the physics community.

15.5.4 Team working and preparation for employment

I have already commented on student attitudes towards teamwork and the possible effect on their individual assessment in project work. Employer surveys always show that teamworking skills and interpersonal skills are highly valued but, in the pure sciences, is there a tendency for physics students to be loners/introverts? Do they have preferred learning styles (see Honey and Mumford, 1992), which mediate against being good team players?

Only a few departments of physics introduce teamworking into some of the first-year and/or second-year undergraduate courses. (At Leeds, for example, the Physics with Electronics and Instrumentation group of students undertake a second year, Industrial Placement Project module which involves small team working.)

15.6 Conclusions

C. Northcote Parkinson (1979) has encapsulated the common view of science education in the following quotation:

> It was assumed (no doubt rightly) that a scientific education would fit a candidate for nothing — except, possibly, science ... Since it is impracticable to decide whether one man is better in geology than another man in physics, it is at least convenient to be able to rule both out as useless ...

This is an interesting time for science pedagogy and the latest Teaching and Learning initiatives. At the time of writing, departments of physics are in the middle of the QAA's Subject Review process and for the first time, all academics within the system are having to come to grips with documenting and proving their commitment to teaching provision. Large sums of money from diverse sources (HEFCE, DTI and DfEE) are becoming available to 'ring fence' for teaching initiatives. In 1998, DfEE announced a fund to sponsor viable projects between the academic Discipline Networks and the National Training Organisations (NTOs) — whose remit is to act as the 'voice of firms in an industrial sector' and influence the Higher Education and further education agenda. The Departments of Physics and Astronomy at Leeds and Leicester were awarded funds to liaise with the e-business NTO and a firm called Univentures Ltd in order to achieve the following objectives:

- survey student attitudes towards IT-related industry;
- map out most important generic skills required;
- raise awareness of career opportunities for physicists;
- audit the skills acquired in honours physics courses;
- define replicable, one-day, business skills workshops;
- adopt a recording/reviewing file or portfolio approach for student development.

The final report of this project will be produced in autumn 2000 but it is clear that much has to be done to raise awareness generally of opportunities for pure science students in industry. Perhaps the students approach to learning could be transformed by making these links?

Now HEFCE is forcing the chemists and physicists to collaborate in a single Physical Sciences Subject Centre rather than support the establishment of two separate Centres. The form of this Centre is still a subject for discussion and debate, but it should be resolved in the near future. This conference session was devoted to chemistry and physics and both disciplines acknowledge that there is a generic pedagogy that could be developed by either discipline and disseminated across to the other, e.g. the 'one-minute lecture' idea of Kee (1999).

Perhaps physical scientists would take more interest in pedagogy if the Fundamental Laws of James and Parkinson could be augmented by other more mathematically based laws. For example, it is amazing how many physical processes show an exponential increase or an exponential decay in their outputs with time. If you are a physicist, you have faith in natural 'time constants' which indicate the rate of change of these physical processes. The time constant related to the electrical charging of a capacitor is given by $\tau = RC$ where R is the resistance of a resistor in series with a capacitor of capacitance, C. One can only hope that the effective time constant for the embedding of novel Teaching and Learning initiatives into Higher Education (which is related to an academic's 'resistance to change' and 'capacity for inaction' — except in research matters) is much shorter than the working life of the average academic.

15.7 References

Hunt, D.N. and Lawson, D.A. (1996) Trends in mathematical competency of A-level students on entry to university, *Teaching Mathematics and Its Applications* **15**(4): 167—73.

Black, P (1997) Aims, assessments and workplace needs, *Physics Education* **32**(5): 351—60.

Thompson (1979) *Studies in Higher Education* **4**(2): 169—80.

Elton, L. (1997) University physics teaching in reduced circumstances, *Physics Education* **32**(5): 346—50.

Clarke, A.R. (1995) *Management of Group Projects*, DfEE First Year Report of the Physics Discipline Network, University of Leeds.

Clarke, A.R. (2000) Final report of DFEE project PUNDIT activities, University of Leeds.

Garratt, J., Overton, T. and Threlfall, T. (1999) *A Question of Chemistry*. Pearson Education.

Honey, P. and Mumford, A. (1992) *The Manual of Learning Styles*. Peter Honey Associates.

Northcote Parkinson, C. (1979) *The Law: Still in Pursuit*, John Murray.

Kee, T. (1999) *The One Minute Lecture and its Variations*, Report for Project Improve, c/o Project Improve Coordinator, Department of Chemistry Education, University of Hull.

16 Disciplinary differences and commonalities across the humanities, arts and social sciences

Ellie Chambers and Andy Northedge
The Open University

16.1 Introduction

Both authors have been with the UK Open University since the early 1970s, working on a variety of projects relating to teaching and learning, Ellie Chambers largely with the Arts Faculty and Andy Northedge with the Faculty of Social Sciences and the School of Health and Social Welfare. We have worked over many years with both interdisciplinary and disciplinary course teams. The two parts of this chapter present our reflections on the implications of disciplinary differences and commonalities for teaching and learning. As will be apparent we have drawn somewhat different conclusions; one of us having been struck more by the commonalities and the other by the differences.

16.2 The social sciences (Andy Northedge)

Though interdisciplinary courses provide occasional opportunities to peep over the fence to watch the teaching rituals of neighbouring sects, academic disciplines have largely functioned as enclosed communities, making comparisons between their teaching strategies difficult. At the OU, however, intermixing of the disciplines is structurally unavoidable and because teaching is done largely through the written word pedagogic strategies are exceptionally open to scrutiny and debate. Also, a course is typically presented for eight successive years, with tutors (who are not the course writers) having all the direct contact with students, so that a body of independent received wisdom quickly accumulates as to what aspects of a course have succeeded, or failed. Consequently the evolution of teaching strategies from one course to another is unusually public, requiring explicit justifications that can withstand challenge from across the disciplinary divides. This part of the chapter presents reflections on the evolution of teaching strategies in successive versions of the OU social sciences foundation course: a course which brings together five disciplines: sociology, political science, economics, social geography and psychology.

The first OU courses had to be produced fast in the absence of an established methodology. The social sciences foundation course was divided into seven blocks: an introduction, a conclusion, and a main body of five blocks, in each of which one discipline did its own thing. In other words, the disciplines simply sat alongside each other and were tackled in sequence by the students. Although the course worked to the satisfaction of many students, it was felt to take little advantage of the opportunities offered by the OU system for radically rethinking teaching. It was replaced after only four years by a course with considerably more ambitious pedagogic aims.

Version Two was structured not around disciplines but around 'society'. Its seven central blocks each dealt with a basic 'dimension' of society, such as 'communications', or 'work'. The disciplines disappeared into the background in favour of 'generic' social science analysis. In practice, units within a block were written by specialists from various disciplines, but without identifying the disciplines. This had the effect that, whilst the course had many admirable features, there was an underlying fragmentation of message. Different 'voices' would speak on the same topic, pursuing very different agendas, and without any obvious connections between their messages, or clues as to why they differed. Theories were glimpsed and then disappeared. What was learned one week often helped little in understanding the following week's study. Students themselves had difficulty establishing a 'voice' in which to write their assignments. The course was experienced as interesting in parts, but a long slog; skipping sections became a widely recommended survival strategy.

Seven years later Version Three set out to address these concerns by positioning 'theory' as the coherent core. A debate was launched in week one and concluded eight months later. This time 'society' played a support role, being brought in as appropriate in explicating the theory. The disciplines again returned to the foreground; each with its own block, but with a remit to work within the core debate, taking up the 'story' from the previous block and passing it on to the next. Questionnaire ratings for this new course far outstripped earlier figures and students' work improved dramatically. Tutors too saw the course as a great improvement. When eventually it was replaced, a similar model was adopted for Version Four. Although 2000 sees the launch of Version Five with a radically new design, the success of which will be debated by thousands more students and tutors, our attention here will focus on the evolution of those first three versions.

16.2.1 The importance of 'storyline'

Why were students able to learn so effectively from Version Three? A major factor, it seems, was its coherence and the cumulative way students built on their insights and understanding from week to week. The 'continuity of framing' enabled students to keep on 'making sense' as they studied. *Making meaning* is the central challenge of studying. The struggle to construct *new* meanings, which is fundamental to learning, is difficult and exhausting mental labour, interrupted all too frequently by collapses into frustrating confusion. Consequently, *maintaining a 'storyline' is always a key element of effective teaching* — a flow of meaning which carries students along. Version Two of the foundation course, in mixing together theoretical perspectives from different disciplines, in effect kept starting up new 'stories', with very little meaning carried over from one story to the next. The students had no underlying plot to work on and make their own connections and conjectures. However many weeks into the course, they were still beginners starting out on another trip into the unknown. The social science disciplines, having been concealed, were not able to develop their own distinctive types of 'story'. Version Three, by contrast, paid close attention to coherence of storyline, allowing disciplines to develop their own sub-plots, so long as they were woven into the overall narrative. The content was, if anything, more intellectually sophisticated and complex, but far fewer students rated the course too difficult. At all levels of ability, students were able to involve themselves in satisfying learning, carried along by the continuity of the debate, and constructing such meaning as they were capable of.

16.2.2 Knowledge as discourse

The shift from Version Two to Three also brought into sharp focus the fact that students were learning not about society *per se*, but about *what social scientists say about society*. 'Society' does not in itself present an intelligible story; it is the disciplines that turn aspects of social experience into coherent accounts. Adult OU students have a lifetime's experience of society and daily see it depicted and discussed in the mass media. However, in taking a social science course they become participants in the systematic debates about various aspects of society carried on within the disciplines. Indeed, the underlying purpose of their studies is to acquire access to the powerful knowledge-producing capabilities of social science discourses. Knowledge does not consist of 'possession' of free-standing facts, concepts and theories, it is a 'capability' for producing effective propositions and arguments within ongoing debates between knowledgeable people. As Bruner puts it, 'Knowledge is what is shared within discourse, within a "textual" community' (Bruner, 1996, p.57). The student's task is to learn how to be a participant within a chosen discourse community. Their objective is to become capable of reading and listening to what is said by accomplished speakers of the specialist discourse and of writing and speaking in ways that carry force within the discourse community. Their goal is to be able to trade meanings effectively within that specialist community.

16.2.3 Impermeability of discourses

There is, however, a fundamental barrier. It is impossible to make sense of a sentence you read, or hear, unless you know 'what it is about'. 'The meaning of any fact, proposition or encounter is relative to the ... frame of reference in terms of which it is construed' (Bruner, 1996, p.13). But students are necessarily newcomers to the specialist discourse and do not know its frames of reference. They find themselves 'locked out' — unable to make sense of utterances they encounter because they cannot place them within the necessary frames of reference — but equally unable to make progress in internalizing the frames of reference because they cannot engage with the utterances through which the frames are made manifest. That is why students need teachers. The teacher, as a discourse speaker, can help students construct meanings they cannot yet produce independently. This enables them to participate in the flow of discourse and thereby come to comprehend its purposes and processes: the nature of the questions being addressed, the forms of evidence and argument employed, the types of conclusions arrived at, and the history of previous debates, in the light of which current debate is conducted. All these are structuring features of a discourse which are internalized primarily through participation, rather than from explicit explanation.

16.2.4 Surface learning

If students are not provided with sufficient support to engage with the frames of reference of the specialist discourse (or are unwilling to engage), their only alternative is to construct the best sense they can using frames of reference they already know. In other words they incorporate propositions and terminology from the specialist discourse into a more elementary form of discourse, losing and distorting much of the meaning in transit. They are then able to produce crude facsimiles of specialist knowledge, but have no access to its analytical and generative power. This is the widely reported phenomenon of surface learning.

16.2.5 Tracing pathways into the specialist discourse

To support 'deep learning' the teacher must develop techniques for leading parties of students into the unfamiliar terrain of the specialist discourse. Two basic properties of human communication offer leverage. One is *'intersubjectivity'*. '[Teaching] rests upon our astonishingly well developed talent for 'intersubjectivity' - the human ability to understand the minds of others' (Bruner, 1996, p.20). When two or more people are engaged in discussion they immediately and unconsciously construct a shared frame of reference — a common consciousness, or intersubjectivity, which enables meaning to be passed between them. Without this shared intersubjective framing the utterances of each would be unintelligible to the others. (A similar state of intersubjectivity is required when reading. The reader has to be prepared to enter into the framing projected by the writer's utterances.) This capacity to construct a situational shared consciousness is central to teaching, in that it allows the teacher to 'lend' students the capacity to frame meanings within the expert discourse. By shaping and supporting a flow of discussion, the teacher enables students to engage with the new discourse and thereby experience how to 'mean' within it.

The other property is the *'intertextuality'* of discourses. Meanings are always constructed upon other meanings and discourses likewise develop out of other discourses. Equally, discourse communities do not usually have tight boundaries. We are all members of a variety of discourse communities, including the general public discourses of the mass media and everyday interactions. Thus a teacher can trace pathways from known discourses into the new discourse. A key teaching manoeuvre is to initiate a discussion within a familiar discourse and then, while maintaining intersubjective framing through ongoing dialogue, to make an excursion into the new discourse. This exploits the powers of intersubjectivity, while at the same time building on intertextuality. In the context of distance education, where the immediate force of directly negotiated face-to-face intersubjectivity is not available, alternative 'literary' devices are required. Hence the importance of 'storyline' in a text, as seen in Version Three of the foundation course. Hence also the value of allowing the disciplines space to construct well-guided excursions into their own discursive framing, rather than dropping students briefly into a series of unidentified locations. The discipline's mode and history of discourse are central to what the student is learning. 'A central learning task for individuals ... is to acquire both the organising conceptual theories and the patterns of discourse that are used by particular reasoning communities' (Resnick et al, 1997, p.4).

16.2.6 The importance of 'discoursing' in the social sciences

Making meaning is particularly challenging in the social sciences (as also in the arts, and humanities), since they deal to a large extent with what von Wright has called Aristotelian, as opposed to Galilean, forms of explanation . As opposed to Galilean forms of explanation (see Feldman and Kalmar, 1996, p.109) offer causal accounts of non-intentional objects, the Aristotelian offer teleological accounts of human action. '[For] accounts of ... [action with] a complex pattern of meaning by virtue of its interpretability within a complex cultural frame — we eschew the Galilean mode as simplistic and reductive' (Feldman and Kalmar, 1996, p.110) in these 'discursive' disciplines is derived through interpretation and argument, rather than through detailed modelling of the physical world. Definitions are never watertight, interpretations never securely pinned down; meanings need to be continually reproduced through debate. Learning is not basically about learning how to select and apply an appropriate model to a concrete aspect of the world, buť about learning how to construct and sustain an analytical framework adequate to the subtleties and ambiguities of the issue at hand. It is less about the skills of applying elaborate techniques in the solving of problems, than about the skills of developing an argument and supporting it. It is not so much about becoming a skilled technician, as establishing an 'identity' as a legitimate participant within the discourse community. Consequently, the activity of 'discoursing' is central to learning in these disciplines, whether in the form of 'live' talk or through reading and writing.

It is helpful to consider how each of the common modes of teaching contributes to the students' experience of engaging with the specialist discourse.

- Lectures enable students to hear the discourse 'live', as spoken by an expert; to get a sense of how meanings are 'framed', to hear what kinds of argument the discourse develops, the starting points, the forms of evidence and their use, the considering of counter-arguments, the drawing of conclusions. All these are valuable clues for projecting meaning on to texts subsequently attempted.
- Group tutorials, or seminars, enable students to participate in the discourse alongside peers, sharing in framing makeshift meanings, learning how to harness the powers of the discourse to generate analyses of their own.
- Reading presents students with the challenge of using the text to generate the discourse on their own. They must supply the momentum, reflect on and control their progress, participate in producing meanings by taking appropriate notes, and make links to other knowledge, so that they will be able to reproduce some of the argument for themselves. Academic disciplines function primarily through 'literate' rather than 'oral' forms of discourse, where literal meanings and formal logic are prioritized. 'Consciousness of the fact ... that utterances can be taken literally ... is at the heart of literate thinking' (Olson, 1996, p.149). Thus grappling with an academic discourse in written form is a central part of coming to understand how it works.
- Writing is where students learn to 'speak' the discourse, taking hold of it to present their own meanings to other members of the specialist community. This is the point at which students really discover how much purchase they have on the 'tools' the discourse offers. It is also where they learn to position themselves as active speaking members of the community, as they develop a 'voice' in their writing. Until students are engaged in writing, and getting some answering feedback from a speaker of the discourse, they may be learning relatively little from a course. Consequently, they need opportunities to write a little, often and starting as early in the course as possible.
- Practical work, field trips, surveys, or experiments can all be seen as aspects of serving an 'apprenticeship' in the practices of the discourse community.
- Scholarship such as undertaking dissertations and theses can be seen as extended exercises in consolidating an 'identity' as a productive member of the discourse community.

To view teaching methods in this 'discursive' light has significant implications for practice. It shifts goals, redirects strategy and tactics and suggests alternative criteria for evaluating success. Though each of the social sciences has its more 'Galilean' aspect (economic calculus, probabilistic statistics, experimental methodology, etc.) to the extent that they can be characterized as 'Aristotelian' (and thus discursive) at heart, they share these pedagogic implications.

This is not to say that the social science disciplines should be lumped together, or 'homogenized'. As we saw earlier, students need opportunities to learn how meanings are distinctively framed within each discipline's discourses. But it is to suggest that much can be generalized across disciplines in terms of basic teaching principles.

16.3 The arts/humanities (Ellie Chambers)

While I agree with Andy Northedge that 'much can be generalized across disciplines in terms of basic teaching *principles*', nonetheless I take the view that there are significant differences between the disciplines that make up the humanities (that is, those subjects usually taught in the Faculty of Arts in universities — Art History, Classical Studies, Cultural Studies, History, Linguistics, Literatures, Modern Languages, Music, Philosophy, Religious Studies and the rest — and excluding the fine and performing arts), that these differences are intrinsic and that, in practice, they matter. To begin with, though, we will look at what these subjects share; the commonalities that account for them being grouped together as 'humanities'.

16.3.1 Commonalities among the humanities

First, the 'what' of study: the scope and focus of these subjects. What unites them is that they all explore, and yield knowledge and understanding of aspects of *human cultures*. In them we study the activities, ideas, beliefs, cultural practices and products of individuals and groups, in our own and other societies, over time. Furthermore, what we study are 'texts', broadly defined to include visual, aural and symbolic as well as written forms. For we cannot gain access to people's ideas, beliefs, intentions and activities in a direct way, but only through studying the texts that 'stand for' these things; texts that represent the conditions of time and place and all the ideas, knowledge and activity that went into their making. (Even a living artist's account of why and how she is painting a portrait is one more text, not to be taken at face value but to be examined and interpreted.) In short, then, humanities subjects are united by their cultural focus and by their 'textuality'.

Secondly, the 'how' of study: methodology. Our task is to interpret the meanings and significance of these texts, to produce understanding and knowledge. This entails *making* meaning — active encounter between object and enquirer (Gadamer, 1989) — through our engagement in processes of textual analysis, interpretation and evaluation. Textual analysis is a quasi-technical process involving knowledge of the 'rules' governing the composition of different text-genres, their subject-matters and formal elements (literary genres such as poems, plays, novels; musical forms of oratorio, sonata, and so on). Such analysis is fundamental to interpretation of the text's meanings, which includes knowledge of the socio-historical circumstances of the text's inception and reception along with the interplay of these contexts. Also implied here is consideration of the text's (possibly changing) status over time, or, acts of appraisal and judgement. These inter-related processes of analysis-interpretation-evaluation are notoriously contentious; subject to theories about why and how we do them — theories which themselves change over time and are part of the contexts that have to be understood. The outcome (for academic and student alike) is our own 'text': literary, musical or art-historical criticism, judgement about the soundness of a philosophical argument and its significance, explanation of historical or religious events and

Subject	Objects of study/text type	Use of/teaching methods
Art history	visual: art, artefacts and buildings; symbolic (plans, sketches, elevations etc.)	• lecture/visual illustration (still & moving image) • seminar: analysis etc. of visual text, debate • other: galleries, buildings
History	written: documents of all kinds; visual & symbolic source material (photos, film, etc.)	• lecture: contexual/propositional/methodical • seminar: analysis etc. of visual text, debate • other: museums, archives
Literature	written: literary texts in all genres; performance (texts in performance)	• lecture: contextual/methodical/performative • seminar: analysis etc. of literary text, debate, workshop-style performance • other: theatre, film
Music	aural ('sounds'); symbolic (scores)	• lecture/sound illustration • seminar: listening, anaysis etc. of sound and score, debate • other: concerts, music making
Philosophy	written: philos. texts ('ideas', theory); oral utterances	• lecture: propositional/methodological/ contextual • seminar: 'philosophising'
Classical studies/ Modern languages	multi-disciplinary - as above, plus critical studies, language study and practice	various (as above, according to object of study) plus language workshop/lab., structured discussion in target language, etc
Cultural studies/ Area studies	multi-disciplinary - as above, plus some social sciences (eg. geography, sociology, politics, economics)	various (as above, according to object of study) plus modern media (TV, film, etc.) and socio-cultural theory and practice

Table 16.1 **Differences between humanities disciplines**

movements, and so forth, which we in turn communicate to others. In short, participants in the humanities learn to make theoretically informed, appropriate interpretations and judgements by studying the primary and secondary texts produced by their predecessors, by making their own enquiries and producing their own texts (Chambers, 1993).

Significant knowledge in the humanities, then, is socially constructed, through our discourse past and present. This type of study is hermeneutic, inter-textual, participatory, value-laden, context dependent, and relatively indeterminate.[1]

16.3.2 Disciplinary differences

Having said all that, there are significant differences between humanities disciplines. Indeed, over time, academic disciplines have been developed precisely as increasingly *differentiated* ways of distinguishing between and mediating aspects of human experience and imagination, following certain traditions of thought and practice.[2] As the ways in which we carve up the very wide range of cultural activity and achievement (our history, languages, art, music, literature ...) — in order to create order among it, to be able to examine aspects of it in detail and, together, come to understand it better — so humanities disciplines pick out and focus on *different* aspects of our 'world'. That is, they have different objects of study / characteristic 'text-types': in Art History we focus mainly on visual objects / texts, in Music on aural, and in Literature, History and Philosophy on written texts of different kinds (see Table 16.1, *Objects of study/text-type* column).[3]

In brief, the disciplines are conventional but they are not arbitrary. They represent the ways in which we 'choose' to carve up our cultural experience, but those choices are far from capricious. Some important implications flow from this.

First, since the disciplines are conventional they are not set in concrete; they are always open to reinterpretation and change. We see this around us today, in a growing tendency towards multi-disciplinary study and in the emergence of new fields such as Cultural and Gender Studies. Single-disciplines too are changed as new intellectual agendas take hold (witness a refocusing and broadening of the literary canon as some English Literature departments re-define the discipline as 'Literatures in English'). The disciplines, then, are *living* traditions of thought and practice. The map of the humanities changes and fresh boundaries are drawn.

Secondly, we saw that although the humanities have a shared methodology — with meaning-making at its heart, dependent upon processes of textual analysis-interpretation-evaluation and communication between people — because the disciplines are non-arbitrary, focusing on different aspects of our culture, they are concerned to explore different text-types. This means that analytical modes and concepts *differ* between them. It is not the same thing to interpret the meanings of a poem and a painting, for example. Even on first encounter these texts are experienced as different and make different demands; a poem is read in linear fashion, so that the process of understanding is inevitably a 'delayed' one, whereas the painting may be apprehended as a whole, 'at a glance'. Then, when studying them closely, we apply different categories in our analyses (identifying patterned uses of language and sound in the poem, involving concepts such as metaphor, alliteration and rhythm; representations of distance and light / shade in the painting, applying analytical concepts such as perspective, mass, and colour density). Ultimately, we may read 'symbolic' and other types of meaning in either form, but the process of arriving at informed, appropriate interpretations and judgements differs significantly. Beginning students have to learn how to analyse a poem *and* a painting; the ability to do the one does not simply carry over to the other, even though both activities are labelled 'analysis'. Similarly, the very purpose of analysing written text differs in History and Philosophy. We study an historical document to assess its reliability as a source of information, otherwise we cannot be sure just what it is 'telling' us; in philosophy we first aim to determine whether what we are presented with is a 'good' argument in itself, logically sound and illuminating.

In summary, I would say two things:

- each humanities subject has (more or less) distinctive: purposes, objects of study, text-genres, central concepts and networks of ideas, uses of evidence, and tests for 'truth'.[4]
- these differences are, at once, conventional and intrinsic.

As such, disciplinary differences have implications for teaching and learning.

16.3.3 Teaching and learning

The first thing to be said about the concepts 'teaching' and 'learning' is that there is no (logically) necessary relationship between them. People can, and do, learn all kinds of thing without being taught them directly — including in educational settings, where students may learn from books, films etc., and from each other. And even in formal courses of study when educational aims and other matters are determined by teachers, there is a wide variety of ways in which education may proceed and those aims can be achieved (Hirst and Peters, 1970). However, we may say that, *depending on the nature of the subject,* some teaching-learning methods will be more appropriate than others, the more likely to result in successful study (i.e. in 'learning'). As regards the humanities, which we have seen are in their nature discursive, a focus on processes of reading with understanding, on speaking and writing is strongly implied, along with teaching-learning methods that enhance students' analytical-interpretive capacities and independence of judgement. Overarching aims of this type of education might be summarized as:

- to learn to read the text-genres of the discipline appropriately and engage in related processes of textual analysis, interpretation and evaluation;
- to engage with the concepts and networks of ideas that characterize the discourse, and learn to think in terms of them;
- to grasp the purposes and assumptions that underlie current debates within the discipline, as well as the systems of belief and value that inform them;
- to understand the way argument is constructed within the discourse, what counts as evidence and how it is used;
- to learn to speak and write within the conventions that apply, taking an independent, critical stance.

Students normally learn these things in lectures and practical workshop, through discussion in seminar/tutorial, by researching in libraries, archives, galleries etc., and in the process of writing essays and undertaking project work. These days, applications of Information and Communications Technology perhaps include discussion via e-conferencing, study of digitized text, often using a 'search' facility, and use of visual, sound and other databases on CD-ROM or the Internet. It is no accident that study via these new media mainly replicate traditional (discursive, text- and research-based) pedagogic forms — although, as we have seen, in principle other teaching-learning methods are not ruled out.

A glance down the *Use of/teaching methods* column in Table 16.1 shows that the lecture and seminar are staples of humanities teaching, teaching-learning methods used in every discipline. But, as with the term 'analysis' applied to the different disciplines, this does not mean that 'the same thing' is denoted in each case. Table 16.1 attempts to show some of the differences between the form they take in, for example, Art History, Music, Literature and Philosophy. An Art History lecture is not mainly an opportunity to transmit information, nor is it simply an illustrated talk, but is predominantly a visual experience; similarly, the relationship of sound to the Music lecture. Here, the representation on slide or CD is the focus of attention, with the lecturer providing some of the context for (later) discussion and/or 'modelling' processes of textual analysis-interpretation and of argumentation in a sustained, uninterrupted way. A seminar in Literature involves discussion of the written text (and/or author, period, style) and may include an element of performance, while the

Philosophy seminar is primarily an opportunity for students to engage in a particular kind of discussion and debate, namely to 'philosophize'. Humanities teachers' preference for the essay as the main means of written communication is not just a matter of tradition (used pejoratively); this form offers students the opportunity to develop and present a sustained argument, including adequate illustration and justification of their points of view — although, again, the *modes* of argumentation and *types* of evidence involved differ between the disciplines.

In short, the requirement that in the humanities students engage actively in reading/viewing/listening, questioning, analysing, interpreting meanings and producing their own verbal performances and written texts, implies teaching-learning practices that focus on discursive processes themselves and, centrally, on negotiation of meaning. But the *ways* in which these things are performed and achieved differ between disciplines that, fundamentally, address different aspects of our culture.

16.3.4 Conclusion

The significance of disciplinary difference is perhaps best appreciated when we consider its practical implications for people like us, who are interested in systematic inquiry into teaching and learning and in staff development. Anyone who has taken the role of teacher-educator knows that it is useless to address academic colleagues in terms other than those they 'speak', or attempt to engage them in discussion of practices they have no experience of — at least, beyond a point that is soon reached. In 'generic' courses, typically they complain that what(ever) is being said does not apply to them, is unhelpful and is not interesting; their needs are otherwise because 'their' subject is particular, and different. Clearly, practitioners themselves believe they belong to different disciplinary sub-cultures, having distinct academic-pedagogic preoccupations and styles. But to acknowledge disciplinary differences is not just a matter of practical expedience; it goes deeper. Such recognition implies that the characteristic features of a discipline should determine the manner and terms in which we conduct research into the teaching and learning of it. The conceptions that guide our inquiry must attune with those of our academic colleagues who work within it, making sense to them — and not just because we want research outcomes to make a difference.

Our focus then shifts towards examination of the languages and practices that constitute particular fields of knowledge and inquiry. That is, as researchers, we ourselves must be 'on the inside of' the disciplines we seek to investigate, acquiring sufficient understanding of their nature and purposes.[6] Only then can we engage fully with our academic colleagues, begin building up wider 'discourse communities' within which a scholarship of teaching and learning may flourish and, indeed, make a difference.

Notes

1. It is these characteristics, particularly the last, that give rise to teachers' vociferous criticism of some current educational orthodoxy as inappropriate to and reductive of the humanities (e.g. pre-determination of 'objective outcomes' of all higher education, the central importance of vocational 'skills' or 'competence'), although such criticism is often mistakenly dismissed as ingrained conservatism on their part.

2. See an account of the development of the modern higher education curriculum over time, from the sixteenth century's 'seven liberal arts', in, for example, Lawson and Silver (1973).

3. This is merely a sketch of the terrain, and a partial one at that — for example, there may well be objections to bracketing together Classical Studies and Modern Languages, and among other subjects Religious Studies is missing. But it illustrates my argument sufficiently, I hope.

4. For the argument in greater detail, see Chambers (1993) and Chambers and Northedge (1997). Successful learning in multi-disciplinary studies involves such understanding and skill applied to the range and variety of text-types involved (as Table 16.1 indicates), which is what makes it so difficult to achieve.

5. I base this observation on many years' teaching in the London Institute of Education annual 'Course for University Lecturers'. After much experimentation, the team settled on a combination of generic sessions and time spent in academic domain-specific working groups.

6. For one such research attempt, with respect to the teaching and study of Philosophy, see Chambers (1994). As to whether the outcome has made a difference, I don't know; the situation was that the paper had to be published in the USA because no appropriate journal (or, discourse community) existed in the UK.

16.4 References

Bruner, J.S. (1996) *The Culture of Education*. Cambridge, Mass.: Harvard University Press.

Chambers, E.A. (1993) The role of theories of discourse in course design for humanities distance education, *Media and Technology for Human Resource Development* **5**(3): 177—96.

Chambers, E.A. (1994) Representing Philosophy, *Teaching Philosophy* **17**(3): 195—221.

Chambers, E.A. and Northedge, A. (1997) *The Arts Good Study Guide* (Chapter 6). Milton Keynes: The Open University.

Feldman, C. and Kalmar, D. (1996) Autobiography and fiction as modes of thought. In Olson, D. and Torrance, N. (eds), *Modes of Thought: Explorations in Culture and Cognition*. Cambridge: Cambridge University Press.

Gadamer, H-G. (1989) *Truth and Method*, 2nd revised edn, transl. J. Weinsheimer and D.G. Marshall. London: Sheed & Ward.

Hirst, P.H. and Peters, R.S. (1970) *The Logic of Education*. London: Routledge & Kegan Paul.

Lawson, J. and Silver, H. (1973) *A Social History of Education in England*. London: Methuen.

Olson, D. (1996) Literate mentalities: literacy, consciousness of language, and modes of thought. In Olson, D. and Torrance, N. (eds), *Modes of Thought: Explorations in Culture and Cognition*. Cambridge: Cambridge University Press.

Resnick, L.B., Pontecorvo, C., and Säljö, R. (1997) Discourse, tools, and reasoning. In Resnick, L.B., Säljö, R., Pontecorvo, C. and Burge, B. (eds), *Discourse, Tools and Reasoning*. Berlin: Springer-Verlag.

17 Musicians' experience of the musical world: relations with teaching and learning

Anna Reid

Centre for Learning and Teaching, University of Technology, Sydney

17.1 Overview

The teaching and learning of instrumental and vocal music have a long tradition where students seek out a master musician and 'learn' the master's style. The tradition assumed that master musicians could naturally 'teach' by virtue of their own experience of learning by watching their master, and by virtue of their own formidable abilities. Instrumental and vocal music is unusual in that there has been no defined pedagogy or curriculum for the field. Some prominent musicians have written 'methods' books that tend to focus on instrumental techniques and style, but none addresses the way that students' learn. Recent research has described the ways in which musicians' experiences of music may be related to their understanding of teaching and learning.

This chapter describes musicians' experiences of the 'world' of music in three distinct ways. These three ways of experiencing focus on the extrinsic technical dimensions of music; the extrinsic but meaningful dimensions of music; and finally the intrinsically meaningful dimensions of music. These ways of experiencing are related to the ways in which musicians and their students understand teaching and learning. The issues explored in this chapter are the relations between their experience of the world of music, the ways that musicians 'create' a teaching/learning content related to these experiences, and their conceptions of teaching and learning music.

17.2 Introduction

Hildegarde Froehlich (1992) observed that 'surprisingly little research exists on what teachers believe to be the purpose of music teaching to be' and that 'there are hardly any investigations on what students themselves consider important to learn' (p. 563). For centuries music students have chosen to study with master musicians usually as a result of hearing the master's performance. It has been assumed that if you can play, you can also teach (Bruhn, 1990; Kennell, 1991; Persson, 1996). It has also been assumed that the quality of a student's performance is related in some way to the teacher's ability (Johnson, 1991).

The teaching of instrumental music has a long and traditional background and teachers today adhere to teaching techniques and philosophies that date back in some instances for centuries.

> Applied music teachers are members of an important oral tradition in which personal experience and historical anecdote form the basis of contemporary common practice. Performance expertise is passed on from one generation of performers to the next through the lineage of personal experience and the applied lesson. (Kennell, 1992, p. 5)

It is well recognized that there are 'schools' of practice that can often be traced back to one notable teacher/performer in each instrumental category. Every musician spends a significant amount of time with a single teacher. In a four-year course a student can expect to be with their teacher for an average of an hour per week, totalling about 160 hours. The relationship and memories that develop are reflected later in the student's own teaching practice.

> They remember how their teachers did it, how their teachers once asked them to play a certain work, movement or phrase, and find an easy solution in recapitulating these truths, inherited as they are through many a generation. (Bruhn, 1990)

Bruhn considers the instrumental teacher/performer and the duality of these roles. Bruhn claims that instrumental teachers lack a conscious knowledge about pedagogy and also the consciousness and knowledge about how to teach interpretational details. Bruhn suggests that instead of knowledge and understanding of pedagogy, teachers teach as they have been taught, passing on attitudes and values that have been established in previous generations. Instrumental teaching in this context is perceived as the transmission of as many musical ideas as possible from the teacher to the student. Bruhn also suggests that well-trained musicians must understand musical and theoretical aspects of performance in order to perform creatively and authentically, and in the process acquire enough resources to teach their own students!

Uszler (1992) suggests that 'the relationship between teacher and students carries on the master-apprentice tradition. The master is the model who demonstrates, directs, comments, and inspires. The apprentice is the disciple who watches, listens, imitates, and seeks approval' (p. 584).

Instrumental teachers also understand that teaching can be a valuable process through which they themselves can refine their own thoughts through the process of passing it on to others. Combined with this is a need to pass on their own knowledge and understanding in deference to the traditions surrounding the art.

> Well let me say that I feel teaching is a very important part of my career, and I am very attached to my own students. Moreover, I think it is our responsibility to pass on to the up and coming generation the violinistic lore and tradition that we have imbibed. Teaching helps me verbalise my own ideas about playing, and I sometimes find myself learning from students what not to do. (Friedman in Applebaum, 1978, p. 16)

Instrumental teaching is seen as an integral part of the responsibilities of the professional musician. Learning an instrument can be seen as a complex initiation in to the values attitudes and secrets of the musical world which are revealed portion by portion as the master musician chooses.

Given that musicians' teach as part of their professional role, and that an understanding of that professional role appears to be related to what is taught, finding out how musicians understand the profession, and the associated teaching/learning role would seem to be important. Ritterman (1999) suggests that students need to have a variety of learning experiences that are supported by teachers that have differing understandings of the professional experience. But where does the difference lie? Is it in the sorts of *work*, such as large, small or solo work? Or is it a difference in musical *style*? Or is it a difference in the way that they understand the value of their professional work? The section that follows describes the outcomes of a qualitative study that sought to describe variation in the way musicians and their students understood teaching and learning music. From this initial research plan the musicians' understanding of their work emerged which can be related to their understanding of teaching and learning.

17.3 The Music Entity

Phenomenographic interviews[1] with 24 musicians and their students about their experience of teaching and learning instrumental and vocal music revealed three distinct ways in which 'music in the professional world' was understood by the group. This constitution has been called the Music Entity. The Music Entity is hierarchical and is related to categories of description of teaching and learning instrumental and vocal music.

The Music Entity is found in the participants' understanding of world of music making. The students' view of 'what is music' informs their understanding of 'what is to be learned', 'how it should be learned', and 'what should my teacher teach me?'. In the same way the teacher/musicians' experience of the musical world informs their understanding of 'what is to be taught', 'how it is to be taught', and 'what should my students learn?'

The Music Entity is a way of describing musicians' (and student musicians') experience of the musical world through which the participants are aware of both what it is to know and understand music and to be a musician. An understanding of music in society, and an understanding of what it is to be a musician, may be related to the way in which the participants are aware of teaching and learning music.

The Music Entity may be defined as having three qualitatively different dimensions:

- Extrinsic Technical (level 1);
- Extrinsic Meaning (level 2);
- Intrinsic Meaning (level 3).

The *Extrinsic Technical* (level 1) dimension describes elements of music making that are literally 'outside' the participant. Music is understood as a combination of technical elements related to either an instrument or to musical notation. Music is understood as a series of technical and notational elements that are joined together physically on an instrument (or voice). The music and the instrument are objects that are considered as external to the musicians. Music is created through a physical act where instrumental/musicological components are prescribed by external forces rather than being interpreted or created from within. For instance, music is limited by the physical/technical nature of playing the instrument and is also limited by the predictive elements of music that are found in the written manuscript (harmony, style, melody and rhythm). The amount to be learned and taught about the instrument and musicology are considered finite.

> As a professional player, playing the kind of music that I have to play, from jazz to classical music, I am competitive. I have a secret, I have accomplished a way of making music that is identifiable with me. It fits into the large scheme of what the orchestra needs or the style of music, or the period of time, but I do it in a special way. I don't give that secret away to anybody because it would cost me work. So I am naturally secretive about it and I would think that anybody who is in a creative field would be that way. But when we are teachers, we give away everything. Every thing I know, my secrets on how I do things, I give them to the students willingly. (Colin)

The *Extrinsic Meaning* (level 2) dimension describes a more integrated view of music making where the focus is the production of meaningful communicative musical sound. The focus is on the inherent meaning of the music described through the textual and stylistic elements. Communication of meaning is important but the meaning is constituted through textual and technical elements and is external to the teacher/student. The instrumental/ musicological elements of music making are considered only as the mechanics of playing, the real Music Entity is the meaning that is ascribed to music. The Extrinsic Meaning Music Entity is not finite. Rather, the meaning of the music can be approached from several different perspectives. The music is understood to have a meaning that is unique to it and it is that meaning that is discovered and performed or communicated with an audience.

> And so you approach it in an intelligent way and you can say, you know, what were their musical (pause), what was their music written for? What instruments were they written for? And did they have a liturgical function? Or was it simply performance music and all these sorts of questions. And you look at that and even down to things like the temperaments that instruments were that they played in and books that they wrote. And you ask why he wrote all these pieces in E minor which sound dreadful on the mean tone organs. There are various questions which interest me and they rise up and you look at them and you think about then hope that by the time you come to play the music you've got some sort of deeper understanding of what it is doing and what it is that you're playing. (Andrew)

The final dimension of the Music Entity is that of *Intrinsic Meaning* (level 3). Music is seen as a vehicle for expressing personal artistic truths. This view of music includes the extrinsic elements of instrumental technique and inherent musical meaning but incorporates them within the broader framework of personal interpretation and meaning. The focus of this dimension is on the relations between personal understanding, or aesthetic, of the world of music and the consequent personal re-interpretation of it through a communicative process. The external meaning of music is re-interpreted as internal as the mechanics of playing the instrument are subsumed in the interpretive aspects. Music is the demonstration of personal meaning. The students/teachers develop personal meanings and a view of the world from their experiences with music and the meaning that is within that music. They reinterpret the music's meaning through their own understanding of the world. The essence of the Intrinsic Meaning Music Entity is the development and expression of artistic truth.

> And because there is such a set standard now, this is just what music is, and there is so much to learn about what there already is, that to experiment is kind of left in the lurch if you don't get time to experiment. You have to learn all there is to learn and then you can experiment. Just a general description would be to know the skills. Lets take an example, say a first movement of a Mozart Sonata, to be able to learn the skills to be able to play all the notes correctly, to have learned (pause) I think within that learning comes a knowledge of the composer, period and the harmony of the piece and all that is involved with the music, the interpretation. If you have learned all that then you come to a performance and on top of all that there is something deep inside that you have to also learn. (Fiona)

The participants' experience of the Music Entity becomes the ground from which they are aware of teaching and learning instrumental / vocal music. Students' experience of the Music Entity allows them to learn aspects of musicality that are consistent with their personal view. The idea of 'what is music?' becomes central to the participants' understanding of teaching and learning 'music'. In essence those who consider that music is simply what the instrument and the manuscript produce can only approach their understanding of teaching and learning from this view. Similarly those who consider music to be the discovery of meaning approach teaching and learning music with a sense of adventure and discovery.

Certain perceptions of the Music Entity allow musicians and student musicians to frame experiences of teaching and learning with an awareness of what should be taught and learned for the profession. The way that people come to a teaching or learning task (or indeed any activity) reflects how and what they have already understood about the phenomenon. To some degree each time that people are involved with a phenomenon their understanding of and awareness of it changes. People's understanding of a phenomenon is related to their awareness of and the meanings they give to their prior experiences of the phenomenon. Meaning or understanding of an experience is developed or changed through the current experience. Marton and Booth (1997) describe this as the 'nature of awareness'.

In this instance the musicians' experience of the musical world can be related to their experience of teaching and learning music. Their experience of music making, the Music Entity, provides a ground from which musicians and their students experience of teaching and learning. In the following section categories of description of teaching and learning music are defined that focus on the variation found within the subject groups' experience of teaching and learning music.

17.4 Teachers' experience of teaching/learning instrumental and vocal music

17.4.1 Disseminating (level 1)

Teaching is disseminating the teachers' musical and performance experience. Students learn through being exposed to the teacher.

Characteristic of this category is the teachers' belief that students wish to emulate the musical and professional life of the teacher. The role of the teacher is to tell of experiences and to demonstrate the craft. Students learn by copying the teacher's performance. Music is seen as a collection of technical and notational packages that need to be transferred to the student. Teaching is seen as a formative experience for the student and the outcome of the teaching and learning experience is to provide a background for the student's future development.

Peter: I tend to concentrate on developing them [the students] through working on specific technical faults as separate items.

The way that students learn is simply by being near and being exposed to a master musician. The intent of the teaching is to provide a 'grounding' for the students. It is assumed that the students will build upon their own experiences using this information when they in turn become master musicians. This is achieved simply by relating personal experiences and hoping that the students will remember them at an appropriate time.

17.4.2 Transferring/adapting (level 2)

Teaching is passing on the teacher's experience of music and performance. Students learn by using the teacher's methods and adapting them for their own particular needs.

As in the previous category, the teacher's performance and musical experience are the focus of the teaching and learning encounter. The difference between this and the previous category is that students are expected to copy their teachers' methods and then adapt them for their own use at some later stage. Learning is acquiring the teachers' ideas and integrating them with the students' ideas. The teachers' ideas are adapted for each student's particular needs and the student learns by copying and practising the ideas. Music is seen as a collection of ideas that need to be given to the students. The outcome of this teaching/learning experience is student success in assessment.

As in the disseminating (level 1) category, information is broken down into component parts.

Peter: My natural inclination is to dump information and give lots of knowledge. But I realised that that doesn't work. So in my piano teaching, I've taken what I have learned from that into my piano teaching. So I will focus usually on one thing each lesson, and in each piece, one thing.
I: Why would you do that?
Peter: So that they can take that away, focus on it and achieve it in a week. And then hopefully it comes back the way I want it the next week and then I can focus on something else (pause) I work idea by idea.

This quote illustrates the intention to teach students a little at a time and slowly build up from a base of knowledge. Students are expected to 'take it away' and do something with the information, but the teacher's main aim is that the student's playing will come back 'the way I want it'. The quality of student learning is gauged on the music sounding similar to the teacher's playing: 'hopefully it comes back the way I want it'. Assessment of learning is based on the teacher's criteria. Each student is recognized as an individual with different problems and experiences from any other and the teacher's repertoire of musical experience is filtered for each different student.

17.4.3 Exchange (level 3)

Teaching is an exchange of experiences and musical ideas with the student.

In this category teaching is seen as recognizing the diversity of student experiences and the teacher's role is to help students build upon their experiences. Students learn by being encouraged to experiment with different solutions to musical problems with a range of ideas that are developed and expressed by both teacher and student. Music is seen as a combination of physical, intellectual and artistic skill. The outcome of the teaching/ learning experience is for students to show an understanding of, and be able to demonstrate, the technical qualities of the instrument combined with intellectual and artistic interpretation in performance.

John: You can guide the students towards self-expression and in the end they have to find their own voice.

Teaching and learning are seen as complementary events. Teachers acknowledge that teaching is dependant on the learning taking place and also that learning is in some way dependent on the teaching. The individuality of students and the discovery and extension of the students' artistry and expression ('their own voice') is fundamental. The professional experiences of the teachers take a background role as the purpose of the teaching/learning encounter is to help the student to develop their own unique sound.

17.4.4 Exchange/mutual change (level 4)

Teaching is an exchange of experiences and musical ideas with the student that change the way both the teacher and the student think about and engage in music making, communicating and how they see the world.

In this category teachers and students work together to develop new ideas on performance and musical understanding. Music is seen as a 'reflection of the world' and the purpose of teaching and learning is to enable both teacher and student to expand and develop their world views. The outcome of the teaching learning experiences is when technique, intellect and musicality are combined to produce a message that communicates with an audience expressing the students' emotions and view of life.

Paul: What I am trying to achieve is that these people go a little further down that pathway of individuality. Since I think that's pretty much all people's main, that is the best you can do, was that you can turn out some of the people from the course who are individuals. Now that is damn difficult to bring about, it is difficult to test, and at the same time I can't think of a more worthy sort of angle for me to be plugging away at. So what I try to do is maybe suggest to people, this is what they need to attend to if they need to know more about a specific areas and that by looking at these areas, and by adventuring in those areas, and by using whatever aspects of trial and error, that they will in fact teach themselves some things and that will begin to sound like their individuality.

Teaching and learning are experienced as inseparable activities and contains elements of mutuality as the teachers learn from their students as they teach. The focus for the music lesson is not the teachers' professional experience, the instrumental technique or the musical meaning, but is rather the personal expression of the student that can be communicated through the playing of music. This category is the most inclusive where attributes of the previous categories are included but are experienced in more sophisticated ways.

Each of the Categories of Teaching/Learning differs in aspects of their description of what is to be taught and learned and how it is to be taught and learned. The variation lies in how professional experiences are constituted into something that can be either taught or learned. The disseminating (level 1) and transferring/adapting (level 2) categories emphasize the technical aspects of performance. These aspects are related to an intended outcome stressing completion of exams, the transfer of knowledge, and 'learning' through demonstration. These categories differ only in the teachers' intention for the students' learning strategy, the disseminating (level 1) category emphasising copying and the transferring/adapting (level 2) category including copying but acknowledging that students should apply and adapt specific techniques.

The teacher's experiences of the music industry is the content that is taught in the disseminating (level 1) category. This understanding is often expressed in the form of 'tips' or 'secrets'.

Colin: I have accomplished a way of making music that is identifiable with me. It fits not the large scheme of what the orchestra needs or the style of music, or the period of time, but I do it in a special way. I don't give that secret away to anybody because it could cost me work. So I am naturally secretive about it and I would think that anybody who is in a creative field would be that way. But when we are teachers, we give away everything. Everything I know, my secrets on how I do things, I give them to my students, willingly, I don't hold anything back, and I hope that my students will be better musicians, brass players, person, breadwinner, citizen that I am.

In higher level categories of teaching and learning technique is described as the vehicle of musical expression which is subsumed by the importance of the communication of the music. In the disseminating (level 1) category however, technique and music are regarded as separate entities, each to be taught separately.

Maria: I tend to concentrate on developing them [the students] through working on their specific technical faults as separate items.

These extracts illustrate the underlying 'ground' of the Extrinsic Technical Music Entity (level 1). This Music Entity in turn is related to 'what is to be learned' by the students. The teachers' view of teaching and learning in the disseminating (level 1) category is that teaching and learning are two separate activities. Teaching is an activity that teachers do, the content to be taught a culmination of their own professional and musical experiences. Learning is an activity that students do, the content to be learned determined by the teachers' experience and understanding of the Music Entity.

17.5 Students' experience of learning instrumental and vocal music

Students' experience and understanding of the musical world, and what music means within this world, forms the foundation for their understanding of learning instrumental/vocal music. Variation found in the students' description of their awareness of learning music constitutes the categories of description of learning instrumental/vocal music. The three ways of understanding the Music Entity form the backdrop from which the distinctions between the five categories of learning instrumental/vocal music can be seen.

In the instrument (level 1) category students focus their attention on the technical aspects of learning the instrument and learn by copying their teachers.

The elements (level 2) category is like the instrument (level 1) category as the students focus their attention on the technical aspects of learning the instrument and learn by copying their teachers. It is unlike the instrument (level 1) category in that some musical elements are also focused upon.

The musical meaning (level 3) category is like the elements (level 2) category in that students still learn an instrument. It is unlike the elements (level 2) category because the focus of learning has shifted to the meaning found within the music and the students learn by reflecting and adapting their teacher's advice.

The communicating (level 4) category is like the musical meaning (level 3) category as the students include learning musical meaning. It is unlike the musical meaning (level 3) category as the focus of learning has shifted to learning to communicate musical meaning. The students learn by experimenting with different styles of playing music, the teacher is only one source.

The express meaning (level 5) category is like the communicating (level 4) category as it focuses on learning how to communicate. It is unlike the communicating (level 4) category as the students' focus on expressing *personal* meanings through the music.

17.5.1 Instrument (Voice) (level 1) Category: Learning an Instrument (Voice)

In this category the object of learning is the physical instrument. The students focus on the technical skills required to play the instrument. They rely on their teachers to organize their repertoire and practice schedules. Written music is seen as a series of technical problems that have to be individually solved. The outcome of the learning experience is the ability to demonstrate technical skill on the instrument and to pass examinations.

Learning is defined as the demonstration of technical speed. In this category the Extrinsic Technical Music Entity (level 1) is evident through the focus on the instrument. This precludes the students from being aware of any other musical aspect associated with instrumental playing.

A characteristic of this category is the acquisition of technical skills that are perceived to be needed in order to play the instrument. Each technical aspect is broken down into smaller components that, once mastered, are added to each other. The music to be learned is treated as a series of technical problems that are isolated and then practised with the intention of building on a logical technical scaffold.

I: Is there anything else that you are looking for as you are learning?

Susan: Yeah, I have to watch my hands to make sure my fingers aren't sticking out. I tend to have sticking outish fingers. I lift my fingers too high. I have to check that I have my fingers in nice and close. I have to check out my fingering. I'll go through a piece and go through it hands separate and I will write all the fingering in, and change what I don't like that the book has. And then the next day I will pick it up where I have stopped and practise all the bits that I am stopping in all the time. I will pick them up and I will just play them over and over. And I will go back a bar and play it just to run it into it. And then I will go past a bar to run out of it again. Because it is pointless having that part really well and not be able to join it with any thing else!
I: Would you learn every piece this way?
Susan: I am going to. Well I normally do. I usually do it hands separately and then put it together. My goal this year is not to have a piece that continually has one little bit that I can't play. That is one of my goals this year is to be able to play a piece well all the way through and not have to stop for anything. You shouldn't have to have that if you practise it enough.

In this category written music (manuscript) is seen as a series of technical problems that have to be individually solved. The manuscript is broken down into technical aspects that can be practised, the manuscript being considered learned when the technical problems have been solved. The intended outcome of the learning experience is the ability to demonstrate technical skill on the instrument and to pass examinations.

17.5.2 Elements (level 2) Category: Learning an Instrument and Some Musical Elements

In this category the instrument still remains the focus of the learning experience but some musical elements are included. The focus is on the acquisition of technical skill and adding musical elements combined with a dependence on their teacher to choose repertoire and organize practice schedules. Written music is seen as a series of individual technical problems that must be solved. Once technical solutions have been found musical elements, such as phrasing or dynamics, are added. The outcome of the learning experience is technical proficiency in an exam situation.

Matthew: I feel that I've got a better understanding in what's involved myself in playing (pause) physically what sort of things will go towards making up the right sound for the right articulation or the right fingering or so on like that. Perhaps it's what she's said in the past has helped me think about these things and now I've been able to apply those thoughts and direct them towards new pieces of music that I'm playing, so that I'm able to interpret the phrasing or the way pieces should be played better than I would've at the beginning. She's told me what things I should look for in the music. And for instance where there's writing scales in a piece I might increase the dynamic so that if the dynamic's increasing getting louder or that sort of thing or if the scale's going down I decrease the dynamic so I'm actually following the contour of the music. And try and shape the phrases around that.

The intended outcome is the correct technical and elemental execution of the music.

17.5.3 Musical Meaning (level 3) Category: Learning Musical Meaning

Learning about the meaning of music is the focus of this category. Students reflect on their teacher's advice on technique and stylistic interpretation of music. Technical proficiency on the instrument is seen as a vehicle to enable correct playing of the music. The outcome of the learning experience is to be able to play the music with correct technique and musical style in a performance situation.

In this category students reflect on teacher's advice about the stylistic interpretation of the music and then choose how to use the advice. This view is qualitatively different from the previous categories as students feel able to make judgements about the appropriateness of the teachers' advice for their own musical situation. The focus of learning is on the sound and meaning of the music. Both the teachers and students are contributors to the development of the sound.

Nathan: Well I guess maybe some more complex harmonic material like passing chords and maybe some counterpoint lines (pause). Maybe some other idea I guess what I want to come to eventually is a whole performance. I'm looking for a complete piece of music and to do that I have to my whole conception of that music.
I: Your 'whole conception of music', what do you mean be that?
Nathan: I have to know the piece as a whole. You can't really, you can take a piece down to its elements, such as melody and harmony but the actual overall effect that's what people hear. It is not something you can put into words, I guess the aim is for me, is to get some sort of feeling across whatever that might be.

As in the lower level categories music is still broken down into its component elements. But unlike the lower level categories, where the reason for breaking the music into simpler elements was to eventually add them together, this category breaks the music into elements in order to develop an understanding of the musical meaning. Each musical work is considered to have a meaning that is ascribed specifically to it. It is for this reason that the students listen to a variety of recordings, their teachers' advice and experiment with their own version of the musical meaning in order to understand the 'feeling' of each work.

The outcome of the learning experience is to be able to play the music with proficient technique and correct musical style in a performance situation.

17.5.4 Communicating (level 4) Category: Learning to Communicate Musical Meaning

In this category music is seen as a means of communicating with the audience. Written music has an implicit meaning that is expressed by the student using the instrument as a medium. Technique is seen only as a tool through which musical meaning is expressed. The intended outcome of the learning experience is to express the implicit musical meaning of a work to an audience.

Andrew: It's absolutely exciting to find out the text of the chorale. So, because it will always be painted in some way in the music and you don't know what the words are then how can you understand the music? I think you've got to be thinking about all these things even in the early stage of learning the notes otherwise I think you're just hindering your ability to communicate the music and eventually to perform.

The meaning of the music and the communication of the meaning to an audience is the focus of this category. Students reflect on their previous experiences with similar music and combine their own musical views with that of their teachers to develop an informed view of the musical meaning to be communicated.

17.5.5 Express Meaning (level 5) Category: Learning to Express Personal Meaning

This category describes learning music as a means of self-expression and communication. Learning is expressed as an experience that requires the student to reflect on musical knowledge and assimilate musical ideas into a performance that both communicates with the audience and expresses personal meaning. The instrument is seen only as a vehicle of self-expression which is subject to the greater need to express personal meaning through music. Engagement with music is seen as a method of continuous personal development. The intended outcome of the learning experience is to communicate personal meaning and interpretation of the music to an audience through performance.

I: What do you plan to achieve through learning the piano?
Fiona: Well personally, first and foremost, I'm a human being and through being human as a way of expression I play the piano. And it's a means of my own expression of myself and what I wish to communicate, be it through other people, playing with other people or through an audience, and through teaching.

Technical and musical aspects of the music are taken into account but a distinction made between the physical requirements of learning an instrument, the historical and theoretical requirements that undergird style and musicality and the 'aesthetic' dimension. The aesthetic dimension is regarded as learning about oneself. Learning is seen as an integration of these three aspects which contains the intention to communicate the students' view of the world.

Simon: I find that a lot of my learning of the piece isn't actually the practice and the playing of it. A lot of it is actually in the mind. And if the piece is in there and has time to, it sort of, I don't know whether you say subconsciously but (pause) your mind sort of works on it as it's sitting in there. And then I have a better idea of how I want to play it. And then when I'm playing, and again music is such a complicated thing you can't always be concentrating on every bar and every thing you do. You can get it across to the more automatic side of the thinking then it seems to be much easier. And if it's sort of settled in there then I find it easy just to (pause), then if I've done the technical parts of it then I can allow that side to take over. Does that make any sense?

Learning is experienced as a way of thinking rather than the acquisition of technical or musical skills. Listening to students practising the technical aspects may sound similar from student to student regardless of their underlying understanding of learning music. The difference lies in the intention of the practice, whether it is to rehearse a physical activity or to rehearse a physical activity in order to interpret and express meaning.

17.6 Students' experience of teaching instrumental and vocal music

Instrumental students described understanding teaching instrumental / vocal music in three qualitatively different ways. Each category supports dimensions of content, focus of critique, inspiration and student reasons for satisfaction with the teaching and the teacher.

The categories of description also appear to be closely associated with the students' understanding of the professional world (the Music Entity).

17.6.1 Demonstrating (level 1) category: teaching is demonstrating musical techniques and experience

In this category students consider that teaching is demonstrating the teachers' instrumental technique and professional experience.

Students suggest that 'good performers are good teachers' and that students will learn by simply being exposed to the teacher. The content of the lesson (repertoire, technique, style and professional experiences) is devised by the teacher as the teachers' experience gives them expert knowledge that is demonstrated to the student. In this category the students describe their role as learners passively. The aim of the teaching is that students are able to demonstrate, in a performance situation, certain techniques and styles that are similar to their teachers'. The main methods of teaching are teacher demonstration and critique of the technical elements of the students' playing. Teachers and teaching are considered to be inspirational because of the quantity of the teachers' knowledge and experience, their reputation and the tradition of respect for their teachers. The students' experience of teaching within this category is one of directed music making.

I: What are your responsibilities?
Susan: To practise, to listen, respect. You have to respect your teacher. I suppose that isn't a responsibility but it is part of the students/ teacher relationship.
I: Could I ask you about the other side. What are your teacher's responsibilities?
Susan: He has got more than I have got really. To motivate, to be motivated himself. To teach and have knowledge. I mean he has to have knowledge, it is a responsibility of him to prepare and have knowledge first and pass it on.

17.6.2 Describing (level 2) category: teaching is expressing musical meaning and experience

In this category students' understand teaching to be about expressing musical meaning and professional musical experience for the students to adapt.

The difference between this category and the demonstrating (level 1) category is twofold. First, teaching content changes from a technical focus to a focus on musical meaning. Secondly, the student is an active member of the partnership as the teacher expresses, demonstrates and explains ideas that students accept and use or reject.

Lesson content is devised by the teachers as the teachers demonstrate musical ideas on their instruments, critique student performances for both technical and some musical elements, and encourage students to question methods and ideas.

Teachers are admired for their playing ability but are at times acknowledged as not being 'good' teachers. Students consider that they can still learn effectively from a good performer despite the teachers' teaching ability, as teaching ability is one of the aspects that is filtered out. Association with an important musician is seen as important for the students' future career. The aim of the teaching experience is to develop technical and stylistic proficiency for an exam or performance. The students experience of teaching within this category is one of semi-directed music making.

In the describing (level 2) category teaching is about expressing musical meaning and professional experience to students. The expression of meaning and experience can be in the form of musical demonstration or dialogue. Unlike the demonstrating (level 1) category, students are encouraged to evaluate and test the information provided by the teachers.

Jane: I've been with Steven the whole time I've been at the School of Music. And the way that I have learned has changed because of his teaching. By the time he teaches me I really (pause) sort of put it in the back of my mind how I'm going to (pause) like I'll think of some comment he's said to me about the music and I'll try the way he's taught me. And I'll think 'Yeah. This really works.' Like with the chordal thing, and like talking about the character of the piece, and just technical things. Just like I said, like not keeping my fingers so close to the piano. He points out little things like that. When he points them out I make a conscious effort to really use what he has taught me. So I learn very much the way he wants me to learn I suppose.
Jane: He usually says these pieces would be good for you to play for the next exam or the next concert practice. And he will play them and if I like a piece I will bring it to him and I'll say I'd like to play this. And that would be OK as well. It's sort of a mixture I think. But mainly I often like the pieces that he picks. One of the pieces I had to do yesterday that I didn't like was a study.

17.6.3 Supporting (level 3) category: teaching is supporting student learning, encouraging independent student expression

In this category teachers are regarded as resources for the students to access.

Teaching is allowing students to access their teachers' knowledge and experience through questioning and discussion that is generated by the students. The content of the lessons is determined by the students' needs and questions. Teachers support students by being free with their musical and professional insight and information and by offering critique on musical performance by discussing and demonstrating several musical alternatives to various musical and technical problems. In this category the teaching and the teachers inspire students by the quality of their information and experience and their willingness to trust students with their personal experiences of music making and of the world. Students learn through questioning their teachers and their own music making and by experimenting with new ideas. The goal of the teaching is to equip students with a high level of technical facility coupled with a depth of musical understanding and to develop students' personal view of the world. The students' experience of teaching is one of independent music making with teacher encouragement and support.

Fiona: It is just wonderful to have a relationship between teacher and student if it is a successful relationship. You come to understand each other you know, and I think that is how you grow. Because you find that by them trying to understand you, you're growing as a person. And therefore it reflects in the music. Therefore there is a lot of communication in the lesson. Rather than just walk in, open your book and what are we going to do today? You know that there is a lot of exchange of ideas as well and not just about the music, he taught about life as well, you know. It was a wonderful series of lessons.
Andrew: I think that he encourages you to find out for yourself how you think about things, and not to tell you. I think that he thinks that if you discover something about the music rather than be just told it, then it will mean a lot more to you and you will retain it.

The teachers' professional experiences are considered to be an important factor in learning from a particular teacher in all categories. All categories describe the teachers' professional experience as part of the lesson content.

Teaching is allowing students to question teachers, experiment with new ideas and to have the new ideas subject to their teachers' criticism in order that the students can make, and learn how to make, artistic judgements about music and communication and how music is integrated with their lives. In this way students develop a depth of musical understanding that is demonstrated in their inclination for independent music making.

17.7 Relations between the categories of description of teaching and learning instrumental and vocal music and the music entity

Both student and teacher groups understand that what is taught and learned is more than the basic instrumental musical content but is related to a professional musical *context*. This notion of professional formation integrated into the content of the music lessons, defines the importance of the Music Entity. The intentions for teaching and learning are constituted from the musicians', and student musicians', understanding of the world of music. The Music Entity does not describe the musical world per se, but the meaning that both teachers and students give to the musical world and the way that they reflect and iterate on the experience to create something about the musical world that can be taught and learned.

More complete ways of experiencing teaching and learning appear to be related to more complete ways of experiencing the Music Entity. For instance, participants who describe their experience of the professional world as the Extrinsic Technical Music Entity (level 1), usually describe their understanding of teaching and learning as focusing on technique. The less complete categories (in all three sets of categories of description) focus on elements that are external. The Extrinsic Meaning Music Entity (level 2) also contains the technical focus but also includes music's inherent meaning.

The most integrated and complete categories of description of teaching/learning (higher levels) move the lesson focus away from the *teachers'* experiences of music towards a focus fostering the development of student independence. Attributes related to less complete categories can be used within the lessons but the intentions for their use are quite different. The Intrinsic Meaning Music Entity (level 3) is related to the more complete categories where students and teachers expect that teaching/learning is about developing the *students'* ability to think musically and interpretively using their own personal view of the world as a basis for artistic interpretation.

Table 17.1 illustrates the relations between the Music Entity, the teachers' and students' understanding of what teaching and learning music is, and what it is teachers/students wish to teach or learn.

From the evidence found in all transcripts it could be argued that the Music Entity represents part of a receding background awareness from which the experience of teaching and learning are brought to the fore. In this way the Music Entity is perceived as part of a life experience on which the categories of description of teaching and learning are dependent. Other elements of the background experience are not perceived as being as dominant as the Music Entity in relation to the participants' understanding of teaching and learning music. The Music Entity is a constant presence as the teachers and students describe teaching and learning.

The nature of instrumental lessons allows a certain amount of flexibility in teaching and learning to be evident, but this flexibility is related to ways in which the participants have experienced the musical world and teaching/learning. Discussing and rehearsing the

Music entity	*Students' experience of learning*	*students' experience of the teaching*	*Teachers' experience of teaching/learning*
Extrinsic technical	Instrumental (level 1)	Demonstrating (level 1)	Disseminating (level 1)
	Elements (level 2)		Transferring/adapting (level 2)
Extrinsic meaning	Musical Meaning (level 3)	Describing (level 2)	Exchange (level 3)
	Communicating (level 4)		
Intrinsic Meaning	Express Meaning (level 5)	Supporting (level 3)	Exchange/mutual Change (Level 4)

Table 17.1 **Relations between the three sets of categories of description and the Music Entity**

technical or musical qualities of a particular phrase, or experimenting with a new hand position to enable greater ease for playing some musical aspect, are examples of this. These examples are the immediate object of learning but the immediate object is underpinned by the participants' understanding of the salient features of music (experienced in the world of music, the Music Entity) and the meaning that they place on these features.

17.8 Implications for teaching and learning

These research findings suggest that the ways in which people experience their profession may have a profound impact on associated teaching and learning. Professionals are often employed within the university system in order to bring in the authenticity of the workplace. These findings in the context of musical professionals suggest that professionals may understand their work in a variety of ways and that what they decide to teach, and how they go about teaching, is related to this understanding. Conversely students are also sent into the workplace, or learn within employment. In these situations students learn with work-place 'mentors' who may have differing experiences of the industry. 'New ways of thinking about knowledge' need to be established (Garrick and Kirkpatrick, 1998, p. 176). In the next chapter (Chapter 18), Ritterman suggests that a 'balanced picture' needs to be shown to students in order for them to understand the profession. Part of this 'balanced picture' is acknowledging the different ways that the profession can be understood and providing learning experiences for students that embrace the variation. Finding out the different ways that a profession may be understood would be a first step in being able to use that variation for student learning.

Note

1. See Bowden (1996) and Francis (1996) for a discussion of phenomenographic interviews. See also Marton and Booth (1997) for a description of phenomenography and the way phenomenographic results may be used for teaching and learning.

17.9 References

Applebaum, S. and Roth, H. (1978) *The Way They Play*. Book 5. USA: Paganiniana Publications.

Bowden, J. (1996) Phenomenographic research — some methodological issues. In G. Dall'Alba and B. Hasselgren (eds), *Reflections on Phenomenography: Towards a Methodology?* Goteborg Studies in Educational Sciences **109**, 49—66.

Bruhn, S. (1990) Reconsidering the teacher—student relationships in the training of the performing musician, *International Journal of Music Research* **15**: 13—22.

Francis, H. (1996) Advancing phenomenography: questions of method. In G. Dall'Alba and B. Hasselgren (eds), *Reflections on Phenomenography: Towards a Methodology?* Goteborg Studies in Educational Sciences, **109**, 35—48.

Froehlich, H.C. (1992) Issues and characteristics common to research on teaching in instructional settings. In R. Colwell (ed.), *Handbook of Research on Music Teaching and Learning*. New York: Schirmer Books, 561—7.

Garrick, J. and Kirkpatrick, D. (1998) Workplace-based learning degrees: a new business venture, or a new critical business?, *Higher Education Research and Development* **17**(2): 171—82.

Hallam, S. (1995) Professional musicians' orientations to practice: implications for teaching, *British Journal of Music Education* **12**, 3—19.

Johnson, N. (1991) Effective professional development: the key to quality teaching and effective learning. Occasional paper for Incorporated Association of Registered Teachers of Victoria, 23.

Kennell, R. (1992) Toward a theory of applied instruction, *The Quarterly Journal of Music Teaching and Learning* **3**(2): 5—16.

Marton, F. and Booth, S. (1997) *Learning and Awareness*. New Jersey: Lawrence Erlbaum Associates, Publishers.

Persson, R. S. (1996) Studying with a musical maestro: a case study of commonsense teaching in artistic training, *Creativity Research Journal* **9**(1): 33—46.

18 Teaching how to learn, learning how to teach: educating musicians for the twenty-first century

Janet Ritterman
Royal College of Music, London

18.1 Defining the territory

For the purposes of this chapter, I am using the term 'musicians' to refer to performers — instrumentalists and singers — and am drawing my examples from research undertaken with musicians whose learning or teaching takes place within the conservatoire environment. In Britain as in many other countries this is not the only way to undertake advanced studies in music. Here there are two main options — either a course which focuses on the study of music through performance,[1] or a course which treats the subject essentially as a humanities discipline, in which the business of writing about music forms the core of the curriculum.[2] The institution of which I am Director, the Royal College of Music in London, an institution with degree-awarding powers to doctoral level, offers courses which fall into the first of these two categories — performance-based degrees. It is on pedagogical issues raised by the conservatoire approach to the education and training of musicians as performers within the Western classical tradition that I intend to focus in this chapter. While I know that the pedagogical issues which I plan to raise are familiar to those working in other countries, on this occasion my examples are drawn only from the British context.

In Britain in the past twenty years there has been a gradual *rapprochement* between the two main types of higher education music curriculum, for reasons part philosophic, part pragmatic. It has become increasingly common for music courses located within arts and humanities faculties to allow students to elect solo performance as a major option, while most undergraduate conservatoire courses have increased the range and significance of so-called 'academic' elements, teaching these generally in lecture and seminar groups.[3] Nevertheless there remain quite properly fundamental differences between the two types of higher education music curriculum in terms of their aims, content and approaches to learning and teaching. These differences are also reflected in the expectations — of students, as well as of those teaching them — of graduates' future career patterns.[4] Students applying to study music at a conservatoire normally do so because they believe that, in some way or other, the performance of music, and a first-hand understanding of what it involves, are likely to continue to play a significant part in their adult lives.

The curriculum which conservatoire students follow has performance at its heart, enriched by relevant supporting studies and ensemble experience. The individual study of one or more instruments, in a programme of work devised specifically for the individual student, undertaken with a teacher of his or her own choice, makes this, by comparison with undergraduate curricula in most other disciplines, a highly personalized educational experience. It is on this distinctive element of the conservatoire curriculum — the one-to-one teaching which forms its core — that I am focusing in this chapter. In doing this, my aim is to reflect on the pedagogical methods which characterize advanced instrumental teaching and to consider what features of these methods help young musicians to develop the skills and personal attributes necessary to establish and sustain careers in a professional world which is predominantly freelance.

18.2 The conservatoire entrant

In the likelihood that, for the most part, they will work on a self-employed basis, conservatoire students are, of course, in no sense set apart from those pursuing other disciplines. However there are, I believe, various ways in which the typical conservatoire entrant differs from those embarking on undergraduate courses in other disciplines. These differences arise, for the most part, from the importance that they attach to their one-to-one instrumental tuition and therefore how they view the learning and teaching process within the conservatoire. It is the one-to one instrumental tuition, for example, that is usually the major factor in the student's choice of institution at which he or she is to study. Many students make their choices of institution principally because of the presence of particular instrumental teachers. In contrast to what happens in most other areas of undergraduate teaching, conservatoire students in this country are usually invited to nominate the instrumental teacher with whom they wish to study. By the time that they enter the institution some students will already have had some lessons with the teacher of their choice.

Even if this has not yet happened, as far as instrumental study is concerned, the student embarking on an undergraduate course at a conservatoire does so with some confidence that in terms of pedagogical method and working patterns much will be familiar. This is not unreasonable: by this stage in their development, many conservatoire entrants will already have had about ten years' continuous experience of formal instrumental learning.[5] Most who succeed to this point will have benefited not only from a strong one-to-one relationship with a teacher but also from parental support and encouragement.[6] In most cases this will have been a major factor in the establishment and maintenance of regular patterns of formal individual practice — routines which will normally have occupied significant amounts of time. Although it is notoriously difficult to generalize over amounts of practice time, it is not unusual for committed young musicians to have averaged 400 hours a year during the teenage years,[7] excluding time spent in lessons and in group music-making, such as orchestral or ensemble playing or choral singing.

Through group activities such as these, as well as through solo opportunities, many conservatoire students begin their undergraduate studies already familiar with the public face of the working world of the professional musician. As a result of contacts encouraged by their instrumental teachers, or by schools that they have attended, many will have taken in solo and ensemble performances — some in recordings and broadcasts — in circumstances which make no significant concessions to their age or student status. The most talented students of orchestral instruments have usually had extensive first-hand experience of the type of performing activities that are the stock-in-trade of the professional musician: the National Youth Orchestra of Great Britain, for example, plays at the Royal Albert Hall in London each August, as part of the Proms season.

Experience of this kind, gained locally, regionally, or nationally — sometimes through concert tours — though normally undertaken on a purely voluntary basis[8] — gives students a familiarity with the professional environment of the concert platform and a taste for what they see as the excitement of the world of music performance. As a result, they are attuned to the professional situations for which they are preparing, and strongly motivated to succeed. Probably the closest parallels can be found among students entering drama schools: the differences seem to me to lie in the proportion of students entering conservatoires for whom this type of performing experience has been regular rather than occasional. Frequent experience of this kind means that conservatoire entrants tend to feel that they know how the musical world works, that they know what opportunities exist for musicians like them within it, and that they recognize the skills, knowledge and experience which they will need in order to succeed professionally. As a result, some have firmly-held beliefs about what they think that musicians do — and do not — need to learn.

Such direct contact with the external environment is valuable, and gives a focus to the advanced studies of many young musicians which those teaching in other disciplines would at times welcome. However it brings with it certain challenges for those who teach them, since this experience tends to lack some of the key pressures of professional life. Although for most conservatoire students early performing experiences are strongly motivating, there is a significant gap between the experience of the talented teenager and the working life of the busy professional. Some students are surprised when they encounter the discipline of rehearsing and performing every day rather than as a welcome break from the routine of schoolwork; others are demoralized by experiencing the lack of visible enthusiasm of professionals, or the effect of financial disciplines on professional music-making; others find the artistic and practical demands of self-promotion uncongenial. In teaching young musicians, one of the key pedagogical challenges is to help them to develop as people as well as performers — to move from the lower levels labelled by Reid (1999; and Chapter 17, this volume) as 'describing' and 'transferring/adapting' to the levels involving 'exchange' and 'mutual change'[9] involving both teacher and student. Students need to make this transition if they are to deepen their understanding of the challenges of professional life for the freelance musician. This needs to be part of their learning if they are to synthesize their self-concepts as musicians with the realities of the external environment. For teacher and student alike, advanced instrumental study needs to be approached in ways that take account of these external demands but are not unduly constrained by them. For most students early performing experience provides little preparation for this. There need to be gradual changes in the ways in which they learn, and what it is that they learn, if they are to make the transition from talented student to successful professional. It is principally during their years in higher education that these changes need to occur.

18.3 Research background

There has been no lack of research by music psychologists into the development of musical talent among young people. In recent years the earlier emphasis on innate musical ability has been tempered by increasing interest in the findings of developmental psychologists and by those focusing on social and environmental influences. Although much of the recent British research has tended to focus on young musicians up to the completion of their secondary schooling, many of the findings from this work are of relevance to the pedagogical questions facing those responsible for the education and training of musicians during their years in higher education. Work by other music psychologists on life-span development, less extensive and in certain respects more questionable in the application of some of its conclusions, also has insights to offer. It is against the background of the findings from these two categories of research and the research outlined in Reid's paper (Reid, 1999 and Chapter 17, this volume) that the work to which I refer in this chapter should be viewed.

There have been several recent studies which have focused on social and cultural influences on the development of young musicians. All emphasize the importance of external support and approval in generating the motivation evident in the early stages of musical development. In one of these, Jane Davidson and her co-authors summarized the features common to those who have successfully developed musical skills as being 'a supportive parent, a friendly teacher, ample opportunities to practise coupled with levels of investment in formal practice, and informal musical engagement'.[10] This I can confirm: it is from this basis, buoyed up by the support that they have received from the environment in which they have functioned to date, that many young musicians embark on their undergraduate studies.

Researchers who have investigated the developmental stages through which musicians progress in becoming established professionals, have stressed the importance of the phase of musical development that corresponds to, or concludes with, the years spent in higher education. It is at this stage that motivation becomes more intrinsic and the sense of self-concept as a musician develops more strongly. This is reflected in the way in which students begin to describe themselves: whereas earlier they tend to refer to themselves as 'playing the violin/the 'cello/the piano', it is noticeable that at this stage they begin more commonly to identify themselves as performers of the main instrument that they play ('I am a violinist/I am a pianist'). Lauren Sosniak, who investigated the development of a group of young American pianists on the brink of professional careers, emphasises the significance of the growth of 'personal commitment' during this stage. Her description of this stage of development is of one during which 'a sense of personal commitment to the pursuit of excellence is developed, and where the musician becomes a member of a musical community to which there is a shared sense of personal commitment'.[11]

In achieving this transition from motivation dependent on extrinsic factors to motivation dependent on internal conviction, the influence of the experienced instrumental teacher is critical. The music psychologist, Maria Manturzewska, who conducted an extensive longitudinal study of the life-span development of professional musicians in Poland,[12] refers to the character of the 'master-student' relationship which emerges during these years, as being 'paramount for the entire future career'. The quality of this relationship and the learning and teaching which the student experiences are of the greatest importance. As Manturzewska acknowledges, at this level the teaching relationship makes considerable demands on the 'personality, musical competence, and personal culture of the teacher'. However she draws attention to the fact that the presence of a teacher fulfiling all aspects of this role is a feature common to all the high achievers in her study, noting also that Sosniak's study of young concert pianists, reports similar trends.[13] It is, in Manturzewska's view, an 'ever-deepening' professional relationship of this kind that each student musician needs if he or she is to develop 'the personality, aesthetic attitudes, life philosophy, professional standards, and attitudes towards his or her own artistic and professional activity and the role of musician in contemporary society'. It is from teaching at the highest of the levels identified by Reid — the level where teaching 'is an exchange of experiences and musical ideas with the student that change the way that both the teacher and the student think about and engage in music making, communicating and how they see the world'[14] — that this is likely to be achieved.

The high standards which this demands of the teacher as role model are clear. But how, in pedagogical terms, is the concomitant deepening of understanding achieved? Some have suggested that the pedagogical methods characteristic of one-to-one instrumental teaching in a competitive environment tend to militate against the development of independence and initiative: some research conducted with successful teenage performers has shown them to display high levels of dependency, conformity and control.[15] However similar forms of research enquiry conducted among successful professional musicians produce a distinctly different profile: among the traits most consistently displayed by successful professional are those of independence, autonomy and self-determination,[16] with a strong tendency to reject external constraints.[17]

The music psychologist, Anthony Kemp, has drawn attention to this trait reversal,[18] noting that it has implications for teaching within higher education. While there has been some general comment on the need for young performers to be given the 'personal space, and freedom in which creativity and autonomy might blossom',[19] and a recognition that, no matter how hard young musicians work, early promise is not always translated into adult success, no studies of which I am aware have focused on what, in pedagogical terms, is likely to support this transition.

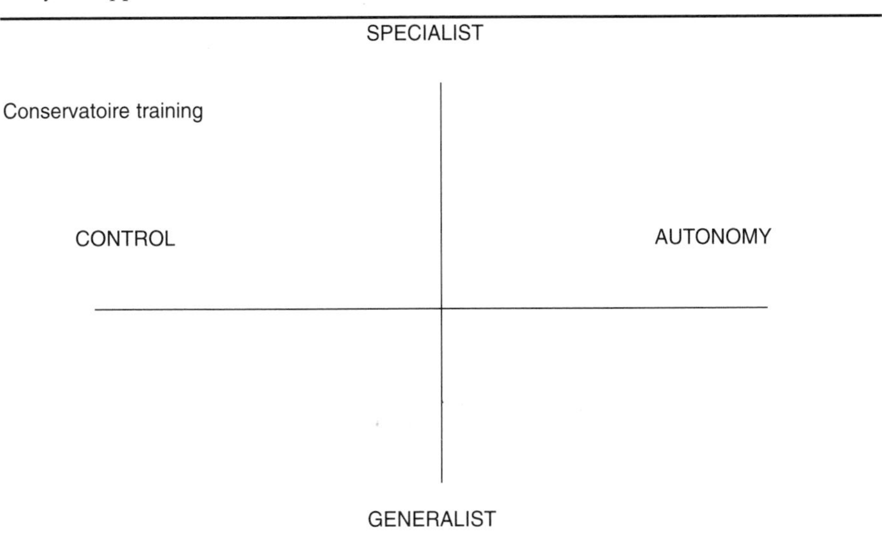

Figure 18.1 Hargreaves's quadrant model categorizing teaching methods in music education

David Hargreaves, a psychologist whose work has emphasized the social and contextual aspects of music, has developed a 'quadrant model' which he has used to categorize teaching methods in music education. The framework of this is reproduced in Figure 18.1.[20]

Hargreaves identifies the 'control-autonomy' polarities with the amount of 'creative control' that rests with the student. Conservatoire education he therefore regards as falling totally within the 'specialist-control' quadrant. The 'specialist-autonomy' quadrant he identifies only with specific music educators known for their contributions to the school music curriculum.[21] For the purposes of this chapter, I am borrowing the terminology of Hargreaves' model but applying it somewhat differently. I am using the 'control-autonomy' axis to focus on the transition which needs to take place in the learning and teaching within the one-to-one teaching relationship. It is, in every sense, an issue of 'creative control'. As

Anthony Kemp has pointed out, it is this trait in particular which differentiates the successful professional from the talented student.

18.4 Pedagogy and the education and training of performers

Individual instrumental study within the conservatoire represents a pedagogical model which is, I believe, unusual within undergraduate higher education. From the outset each student's programme is distinctive. The instrumental study which lies at the heart of the student's programme takes place with an experienced performer and teacher of that instrument — a teacher who is probably a part-time member of staff — from whom the student receives weekly individual tuition for between one and two hours per week, and for which individual practice of between 15 and 30 hours a week is the norm.[22] While there are parallels in other practice-based disciplines, these tend to involve students in group rather than in individual work. Instrumental study appears to me to differ in the focus which it maintains on the individual student's development: as any music student will readily acknowledge, in the individual lesson there is no place to hide. Although students attend regular performance classes, these supplement, rather than replace, the one-to-one lesson.

In other respects, however, one-to-one instrumental study offers parallels with the pedagogical approaches characteristic of many other disciplines. The learning undertaken by performers is typically problem-based and project-based: expertise develops through the individual study and mastery of repertoire and the appropriate techniques necessary to perform it with security and confidence. Each new piece of repertoire studied presents an unique combination of problems, technical and artistic, which need to be identified, analysed by some means or other, and mastered by the performer through individual practice. As in other disciplines, the study of performance demands theoretical understanding and practical skill. While certain theoretical elements are normally taught discretely, performance demands the translation of theory into practice and it enables it to be internalized through repeated opportunities for its application and refinement.

The portfolio approach characteristic of the visual arts also has its parallel for the musician. Most professional performers involved in solo or small-scale chamber work consciously build up their repertoire lists, from which they are readily able to select works for particular performances. This informs the approach taken with students: each student performer is expected at the end of each year to present a solo recital — the expectations in terms of length, difficulty, audience and location usually increasing with each year of study. From a fairly early stage these recitals are open to members of the public: the open, public nature of performance assessments provides one of its major challenges, as well as one of its great potential strengths.

In general, strong and supportive relationships develop between teacher and student, and teachers almost invariably do whatever they can to help their students to succeed in the tasks which immediately face them. Performance before one's peers and before the public is a regular occurrence in the conservatoire environment, so the expectations which surround these performances exert pressure on the learning and teaching relationship, no matter how dedicated or how gifted the teacher and the student. In this respect, the demands on the instrumental teacher are different from those of the lecturer responsible for teaching a class. Whereas the lecturer will normally have a spread of ability among the students in the group, the one-to-one instrumental teacher will usually have only a few students from a given cohort — normally a maximum of about four, a minimum of one, or none in certain years.

In such situations it is difficult not to want all one's geese to become swans. Yet both teacher and student need to take certain risks if there is to be increasing opportunity for the student to have some 'personal space' as a performer and to have the freedom to explore and to make musical decisions for him- or herself.

Among the most familiar features of instrumental teaching — those which typify the 'control' aspect of Hargreaves' model — are modelling and imitation. These are the terms used for the procedures where the student imitates the playing, vocalization or gestures of the teacher — or repeats passages in response to spoken corrections by the teacher. These methods, standard in the early stages of instrumental learning, and key to the acquisition of a secure technical and musical grounding, can, if continued unvaryingly, contribute to the high levels of dependency and to the lack of autonomy observed among some young musicians. Students continually 'spoon-fed' in this way may do well initially, but then may lack the initiative or confidence to take the leap needed to become less dependent and more self-directing. As the model presented in Reid's paper (Chapter 17, this volume) suggests, pedagogical methods which rely on disciplined acceptance rather than critical scrutiny, need gradually to be modified with more advanced students if they are to develop the independence and autonomy characteristic of successful professionals.

One key to this lies in the spoken dialogue between teacher and student. In his book, *The Inner Game of Music*, Barry Green focuses on the way in which instrumental teachers provide verbal instruction, distinguishing between 'do this' instructions, 'try to' instructions and 'awareness' instructions. While he discourages 'try to' instructions on the grounds that they tend to create uncertainty and anxiety, he focuses on 'do this' instructions as making students dependent, by allowing them to follow instructions instead of taking responsibility for solving problems for themselves. His examples of 'do this' instructions — a list with a very familiar 'ring' — include:

> Do such and such.
> This is difficult, but . . .
> Play it this way.
> Make it better.
> Please try harder.
> Now relax.
> Let's get it right this time.23

As he demonstrates, by presenting the task in such a way that the student has to take responsibility for discovering how the music feels or sounds, it is possible to replace 'do this' instructions with 'awareness' instructions. His 'awareness' examples include:

> Be aware of . . .
> Listen for . . .
> How does it feel when you . . .
> Tell me the difference you notice between . . .
> What do you hear when you . . .
> Pay attention to the . . .
> Let's see if . . .
> Notice the feeling you get when . . .

My observations of those teachers who are particularly successful in the teaching of advanced performers confirm that they tend to use 'awareness', rather than 'do this' or 'try to' instructions. They provide opportunities for students to make judgements on their own performance, rather than immediately offering judgements themselves. They tend to question rather than only to instruct. They encourage students to listen to performers on instruments other than their own, to refine their sense of phrasing, tone and musical shaping. They create opportunities for students to begin to choose repertoire for themselves, rather than waiting to be told what pieces to study. They encourage their students to develop specialisms of their own, even where these do not naturally reflect their personal areas of interest or expertise. Sosniak sums up this change — when students begin to find and solve 'their own musical problems, rather than those posed by the teachers' — in the phrase, 'teachers' become 'coaches'.[24]

18.5 Learning and teaching within the conservatoire

In my own institution there is abundant evidence on a daily basis of the importance of the 'master-student' relationship — the relationship with the individual instrumental teacher — in the formation of young professional musicians. I have recently been conducting a series of discussions with student pianists and their teachers. Some of the students are about to embark on postgraduate study, others are just beginning to establish themselves professionally.

In these conversations, all of the student pianists referred spontaneously to the key role which their individual teachers were playing in their artistic development. One described his teacher as 'far more than simply a teacher' — he provided, he said 'a type of spiritual family' and acted as a 'type of mentor'. Echoing some of the observations of Manturzewska on the personal development of the musician and the comments of young pianists reported by Sosniak, this student commented that when he was younger, he thought he 'knew what being a musician is', but that under the guidance of his present teacher he had 'started again on a new level, with a new view'. His teacher, he said, had changed the way he sees his personal life. It was not only the lesson but 'the things that happened between the lessons' that had helped him to acquire the outlook and values which were now shaping his musical life. Another said that it was his teacher who was helping him to develop his moral strength, and enabling him 'to learn to be tough'. Yet another spoke of his teacher as helping him to discover how to 'go for it' and encouraging in him the entrepreneurial qualities that he now realized were necessary for those who wished to develop a career as a freelance performer. Another commented on the fact that the world of the freelance professional musician was, by comparison with other professions, lacking in the type of structure that helped you to know where you 'know where you should be up to'. He observed that this was among the things that he felt that his teacher was now in particular helping to provide, by sharing with him experiences from his own career, including some where he (the teacher) now felt that he had not necessarily made the wisest decisions in career terms. The experience of teaching which all of these students described corresponded with the features which Reid identifies with the category of 'supporting' (level 3), where teaching 'is supporting student learning, encouraging independent student expression' and where teachers act 'as resources for the students to access'.[25]

In my conversations with these advanced students, all referred to ways in which their teachers were encouraging them to develop their self-reliance, their confidence and their independence, and were expecting them to function more autonomously as learners. One, reflecting on the changes in the type of advice which his teacher now provided, commented on the fact that, instead of simply telling or showing him how to play something, his teacher often challenged his imagination by allusion and by reference to works of art or literature, and expected him to try out various possibilities for himself. Several students welcomed the fact that their teachers encouraged them to perform to other people, or to have some lessons with other specialists, recognizing that this was another way of requiring them to function more independently as learners.

A number of the students had, with encouragement, discovered for themselves distinct areas of repertoire in which they intended to specialize, which were not areas of repertoire for which their teachers were known. Among the group there were several who show promise as composers, and who have written pieces for piano which they performed themselves. These are pieces which these students include in their concert performances without teacher or student feeling that they needed to be 'learnt from the teacher' before being performed in public. As the students recognized, all of these are ways in which, through making them find answers for themselves, their teachers were helping them to develop the skills and personal attributes necessary to establish and sustain freelance professional careers. All offered examples of the progression from 'specialist-control' to 'specialist-autonomy' — to a relationship in which the students' experience of teaching is 'one of independent music making with teacher encouragement and support'.[26]

But how can an institution such as mine ensure, in relation to its one-to-one teaching — its lifeblood — that all students are receiving teaching of similar quality — teaching which is helping them to develop as people as well as musicians, and supporting them in achieving for themselves the synthesis to which I referred at the opening of this chapter — the synthesis of their self-concepts as musicians with the realities of the external environment? How can one guarantee that the experience for different students is comparable in quality and appropriately judged and sequenced in terms of level of challenge? Not all teachers have the same level of skills or range of professional experience; not all feel able to 'let go' and encourage the student to take greater responsibility for his or her own learning; not all students are necessarily as gifted or as ready to take responsibility for themselves as the individuals whom I was interviewing.

Apart from the obvious answers to this question, within the conservatoire system one safeguard lies with the element of student choice. Students who feel that they are not making appropriate progress or where the relationship between teacher and student has broken down will normally request a change of teacher. Teachers make available biographical information about their careers, interests and specialisms. Students tend to choose teachers whose career pattern mirrors their own aspirations, and do this with considerable realism and self-awareness, knowing that teachers tend to teach from their own professional experience, and to emphasize the skills, personal qualities and values appropriate to the situations with which they are personally familiar.

In the past this may have been sufficient. However for the musicians of the twenty-first century this is unlikely to be enough. The professional world for musicians is changing rapidly. Fewer agents are now taking on young artists; most young musicians need to be able to manage their careers, including their financial affairs, for themselves. Most musicians are now expected to be able to communicate in words, not only in music — to be able to talk about the work that they are doing, not only to perform it — and to be able to organize and take part in education and outreach programmes. Young performers are facing challenges not personally experienced by those who teach them. Musicians need to be far more versatile and more resourceful, in ways which challenge the traditionally accepted stereotype of the introverted musician[27] and which range beyond the expertise that any one instrumental specialist is normally able to provide, even if the time were available to do so. Reid refers to higher education's employment of professionals as a way of bringing in 'the authenticity of the workplace'.[28] In the case of performing musicians, there is no simple model for the 'workplace'. It is becoming less reasonable to expect that even experienced instrumental teachers will be able to assist their students to acquire all the skills for the types of 'portfolio' careers that they will need. For this reason, some of the experiments taking place in instrumental pedagogy at an advanced level are exploring ways of sharing between teachers the responsibilities for the type of development of professional understanding to which this chapter has referred. With such sharing it is possible to ensure that students are exposed not only to a wider range of music — different styles, techniques, genre, repertoire — but also to a wider range of professional expectations and experience and, through this, to different perceptions of the musical world.

But although the responsibility for providing the support, advice and guidance for the emerging young professional is increasingly shared, rather than individual, the special relationship between the student and his or her main instrumental teacher will, I believe, remain central to the learning which the performer needs in order to develop as a person with the qualities needed to communicate effectively through music. Maria Manturzewska, concluding her analysis of the conditions necessary to the development of the successful musician at all stages of life, identifies as 'one of the fundamental conditions'

> the 'musical dialogue' with someone who believes in the talented individual's potential, who understands his or her musical ideas and accepts them, who supports him or her emotionally in these endeavours and helps to overcome the stresses of life.[29]

It is now several decades since the American occupational psychologist, Schein, developed the concept of 'career anchors'.[30] In helping the young musician to develop the strength of purpose to gain from the experience of performance a 'career anchor' for life, the one-to-one instrumental teacher plays a unique role.

18.6 Conclusion

In the context of this symposium, I feel that I should conclude by offering some thoughts on whether there are features of the pedagogical approaches which characterize the study of advanced performance which can be applied more generally to enhance student learning. Where this works best, it seems to me that the features which contribute most effectively to student learning in performance derive from the supportive nature of the one-to-one teacher-student relationship, the development of a strong sense of self-identity by the student, the emphasis on 'mastery' learning, the increasing emphasis on students identifying and solving their own problems, the contact with strong and diverse role models within and without the institution, and the requirement to present what is learnt in 'real-life' situations. Most of these are already applied to good effect in other disciplines.

But beyond this, the study of performance encourages a striving for excellence and for self-realization which contributes to a sense of personal fulfilment and can give meaning and purpose to individuals' lives. Pedagogical approaches which similarly emphasise the development of human potential — whatever the discipline — are, I believe, key to the development of society as a whole.

Notes

1. In most institutions composition is available as an alternative to performance. For the purposes of this chapter, I am excluding reference to the study of composition.
2. About a quarter of British music undergraduates are enrolled on conservatoire courses (see HEFCE, *Review of Music Conservatoires*. HEFCE Conservatoires Advisory Group chaired by Sir John Tooley (March 1999), 36, paragraph 6.1
3. Ibid., 37, paragraph 6.6.
4. Ibid., 37—8, paragraphs 6.7—6.10.
5. J.A. Sloboda and M.J.A. Howe (1991) Biographical precursors of musical excellence: an interview study, *Psychology of Music* 19(10) gives six years as the mean and median age for starting formal study on an instrumental for the group of instrumentalists in this study. Ten years' continuous study is the norm for pianists and violinists, and is often the case for other instrumentalists, who may well have begun on one instrument and changed to another in their teenage years.
6. J.W. Davidson, M.J.A. Howe and J.A. Sloboda (1997) Environmental factors in the development of musical performance skill over the life span. In D.J. Hargreaves and A.C North (eds), *The Social Psychology of Music*. Oxford: Oxford University Press, 197—8.
7. Davidson *et al.* (in Environmental factors in the development of musical performance skill, 192) cite work by Ericsson, Krampe and Tesch-Romer (1993) The role of deliberate practice in the acquisition of expert performance, *Psychological Review* 363—406, which reports that 'the best students in the performance class of the conservatory had accumulated around 10,000 hours of practice by the age of 21'.
8. Some students may already have undertaken fee-paid work. It is certainly not unknown for young musicians to enter higher education already holding membership of the Musicians' Union.
9. A. Reid (1999) Musicians' experience of the musical world: relations with teaching and learning. Paper presented at the 7th Improving Learning Symposium, University of York, September, 6. (Note: Chapter 17 of present volume is based on this paper.)
10. Davidson *et al.* (1997) Environmental factors, 203.
11. A.E. Kemp (1996) *The Musical Temperament*. Oxford: Oxford University Press, 243.
12. M. Manturzewska (1990) A biographical study of the life-span development of professional musicians, *Psychology of Music* 18, 112—39. The study — the initial research for which was conducted in 1976—80 — was based on 165 Polish musicians, aged from 21 to 89.
13. Ibid., 134—5. Sosniak's study, 'Learning to be a concert pianist', is included in B.S. Bloom (ed.) (1985) *Developing Talent in Young People*. New York: Ballantine, 16—67.
14. Reid, op. cit., 6.
15. A.E. Kemp (1997) Individual differences in musical behaviour. In D.J. Hargreaves and A.C. North (eds), *The Social Psychology of Music*, 30—1.
16. Ibid., 29 *et seq*.
17. See A.E. Kemp (1995) Aspects of upbringing as revealed in the personalities of

musicians, *Quarterly Journal of Music Learning and Teaching* 5: 34—41.

18. Kemp (1996) *The Musical Temperament*, 243 (cf. also Kemp (1997),'Individual differences', 40).

19. Kemp (1997), 'Individual differences', 41.

20. For discussion of the model, see D.J. Hargreaves (1995) Oxford: Oxford University Press, The development of artistic and musical competence, in I. Deliège and J.A. Sloboda (eds), *Musical Beginnings: The Origins and Development of Musical Competence*, 148—9.

21. Hargreaves refers only to John Paynter, Murray Schafer and Karl Orff.

22. This figure excludes ensemble activity, such as chamber music and orchestral playing.

23. Barry Green with W. Timothy Gallwey (1987) *The Inner Game of Music*. London: Pan Books, 151.

24. Sosniak (1985) *Learning to be a concert pianist*, 66.

25. Reid, op. cit., 12—13.

26. Ibid., 13.

27. See Kemp (1996) *The Musical Temperament*, 35—50.

28. Reid, op. cit., 15.

29. Kemp (1996) *The Musical Temperament*, 138.

30. E.H. Schein (1980) *Organisational Psychology*, 3rd edn. New York: Prentice-Hall, 83.

19 Phenomenography and the disciplinary basis of motivation to learn

Rosanna Breen[1], Roger Lindsay[2] and Alan Jenkins[1]

1. Oxford Centre for Staff and Learning Development, Oxford Brookes University; 2. Psychology Department, Oxford Brookes University

19.1 Overview

In-depth interviews of two undergraduate students were used to investigate the interplay between conceptions of disciplinary knowledge and motivations for learning. Both were students of Planning Studies at Oxford Brookes University, one first year, and one final year. Categories used to analyse each student's learning motivations in their discipline were derived from learner characteristics elicited in an associated pilot study (Breen and Lindsay 1999a). Conceptions of disciplinary knowledge were categorized separately under three headings: 'Beliefs about skills being developed', 'objectives/ purpose of the discipline' and 'the nature of knowledge in the discipline'. The findings indicate that the links which exist between learning motivations and conceptions of disciplinary knowledge suggest that it is the *process* of constructing knowledge conceptions, rather than conceptions of knowledge *per se,* that are of key importance in understanding learning motivations. Some tentative suggestions are made about student intellectual development in Planning.

19.2 Introduction

19.2.1 Student motivation to learn

The present study addresses the question: 'is there a relationship between student motivations to learn and conceptions of disciplinary knowledge?' The nature of motivation to learn is a problem fraught with complexity to the extent that the usefulness of the concept itself has been questioned (Peters, 1960). The main problem is that of characterizing the learning environment *within* which the student is oriented in order to establish towards *what* they are oriented. It has been suggested elsewhere (Breen and Lindsay, 1999b) that in Higher Education, it is important to 'establish the specific content of a student's goal, i.e. what the student believes the purpose of his or her presence at University to be — and the reasons which led to the choice of this goal'. By establishing these beliefs and reasons for choice it may be possible to understand what the salient features of the learning environment are for students and the degree to which we can influence their experience of it.

A common assumption behind many attempts to understand the academic environment lies in the widespread acceptance by both staff and students, that undergraduate education is a period of enculturation into a way of thinking and behaving (Akerlind and Jenkins,

1998; Kolb, 1981; Newton, Newton and Oberski, 1998). Kolb (1981) postulates that for students:

> Education in an academic field is a continuing process of selection and socialisation to the pivotal norms of the field governing the criteria for truth and how it is to be achieved, communicated and used, and secondarily, to peripheral norms governing personal styles, attitudes and social relationships ... over time these selection and socialisation pressures continue to produce an increasingly impermeable and homogenous disciplinary culture and correspondingly specialised student orientations to learning. (pp. 233—4)

An understanding of effective student motivation thus requires a theoretical understanding of the academic environment. Because the acquisition of disciplinary knowledge is the goal towards which the student is oriented and which Higher Education seeks to facilitate, the academic environment clearly exists independently of student phenomenology. However, the objective existence of the academic environment is no guarantee that students perceive it objectively. A pilot study designed to elicit the salient features of the learning environment for students indeed found that the disciplinary culture does not feature on its own in student phenomenology, but exists alongside, and mediates students' experiences of the social and institutional cultures (Breen and Lindsay, 1999a).

19.2.2 Conceptions of disciplinary knowledge

Research on disciplinary conceptions of knowledge has centred predominantly on attempts to find out what concepts are used to categorize knowledge. For example, Biglan (1973) interviewed academics about the similarities between the content of different disciplines. Three dimensions underlying shared conceptions of disciplinary knowledge were elicited and were labelled 'knowledge structures'. They are the 'hard/soft dimension', the 'pure/applied dimension' and the 'life-systems/non-life systems dimension'. Lodahl and Gordon (1972) asked academics to rank disciplines on pre-defined bipolar constructs, such as their level of paradigmatic maturity. In order to explain unexpected discrepancies in their findings Lodahl and Gordon were led to postulate two further constructs thought to differentiate disciplinary knowledge. These were first, the degree of current paradigmatic stability and secondly, the extent to which the knowledge comprising the discipline is internally differentiated.

More recently, Lattuca and Stark (1994) investigated the influence of disciplinary knowledge on faculty planning of undergraduate courses. They analysed reports produced by 'teaching scholars' in ten disciplines which had been written in response to a challenge by the AAC (Association of American Colleges) National Advisory Committee, for disciplines to address specified aspects of quality in their curriculum content. Their method of enquiry was directed not towards conceptions of disciplinary knowledge *per se*, nor towards shared conceptions of what differentiates disciplinary knowledge. Rather, their interest was in the empirical investigation of what they and others believe to be excessively narrow conceptions of teaching which focus the curriculum on specific areas of knowledge instead of on how knowledge can be organized (see also Kolb, 1981; Dressel and Marcus, 1982; Sheppard and Gilbert, 1991; Becher, 1994). Content analysis of the written reports thus aimed to elicit the disciplinary norms and rules manifest in approaches to course planning.

It was from these elements that teacher conceptions of disciplinary knowledge at the undergraduate level were inferred. Four main issues of quality in the curriculum were addressed in the reports; 'curricula coherence and sequencing', development of a 'critical perspective' in students, 'connecting' learning material to other disciplines and levels of 'inclusiveness' of student minorities. They found that disciplines differed in their responses to the challenges of the AAC both in the meaning and importance attached to the four quality issues and also in their self-reported ability to respond to them.

An important element of the work by Biglan (1973), Lodahl and Gordon (1972) and Lattuca and Stark (1994) is their struggle to analyse and describe disciplinary conceptions of knowledge. Their contrasting perspectives provide a useful starting point for the present study. The first two investigations were concerned with eliciting the dimensions underlying shared cognitions of disciplinary knowledge. Lattuca and Stark (1994) were more concerned with the attitudes, beliefs and values differentiating disciplinary cultures. From their investigations of attitudinal variables, Lattuca and Stark were able to infer some dimensions along which conceptions of knowledge differed by discipline, which were comparable to those of Biglan (1973). This suggests that in addition to 'pure knowledge', social norms and values are an important part of the conceptual framework of academic disciplines. In conclusion, conceptions of knowledge can be understood via typologies comprising several dimensions. These conceptions are partially defined by, and may be inferred from the social rules and norms through which the knowledge is communicated and used, for example through attitudes, values, beliefs, ways of behaving and using language. These latter elements are also likely to constitute aspects of the learning environment within which students develop disciplinary conceptions of knowledge.

19.2.3 Phenomenography and 'conception'

Phenomenography is a recent research tradition, which aims to elicit and interpret people's interpretations of the world around them. Its non-dualist philosophy of consciousness meshes well with the assumption that through the investigation of the *relationship* between student and discipline, insights may be gained into the motives behind the choices students make and the behaviours they exhibit. The phenomenographic position also aims 'to seek out the critical ways of experiencing the world that make people able to handle it in more or less efficient ways' (Marton and Booth, 1997) and assumes that experience is organized in terms of a limited number of 'categories of description' (Marton, 1981, 1994) which are stable, generalizable and apply to all situations.

Discussion of the nature of 'conceptions' has been prevalent in the recent phenomenographic literature. This is probably because, the lack of clarity in the notion of a 'conception', makes it 'difficult to discuss changes in individual subjects' ways of experiencing, i.e. learning, in a theoretically interesting way' (Uljens, 1993, p. 128). Säljö (1993) suggests that this problem leads to insufficient effort to ensure the establishment of a shared communicative context between interviewer and interviewee in the actual practice of phenomenographic data collection. He claims that a common understanding of what is being talked about in the interview can be made clear by either posing problems, or by referring to shared topics of discourse. Ashworth and Lucas (1998) call for more rigour in the reporting of the phenomenographic research process by giving active consideration to the *process* of research in revealing the actual 'lived worlds' of students. Implicit in this is the demand for a theoretical contribution on the part of the researchers to the notion of 'conception'.

Investigations of learning in the domain of cognitive psychology have contributed to elucidating the nature and status of conceptions. Some of this research has predominantly been concerned with the development of conceptual change models of learning. The assumption behind such models is that learning constitutes a change in the conceptual framework. The impetus behind this research is well captured by Strike and Posner's (1992) suggestion that it may be 'more important to understand what it is that produces [conceptions] than it is to understand the character of the misconception itself' (p. 158).

The conceptual framework functions as a 'heuristic for the interpretation of isolated facts and make[s] them possible to assimilate within a given conceptual structure and *inter alia,* affect this structure' (Hallden, 1993). Hallden's 'alternative frameworks' seem to resemble closely the 'conceptual ecology' of Strike and Posner (1992) and Säljö's distinction between 'specific problem solving' and 'shared topics of discourse' as phenomenographic data. The first level of Hallden's alternative frameworks is described as the 'beliefs about specific concepts and phenomena presented in the instruction' and the second as 'a *meta* level: ... the set of beliefs which can be defined as the sum total of beliefs which determine what kind of questions can be meaningfully asked in the realm of a specific topic' (p. 324). It is the latter level with which the present study is concerned.

In the light of this previous research it seems reasonable to seek to investigate the links between student motivation and conceptions of disciplinary knowledge, via phenomenographic interviewing. However, special attention will be given to the appropriateness of the notion of 'conceptions' of disciplinary knowledge in understanding student learning motivations.

19.2.4 The Oxford Brookes University context

Degrees in Planning Studies form part of the Undergraduate Modular Programme (UMP). The UMP is a modular course-credit system which allows students to study one or two academic disciplines to degree level by accumulating credits from modules which are predominantly taught and assessed within a single academic term.

19.3 Method

Participants in the study, were recruited via emails and posters advertising the research and offering £10 for participation. The interview schedule employed was a refined version of one used in an earlier pilot study (Breen and Lindsay, 1999a).

The interview began with some introductory questions designed to elicit student motivation to study at Oxford Brookes and general impressions of the university learning experience. Then the interviewee was asked to describe some specific experiences which they think influenced their motivation to learn, in positive or negative ways. Departmental and discipline-related experiences were then elicited before exploring conceptions of the discipline itself. At the end of the interview, students were asked what they thought of the interview and whether they would like to bring up anything that had not yet been discussed. The interview schedule was flexible; containing some subsidiary questions such as 'What was that like then?' and 'What did you do about it?' A consistent attempt was made to:

1. elicit accounts of experiences which exemplified student perceptions of the influence of the learning environment upon them;
2. explore student feelings about these episodes;
3. discover what behaviours resulted;

4. get students to identify those attributes of the situation and themselves that contributed to their response to the situation.

The interview length was around an hour and a quarter.

19.4 Analysis

The central aim of the analysis was to itemize the main features of the students' learning motivations and their conceptions of the knowledge comprising their discipline, and to discover any relationships between them. A tight framework for the categorization of interview content was required to ensure that the interviews were treated in the same way.

A grounded theory analysis performed on the pilot study interview transcripts provided a framework for categorizing the main features of student motivation to learn. Themes elicited in the pilot study allowed extraction of common elements underlying the learning experiences of students studying in different knowledge domains. Four themes — 'Individual aims, goals and objectives', 'Individual learning preferences', 'Individual motivations' and 'Individual competencies' — had been elicited from the interviews as salient features of learner characteristics that interacted with their perception of the learning environment. Students perceive their experiences of the learning environment in different ways depending on the characteristics encompassed by this dimension. The four themes in this dimension describe the different factors believed by the interviewee or the analyst to have influenced the behavioural reactions students associated with experiences described in the interview. 'Individual aims, goals and objectives' describe the nature of students' long term goals, their clarity and the value placed upon attaining them. 'Individual motivations' describes the nature and importance placed upon certain self-ascribed, trait-like attributes. 'Individual learning preferences' describes students' beliefs about what kinds of university learning experiences they believe they benefit from and those they find satisfying and enjoyable and 'Individual competencies' reflect student's explanations for their self-perceived competence.

It became apparent on reading through the Planning Studies interview transcripts that learning motivations linking the student to the *discipline* are more frequently assigned to 'Individual aims, goals and objectives' and 'Individual learning preferences' and less frequently assigned to 'Individual motivations' and 'Individual competencies'. The categories: 'Reasons behind subject choice and for doing a degree' and 'Future possible roles' were thought to capture the type of student characteristics that relate the student specifically to their discipline within the 'Individual aims, goals and objectives' category.[1] Similarly, 'Motivating experiences in discipline' and 'Personal learning preferences', describes the type of data describing the student-discipline relationship within the 'Individual learning preferences' category.

The smaller category; 'Individual motivations' was retained, but renamed as 'Self-ascribed traits' to better capture the meaning of the category and again, to reduce ambiguity in assigning items to it. Finally, because material assigned to 'Individual competencies' consisted of student's beliefs about the skills required of them in the discipline, this category was renamed 'Beliefs about skills being developed'. This category was treated as a component of students' conception of the discipline, rather than a feature of student motivation to learn. Two additional categories were formulated to capture students' conceptions of disciplinary knowledge: 'Objectives/purpose of the discipline' and 'The nature of knowledge in the discipline'.

Category	Statement
Reasons behind subject choice and for doing the degree	I decided to study [discipline]/go to university because .....
Future possible roles	I see myself/expect to/ intend to .....
Motivating experiences	I believe that ..... makes me feel motivated
Self-ascribed traits	I am the sort of person who .....
Personal Learning preferences	I need/would like/prefer the experience of .....
Beliefs about skills being developed	My discipline demands that you are able to/is teaching me to .....
Objectives/purpose of the discipline	The objective/purpose of my discipline is .....
The nature of knowledge in the discipline	My discipline is characterized by knowledge which is .....

Table 19.1 Statements used to check summary note suitability to categories

A final measure taken to increase the reliability of the qualitative analysis, was to set out statements which each summary note had to be able to complete in a comprehensive way, for the note to be assigned to the category. Table 19.1 shows the statements against which each summary note was compared before it was assigned to its category:

19.4.1 Results

The summary notes taken to encapsulate the Planning students' motivation to learn and conceptions of disciplinary knowledge are shown in Tables 19.2 and 19.3. Following each table is a summary of the links between these variables. 'Sally' is a first-year student and 'John' is in his final year.[2]

Sally is motivated by the challenge of presenting to a big audience and also by the experience of receiving recognition of her efforts from tutors. She is interested in political planning and economics and enjoys getting good grades. She went to university because she felt that it was expected of her, and does not yet have any plans for the future. However, she thinks that university will help her to gain contacts and independence and other generally useful experiences for the future.

The single feature of Sally's learning motivations that relates to her conception of planning knowledge is the satisfaction she gets from the challenge of presenting to a large audience. This activity is also one which she believes she will encounter in public inquiry as a planner and the ability to think quickly under pressure is the challenge she takes on in preparation for it.

Thus the relationship between Sally's learning motivation and conception of planning knowledge is centred around her beliefs about what will be expected of her as a planner — around the *operations* and *activities* involved in planning. There is no association between her learning motivations and her beliefs about the *objective* of planning (i.e. she does not report any learning motivations that might be associated with achieving a best fit / answer in doing planning). Further, the learning motivation associated with her belief about the operations and activities involved in planning, is characterized by the feeling of *satisfaction* she gets from the activity of presenting to a large audience, and is not associated with any particular goal she seeks to attain by getting involved in the activity.

Motivations to learn planning	Conceptions of planning knowledge
• Reasons behind subject choice and for doing a degree	**• Beliefs about skills being developed**
1. It is expected to go to Uni. 2. Uni. helps to gain contacts, experience and independance, gain new perspectives	1. Thinking qickly in preperation for public inquiry 2. Being aware of peoples situations 3. Communnication is central
• Future possible roles	**• Objectives/purpose of the discipline**
1. No clear plans	1. Its about finding the best fit/answer
• Motivating experiences	**• The nature of knowledge in the discipline**
1. Political planning, economics 2. Getting good grades 3. Recognition from others	Discussion and debate is important, it is not a black and white discipline
• Self ascribed traits	
1. Needs to have a personal aim to target focus on	
• Personal Learning prefences	
1. The challenge of presenting to a big audience	

Table 19.2 Overview of summary notes of Sally's motivation to learn and conceptions of disciplinary knowledge (first-year student in Planning) from the interview transcript.

Sally believes that the objective of planning is to find the best solution to problems which affect many different sectors in different ways. She believes that the central operations and activities one is involved in, in applying planning knowledge are; communication and debate, exercising understanding and retaining an awareness of other people's situations, and thinking quickly in public inquiry.

In summary, Sally's learning motivation in planning is characterized by the satisfaction she gets from presenting to a large audience and is not associated with any particular goal she seeks to attain. It is also very specific to one planning activity — that of participating in public inquiry.

John is motivated by peer interaction and the opportunity for gaining some hands-on, practical experience in planning. He wants to get a degree in order to get a job, and is able to describe many situations he expects to find himself in, in the future: He expects to perhaps work in a planning office to start out as a 'general dogsbody', but one day he would like to work for a consultancy researching the impact of big planning projects on the society and the economy. He has also considered working for the Council for the Protection of Rural

Motivations to learn planning	Conceptions of planning knowlegde
• Reasons behind subkect choice and for a degree	**• Beliefs about skills being developed**
1. Useful to have a degree as a qualification for a job 2. Planning helps you to get a specific job, unlike geography	1. Critical awareness of own environment 2. Presentations/confidence 3. Strong arguments 4. Learning what people from disadvantaged areas have to go through - understanding people and their lives
• Future possible roles	• Objectives/purpose of the discipline
1. Expects to work in a Planning office as a general dogsbody 2. Might work for a consultancy, researching the impact of big projects on environment, society and economy 3. Expects to work for the council for the protection of Rural England 4. Expects to help people in a certain way 5. Expects to be in court for public inquiries	1. It's about safeguardingthe environment 2. Its about finding the best fit • The nature of knowledge in the discipline 1. Knowledge is always changing with new government legislation
• Motivating experiences	
1. Group, student support	
• Self-ascribed traits	
1. Tries to be positive and persits at projects he doesn't enjoy	
• Personal Learning Preferences	
1. Needs hands on work experience to become aware of all the different issues out there	

Table 19.3 Overview of summary notes of John's motivation to learn and conceptions of disciplinary knowledge (final year student in Planning) from the interview transcript.

England. Whichever avenue he takes, he expects to end up helping people in some way and, like Sally, to be involved in public inquiries.

John also believes that one objective of planning is to find the best solution to a problem. However, planning to him, is also about safeguarding the environment. He believes that the operations and activities involved, include understanding people and their lives and learning about what disadvantaged people have to go through. He also thinks that the building of strong arguments and confidence in presentation are important abilities, as is having a critical awareness of one's own environment.

Many more associations between John's learning motivations and conceptions of planning knowledge are evident in comparison with the first-year student. First, his belief that the objective of planning is to safeguard the environment links with his goals to work in consultancy, researching the impact of big research projects on society and the economy, and also to work for the CPRE. Thus there is a close link between the discipline's objectives and his own. Secondly, he believes that operations and activities in planning require an understanding of people and their lives and this links well with another of his own goals; to be help people in some way in the future. It may also be postulated that this learning motivation links with his goal to research the impact of projects on society. The third and final link between his conceptions of Planning knowledge and his own goals is between his expectation that he will be involved in public inquiry, and his beliefs both that the operations and activities in Planning demand confidence in presentations and strong argumentation.

19.5 Discussion

The present analysis of learner motivations and conceptions of disciplinary knowledge allocated interview content to mutually exclusive categories developed over the course of the research so far. Exploration of the interactions between these variables made it possible to re-formulate these categories, in a manner which better captures the links between them. The two types of learning motivation, which relate to conceptions of disciplinary knowledge are: *goal-oriented* and *activity-oriented*. Disciplinary knowledge conceptions linking with student motivations to learn are also twofold: the *process of forming conceptions* and *internalizing the objectives of the discipline*.[3] A comparison between the two students allows for elaboration and exemplification.

The first-year and the final-year students differ in both the *number* and the *nature* of the links between their learning motivations and their conceptions of planning knowledge. John's learning motivations, which may be said to link with his conceptions of planning knowledge, are all goal-oriented. In contrast, the only possible link between Sally's learning motivations and conceptions of planning knowledge lies in the feeling of satisfaction she expects to get from the activities associated with public inquiries. Sally, in comparison with John, has as yet developed no goals associated with planning.

On the other side of the interaction, one of John's beliefs about the objective of planning knowledge and several of his beliefs about the operations and activities involved, relate to his learning motivations. Sally's belief about the objective of planning knowledge does not, however, relate to her learning motivations and, the findings suggest that there is only one process feature of planning knowledge that does.

Some conclusions concerning intellectual development in planning may be tentatively drawn from the analysis of these two interviews. The main feature of the analysis, which clearly differentiates the first-year and the final-year students, is the extent to which they articulate their possible future roles they expect to hold. Although John was not completely clear about where he saw his future heading, he had a more elaborate repertoire of contexts he could expect to encounter as a planner available to him, and was able to identify features of those contexts matching his own future goals. This implies that the perceived usefulness of disciplinary knowledge in action contexts, which the student perceives to fulfil some motivational goal s/he holds, is an important feature of intellectual development in planning. Since the features of the contexts matching John's goals all require an understanding of the operations and activities required by the discipline, this also implies that it is the process of conception formation that is more relevant to student learning, than conceptions of knowledge per se.

The case studies both support and add substance to the findings of the associated pilot study (Breen and Lindsay 1999a), confirming that perceptions of the learning environment differ according to student characteristics. The pilot study also supported the idea that it is the *process* of knowledge conception, rather than conceptions of knowledge *per se*, that are relevant in understanding learning motivations. Additionally, the pilot study suggested that the social and institutional cultures mediated by the disciplinary culture, play a prominent role in the process of knowledge conception and revealed that the social culture is more prominent in planning than in other subjects investigated. It seems that this culture could function to support one element of students' process view of planning: that of understanding where others are coming from and maintaining an awareness of other people's situations (the *empathic* element). Similarly, the emphasis on developing an ability to communicate in a confident and competent way in preparation for the work-place, may be supported by Planning's institutional culture, which was found in the pilot, to emphasize strongly the preparation of students for the workplace in comparison with other subject domains.

The present study has further assisted our understanding of student enculturation into their disciplines by analysing two case studies. In the final year student's case, Kolb's (1981) 'norms' which govern the criteria for truth and how it is to be communicated and used, appear to be a more prominent feature of disciplinary socialization in planning, than in how truth itself is to be achieved. 'Peripheral norms' governing personal styles, attitudes and social relationships will be the subject of continuing research.

Notes

1. Note that this category, derived in the pilot study, captures the characteristics relating the student to their learning environment more generally.
2. Names have been changes to protect their identities.
3. Process and objective elements of disciplinary knowledge are jointly referred to below as 'conceptions of disciplinary knowledge'.

19.6 References

Akerlind, G.S. and Jenkins, S. (1998) Academics' views of the relative role of responsibility of teachers and learners in a first-year university course, *Higher Education Research and DevelopmentI* **17**(3): 277—89.

Becher, T. (1994) The significance of disciplinary differences, *Studies in Higher Education* **19**(2): 151—61.

Biglan, A. (1973) The characteristics of subject matter in different academic areas, *Journal of Applied Psychology* **57**(3): 195—203.

Breen, R. and Lindsay, R. (1999a) *Student motivation and the phenomenography of knowledge.* Paper presented at the Annual International Conference of the Higher Education Research and Development Society of Australasia. University of Melbourne: Australia, 12—15 July. http://herdsa.org.au/vic/cornerstones/authorframeset.html

Breen, R. and Lindsay, R. (1999b) Academic research and student motivation, *Studies in Higher Education* **24**(1): 75—93.

Dressel, P.L. and Marcus, D. (1982) *On Teaching and Learning in College — Reemphasising the Roles of Learners and the Disciplines. London: Jossey-Bass.*

Hallden, O. (1993) Learner's conceptions of the subject matter being taught: a case from learning History, *International Journal of Educational Research* **19**(3): 277—300.

Jenkins, A. (1996) Discipline based educational development, *International Journal for Academic Development* **1**: 50—62.

Kolb, D.A. (1981) Learning styles and disciplinary differences. In A.W. Chickering (ed.), *Modern American College — Responding to the New Realities of Diverse Students and a Changing Society.* London, Jossey-Bass.

Lattuca, L. and Stark, J. (1994) Will disciplinary perspectives impede curricular reform?, *Journal of Higher Education* **65**(4): 401—26.

Lodahl, J.B. and Gordon, G. (1972) The structure of scientific fields and the functioning of university graduate departments, *American Sociological Review* **37**(Feb.): 57—72.

Marton, F. (1981) Phenomenography — describing conceptions of the world around us. *Instructional Science* **10**: 177—200.

Marton, F. (1994) Phenomenography. In T. Husen and N. Postlethwaite (eds), *International Encyclopaedia of Education.* Oxford: Pergamon.

Marton, F. and Booth, S. (1997) *Learning and Awareness.* Mahwah, New Jersey: Lawrence Erlbaum Associates.

Newton, D.P., Newton, L.D. and Oberski, I. (1998) Learning and conceptions of understanding in history and science: lecturers and new graduates compared, *Studies in Higher Education* **23**(1): 43—58.

Peters, R.S. (1960) *The Concept of Motivation.* London: Routledge & Kegan Paul.

Säljö, R. (1996) Minding action — conceiving of the world versus participating in cultural practices. In G. Dall'Alba and B. Hasselgren (eds), *Reflections on Phenomenography.* Göteborg: Göteborg Studies in Educational Sciences.

Sheppard, C. and Gilbert, J. (1991) Course design, teaching method and student epistemology, *Higher Education* **22**: 229—49.

Strike, K.A. and Posner, G.J. (1992) A revisionist theory of conceptual change. In R.A. Duschl and R.J. Hamilton (eds), *Philosophy of Science, Cognitive Psychology and Educational Theory and Practice.* New York: State University of New York.

Uljens, M. (1996) On the philosophical foundations of phenomenography. In G. Dall'Alba and B. Hasselgren (eds), *Reflections on Phenomenography.* Göteborg: Göteborg Studies in Educational Sciences.

20 What do professional skills mean for different disciplines in a business school? Lessons learned from integrating professional skills across the curriculum

Barbara de la Harpe, Alex Radloff and John Wyber
Curtin University of Technology, Western Australia

20.1 Introduction[1]

Employers are seeking graduates who possess both the professional and lifelong learning skills which enable them to meet the needs of the changing workplace, to continue learning and to be successful in their professions. However, there is concern worldwide that existing undergraduate programs are not producing graduates with such skills (Australia, Higher Education Council, National Board of Employment, Education and Training, 1992; Australia, NBEET, 1992; Australian Association of Graduate Employers, 1993; Business/Higher Education Round Table, 1992; Candy and Crebert, 1991; Candy, Crebert and O'Leary, 1994; Harvey, 1993a, 1993b; Institute of Chartered Accountants in Australia, 1994; The Association of Graduate Recruiters, 1995). The feedback from employers nationally and internationally highlights the skills which graduates are considered to lack — skills typically include communication, problem-solving, teamwork and interpersonal skills and information literacy (Candy *et al.*, 1994; Mayer, 1992; Guthrie, 1994; Harvey, 1993a). Their concerns are illustrated by the following quotes:

> They come out with a lot of academic theory but can't present, they can't write, they don't understand what business is about. While they are made to present assignments at university, they are not actually taught how to do them. (ACNielsen, 1998, p.8)

> Both technical and non-technical entry-level employees [are] deficient in basic skills such as thinking abstractly, establishing priorities and setting goals, and using interpersonal skills to handle conflict or criticism. Employers [are] particularly concerned about writing and presentation skills of technical graduates (scientists, accountants, engineers). (O'Brien, 1997, p. 9-10)

Many graduates themselves, regardless of discipline, report that their undergraduate study did not improve their generic skills (Johnson, 1998). In Australia, data from the Generic Skills scale of the Course Experience Questionnaire (CEQ), which all new university graduates are asked to complete, shows that for problem-solving, writing and team work, only 67%, 68% and 46% of the almost 58,000 graduates respectively agreed or strongly agreed that these skills had been developed during their undergraduate study (Johnson, 1998).

Although the skills needed for successful employment are often referred to as 'generic skills' in the literature, the term 'professional skills' has been used in this chapter. This term has been chosen because of the possible misconstruction of the term 'generic skills', first, through meaning slippage, so that, as Clanchy and Ballard (1995) point out, 'generic skills' are used interchangeably with 'attributes', 'characteristics', 'values', 'competencies' and 'qualities', and, secondly, because the word 'generic' suggests that such skills are independent of a learning context and, therefore, can be developed in a vacuum, a view not supported by current research on learning (Hattie, Biggs and Purdie, 1996; Hadwin and Winne, 1996).

In this chapter, we discuss how students can be helped to develop the skills which employers and professional bodies value and require, suggest how this is best done, and describe a project within a Business School aimed at helping students develop these skills in the context of their undergraduate programme. We explore whether the discipline influenced the choice of skills and how they were taught and assessed and how such differences may be related to the instructors' conceptions of their discipline. We discuss the findings in terms of students' skill development, explore the implications of the findings for integrating professional skills into disciplines, and share lessons learned for changing the curriculum.

20.2 Developing students' skills[1]

Professional skills, despite their recognized importance for employment, have rarely been explicitly taught as part of undergraduate courses, where the focus is on the content of the discipline (knowledge objectives) rather than on learning outcomes and processes (Business/Higher Education Round Table, 1992; Rosenman, 1996). When such skills have been taught, they have usually been presented as ad hoc, stand alone, out of context, and add-on, and have often been designated as 'remedial' and, therefore, of limited value (see Hattie, Biggs and Purdie, 1996 for a review).

Evidence from educational research suggests that learning is most likely to be effective when it occurs in context, since knowledge is fundamentally situated; that is, it is a product of the activity, culture and context in which it is developed. In addition, the transfer of knowledge and skills from the classroom to the workplace is most likely to occur when the classroom situation closely resembles the work situation; in other words, learning is situated (Brown, Collins and Duguid, 1988). Thus, professional skills should permeate the whole curriculum rather than be isolated in a single or specialized course, avoiding the 'one-shot' or inoculation model of teaching.

Moreover, research suggests that learning support is more effective when provided in the context of students' subject learning by the discipline instructor. Weinstein refers to providing support in-context as implementing a metacurriculum which involves the teaching of skills while teaching the content area of the discipline. Contrary to many instructors' opinions, she believes that they have many opportunities to teach skills while simultaneously teaching the content area of the discipline. Biggs (1987) believes that effective instruction requires instructors to teach metacognitively, that is to provide students with appropriate information on when, where and why they should learn and use the skills being taught.

Given the above, it is imperative that students have the opportunity to develop professional skills in all courses and, since each discipline has its own language and culture, the teaching of such skills should be the responsibility of the discipline instructor (Hattie, Biggs and Purdie, 1996).

20.3 The Professional Skills Project

In line with the research findings outlined above, a project aimed at developing the professional skills of approximately 3000 undergraduate business students enrolled in one of 23 majors of a Bachelor of Commerce degree is currently being implemented in a business school of a large technological Australian university. The project commenced in February, 1999, and will be 'rolled in' over three years (CBS Professional Skills Taskforce, 1999).

A Task Force comprising instructors from each of the disciplines, students, employers, professional development and library staff identified a set of professional skills, namely Communication (divided into three components, Writing, Presenting, and Speaking Out), Computer Literacy, Information Literacy, Team Working and Decision Making. A definition of each skill was also developed.

The Unit Outline, handed out at the beginning of the semester, was standardized and contained:

- the selected skill learning objectives as well as content learning objectives;
- a program for the semester showing where each skill is to be taught and assessed;
- assignment marking guides showing assessment criteria and allocation of marks for both the skill and content components of the task; and
- an icon identifying each professional skill placed next to the skill learning objective, teaching and learning activities and assessment tasks.

First year Unit Coordinators from each of the five core subjects — Information Systems, Business Law, Management, Accounting and Economics — were asked to select from the skills those they considered most appropriate to their discipline and integrate them into the undergraduate programme through changes to curriculum materials, instructional strategies and assessment tasks. They were supported in integrating the skills by an educational consultant and/or a discipline specialist. An important feature of the integration process was the expectation that the professional skills be taught and assessed in the context of the discipline. Moreover, in line with Biggs (1996), there was a requirement that the learning objectives, teaching activities and assessment tasks be closely aligned.

Did the discipline make a difference to the professional skills which the Unit Coordinators integrated into their subjects and was their choice of skills related to their conceptions of the subject? We explored these questions in relation to the professional skills that the Unit Coordinators chose to integrate and how they conceptualized the teaching and assessment of them.

20.4 Methodology

In order to address these questions, we collected, as part of the on-going evaluation of the larger Professional Skills Project, data from three sources, namely semi-structured interviews, Unit Outlines and, where available, session outlines. At the end of the semester, the Unit Coordinators were interviewed by the first author about which professional skills they selected and why, their approach to teaching them, and their conceptions of their subject. The questions asked were:

1. 'Which of the professional skills did you select for your unit and why? (i.e. how are the skills relevant to your discipline?)'
2. 'Describe how you are teaching the skill(s) you have selected.'

3. 'How do you conceptualize ... as a subject in the undergraduate degree? (In other words, ... is about ...)'

Interviews were taped, transcribed and analysed. A copy of their transcribed interview was sent to each of the Unit Coordinators. The authors, working individually, read the transcripts and identified themes. They then compared and validated views. When analysing the responses, they adopted a bottom up or data-driven approach.

Responses to the third question, dealing with conceptions of the subject, were also categorized using Kember's (1999) two-level categorization model. According to Kember, instructor beliefs about teaching can be organized into two orientations — teacher-centred / content-oriented, and student-centred / learning-oriented — each with two subordinate conceptions. The two subordinate conceptions for the teacher-centred / content-oriented orientation are imparting information and transmitting structured knowledge. The two subordinate conceptions for the student-centred / learning-oriented orientation are facilitating understanding and conceptual change / intellectual development. A further subordinate conception, student-teacher interaction/ apprenticeship, links the two orientations. These orientations and subordinate conceptions vary along a continuum from teacher-centred / content-oriented to student-centred / learning-oriented.

20.5 Findings

The findings are reported in terms of first, the professional skills selected by each of the Unit Coordinators and why, using data from unit outlines and the interviews, second, how the professional skills were taught and assessed, using data from the interviews and session outlines, and third, Unit Coordinators' conceptions of their subject, using data from the interviews.

20.5.1 Who selected which skills and why?

Table 20.1 shows the professional skills that Unit Coordinators chose to integrate into their subject as indicated in their Unit Outlines at the beginning of the semester. As already mentioned, we defined integration to mean the teaching and assessing of the skill.

	Professional skill integrated						
Subject	*Writing*	*Speaking Out*	*Presenting*	*Computer Literacy*	*Info. Literacy*	*Team Working*	*Decision Making*
Information Systems	•*		•*	•	•*		
Legal Framework	•						•
Management	•	•*	•*		•	•*	•*
Accounting				•	•	•*	
Economics	•	•		•*	•*		

Note: The professional skills marked with an * indicate that the skill was in the Unit Outline but was either not taught or not assessed.

Table 20.1 Professional skills selected by Unit Coordinators by subject

As shown in Table 20.1, at the beginning of the semester, each Unit Coordinator selected a different combination of professional skills and none selected all seven. When the same professional skill was selected, it was conceptualized differently by Unit Coordinators in the different subjects. Thus, for example: Writing in Economics focused on steps in writing Economics essays and Harvard referencing; in Legal Framework, it focused on legal writing and citing legal acts; in Management it focused on a report on working in a Learning Set team; and in Information Systems, it focused on writing short explanations of developments in the technological field. Similar subject differences were evident for the other Professional Skills.

The skills shown in Table 20.1 were selected at the beginning of the semester and included in the Unit Outlines; however, by the end of the semester, over half of the skills selected were not fully integrated into the unit in that they were not both taught and assessed. Moreover, the Information Systems Unit Coordinator did not believe that he had in fact chosen any of the professional skills but, rather, that these were already in the unit. He commented that he did not select the skills 'because those components were part and parcel of what we did and now they were being identified as being appropriate to being labelled professional skills and with some adjustment they could be incorporated into the program'. In addition, the Management Unit Coordinator found that, except for Writing and Information Literacy, it was impossible to teach and assess the skills selected because they were 'too close to the content ... so embedded it became difficult to separate it all, so I took all those [skills other than Writing and Information Literacy] out'.

The reasons Unit Coordinators gave for selecting the professional skills which they did are outlined below.

For *Information Systems*, the Unit Coordinator selected presentation skills specifically for historical reasons (the skill was already in the unit since it had been included by the previous Unit Coordinator). However, it was not formally taught although it was assessed. Further, as mentioned, the Unit Coordinator believed that the inclusion of the skills was 'just current practice' which reflected how things are done in the unit.

For *Legal Framework*, the Unit Coordinator selected problem-solving as a component of Decision Making skill because 'the truth is, lawyers are problem-solving all the time ... it's the style of thinking that we want them to develop ... [even though they are not going to be lawyers but accountants, economists etc.] that process of thinking will still be useful in those sorts of subjects'. He selected Writing because it reinforced this problem solving approach 'writing is essential to being a lawyer ... we want them to write in a particular way, so writing for law was something I chose'.

For *Management*, the Unit Coordinator selected Writing because 'there is scope for that one to fit into the model that was put forward' by the project. She selected Team Work because she saw it as 'part of the structure of the unit so that students have to work in teams to be able to complete the unit' and because it is part of the content. She also wanted students to be able to 'go into the next unit and be confident in writing essays and reports, and so on, referencing their work, writing at a professional standard and that can include things like grammar and spelling and presentation'.

For *Accounting*, the Unit Coordinator selected Decision Making because of his own interest in the area. He commented that in terms of Information Literacy, Computer Literacy and Team Working 'professional accountants would need to have an ability to find information using computers, making appropriate decisions and working well with other people'. He saw the integration of professional skills as giving him 'formal permission or formal encouragement to introduce some different stuff' and to 'get students to reflect on their experiences'.

For *Economics*, the Unit Coordinator selected Writing because 'part of the key assessment was a written assignment ... I mean writing is always viewed as an important aspect of communicating Economics, writing Economic reports, writing Economic analyses, so it was probably the main reason for selecting writing and referencing'. He saw Information Literacy and Computer Literacy as 'subskills that are part of writing an assignment'. In terms of Speaking Out, he considered that 'students should be confident to be able to explain or demonstrate answers to the rest of the class by using the right word or simply explaining the question, participating in discussion'.

In terms of the reasons which Unit Coordinators gave for selecting the professional skills they did, Unit Coordinators in all the disciplines, with the exception of Information Systems, mentioned the link to the discipline. Other reasons given included project requirements and academic enabling skills for Management, personal interest for Accounting, and academic enabling skills for Economics, and historical reasons for Information Systems.

20.5.2 How were the professional skills taught?

How the Unit Coordinators described how the professional skills included in their units were taught, is outlined below.

For *Information Systems*, the Unit Coordinator's view of the teaching and assessment of professional skills was by self-discovery. For example, he did not teach presentation skills directly but set a presentation assignment and provided global feedback to the class after each student had done a presentation. The approach he took, thus, was to 'provide information to the tutors and the students as background, either verbal or on the web'. Information was 'not in step 1, step 2, it's rather more like a set of tips for people to follow'. The apparent purpose of this 'information' was to enable the students and the tutors to 'use' it in preparation and/or review. This 'teaching process' was, according to the Unit Coordinator, supplemented in relation to the professional skill of presenting by detailed verbal feedback to the students undertaking presentations so that the recipient and other students 'can learn from it'. The Unit Coordinator was of the strong opinion that this method of teaching was 'a far better model than giving them a dollop of training or education in week one or week two and then letting them all do their assignments'. The Unit Coordinator did not describe how he taught Computer Literacy, Information Literacy or Writing skills.

The approach adopted by the Unit Coordinator in Information Systems to teaching and assessing the skills reflected his view of his role as a lecturer which was to teach the subject content. He said,

> I have to concentrate on the content ... I don't feel as though it is appropriate for me to be spending my time doing that [teaching and assessing English]. I have to concentrate on the content ... and here am I and all the tutors spending all our time working on that and not on the content, and one of the things that I thought was going to come out of this professional skills project was the fact that we could refer students for help [and that] a lot of our work is geared towards helping the strugglers struggle through or muddle through ... I am looking after the high performers.

For *Legal Framework*, the approach the Unit Coordinator took to teaching the skill of problem solving as a component of Decision Making was quite 'formal' with both the lectures and tutorial sessions being used to teach, reinforce, model and practise (both verbally and in writing) the skill. The importance to the Unit Coordinator of teaching students the problem-solving skill was clearly manifested by its inclusion as the first teaching topic of the unit, 'the first topic is actually on the skill of writing and the problem solving process. So we have integrated it into the course as topic 1'. The skill forms the subject matter of one hour of the first two hour lecture, and then regularly throughout the semester where in 'almost every lecture their attention is drawn to the 4 step process'.

Additionally, the process is reinforced in the weekly one hour tutorial sessions, where 'two or three times in the tutorial ... the tutors will ask them to specifically address that [the 4 step process]'. This is possible because the tutorials require the use of the process in the discussion of 'hypothetical problems'. Reinforcement of the skill in the tutorials is by way of both discussion and by requiring the students to write an answer and then show it to other students.

For *Management,* the approach the Unit Coordinator took to teaching and assessing Writing involved setting aside time during the second week of semester, where staff 'spend quite a bit of time going through a quality report, and how it should be written, explaining this, this and this'. A video was also used that 'takes them through the steps of writing up an assignment or report'.

Information literacy was taught by getting the students to complete a self-paced 'introduction to the library' exercise, where they 'learn to find their way around the library'. The involvement of the Unit Coordinator in this 'teaching process' was to provide 5 per cent 'to encourage them to do it'.

For the other skills, the Unit Coordinator pointed out that 'they are still in there, but they don't come under the umbrella — I am still doing Team Work and assessing it and all that' because she was unable to assess them independently of the content, since, as she commented, 'having to break it up into the mark for professional skills and the mark for content ... that's where I came unstuck ... my unit is more holistic than that ... and I found it very difficult to do that ... it was painful'.

For *Accounting,* the approach the Unit Coordinator took to teaching skills emphasized having students 'doing' rather than being taught or told, by having them to 'engage' in certain behaviours. This was clearly illustrated with respect to Computer Literacy, where the teaching involved 'setting a goal and hoping the students could figure it out ... giving a little bit of guidance, not much formal saying what to do'. The development of Information Literacy skills was described as 'trying to promote a particular aspect of that in terms of navigating through the Internet to find an annual report and navigating through the installation instructions of a CD ROM' rather than as a taught skill.

For *Economics,* the approach the Unit Coordinator took to teaching skills emphasized showing students models of the skill, so that 'all students would be given models to look at so they can see ... the way to prepare for a tute class and to prepare notes, and to get ready for discussion, how to write out an economics answer to a particular issue ... how to write essays, the structure of essays, how to reference'. Time was set aside in tutorials to teach skills so that 'in about a third of the tutorials there is something specifically taught about professional skills'.

In summary, in terms of the approaches adopted by the Unit Coordinators to teaching the skills, a number of approaches were reported. For Information Systems and Accounting, teaching of skills was unstructured and emphasized students being set tasks which required them to discover for themselves how to develop the skills. For Legal Framework, Management and Economics, teaching of skills was structured with time being set aside in class to address skills specifically. In addition, for Legal Framework, practice and peer and instructor feedback; for Management, videos and external services (the library); and for Economics, models were used.

20.5.3 What were the Unit Coordinators' conceptions of their subject?

How each Unit Coordinator conceptualized his or her subject is presented using quotes from the interview transcripts.

> **Information Systems**
> Information Systems is the study of the tools, techniques, methods, of analysing, designing, creating, implementing, evaluating mainly computer based information systems ... it introduces students to the terminology, and the concepts that are related to that ... so, along the way, students sort of learn how to use some of the tools.

> **Legal framework**
> I realise that it is important for the students to get the taste of things to come and it should be delivered so that the taste is something they enjoy ... [Legal Framework 100] is a vehicle for getting students to think about doing law for the future ... I want to make it a journey that they can cope with.

> **Management**
> I see [Management 100] as an introductory unit ... that introduces them to some of the key areas of management ... but I also see it as being a unit that will develop them in certain skills ... I guess I also see it a little bit as a sort of promotional unit as well.

> **Accounting**
> Accounting 100 is enabling students to understand how accounting information is used and not the process of generating information, but the process of using the information.

> Economics
> [Economics 100] focuses on students understanding how a market price system works ... all students should have a good understanding of how a marketing economy functions, how the price system works, so understanding the economical environment, I would think is a key aspect of understanding the business environment.

In summary, it appears that Unit Coordinators held a range of conceptions about their subjects. Lecturers in Information Systems, Management and Economics saw their subjects in terms of the content; Lecturers in Legal Framework and Management in terms of 'selling' or promoting the subject to students and helping student manage the subject and university study, respectively; and Lecturers in Accounting, in terms of the application of knowledge.

Unit Coordinators' responses relating to how they taught professional skills and to their conceptions of their subject were categorized using Kember's (1999) model as shown in Table 20.2.

As shown in Table 20.2, Unit Coordinators appeared to hold conceptions which varied from teacher-centred to student-centred.

	Teacher-centred/content-oriented		**Student-centred/learning oriented**		
Subject	Imparting information	Transmitting structured knowledge	Student-teacher interaction/ apprenticeship	Facilitating understanding	Conceptual change/ intellectual development
Information Systems		**3**			
Legal Framework			**3**		
Management			**3**		
Accounting				**3**	
Economics				**3**	

Table 20.2

20.6 Discussion

Did the discipline make a difference to the professional skills which the Unit Coordinators integrated into their subjects and was the choice of skills related to their conceptions of the subject? The findings suggest that the discipline did make a difference in the choice of skills in that Unit Coordinators in the different disciplines selected different combinations of skills to integrate into their units. Moreover, analysis of data suggests that the role and integration of the same skill was described differently by Unit Coordinators in the different disciplines.

These descriptions, in turn, were related to their conceptions of the subject and the way the skills were taught. Information Systems was conceptualized in terms of transmitting content and thus, the Unit Coordinator found it difficult to teach professional skills directly if at all. Legal Framework was conceptualized as helping students to think like lawyers as well as to enjoy the study of law. Thus the professional skills selected by the Unit Coordinator in Legal Framework were Decision Making and Writing, both of which focused on the style of thinking and writing used by lawyers. Management was conceptualized in holistic terms including both a marketing and academic enabling focus. Thus, the Unit Coordinator found it difficult to separate professional skills from content while teaching and/or assessing many of them as well as academic enabling skills such as 'learning-to-learn'. Accounting was conceptualized as the application of accounting information. Thus, the professional skills selected included Information Literacy and Computer Literacy aimed at locating information on the web and a CD-ROM related to its application in accounting. Economics was conceptualized as understanding economic concepts, and thus, the professional skills selected focused on Writing and Speaking Out about economic ideas.

Unit Coordinators' descriptions of professional skills and their conceptions of their subject reflected an academic orientation to teaching their subject rather than a business or real world focus on skill development. This finding suggests that academics may see their role more as teaching the content of their subject rather than as helping students to develop professional skills which they will need as graduates. Moreover, our findings support the view that the conceptions which an instructor holds may be influenced by the context resulting in each teacher having 'a unique perception of his or her teaching situation' (Prosser and Trigwell, 1999, p. 23).

How Unit Coordinators described the teaching of professional skills and their views of their subjects reflected their conceptions of teaching. This finding is in line with other research on the role of conceptions in teaching which suggests that how instructors conceptualize teaching and their roles as teachers impacts on their approach to teaching and assessing (Kember, 1998). According to Kember, instructors at the teacher-centred / content-oriented end of the continuum and adopting the information transmission orientation, rely almost exclusively on a 'unidirectional lecture approach' and are unlikely to engage 'in more interactive teaching methods such as dialogue or role play' (p. 20). Those at the other end of the continuum use more interactive and learner-centred approaches. However, Kember cautions that 'there will not, though, always be an automatic relationship between underlying beliefs and observable teaching approaches at this end of the spectrum ... [teachers] may at times still have to employ approaches which appear inconsistent with that belief' (p. 20).

These beliefs about teaching are important since, as Kember (1998) points out 'there is evidence of links between the teaching beliefs and teaching strategies and, more significantly, with the learning approaches of students' (p. 17). In addition, research by Trigwell, Prosser and Taylor; Gow and Kember; and Sheppard and Gilbert (cited by Kember, 1998) suggests that instructor conceptions influence the teaching approaches and strategies they adopt, and these, in turn, influence their students' learning approaches and the quality of their learning outcomes.

20.7 Implications for integration of professional skills

The findings of the present study have implications for how professional skills are integrated — taught and assessed — within the disciplines and for professional development of staff in order for this to occur.

Developing professional skills requires approaches to curriculum planning, teaching and assessment which are associated with effective learning. In terms of the curriculum, the focus needs to shift from an emphasis exclusively on discipline content to one which includes also a focus on skill development. Thus, the curriculum must be modified to encompass process as well as content goals. Since skill acquisition is progressive, the inclusion of skills in the curriculum should reflect this. Skills should be integrated across the curriculum and students should be given the opportunity to develop higher levels of skill as they progress through the course.

In terms of teaching, the instructor should ensure that students are informed learners and active participants in teaching and learning activities, and have opportunities to practise skills and obtain feedback on skill development. Furthermore, the lecturer should use modelling, group work and discussion strategies, and encourage students to be metacognitive about their skill development — that is, plan, monitor and adapt their learning. The lecturer should also provide opportunities for students to develop their abilities to reflect on their learning and to reinforce their progress.

In terms of assessment, professional skills should be assessed as an integral part of the unit. As Biggs and Moore (1993) point out, assessment should be a cooperative act between lecturer and students. Moreover, they suggest that if educators are serious about getting students to become autonomous learners, then students should be encouraged gradually to self-assess, something which is 'a rarely cultivated process in the classroom' (p. 380). Assessment tasks which encourage students to engage continuously in learning and which foster deep learning, for example peer review and portfolios, should be used wherever possible (Dochy and Dowell, 1997).

Teaching and assessment of professional skills should take into account the nature of the discipline, and the skills selected for integration should be discipline-specific rather than generic and located in the discipline content, context and approach to teaching and learning.

> In order to achieve the changes in curriculum, teaching and assessment as described, significant investment in professional development of staff involved in skill development is needed. Regardless of the discipline, professional skill development should be underpinned by principles of effective teaching and learning. Any differences between disciplines are less important than effective teaching and learning. Therefore, rather than focusing on disciplinary differences staff should, according to Smart and Ethington (1995, p. 55)
>
> accept the entrenched nature of existing [disciplinary] goals and to focus their energies and resources on assisting faculty to improve their instructional effectiveness which ultimately with benefit student learning. Such an orientation would benefit both the general education and the specific academic major component of students' undergraduate experience'.

Moreover, as Murray and Renaud (1995) point out, 'research to date on specific low-inference teaching behaviors indicates that what makes an effective teacher, at least in the eyes of students, is pretty much the same regardless of academic discipline' (Murray and Renaud, 1995, p. 38). Therefore, professional development should focus on helping staff in whatever discipline they teach, to 'increase the frequency of teaching behaviors that are positively correlated with student ratings, but tend, for whatever reason, to occur relatively infrequently in that discipline' (Murray and Renaud, 1995, p. 39).

Instructors need to have or to develop approaches to their teaching which are learner-centred learning-oriented, if they are to be able to develop their students' professional skills. They may require support which should focus on helping them 'to think of themselves as teachers as well as specialists in their discipline area ... The message is that an academic needs to be a discipline expert and a teacher' (Kember, 1998, p. 23). This view is supported by Speck (1998, pp. 25—6) who states that '[c]learly, one of the most pressing needs in higher education is the linking of training in teaching effectiveness with expertise in an academic discipline'.

However, while there is evidence to suggest that instructors can change their conceptions of teaching, this is not always an easy task (Gallagher, 1994; Kember, 1998; Pajares, 1992; Trigwell and Prosser, 1996) and is especially difficult when traditional practices and 'deep-seated' beliefs are involved (Kember, 1998, p. 22). In addition, concerns about academic freedom and feelings of pride and insecurity (Speck, 1998) may make any changes difficult. Changes are unlikely to occur by *ad hoc* attendance by instructors at seminars aimed at professional development (Trigwell and Prosser, 1996). Gallagher (1994, p. 187) suggests that '[t]he idea that beliefs are difficult to change and are resistant even in the face of facts can explain why inservice and preservice training rarely modify belief systems of teachers'.

Nevertheless, professional development should assist staff to revise their curricula and teaching and assessment practices in line with best practice. Professional development support should recognise the different needs and preferences for support by different staff. It may include: one-on-one assistance; group activities (within and across disciplines), such as seminars and workshops, staff meetings, special interest groups and web-based discussion groups; and the provision of a variety of instructional resources which can be adapted by lecturers to suit their discipline and to ensure ownership of ideas and strategies.

20.8 Lessons learned

In an academic environment, at least in a business school where a large proportion of the staff are likely to have come from practice, to have had no training in teaching, and to be at a formative stage in their research careers, given the perception that the university reward system most values research and publishing, changes to staff attitudes towards teaching require, on the part of management, a new commitment to teaching and learning, a recognition that good teaching does not come naturally but requires training and practice, incentives for staff to teach better, and patience. On the part of staff it requires a recognition that change will be beneficial to the institution and to themselves, and that it is possible if there is collaboration among colleagues; it requires an acceptance that there are proven, more effective, teaching strategies which require moving out of the 'comfort zone' to experiment with different methods.

As a result of our experiences in supporting the integration of professional skills across the curriculum, we have learned a number of lessons. In terms of ownership, academic staff in each discipline have to be encouraged to accept responsibility, as a team, for their graduates since no one academic is responsible for the low level of professional skills in graduates. Nor can individual staff, working independently be expected to achieve a measurable improvement in the overall level of professional skills. Academics must work together as a team to plan where in their course each skill is introduced, taught, practised, improved and assessed.

The issue of staff conceptions of teaching and learning of skills and the impact of these on their roles and responsibilities as lecturers must be addressed. Specifically, conceptions of teaching which reflect a teacher-centred and content-focused transmission model of teaching and learning need to be recognized as obstacles to the development of professional skills (Boulton-Lewis,1998; Kember, 1998) and that conceptions which reflect a student-centred and process-focused constructivist model of teaching and learning are essential for skill development. Thus, it is essential that staff be made aware of their current conceptions and where necessary, be assisted to change these. It needs to be recognized that such changes may be associated with negative feelings and cognitive conflict. Changing conceptions is very difficult and requires time and effort, and there have been few attempts to do so with university lecturers (Kember and Gow, 1994).

Like effective learning, good teaching requires commitment, an appropriate conception and time and effort to develop quality curricula, teaching activities and assessment tasks which support the development of professional skills. Thus, there must be appropriate recognition and reward mechanisms in place to encourage good quality teaching.

In terms of leadership, the first step in a programme to develop professional skills is for the senior staff to convince the academics involved that these skills need to be taught; that the skills can be taught; and that they can teach them. It is important to recognize and deal with staff comments such as:

- 'I shouldn't have to teach this — it should be taught in a specific skills unit.'
- 'I don't know how to teach this. I'm an expert in X and can't be expected to teach anything else.'
- 'If we had decent students in the first place, there would be no need to teach these skills.'

If there is effective leadership, appropriate resources, reward and recognition, and support and encouragement, change can be achieved. In our experience, academics who genuinely make the mind shift to include a focus on professional skills find their new approach to teaching and learning to be rewarding. The lessons discussed above are similar to those reported about a programme to teach 'world of work' skills in an Agricultural degree (Auger, 1998).

Staff should be encouraged to form working groups within their disciplines to discuss issues and plan for change, since sharing ideas and strategies and working collaboratively encourages and supports integration of skills. In order to encourage change, leaders should invite those currently working in the business world to participate in the early stages of the debate about the importance of and need for skill development within the curriculum. Moreover, in order to reach all staff, a model of skill development in which professional development is an integral and essential component of teaching in universities should be adopted. It is only in this way that all staff will take seriously the need for ongoing professional development and use the support provided. Thus, as Speck (1998, pp. 25—6) notes, 'one of the most pressing needs in higher education is the linking of training in teaching effectiveness with expertise in an academic discipline'.

Finally, whatever the discipline, staff should acknowledge and value professional skills, take ownership of student skill development as an integral part of their subject and recognize the need to adopt appropriate teaching and assessment approaches since

> certain skills that are valued by employers, in particular the ability to work in teams and oral communication skills, are not perhaps well developed through traditional university teaching approaches, based on students receiving lectures as a one-way flow of information. Again institutions that rely on this approach should consider how well they are fitting their students for their future working lives...all institutions need to give some consideration to the skills of the future: that is, the need for adaptability and flexibility in the workforce and for continuous training and learning throughout a graduate's working life. (EIP Report, 1998)

20.9 Conclusion

This study took places in the early stages of the integration of professional skills into the majors of an undergraduate business degree. Based on the research literature, skills were integrated in the context of the discipline and explicitly taught and assessed in each unit. In the paper, we examined how Unit Coordinators decided on which professional skills to include in their first semester units and how these choices related to their conceptions of their disciplines. We also explored Unit Coordinators' approaches to teaching and assessing the skills they had integrated in their unit.

We concluded that the combination of skills integrated varied across the disciplines. Further, the choices which Unit Coordinators made about which skills to include were determined largely, but not exclusively, by their conceptions of their discipline. Other factors which influenced their choices included what they inherited from previous Unit Coordinators, their preferences based apparently on what they were willing to teach, and their beliefs about what students needed and enjoyed, based on their perceptions about what made the discipline attractive to students.

Some Unit Coordinators had difficulty in separating the skills from the content or seeing the need explicitly to teach and/or assess them. Thus, the teaching or assessment of some skills was abandoned as too difficult or unnecessary. This finding emphasized the role of the

Unit Coordinators' conceptions of teaching and learning. Teaching of professional skills requires a student-centred/learning-oriented approach which not all the Unit Coordinators held. Therefore, there is a need for professional development of staff so that they can change their conceptions, as appropriate, if the project is to be successful in its objectives of implementing the teaching and assessment of professional skills across the disciplines.

Acknowledgements

We thank our five colleagues who agreed to share their views on integrating professional skills into their units and on their teaching and learning. We also thank Judy McGowan for her help in analysing parts of the interview data.

Note

1. Parts of this section are adapted from the Curtin University of Technology (1998) CUTSD application prepared by Radloff and de la Harpe.

20.10 References

ACNielsen. (1998).Research on employer satisfaction with graduate skills–interim reports, Evaluations and Investigations Report 98/8, Canberra, Australia: DETYA. Available: http://www.deetya.gov.au/highered/eippubs1998.htm

Auger, A. (1998) Teaching world of work skills within a degree program: Ontario Agricultural College. In F.T. Evers, J.C. Rush and I. Berdrow (eds), *The Bases of Competence: Skills for lifelong learning and employability*. San Francisco: Jossey-Bass.

Australia, Higher Education Council, National Board of Employment, Education and Training (1992) *Higher Education: Achieving Quality*. Canberra: Australian Government Publishing Service.

Australia, National Board of Employment, Education and Training (NBEET) (1992) *Skills Required for Graduates: One Test of Quality in Australian Higher Education*. Higher Education Council Commissioned Report No. 20. Canberra: Australian Government Publishing Service.

Australian Association of Graduate Employers (1993) *National Survey of Graduate Employers*.

Biggs, J.B. (1996) *Enhancing teaching through constructive alignment*, Higher Education **32**: 347—64.

Biggs, J. (1987) *Student Approaches to Learning and Studying*. Hawthorn, Victoria: ACER.

Biggs, J. B. and Moore, P. J. (1993) *The Process of Learning*. Sydney: Prentice Hall.

Boulton-Lewis, G. (1998) Applying the SOLO taxonomy to learning in higher education. In B. Dart and G. Boulton-Lewis (eds), *Teaching and Learning in Higher Education* 201—21. Camberwell, Victoria: ACER Press.

Brown, J. S., Collins, A. and Duguid, P. (1988) *Situated Cognition and the Culture of Learning*. Report No. IRL88-008. ERIC Document Reproduction Service No. ED 342357.

Business/Higher Education Round Table. (1992) *Educating for Excellence*. Commissioned Report No. 2. Camberwell: Author.

Candy, P. and Crebert, G. (1991) Ivory tower to concrete jungle, *Journal of Higher Education* **62**(5): 572—92.

Candy, P., Crebert, G. and O'Leary, J. (1994) *Developing Lifelong Learners through Undergraduate Education*. Report to the NBEET. Canberra: Australian Government Publishing Service.

CBS Professional Skills Taskforce (1999) *Integrated Professional Skills Project: Report of the Phase One Task Force*. Perth: Curtin Business School, Curtin University of Technology.

Clanchy, J. and Ballard, B. (1995) Generic skills in the context of higher education, *Higher Education Research and Development* **14**: 155—66.

Curtin University of Technology (1998) Preparing Curtin Business School graduates for successful employment: an integrated approach to developing professional skills. Application for a 1998 CUTSD National Teaching Development Grant (Organisational).

Dochy, F.J.R.C. and McDowell, L. (1997) Introduction: assessment as a tool for learning, *Studies in Educational Evaluation* **23**(4): 279—98.

Guthrie, B. (1994) *Graduate Labour Market Survey*. Report for DEET. Canberra: Australian Government Publishing Service.

Gallagher, J.J. (1994) Teaching and learning: new models, *Annual Review of Psychology* **45**: 171—95.

Hadwin, A.F. and Winne, P.H. (1996) Study strategies have meager support: a review with recommendations for implementation, *Journal of Higher Education* **67**(6): 1—17.

Harvey, L. (1993a) *Employer Satisfaction: Interim Report*. Coventry: Quality in Higher Education, University of Warwick.

Harvey, L. (ed.) (1993b) *Employer Views of Higher Education*. Proceedings of the Second QHE 24-Hour Seminar. Birmingham: University of Central England.

Hattie, J., Biggs, J. and Purdie, N. (1996) Effects of learning skills interventions on student learning: a meta-analysis, *Review of Educational Research* **66**(2): 99—136.

Institute of Chartered Accountants in Australia (1994) *Chartered Accountants in the 21st Century* Sydney: Author.

Johnson, T. (1998) *The 1997 Course Experience Questionnaire*. A report prepared for the Graduate Careers Council of Australia, Parkville, Graduate Careers Council of Australia Ltd.

Kember, D. (1998) Teaching beliefs and their impact on students' approach to learning. In B. Dart and G. Boulton-Lewis (eds), *Teaching and Learning in Higher Education* (1—25). Camberwell, Victoria: ACER Press.

Kember, D. and Gow, L. (1994) Orientations to teaching and their effect on the quality of student learning, *Journal of Higher Education* **65**(1).

Mayer, E. (1992) *Putting General Education to Work: The Key Competencies Report*. The Australian Education Council and Ministers for Vocational Education. Canberra: Australian Government Publishing Service.

Murray, H.G. and Renaud, R.D. (1995) Disciplinary differences in classroom teaching behaviors. In N. Hativa and M. Marincovich (eds), *Disciplinary Differences in Teaching and Learning: Implications for Practice* (pp. 31—9). San Francisco: Jossey-Bass.

O'Brien, T. (1997) Life after college: employment, further education, lifestyle for recent grads, *AAHE Bulletin* **50** 7—10.

Pajares, F. (1992) Teachers' beliefs and educational research: cleaning up a messy concept, *Review of Educational Research* **62** 307—32.

Prosser, M. and Trigwell, K. (1999) *Understanding Learning and Teaching*. Buckingham: SRHE and Open University Press.

Rosenman, L. (1996) *The Broadening of University Education: An Analysis of Entry Restructuring and Curriculum Change Options*. Evaluations and Investigations Report 96/12. Canberra: Australian Government Publishing Service.

Smart, J.C. and Ethington, C.A. (1995) Disciplinary and institutional differences in undergraduate education goals. In N. Hativa and M. Marincovich (eds), *Disciplinary Differences in Teaching and Learning: Implications for Practice*, 49—57. San Francisco: Jossey-Bass.

Speck, B.W. (1998) Unveiling some of the mystery of professional judgement in classroom assessment. In R.S. Anderson and B.W. Speck (eds), *Changing the Way We Grade Student Performance: Classroom Assessment and the New Learning Paradigm*, 17—31. San Francisco: Jossey-Bass.

The Association of Graduate Recruiters (1995) *Skills for graduates in the 21st Century*. Cambridge: Author.

Trigwell, K. and Prosser, M. (1996) Congruence between intention and strategy in university science teachers' approaches to teaching, *Higher Education* **32**: 77—87.

Weinstein, C. (1987) Fostering learning autonomy through the use of learning strategies, *Journal of Reading* **30**(7): 590—5.

21 Traditional teaching of music and dance as a generic model for education

Mo Dodson

London Guildhall University

This chapter is part of an ongoing research project that involves the study of the techniques of 'traditional' dance teachers. The question of what constitutes traditional dance, however, is extraordinarily vexed. As a category it can include anything from the High Courtly Dancing of ancient kingdoms to the dances of small gatherer hunting societies who have no experience of class differentials, in the Marxist sense of the word, nor any concept of High Art (in opposition to folk or Low Art). Social scientists amuse themselves, when they feel bored enough to resort to such easy work, by pointing out the difficulties inherent in a 'category' like traditional that includes such a wide range of phenomena (for instance Mary Douglas in *Natural Symbols*). However, there are distinctions that can be made between traditional and non-traditional forms of culture and society (see for instance, Stocking, 1968; Gellner, 1988; Berman, 1982). As a preliminary to the main argument, we would suggest that the following might be a useful, if slightly idiosyncratic, working definition of traditional dance.

Traditional in this context could be used to refer to those practices that are transmitted primarily in the form of an 'oral culture' in the sense of oral culture established by J. Goody, W. Ong and other authors. Oral in this context does not mean what it seems to mean. Oral cultures emphatically use all the senses and channels of communication available to humans who do not use writing and, in particular, powerful combinations of speech, song, instrumental music, gesture, movement, dance, and visual signs and symbols. This raises a number of problems. Many ancient 'traditional' societies were literate, and would therefore be excluded from the category of 'oral cultures'. We would contend, however that important elements of their culture were passed on in a way that was structurally in the form that oral cultures use (Dodson, 1996; Dodson and Monaghan, 1995). Not until the late seventeenth century in Europe do we witness a substantive transition to non-traditional forms of cultural transmission in many of the arts (including dance, the visual arts, grooming and dress, music). We realize that this definition creates problems. To lump together the open-minded flexibility of some so-called primitive (gatherer hunting/small band) societies with the rigidly fixed nature of other traditional societies (see, for instance, Turnbull 1961 and Douglas, 1970) is dangerous to our argument in two senses.

First, the practices are sometimes very different in terms of the way in which culture is transmitted: this requires a justification for lumping them together under one category. Secondly, these practices are sometimes extraordinarily punitive and cruel especially in the more rigidly fixed societies; we would not be advocating the use of these punitive teaching strategies. What is it, therefore, in the traditional techniques that can be said to be common to all of them, within the context of our argument?

We would suggest the following:

1. A sense of familial or personal connectedness to the tradition that is unbroken, and by implication a sense that this tradition lives on in the bodies of those who are being taught that tradition.
2. Learning by imitation of an accomplished practitioner. This is important in the context of modern primary and secondary education. In modern schools, teachers of a discipline often posses a problematic relationship to competence in that discipline: teachers very rarely engage in the real practice of the discipline they teach, whether that be in humanities, the sciences, sports, or the arts. Teachers of, for instance, history are not typically practising historians; and the same applies to almost all of the disciplines taught in schools. The situation is of course complicated. A maths teacher must be able to do the calculations that the students practise; a language teacher must be able to speak and write the language they are teaching, and so on. Very few of these teachers, however, have the opportunity to engage in the research, professional or creative activities that would allow them to call themselves practitioners of the discipline they are teaching. This is encapsulated in the caricature: 'Those who can, do; those who cannot, teach; and those who cannot teach, teach teachers.' This is indeed a caricature, but it is uncomfortably near the bone, and it is now becoming more and more applicable to tertiary education as well, as that sector enlarges its audience and subject range to include vocational courses taught by lecturers who no longer, if they ever did, practise the professions that they teach.
3. A specific type of encouragement from the teacher. The traditional teacher assumes that the learner will reach a real and appropriate competence in the tradition as a normal part of the learner's human development, a human development that is part of the birthright of the learner, and of all the potential learners of this tradition. Again, there is often a very different assumption working in modern education at every level. In modern education it is assumed that most students up to secondary level will not become professionally competent in the disciplines they are being taught. The assumption is that most of the population is excluded from professional practice of these disciplines by lack of relative or absolute talent or ability, including the very teachers themselves (by this we mean that in some instances a learner may be able to achieve a minimum competence in a field - e.g. sports - but will be excluded from professional practice of that skill because of the competition; whereas in other instances, the assumption is that the learner has not even the minimum ability to achieve competence - e.g. is unmusical, physically uncoordinated, mentally challenged in maths etc.).

If universities are there to produce research and scholarly knowledge, then the same assumption applies to university students: most of them will not be competent to do research by the end of their undergraduate studies. Even worse, a substantial minority will not even succeed in acquiring the core skills that education is supposed to guarantee for students; reading, writing, numeracy and use of information technology. Academics expect failure as a normal and indeed often a necessary result of their work. Failure to fail students indicates slipping academic standards. Even worse, academics very rarely take any blame for failing to bring the majority of their students up to research standards of work - most students are, according to the ideology of academia, incapable, of this. Thus, academia puts most of its students in the double bind of coming to university to learn, but the teachers have already assumed that most of them will not be able to learn the most important thing that goes on in universities - research and scholarship. In effect, most students are there to provide funding for the academics, and end up learning lower level skills looked down on by most academics. As Jules Henry says in *Culture Against Man*, 'in our culture one must learn to dream of failure' (Henry, 1963 p.27).

4. The teaching assumes that the learner will be part of a powerful and well defined collective in two senses:

(a) First, the tradition has been, is, and will be practised by large numbers of people in well-defined and frequently repeated forms. These recognizable patterns are organized in a way that is similar to natural language in that the patterns and organization seem to obey rules that are known/felt by all those in the tradition as generating meaning in some sense of the word. Threshold competence is recognized by all those who practise the tradition, and there is little disagreement about this. Those who are outstanding are also easily recognized, and there is little disagreement about this. In practising the tradition, any single practitioner is guaranteed a place in the present and temporal community of practitioners of this tradition, and the criteria for achieving competence are clear to all those in this collective. The analogy with language is here important. Much of the above could be used to describe non-traditional art forms such as avant-garde art, but if we keep in mind the way in which a language community operates, it will be clear that a speaker of a language recognizes competent speech in a very different way than an appreciator of modem avant-garde 'art' often fails to recognize any hard and fast distinction between competence and incompetence in that 'art' form; the numerous hoaxes perpetrated on so-called expert critics is quick proof of this. The failure of the 'expert' interpreters of avant-garde art to arrive at any consensus as to what is competent, good, meaningful is a longer story, but one worth telling if the audience has the time. In language, however, competence cannot be faked. Our argument is that, as with language competence, competence in traditional dance and music cannot be faked either.

(b) Secondly, the form is practised in groups, or at least in contexts that imply the possibility of a group of participant observers, with emphasis being placed in a variable way on the participant or observer status of the practitioners depending on the context of performance. Again, this is very different from the assumptions that often guide us in modern education. Here the individual is expected to produce 'work' that is different from anything that has been produced before or contemporaneously. With some notable exceptions, if work is produced in groups. and/or if the work resembles other work produced, then it is accused of plagiarisms, cheating or lack of originality, and is normally failed.

I once challenged a group of art students to behave as if they were practising a traditional form of art and to ensure that they all painted in the same representational style using the same iconography. The students were amused, but declined the challenge as they realized that they would all receive low grades for lack of originality and other similar crimes against the ideology of the creative individual.

I make a claim here to be in a kind of oral/traditional continuity with my teachers that is not entirely unlike that which I have been describing above. I have learnt traditional dance and music from teachers who were themselves extraordinarily competent practitioners of their art, even though my own skills here remain largely latent (but better latent than never, as we used to say in the 1960s!). The theory that I learnt from these teachers has, however, been a most powerful influence on me, as these teachers were themselves also theorists of some importance. One of my teachers has already died and another is now suffering the many ills that all flesh is heir to. I am still learning from them and from a man whom I never met - John Blacking, who died only relatively recently. Blacking taught my Ph.D.

supervisors, John Baily and Andrée Grau, who are both not only anthropologists of some distinction but also, respectively, accomplished musician and dancer. Their teaching is informed by many of the principles I have described above, partly because, I think, of their practice of music/dance. They also feel, I believe, that there is a kind of physical continuity between what they are doing and what they learnt from Blacking. This sense of physical continuity that is of course much more then 'physical' is also part and parcel of the heart of Blacking's theory of the nature of dance itself (see Blacking, 1977; Dodson, 1993).

In a paper published in 1942/3 that should be resuscitated for its many insights, Margaret Mead writes:

> Perhaps the most striking [difference between our concept of education today and that of any contemporary primitive society] is the shift from the need for an individual to learn something which everybody he [sic] would wish to know, to the will of some individual to teach something which it is not agreed that anyone has the desire to know.

She goes on to comment on the way in which this traditional form of transmitting skills and knowledge was able to hold a focus on the 'desirability of learning' as opposed to that of 'teaching': 'the master did not go seeking pupils; the pupils ... went to seek the master'. In a further logical pirouette, Mead highlights the way in which the need to teach (convert) is part of a wider cultural insecurity: 'active proselytising was [it might be found] the necessary condition of the preservation of the essential belief in one's own revelation ... [and thus] education becomes the concern of those that teach rather than those who learn'.

Andrée Grau has a beautiful example of the consequences of this movement from learning to teaching among a group of her friends from whom she has learnt much, the Tiwi of northern Australia. When Tiwi youngsters and youth live among their family and clan, they are reasonably well behaved, and learn the traditional arts and skills with no difficulty, and they learn them in the act of doing them. A dance for a deceased relative, for example, is learnt in the doing of it until they reach adulthood and their skill is fully accomplished. Recently schools for 'aborigines', originally a movement instigated by the white authorities, have been attempting to help the Tiwi to preserve their culture, and so there is a compulsory traditional dance class, taught by an elder who is especially brought in. In the school environment, these well-behaved and quick-to-learn Tiwi youngsters become recalcitrant and naughty school children who rebel against their teachers, resisting being taught even dance and music which in their home camp they would find it enjoyable to learn. Andrée Grau herself has danced with the Tiwi to learn their dances as well as having recorded and studied their dances with full-blooded scholarly techniques, from choreology and ethnographic cinematography to kinship analysis.

Many of these lessons are hard to apply in a social context which is very different from that of the relatively homogenous and self-sufficient cultures of traditional societies. Most of all it is difficult to imagine the possibility of a consensus among us about what it is desirable to learn. The extraordinary variety of ideologies and value systems of our professional teachers alone is mind boggling, and must in part explain the blandness of much of what is passed off as curriculum development: in order not to offend each other, we stick to a conventional middle of-the-road approach, tweaking at the edges of the delivery methods rather than striking at the core of the substantive content, which must embody the relation between learner and teacher at the deepest ontological level.

The implications for education in general of what I have learnt so far include the following:

- the relation between the learner and the teacher must be voluntary at the deepest level possible;
- because up to secondary level, education is compulsory in a variety of ways, there is already a backlog of problems that we face when our students arrive at the doors of academe;
- the teacher must have a sense of their own relation to a tradition of knowledge or skills that is both vigorous and relaxedly confident: they must be masters or mistresses of their art;
- the form that the teaching takes is not important in its surface details, and to focus on teaching techniques as separate from the tradition of skills and knowledge that the student wants to learn is at best a *temporary* moment for self-reflection;
- but the teacher must be willing to change what they do radically in order to ensure that their relationship to the student is preserved as one of voluntary and benign transmission of important skills and knowledge;
- the teacher is above all one who provides examples of the art to which the student can aspire and which can be imitated;
- the immediate problem here is that most teachers and students have radically different views as to what should be imitated out of desire (as Raymond Williams said, what we have to do in the Modern age is to learn, all of us, to educate our desires);
- therefore, unless the teachers can be seen to be capable of re-educating their own desires, the students will not have an example of this to emulate (I do not mean that us wrinklies should try to recapture our own misspent youth by learning to go clubbing - re-education would here mean the relearning of new approaches to our subject, and to our way of relating to the world in general, in order to include the experiences of our students as important);
- it is here that traditional cultural forms often have much to teach us, as they are capable of extraordinary flexibility and receptivity to innovation while preserving a continuity with what is valuable from the past see for instance the traditional in a Modern form, the street dances of the twentieth century, and in particular the African American dances that include both the Authentic Jazz Dance and the Latin American dances - these dances showed both extraordinary innovation while preserving amazingly robust continuities with the past.

Note:

This chapter is an adaptation of a paper that was co-authored by Terry Monaghan (co-founder of the Jiving Lindy Hoppers) and myself for the conference 'Continents in Movement' held in Portugal in October 1999. As Terry has not had a chance to edit what I have rewritten and added, I dare not impose responsibility for whatever mistakes I have made on his shoulders, but I will say that the core of this paper derives from what he and I originally wrote and that much of the research that I rely on is that which Terry has collected and analysed himself, or that which he has put me into contact with.

References

Berman, M. (1982) *All That Is Solid Melts into Air*, London: Verso.

Blacking, J. (1995) *Music, Culture, Experience: Selected Papers of John Blacking*, ed. Reginald Byron, Chicago: University of Chicago Press.

Czakanowska, A. (1994) unpublished paper read at Goldsmith's College.

Dodson, M. (1996) *Design and Aesthetics*, London: Routledge.

Dodson, M. and Grau, A. (1993) Dancing, *British Journal of Ethnomusicology* **2**, 166—9.

Dodson, M. and Monaghan, T. (1995) Taxonomies of dance and powers of exclusion: the case of Jazz Dance. In *Border Tensions: Dance and Discourse*, Guildford: Surrey University.

Dodson, M. and Monaghan, T. (1996) unpublished paper read at CORD Conference, University of Illinois, 26 April, 'Modernism and African-American Dance'.

Douglas, M. (1970) *Natural Symbols*, London: Barrie and Radliff.

Gellner, E. (1988) *Plough, Sword and Book*, London: Collins and Harvill.

Goody, J. (1986) *The Logic of Writing and the Organisation of Society*, Cambridge: Cambridge University Press

Grau, A. (1999) unpublished paper given at Goldsmith's College.

Henry, J. (1963) *Culture Against Man*, New York: Random House.

Howe, M. (1995) *Shades of the Dancing English*, London: The Terrace
Trust.

Mead, M. (1942/3) Our educational emphases in primitive perspective, *American Journal of Sociology* **48**: 633—9; reprinted in Keddie, N. (ed.) (1973) *Tinker Tailor: The Myth of Cultural Deprivation*, London: Penguin Education.

Ong, W.J. (1982) *Orality and Literacy*, London: Methuen.

Quirey, B. et al. (1976, 1987) *May I Have the Pleasure?*, London: British Broadcasting Corporation (recently republished by Dance Books, London).

Stocking, G.W. (1968) *Race, Culture and Evolution*, Toronto: The Free Press

Turnbull, C. (1961) *The Forest People*, London: Chatto & Windus.

22 Do development interventions shape conceptions of teaching in Art and Design?

Linda Drew

London Institute (London College of Fashion and Chelsea College of Art and Design)

22.1 Introduction

A body of research has developed around lecturers' conceptions of teaching; although not as broadly explored as the research into students' conceptions of (and approaches to) learning. Studies have differed in approach, as have the contexts, some compare conceptions held by different discipline groups of lecturers. This chapter concerns itself with discerning Art and Design lecturers' conceptions of teaching in the discipline. The group of staff who are the focus of the study had just completed a two-year Institutional educational development activity leading to SEDA (Staff and Educational Development Association) accreditation. The overall aim is to establish a situated application of teachers' conceptions and to measure data against an existing model (Kember, 1998). A further aim of the study is to explore influences or shaping factors in the formation of those conceptions in order to evaluate the impact of educational development interventions as well as other aspects of the teachers' experiences. Staff in the study often referred to their *beliefs*; this term is considered generally interchangeable with the more commonly used term, *conceptions* of teaching.

> Conceptions are specific meanings attached to phenomena which then mediate our response to situations involving those phenomena. We form conceptions of virtually every aspect of our perceived world, and in so doing, use those abstract representations to delimit something from, and relate it to, other aspects of our world. In effect, we view the world through the lenses of our conceptions, interpreting and acting in accordance with our understanding of the world. (Pratt, 1992, p. 204)

Teaching conceptions have been shown to be related to approaches to teaching, which, in turn, affect students' approaches to learning and the quality of student learning outcomes (Trigwell, Prosser and Waterhouse, 1999). If a link can be established between educational development activities and the formation of a student-centred / learning oriented conception of teaching, then the role of those activities cannot be underestimated in the pursuit of enhancing the quality of student learning outcomes.

> Measures to enhance the quality of teaching should take account of teaching conceptions if they are to be effective, as teaching approaches are strongly influenced by the underlying beliefs of the teacher. (Kember, 1998)

22.2 Research on beliefs and conceptions of teaching

Earlier research studies exist on teachers' conceptions in schools (Pajares, 1992) and many of the findings bear relevance to the higher education context, but all school teachers have to undergo specific training and development for the teaching role and often do not have such a focused discipline based identity as in higher education. Kember (1998) produces a comparative review of all research into conceptions of teaching in higher education which describes the work of others in creating models for categorizing conceptions. The categorizations identified broadly fall between an ordered set of qualitatively differing conceptions and a nested hierarchy of conceptions. A significant number of studies adopt a phenomenographic approach, in which a limited number of categories emerge describing the subjects' perception of a phenomenon (e.g. Trigwell *et al.*, 1994, 1996, 1999). Some studies went on to develop quantitative instruments (Gow and Kember, 1993) but in the main a grounded approach is adopted to analyse the data aiming for categories to emerge (Glaser and Strauss, 1967). The categories as defined in many of these studies bear many similarities in use and in choice of terminology; some studies describe the categories as a 'spectrum' with two ends (Prosser *et al.*, 1994), or as a 'continuum' of categories of conceptions (Samuelowicz and Bain, 1992). It is as a result of this study that I have chosen to adopt Kember's model to position the subjects along the spectrum of conceptions of teaching (Figure 22.1).

> The model posits two broad higher level orientations labelled teacher-centred / content-oriented and student-centred / learning oriented. Subordinate to each orientation are two conceptions. The boundary between each pair of conceptions is shown as diffuse, implying a relatively easy development across each pair. Transitions between the two orientations are envisaged as requiring a more significant change. A fifth intermediate conception, in which teacher-student interaction is first recognised as necessary, is included as a transitionary bridge between the two orientations and their subordinate conceptions.

In the main, of the studies reviewed, largely non-UK universities were chosen due to the location of many active educational developers and researchers in Australian and Far East universities, where measures to evaluate and enhance the quality of student learning and of teaching have been embedded for considerably longer in HE practice. In these studies the influence of development activities in the formation of beliefs and conceptions is not formally addressed; one paper reviewed by Kember (Martin and Ramsden, 1992) reports outcomes of a one-year course for tertiary teachers and monitors their changing conceptions over time, clearly showing that during the course lecturers change their conceptions of teaching; they conclude that for conceptual change to take effect, a higher education development activity should take place over at least one year.

Teaching context or discipline frameworks are another area that the literature suggests can influence teachers' conceptions of teaching. One such study did begin to categorize conceptions from two broadly different discipline areas, the sciences and social sciences, however no conclusions could be drawn from the findings that bear a direct relevance to either teaching context or discipline frameworks for teaching and learning (Samuelowicz and Bain, 1992). The work of Prosser *et al.* concentrates on empirical studies of science teachers (physics and chemistry), and as such they are clear in conveying that although some findings will have generalizable applications, in the main the findings may only be pertinent to science teaching.

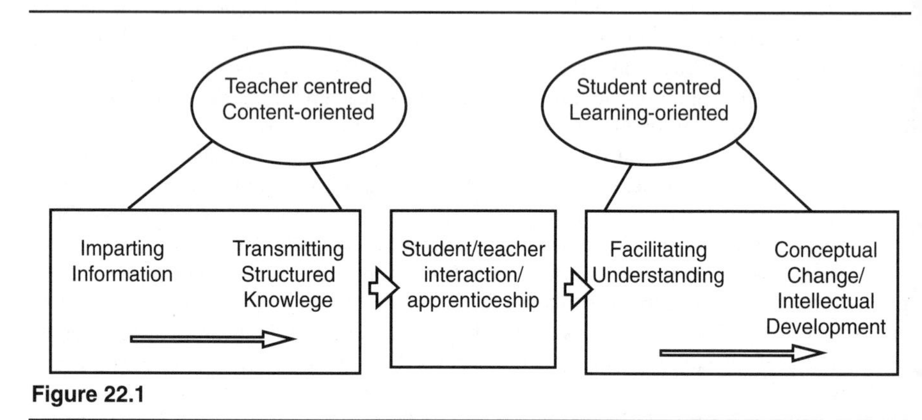

Figure 22.1

22.3 Methodology

Given that methods used in previous studies of conceptions vary in complexity and approach, mainly using semi-structured interview techniques to construct empirical data, I felt the need initially to use a method which would elicit lecturers' own constructs, using their own terms about teaching and learning. Some other studies have used specific instruments to measure approaches to teaching (Prosser and Trigwell, 1999) which offered some scope, but are bound in a particular vocabulary of teaching and learning which may not mesh well with Art and Design lecturers' conceptions of teaching. Art and Design as a discipline area, although it can be said to have a knowledge base, is often constructed from the practice itself and is a therefore a prime example of situated cognition. Lecturers in this discipline area when asked about their practice will often refer you to their exhibiting, curating or design consultancy work rather than to their teaching practice, which some see as a nested part of their identities as creative practitioners. The objective of this research is to measure art and design lecturers' conceptions of teaching against a model (Kember, 1998) and to explore further the influences on the formation of those conceptions.

22.3.1 Repertory grids

Seven art and design lecturers from across a broad spectrum of specialisms (fine art — sculpture, design studies, fashion design, graphic design, make-up styling, product design) were brought together to explore their constructs using a repertory grid method. The repertory grid method is derived from Kelly's (1955) Personal Construct Theory, and it aims to identify personally meaningful distinctions with which a view of the world is constructed. This seemed highly appropriate given that a stated aim of the research was to situate the conceptions of art and design lecturers, this method would allow for any range of personally constructed language or way of conceiving of something. The subjects were all participants in a two-year SEDA programme at the London Institute, and teaching at its constituent colleges. Small groups were formed and, in turn, each member of the group acted as the research subject. The subject first lists teaching methods used or preferred for their teaching practice. For some subjects this process was very brief; some displayed a broad repertoire of preferred teaching methods. The methods described are then written on cards and the subject goes through an *elicitation* procedure. Three cards are chosen at random (this is known as a *triad*) and the subject is asked to say what is the most important attribute that distinguishes the two most similar methods in the triad from the third 'outlying' method. For example, studio and sample room encourage independent learning. This *discriminating construct* is then recorded by another member of the group. The subject is also asked to provide an *opposing construct* (if they can) to define further what the distinguishing attributes are. For example, if the discriminating construct was 'encourages independent learning', the subject might offer 'dependent on tutor involvement and guidance'. The opposing construct, where defined, is recorded too. The subjects continue eliciting constructs about their teaching methods until no new constructs emerge. The subjects then go through a *rating grid* procedure; on the top row of the grid the teaching methods are written across the columns and the discriminating constructs are recorded in the left-hand column. The subject ranks each teaching method recorded against each construct on a scale of 1 to 5, 1 being a low and 5 being the highest correspondence between method and construct. For example, if the discriminating construct is 'encourages independent learning', then studio practice could be ranked at 5 and lecture method could be ranked at 1.

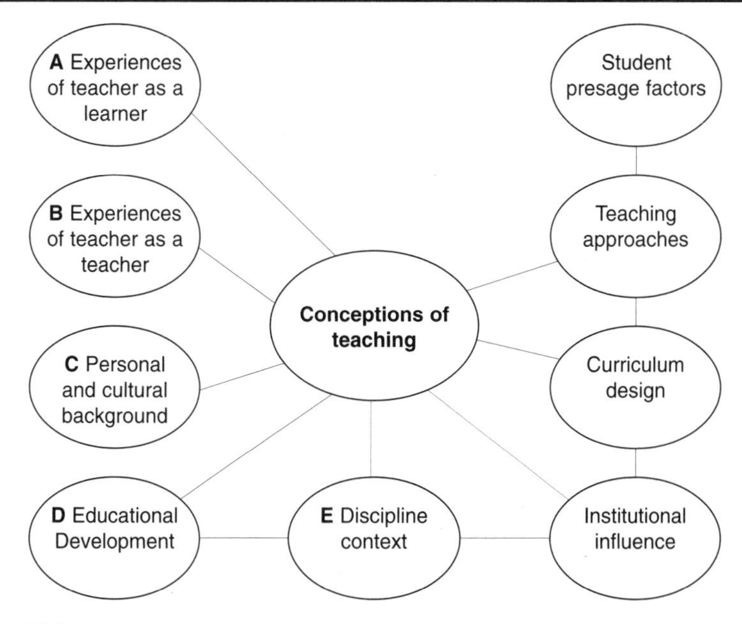

Figure 22.2

22.3.2 Interviews

Three of the original subjects were followed up with individual interviews. Following a desire to reflect the subjects' situated understanding of their conceptions and related practice, a 'storytelling' approach was encouraged. The subjects were asked to relate how they felt their beliefs or conceptions of teaching were formed or shaped. The three interviews lasted between one half and one and a half hours each. The interview tapes were transcribed and rigorously analysed. A constant comparative method of analysis was used (Glaser and Strauss, 1967). The verbatim transcripts were read and re-read and any emerging categories of influences on conceptions were noted. When an emerging category of influence was provisionally identified it was compared to an established one, especially to see where it varied significantly. For example, if the meaning rather than the choice of language used actually differed. This process continued until no new categories of influence

Constructs	**Method 1** Model workshop	**Method 2** Portfolio construction	**Method 3** Assessment crit	**Method 4** Library research	**Method 5** Interview for prior learning	**Method 6** Reflective practice
Encourages a student to collect or collate information	2	5	5	5	3	1
Enables student to reflect on learning	3	4	3	2	3	5
Encourages learner feedback	4	1	5	2	2	1
Gives evidence of students' prior learning, experience or skills	4	5	5	4	5	5

Table 22.1

emerged. Using this method four main categories of influence and one adjunct category were identified and these categories were used to code the original transcripts. A model of these categories and their interplay with conceptions and approaches to teaching was also devised to illustrate the relationships (Figure 22.2).

22.4 The findings and discussion

For the repertory grid analysis, as there was a small group of subjects, each one shall be described separately. Because the subjects were working in groups to elicit constructs, there is evidence of a shared use of language to express those constructs. None of the sets of data enables the subject to be neatly placed along Kember's spectrum of conceptions. It is of course possible for someone who displays a student-centred conception for the most part also to demonstrate teacher-centred conceptions sometimes according to context. This was certainly an emerging factor in the work of Samuelowicz and Bain (1992). The two groups

Constructs	**Method 1 Design workshop**	**Method 2** Portfolio construction	**Method 3** Assessment crit	**Method 4** Library research
Encourages a student to collect information	2	5	5	5
Enables student to reflect on learning	3	4	3	2
Encourages learner feedback (oral or written)	4	1	5	2
Evidencing students' prior experience or skills	4	5	5	4

Table 22.2

of research subjects, although using broadly similar terms to describe the different attributes, tended to articulate a varied range of teaching and learning methods, which did not include lecture or seminar as the art and design discipline concentrates on learning through practice.

Constructs	**Method 1** Model workshop	**Method 2** Portfolio construction	**Method 3** Assessment crit	**Method 4** Resource based learning	**Method 6** Reflective feedback session
Encourages a student to collect and/or collate information	2	5	5	5	1
Enables student to reflect on learning	3	4	3	2	5
Encourages learner feedback	4	1	5	2	5
Gives evidence of students' prior experience and/or skills	4	5	5	4	5

Table 22.3

This subject (Table 22.1) uses a variety of student-centred approaches, if there is an acceptance that in an assessment crit there is an interaction between student/teacher and student/student to balance peer and tutor assessment feedback. All of the constructs define the methods in terms of learning outcomes for the learner or learner activity. The highest ranked method in student-centred learning is the assessment crit. As this subject evidently values prior learning experience and reflection on practice as part of the teaching repertoire, it could be said that they demonstrate a student-centred/learning oriented conception of

Constructs	**Method 1** Studio teaching	**Method 2** Tutorial (with portfolio)	**Method 3** Group crits	**Method 4** Reflective journal	**Method 6** Self assessment
Encourages group based learning	5	1	5	1	1
Promotes active learning	5	1	5	3	3
Encourages practical activity	5	5	3	1	2
Encourages personal reflection	2	5	5	5	5

Table 22.4

teaching with the emphasis on conceptual change and intellectual development of the learner.

This subject (Table 22.2) has a narrower range of teaching methods but professes to demonstrate similar constructs about teaching and learning. The highest ranked method in student-centred learning is Assessment crit. As this subject does not include reflection or other conceptual tools which are also student-centred it is more likely that they demonstrate a student-centred/learning oriented conception of teaching with the emphasis on facilitating understanding.

Constructs	**Method 1** Reflective journal	**Method 2** Interviews/ primary research	**Method 3** Presentations	**Method 4** Library / secondary research
Encourages group based learning	1	2	5	1
Promotes active learning	3	1	5	5
Encourages practical activity	1	1	5	1
Encourages personal reflection	5	5	5	1

Table 22.5

This subject (Table 22.3) has a broad student-centred repertoire and also demonstrates a similarly defined set of constructs, all of which define the methods in terms of learning outcomes for the learner or learner activity. The highest ranked methods in student-centred learning are reflective practice and assessment crit. As this subject evidently values reflection on practice as part of the teaching repertoire in an interactive mode, it could be said that they demonstrate a student-centred/learning oriented conception of teaching with the emphasis on conceptual change and intellectual development of the learner.

Constructs	**Method 1** Design projects	**Method 2** Portfolio construction	**Method 3** Self assessment	**Method 4** Group crits	**Method 6** Reflective journal
Encourages group based learning	5	1	1	5	1
Promotes active learning	5	1	3	1	3
Encourages practical activity	5	5	2	3	1
Encourages personal reflection	2	5	5	5	5

Table 22.6

It is interesting to note that this subject (Table 22.4) ranks studio-based teaching and group crits highest as a studio-based practitioner, but still places a value on the place of self-assessment and reflective practice as part of the role of the critical reflective practitioner. The groups' construct of *encourages practical activity* was further defined by the recorded opposing construct which was *encourages a theoretical position*, which can explain why the reflective journal would be an ideal place for underpinning theory rather than practical

Constructs	**Method 1** Styling workshop	**Method 2** Portfolio construction	**Method 3** Work placement	**Method 4** Course assessment
Encourages group based learning	5	1	5	3
Promotes active learning	5	1	1	3
Encourages practical activity	5	5	5	2
Encourages personal reflection	2	5	5	4

Table 22.7

activity. This combination of articulation of student-centred activity and reflection indicates a conception of teaching which is student-centred/learning-oriented through conceptual change/intellectual development.

This subject (Table 22.5) has an interesting range of methods, ranking presentations the highest in relation to the constructs. Research based, and therefore student directed, methods are also included in this grid which, although not ranked high by the subject, make an appearance alongside reflective journal. This subject could be either placed with the central conception, transitional in nature, of student/teacher interaction/apprenticeship, or along the spectrum toward a student-centred/learning oriented conception characterized as facilitating understanding.

This subject (Table 22.6) is an active design practitioner, and places the highest ranking on the use of design projects, but also uses group crits and portfolio construction. The reflective activity is present if not ranked particularly highly. This mix of student-centred activity and reflection indicates a conception of teaching which is student-centred/learning-oriented through facilitating understanding.

This subject (Table 22.7) regards the relevance of the workplace in learning so highly that, alongside styling workshop, it is the highest ranked 'method'. This implies a conception where teaching is believed to be preparation for a particular profession or skill, therefore the subject engages with the conception of interaction/apprenticeship and has not included any aspect of reflection or critical engagement in the repertoire.

The majority of subjects demonstrated a student-centred conception of teaching, with at least one also demonstrating features of the transitional conception of student/teacher interaction/apprenticeship. All of the subjects were asked if they would agree to be interviewed for the second stage of the research about influences on formation of conceptions. Three were pursued who each took a different position on Kembers' model of conceptions (Subjects 1, 6 and 7) and were therefore likely to provide data which was both varied and, for the size of the original study, as valid as possible in this context.

22.5 Influences on conceptions of teaching (Figure 22.2)

The analysis of the interviews highlighted a number of distinct categories of influence for the teachers interviewed. The influence of the discipline context was not prominent in their descriptions of how they conceptualized or approached their teaching. Given that all seven subjects teach in a similar area this result is expected, however it is of interest that the proportions describing student-oriented conceptions are much greater than the proportions of science teachers who describe this conception (Trigwell and Prosser, 1996).

The findings are consistent with research in the school sector (Pajares, 1992), but there is not much equivalent evidence in Higher Education.

> little in the research literature to explain how staff acquire and develop their conceptions of teaching. It is clear, from psychological research findings, that such conceptions will be established from a succession of experiences which build up into a particular view of what teaching involves and how it affects learning. (Walker and Entwistle, 1999)

22.5.1 Influence A: Experiences of teaching — as a learner

Earlier experiences of learning and the learning context, especially when they were recently experienced, seem to influence the teachers' formation of conceptions. The nature of the experience in this case was a positive one. This teacher had come to teaching design after completing a Masters degree in Design.

> ...my MA very much, especially design processes and research based projects, and putting more of a research input into design-based projects. That is fed into my teaching very much, especially getting students involved in a project from day one. They can understand it from the beginning and be absolutely involved in it. You can develop the research angle of it and not just restrict it to students going to the library.

When the experience of learning is a negative one, the influence is reactive in the sense that the teacher is looking to counteract or anticipate that for her own learners.

> What sticks with me very much is my memory of my own teachers and some very bad practice; people yelling and shouting at you, especially as a dyslexic student I was led to believe that I would never make anything of myself and all that stuff which rather kinks the way I approach students.

The art and design discipline does encourage independent learning as part of an experiential approach to practice, but this can be interpreted differently as this excerpt implies. This teacher was influenced by the lack of support within the learning environment.

> As a BA student I would say lack of teaching, certainly not student-centred learning. Their idea was great, yeah, fantastic, off you go — do that, come back in a few weeks' time with the project. When I am working now I am quite conscious that I try to kind of over-compensate and get really, really involved and go 'oh wow' with the student's work. That is what I would say about my degree course.

The experience of learning characterized in this influence is equally shaped by good experiences, which can be emulated and aspired to, and bad experiences, which are consciously not reproduced for the teachers' learners.

> Most of my personal experience has been formative in the shaping of my beliefs. Mainly best and worst practice — tutors I have got nothing from. I would hate the idea of wasting a student's time and I hate the idea of leaving something or someone completely turned off.

22.5.2 Influence B : Experiences of teaching — as a teacher

With this influence, teachers can build a knowledge base by reflecting on experiences and becoming aware of the various demands on there role, shifting from a content focus to an enabling role. Teachers' reflection on this experience is dependent on their acquisition of a technical language and a knowledge base with which it is contextualized. The teachers interviewed did not use the language of the researcher, or indeed of pedagogy, but were aware (in some cases) of specific terminology relevant to their practice of teaching. The other noticeable factor in this influence was the ability to express how experience had helped the teacher to develop a strategic alertness to the relationships between teaching and learning, this enables teachers to build learning opportunities from chance events, remarks and incidents. In other words, their experience influences their ability to use reflection to highlight instantly a possible action by 'thinking on your feet'.

The ability to discuss the experience of teaching is a very important part of this influence, whether as part of an educational development support structure, or in the staff room informally. For this reason peer observation of teaching could also be included in this influence.

> The ability to think about how I am teaching and why I am doing it, and the ability to understand how other people see me. Things like being able to expose your teaching to other people, having space in which to do it.

This teacher uses reflection on her earlier teaching experiences to realize that she has shifted her conception from a teacher-centred conception to a student-centred conception. The range of excerpts illustrate how she stages her view of that influence, in the beginning she had an instinct to transfer knowledge to the student, which she now calls spoonfeeding, and now she encourages students to self-develop by guiding them.

> All I had in the beginning was an instinct about transferring knowledge. I call that naive teaching.
>
> I was influenced by previous teaching and learning methods. Going away from that I thought I'll repeat that, improve it and if I didn't like them — I will avoid that.
>
> I look at other practitioners and my own self development and my own practice so then I realized students need to be encouraged, offered support and guidance. I will be helpful to them if I allow them to self develop by guiding them.
>
> I reflected on students saying what was good and what wasn't. What worked and what didn't, but I didn't reflect only on this — I was being such a spoon feeder. The students they never took any responsibilities.

The strategic alertness to situation is present and gives the teacher the ability to improvise with confidence, this influence has given her conceptions some points of reference, not fixed in each case, but which act as a conceptual toolbox.

> In a way what I do is to remove myself from the picture. When you are teaching you are very much in action so you have to programme a lot and experience gives you the ability to improvise. You have to look at the whole course, the Handbook integrated with the other subjects of the course. You have to look at the context and the values then you get the whole picture, then you can be flexible.

22.5.3 Influence C: Personal and cultural background

There was more tacit evidence for this influence, those interviewed coming from a diverse range of personal and cultural backgrounds. It can be acknowledged that this influence may not be as clearly voiced as it may not present as an obvious source.

Evidence that some teachers have had learning difficulties themselves.

> as a dyslexic student I was led to believe that I would never make anything of myself.

Evidence that some teachers have had negative experiences of learning.

> A lot of people in my environment (teaching design) don't have a successful experience of the school environment.

Evidence that some teachers come from different cultural backgrounds where received interpretations of teaching, and the role of teaching, mean that although afforded respect, the teachers are expected to conform to a particularly formal style of engagement and with little variation across all teachers. This could be illlustrated here.

> Some of the learning was by watching other people, many other people and they would observe how other people do it and they will just copy the action.

22.5.4 Influence D : Educational development

Initially it seemed possible that this could be the central influence, but on balance, and with reference to all the data, it is no more influential than the teachers' recent experiences of teaching and learning. The way in which educational development is viewed however, is most interesting, it also seemed feasible that teachers could react to specific development interventions, and in doing so incorporate changes to their conceptions of and approaches to teaching. The teachers did not see it this way and indeed saw the educational development activity as an holistic event, something which had affected them in all it's parts, not in any small isolated incidents. This influence also incorporates the notion, linked to the experience of teaching : as a teacher, that the educational development can inculcate the teacher into the language of learning and teaching. In engaging with the educational development activity, the teacher becomes a learner also and uniquely sees what it is their own students are experiencing with a new focus.

> teachers mould experiences for their students with the aim of bringing about learning, and the essential feature is that *the teacher takes the part of the learner*, sees the experience through the learner's eyes, becomes aware of the experience through the learner's awareness. (Marton and Booth, 1997)

> ...things like SEDA. It is really relevant in lots of different little ways, it affects lots of things all over — and the way you think. It is this thing about reflecting on your practice that is really important because it is really difficult to get into how the way you are doing that but once you start doing it you can get in and understand what you are doing from both angles. You can see yourself as a student which can be really difficult to handle.

> When I was at (XXX University) I had to do a teaching and learning course which was very odd because I don't think anybody knew exactly what it was they were looking for and it had in it all the things we look at in SEDA and was relevant to teaching but I don't think anybody looked at it. I hated doing it at the time but now I think about it I have the ability to think about my teaching and how I am doing it.

> SEDA offered new aspects of teaching for me, how people learn and why people learn.

> Being able to have the language to talk about your teaching and therefore to be able to operate on that level. And you feel sort of a bit of an outsider before you can do that, but there is a language — oooh err — there is a language.

> I have to be careful about the criteria because it's dangerous to assess based on personal opinion. I would always refer to the criteria. That was because I had to write about a project and when I came to SEDA I learnt that a project is more than just techniques, it includes a level of creativity based on parameters from low to high, otherwise it would go into personal opinion. Look at the work, look at the criteria, what should they be learning?

22.5.5 Influence E: Discipline context

The discipline context was present in all that the teachers talked about, but specifically, there were few mentions that this was the main (if any) influence in the teachers' practice in teaching art and design. Because the discipline context is a genuine part of the educational development activity and is also a major institutional factor, this influence is considered valid but adjunct to the other influences. It is most likely to be expressed as a contextual influence in tandem with another, e.g. educational development.

> We were at that session the other day and (he) talked about deep and surface learning and I was really interested with that because the crit assessment methodology I believe encourages surface thinking. If you are used to doing presentations, this is a little bit different to doing good designs. You can do a good sketch but it is not necessarily going to be a good product. You have got to realize its limitations. What's the crit going to do? A slick illustration can often carry more weight than the finished design concept. This could do with some challenging. This can also limit the scope of good design, not just the scope of good design teaching.

> The teaching I do — I like doing. It is more, well — less chalk and talk, what's it called? An enabler? — but I'm already teaching practitioners so I am talking to people and it already triggers off ideas. Not so much creative links in talking with them, more like creative bridges. It is not a miraculous process. I think art and design ideas can be firmly linked. It is a creative act based on hard work. I'll have a methodology up my sleeve but if the student says ... mmm ... I want to do it like this then yeah, as long as they view it as a learning process I am happy to go with that. I see teaching as a design process.

Figure 22.2 summarizes the relations between these five influences on conceptions of

22.6 Conclusion

While there has been some substantial research into university teachers' conceptions and approaches to teaching, there is still little work to date on the development and formation of those conceptions as previously discussed. From the interviews conducted for this study at least four influences (A—D) on art/design teachers conceptions of teaching have been identified. There can be little doubt from the nature of the comments included above that educational development activities influence teachers' beliefs about teaching, but there is insufficient evidence from this study to suggest that changes between categories as broad as those described by Kember (1997) are brought about by such development activities. Changes of this magnitude are difficult to achieve, but making teachers aware of the possible influences may facilitate this process. The model of relationships between conceptions of teaching, teaching approaches and learning outcomes (Kember, 1997) is further developed (Figure 22.2) to include the influences and their interrelationship with conceptions and approaches to teaching, illustrating just how important awareness of these influences can be.

> awareness is arguably a necessary precondition for a qualitative change in conceptions to occur, given the symbiotic relationship between conceptions and experience. One has to become aware of the possible existence of conceptions to begin with, and their pivotal influence on experience and action ... (Walker and Entwistle, 1999).

Further studies may be necessary to illustrate these links from influences to conceptions of teaching, approaches to teaching and learning outcomes, but they would benefit the HE community given that educational development is more focused on improving student learning through teachers' awareness.

22.7 References

Glaser, B.G. and Strauss, A.L. (1967) *The Discovery of Grounded Theory*. Chicago: Aldine.

Gow, L. and Kember, D. (1993) Conceptions of teaching and their relationship to student learning, *British Journal of Educational Psychology* **63**, 20—33.

Kelly, G.A. (1955) *The Psychology Of Personal Constructs*. New York: Norton.

Kember, D. (1997) A reconceptualisation of the research into university academics' conceptions of teaching, *Learning and Instruction* **7**: 255—75.

Martin, E. and Ramsden, P. (1992) An expanding awareness: how lecturers change their understanding of teaching. Paper presented at the 1992 HERDSA Conference, Gippsland.

Marton, F. and Booth, S. (1997) *Learning and Awareness*. Mahwah, NJ: Lawrence Erlbaum.

Pajares, M.F. (1992) Teachers' beliefs and educational research: cleaning up a messy construct, *Review of Educational Research* **62**, 307—32.

Pratt, D. (1992) Conceptions of teaching, *Adult Education Quarterly* 42: 203—20

perspective, *Studies in Higher Education* **21**: 275—84.

Prosser, M. and Trigwell, K. (1999) *Understanding Learning and Teaching: The Experience of Higher Education*. Buckingham: SRHE/Open University Press.

Prosser, M., Trigwell, K. and Taylor, P. (1994) A phenomenographic study of academics' conceptions of science learning and teaching, *Learning and Instruction* **4**: 217—32.

Samuelowicz, K. and Bain, J.D. (1992) Conceptions of teaching held by academic teachers, *Higher Education* **24**: 93—111.

Trigwell, K. and Prosser, M. (1996) Changing approaches to teaching: a relational Trigwell, K., Prosser, M. and Taylor, P. (1994) Qualitative differences in approaches to teaching first year university science, *Higher Education* **27**: 75—84.

Trigwell, K., Prosser, M. and Waterhouse, F. (1999) Relations between teachers approaches to teaching and students' approach to learning *Higher Education* **37**: 57—70.

Walker, P. and Entwistle, N. (1999) Conceptions of teaching and levels of understanding: emerging structures and shifting awareness. In Rust, C. (ed.), *Improving Student Learning: Improving Student Learning Outcomes* (pp. 309—18). Oxford: Oxford Brookes University, Oxford Centre for Staff and Learning Development.

23 Modelling the student experience of studying mathematics

Malcolm G. Eley[1] **and Jan. H. F. Meyer**[2]

1. Centre for Higher Education Development, Monash University; 2. Centre for Learning, Teaching and Research in Higher Education, University of Durham

23.1 Overview

An ongoing project aimed at a more detailed description of student learning, specifically within the context of mathematics studies at tertiary level, is described. The project's intended outcome is the construction of a conceptual model, manifested in the development of two complementary inventories, designed to reflect variation in students' affective reactions and preferences relative to mathematics study, and in the learning processes employed in mathematics study.

The already developed *Experiences of Studying Mathematics Inventory* (ESMI) focuses on affective aspects. The five scales that comprise the ESMI are described, and the psychometric properties of the inventory are outlined. The potential uses of the ESMI in distinguishing among the motivations and preferences of different student cohorts are illustrated. The role of the inventory in diagnosis and inference is discussed.

The partially developed *Mathematics Study Processes Inventory* complements the ESMI. The initial generation of potential item stems, and their systematic culling and trialling is described. Analyses of trial responses suggest seven conceptually distinct scales. These scales are described, and some preliminary indication of their psychometric properties is given. The projected use of the inventory in detecting students potentially at risk of failure is illustrated.

23.2 Introduction

The modelling of student learning requires the description and isolation of dimensions of explanatory variation that exhibit some structural relationship with learning outcomes. Such modelling is not a new enterprise, with commonly considered dimensions being of two broad classes; those representing variation in the student's engagement with the learning materials, and those representing contextually determined variations that influence the student's willingness to commit to that engagement in a particular manner. Further, the relationship of commitment and context dimensions with learning outcomes is indirect, being via learning process dimensions (see Figure 23.1, adapted from Meyer, 1999; the depicted relationships represent general patterns of directional association that are not necessarily invariant across different contexts).

At the core of the first broad class, and indeed any model of student learning, are the specific cognitive processes evoked by students as they interact with particular learning material. Learning outcomes, the changes in students' knowledge and capabilities, are most directly a function of how students mentally operate on the detail of the material studied. However, less direct processing could also be involved (*meta capacities* in Figure 23.1). Students vary in their awareness of their immediate learning processes, in the strategic control consciously exercised over those processes (Iran-Nejad, 1990; DiVesta & Moreno, 1993), and in the broad management of their study activities generally.

The second broad class of dimensions is essentially about contextually associated commitment. Students do not learn in a vacuum. They have particular goals and interests. They have affective reactions and predilections related to content material. They react to the situations within which their learning occurs. They interpret the demands implied by how their courses are presented (Biggs, 1989; Eley, 1992). As much as learning outcomes might be a function of specific learning processes, if those processes are not evoked, and the student does not engage with the material, then the learning outcomes do not result. Variation in these contextually influenced dimensions seems to determine that necessary student commitment to engage and thus learn (*motivation* and *intention* in Figure 23.1).

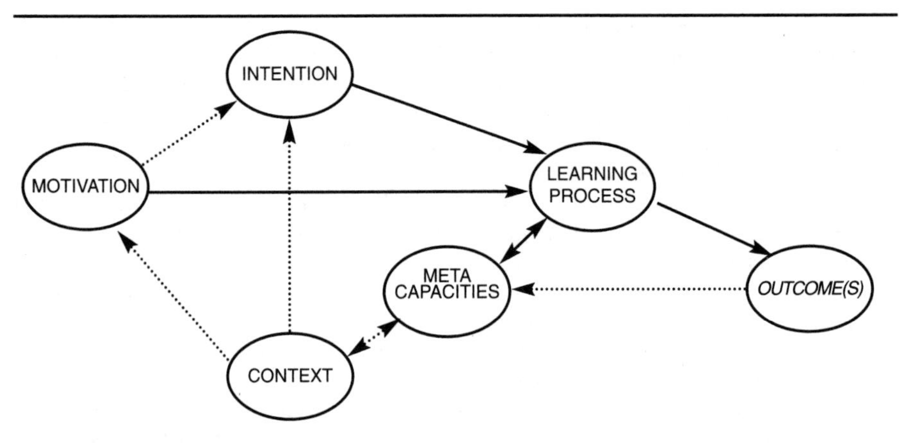

Fig. 23.1 A model of generic observables and some likely structural relationships

Much previously reported modelling of the student experience of learning has reflected these two broad dimensional classes (e.g. Biggs, 1987; Entwistle and Ramsden, 1983). The now classic distinction between 'deep' and 'surface' approaches is commonly described as comprising both a process component and a motivational or affective component. This modelling is operationalized in inventories such as the *Study Process Questionnaire* and the *Approaches to Study Inventory*. The application of these models is well established, and has led to much improved understanding of the learning of higher education students (e.g. Entwistle, Meyer and Tait, 1991; Entwistle and Waterston, 1988; Harper and Kember, 1989; Tait and Entwistle, 1996).

However, much of the student learning modelling to date has been general in its focus. The concern here is that the epistemology of a particular subject discipline might prompt learning process requirements, and affective and motivational reactions, that are peculiar to it. The specifics of any derived student learning model might vary dependent upon the subject discipline within which it was developed. This is more than a simple application of generally derived learning approach instruments within the context of a specific discipline. The point is that general models and their accompanying instruments are, simply because they are general, unable to reflect directly variation that is peculiar to a particular discipline. Models developed within the context of studying a particular discipline might be expected to enable diagnoses and inferences that are more targeted and discriminatory, and thus more practically useful to *teachers* in that discipline.

In the present work the intent has been to model student learning, but within the specific context of studying mathematics. The prime focus has been on the development of two complementary inventories, one targeting affective or commitment aspects of studying mathematics, and the other the cognitive processing aspects of what students actually do when they study mathematics. Together these inventories should provide measures that enable mathematics study to be more effectively modelled, and in a manner that is of more direct practical use to mathematics teachers. The first of these, the *Experiences of Studying Mathematics Inventory* (ESMI), is now developed, trialled, and validated (see Meyer and Eley, 1999). The second, the *Mathematics Study Processes Inventory* (MSPI), although well advanced, is nonetheless still under development. The present chapter describes both of these inventories, gives an indication of their respective psychometric characteristics, speculates on their potential complementary application, and discusses work in train.

23.3 Affect and preference: The *Experiences of Studying Mathematics Inventory*

The ESMI grew out of an interest in elaborating what seemed to be an affective dimension of variation peculiar to studying mathematics, namely a predilection for the manipulation and study of essentially mental constructs (Meyer and Parsons, 1996). Its development proceeded in research studies over a period of some four years, and the outcome is an inventory comprising five six-item component scales. These scales capture variation in the extent to which students find enjoyment in mathematics and its study (Enjoyment), see mathematical entities as objects of beauty (Beauty), prefer certainty and integrity in decision rules (Truth), prefer systematic, logical, and ordered approaches to study and problem-solving (Procedures), and engage in mathematically oriented recreation (Recreation).

The final version of the ESMI (see Appendix 23.1) was developed in four distinct trialling cycles, using the responses from samples of undergraduate mathematics students (ranging from approximately 300 to 1,400) in Australia, South Africa and Britain. Using a separate and subsequent sample of 969 undergraduates, the scale reliabilities of the final version were determined. Those reliabilities ranged from 0.71 to 0.89, and were consistently greater than related interscale correlations; indicating the scales to be both reliable and distinct. Using a further separate sample of 174 undergraduates, a confirmatory factor analysis established the robustness with which the underlying empirical structures conform to a five-dimensional conceptual model.

Following its development, the ESMI was field trialled to determine whether it could provide interpretable findings in applied contexts. Specifically, the trialling sought to determine whether first year students varied over the academic year in their levels of affect and preference as manifested in the ESMI scale scores, whether such variation was statistically associated with measured learning outcomes in mathematics, and whether such variation reflected the different mathematics study goals held by discernible student cohorts. Were the ESMI to prove incapable of detecting such variation, then its potential utility would be in serious doubt. This trialling required the administration of the ESMI to an entire first-year mathematics enrolment at both the beginning and end of an academic year, and the collection of mathematics marks matched to those two sets of ESMI scale scores. More than 1,100 first-year undergraduates were involved in this field trialling.

In summary, the ESMI performed well. There were significant score changes over the year on each of the five ESMI scales, and those changes were negative overall. ESMI scores did generally correlate positively with mean mathematics marks, and the lowest mark levels were associated with the largest drops in ESMI scores over the year. Interestingly however, the relationship of the ESMI scores to marks was not a simple linear one. The ESMI proved capable of identifying a group of students who performed well in their mathematics studies, but nonetheless exhibited ESMI scores more akin to low performing students. It was speculated that this group comprised students who were proficient in, but not motivationally committed to, mathematics study, or alternatively, students who performed well yet below their perceived capabilities and thus experienced disenchantment. Finally, the ESMI differentiated between groups of students defined by their enrolments. Engineering students and intending mathematics majors tended to evidence higher ESMI scores than students studying mathematics simply to satisfy minimum degree rule requirements, with intending majors actually showing negligible ESMI drops over the year. The ESMI clearly proved itself sensitive to conceptually interpretable variations in the context of mathematics studies. A full description of the ESMI's development and trialling is given in Meyer and Eley (1999).

23.4 The student's engagement: The *Mathematics Study Processes Inventory*

The ESMI operationalizes affective and aesthetic variation in the context of studying mathematics. However, as argued earlier, dimensions like preference and motivation influence learning outcomes only through the specific learning processes that they might prompt the student to evoke. Therefore, the ESMI needs to be complemented by operationalizations of variations in learning *processes*, but also focused specifically on mathematics study. The intent that general models of learning be applicable across a broad range of contexts necessarily constrains them to definition in terms of broad, global dimensions of variation. When that requirement for broad applicability is replaced by a focus on a particular study context, it becomes possible to develop learning models defined in terms of larger numbers of more specifically sited dimensions. It is more than a simple translation of 'deep' and 'surface' into the context here of mathematics study. Rather, it is that those singular, global constructs might be replaced by more numerous, more elaborated constructs, each related to distinguishable aspects of mathematics study. The resultant model could be defined in terms of more differentiated dimensions, and thus be capable of greater discrimination in describing students' learning processes.

There is another aspect to this argument. When they think about their students' learning processes, academic mathematicians are unlikely to do so in terms of the generic constructs of general models. Rather, they are more likely to speculate on how their students might respond in quite particular mathematical contexts. Indeed, much of the academic mathematician's thinking about student learning might be very tightly sited around the specific topics under current study. Much of this thinking might well be derived anecdotally from personal experience with students, or part of the folklore surrounding the study of mathematics, but it is almost certainly firmly embedded in mathematics. The more that a model's dimensions can be defined in mathematically sited ways, the more likely that those definitions will reflect academic mathematicians' accustomed ways of thinking about student learning, and that those mathematicians will find those dimensions interpretable and practically useful.

23.4.1 The initial item pool

The development of the *Mathematics Study Processes Inventory* (MSPI) began with the generation of potential item stems. This generation proceeded from a number of sources. First, in focus group interviews mathematics students ranging across undergraduate and postgraduate levels described their typical approaches to learning mathematics and solving presented mathematics problems, and how such approaches might have changed over the years or been influenced by different topic areas. The recorded responses were used to generate potential item stems.

Secondly, in the mathematics learning literature individuals more experienced and expert in mathematics have variously been found to approach problems on a schema or principled basis, to set themselves subgoals to guide their working, to monitor their progress during mathematical work, to spend relatively more time conceptualising than actually working problems through, to reflect explicitly on their problem approaches, more so than those of lesser experience and expertise (Cai, 1994; Garofalo and Lester, 1985; Bookman, 1993; Schoenfeld and Herrmann, 1982). Work on mathematicians' perceptions of mathematics has emphasized the importance of abstraction, of the application of systems of rules, and the modelling of reality (Mura, 1993; 1995). Such findings were also translated into item stems.

Thirdly, findings from the more general literature on learning could be translated into mathematical contexts. Considered was the work on surface versus deep approaches, that on procedural learning and practice effects (Anderson, 1982; Eley and Cameron, 1993; Kieras, 1988), and that recently indicating that apparently surface approaches can sometimes be a precursor to deeper understanding of complex material (Chalmers and Volet, 1997; Biggs, 1999). Finally, other generally oriented inventories (the *Study Process Questionnaire*, the *Approaches to Study Inventory*, and Weinstein's (1988) *Learning and Study Strategies Inventory*) were considered, with a view to translating non-specific items into particularly mathematics directed forms.

The result was a starting pool of some 136 potential item stems. An essentially editorial process of deletion and combination based on similarity and redundancy culled this initial pool down to 87 items for trialling.

23.4.2 Initial trialling and scale development

The resultant 87 items were random ordered, with item stems phrased as descriptions of things that students might do or experience as part of their studies. A five-point response scale asked students to indicate the extent to which an item described something that was true of their mathematics studies (ranging from 'recognize as immediately and consistently true' to 'not recognize as true at all'). Three versions of the inventory were used, each having the items in the same cyclical sequence but beginning with a different first item. This was to spread the potentially confounding effects of item order and fatigue.

This 87-item inventory was administered to 165 students at Monash University, Australia, and 741 at the Cape Technikon, South Africa. The Monash sample were all volunteers from the first year enrolment. The Cape sample was spread from first year (some 66%) through fourth year, with the inventories completed in class. The total sample was thus likely quite heterogeneous on approaches, goals, and experiences in mathematics study, and motivation to complete the inventory.

Exploratory factor analyses (Maximum Likelihood, Varimax) on the pooled responses from all students yielded four clear initial factors defined by 21, 20, 10, and 11 items respectively. Beginning with those loading highest on a factor, items were retained if they related well conceptually to the other loading items while yet being minimally redundant, if they loaded minimally on other factors, if their responses distributed approximately normally across the entire possible range, and if they contributed positively to overall scale reliability (Cronbach). From this sequential culling process the initial four factors suggested four well-defined 7-item scales.

The first scale seems to reflect variation in students' adoption of general, broad level metacognitive and strategic approaches to their mathematics studies (META). Illustrative items are 'I set myself goals related to the main overall parts of a problem, but I also break those down further into more specific subgoals' and 'I think back on the approaches that I have taken to a problem, to see if I can find alternative ways'. The second scale also seems to relate to strategic approaches, but now directed at specific procedural approaches taken in problem solution (PROC). Illustrative items are 'I will apply a general approach that I used in one topic area to other different topics' and 'When I learn some new mathematical procedure I attend just as much to the "when to use it" as to the "how to do it"'. The third scale seems to reflect variation in the use of real world applications, and in the adoption of particularly principle based approaches to those applications (REAL). Illustrative items are 'To decide whether two real world problems are similar I look at the mathematical principles or approaches used in their solution' and 'I need to reduce a real world problem to an underlying mathematical problem before I can decide which specific solution procedures to apply'. The fourth scale seems a counter to the others, reflecting variation in the adoption of inhibiting, surface oriented, non-purposive approaches (INHI). Illustrative items are 'I just substitute values into formulae and work them through without thinking too much about what the symbols represent' and 'I begin by applying anything that seems related to a problem in the hope that something will work'.

	META	PROC	REAL	INHI
N	859.0	861.0	862.0	866.0
Mean	22.05	26.07	21.40	21.48
Median	22.00	26.00	21.00	21.50
Std Deviation	4.66	3.82	4.83	4.61
Minimum	9.0	12.0	7.0	7.0
Maximum	35.0	35.0	35.0	34.0

Table 23.1 Distribution statistics for scale scores calculated on the first four scales to emerge from the initial item pool trialling

The psychometric characteristics of these four scales are summarized in Tables 23.1 and 23.2. Assigning point values of five (... consistently true ...) through to one (... not ... true at all ...) gives possible scale scores of 7 through to 35 with a mid-scale of 21. Scores for each scale show good spread across the possible range, and good normal approximation, especially for META, REAL and INHI (means and medians close to the mid-scale). That

PROC seems to show some positive linear translation along the scale (negative skewing) could be an artifact of the response scale definitions being set too hard at the minimal extreme and too soft at the maximal; this point is taken up in further trialling discussed later. The scale reliabilities show quite acceptable values, and each is clearly greater than any of the associated inter-scale correlations. That INHI correlates marginally negatively with each of the other three scales fits well with its conceptual alignment of reflecting non-metacognitive and non-strategic approaches. In summary, there seem strong grounds for claiming these first four scales as established. Although it may yet prove sensible to fine tune these scales further, their emergence from this initial trialling is very encouraging in modelling terms.

	META	PROC	REAL	INHI
META	**0.709** (859)†	0.429** (825)	0.480** (832)	-0.053 (832)
PROC		**0.643** (861)	0.344** (831)	-0.078* (832)
REAL			**0.757** (862)	-0.090** (836)
INHI				**0.644** (866)

** Significant at p<.01 (2 tailed); * significant at p<.05 (2 tailed); † N in parentheses

Table 23.2 Scale reliabilities (bold values on the diagonal) and between scale correlations for the first four scales to emerge from the initial item pool trialling

In the next analysis stage responses to 36 items that did not contribute to the initial four scales' derivation were factor analysed (Maximum Likelihood, Promax). Three further 'conceptually consistent groupings' of 12, 8 and 9 items, which seemed to have scale development potential, were indicated. Sequential culling of the first two of these groupings suggested two tentative 7-item scales. One of these seems to reflect establishing and maintaining a conceptual overview or mind image of a problem (OVER). Illustrative items are 'To understand a problem type, I see how the whole process develops as I work it through step by step', and 'As I work through the detailed steps of a problem, I also keep in mind its main overall parts or stages'. The second scale seems to reflect the use of examples specifically to develop a more conceptual understanding of a problem type or topic (EXMP). Illustrative items here are 'I think through worked examples in order to develop a more general understanding of a topic' and 'I work through lots of examples to make it easier to use bigger steps in solving similar problems'.

	OVER	EXMP	ROTE
N	136	136	245
Mean	23.26	23.75	21.16
Median	24.00	24.00	21.00
Std. Deviation	4.83	5.42	4.83
Minimum	10	9	8
Maximum	35	35	33
Scale reliability	0.781	0.830	0.705
OVER-EXMP correlation	0.489		

Table 23.3 Scale reliabilities and distribution statistics on scale scores for scales OVER and EXMP, and ROTE, derived from responses in separate follow-up triallings

These two tentative scales were administered to a new sample of 136 volunteer Monash first- year students. In consideration of the possible influences mentioned previously, the response scale definitions used here were modified. For example, the minimal extreme 'not ... true at all' became 'very rarely true', and the maximal extreme 'very commonly do' became 'always or almost always do'. A factor analysis (Maximum Likelihood, Promax) of responses showed a perfect match between posited scales and primary loadings in a two-factor solution. The reliabilities of both scales proved to be relatively high, and unambiguously greater than the between scale correlation (see Table 23.3). Further, scale scores showed good spreads and approximations to normal, even though there was yet some positive translation away from the mid-scale. Clearly, this subsequent trialling provides strong indication for a further two 7-item scales.

For the third 'suggested grouping', the common theme seemed to be a non-thinking approach to learning and to the use of examples (ROTE). The items referred to learning things by simple repetition, to solving problems by the direct copying of steps from worked examples, and to a reliance on rote memorization as a means of learning problem solution procedures. Eight of the items were rephrased to tighten their focus on this apparent theme. The nine resultant items, again with modified response definitions, were subsequently administered to a new sample of 245 volunteer first-year students at the University of Cape Town, South Africa. Factor analyses and scale reliability analyses of the responses were used to derive a single 7-item scale. Illustrative items are 'I work on problems or exercises by copying the steps from other examples of the same sort' and 'I learn problems and proofs by just going over the steps until I know them off by heart'. From Table 23.3 it seems that the more focused phrasings together with the modified scale definitions resulted in good scale reliability, and in a distribution of scale scores that sits centrally on the mid-scale. A seventh 7-item scale can now be claimed as well indicated.

23.4.3 A speculative diagnostic usage scenario

There seem three prime uses for a *Mathematics Study Processes Inventory* (MSPI). First, it could be used as a research instrument. If they prove predictive of mathematics learning, then scale scores could be used in testing for relationships with student study experiences and background, and with teaching and curricular variables. Second, the MSPI could provide class profiles that could inform teachers of approaches to mathematics study that might be expected of those classes. But perhaps most important, the MSPI could be used to detect early those students at risk of failure. Students scoring minimally on META, PROC, REAL, OVER and EXMP, and coincidentally at the maximal extremes on INHI and ROTE, might be expected to experience considerable difficulty in their studies. Once detected such students could, for example, be targeted for special tutorial attention. If complemented by minimal ESMI scale scores, such detection could be of high diagnostic validity.

To illustrate, two classes from the Cape Technikon sample seemed to present something of a contrast. Class X scored generally lower than Class Y on META, PROC, and REAL, but higher on INHI. When simple proportions of students above and below mid-scales are considered, majorities of Class X students scored above the mid-scale for INHI but below for REAL compared to the reverse for Class Y, and there were no Class Y students below mid-scale for PROC. These two classes would be very different to teach. In overall terms, Class Y seems clearly oriented towards 'deep' approaches, and Class X towards 'surface'. However, expressed in terms of these MSPI scales these characterizations are much more elaborated, and reference experiences peculiar to mathematics. From the items comprising the MSPI scales the teachers would have direct indications of specific mathematically oriented processes likely (or not) to be adopted.

To illustrate the use of scale scores on an individual basis, three particular Class X students combined high INHI scores with middling or low scores on each of META,PROC and REAL. If the INHI scale reflects variation on unthinking, compartmentalized, non-purposive and surface oriented approaches to study and problem solving, then these students' large INHI scores could indicate potential study disadvantage, especially when combined with lower scores on the more positively cast META, PROC and REAL scales. The teacher of these Class X students could well use these 'extreme' combination patterns as a means of detecting these 'at risk' students, enabling early, targeted intervention. In comparison, no Class Y students showed this same 'at risk' pattern. Instead, two students showed an 'opposite' pattern of high scores on each of META, PROC and REAL combined with low scores on INHI; they would be very different individuals indeed.

23.5 Conclusions

The base intent in the present work is to model student learning specifically in higher education mathematics, in a more differentiated and elaborated fashion than is possible through the application of general models. Five scales reflecting affective sources of variation have been successfully defined, and validated in field trials. These five scales together comprise the ESMI, and provide indications of students' experiences of enjoyment in their mathematics studies, of their perceptions of mathematical constructs as beauty objects, of their preferences for truth rules, and for problem solving approaches, and of their engagement in mathematically oriented recreation.

Considerable progress has been made in developing process oriented scales to complement the ESMI. Seven such scales can now be taken as established, or at least strongly indicated. These seven seem to represent variation in students' tendencies to be generally metacognitive and reflective, to be deliberately strategic in their problem approaches, to be principle based in their interpretation of real-world applications, to develop conceptual overviews or mind models when solving problems, to use examples specifically to derive deeper understandings of topics and, in a contrary direction, to adopt surface-oriented, short-term approaches, and to rely on rote repetition and mindless copying of procedural steps. Following further work in scale fine tuning and field testing, a seven-scale MSPI is expected to result.

The eventual outcome will then be some 12 defined scales, manifested as two validated inventories. Those scales will be capable of detecting dimensional variation both in the processes of learning mathematics and in the affective and aesthetic components of that experience. Those scales will enable fuller, more detailed modelling of the student experience generally and more elaborated characterizations of defined groups or classes, and diagnostically will allow individual students at real risk of study failure to be detected from combined patterns of both ESMI and MSPI scale scores known to be predictive of poor mathematics performance, especially at the extremes.

A further expected outcome, perhaps incidental but also important, is that the ESMI and MSPI might have broader utility. Interpreting how the study approaches indicated by general inventories such as the *SPQ* and the *ASI* might manifest in a specific subject requires familiarity with their underlying learning models. But subject teachers' understandings of educational constructs are often undifferentiated, and derived from personal and practical experience with teaching those subjects, rather than from theoretical study. For many of these teachers the need to interpret general model scores relative to their own discipline is too big a jump, and can constitute a disincentive to the use of such general inventories. However, the ESMI and the MSPI have been developed within the specific context of mathematics study. Their component scales are defined in terms sited in mathematics. For the mathematics teacher, no intermediate interpretation from the general to the specific should be needed. The expectation is that the ESMI and the MSPI will thus be both practically useful to and usable by the mathematics teacher.

Acknowledgements

The authors wish to acknowledge Professor Philip Parsons, Director of the Teaching Development Unit, Cape Technikon, Professor John Webb, Department of Mathematics and Applied Mathematics, University of Cape Town, and Dr Pam Norton, Department of Mathematics and Statistics, Monash University, for their interest in the present work, and for their valuable practical assistance in gaining access to samples of students.

23.6 References

Anderson, J.R. (1982) Acquisition of cognitive skill, *Psychological Review* **(89)**: 369—406.

Biggs, J.B. (1987) *Student Approaches to Learning and Studying*. Melbourne: Australian Council for Educational Research.

Biggs, J.B. (1989) Approaches to the enhancement of tertiary teaching, *Higher Education Research and Development* **8**, 7—25.

Biggs, J.B. (1999) *Teaching for Quality Learning at University*. Buckingham: Open University Press.

Bookman, J. (1993) An expert novice study of metacognitive behavior in four types of mathematics problems, *Primus* **3**, 284—314.

Cai, J. (1994) A protocol-analytic study of metacognition in mathematical problem solving. *Mathematics Education Research Journal* **6**, 166—83.

Chalmers, D. and Volet, S. (1997) Common misconceptions about students from south-east Asia studying in Australia, *Higher Education Research and Development* **16**, 87—98.

DiVesta, F.J. and Moreno, V. (1993) Cognitive control functions of study activities: a compensation model, *Contemporary Educational Psychology* **18**, 47—65.

Eley, M.G. (1992) Differential adoption of study approaches within individual students, *Higher Education* **23**, 231—54.

Eley, M.G. and Cameron, N. (1993) Proficiency in the explanation of procedures: a test of the intuitive understanding of teachers of undergraduate mathematics, *Higher Education* **26**, 355—86.

Entwistle, N.J., Meyer, J.H.F. and Tait, H. (1991) Student failure: disintegrated patterns of study strategies and perceptions of the learning environment, *Higher Education* **21**: 249—61.

Entwistle, N.J. and Ramsden, P. (1983) *Understanding Student Learning*. London: Croom Helm.

Entwistle, N.J. and Waterston, S. (1988) Approaches to studying and levels of processing in university students, *British Journal of Educational Psychology* **58**, 258—65.

Garofalo, J. and Lester, F.K. (1985) Metacognition, cognitive monitoring, and mathematical performance. *Journal for Research in Mathematics Education* **16**(3): 163—76.

Harper, G. and Kember, D. (1989) Interpretation of factor analyses from the Approaches to Studying Inventory, *British Journal of Educational Psychology* **59**: 66—74.

Iran-Nejad, A. (1990) Active and dynamic self-regulation of learning processes, *Review of Educational Research* **60**: 573—602.
Kieras, D.E. (1988) Towards a practical GOMS model methodology for user interface design. In M. Helander (ed.), *Handbook of Human-Computer Interaction*. Amsterdam: Elsevier, pp. 135—57.
Meyer, J.H.F. (1999) Assessing outcomes in terms of 'hidden' observables. In C. Rust (ed.), *Improving Student Learning; Improving Student Learning Outcomes*. Oxford: OCSD, Oxford Brookes University, pp. 25—37.
Meyer, J.H.F. and Eley, M.G. (1999) The development of affective subscales to reflect variation in students' experiences of studying mathematics in higher education, *Higher Education* **37**: 197—216.
Meyer, J.H.F. and Parsons, P. (1996) An exploration of student learning in mathematics, *International Journal of Mathematical Education in Science and Technology* **27**: 741—51.
Mura, R. (1993) Images of mathematics held by university teachers of mathematical sciences, *Educational Studies in Mathematics* **25**, 375—85.
Mura, R. (1995) images of mathematics held by university teachers of mathematics education, *Educational Studies in Mathematics* **28**: 385—99.
Schoenfeld, A.H. and Herrmann, D.J. (1982) Problem perception and knowledge structure in expert and novice mathematical problem solvers. *Journal of Experimental Psychology: Learning, Memory, and Cognition* **8**: 484—94.
Tait, H. and Entwistle, N.J. (1996) Identifying students at risk through ineffective study strategies, *Higher Education* **31**: 97—116.
Weinstein, C.E. (1988) Assessment and training of student learning strategies. In R.R. Schmeck (ed.), *Learning Strategies and Learning Styles*. New York: 1988, pp. 291—316.

Appendix 23.1 Experiences of studying mathematics

The purpose of this inventory is to gain an indication of your feelings and experiences in relation to your **present** studies in Mathematics.

The following are some comments that have been made by students of Mathematics about their study experiences. The comments are necessarily rather general, but each relates to a different aspect of studying to which we would like your personal reaction. We would like to know to what extent you agree or disagree with these comments, but in terms of **your** Mathematics studies specifically.

Answer each of Questions 1 to 30 using the following defined responses.

A = I **definitely agree**

B = I **agree**, but with **reservations**

C = I am **not sure**, or the comment **doesn't apply**

D = I **tend to disagree**

E = I **definitely disagree**

Read each comment **quickly**, and indicate your **immediate** reaction by marking the appropriate box on the accompanying Response Form. This is not a test and there are no 'right' or 'wrong' answers. We are simply interested in your own experiences and feelings about your present studies in Mathematics.

1 I spend a lot of my spare time thinking about mathematics.

2 I enjoy the rigour and precision of mathematics.

3 I try to understand new mathematical ideas by building on things that I already know.

4 I prefer topics where there are clear and well understood ways of judging whether an idea is good or true.

5 Some mathematical arguments or proofs are objects of real intellectual beauty.

6 I prefer problems that can be understood as direct applications of a set of underlying principles.

7 I get real enjoyment from what I see as the timelessness of mathematics.

8 The rigour and precision of mathematics is actually quite beautiful.

9 I try to start a problem's solution by deciding whether it belongs to a more general class of problems.

10 I attend talks and seminars on mathematical topics, out of general interest.

11 I study mathematics because I enjoy the intellectual challenge.

12 In my spare time I play games and do puzzles that have a mathematical flavour or basis to them.

13 When deciding how a problem might be solved I try to think through as many possibilities as I can.

14 Mathematics is a universal language of beauty.

15 I prefer learning things that I know are true, and will always be true.

16 I approach problems by trying to recall similar problems that I have successfully solved in the past.

17 I will sometimes tackle extra mathematical problems or exercises, just for fun.

18 There is a sense of beauty in how mathematical ideas can develop, and build on each other.

19 I prefer solving problems in which there is a well established procedure to follow.

20 I enjoy using the abstract concepts that are part of mathematics.

21 Much of mathematics is intellectually beautiful regardless of whether it can be applied in some way.

22 I enjoy making my mathematical proofs and solutions as elegant as I can.

23 I approach problems by trying to decide what principles or concepts might be applicable.

24 I read books about mathematics, for recreational purposes as well as study.

25 I prefer problems that can be fully solved by applying rational and logical analyses or approaches.

26 Studying mathematics is a source of real enjoyment.

27 I prefer those topics in mathematics where the knowledge essentially consists of logically derived truths.

28 I usually check whether my solutions or results fit with my broader knowledge of mathematics.

29 I like finding out about the lives of famous mathematicians.

30 I find the conceptual interrelatedness within mathematics to be intellectually beautiful.

Thank you very much for your assistance in completing this inventory.

Table 23.A1 ESMI scoring

The questions that define each of the scales are:

Enjoyment	2	7	11	20	22	26
Beauty	5	8	14	18	21	30
Truth	4	6	15	19	25	27
Procedures	3	9	13	16	23	28
Recreation	1	10	12	17	24	29

Score each question by assigning points according to:

A = 5 B = 4 C = 3 D = 2 E = 1

Scale scores are the sum of the point scores for the questions defining a scale.

Eley, M. G. & Meyer, J. H. F. Modeling the student experience of studying mathematics.

24 Developing epistemological pluralism through a web-based post-graduate science and mathematics education course

Robert Fox, Allan Herrmann and Peter Taylor
Curtin University, Western Australia

24.1 Introduction

The pedagogical practice in school-based science and mathematics is dominated by portraying the outcomes of past inquiry as standing freely outside human enquiry, as though their genesis were that of immaculate conception and their textual representation could be equated with knowledge *per se*. In reinforcing this image, *canonical epistemology* privileges the teacher's perspective and largely overlooks the learner's active involvement in making sense of their experiences of the phenomenological world impacting on their senses.

In this study, constructivism and feminism have been brought together to form a *connected epistemology* for a teacher education pedagogy that engages teachers of school science and mathematics in reflecting self-critically on their epistemological assumptions, valuing and taking account of the personal perspectives of their colleagues and expressing in writing their own thoughts and feelings within a computer mediated learning web-based environment.

This chapter reports on the two-year study, providing practical implications of this research for science and mathematics education with indicators of how the findings may be useful to teachers and students in other disciplines.

24.2 Research is a voyage of discovery with most of the time spent at sea

David Hamilton once said 'research is a voyage of discovery with most of the time spent at sea' (1992). Studying and using computer mediated communications (CMC) in distance education is also a voyage of discovery and as Bates indicates, this often requires a 'leap of faith' (1997) in the sense that we do not know nor can we predict how things will pan out in this environment: there are a multitude of varied, though interrelated factors playing significant roles in whether the 'outcome' and indeed the process is considered a success or a failure by individuals and by groups involved.

Nevertheless, in higher education, the Web has been heralded widely as a panacea for overcoming the traditional problems of delivery of distance education programs to geographically and socially isolated learners. The new technology has been touted as the ultimate means of speeding up the exchange of study materials between teachers and remote students, and also as an unparalleled provider of online interactive learning opportunities via bulletin boards, chat groups and email. But in the rush for universities to market Web-based teaching, the traditional teacher-centred approach of efficient delivery often prevail, leading to the use of the web as a convenience technology that allows the transfer of study materials, designed for print to online environments, producing 'Shovelware' (Hopper, 1999). Yet the new technology offers unique prospects for promoting collaborative learning (Stacey, 1998; Bates, 1997; Eastmond, 1995).

The significance of web-based university distance teaching and of research on web-based distance learning from a social constructivist perspective is well established in the current research literature (Blanton, Moorman and Trathern, 1998; Jonassen and Reeves, 1996; Owston, 1997). Of particular note are elaborate theories for using the Web to form learning networks (Harasim, Hiltz, Teles and Turoff, 1995) and non-linear cyberspatial environments (Kitchin, 1998).

Research has shown that online learning in higher education can be an advantage to students who are geographically or socially isolated or who need more flexible learning opportunities (Hipp, 1997; Owston, 1997). However, online learning also can present teachers and students with problems of connectivity and the challenge of establishing educative relationships via a new and somewhat restrictive medium of communication (Burge, 1994; Tolmie and Anderson, 1998). The following section of the paper offers an account of a two-year study in teaching science and mathematics, and raises some of the problems and findings in teaching and learning in an online environment.

24.3 Science and mathematics teaching of teachers

Peter is responsible for a postgraduate professional development unit for teachers in the distance mode. The main aim of this unit is to enable students to develop 'the ability to reflect critically on their beliefs and values as they struggle to make sense of new ideas that urge them to break with traditional teacher-centred approaches to teaching'. Peter wanted to adopt a critical pedagogy, which promotes communicative and critically insightful learning (Taylor, 1998). As Peter said:

> Our critical pedagogy aims to engage teachers with their colleagues in a discourse of possibility for transforming their professional practices; to stimulate teachers' critical awareness of restrictive cultural beliefs and assumptions, which blind many to the possibility of re-visioning their practice; and to inspire teachers to develop their own critical pedagogy.

As a teacher of this postgraduate unit Peter felt that he should model a teaching methodology which empowered his learners in the belief that the teachers participating on the course would then reflect this methodology in their own classrooms with their own learners. However Peter felt constrained and believed his students' learning was impeded by the intellectual and social isolation of distance learners. It was almost impossible to empower his learners within the constraints of the print medium of the unit, which he believed could only reinforce 'a passive and compliant learning style'. His students needed to be able to contact each other easily to discuss ideas and work through critical issues. He wanted to encourage students to collaborate with each other, by exchanging drafts of their assignments and he wanted to provide immediate feedback to students' work in their assignments. However, delays associated with the postal service restricted the number of possible exchanges he could make with his students and those they could make between themselves. Peter also found that phone contacts, instead of initiating reflective discussions, made it relatively easy for students to reject prematurely, the viability of new ideas that did not seem to fit comfortably with their own thoughts and practices. In effect Peter's desire to empower his students was thwarted by paper and distance.

The solution took the form of an online learning community developed by Peter and David (then a full time PhD student and tutor in the unit). Within this learning community the students and tutors could engage in public and private reflective discussions via the Internet. Students were given opportunities to: take part in public discussions with fellow students; send and receive private email communications between the tutor and students and from student to student; access study materials as well as links to computer-based services, including the library information and retrieval service and world-wide educational databases. This gave the students an opportunity to receive different points of view and time to digest and respond to the differing opinions on a more considered basis, and this improved the quality of ideas and opinions shared. The Web, and in particular, the discussion, resource and module sections, have become core components. Peter feels this shift in unit development and delivery has the potential to empower students participating in the unit and to position their 'knowledge at the heart of the learning process'.

The web site in 1996 for the Masters level curriculum unit, was designed to provide electronic access to the study materials, a *Discussion Room* and email for private correspondence. A series of (not-for-assessment) online discussion activities, related directly to three assignments (to be submitted individually) were developed, and it was hoped that students would find irresistible the opportunity to enrich their learning in this innovative 'high tech' manner. However, by the end of semester, and despite our enormous efforts to facilitate online dialogue, the results were disappointing (Taylor, 1998). Although the degree of online interaction among students varied widely, at the end of semester the log-file of the Discussion Room revealed an average of only ~3 messages per student.

For 1998, Peter decided to make the online discussion an assessable learning activity, worth 25 per cent of the overall grade (the remaining 75 per cent was allocated to the three assignments; in 1999, online discussion constituted 60 per cent of the unit's assessment). Within the Discussion Room, students were assigned to small groups and each student was required to post at least one online message in response to each of six sequential discussion activities, and to reply within their group to at least two other students' online messages. The tutors also prescribed assessment criteria for the quality of online dialogue, criteria that, they believed, would ensure the co-construction of a community of learners who learned collaboratively, compassionately and critically about their own curriculum-related beliefs, values and practices.

In contrast to the first year trials, almost 500 individual messages were posted during the 14-week teaching period; over 75 per cent of these originated from students. Averaging across the seven students, this represents an astonishing increase over the previous year. The tutors' messages account for an additional 21 per cent of postings and other students' messages account for the remaining 9 per cent (Stapleton *et al.*, 1999).

24.4 Reflections on what worked online

Students reflecting on their experiences in using CMC indicated that they had not previously felt part of a community of learners, using predominantly print-based materials and that the online environment had provided opportunities to: break feelings of isolation, communicate regularly with fellow students and, learn from each other. However, for the more isolated student who incurred higher Internet Service Provider (ISP) costs, he felt disadvantaged, as he could not afford the rate of online interaction he perceived he needed:

> Replying to the set activities and responding to follow up comments is hard enough at all times due to the financial constraint, let alone being able to surf happily and read everyone's opinions. I would love to jump online for an hour everyday to see what people have to say, and reply, but it is not possible, so I hope people can understand the situation for more isolated users. [Doug], DR, October 21, 1998 at 16:13:12:

For another student, Sally, another significant factor that restrained her participation was the occasional lack of opportunity to engage dialogically in some of the messages posted in the Discussion Room, a problem that she 'spoke about' in a very empathic manner to a student who was a very frequent online participator, Mari:

> [Mari] ... your postings were hard to respond to. You did sound like an expert and you didn't sound like you needed any input from me. For you the issue/idea was already resolved and no grey areas, which we could mutually explore, existed. You wrote really well and I envied your touch with words, but for you I felt I was useless. I do understand your sense of frustration when no one replied to you quickly as I'm very sure you put a lot of thought into your replies. You probably thought "@#$% ^*@ no one else puts as much work into this as me " and your probably right. [Sally], DR, October 28, 1998 at 14:45:50:

24.5 Online tutoring

In setting up the web environment, the tutors were unsure how best to use the online discussion forum to attain 'the pedagogic goals we had set ourselves'. The tutors valued student discourse from a social constructivist perspective; that students would construct their own knowledge, more effectively if they communicated with each other and with their tutors. But it was recognized that the online environment is a hybrid form of 'talking-by-text' combining some of the linearity of text with the interweaving of open and critical forms of conversation: in this sense, CMC is different and as such privileges a different and quite unique discourse (Geelan *et al.*, 1999). As one tutor pointed out:

> This is a very distinct and fertile environment. ... it requires a different way of working as a teacher and a different way of studying for students. ... We started not knowing how we would go about doing what we wanted — to get students involved in a rich discourse ... we weren't sure how best we could facilitate appropriate discussion ... not quite understanding the quality of that discussion or what it would require to keep it going. It's been very much a learning process for all involved — for the tutors and the students. Our experiences in particular incidents of discourse have provided us with new understandings and insights. Last year the richness of the discourse was limited in part this was due to the way we as tutors lead the discussions rather than stimulating and facilitating the discussions, I think we lead too strongly. ... this year we've done things differently and students have taken far more responsibility for the interactions online. ... students have a strong commitment and desire to participate in the discussions.

The sheer volume of interactions in second semester 1998, as David, one of the tutors pointed out 'compares very favourably to the 30 interactions in the entire unit in the earlier offering in 1997. This semester 60—80 interactions often followed any single discussion activity' and this was between seven students and two tutors. David felt the main reasons for this disparity were first, that students were required to post and interact online: this compulsory requirement constituted 25 per cent of the total semester mark for the unit. Secondly, the set activities during the semester required student responses. Thirdly, the various 'hot button' issues, topics that everyone wanted to comment on stimulated interaction. For example, one student raised the issue of whether classes should be streamed by ability and with students as practising teachers, all had a view to express.

24.6 Searching for a balance — moderating online

Searching for appropriate models in the use of CMC has been the focus of discussion and research for more than ten years, for example Mason and Kaye (1989) and Eastmond (1995) describe CMC offering new opportunities for dialogue and debate as well as offering a real sense of community and interaction, stimulating active learning. But getting the right balance in attaining the required levels of interaction is not easy. In the first year, the tutors encouraged students to participate by providing a model of how they hoped students would interact. Early discussions tended to be dominated by the tutors whereas in the second year, the students were dominant and lead informal open discussions. The tutors monitored these interactions and noted that students were forming mutually supportive groups. Student interactions were typified by: sharing and comparing ideas, providing feedback to each other's ideas, and searching for group solutions to issues. But there was little contestation and critical discourse between students. Peter outlines the open discussions were often along the lines of: 'This is what I think' ... 'What did you mean by that? Do you mean this?' ... 'Oh yes, sorry, I wasn't clear' variety. By critical discourse, Peter continues, 'I mean being critical of other people's standpoints, other readings, previous students' assignments posted online and being critical of themselves.' At this point in the semester, Peter was concerned that critical discourse was not occurring (Geelan *et al.*, 1999). Later he reflected that these open discussions were a necessary precursor to more critical discourse. To engage students in critical discourse, the tutors decided to role model a dialogical discourse — the intertwining of open and critical aspects of discourse in a friendly and supportive manner. In this way, the tutors had to select when to interject into the discussions and at what level should their input be made. Choosing an appropriate time, level and language to use was not straightforward and could not be successfully produced in any simple recipe style format.

24.7 Separate and connected knowing

Central to studying this unit were the terms separate and connected knowing and understanding. 'Separate knowing is characterised by an objective, critical and adversarial stance whereas connected knowing is based on empathy and a willingness to suspend judgement' (Dawson and Taylor, 1998). The tutors through dialogical discourse online aimed to help students enrich their world view, their rationality, epistemology and values. The aim of the tutors is to broaden and enrich students' experiences and the sense they make of their experiences as learners and as teachers, moving them toward an epistemological pluralism of constructed knowing, an integration of separate and connected ways knowing. The big question is how to create a truly pluralistic epistemology in the web-based environment and not simply to provide a forum for students to reinforce their extant standpoints.

Another member of the team was more sceptical about the possibilities and wonders whether students can embrace multiple epistemologies . and whether it is desirable in the first place, or ethical, since shifting how individuals think and learn 'can be very uncomfortable and destabilising', especially working in this 'sensory deprived environment, disconnected from the real world. ... There's something very disturbing about being so fundamentally challenged. ... The very basis of one's understanding of the world is questioned. ... It's like pulling the rug from under people's feet'.

Is this as one researcher pointed out 'the worst medium for communicating' complex and sophisticated discourse? Is trying to shift student's epistemological underpinnings just too big a task, especially at a distance using this very new, mostly unknown and very different way of communicating? Do the combination of new online learning environments and the aim to enrich students' ways of knowing just too radical and does it put students under too much pressure?

24.8 Time involvement and marking balances

Time involvement, both on the part of tutors and students in the online discussions was very high. The present combination of marked activity in the unit is 25 per cent Discussion Room interactions and tasks and 75 per cent written assignment. But since interactions have been and continue to be so rich and so time consuming, requiring more writing, thinking and reflecting than conventional print-based assignments, is this mix unfair and inappropriate?

Among the online class, there was a divergent range of expectations about the optimum amount of online student-student interaction. Although the tutors had set a minimum standard, they had, by default, left the students to decide a suitable upper level. Nearly everyone rose to this challenge by interacting well in excess of minimum requirements. But the intensity was problematic, especially for busy teachers with out-of-school and family commitments, and for those with less than adequate connectivity. Inexperience with online distance learning contributed to an inability by highly interactive students (with excellent connectivity and computing experience) to delimit their Discussion Room activity in the interests of other students. Towards the end of the semester, Peter recalls asking himself: 'Do I really want to teach this way if it involves so much more hard work than the traditional print-and-post mode?' 'Will I continue with this innovative teaching approach beyond the initial funding period?'

24.9 Conclusion

Working successfully in an online environment where tutors and students interact frequently and regularly is complex and requires participants to acquire many new and unique skills in writing conversationally and interacting carefully in a 'sensory deprived' communications environment. 'Knowledge evolves in dialogue.' When the dialogue fails or isn't progressing at appropriate levels then a stimulus is needed to guide learners into more productive ways of interacting. Four suggestions in considering productive online discussions are offered:

- Provide clear guidelines regarding the tutor's expectations of online interactions.
- Provide good reasons for students to engage online, in this case, allocating 25 per cent of the total marks for the unit to online interactions.

- Offer 'red button' topics that stimulate or inspire students to react and interact.
- Provide some input by tutors, assuring students that the tutor is reading and where necessary, participating in the discussions.

The description within this chapter has attempted to exemplify the pedagogical style of teaching, which we believe can be transferred to other disciplines, especially within a CMC environment.

24.10 References

Bates, A.W. (1997) The impact of technological change on open and distance learning, *Distance Education* **18**(1): 93—109.

Blanton, W.E., Moorman, G. and Trathern, W. (1998) Telecommunications and teacher education: a social constructivist review, *Review of Educational Research* **23**: 235—75.

Burge, E.J. (1994) Learning in computer conferenced contexts, the learner's perspective, *Journal of Distance Education* **9**(1): 19—43.

Dawson, V. and Taylor, P.C. (1998) Establishing open and critical discourses in the science classroom: reflecting on initial difficulties, *Research in Science Education* **28**(3): 317—36.

Dawson, V. (1998) SMEC 612 evaluation: connected knowing, unpublished report, Curtin University Perth, WA.

Eastmond, D.V. (1995) *Alone but Together: Adult Distance Study through Computer Conferencing*. New Jersey: Hampton Press.

Geelan, D.R., Taylor, P.C.S., Fox, B. Herrmann, A., Stapleton, A. and Dawson, V. (1999) Arcs, braids and webs: exploring constructed narratives in a web-based distance education unit. In K. Martin, N, Stanley, and N. Davison (eds), *Teaching in the Disciplines* (pp. 138—42), the University of Western Australia, Perth.

Hamilton, D. and Holly, M.L. (speakers) (1992) *Research Methodology*. (Cassette recording No. M1044). EdD901 Professional doctorate., Deakin University, Geelong, Victoria.

Hipp, H. (1997) Women studying at a distance: what do they need to succeed?, *Open Learning* **12**(2): 41—9.

Hopper, K. (1999) IT Forum Listserve discussions, ITFORUM@uga.cc.uga.edu.

Jonassen, D.H. and Reeves, T.C. (1996) Learning with technology: using computers as cognitive tools. In D. H. Jonassen (ed.), *Handbook of Research for Educational Communications and Technology (pp. 693—720). New York, NY: Macmillan Press.*

Mason, R. and Kaye, A. (eds) (1989) *Mindweave: Communication, Computers, and Distance.* Oxford: Pergamon Press.

Owston, R.D. (1997) The world wide web: a technology to enhance teaching and learning, *Educational Researcher* **26**(2): 27—33.

Stacey, E.A. (1998) Study of the enhancement of learning through group interaction by computer mediated communication, PhD dissertation (unpublished).

Stapleton, A., Taylor, P., Dawson, V., Geelan, D., Fox, R., Herrmann, A. and Parker, L. (1999) Analysing hypertextual discussion for connected knowing: units of analysis. In K. Martin, N, Stanley and N. Davison (eds), *Teaching in the Disciplines* (pp. 391—400), the University of Western Australia, Perth.

Taylor, P.C. (1998) Constructivism: value added. In K.G. Tobin and B.J. Fraser (eds), *The International Handbook of Science Education* (pp. 1111—23). Dordrecht, the Netherlands: Kluwer Academic Publishers.

Tolmie, A. and Anderson, T. (1998) Information technology and peer-based tutorials. *The Psychologist*, 381—4.

25 Reconciling pedagogies in interprofessional shared learning — exploration of the value of interprofessional learning strategies from the educators' perspective

Peter Funnell[1] and Melanie Jasper[2]

1. Suffolk College; 2. University of Portsmouth

25.1 Introduction

From the mid-1970s there has been a surge of interest in, and critical study of, interprofessional shared learning (IPSL) in health care and related areas of social welfare. In this context, shared learning may be identified as a means of promoting effective learning outcomes and securing value-added from structured learning interactions:

> A shared learning interaction brings together learners who would not otherwise meet in a structured learning context, and does so with the intention of enhancing learning outcomes. Usually such interactions are designed in recognition, or as a consequence, of contemporary occupational and employment behaviours which promote a holistic and non-fragmented quality response to market or service demands rather than one based on individual or occupational group specialisation. (Funnell, 1990, p. 151)

The current development of interest in IPSL may be tracked to the 1974 investigation into the tragic death of Maria Colwell, and to the painful recognition that insufficient attention had been given to interprofessional co-operation or the embedding of such co-operation into the pre- and post-qualificatory training of health and social welfare professionals. Subsequent developments in the service areas such as child protection and community care reaffirm this view.

The perceived significance of 'learning together' to facilitate 'working together' has been recognized and promulgated across a wide range of primary, secondary and community care provision both in policy and practice. In all cases the development of teaching and learning strategies to facilitate interprofessional shared learning, the creation of new and specific interprofessional undergraduate and post-graduate provision, and the establishment of national networks to promote and encourage interprofessionalism, have been based upon a set of assumptions about its value. However, evidence suggests that such assumptions may themselves be problematic. Indeed, underpinning such assumptions of value is often a failure, or unwillingness, to acknowledge that at the heart of discussion about shared learning lies a contradiction between professionalism (and a notion of professional autonomy in particular), and the pluralism which forms the ideological bedrock of shared learning (for a fuller discussion of these issues, see Funnell, 1995).

25.2 Research issues and methodology

Within this problematized context, this research activity has sought to gain a deep understanding of the rationale for, and implementation of, IPSL as identified by a sample of course leaders and external examiners of IPSL post-graduate programmes of study. The project was designed as the first of a developing series of research activities designed to elicit an understanding of the views of educationalists on the value of IPSL. The research adopted an action research approach with its underpinning principle of 'collaborative intent':

> Action research is a form of collective self-reflective enquiry undertaken by participants in social situations in order to improve the rationality and justice of their own social or educational practices, as well as their understanding of these practices and the situations in which these practices are carried out. (Kemmis and McTaggart, 1982, p. 5)

As such the research was explicitly embedding into a value system designed to promote and inform positive action.

A micro-ethnographic approach designed to allow the view of practitioners to emerge through peer discussion was employed. A facilitated conversation regarding the value of IPSL involving five experienced practitioners (course leaders and external examiners) held over a single day was audiotaped. The participants reviewed a transcript of the conversation and made additional comments, amendments and clarifications and these were added to the text. Permission was granted to use the resulting text as the basis for analysis and to draw out inferences about the perceived and identified value of IPSL.

Lines of enquiry remained open throughout the research activity. In particular, the precise nature and focus of the conversation was determined in situ. Specifically while the participants were clear about the purpose of the conversation only the general nature of the issues to be discussed were pre-determine. This was intended to support a naturalistic approach, one primarily determined by the interests, views and stories of the participants, rather than by pre-constructed research needs. Consequently the research acknowledges the explicit subjectivity within its findings. This acknowledgement is intended both to support the reader make judgements on the validity and reliability of the data and to allow the recorded statements of participants to 'speak for themselves'. As such while the analysis which follows does not support generalization it does provide a story which, put alongside other stories, may inform understanding. To quote Miller and Glasner:

> All we sociologists have are stories. Some come from other people, some from us, some from our interactions with others. What matters is to understand how and where the stories are produced, what sort of stories they are, and how we can put them to honest and intelligent use in theorising about social life (1997, p. 111)

25.3 Analysis: an overview

The conversation addressed four main themes. Much of the discussion addressed the issue of value and how such value might be evidenced through outcomes. While the value of learning from and with others has many facets, the barriers to IPSL were identified as diverse and numerous. However, the overwhelming conclusion from the participants was that there is definite value to be gained from different professionals sharing a learning environment. These are explored below through an expansion of the themes.

25.4 The context of IPSL

A combination of stimuli for IPSL seems to be the norm. Like most educational initiatives it is not a value-free development solely motivated by altruism or the public good. Rather it appears to have arisen countrywide in response to a combination of economic expediency resulting from a growing crises of recruitment into higher education; the movement of the paramedical occupations into higher education; the broadening context of the educational curricula; and moral panics in health and social care recognizing the need for interdisciplinary working — particularly between social work and health care professionals.

The first issue to arise during the conversation was the question of how we define IPSL as distinct from interprofessional learning (IPL), and establishing some commonality to what was being discussed. Just how were participants differentiating between interprofessional learning and interprofessional shared learning? Initially the difference seems to lie in learning between professionals (IPL) and learning with professionals (IPSL). Specifically, IPL involves learning about the other's perspective, what they do and how they operate, whereas IPSL requires learning together, arriving at an understanding of an issue from a range of perspectives in an interdisciplinary forum.

It is recognized that each professional / occupational group arises from a particular ethical and philosophical value base that defines its perspective on, and to, the world. This includes the conceptual definitions that inform action in terms of working with others, including the value placed on members from other professional groups and the clients of their services. Other differences identified between the disciplines are the language base that is used, and the educational pedagogy that directs early learning experiences within professional preparation for practice. IPSL is viewed as a strategy for enabling understanding of these differences and learning to work in a team within that understanding. It is seen as a way of identifying and valuing one's own professional foundations, while recognizing and valuing those of others for a mutually agreed purpose. As one participant said:

> it's about an acknowledgement that other professional bases not only exist, but have a right to exist, and they have a right to be different. And once you can acknowledge the different rights to exist, you acknowledge the right for yours to exist within that environment. It becomes more than just an understanding of their role, but an understanding of how you can share.

The educational methodology between the two differs too, in that IPL often involves being taught; for instance by a member of a profession addressing a group of students about what they do, as such sharing their perspective so that the students see where they are coming from. IPSL, however, is seen as arising from a student-centred pedagogy of problem-solving, discussion and group working to facilitate understanding. In summary:

> IPSL almost becomes synonymous with the teaching style that is interactive.

Arising from the interdisciplinary composition of an IPSL student group is the issue of professional boundaries. One participant suggested that:

> I think there is something called Interprofessional Learning which is not necessarily about that, but actually is awareness raising about barriers, or whatever, that actually goes on as well.

It was acknowledged that an interdisciplinary group of students brings with it particular challenges for teachers in facilitating learning because of the differing pedagogical experiences of the professions involved. Achieving a compromise where all students can participate, feel comfortable and learn as a result is especially difficult when students from diverse pedagogical backgrounds are expected to adapt to different teaching and learning strategies to those with which they are familiar.

A further issue to arise during the conversation was whether there is an optimal educational level for IPSL to operate successfully. While all participants had experience of attempting IPSL across a range of undergraduate and postgraduate courses, it was acknowledged that the outcomes at each level, in terms of learning, can be qualitatively different:

> at the undergraduate level, the professional qualifying level, at the end of the course the students are actually very enthusiastic and they say things wholeheartedly like 'this will change the way I work'. Those at masters level however, who are far more sophisticated and have been in the job longer say ' this was really worthwhile, but it doesn't mean to say that things will necessarily change in practice because the systems are not there in order to enable us to take that on.'

A further distinction appears to arise at masters level between initial registration through a post-graduate route, and continuing professional development for experienced professionals. It is almost as though to be able to appreciate the perspective of others there needs to be an emotional maturity and confidence in one's own value base and practice before a community of shared learning can be achieved:

> I think it [IPSL] actually fits well with the Masters model because individuals need to be comfortable with their own roles and then be able to challenge what they think are the boundaries of those roles. What I'm talking about is not necessarily getting individuals very young or early on in their careers and saying 'think broadly first'. I think they must become confident in their own roles, because we want to protect the roles ... But if we are able to have people who are developed in their own roles to then challenge those boundaries sufficiently, to be able to acknowledge the other realities.

This seems to be the essential value of IPSL, namely its ability to transcend professional boundaries whilst at the same time maintaining an individuals own professional integrity. The purpose of attempting to achieve this lies in the perceived value of the outcomes of IPSL.

25.5 The outcomes of IPSL

The outcomes of IPSL were identified by participants in relation to practice outcomes; multidisciplinary ways of working; and individual growth and development. It must be acknowledged however, that the first two categories represent *perceived* outcomes on the part of the participants rather than any for which evidence could be provided to support such perceptions. This represents a paradox for many educationalists, and to some extent a frustration: one of being in a position to challenge and enable individuals to review their own practice, without having the power to enable that change to impact on operational practice through direct mechanisms.

The overwhelming view of participants was that IPSL should facilitate change in professional practice with a direct improvement in patient/client care, and possibly outcomes. As one person said:

> I think the value must lie in outcomes for patient or client care because if we understand more about what we're doing in relation to other people and why other people make decisions, that will facilitate better teamwork; and what you should see is that being translated into more effective practice.

However, the conversation also introduced an alternative reality in terms of an awareness of the barriers to change ways of working in the form of policies and procedure; management strategies and intransigent colleagues who may unintentionally (or even intentionally) sabotage attempts to initiate change. As one person suggested:

> I think the difficulty for evaluating IPSL in terms of its effectiveness is the fact that the policy and organisational context within which the outcome has to be seen is completely alien from the educational setting. The educational setting almost provides a little secure environment to practice your skills and you go out into the big bad world which has a completely different agenda, which is structured completely differently, with very different goals and objectives. IPSL, while it's in all the policy documents, it's open to more rhetoric than practice in terms of how organisations are.

However, IPSL may change practice as a consequence of two factors. The first is that of facilitating multidisciplinary team working. This may arise not only from the understanding of others' roles developed through learning together, but also from the ability to appreciate different conceptual backgrounds thus facilitating communication between the different professionals and a willingness to respect differing viewpoints and value bases.

The second relates to the valuing of professional boundaries and limitations. To quote one participant:

> It's a case of 'I've got a problem, I don't know how to handle this, but I know a person who does', and I can go down the corridor and knock on their door; or pick up the phone. To me, that is interprofessionality. It might well be about networking, whereas before we've educated people in completely different professions and different places ... so one of the characteristics of effective IPSL is a collaborative learning style because

that develops in individuals not simply an understanding of the content of the course, but actually an ability to apply that content in a collaborative way.

This outcome appears to arise from the process of learning together; of being challenged to identify and defend one's own position while developing the interpersonal skills of valuing those of another's; and of having the confidence to acknowledge those different realities that define the way that other professionals work.

In this context the successful outcomes of IPSL are located in the ability of the individual student to develop and grow as a professional as a result of the educational process. The participants believed that they could provide substantive evidence to support this outcome as a result of their own observations, their assessment of students and evaluation of courses in a variety of roles and contexts.

25.6 Learning from and with others

Key skills arising from the process of learning with others were identified as learning to negotiate; developing dialogue with others; understanding differing viewpoints; constructing sound arguments and participating in discussions from an analytical viewpoint; and recognizing the limitations of professional socialisation.

The first four of these were seen to arise primarily from the use of interactive teaching and learning strategies. These were judged to stem from a student-centred perspective and to challenge the use of traditional pedagogical styles that arise from one professional educational approach. The value of this type of style, seen to encourage discussion and listening to others, was to enable understanding of others' perspectives, and the possibility of creating dialogue between professionals, which would ultimately result in:

> getting people to think differently from the way they would normally think — we are actually trying to facilitate change in some way or move things forward.

This notion of facilitating change was identified as a significant outcome of IPSL and acknowledged as a function of individual professionals being able to acknowledge the multiple realities of others delivering health care and social welfare support. Once these multiple realities are understood, through the recognition of differing values and language usage among and between professions it becomes possible to function from a wider, more inclusive perspective. To some extent this was seen as the first stage of overcoming professional barriers.

Professional differences were seen as having both positive and negative effects. From a negative viewpoint, professional boundaries were seen to inhibit patient care, such as the problems of territoriality, accountability, language and conceptual differences. However, professional identification in terms of valuing philosophical underpinnings, and being able to work from within the security of a familiar framework was seen as facilitating confidence and enabling students to enter dialogue with each other. As one person explained:

> you've got an understanding of everybody's rights to exist in their own professional form.

25.7 Barriers to IPSL

While the values and outcomes to IPSL were identified, it was also acknowledged that there are significant barriers that need to be addressed and managed if IPSL is to be successful. Initially, problems were seen to arise from each profession having a different value base that involves alternative philosophical and ethical frameworks, differing conceptual definitions, and often a separate language base. Part of the dialogue illustrates this problem:

> if they are technical terms and people don't understand them that's fine — they'll say 'what does that mean?'. The problem arises when a term carries with it connotations of certain values with it, and that's why I used individualism as an example, because some professions see that as positive and others see it as slightly negative, and so people can be talking about the same thing but also thinking, 'yes, that for me it epitomises that profession and it's wrong' attitude when people think they are actually talking positively.

> I'd agree totally in terms of language — it's not the terms because technical terms are there supposedly to reduce confusion. However, it's the interpretation — whether it's seen as positive or negative — that is the issue. One example I was thinking of is when someone says 'patient' — other people may wince at that, whereas when other people say 'client' you may find the medical profession wincing at that.

> There are also the terms 'empowerment' or 'informed consent' or 'patients having the right to choose'. One of the ones that has been highlighted to me has been the notion of women in labour being allowed to take the decision to refuse treatment and where the different professions come down on the side of the discussion. If you talk to an Obstetrician or Gynaecologist they are going to have very different views from a Social Worker or a Midwife or someone who is teaching medical ethics.

Not only do the barriers of language and conceptual differences have to be overcome when forming interprofessional groups, but so also do those arising from the students' previous experiences of different pedagogical styles. Interactive teaching styles were identified as being those most likely to be effective in facilitating IPSL. However, it was recognized that teaching using this sort of style presented some students with significant challenges in adapting to a different pedagogy to the one(s) they were familiar with. This is particularly apparent for students who are used to 'talk and chalk' or formal lecturing, such as in medicine or science. One participant made the following insightful observation:

> I think it's important throughout the learning experience [to identify] how we learn best, and we all learn in different ways. So it could well be that those who gravitate towards a medically dominated profession would be more into didactic type approaches, whereas those who go into more vocational, more interactive professions will be more likely to be those personalities that learn more experientially.

This suggests that students with a different value base select different types of professions as their career choice. If so, any IPSL group is likely to comprise students from a range of pedagogical backgrounds. It could even be that the range of students is limited because of the challenge of learning in a different sort of way and many prospective students are uncomfortable with teaching and learning strategies with which they are unfamiliar. As one participant said:

> There is a difference in the way the different professions are educated, that they actually have a value around their own educational processes ... different professions have their own pedagogies ... how do you put people who are 'touchy feely' in the same room as people who want overheads to copy and handouts?

Another challenge to arise from the student group is that of the balance between the professions represented, and just what constitutes 'interprofessional':

> sometimes, for instance, we have two social workers and 18 nurses — those social workers are the dominant force in that group and so it does not have to be nine of each we know when it doesn't work — the balance of the group, the tyranny of the vociferous, the two social workers dominating the 18 nurses, the person who shouts the loudest.

This may be compounded by the teaching style adopted. Not only does the students' approach need to be interactive and receptive, but the attitude and style of the teacher also needs to facilitate and encourage this. It was suggested that:

> the teacher component is more of a problem than the student component. In my experience, if you can conquer the teacher barriers you can begin to make progress with the students.

This was seen as being another problem related to the professional boundaries between students, and teachers, in a group. Professional socialization was seen to encompass most of the barriers to successful IPSL, ranging through not only the different ways in which people think and conceptualize their everyday realities, but also in how these are enacted through education, and professional attitudes and practice.

Finally, issues related to the theory-practice gap loomed large in the conversation. There was an acknowledgement of the problems of creating dissonance and anxiety for students in envisioning a reality for interprofessionality that does not exist in practice. This was perceived as being contributed to by employer organizational policies and management expectations, as well as the operational barriers of attempting to work in an interprofessional manner within hierarchical institutions where the issues of power and finance may interfere with the most effective, appropriate and efficient care for service uses.

25.8 A final word

The data presented does not support generalization. Indeed it was not designed to do so. Rather the data opens up opportunities for summarization, further interpretation, and new lines of enquiry in the search for understanding about the value of IPSL. The presented views of experienced educationalists suggest new areas for research and problematized the simplistic assumption that IPSL has value.

25.9 References

Funnell, P. (1990) Maximising the value of shared learning interactions. In Farmer, B. *et al.* (eds), *Making Learning Systems Work (Aspects of Educational and Training Technology XXIII)*. London: Kogan Page.

Funnell, P. (1995) Exploring the value of interprofessional shared learning. In Soothill, K. *et al.* (eds), *Interprofessional Relations in Health Care*. London: Edward Arnold.

Kemmis, S. and McTaggart, R. (1982) *The Action Research Planner*. Australia: Deakin University Press.

Miller, J. and Glasner, B. (1997) 'The 'inside' and the 'outside': finding reality in interviews'. In D Silverman (ed.), *Qualitative Research: Theory, Method and Practice*. London: Sage.

26 Researching the role of group work in learning, teaching and assessment: a comparative case study of two degree programmes

Carole Leathwood, Linda Johnson, Simon Moore
University of North London

26.1 Introduction

Group work is increasingly seen as a vital element of teaching and learning in UK higher education. It is thought to enhance student learning by encouraging an active and deep approach (Falchikov, 1988; Bruffee, 1999; Thorley and Gregory, 1994), potentially encompassing all the elements of Kolb's learning cycle (Stone and Pashley, 1997). It is seen as a way to develop independent learning (Nias, 1995), student capabilities (Falchikov, 1988), enterprise (Hindle, 1993), and transferable skills (Butcher, Stefani *et al.*, 1995). Its increasing importance partly reflects employer demands for skilled and capable graduates able to work in a team (Harvey, Moon *et al.*, 1997) and it is seen as a way of enabling students to develop the skills and capabilities required for their future careers. On a pragmatic note, the current emphasis on group work may also be a response to rising student numbers and the increasing pressures on academic staff. Students in higher education are having to work more on their own (NCIHE, 1997), and a variety of self-study groups, student run seminars and project teams may be emerging as one way of dealing with these pressures (Thorley and Gregory, 1994).

It is not surprising then, as Stone and Pashley (1997) note, that group work has taken on the status of 'a good thing' irrespective of the different models and practices adopted. Despite the extolled virtues of group work in much of the literature, and the lack of reference to problems or difficulties in some texts, the benefits claimed are not automatic (Jaques, 1991). Group work can be fraught with difficulties, and indeed a 'stormy' stage is recognized in Tuckman's well-quoted 'form, storm, norm and perform' stages of group development (Tuckman, 1965). This model suggests, however, a rather neat and orderly linear progression, something which is not always born out by the authors' experiences of group work with students. Among the more common explanations for the difficulties groups encounter are levels of commitment and differential contributions (Cuthbert, 1994; Falchikov, 1988), the skills and time demanded of staff (Hindle, 1993), unbalanced team membership (Belbin, 1981) and lack of group work skills and/or training (Johnson and Johnson, 1975; Jaques, 1991). It is clear that the term 'group work' encompasses a wide range of conceptualizations and practices, and it is with some of these differences that this chapter is concerned.

26.2 The research

This study emerged from the pilot phase of a longitudinal programme of research into student learning involving two undergraduate programmes: Business Studies/Administration and Applied Psychology. It became apparent that there were differences between these programmes in the ways in which group work was conceptualized and practised, and this research was designed to explore this.

The context is a post-1992 inner-city university which prides itself on its access policies and the diversity of its student body. 73 per cent of the students are mature students on entry, and 56 per cent are women. In terms of ethnicity, 49 per cent are white and 36 per cent black (the rest are unknown), although such broad grouping disguises the diverse ethnic profile of the student body.

The University has developed a new 'capability-based' undergraduate curriculum as part of its commitment to developing not only subject knowledge and understanding, but also a broader range of 'generic' skills and capabilities to ensure students are well prepared for their future careers. The curriculum encompasses a set of core capabilities which are integrated into the subject modules and include working with others, effective communication, self-organization and problem-solving. Group work activities are seen as an important vehicle for the development and assessment of these capabilities.

Questions about group activities were included in student and staff focus groups, and students were asked to provide written evaluations of a specific group work project. In practice it proved to be very difficult to persuade students to attend focus groups, with only one group of business studies students and two groups of psychology students taking place. Only one male student attended, although a better balance was achieved in terms of ethnicity and age. The responses to the request for written evaluations were also patchy, with the majority received from the business students. The difficulties of encouraging students to take part in research activities outside class time, especially when most work and many have family commitments, need to be acknowledged. It is perhaps not insignificant that these same time pressures emerged as a major impediment to group work. Focus groups were also conducted with each staff team. Although some clear differences of emphasis and practice were evident, the relatively low numbers of students who contributed to the focus groups mean that any conclusions must remain tentative.

26.3 The role of group work

The BA Business Studies and BA Business Administration programmes are located in the University's Business School, and, like other business degrees, have been shaped and influenced by developments in transferable skills, including BTEC core skills and the perceived needs of employers. The BSc Applied Psychology pathway is provided across the Faculties of Environmental and Social Science, and Science, Computing and Engineering. Psychology degrees have traditionally been shaped and guided by the influence of the professional body, The British Psychological Society.

Group work is conceptualized and practised rather differently in the two disciplinary areas. On the business programmes, when students and staff referred to group work they were mostly talking about task-based or project-based groups, often involving some aspect of group assessment with students engaging in a variety of both formative and summative group work. Students working in groups are often given the same grade regardless of effort or ability, although in some assignments individual grading is possible with the production of a group diary.

Staff saw group work as important in preparing students for the 'real world' of business and developing a number of skills and capabilities such as communicating, thinking creatively, and managing time. Working with others was identified as a vital employment skill with staff making comments like 'there are very few professions that people move into when they are in complete isolation ... the majority of students want to be managers and have to have some idea about how to make groups work and help motivate them.' Another lecturer emphasized that it is about 'skills development and they're actually learning how to work with other people and how to listen and to take on board other people's comments'.

Group work was also identified as a useful tool for encouraging student interaction and peer support, with one lecturer saying, 'as a teacher you should not set yourself up as the fount of all knowledge, you've got to let them appreciate that they can learn from other students'.

Some staff suggested that a few of their colleagues 'cynically' use group assessment to cut down their workload, and 'survival' was also mentioned in a context of increasing student numbers, particularly in Business Schools. This research and the work of Hindle (1993) suggest, however, that group activities can be more demanding.

On the Psychology programme, the term 'group work' was mostly used to refer to small group discussions in seminars, where students are encouraged via problem setting to discuss the topics and issues raised in the lecture prior to reporting their discussions to the whole seminar class. This group work is not assessed. In experimental psychology, students conduct experiments and collate data in small groups before writing up reports for individual assessment. Students also used the term 'group work' to describe their own informal discussions outside classes. Psychology degrees do not tend to have a tradition of assessed group work. Although students gain experience of working in groups throughout this programme, both the influence of the professional body and the attitudes of the staff and the students mitigate against it being used as a formal assessment tool.

In Psychology, the academic and educational benefits of group work were particularly stressed: 'I think its about facilitating learning' and 'it is a useful tool to encourage students to discuss and develop their ideas and approaches in an informal environment'. Several staff emphasized that group work was a motivation tool that encouraged students to take responsibility for their learning, thereby facilitating independent learning (Nias, 1995). One lecturer said: 'some students choose to be completely passive and learn everything from the lecturer and you want ways to challenge that and to encourage the students to become more active in their own learning'.

Group work as a work-related skill was not the main emphasis, although a Counselling Psychology lecturer felt that 'the whole group process is important because it's a reflection of how you should be as a counsellor in a counselling situation — so for me the group is where most of the learning happens'. Group work was, though, generally thought to encourage personal as well as academic development. Another lecturer said 'it is very important for their self-esteem, for their communication, for their social interaction ... it will prepare them (for) live situations where they will have to overcome their shyness and their anxiety'.

To some extent, the different emphases of these two disciplinary areas reflect Tribe's (1994) distinction between two main purposes of group work, one which stresses the acquisition of a range of interpersonal and employment skills, and the other focusing on academic aims.

26.4 Student responses to group work

According to the University's student satisfaction survey for 1997—98, 65 per cent of students who responded were satisfied with group work as a teaching and learning activity.

This compares with 69 per cent who were satisfied with lectures, 70 per cent with seminars and 75 per cent with practical work. Satisfaction drops considerably, however, when asked about group assessment, with only 45 per cent of students reporting that they were satisfied with being assessed on group work compared to 82 per cent for individual coursework and 58 per cent for examination.

The business students in the focus group were initially very negative about group work, commenting 'it is not effective', and 'I don't think anybody likes doing group work'. After some encouragement to think positively students acknowledged the benefits, commenting 'two heads are better than one', 'I think it helps the communication skills' and 'not all groups are bad, one of the groups was very productive ... if you have a good group you can move mountains'.

Students' written evaluations were more positive. Comments included: 'I thought it was good working as a group, because that way we can help each other out', 'I felt more comfortable and felt that I was being recognized in the group' and 'It was a great experience, me and other members of the group hardly knew each other in the beginning and turned out to be really good friends'. However, problems relating to poor attendance at group meetings, motivation and assessment, all of which are discussed below, were identified.

In Psychology, students were very positive about the informal use of group work in seminars with one describing it as 'really useful', and another adding 'I really like group learning'. The more formal group research activities were also appreciated with another stating 'if it's a good working group then its just great — you can't ask for anything more really'. The only complaint was when a lecturer was 'a bit too obsessed with it' requiring students to 'get into groups of two, now get two groups of two together and now get in a bigger group'.

Students emphasized the benefits of their own informal 'self-study' and 'social groups', commenting 'if you're walking from one building to another you just discuss something' and 'throw ideas about'. They stressed that they formed these groups themselves out of choice, because it helped their learning. Negative comments from a few psychology students relating to the differential commitment and motivation of group members and 'personality differences' were largely directed towards non-psychology option modules which had included group assessment.

Most of the benefits described by Psychology students were academic ones to do with helping their learning, but in reflecting on the difficulties of the formal assessed group work in other modules, two students did stress work-related benefits, with one saying, 'I've worked before coming here you know you always work in a team ... so you have to learn how to relate to others'.

26.5 Group work training and support

Much of the literature emphasizes the importance of training in group work skills (Jacques, 1991), and support from lecturers (Hindle, 1993).

On the business programmes, all students receive input on group processes in two compulsory modules in the first year and are familiarized with Tuckman's 'forming, storming, norming and performing' (Tuckman, 1965). This was identified as an important feature of the programme as, in the words of one lecturer, it 'sets the ground rules for lots of other group work they'll be doing on the course'. Practice varied as to how far staff were prepared to help students with 'group problems'. In one first-year module, the assignment stated that students must resolve their own problems, but inevitably this was not uniformly enforced by all seminar tutors which caused some student dissatisfaction. This issue of support raises questions about the extent to which lecturing staff take on supportive or 'nurturing' roles, and the gender issues related to this (Cotterill and Waterhouse, 1998; Williams, 1993). Student views were mixed in terms of their own stated expectations of support.

In psychology, there is no formal input on group processes other than where this is part of the subject matter of the module (e.g. counselling psychology), and again there are differences in staff support. One lecturer said she would draw attention to group dynamics, but stressed that the emphasis of the seminar is the subject matter being discussed, not how the group is working.

The Business students acknowledged that they had been given some theoretical input on group processes but were critical of their ability to apply this with one student commenting 'but how much of it was actually put into practice?', and another saying 'even if they give you guidelines then you have to apply it'. Some students felt that staff could do little more as 'it depends on students behaviour, they do have to be serious', although others from both programmes felt that lecturers could do more to assist and that guidelines would be helpful. This gap between theory and practice is recognized by Schadler and Wolfgang (1994) who noted students' difficulties transferring what they had learnt about group processes to the groups they were later working in. Often there is an implicit assumption of a straightforward linear relationship between knowledge and conduct, i.e. that students given knowledge and skills in group dynamics will automatically be able to apply those in practice. There is a danger of assuming that technical procedures can solve what are often the complex and messy realities of groups in practice. Experience on the business courses suggests that this is not necessarily the case, and Thorley and Gregory (1994) warn that 'groups are unpredictable', arguing against prescriptive methods of working with groups.

One possible explanation for this gap between theory and practice is the extent to which the power relations embedded in interpersonal and institutional contexts impact on group work — something rarely touched upon in standard group work training. Several studies have noted gender issues in groups (Halterman, Dutkiewicz *et al.*, 1991; Alexander and Stone, 1997), and Hayes and Walter (1995, p. 148) suggest that 'we need more consideration of how gender, race and class differences may create power differentials that affect group dynamics and learning'. Bosley (cited in Hayes and Walter, 1995), argues that the models of group behaviour used tend to be based on the norms and values of the dominant white culture, and may not reflect the learning preferences, experiences and cultures of the students. This may in part account for students' frequently stated preferences for choosing who they work with, although this could also reinforce differential power relations within the student group, something that was commented on by business staff.

26.6 Issues of group selection, commitment and contributions

Many of the group work difficulties identified related to differential commitment and contributions, and the issue of group selection.

On the Business programmes where group assessment was a regular feature, these difficulties were repeatedly referred to. One student said: 'the only difficulty I encountered was lack of enthusiasm within my group — I had to motivate and pressure them to complete tasks'. Another student added: 'Some people abused group work and left their work up to others', while another said 'the group never met'. One of the problems acknowledged was that meeting outside class time was often difficult due to family and work commitments.

Business staff sometimes allocate students to groups in the hope of achieving a balance, including a mix of students with different cultural backgrounds. Some students, however, complained that they have 'lazy' or 'weak' students in their group and that lecturers should let the students choose the people they want to work with. This created other difficulties though, as they often chose friends, causing problems for students who were new to the group. It was described as 'like being at school' and on a par with not being picked for the football team, resulting in some students feeling isolated and 'second rate' from the outset. Cultural differences were also highlighted as sometimes creating barriers, although the positive benefits of inter-cultural learning contexts were also acknowledged (Tomlinson and Egan,1999; Volet,1998).

In Psychology, students mostly chose their own, often friendship, groups. The value of working with friends and people they knew was repeatedly emphasized by these students. Only one student disagreed with this, saying 'you stay with your friends ... stay with what's comfortable which isn't right'.

The consensus among the other students, however, was that 'it's great if you're with like minded people', 'it's easier if you're with people that are of similar abilities as you' and 'we knew each other and can also sort of listen to each other and suggest something without feeling maybe I shouldn't have said that or done it differently'. Some students claimed that working with others you have not chosen or do not know can be 'hazardous' or 'frustrating'. One student who had chosen a module outside the core psychology programme involving group assessment explained: 'I worked in a group last semester for the first time, a sort of proper group, and it freaked me out to tell you the honest truth ... eventually it just made me ill'. She described problematic group dynamics and the difficulties of challenging other group members who she did not really know. Another said 'it's 'very demoralising, very demotivating I think, to have to work with people that you don't want to work with'.

26.7 Assessment

The main difference between the two programmes related to the use of assessment. For the business lecturers, group assessment is accepted as the norm. Staff acknowledged students' complaints about group marks and expressed concern that an increasing number of students now seemed happy to 'carry' individuals who were not pulling their weight, rather than spend time and energy challenging them, but the benefits of group assessment per se were not generally questioned.

For the business students, the use of a single group grade caused the greatest anxiety with several students recommending more individual assessment. Even students reporting fairly positive group experiences expressed reservations about 'fairness' with group assessments. Typical comments included 'others have not contributed the same amount of work' and 'I think its good for those who didn't do too well but unfair for those who did well individually by having their grades slip due to less capable individuals — but that's life'. For another student, 'it can be unfair because sometimes not everyone contributes, but if everyone works properly and contributes then I think it is fair that everyone gets the same grade'.

Psychology staff strongly rejected the idea of group assessment. One lecturer questioned it by saying 'the whole nature of any degree in our higher education system is rightly or wrongly based on the principles of independent learning, thus based on this assumption should we really be incorporating the contribution of assessed group work into students final degree classifications?'. It was felt that students would get just as much valuable experience through non-assessed group work assignments. Indeed Butcher *et al.* (1995) suggest that group work does not necessarily have to be assessed to have a positive effect, and Lejk, Wyvill and Farrow (1997, p. 88) found that computing staff also had some reservations about group assessment with most strongly agreeing that 'it is more important to expose students to learning in groups than to assess them in groups'.

While staff realized that non-assessed group work can cause problems relating to student attendance, it was suggested that assessing such work could actually serve to demotivate students and detract from their enjoyment, 'if you are stressed you merely concentrate on removing the source of the stress and under such circumstances you gain nothing positive from participating in assessed group work'. Formal assessment might also provoke anxiety 'if its too big or important I think some of the students find it too fearful an environment'.

There was a feeling that giving a single group mark was unfair, echoing the views of Crick (1992). One staff member said: 'Surely the only mark you get in an assessed group is an average ... by using this method you might not get as many fails but you also don't get many first class marks either'. The staff considered other marking systems such as peer marking but this also attracted criticism with comments such as 'where I have had experience of peer assessment it was "if I give you 10 points you give me 10 points" — they all worked out the points before they went in the room and it didn't work so well'. Psychology staff also felt that group assessment would create additional difficulties of group selection, with one saying 'Do you put all the good students together and all the weak ones together to protect their grade standing or do you mix them all up and risk getting average marks overall? It is a very difficult and sensitive issue.'

Psychology students similarly argued strongly for individual assessment for group work. In particular, those who had experienced group assessment on other modules were very opposed to it. One said 'I don't see the problem of assessing people as individuals even when they are within a group because they still have to individually produce something.'

26.8 Evaluation of practice and ways forward

On the Business programmes, a number of recurring issues have emerged, and staff have continued to question and evaluate their practice. Some of the difficulties are felt to be at least partly attributed to modularity. One such issue is the amount of group work students encounter, which has been raised by students and has been the subject of comment by some external examiners. In the early days of assessed group work, course tutors assumed some responsibility for monitoring the student experience to ensure that students were not overloaded with group assessment, but modularity makes this very difficult.

A few staff remarked that they now use group work less often due to practical problems, such as 'you identify groups in week two and additional people join for one reason or another'. Some subject areas now allow students to work together in groups but be assessed individually, partly due to the nature of the subject but also because students 'find it increasingly difficult to meet because they've all got part time jobs and so I regard group work as something that would be nice but couldn't face the hassle and because I don't think in this subject they gain that much as they do in other subjects'.

The increasing difficulties associated with assessed group work resulted in the Business School Quality Group drafting guidelines for group work across the Faculty. These state that tutors should normally allocate students to groups, students in a group should be required to sign up to one of three options for assessment: equal shares, peer assessment, or that there had been no agreement, and that a group assignment should not exceed 50 per cent of the total marks for any module. It is too soon to evaluate the impact and effectiveness of these guidelines, though one issue that is already apparent relates to the need for preparation for peer assessment for students and, in some cases, staff (Cheng and Warren, 1997; Falchikov and Magin, 1997), which has not yet been systematically addressed.

In Psychology, some staff felt that group work was an area that could be further developed and there was a sense that it has become slightly marginalized, almost as an extra-curricular activity. The further use of group work to support and encourage student learning was emphasised, although group assessment was likely to continue to be resisted.

26.9 Conclusions

There are clear differences between the ways in which group work is conceptualized and practised in the courses that took part in this research.

Group assessment remains a contentious area, and it may be, as Thorley and Gregory (1994) suggest, that some of the difficulties with assessment are insurmountable as there is a contradiction between assessing individuals' performance and requiring that they work effectively as a team. However, pressure to assess capabilities in part through group work may come from within the University, and Psychology staff could be forced to return to this issue. Further discussions of self and peer assessment are also taking place.

The selection of groups, power relations and the gap between theory and practice have all been problematized, and further research to explore the inter-connections between these issues could help to illuminate some of the difficulties often experienced in group work. Increased student numbers, pressures on staff and modularity also appear to present difficulties, suggesting that more group work is not necessarily a simple and straightforward solution to the challenges of mass higher education.

Despite the difficulties, both staff and students in these two disciplinary areas felt that students benefited and learnt from group work. As this research is disseminated and discussed within and between these course teams, further discussions of practice will inevitably be initiated, and the effective use of group work to enhance student learning will continue to be developed.

26.10 References

Alexander, M.W. and S.F. Stone (1997) Student perceptions of teamwork in the classroom: an analysis by gender, *Business Education Forum* **51**(3): 7—10.

Belbin, M.R. (1981) *Management Teams: Why They Succeed or Fail.* Oxford, Butterworth-Heinemann.

Bruffee, K.A. (1999) *Collaborative Learning: Higher Education, Interdependence, and the Authority of Knowledge.* Baltimore, The John Hopkins University Press.

Butcher, A.C., Stefani, L.A.J., Tariq, V.N. (1995) Analysis of Peer -, self- and staff-assessment in group project work, *Assessment in Education* **2**(2): 165—85.

Cheng, W. and M. Warren (1997) Having second thoughts: student perceptions before and after a peer assessment exercise, *Studies in Higher Education* **22**(2): 233—9.

Cotterill, P. and R.L. Waterhouse (1998). Women in higher education: the gap between corporate rhetoric and the reality of experience. In D. Malina and S. Maslin-Prothero (eds), *Surviving the Academy: Feminist Perspectives.* London: Falmer Press: 8—17.

Crick, M. and L. Thorley (1992) Peer assessment forms for group work: an evolutionary story, *Innovative Assessment in Higher Education,* Bangor.

Cuthbert, P. (1994) Self-development Groups on a Diploma in Management Studies Course.

In L. Thorley and R. Gregory (eds), *Using Group-based Learning in Higher Education.* London: Kogan Page.

Falchikov, N. (1988) Self and peer assessment of a group project designed to promote the skills of capability, *Programmed Learning and Education Technology* **25**(4): 327—39.

Falchikov, N. and D. Magin (1997) Detecting gender bias in peer marking of students' group process work, *Assessment & Evaluation in Higher Education* **22**(4): 385—95.

Halterman, C., J. Dutkiewicz *et al.* (1991) Men and women on the job: gender bias in work teams, *Journal of Business and Technical Communication* **5**(4): 469—81.

Harvey, L., S. Moon *et al.* (1997) *Graduates Work: Organisational Change and Students' Attributes. Birmingham: Centre for Research into Quality.*

Hayes, E. and P.G. Walter (1995) A comparison of small group learning approaches in adult literacy education, *Adult Basic Education* **5** *(3): 133—51.*

Hindle, B.P. (1993) The `Project': putting student-controlled, small-group work and transferable skills at the core of a geography course, *Journal of Geography in Higher Education* **17***(1): 11—19.*

Jaques, D. (1991) *Learning in Groups.* Houston: Gulf Publishing Company.

Johnson, D.W. and F.P. Johnson (1975) *Joining Together: Group Theory and Group Skills.* Needham Heights: Allyn & Bacon.

Lejk, M., Wyvill, M. and Farrow, S. (1997) Group learning and group assessment on undergraduate computing courses in higher education in the UK: results of a survey, *Assessment & Evaluation in Higher Education* **22***(1): 81—91.*

NCIHE, National Committee of Inquiry into Higher Education (1997) Higher Education in the Learning Society (The Dearing Report). *London: HMSO.*

Nias, J. (1995) Developing intellectual independence, *The New Academic* **4***(No. 2, Summer): 8—9.*

Schadler, U. and J. Wolfgang (1994) Improving group work of students in seminars through team training. In G. Gibbs (ed.), *Improving Student Learning: Through Assessment and Evaluation.* Oxford: The Oxford Centre for Staff Development: 493—98.

Stone, B.W. and J. Pashley (1997) The Application of theory to practice in student group business projects, *Capability Volume* **3***(1): 21—6.*

Thorley, L. and R. Gregory (eds) (1994) *Using Group-based Learning in Higher Education.* London, Kogan Page.

Tomlinson, F. and S. Egan (1999) Learning in the context of cultural diversity: explorations of task group working and friendship networks amongst international MBA students. Paper presented at the British Academy of Management Conference 1—3 September, Manchester.

Tribe, D.M.R. (1994) An overview from higher education. In L. Thorley and R. Gregory (eds), *Using Group-based Learning in Higher Education.* London: Kogan Page.

Tuckman, B.W. (1965) Development sequence in small groups, *Psychological Bulletin* **63**(6): 384—99.

Volet, S.E., Ang, G. (1998) Culturally mixed groups on international campuses: an opportunity for inter-cultural learning, *Higher Education Research & Development* **17***(1): 5—23*

Williams, C. (1993) The politics of nurturant teaching, *Studies in Continuing Education* **15**(1): 50—61.

27 Information skills: do we help our students enough?

Lin Norton and Bill Norton
Department of Psychology, Liverpool Hope University College

Keywords
Information skills; library induction; library skills; catalogue usage; WWW usage

27.1 Overview

This chapter presents findings from a study designed to examine the provision made for undergraduate students to help them with two key skills: seeking information and evaluating it. Students from four different subjects in a university college were given a simple quiz to test how well they knew how to find different sorts of information in their college library. At the same time, tutors were also given a questionnaire asking them to estimate how many of their students would be able to correctly answer the library quiz and to outline the procedures that their subject provided to help their students. The results showed that on the whole most students were not very good at using the computer catalogue or in knowing about the library classification scheme, but were better at locating journals and CD-ROM databases and using the Internet. There appeared to be considerable tutor differences both within and between subjects on their expectations about what their students would know about information-seeking and what provision their own subjects set up to help their students acquire these skills. The implications of the research findings are discussed in the framework of the Conference issues about improving student learning through the disciplines.

27.2 Introduction

In Higher Education today students are increasingly expected to acquire skills which will equip them to be lifelong learners (Knapper, 1995). Pedagogy embraces conceptions of teaching as learning facilitation rather than knowledge transmission (Kember, 1997) and learning as taking a deep rather than a surface approach (Marton and Säljö, 1976). Part of this gradual change in the emphasis of tertiary education has come from the explosion of information through electronic means at the end of the twentieth century. Employers are increasingly looking for graduates who not only have generic skills of finding information from a wide range of sources but also have evaluative skills in order to separate the 'gold from the dross'.

Recent evidence by Norton, Brunas-Wagstaff and Lockley (1999) showed that final year psychology undergraduates clearly understood the importance of using up-to-date research in their coursework assignments. Students correctly expected that the number of journals they used in a coursework essay would be related to the mark they obtained and yet relatively few of them actually used journals when writing their essays. In an Australian study, Wells (1995) compared undergraduates' usage of the library with their academic results and found a positive correlation. Such findings would seem to suggest that students are not unclear about assessment criteria that tutors use so their lack of using appropriate resources must presumably be due to something else. Of course it may be a lack of motivation but perhaps the real explanation is simpler — students are not skilled in resource searching and using the library. In a recent qualitative-interview based study undertaken at Sussex University, Jacobs (1996) found that students were extremely cautious about using material that had not specifically been recommended by their tutors, so reading lists were of prime importance and if a source was not on the reading list, students tended to assume that it wasn't any good. This assumption by students together with the high occurrence of library anxiety, particularly with inexperienced undergraduates (Jiao, Onwuegbuzie and Lichtenstein , 1996; Mech and Brooks 1997) suggests that maybe academic tutors need to do more, rather than leave it to the usual library induction classes run by most university library staff at the start of each academic year. Williams (1995) found that a strong predictor of library use was the extent to which it was incorporated into assignments and classroom discussion.

The study reported here was designed to compare the induction procedures made by the departments of English, History, Psychology and Environmental Studies (representing the disciplines of the Arts, the Social Sciences and the Sciences) to establish what information-seeking skills undergraduates were expected to have at the start of their degree and what help was given to them. It was also designed to provide a measure of how effectively the different subject provisions were working by testing students' knowledge about different sources of material available in their university college library.

27.3 Methodology

27.3.1 The students' library quiz

Students from the four participating departments were set a library quiz relating to their subject. The questions were devised by the second author, a recently retired librarian with thirty years experience. The questions were about classification numbers, location of journals in the library, computer databases, the computer catalogue and the Internet/WWW and were individually tailored to each department. Before giving the quiz to the students, it was sent to the head of each subject for comments and certain amendments were made. A case in point was the English department where it was suggested that we use second years and not first years as students were expected to concentrate mainly on their texts and use a handbook called *The Student Companion*.

This procedure produced four subject-specific versions of the same basic library quiz. Students were given the quiz in class time. The responses to the quiz were completely anonymous and took no more than ten minutes to complete. All students who were present completed the quiz, but attendance in some subjects was rather low — presumably because of the timing when students were coming to the end of their modules.

An example of the type of questions asked in the quiz can be seen in Table 27.1.

27.3.2 The tutors' questionnaire

The second author also devised a questionnaire for the tutors in each of the four subjects

Question	Answer choice
At which classification numbers would you find books relating to English?	15 numbers were given of which three related to English
Where would you find current journals (i.e. less than 5 years old) on English?	Three locations given, of which one was the correct location
Where would you find back copies of journals over 5 years old on English?	Three locations given, of which one was the correct location
How many journals on English do you think the library has in stock?	Six numbers given, of which one was the correct answer
Which of the following are English databases available on the computers in the library?	12 were given of which two were genuine and one was a spurious database in English.
How would you search the computer catalogue to find books on a particular topic on English in the library?	8 were given of which 4 were correct
Do you use the Internet/WWW to get information to help you in your studying?	Yes/No
Which source might cause you to question the worth of such information?	Four sources were given of which two were questionable

Table 27.1 Questions asked in the library quiz to students in English

How are students helped in * to:**

Find books using the Library classification scheme?
Find current journals in the Library?
Find back copies of journals (over 5 years old) in the Library?
Be aware of the scope and number of journals available in the Library?
Use the databases available on the computers in the Library?
Search effectively on the computer catalogue for books on a particular topic?
Use the Internet/WWW to obtain information?
Evaluate information obtained from the Internet/WWW?

Figure 27.1 Tutors' questions about the help provided for students in their department

asking them whether they would expect their students to know the answers to the library quiz questions and to estimate what proportion of their students they thought would answer correctly. A copy of the students quiz (with the correct answers identified) was attached to each tutor's questionnaire. In addition they were asked to comment on how students were helped in their subject to know about these various resources. (See Figure 27.1.)

27.3.3 Participants

249 students took part in the study consisting of 190 first years and 59 second years and 13 tutors (see Table 27.2).

Subject	Students	Tutors	Ratio of tutors to students
Psychology	127 (1st yrs)	5	[25.4]
Environmental Studies	22 (1st yrs)	3	[7.3]
History	41 (1st yrs)	3	[13.7]
English	59 (2nd yrs)	2	[29.5]

Table 27.2 Participation numbers

27.4 Induction procedures by the departments

The following information has been obtained from documentation such as the handbooks that most subjects provide, from personal communications via email with the heads of each subject and from participating tutors' comments on the questionnaire used in this study.

27.4.1 Psychology

The first year of psychology is run with a firm pedagogical philosophy of encouraging independent reading, group work and increasing independence on part of students — the aim is based on the concept of teaching as facilitating learning rather than transmission of knowledge, but given the fact that the discipline may be entirely new to many of our students, there is inevitably an amount of transmission of knowledge.

Students are given a handbook and are expected to read widely before as well as after lectures and are given extensive reading lists to guide them. Information-seeking skills are incorporated into the seminar and workshop programme which are designed to incorporate a range of generic skills into the study of psychology (essay-writing, journal-using, debating and defending your viewpoint, taking a deep approach). One example is where students are given a simple library orientating task which they are expected to complete in their own time. Many of the skills introduced in the seminars and workshops are reinforced as the course progresses in coursework assignments.

27.4.2 Environmental Sciences

No information received

27.4.3 History

The subject head of history told us that they had tried for the first time a seminar programme attached to skills. The idea is that seminar tutors use something appropriate from the content of the lecture programme to very specifically discuss, identify, examine, find, examples of, the particular skill under consideration that week. An example is a seminar on Reading skills: using bibliography, finding reading, styles of reading, (survey, monograph, chapter, article), identifying main argument (acquiring University library ticket). The aim of this programme is to reinforce the various skills as students go through their first year.

27.4.4 English

The head of English said that students were discouraged from using secondary sources in their first year; instead they were encouraged to concentrate on looking at primary materials. In the first year students are provided with a handbook called *The Student Companion* — a ring binder to which they are encouraged to add information. There is no formal induction apart from this but the department makes a point of teaching all first years in groups no larger than 12. The head added that because of this pedagogical philosophy, the department was thinking of asking for their students' library induction to take place at the beginning of the second year, rather than in the first year so that it would be more relevant and subject specific to them.

27.5 Results

These will be presented subject by subject and the statistical findings will be interpreted in the light of the tutors' comments. In the tables that follow, the columns show the four subjects and in each cell we show the numbers of students who were able to correctly answer the quiz question plus the mean of their tutors' estimations in brackets.

English	Psychology	History	Environmental Studies
85 (65) (Novel)	36 (44) (Psychology)	88 (63) (Modern English history)	59 (20) (Physical geography)
71 (65) (Poetry)	17 (28) (Social psychology)	61 (37) (French history)	0 (23) (Environmental science)
0 (35) (Language)	9 (24) (Abnormal psychology)	27 (23) (Americanhistory)	45 (20) (Human geography)

Table 27.3 Comparison of identification of classification numbers in the four different subjects

27.5.1 Using the library classification scheme

Comparison data are shown in Table 27.3.

Looking at this table we can see that English and History students appear to do the best and, in both cases, better than their tutors expected. (The single exception was English Language where none of the students picked out this class number.)

Of course we might expect that the English students would do well as they are second years, but the History students did equally well and they were only first years — so why should they do better than EVS students and much better than psychology students who did rather badly?

The tutors' comments suggested disciplinary differences in provision — with History giving task-related work which means students *have* to know how to find books. One of the psychology tutors made a similar point but perhaps the reason why the psychology process wasn't so successful as History was because of the rather bolt-on nature of how information-seeking skills are dealt with in psychology, where the students are set a library orientation exercise but this isn't related specifically to their coursework.

> They are requested to complete a library quiz but this is without the guidance of their tutor so if they can't figure the library system out, help in the classroom is rather detached, anxieties already high. (Psychology tutor 7)

A bolt-on provision of providing study skills seminars and indirect help also seems to characterize EVS support.

> Helping is indirect rather than direct: we don't refer them to the number classifications. Students have seminars that focus on study skills — at the beginning, several are about finding & extracting information — they need therefore to use the library catalogue (EVS tutor 12)

27.5.2 Using journals in the library

A different pattern emerged when we looked at how good the students were in using and knowing about journals in their subject (see Table 27.4). Clearly English students are the best and far outperform their tutors expectations. This is rather odd because their tutors' comments highlighted again the need to work with primary sources:

> We help them in English to read texts and to talk and think about them. If we've done this we're doing well — with the best will in the world back copies of journals can't be a priority (English tutor 2)

One reason why English students know more about journals than their tutors estimated may be because they are second-year students and do combined honours degrees. So their training in their other main subject may well spill over into English.

Both Psychology and Environmental Science students did well on these questions, better than their tutors predicted, but what was particularly interesting was the very wide variation between individual tutors in knowing how to help their students. For example when asked about how students are helped to find out how many psychology journals there are in the library, one psychology tutor said:

> I don't know the answer to this, I have never been asked this question myself; — also not sure how relevant it would be to actually know. Students (and self!) mainly concerned with single journals which are required at the time. (Psychology tutor 8)

Other psychology tutors were somewhat more knowledgeable and the same variation between tutors was found in EVS with one being very knowledgeable and the other one not. The third tutor expressed a similar opinion to the psychology tutor quoted above by questioning whether it was in fact important for students to know how many journals were stocked in the library in their subject area. [While not wishing to digress too much, it is an interesting and fairly recurrent feature of student evaluation to criticise library provision — how much of this criticism is justified and how much is due to lack of knowledge by the students was one of the research questions that instigated this study]. In History two of the three tutors said that using journals was not a priority in the first year, which might account for why they underestimated their students' knowledge in the location of older journals.

27.5.3 Using the computer databases in the library

This question was asked as we were very interested to see how the different academic disciplines would respond to this relatively recent source of material. The spurious databases were included in the student quiz to provide some check against students simply guessing, for example they might have selected a database that had their subject mentioned in it.

It is quite clear from these tables that a number of students must have been guessing. In English and EVS the percentage of students identifying the spurious databases was bigger than the percentage identifying the genuine ones, and in History it was almost as big. The only exception was Psychology where the genuine database was correctly identified by a massive 98 per cent and the spurious one selected by only 40 per cent.

When tutors were asked about how students were helped to use databases, again there was a wide variation in response. In psychology for example, two said they gave personal advice and referred to a class session in Research Methods, two tutors weren't sure and one tutor didn't answer the question at all. In contrast, in EVS all three tutors were in accord and stated that information relating to databases was given as part of EVS students' practical classes in information technology. But perhaps the most interesting discrepancy between

English	Psychology	History	Environmental Studies
71 (30) (English Poetry)	98 (54) (Psychlit)	66 (30) (Historical Abstracts)	45 (53) (Life Sciences)
8 (60) (MLA Bibliography)			

Table 27.4 Comparison of computer database skills in the four different subjects: identifying genuine databases

staff and students came in English where the tutors expected 60 per cent of their students to know about the MLA bibliography and yet only a tiny percentage of 8 per cent actually did. This is a difficult finding to explain especially as one of the tutors said that most colleagues discuss the use of this database in class.

27.5.4 Searching effectively for books on the computer catalogue

When looking at how the students did, we can see that there's a remarkable similarity between the departments (see Table 27.6).

About two-thirds of students know to use a keyword, and about a third know to use titles and subjects, but hardly any student knows how to use the classmark. This came as a surprise to us as ex-librarians as we both know the value of not only searching by classmark on the catalogue but also on the shelves, as it is so much more precise than any of the other three ways, but clearly the tutors didn't expect their students to know about this way as they all predicted low percentages to get this right.

Looking at the difference between the departments, we can see that the History tutors thought their students would be better than they were, which is not surprising given the amount of support they give. One tutor makes special mention of the advice given in history seminars plus the necessity for knowing how to find books as they are needed for specific tasks — namely an exercise, an essay and a group project.

English	Psychology	History	Environmental Studies
81 (30) (Literature Online)*	40 (54) (Psychology Online)	59 (50) (HistLIT)	59 (37) (EnviroInfo)
59 (30) (English Abstracts)			55 (23) (Earth Sciences)

*Note: A database of this name later became available commercially but was not installed at the time of this research.

Table 27.5 Comparison of computer database skills in the four different subjects: wrongly identifying spurious databases

All three EVS lecturers thought students would know how to search effectively for books on a topic, but their estimations were not accurate — they grossly under-estimated percentage of students who would search by keyword (30 per cent as opposed to 73 per cent); their other estimations were over. Interestingly, when they were asked how students were helped to use the computer catalogue, their responses showed that they did not think such information was the responsibility of the subject tutors.

In psychology, library induction and the library orientation quiz appeared to be the biggest source of help and tutor advice was also mentioned but only by three of the five tutors. One tutor thought students probably worked it out by trial and error or by helping each other! Again we have a big variation in provision which may indicate discipline differences.

Searching for books on a particular topic by:	English	Psychology	History	Environmental Studies
Keyword	68 (50)	67 (60)	63 (67)	73 (30)
Subject	36 (90)	43 (50)	32 (70)	32 (57)
Classmark	2 (10)	0.6 (16)	0 (23)	0 (10)
Title	36 (10)	30 (58)	44 (57)	23 (57)

Table 27.6 Comparison of catalogue searching skills in the four different subjects

27.5.5 Using the Internet/WWW

The last question we asked in our quiz related to the Internet where we expected that there might be some differences between the departments. Looking at Table 27.7, we can see that English students use the Internet least (36 per cent) and Environmental Studies use it the most (86 per cent).

Perhaps unexpectedly, both History and EVS students used the Internet more than Psychology students. This may be because both these subjects made formal provision in their seminar system for WWW use. Where Psychology was concerned, 4 of the 5 tutors thought students should *not* be using the Internet. Psychology was an interesting case because again there were very different comments about what help students were given with two tutors claiming they weren't helped, one not sure and two being very knowledgeable about the sort of information students were given.

	English	Psychology	History	Environmental Sciences
Proportion of students using the Internet/WWW	36 (55)	54 (50)	66 (57)	86 (83)
Questioning the worth of information from an Individual's home page	31 (no response)	45 (52)	44 (73)	59 (27)
Questioning the worth of information from a Commercial organisation	22 (no response)	29 (30)	32 (73)	41 (23)

Table 27.7 Comparison of computer searching skills in the four different subjects

In English there was also a big difference of opinion, but as only two tutors were involved, we have to be cautious about making too much of this. Certainly, one of the two tutors was for the Internet but the other was strongly against it:

> We strongly suggest that they avoid it like the plague — soundbites are worthless and misleading and create endless possibilities for undetectable plagiarism. (English tutor 1)

Using the Internet seemed then to reveal distinct subject differences, but when it came to asking tutors about evaluating the worth of such information, they tended to all raise very similar concerns. One of the EVS tutors puts the problem very well:

> Discrimination and lack of it about quality of WWW materials is a major issue. Mostly students don't seem to be filtering info. — most seem to gather it on the 'more is better' principle. There's also the problem that you can 'collect' WWW info and *not actually read it*. I think this is even *more* of a problem with Internet stuff than stuff from other sources. (EVS tutor 3)

One of the English tutors was also concerned and said:

> Students tend not to question (English tutor 2)

Psychology and History tutors also sounded similar views. One of the psychology tutors said:

> Warnings that information is NOT peer-reviewed, often unscientific and non-academic (Psychology tutor 7)

and one of the History tutors said:

> advice is geared towards warning about excessive and indiscriminate use (History tutor 5)

27.6 Conclusions

First of all, it must be pointed out that this is a small-scale study, particularly with regard to the number of academic tutors that responded to our questionnaire, therefore we cannot be sure that their views represented each department accurately. Having said that we want to focus on four points:

1. One of the main finding from this research was that even though the students quite often outperformed their tutors expectations nevertheless the number of students getting the right answer to these very basic questions was often worryingly low. Our evidence then would seem to suggest that undergraduate students are *not* skilled in finding information from the library.
2. This finding coupled with what appear to be quite considerable differences between tutors about the amount of help students are given by their subjects would suggest that perhaps disciplines need to think more carefully about this aspect of student support.
3. A third finding seemed to suggest that any bolt-on provision was less useful than skills being integrated into the actual teaching of the subject itself. The departments providing the more formal in class/seminar provision with explicit links to the curriculum seemed to have more knowledgeable students.
4. In this study, we have shown that some of the tutors relied quite heavily on the library staff to help their students and there was a wide variation about how much they themselves knew about library provision. It may well be the luck of the draw then on how much help a student gets at the start of their academic degree. This is particularly so in view of the fact that library induction for students was optional, not compulsory.

These findings raise pedagogical issues about the nature of learning and knowledge. In Higher Education should we be mainly concerned with giving our students subject knowledge? Or should we be more concerned to give them generic skills to equip them as expert learners which they can then apply to any sphere of knowledge? It is beyond the scope of this research study to answer these questions, but clearly there is enough evidence here to indicate that further research needs to be carried out on the provision made by departments to help students with their information-seeking skills.

27.7 References

Jacobs, N.A. (1996) Students' perceptions of the library service at the University of Sussex: practical quantitative and qualitative research in an academic library, *The Journal of Documentation* **52**(2): 139—62.

Jiao, Q.C., Onwuegbuzie, A. and Lichtenstein, A. (1996) Library anxiety: characteristics of 'At Risk' college students, *Library and Information Science Research* **18**(2), 150—63.

Kember, D. (1997) A reconceptualisation of the research into university academics' conceptions of teaching, *Learning and Instruction* **7**(3), 255—75.

Knapper, C. (1995) Approaches to study and lifelong learning; some Canadian initiatives. In G. Gibbs (ed.) *Improving Student Learning: Through Assessment and Evaluation*. Oxford: The Oxford Centre for Staff Development.

Marton, F. and Säljö, R. (1976) On qualitative differences in learning: 1. Outcome and process, *British Journal of Educational Psychology* **46**, 4—11.

Mech, T.F and Brooks, C.I. (1997) Anxiety and confidence in using a library by college freshmen and seniors, *Psychological Reports* **81**, 929—30.

Norton, L., Brunas-Wagstaff, J. and Lockley, S (1999) Learning outcomes in the traditional coursework essay: Do students and tutors agree? in C. Rust (ed.), *Improving Student Learning: Improving Student Learning Outcomes*. Oxford: The Oxford Centre for Staff and Learning Development.

Wells, J. (1995) The influence of library usage on undergraduate academic success, *Australian Academic & Research Libraries* **26**(2): 121—8.

28 Disciplining interdisciplinarity: the design studio and the scholarship of integration

Dave O'Reilly, Nick Weaver and Mary Caddick
University of East London

28.1 Overview

Architectural education stands in the paradoxical position of being both opaque to most colleagues in other University departments and at the same time proposed by two such eminent educationalists as Donald Schön and Ernest Boyer as a model which other subjects might do well to emulate. This chapter seeks to identify the features of architectural education which generate these tensions, looking first at architecture's epistemological standing in relation to typical academic disciplines. We then present a more detailed analysis of a key feature of architectural education — the design studio or atelier — derived from the Atelier Principle in Teaching (APT) project. An important element of the APT project has been the articulation of tacit features of the design studio experience, not least through an experimental tutor training programme, which involved detailed observation of the learning process and critical reflection upon it by trainee tutors. We consider also how far architectural education might be considered a form of problem-based learning, or some other generic approach, in contrast with developing a discipline-based understanding within its own discourses and metaphors. Drawing upon Boyer's call for a wider conception of scholarship, including a scholarship of integration, we suggest that both the atelier method and the associated tutor training programme may have features of interest to other disciplines, but more importantly may offer adaptable models for interdisciplinary learning.

28.2 Introduction

Edward: And since then, I have realized that mine is a very unusual case.
Reilly: All cases are unique, and very similar to others.

(T.S. Eliot, *The Cocktail Party*)

Though it perceives of itself as a distinctive discipline and profession, architecture is remarkably interdisciplinary in practice, which is reflected in turn in the professional formation of architects and in the curriculum of architectural education. The resulting epistemological and disciplinary tensions have generated much debate within architecture and have attracted the attention of both Donald Schön and Ernest Boyer, two influential commentators on learning in professional and higher education, as we shall discuss below. In the first section below, following Schön (1985), we will argue that architecture occupies an anomalous position relative to typical academic disciplines, in that it remains rooted in an epistemological tradition that predates the technical rationalist model dominant in higher education and professional education. Yet, despite its anomalous position, or even precisely because of it, Schön (1985, 1987) and later Boyer (Boyer and Mitgang, 1996) both argue that architectural education offers an appropriate model of learning in a world of increasingly messy problems which do not recognize neat disciplinary boundaries.

We will then explore what might be distinctive about architecture as a discipline (or what it means 'to think like an architect') and how that epistemological stance is typically cultivated in the education of architects. We comment on the interplay of different disciplines in the architectural curriculum and how they are integrated through the design project. Our discussion acknowledges diversity in schools of architecture, while reporting findings from research on the staff and student experience of the atelier (or unit or design studio) method of teaching and learning at one university in the UK.

The School of Architecture at the University of East London has been funded by HEFCE (the Higher Education Funding Council for England and Wales) from 1996 to 1999 under the Fund for the Development of Teaching and Learning (FDTL) to disseminate its version of the atelier method for teaching architecture. One method of dissemination of the atelier method has been the development of a tutor training programme, based on placement of a trainee tutor in an atelier unit supported by weekly reflective seminars. Discussion in the seminars not only contributed to articulating more clearly aspects of atelier teaching in practice, but also generated a wider and deeper conversation about architectural education, including a series of staff colloquia within the School of Architecture.

A feature of the training programme has been the extent to which discussion in the seminars has often resisted generic models of learning and teaching in higher education, tending instead to develop understanding of the learning process through personal metaphors and a distinctively architectural educational discourse. We reflect also upon our own attempts, as project collaborators with diverse academic backgrounds, to contain the atelier method as a form of problem-based learning and the unease we have felt at times with that.

In conclusion we suggest that there may be features of the atelier and the experimental tutor training programme that may be of interest to other disciplines and, more importantly, to developing ways of working between and beyond disciplines: to contribute, in Boyer's terms, to the scholarship of integration (Boyer, 1990).

28.3 Architectural education, interdisciplinarity and integrative learning

In a brief historical survey of architectural education, Broadbent (1995) quotes from the classical work of Vitruvius (c. 80 BC):

> Let [the student of architecture] be educated, skillful with the pencil, instructed in geometry, know much history, have followed the philosophers with attention, understand music, have some knowledge of medicine, know the opinions of the jurists, and be acquainted with the theory of the heavens.

Two millennia later, the scope of the architectural curriculum is no less demanding, though the details might vary, with current requirements ranging from principles of structural engineering to issues of sustainability and social inclusion. It is no wonder that architectural training in the UK takes seven years (three years for Part One, equivalent to Honours Degree; two years in practice; then two years for Diploma) and that there is debate about the disciplinary status of architecture.

Teymur traces the roots of debate to the dual nature of architecture as both design discipline and vocational practice:

> The desire to identify architecture as, say, technology and/or craft and/or science and/or art throughout the centuries betrays the very paradox of the idea of architecture *both* as a multi-disciplinary, multi-skilled, multi-dimensional and multi-media practice *and* as a self-sufficient profession that behaves as if it already possesses all the knowledge it needs. (Teymur, p. 17)

The duration and intensity of debate reflects the importance of disciplinary identity within academia (O'Reilly and Wareing). For Schön (1985), the identity crisis for architecture resides in its rootedness in an epistemological tradition of professional artistry that predates the now dominant technical rational model of expertise, in which knowledge is generated primarily through disciplinary research in universities, to be applied by professional experts to the rational solution of technical problems. The core of the architect's training in the design studio derives from the *Beaux Arts* method of training artists through apprenticeship in the atelier of a master. Through his study of student—teacher interaction in the design studio, Schön (1985, 1987) identified an educational process which gave an appropriate preparation for dealing with the swampy ground of architectural practice and 'the indeterminate zones of complexity, uncertainty, uniqueness and value conflict' in professional practice generally (1985, p. 83). Herein resides a challenge:

> Not only students of design, but all those who seek to learn the artistry of a practice new to them, face an epistemological paradox and psychological predicament. They need to educate themselves to a new competence when they don't know yet what it is they need to learn. And they must therefore plunge into *doing* before they know what to do. Similarly, those who try to help these students need an artistry of coaching similar in its essentials to the artistry they want to help students to acquire. (p. 88)

Yet Schön was still optimistic that the 'reflective practicum' modelled on the design studio/atelier could usefully be extended to other professions, where design may be taken as a powerful metaphor for 'constructionalist' conceptions of world making (Goodman), a model for professional education (O'Reilly, 1998) or a mode of general education (Schön, 1985, pp. 92—7).

Schön's study was commissioned by the Royal Institute of British Architects in the UK. A cognate study commissioned in the USA by the five major national architectural professional bodies echoed this suggestion of the design studio as a general model, emphasizing the *integrative* dimension:

> Making the connections, both *within* the architecture curriculum and *between* architecture and other disciplines on campus, is, we believe, the single most important challenge facing architectural programs.
>
> The good news is that architecture, by nature and tradition, holds vast potential as a model for the integration and application of learning, largely because of its most distinctive feature — *the design studio*. The integrative possibilities of studio extend far beyond architecture. MIT's architecture school, for example, recently began an experimental course that applies the studio methods of architecture to teaching software design. Beyond question, the design studio is a model that many other disciplines on campus, as well as elementary and secondary schools, could well profit from. (Boyer and Mitgang, p. 85)

Like Schön, Boyer was critical of the over-dominance of research in higher education, arguing instead for a re-visioning of scholarship which recognizes the scholarship of discovery on a par with scholarships of teaching, application and integration (Boyer, 1990). It is interesting that in architecture, which is relatively weak in the scholarship of discovery (at least in Research Assessment Exercises), Boyer should have found a community of '"engaged scholarship", which if combined with civic commitment, holds virtually endless possibilities for renewing communities or even nations' (Boyer and Mitgang, 1996, p. xiii).

However, before we get carried away by the vision, let us refocus on how the atelier works, taking the UEL system as our exemplar.

28.4 Distinctive features of the pedagogy of architecture at UEL

In this section we do not intend to give an exhaustive account of the atelier method. (For a more detailed account, see Weaver, 1997.) Our purpose is to note some distinctive features to consider in relation to methods of teaching and learning and appropriate forms of tutor training for those methods.

The aim of architectural education is to induce the student to 'think like an architect'. At UEL this is interpreted as being :

> to develop the conceptual, analytical, imaginative and practical skills necessary for the student to determine human needs and aspirations and to meet and express these in space and form (BA Architecture Student Handbook, UEL, 1998)

The architect is someone who does something, so the definition is couched in terms of actions, procedures, processes or performance, rather than a fixed body of knowledge. As Schön remarked, 'The architectural studio is one of the few forms of traditional higher education centred on making things' (1985, p. 94) (though we shall qualify this below).

Two kinds of activity are indicated: the architect finds out what is required and then makes a proposition. Thus 'thinking like an architect' involves periods of analysis and periods of synthesis. One of the features of architectural education that distinguishes it on the one hand from library-based subjects like history and on the other from studio-based subjects like painting, is the weight given in the learning process and the final assessment to both the quality of the analysis — the formulation of the problem, what needs have to be met, what are the conditions obtaining — and the quality of the synthesis. The final result is often called the architect's design, but in fact designing embraces the whole process of analysing the problem and synthesizing into a building proposal. The process is iterative, cycling repeatedly between analysis and synthesis, and perhaps should be understood as a process of increasingly precise problem formulation, to whose definition the solution contributes.

Architecture is both a science and an art. Every architectural design is the solution to a problem, and to some extent every design is a new problem requiring a new solution. 'Thinking like an architect' cannot be learnt by demonstration or by rote, it can only be learnt through the repeated experience of the process of analysis and synthesis that constitutes designing. An essential task in teaching consists in organizing the situation so students will have the necessary experience of analysis and synthesis. Traditionally the main armature to organize this experience is the design project. The design project involves the student in formulating the problem and proposing a solution. The design project is a streamlined version of what students will later do in an office, but shorn of the educationally less useful interruptions and distractions of the 'real world'.

When schools of architecture first started, the final output tended to be similar to the descriptive drawings architects produced for their clients and the instructions architects produce for the contractor. The fact that the output of architecture students, unlike students of painting or music or history, is surrogate (not actual buildings but descriptions of something that does not yet exist) imparts a particular quality to the education. Though the ultimate aim of the architect is to organize space and form, characteristically as buildings, a peculiarity of the output of architectural students is that they are not the buildings themselves but evocative/descriptive of what the context is, as well as what the building would be like, its spatial arrangement and materials, and of the process by which it would be constructed. Thus the proposition has always to be understood conceptually and even the synthetic stage of the design process is shot through with analysis, since the building in order to be understood has to be broken down conceptually into its significant aspects: it is developed, described and understood in plans and section and axonometric projection.

Thus the analytical faculties are being exercised at all stages. Developing the capacity to decide what is significant makes up a large part of the education. A peculiarity of architectural education is that teachers are making an assessment on the basis of descriptions, of various kinds, of something which does not yet exist, and which if it did exist would have all sorts of unexpected qualities and attributes and consequences that are not explicit in the drawings and models.

As architectural education has developed, the characteristic output of students has tended to evolve into something (drawings, wire and plaster models, collages, photos, snippets of video) less intelligible to either client or contractor but which can form the basis of discussion in the academy. These discussions appear arcane to the outsider partly because they are concerned with the development of the students' creative processes, how they might think about the architectural problem, as much as the architectural proposition itself as it would appear in the real world if it were built. Often what is produced for discussion is not intended to be built: it is (to borrow a phrase from science) a thought experiment.

Each atelier is led by one or two part-time tutors who are practising architects. The tutors present their theme for the year at a Market Day in September, then negotiate with students to form units of about 15 people, which stay together for the year. Themes proposed by tutors might be 'the understanding of distinctive relations of ground, structure and level' (UEL, 1999, p. 60) or 'the desires and values that organise domestic space, their inscriptions in the assembled interior of the house and in the placement of objects in and around it' (p. 48). What this might mean in terms of a programme for the year may be little understood at the start by the students and it will be unclear even to the tutors where the group will end up or even how it will get there week by week. In this respect the studio replicates the features of uncertainty and indeterminacy that Schön identified as typical of professional practice.

This indeterminacy in the atelier unit's programme leads to some distinctive features in formative and summative assessment. At regular stages in the year each student's propositions are made public, displayed on the wall, for commentary by a combination of the unit tutor(s), tutors of other units and visiting critics. These are emotionally charged events and this may be the feature most obvious to the non-architect. However, the mode of presentation is also interesting, as information is conveyed in way that is non linear — several drawings can be looked at simultaneously — which may become more prevalent in other disciplines with the incursion of hypertexts into the realm of the traditional essay. Also interesting is the intensity of public debate between members of the panel or jury, in which to some extent the precise parameters of assessment or outcomes of learning are being formulated right up to the last moment. This process reveals clearly the collegial dimensions of assessment, yet it may appear very strange to disciplines which have other ways of arriving at assessments.

A further contrast with other disciplines at UEL is that architecture is the only undergraduate programme that is not modularized. The School has insisted on the possibility of making an integrated course, as represented schematically in Figure 28.1, which also shows the basic distinction between (K) the knowledge and skills underlying any discipline and (A) their application in practice. As we have noted earlier, a particular feature of the knowledge base in architecture is that it is almost entirely drawn from other disciplines, which are then synthesized and applied in practice. These disciplines include technical subjects (such as structural mechanics), practical skills (such as photography, drawing, and computing) and contextual studies (such as architectural history and theory). The Applied side of the diagram represents studio-based design work. The curve shows that in the early years there is a greater proportion of K to A, while as the student progresses through the course and becomes more effective the proportion of A to K increases. Final degree classification is based on the student's atelier work, though the various supporting studies must also be passed.

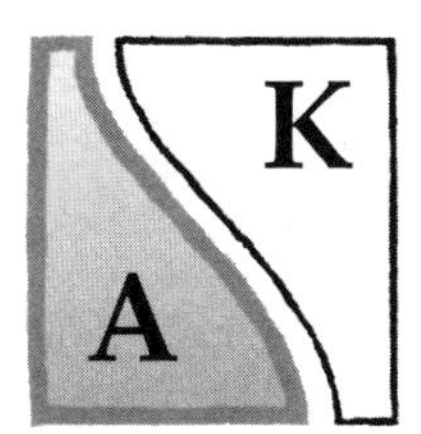

Figure 28.1: Application/Knowledge (A/K)

The rationale for this is that architects need to draw on these disciplines, they are not required to be historians or engineers. They need the knowledge only in so far as it supports their own practice as architects. Because every problem is a new problem, one of the important things they are learning is how to decide when they need to know something, what it is significant to know in any particular case, and how to communicate with specialists. At UEL most of the teaching of supporting subjects is modelled on the way design is taught. For instance in History the site of learning is the seminar, to which each student makes a formal contribution, and the lecture is less a way of imparting specific information than the opportunity to watch a trained mind think. In technical subjects such as structures, students learn through making experiments from which principles are derived, and so on.

In summary, we have highlighted features of the atelier method that can be related to Schön's notion of the reflective practicum and Boyer's notion of integrative learning. We have also portrayed the atelier as a form of problem based learning (PBL). Previous studies, particularly at the University of New South Wales (de Graaff and Cowdroy, 1995; Maitland, 1997) have already established this connection. However, we note that the very open-endedness of both problem and solution in the atelier sits uneasily with some approaches to PBL which favour the use of well-defined problems with more determinate solutions. We have recently established contact with colleagues in architecture at NSW to explore such issues, but it may be that a wider spectrum of PBL typologies will emerge only from fuller consideration of design disciplines alongside medicine, law and engineering.

In the next section we will return to Schön's remark about teaching in the design studio, 'Similarly, those who try to help these students need an artistry of coaching similar in its essentials to the artistry they want to help students to acquire' (Schön,1985, p. 88), and consider features of an experimental atelier tutor training programme.

28.5 Outline of an Atelier tutor training programme

At an early stage in the APT project, the authors of this paper decided to offer an experimental atelier tutor training programme as a means of dissemination of the atelier method (O'Reilly, Weaver and Caddick). Such a programme would be an innovation in architecture. As Rhowbotham has remarked:

> It is customary among practising architects to assume that those who have achieved some degree of experience are automatically equipped with all that is necessary to teach. Nothing could be further from the truth. The skills which are required to teach successfully cannot be acquired in the context of practice. Teaching is a separate order of things, tied to practice certainly, but by analogy, not by stricture ...
>
> Practitioners construct the world from pragmatic instrumentalities, and necessarily so, since their context demands it. Teaching, on the other hand, engages a separate discourse in which its conditions of operation are always analogous to the act of building. What must be taught is a process of thinking, an articulacy of speculation and reflection.
>
> The materiality of teaching is conceptual. (Rhowbotham, 1995)

We have quoted this at some length to illustrate the ways architects talk to each other about teaching architecture, using an architectural discourse and metaphors that would not typically be found in the learning and teaching literature. From the beginning we were aware that translation between the generic and the disciplinary discourses would be problematic.

Another problem was that we really did not know what made good atelier tutoring. Of the three authors, one had some idea, from teaching in the system and from managing it, but it was less accessible to the others, who are not architects. Even for an architect much of the skill of tutoring remained implicit knowledge. To quote Schön again:

> In a reflective practicum, it is assumed that both instructor and student know more than they can say. The instructor seeks to reflect aloud on the reflection-in-action implicit in her demonstrations, and on the assumptional basis of her judgement of the student's work. The student is encouraged to reflect on what he already knows, on the difficulties he experiences, and on the emergent understanding implicit in his performances. (1985, p. 90)

In hindsight, we might claim to have constituted the tutor training as a reflective practicum, where the central element is a placement in an atelier unit one day a week supported by a weekly seminar for critical reflection and discussion. In truth it was more a pragmatic response to enabling the tutor trainees to learn something we could not tell them and to do so by experiencing it and articulating it in their own words.

Though there were also weekly inputs on key concepts from current approaches to learning and teaching, the trainees made little spontaneous use of these generic ideas either in the seminars or in the written work submitted in a portfolio for assessment. Instead each trainee seemed to find a personal metaphor, which also acted almost as a mantra — a case of 'naming the process' (Griffin, 1987). For example, one trainee worked repeatedly around the notion of 'throwing off balance', as he explains:

> The intention of the teaching method referred to here as 'throwing the students off-balance' is to confront the students with a learning environment where the familiar rules no longer apply. In this unstable situation, a state of confusion sets in among the students, one in which their preconceived ideas and existing beliefs start to become suspect. Through this process, they are forced to re-examine their existing value systems and methodologies, and from this a new synthesis may emerge.
>
> What of the students' experience of being thrown off-balance? How do they respond to this? Does it serve to stimulate them into deeper learning, or does it make it a greater struggle to achieve the tangible goals of the unit (producing required work, completing projects etc.).
>
> It is difficult to address this from the observations and reflections recorded in the first term. It is possible to make some generalizations. The students have struggled to gain a secure foothold on their new and unstable ground. They have shown signs of frustration at all the various incidents of being thrown off balance, evidenced by facial expressions, body language, comments, discussions during tutorials and perhaps even by their sporadic attendance. Their difficulties with this situation come through in their work, both in the amount produced and nature of it.
>
> That they have had difficulty with the initial project of identifying their architectural touchstone is both understandable and puzzling: understandable in that it is a new way for most of beginning the design process, and puzzling in that to an outsider it seems so clear how they can push forward their ideas that they themselves are so unsure of. (quoted in University of East London, School of Architecture, 1999, p. 20)

While there is an allusion here to the generic concepts of deep and surface learning, it is not foregrounded. The account develops the personal metaphor (which Bob traced elsewhere to a transformative experience he had had as a student) in a way which is true to the student experience in the atelier unit. Like the other trainees' portfolios, it demonstrates rich and insightful reflection on the learning and teaching process on a tutor training programme with very little didactic input.

More recently we have come to think of the tutor training group as another atelier, in which we grapple with tutoring an atelier as another form of design activity and performance. As in the architectural design studios, our trainee tutors go through cycles of analysis and synthesis, culminating in the grand synthesis for the year, a proposition for 'an atelier of my own'.

28.6 Conclusions

This chapter has asked, first, whether there are distinctive features of architectural education that might be of relevance to other disciplines; and, secondly, how these features might derive from the interdisciplinary aspects of architecture. Further, we have reflected on what this might mean for a tutor training programme in architecture.

On the first issue we would agree cautiously with Schön that the design studio offers a rich learning environment for reflective professional practice and with Boyer that it offers a model for integrative learning. Both writers based their assessments on a critique of dominant modes of discipline-based research and knowledge production in universities. We have suggested that while architecture is relatively weak in the scholarship of discovery as conventionally measured in Research Assessment Exercises, it is strong in the scholarships of integration and application.

The atelier tutor training programme at UEL has been an experiment in finding a form of tutor training consistent with the atelier principle in teaching. To the extent that we have succeeded the experience has been no less messy and frustrating at times than in any other indeterminate zone of professional practice. We have found that trainees find their way through the zone using personal metaphors and architectural discourses in preference to generic models and concepts. Perhaps this form of ownership is necessary for deep learning to take place.

We have also expressed our unease at categorizing the design studio too readily under any generic umbrella, such as problem based learning (PBL). This is not to deny that PBL has been and continues to be a very useful bridging concept from architecture to other disciplines. Rather it is to note that there are features of the design studio, such as the very open-ended nature of the problem and the possible solutions, that do not square easily with some schools of thought about PBL, which favour problems for learning which are much more well-defined. This may be remedied if wider consideration is given to design disciplines as forms of PBL.

Address for correspondence

Dave O'Reilly, University of East London, Manbey Park Road, London E15 1EY. e-mail: d.oreilly@uel.ac.uk

28.7 Bibliography

Boyer, E.L. (1990) *Scholarship Reconsidered*. Washington, DC: Carnegie Foundation for the Advancement of Learning.

Boyer E L. and Mitgang L.D. (1996) *Building Community: A new future for architectural education and practice*. Princeton, NJ: Carnegie Foundation for the Advancement of Learning.

Broadbent, G. (1995) Architectural education. In Pearce, M. and Toy, M. (eds), *Educating Architects*. London: Academy Editions, pp. 10—23.

de Graaff, E. and Cowdroy, R (1995) Theory and practice of educational innovation: a case study on the introduction of problem-based learning in architecture. In Little, P, Ostwald, M and Ryan, G (eds), *Research and Development in Problem Based Learning. Vol 3*. Sydney: Australian Problem Based Learning Network, pp. 125—36.

Goodman, N. (1978) *Ways of Worldmaking*. Hackett Publishing.

Griffin V. (1987) Naming the process. In Boud, D. and Griffin, V. (eds), *Appreciating Adults Learning: From the Learner's Perspective*. London: Kogan Page.

Maitland, B. (1997) Problem-based learning for an architecture degree. In Boud, D. and Feletti, G. (eds) *The Challenge of Problem-Based Learning*, 2nd edn. London: Kogan Page, pp. 211—17.

O'Reilly, D. (1998) In conversation with Donald Schön: learning through reflection on conversations. In O'Reilly, D., Cunningham, L. and Lester, S. (eds) (1998) *Developing the Capable Practitioner: Professional Capability Through Higher Education*. London: Kogan Page, pp. 9—15.

O'Reilly, D. and Wareing, S. (1999) Alien cultures: transgressing the boundaries of academic tribes. Paper to joint Society for Research into Higher Education (SRHE) and Staff Educational Development Association (SEDA) Conference: *Research and Practice in Educational Development(s): exploring the links*, Stoke Rochford, April 1999.

O'Reilly, D., Weaver, N. and Caddick, M. (1999) Developing and delivering a tutor training programme for problem based learning: a case study in architecture. In Conway, J., Melville, D. and Williams, A. (eds), *Research and Development in Problem Based Learning: Volume 5*. University of Newcastle, NSW: Australian Problem Based Learning Network, pp. 194—202.

Rhowbotham, K. (1995) *Form to Programme*. London: Black Dog Publishing.

Schön, D.A. (1985) *The Design Studio: An Exploration of its Traditions and Potentials*. London: RIBA Publications.

Schön, D.A. (1987) *Educating the Reflective Practitioner: towards a new design for teaching and learning in the professions*. San Francisco: Jossey-Bass.

Teymur, N. (1992) *Architectural Education: Issues in educational practice and policy*. London: ?uestion Press.

UEL School of Architecture (1999) *Book of the Year No 5*. London: University of East London.

Weaver, N. (1997) The atelier principle in teaching. In Knudsen, M. and Vinther, T.S. (eds), *Project Work in University Studies*. Roskilde, Denmark: Roskilde University, pp. 97—105.

29 Qualitative aspects of teaching and assessing in the chemical engineering curriculum: applications of the SOLO taxonomy

Thomas Olsson

Lund Institute of Technology, School of Engineering in Helsingborg, Lund University, Sweden

29.1 Introduction

Learning in higher education involves both quantitative and qualitative aspects. Traditionally, especially in science and technology, quantitative aspects of teaching and assessing have been emphasized at the expense of qualitative aspects. Some important questions raised in this chapter deal with this problem.

What do existing examination papers from the different courses within the curriculum look like? Do they make it possible for students to demonstrate learning at qualitatively high levels? Section 29.2 presents an investigation of examination papers within the chemical engineering curriculum.

What happens if students are presented with an assessment designed especially to measure the qualitative level of learning? Is it important if the examination is written or oral? Do the students show a deep, holistic approach or a surface, atomistic approach to learning? Section 29.3 presents a qualitative examination in chemical engineering.

What characteristics of a teaching method are important if you want to enhance the quality of learning? This question is discussed in connection with a presentation of a special teaching method used in chemical engineering called 'Solving Practical Problems'. Section 29.4 presents the method and its qualitative features.

The SOLO (Structure of the Observed Learning Outcome) taxonomy is a model for qualitative evaluation of teaching and assessing (Biggs and Collis, 1982). It consists of five levels of increasing structural complexity. These levels are called the prestructural, unistructural, multistructural, relational and extended abstract levels. The SOLO taxonomy is applied in the analysis of the different aspects of quality in teaching and assessing presented in this study.

29.2 A solo analysis of examination papers within the curriculum

29.2.1 Overview of the investigation

What kind of assignments you present to your students are crucial to the answers you get. Not only the content of the questions but also how they are formulated can result in quite different answers at qualitatively very different levels. You get what you ask for and nothing more. This is especially true regarding the answers you receive from students studying only to pass an examination.

This study presents a thorough investigation of 80 examination papers within the Chemical Engineering Curriculum (Bachelor of Science level) at Lund University. The papers represent the following subjects: food engineering, food technology, applied nutrition, analytical chemistry, biochemistry, general chemistry, microbiology and chemical engineering. Of the papers investigated about 60 per cent were given during the years 1991—94 and 40 per cent from 1997 to 1999. Major revisions of the curriculum were performed between the two periods investigated.

In the study all relevant questions were categorized according to the possibility of reaching and identifying different SOLO levels when answering the questions.

29.2.2 Examples of questions inviting answers at different SOLO levels

A representative selection from the more than 1050 analysed questions and tasks is listed below. It gives a good picture of the various questions of the examination papers and the maximal SOLO levels that can be expected from the corresponding answers.

Questions inviting unistructural responses

•Which are the Latin names of the families' wheat, barley, maize and oats? (Food Technology)

- What factors are important to consider in connection with cold storage of foodstuff? (Food Technology)
- What is gluten? (Food Technology)
- Which membrane processes would you suggest if you should

(a) separate fat from wastewater?
(b) recover proteins from whey?
(c) desalinate seawater? (Food Engineering)

- Many of our choices of different foodstuffs have changed during the 20th century. Give two examples of foodstuffs that we have increased and decreased our consumption of respectively. (Applied Nutrition)
- Give two examples of metabolic fibres. (Applied Nutrition)
- Which two rules for the solvents are important to consider in LSC-separations (adsorption chromatography)? (Analytical Chemistry)
- Explain the following terms

(a) primary structure of a protein
(b) transcription
(c) translation
(d) feed-back inhibition
(e) induced-fit theory
(f) essential amino-acid (Biochemistry)

- State six important differences between procaryotic and eucaryotic organisms. (Microbiology)

- Explain the following terms

(a) D-number
(b) pasteurisation
(c) BOD
(d) restriction enzyme
(e) secondary metabolite (Microbiology)

- Name five different bacteria that can be found in milk. (Microbiology)

Questions inviting multistructural responses

- Explain why bread baked with rye flour is more compact than bread baked with wheat flour. (Food Technology)
- Describe the manufacturing of soured milk. (Food Technology)
- What purpose has selenium in the body? (Applied Nutrition)
- What is the characteristic of the composition of olive oil, maize oil and coconut butter respectively? (Applied nutrition)
- Describe the construction and the characterisation of the different sources of light that are used in UV-VIS-spectrophotometers. (Analytical Chemistry)
- Describe two different principles of building up a mobile phase gradient in HPLC. State advantages and disadvantages. (Analytical Chemistry)
- Describe the different RNA-types of a cell and their tasks in the protein synthesis. (Biochemistry)
- Describe schematically the cycling of carbon in nature. (Microbiology)
- There are three distinct mechanisms for DNA-transfer. Describe them briefly. (Microbiology)

Questions inviting relational and extended abstract responses

- What is food quality? Discuss the question from the point of view of the consumer, authorities, distribution system, processing industry and food security. (Food Technology)
- A company that exports pharmaceuticals to tropical countries has received several complaints that the tablets absorb moisture and therefore cannot be used. As a newly employed engineer you are asked if you know anything about 'sorption isotherms'. The product development department claims that the problem might be better understood if you know something about sorption isotherms. Can you help them? (Food Engineering)
- You can nowadays find several fermented milk products sold in ordinary grocer's shops with health promotive arguments published in scientific journals. The products contain living cultures that are good for your health and stomach. Make a proposal of how you should best quality-secure a fermented milk product. Follow the production line from the milk entering the Pasteur to the packed milk product in the refrigerated display case in the shop. (Food Technology)

- You are working with product development within a large food company. The market department has received information about a possible market for products promoting the blood lipids. There is already a proposal to introduce a cholesterol-free oil on the market. Answer this and make other proposals. (Applied Nutrition)
- 'Line spectral sources of light must be used in AAS-instruments.' Discuss this statement. (Analytical Chemistry)
- 'Using AAS with a flame the sample is used ineffectively.' Analyse this statement. (Analytical Chemistry)
- You work in a food laboratory where an optimal pasteurisation process for a foodstuff is to be designed. Your task is to propose an experiment for this purpose. How would you design the experiment? State what you think is especially important to consider. (Microbiology)
- There are several different methods that can be used to identify and classify micro-organisms. You receive a completely unknown micro-organism that you should try to characterise. How would you proceed? What characteristics would you consider to be most important to determine? The investigations are to be conducted in a normally equipped microbiological laboratory. (Microbiology)

Examination paper	**Total of points**	**Relevant points**	**SOLO levels**					
			unistructural		*multistructural*		*relational and extended abstract*	
			points	*%*	*points*	*%*	*points*	*%*
Food Engineering, 5 credits								
fall' 92	72	36	18	**50**	14	**39**	4	**11**
spring '93	61	29	13	**45**	14	**48**	2	**7**
summer '93	68	38	15	**39**	23	**61**	0	**0**
fall '93	56	25	0	**0**	21	**84**	4	**16**
spring '94	58	31	4	**13**	27	**87**	0	**0**
Food Technology, 3 credits								
summer '91	50	36	16	**44**	17	**47**	3	**9**
spring '92	107	72	20	**28**	52	**72**	0	**0**
summer '92	87	58	22	**38**	32	**55**	4	**7**
fall '92	32	32	15	**47**	14	**44**	3	**9**
spring '93	59	38	8	**21**	24	**63**	6	**16**
summer '93	61	38	13	**34**	23	**61**	2	**5**
Applied Nutrition, 3 credits								
fall '92	108	104	66	**63**	38	**37**	0	**0**
fall '93	112	112	72	**64**	40	**36**	0	**0**

Table 29.1 Food Technology Courses, 1991-1994

- A chemical engineer performs a batch distillation using a glass tube filled with crushed glass connected as a column directly above a boiler. All vapour that leaves the column is condensed and withdrawn as a distillate. The condenser is connected in such a way that there is no reflux. Despite this the engineer succeeds in concentrating the volatile component much more than would be expected from an ideal tray (the boiler). Try to explain this. (Chemical Engineering)

29.2.3 Results

29.2.3.1 Tables with a complete presentation of the results

Only relevant questions were analysed with regard to possible answers at different SOLO levels. Relevant questions are theoretical and explorative problems. Questions testing methods of calculation and design were regarded as non-relevant for a SOLO analysis.

The sizes of the different courses are given as credits. In the Swedish higher educational system one credit represents one week of full-time studies.

Examination paper	Total of points	Relevant points	SOLO levels					
			unistructural		*multistructural*		*relational and extended abstract*	
			points	*%*	*points*	*%*	*points*	*%*
Unit Operations, 4 credits								
fall'97	49	17	4	**24**	8	**47**	5	**29**
spring "99	58	29	10	**34**	9	**32**	10	**34**
Production Technology, 4 credits								
spring '98	46	46	0	**0**	31	**67**	15	**33**
spring '99	46	46	0	**0**	23	**50**	23	**50**
Raw Materials, 2 credits								
fall '98	97	97	36	**37**	54	**56**	7	**7**
Applied Nutrition, 5 credits								
spring'98	75	75	15	**20**	24	**32**	36	**48**
Final Examination, 20 credits								
spring'98	-	-	-	**0**	-	**0**	-	**100**
spring '99	-	-	-	**0**	-	**0**	-	**100**

Table 29.2 Food and Drug Technology Courses, 1997-1999

Examination papers from different food (and drug) technology courses are presented in Tables 29.1 and 29.2. Before the revision of the curriculum these courses comprised a total of 11 credits (Table 29.1). After the revision a single course in food and drug technology (20 credits) was introduced (Table 29.2). Except for applied nutrition the same teachers were

Examination paper	Total of points	Relevant points	SOLO levels					
			unistructural		*multistructural*		*relational and extended abstract*	
			points	%	*points*	%	*points*	%
Analytical Chemistry, 3 credits								
fall'92	40	10	0	**0**	10	**100**	0	**0**
spring "93	35	12	3	**25**	9	**75**	0	**0**
Analytical Chemistry with Food Analysis, 4 credits								
fall '92	27	16	0	**0**	16	**100**	0	**0**
fall '93	25	16	5	**31**	8	**50**	3	**19**
fall '94	28	21	2	**10**	6	**28**	13	**62**
spring '94	28	24	4	**17**	9	**37**	11	**46**
fall '94	30	16	3	**19**	10	**62**	3	**19**
fall '95	30	16	0	**0**	12	**75**	4	**25**
Instrumental Analytical Chemistry, 5 credits								
spring '97	80	50	3	**6**	19	**38**	28	**56**
summer '97	70	54	2	**4**	20	**37**	32	**59**
fall '97	70	42	4	**10**	24	**57**	14	**33**
Analytical Chemistry - Modern Separation Methods, 5 credits								
fall '96 (1)	80	80	6	**8**	62	**77**	12	**15**
fall '96 (2)	80	80	0	**0**	51	**64**	29	**36**
fall '97	80	80	15	**19**	48	**60**	17	**21**
spring '98	80	77	18	**24**	49	**64**	9	**12**
summer '98	80	80	8	**10**	38	**47**	34	**43**
Food and Drug Analysis - Quality Assurance, 5 credits								
fall'98 (1)	60	60	4	**7**	17	**28**	39	**65**
fall '98 (2)	60	60	0	**0**	26	**43**	34	**57**

Table 29.3 Analytical Chemistry, 1992-1998

responsible for the courses both before and after the revision of the curriculum.

Analytical chemistry is presented in Table 29.3. New courses were introduced and different teachers were responsible for the courses before and after the revision of the curriculum. The course 'modern separation methods' was exchanged for 'food and drug analysis — quality assurance' in 1998.

Biochemistry and general chemistry are presented in Tables 29.4 and 29.5. The same teachers were responsible for the courses during the entire period investigated.

Table 29.6 presents different courses of microbiology. The content of the courses is the

Examination paper	Total of points	Relevant points	SOLO levels					
			unistructural		*multistructural*		*relational and extended abstract*	
			points	*%*	*points*	*%*	*points*	*%*
Biochemistry, 5 credits								
spring '93	49	49	32	**65**	17	**35**	0	**0**
summer '93	49	49	32	**65**	17	**35**	0	**0**
fall '93	49	37	31	**84**	6	**16**	0	**0**
spring '94	48	43	27	**63**	16	**37**	0	**0**
summer '94	50	40	20	**50**	20	**50**	0	**0**
Biochemistry and Physiology, 10 credits								
spring '98	87	77	27	**35**	50	**65**	0	**0**
fall '98 (1)	86	78	38	**49**	40	**51**	0	**0**
fall '98 (2)	92	82	34	**41**	48	**59**	0	**0**
spring '99	81	63	23	**37**	40	**63**	0	**0**

Table 29.4 Biochemistry, 1993-1999

Examination paper	Total of points	Relevant points	SOLO levels					
			unistructural		*multistructural*		*relational and extended abstract*	
			points	*%*	*points*	*%*	*points*	*%*
General Chemistry, 5 credits								
fall '92 (1)	80	28	12	**42**	8	**29**	8	**29**
fall '92 (2)	80	30	10	**33**	10	**33**	10	**33**
fall '93	100	16	4	**25**	8	**50**	4	**25**
General and Inorganic Chemistry, 10 credits								
fall '97 (1)	108	32	0	**0**	13	**41**	19	**59**
fall '97 (2)	108	31	0	**0**	10	**32**	21	**68**

Table 29.5 General Chemistry, 1992-1997

same before and after the revision of the curriculum. Different teachers were responsible for each of the courses analysed.

The courses of industrial chemistry and chemical engineering had all the same responsible teacher (Table 29.7).

Examination paper	Total of points	Relevant points	SOLO levels					
			unistructural		*multistructural*		*relational and extended abstract*	
			points	%	*points*	%	*points*	%
			Microbiology, 2 credits					
fall '90 (1)	44	40	16	**40**	24	**60**	0	**0**
fall '90 (2)	46	42	8	**19**	34	**81**	0	**0**
spring '91	48	48	20	**42**	18	**38**	10	**20**
fall '91	42	42	25	**60**	17	**40**	0	**0**
fall '92	41	41	20	**49**	21	**51**	0	**0**
fall '93	45	45	26	**58**	19	**42**	0	**0**
			Food Microbiology with Hygiene, 3 credits					
spring '93	60	60	23	**38**	29	**49**	8	**13**
summer '93	60	60	25	**42**	27	**45**	8	**13**
fall '93	60	60	21	**35**	17	**28**	22	**37**
spring '94	60	60	20	**33**	32	**54**	8	**13**
			General Microbiology, 5 credits					
spring '98(1)	100	95	28	**29**	57	**60**	10	**11**
spring '98(2)	100	98	17	**17**	44	**45**	37	**38**

Table 29.6 Microbiology, 1990-1998

29.2.3.2 Analysis of the reported results and some concluding reflections

An analysis of the reported results shows that the number of questions inviting answers at the relational and higher levels have increased considerably in recent years for many of the subjects investigated.

A comparison of papers from the first half of the 1990s with those from the second half of the decade illustrates this increase. This can be exemplified by general chemistry with an increase from an average of 30 to about 60 per cent questions at the relational level, chemical engineering from 30 to 60 per cent, food technology courses from less than 10 to 40 per cent, applied nutrition from 0 to 50 per cent and analytical chemistry from 20 to 40 per cent questions at the relational level.

Correspondingly questions at the unistructural level have decreased and for some subjects, such as applied nutrition, general chemistry and chemical engineering, there are no longer any examination tasks that only require answers at the unistructural level.

Examination papers of microbiology show the same tendency and in biochemistry the questions at the multistructural level have increased from 35 to 60 per cent although still no questions requiring answers at the relational level can be found.

The reason for this positive development is probably to be found in the major revisions of the curriculum performed in 1996—97. This stimulated the pedagogical discussions among

Examination paper	Total of points	Relevant points	SOLO levels unistructural points	%	multistructural points	%	relational and extended abstract points	%
Industrial Chemistry, 2 credits								
fall '92 (1)	60	60	34	**57**	18	**30**	8	**13**
fall '92 (2)	60	60	31	**52**	27	**45**	2	**3**
Chemical Engineering, 4 credits								
fall '92	60	27	4	**15**	12	**44**	11	**41**
spring '93(1)	60	16	0	**0**	12	**75**	4	**25**
spring '93(2)	60	23	10	**43**	8	**35**	5	**22**
spring '93(3)	60	19	4	**21**	6	**32**	9	**47**
summer '93	60	21	4	**19**	10	**48**	7	**33**
fall '93(1)	60	22	8	**36**	10	**46**	4	**18**
fall '93(2)	60	16	4	**25**	10	**62**	2	**13**
fall '93(3)	60	22	8	**36**	9	**41**	5	**23**
Chemical Engineering, 5 credits								
fall '96	60	15	0	**0**	7	**47**	8	**53**
fall '97	60	16	0	**0**	2	**13**	14	**87**
spring '98	60	29	2	**7**	12	**41**	15	**52**
fall '98	60	13	0	**0**	6	**46**	7	**54**
spring '99	60	14	0	**0**	8	**57**	6	**43**

Table 29.7 Chemical Engineering, 1992-1999

the teachers at several departments who take part in the teaching within the curriculum. Another aspect of the revision is the new structure of the curriculum. It comprises a total of only 14 courses, which favours a deep holistic approach in teaching as well as learning.

Another important factor is most certainly the increased pedagogical activities at the university. Many teachers have participated in advanced pedagogical courses in recent years.

29.2.4 Design of examination papers that measure more advanced SOLO levels

What should be tested in an examination paper? Is it important to ask about definitions, Latin names of cereals or names of vitamins and bacteria? It may very well be of importance but then why not broaden the questions so that names and definitions must be understood to be able to answer the wider questions (at more advanced SOLO levels)?

An example from section 29.2.2 illustrates this:

Instead of asking, 'What is gluten?' at the unistructural level ask the question 'Explain why bread baked with rye flour is more compact than bread baked with wheat flour' at the multistructural level. The last question cannot be answered if you do not have any knowledge about gluten.

How questions are formulated can be crucial to the SOLO levels of the answers you get. If you use words like *exemplify, describe* and *explain* you invite answers at the unistructural or multistructural levels. Whereas words like *discuss, compare, relate, analyse* and *judge* invite answers at the relational or extended abstract levels.

More examples from section 29.2.2 illustrate this last and very important aspect:

'What factors are important to consider in connection with cold storage of foodstuff?'

This unistructural question can easily be reformulated by adding

'and discuss their relative importance.'

Now you have a question requiring at least a multistructural, probably a relational, response.

Another unistructural question is:

'What membrane processes would you suggest if you should

(a) separate fat from waste water?
(b) recover proteins from whey?
(c) desalinate sea-water?'

Add words like *discuss, motivate* or *argue* and the expected responses will be at the relational level.

'Which two rules for the solvents are important to consider in LSC-separations (adsorption chromatography)?' is a unistructural question that becomes multistructural by adding, 'explain why'.

Several of the multistructural questions presented in section 29.2.2 begin with the word *describe*:

'Describe the manufacturing of soured milk.'

'Describe the construction and the characterisation of the different sources of light that are used in UV-VIS-spectrophotometers.'

'Describe the different RNA-types of a cell and their tasks in the protein synthesis.'

'Describe schematically the cycling of carbon in nature.'

If you use words like discuss, compare and analyse in the questions the expected SOLO levels of the responses is raised to at least the relational level.

29.2.5 Conclusions and comments — based on interviews with university teachers responsible for the different courses

The investigation shows that many of the theoretical and explorative problems in the examination papers only require answers at the unistructural or multistructural levels. Examination problems in higher education should normally be of such a quality that it is possible to demonstrate at least the relational level. At this level students are able to integrate the task components into a coherent structure and this should be a desirable level of outcome for learning at a university. Extended abstract responses are not likely to be found if the students have not been given specific instructions about the SOLO taxonomy and qualitative examination.

Interviews with some of the university teachers responsible for the different courses lead to three major conclusions relative the reported results.

- Some teachers perform their assessment of students as they always have done. They have never reflected about what kind of questions they give in their examination papers. This is hopefully a rapidly diminishing category of teachers.
- Some, especially inexperienced university teachers, feel that they must cover the whole course by asking many unistructural and multistructural questions. They also feel more insecure in marking answers at the higher levels. This is a problem easily solved by professional training and advice.
- Many teachers are quite aware of the problem but feel that they are prisoners of the higher educational system. It is quite easy to alter the examination papers so that they require more answers at higher SOLO levels but then the time for marking the papers increase considerably. And they just do not have that time. Because a university teacher not only has to teach but also develop the teaching, develop courses and the curriculum, perform own research, participate in the administration etc. There are no simple solutions to this problem ...

The third and last conclusion is of course very serious and a solution would require appropriate measures to be taken from the university management.

29.3 Qualitative examination in chemical engineering

29.3.1 Introduction

This part of the study deals with methods of qualitative examination in chemical engineering. Criteria for different SOLO levels have been set up and a task analysis is presented in section 29.3.3.

A combined oral and written examination is presented. The 28 participating students have studied basic fluid mechanics, engineering thermodynamics, heat engineering and mass transfer separation processes. The students have also been given some information about qualitative assessment and the different qualitative levels of the SOLO taxonomy.

29.3.2 Assessment design

The qualitative examination is presented in Figure 29.1. Each student was given six out of the nine questions presented. They worked with the assignment for about four hours.

29.3.3 Criteria for different SOLO levels and task analysis

At the prestructural level students show that they do not understand the context of the problem. At the unistructural level at least one relevant aspect of the problem must be discussed and a correct explanation or conclusion presented. The multistructural level requires several relevant aspects of the problem to be treated although independent of each other. At the relational level these aspects are integrated into a coherent structure. Finally extended abstract responses introduce a general principle from which deductive conclusions can be drawn. The two highest levels of the SOLO taxonomy are qualitatively different from the lower levels since students must integrate their knowledge and skills into a coherent structure (Biggs and Collis, 1982). This should always be the aim of higher education.

A task analysis has been made for the qualitative examination and three examples are presented below:

Qualitative examination in Chemical Engineering
February 1999

Answer the following questions. Your written answers will be analysed qualitatively using the SOLO taxonomy. This means an evaluation of structural complexity according to the written and oral directions you have received. Have this in mind when you work with the questions.

For all questions you should:

- describe
- explain
- discuss
- exemplify
- compare
- relate
- generalise
- hypothesise
- conclude
- analyse
- judge

1. The equation of continuity
2. Flow measurement using flow meters based on the principle of variable head
3. Methods to separate particles from a gas or a liquid
4. Mechanisms of heat transfer
5. Heat transfer by convection
6. Heat engine (from a general point of view)
7. The first law of thermodynamics
8. Refrigeration process
9. Diffusion and separation processes based on diffusion

Figure 29.1 Qualitative examination in Chemical Engineering

Flow measurement using flow meters based on the principle of variable head

This kind of flow meters comprise orifice meters, venturi meters, flow nozzles, elbow meters etc. Answers at the unistructural level discuss only one method correctly. Multistructural responses include several methods but they are treated independently. At the relational level these methods are compared and analysed with respect to pressure differences, accuracy, flows, energy losses, costs etc. An extended abstract discussion might introduce a general equation valid for all flow meters based on the principle of variable head.

Mechanisms of heat transfer

The mechanisms of heat transfer are conduction, convection and radiation. Unistructural responses treat one and multistructural responses all mechanisms correctly. At the relational level the mechanisms are compared and analysed with respect to magnitudes, temperature levels, interactions etc. Extended abstract responses might introduce general discussions including the second law of thermodynamics.

Heat engine (from a general point of view)

Examples of heat engines are the steam process, the Otto and the Diesel processes (internal combustion engine processes), the refrigeration process and the gas turbine process. One or several treated correctly result in unistructural or multistructural responses. Discussions and comparisons of thermal efficiencies, temperature levels and working media are necessary for a relational answer and extended abstract responses could introduce a general principle for all heat engines and discussions with respect to the first and second laws of thermodynamics.

Similar task analysis must be set up for all questions (written or oral) in a qualitative examination that is evaluated using the SOLO taxonomy.

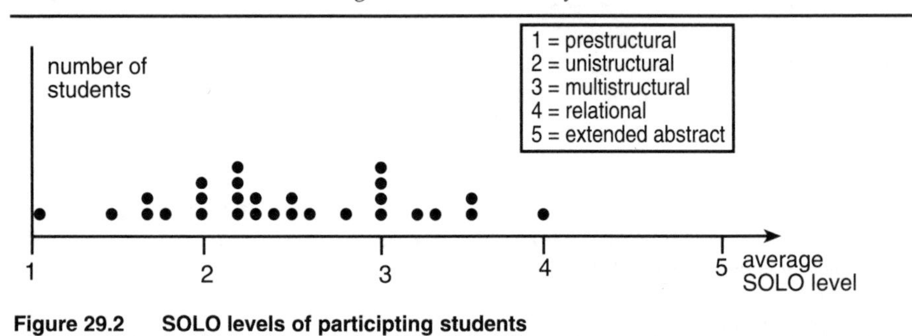

Figure 29.2 SOLO levels of participting students

29.3.4 Results

29.3.4.1 Presentation of results focusing on either students or questions

Figure 29.2 shows the average SOLO levels of each of the 28 participating students and Table 29.8 shows the average SOLO level for each question of the qualitative examination. The result in the second column is based on the entire student group whereas the third column is based only on students with an average SOLO level above 2.0.

29.3.4.2 Comments and discussion of the results

The SOLO levels reached by this student group are quite low. There are several possible explanations. Students presenting unistructural and prestructural responses are obviously not prepared for the examination. Some of the questions were not very suitable for a qualitative examination (for example 5, 7 and 8). The students were probably not prepared enough for this kind of examination. Results from the oral part of the examination (section 29.3.5) and interviews with students (section 29.3.7) indicate this.

Question number (1-9) (Qualitative Examination in Chemical Engineering)	Average SOLO level for each question (based on the entire student group)	Average SOLO level for each question (based only on students with individual average SOLO levels above 2.0)
1	2.9	3.0
2	3.0	3.4
3	2.7	3.2
4	2.6	2.8
5	1.3	1.5
6	2.4	2.6
7	2.2	2.2
8	1.7	2.0
9	2.2	2.4

Table 29.8 SOLO levels for different questions

29.3.5 Oral examination

29.3.5.1 Description

After the written part of the examination followed an oral part. The students were examined individually and in groups of seven students. The questions of the written examination were discussed again together with new aspects.

29.3.5.2 Results

Students presenting multistructural responses during the written examination with few exceptions presented discussions at the relational level during the oral examination. They just needed some minor input. Even some positive attempts at the extended abstract level were made. This shows that qualitative assessment is better to perform orally than in written examinations. Many students have the ability to present relational solutions although they do not show it in written examinations.

29.3.6 Investigation of different approaches to learning within the student group

29.3.6.1 Procedure

An investigation of the participating students deep or surface approaches to learning (Ramsden, 1992) was performed using parts of the course experience questionnaire presented by Ramsden (Ramsden, 1991 and 1992). A total of 17 statements regarding deep or surface approaches were used. Some examples are shown below:

> I try to relate ideas in this subject to those in others wherever possible.

I usually set out to understand thoroughly the meaning of what I study.

Although I generally remember facts and details, I find it difficult to fit them together into an overall picture.

I usually don´t have time to think about the implications of what I have read.

The investigation was performed in connection with the oral examination and the following question was asked: 'How do the statements (1—17) correspond with your opinions?' In this investigation only four options were possible: *not at all, hardly, quite good* and *very good.* This means that for each statement the students had to make a choice between a surface and a deep approach.

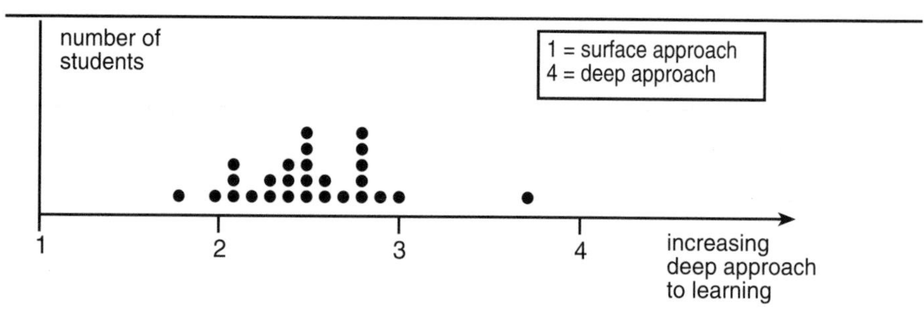

Figure 29.3 Deep or surface approach to learning

29.3.6.2 *Results*

The four options were given numbers (1—4) where 4 always indicates a deep approach. The answers were analysed and are presented in Figure 29.3. The result shows that these students neither are very deep oriented nor especially surface oriented in their approaches to learning.

29.3.7 Comments and conclusions — based on the presented results and interviews with students

The written examination shows responses mainly at the multistructural and unistructural levels. Interviews with students resulted in explanations like: 'I was so pleased just to be able to write down all I know about flow meters that I did not think about the relational level.', 'I just don't think like that', 'I would have needed more experience with this kind of examination.' The last reflection is of course very serious and might explain why some of the students did not reach the relational level.

Oral examinations help the students demonstrate more advanced SOLO levels. Biggs and Collis already stated this when they presented the SOLO taxonomy (Biggs and Collis, 1982).

Interviews with students indicate that they would want to study with a deeper approach to learning and they are surprisingly aware of the problem. The reason why they are not doing so is to be found in the higher educational system. There is just not time enough when you study two or even three subjects in parallel and have to do laboratory experiments, hand in different exercises and projects in time and finally pass the examinations. It is an interesting result worth considering especially if you compare it with the results from the interviews with teachers presented in section 29.2.5.

29.4 Solving practical problems — a teaching method that increases the quality of learning

29.4.1 Presentation of the method

Solving practical problems is a special teaching method used as an alternative in the chemical engineering laboratory. The method introduces problem-solving and creative thinking in the undergraduate courses of chemical engineering (Master of Science and Bachelor of Science levels) at Lund University. It has been used since the beginning of the 1980s and it has been further developed in a recent research project funded by the Swedish Council for the Renewal of Undergraduate Education (Axelsson, 1995).

Some of the most important objectives of the method are:

- the problems should illustrate interesting physical phenomena or important engineering problems;
- the problems should preferably be able to solve both practically and by using theoretical reasoning;
- the problems should enhance the ability to suggest new solutions and ask new questions;
- the problems should stimulate students to propose creative ideas.

The problem is presented by the teacher together with a brief written description. The students (in groups of four students) discuss and do experiments for about 20 minutes trying to reach a solution. During a final discussion together with the teacher the students present their solutions and new aspects and questions are raised and discussed.

We have long been aware of the qualitative advantages of the method and in this investigation some qualitative aspects of the effects of the method based on a SOLO analysis are presented. Using this method as a complement to lectures, tutorials and traditional laboratory work it is possible to encourage students to reach high SOLO levels. Discussions at the relational and even extended abstract levels are common in the solutions of these problems.

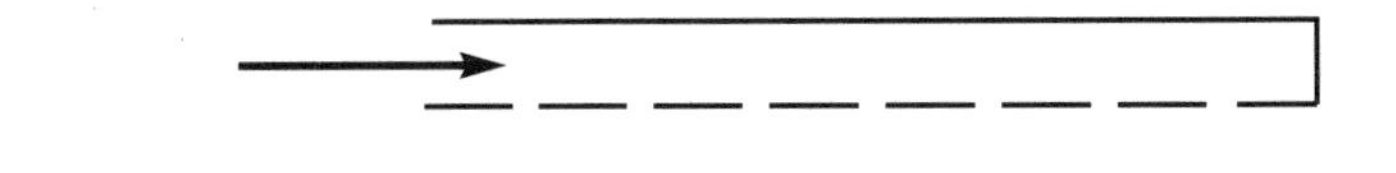

Figure 29.4 Flow in a manifold

29.4.2 Examples of practical problems with corresponding solution strategies at different SOLO levels

Manifold

The distribution of flows in manifolds is a challenging problem both theoretically and practically. It is a typical example of a practical problem.

Water flows to a manifold with circular holes as shown in Figure 29.4.

From which hole is the flow of water highest? Explain why. Sketch the pressure profile in the figure.

What happens if the holes are smaller?

What happens if the manifold is longer?

What happens if the inner surface of the manifold is rougher?

How can we get a uniform distribution of water?

Solution strategies at the unistructural/multistructural levels lead to a correct answer and possibly a theoretical explanation. At the relational level the students handle different alterations (smaller holes, longer tube, rougher surface) without problems. An extended abstract solution might comprise correct ideas and theoretical explanations for a uniform distribution of water. A mathematical treatment of the problem is very complex and involves difference equations but students that master this are demonstrating the extended abstract level.

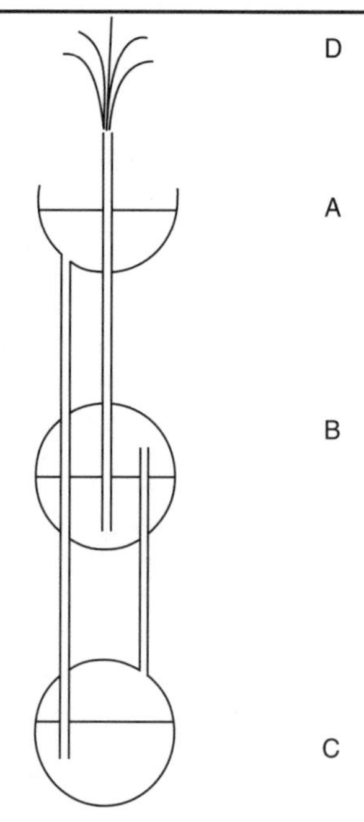

Figure 29.5 Heron's fountain

Herons fountain

Heron of Alexandria, a Greek mathematician and physicist, invented this fountain about 2000 years ago. It is a fascinating illustration of fluid statics (Figure 29.5). It might be necessary to think twice to realize why it is not a *perpetuum mobile*.

Water is flowing from level A through a glass tube to a lower level C. As a result water squirts from D to a higher level than A.

Explain how the fountain works.

What is the maximum height the water could squirt? How can you alter this height? Does the actual height differ from the theoretical?

Discussions at the unistructural/multistructural levels lead to a correct explanation. At the relational level different situations and alterations are explained correctly. An extended abstract solution is perhaps not quite applicable in this case but a discussion of other phenomena based on the same principle as Heron's fountain is at least at the upper relational level.

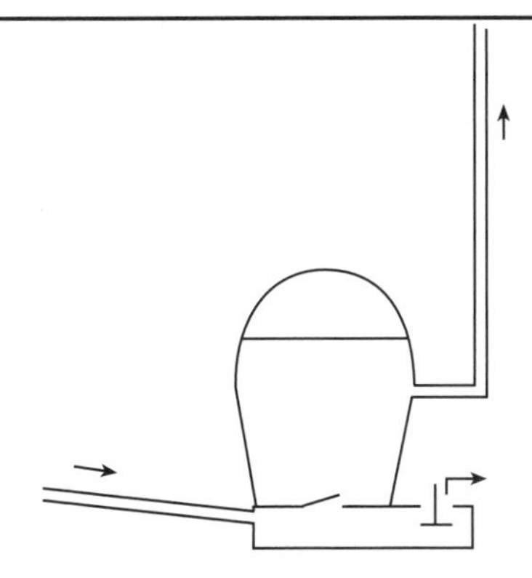

Figure 29.6 Hydraulic ram

Hydraulic ram

In this water pump, invented in the late 18th century by the Montgolfier brothers, water is pumped from a lower to a higher level without any external supply of energy (Figure 29.6)

Explain how the pump works.
How can you alter the delivery head?
How can you alter the flow of water?
How do you start and stop the pump?

Unistructural/multistructural solutions explain how the pump works. Relational discussions also include correctly how the delivery head and water flow can be altered. At the extended abstract level the students realise that a pressure transient known as water hammer is the reason why the pump works and they are also able to give other examples where and why this phenomenon occurs.

Mariotte's bottle

This useful little device is named after the French monk and physicist Edmé Mariotte (1620—84). It is used as a practical problem to illustrate basic equations of fluid mechanics (Fig. 29.7)

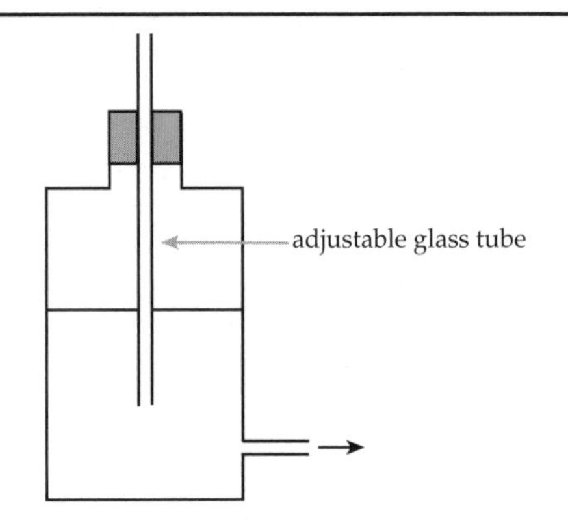

Figure 29.7 Marriotte's bottle

What happens to the flow of water from the bottle when the adjustable tube is held at a constant position?

What happens when the tube is moved upwards or downwards?

Discuss the magnitude of the pressure of air inside the bottle.

Discuss other types of bottles (not shown in Figure 29.7).

Discussions at the unistructural/multistructural levels lead to a correct explanation of the first and second questions above. At the relational/extended abstract levels different situations and alterations are explained. Theoretical explanations and considerations are handled correctly.

Thermos®flasks

Ordinary thermos® flasks are used in a practical problem illustrating fundamentals of conduction and convection at different pressures.

Three flasks are used. One original from the manufacturer, one that is punctured so that the space between the double walls of the flask is filled with air at atmospheric pressure and one that has been provided with a connection to a vacuum pump so that the space between the walls can be evacuated and maintained at different pressures.

The thermos® flasks are filled with boiling water. The temperature of the water and the temperature of the outside walls were measured continually during the cooling of the water.

Why does the water cool at different rates?

Can the heat losses be eliminated?

Why are the surfaces of the walls silver-plated?

Discuss the heat flow at different pressures.

How should the insulation be designed to be as effective as possible?

Unistructural/multistructural solutions explain the experimental results. Relational

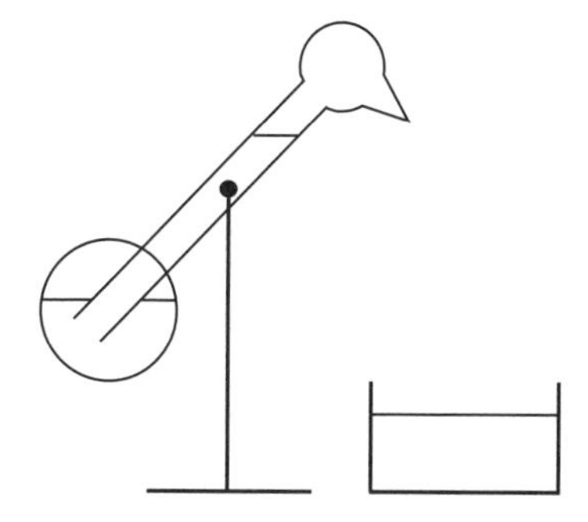

Figure 29.8 The drinking bird

answers also include discussions of different kinds of insulation, different pressures and different designs of the flasks. At the extended abstract level the students extend their discussions to a more general reasoning about heat transfer in gases at low pressures and the relative importance of conduction, convection and radiation for different thermos® flask designs.

The drinking bird

This toy from the 1970s can be used to illustrate important principles of heat and mass transfer (Figure 29.8).

The bird is filled with a volatile organic solvent.

Why does the bird swing up and down so that it appears as if it is drinking from the small cup filled with water beside it?

Unistructural/multistructural solutions explain what happens. Relational discussions also include problems like the use of different solvents in the cup beside the bird and what happens if the bird is enclosed in a glass cover. At the extended abstract level the discussions are extended to a more general reasoning about heat and mass transfer.

The six presented practical problems illustrate the method. More than 40 practical problems have been developed at the Department of Chemical Engineering, Centre for Chemistry and Chemical Engineering at Lund University.

29.4.3 Comments and conclusions

This is an interesting teaching method used as a complement to other methods in the chemical engineering undergraduate courses (Axelsson, 1995). It has many advantages and this study has pointed out some qualitative features of the method.

The most important conclusion is that the oral discussions among the students and between teachers and students increase the quality of learning and help students to reach more advanced SOLO levels.

This teaching method is easily transferable to other experimental disciplines of science and technology

29.5 Final conclusions and recommendations

Pedagogical discussions, seminars and pedagogical training and advice stimulate teachers to design examination papers that measure more advanced SOLO levels. However, many questions are still inviting answers at the unistructural and multistructural levels and this is to some extent a problem due to the organization of the higher educational system itself.

Oral teaching and examination methods may help students to reach the relational and extended abstract SOLO levels. It is especially the scientific discussions among students and between students and teachers that are important.

Many students would want to study with a deeper approach to learning. They are surprisingly aware of the problem and their reasons for not doing so is to be found in the educational system.

Finally, and most important, pedagogical discussions within the faculty increase the knowledge of the importance of qualitative aspects of teaching and assessing in higher education.

29.6 References

Axelsson, A. (1995) *Solving Practical Problems — an Alternative in the Chemical Engineering Laboratory*, Proceedings at the Conference on Teaching Science for Technology at Tertiary Level, 7—9 June 1994, Stockholm.

Biggs, J.B. and Collis, K.F. (1982) *Evaluating the Quality of Learning. The SOLO Taxonomy (Structure of the Observed Learning Outcome)*, Academic Press, New York.

Ramsden, P. (1991) A performance indicator of teaching quality in higher education: the course experience questionnaire, *Studies in Higher Education* **16**(2).

Ramsden, P. (1992) *Learning to Teach in Higher Education*. Routledge, London.

30 Does what students experience in their first class depend on the subject they are studying? Exploring the goals lecturers set and the instructional activities they use in the first class in different discipline areas

Barbara de la Harpe and Alex Radloff

Centre for Educational Advancement, Curtin University of Technology

30.1 Introduction

The first class in any subject is important in setting the tone for the rest of the semester. As Brent and Felder (1999, p. 14) point out, it is during the early part of any course that 'students frequently acquire (or fail to acquire) the motivation to learn that they will carry for the rest of the term'. Similarly, as Jennings (1993, p.1) says , 'what transpires in those first fifty minutes will set the pace, mood, and student attitudes and performance for the rest of the semester'. Furthermore, students are often anxious about what the demands of learning will be and what they will have to do in order to be successful in their studies . Therefore, what happens in the first class — the first formal encounter with a lecturer and peers — is important for making explicit the roles and responsibilities of student and lecturer, and in setting the scene for learning and teaching in the discipline. As Allen (1994, p. 382) notes,

> [t]he first lecture to any class is of utmost importance to achieve success in that class. Students will work harder and perform better if they become immediately interested in the subject matter of that class. They will also feel better about the class if they know how it will be run and what is required of them.

Further, the experiences of students during the first few weeks of the semester affect their decision to stay or withdraw from a course. Students who feel that they are part of the course and the institution, who are satisfied with their subject choice, and who make friends and connect with their peers, are less likely to consider deferring or dropping out (McInnis, James and McNaught, 1995) and are thus, more likely to remain at university and to report greater satisfaction with learning.

When planning the first class, lecturers will have ideas about what they want to achieve and what they will do during class to try to meet their goals. Their goals and instructional activities may vary depending on the discipline in which they teach. It is possible that students too may expect different forms of teaching in different disciplines and may prefer different approaches to teaching and learning. For example, students in the Sciences may perceive the subject as more dependent on covering content which requires memorizing facts rather than discussing or understanding concepts. What might lecturers' goals and instructional activities be for the first class in their subject? Do they differ across subjects?

Are there some goals and activities which are the same irrespective of the subject being taught? The literature suggests that there may be differences in goals and instructional activities in terms of the discipline.

Disciplines can be defined in terms of the ways in which they derive and validate knowledge, and the criteria used for this process (Donald, 1995; Donald, 1997). Based on a typology developed by Biglan in the 1970s, Braxton (1995) describes those disciplines which are well structured or paradigmatic such as the physical sciences, as 'hard', while those which are less well structured such as the social sciences and humanities, as 'soft'.

Smart and Ethington (1995) suggest that there are differences between so-called hard and soft disciplines in approaches to teaching. Hard disciplines are more likely to focus on knowledge acquisition, whereas soft disciplines are more likely to focus on knowledge application (life) and on knowledge integration (nonlife). Moreover, goals for teaching may vary in the hard and soft disciplines (Braxton, 1995). Hard disciplines have as goals, career preparation and content knowledge (facts, principles and concepts), whereas soft disciplines have as goals a broad general education, self-knowledge, personal development, and thinking in addition to content knowledge. Instructional activities also vary across disciplines (Angelo and Cross, 1993; Braxton, 1995; Donald, 1997) in that hard disciplines emphasize teaching research skills and, according to student reports, use fewer student-centred methods. Soft disciplines, on the other hand, emphasize thinking and communication skills and use more student-centred approaches such as small group work and class discussions. Lecturers in soft disciplines are also more likely to adopt a scholarly approach to their teaching by using current literature to prepare their lectures and for student reading assignments.

To what extent are these disciplinary differences evident in the first class of a subject? Surprisingly little appears in the literature about what happens in the first class in any discipline despite the fact that, as already mentioned, evidence would suggest that what happens in the first class is important in terms of influencing student motivation, affect, approaches to learning, learning strategy use, and learning outcomes.

While there has been a growing body of research into lecturers' conceptions of, and approaches to, teaching and their relationship to student approaches to learning and learning outcomes, there has been less research into the relationship between different disciplines and conceptions of teaching. As Hativa and Marincovich (1995, p. 2) point out, 'the issues related to disciplinary differences continue to be vaguely defined and underexplored. Of the literally thousands of studies of teaching, learning, and teacher evaluation in higher education, very few have examined disciplinary differences'. Smart and Ethington (1995, p. 56) agree and suggest that 'there is a strong need for discipline-specific research on pedagogical practice at the college and university level that goes beyond low-inference practices and considers the nature of the subject-matter and disciplinary and institutional goals'.

In this chapter, we explore whether the discipline makes a difference to the goals and instructional activities used in the first class across four discipline areas — Humanities, Social Sciences, Sciences and Health Sciences. We discuss our findings in terms of lecturers' conceptions of teaching and learning, relate them to the literature on student learning and consider the impact on students of learning in different disciplines. We explore the practical implications for teaching the first class in a subject and offer guidelines which lecturers can follow to make the first class a happy, intellectually engaging and active learning experience for both students and lecturers in any discipline.

30.2 Methodology

We initially undertook a study to look at what lecturers did in their first class with first-year students (Radloff and de la Harpe, 1998). We undertook this study because of our interest in the experiences of first-year students across disciplines and because of our belief about the importance of the first class for student learning. Specifically, we were curious about what goals lecturers set for their first class and what activities they planned for the class in order to meet these goals. As academics engaged in providing professional development, we hoped that the information we obtained would help us in our work with academic staff. We, therefore, in the second week of first semester, sent out an invitation via email to all academic staff in a large technological university inviting those who had taught a first-year class the previous week to respond to a brief survey.

The survey comprised six items: subject taught, type and length of class, number of students attending, goals for the class, activities undertaken during the class, and the number of years of university teaching. Respondents replied either by emailing their completed surveys to us or anonymously by returning a completed hard copy of the survey via the internal mail system. Thirty-five staff responded to the survey.

We analysed the responses in terms of goals and instructional activities using a bottom-up approach (for more details on the methodology, see Radloff and de la Harpe, 1998). Categories of goals and instructional activities which emerged are presented in Tables 30.1 and 30.2.

Category	Definition	Example statement
Administration	Dealing with organisation of course in terms of content, format and requirements	*'Outline the program, establish tutorial groups and explain the assessment.'*
Content	Presenting course content	*'Introduce the students to the concept of Marketing.'*
Process	How to go about learning in the course	*'How to take useful notes.'*
Affective	Establishing a positive learning climate	*'Start to know/remember their names ...introduce them to each other (foster their out of class socialising at uni).'*
Information	Getting information about students' background/knowledge	*'I wanted some idea of their Maths and Physics background.'*

Table 30.1 Goal categories with definitions and example statements (N = 35)

Based on the findings of this study which suggested that there were disciplinary differences in the types of goals mentioned by staff and the instructional activities they

Category	Definition	Example statement
Teacher-centred	Teacher active, students passive	*'A 50 min. lecture with lots of illustrations (colour slides and overheads)...*
Student-centred	Students active	*'Ask them to briefly talk with person sitting next to them about what might make for a good tutorial.'*

Table 30.2 Instructional activity categories with definitions and example statements (N = 35)

reported using in the first class, we further analysed the data in terms of four discipline areas, namely Humanities (n = 6), Social Sciences (n = 10), Health Sciences (n = 10) and Sciences (n = 9). In order to explore whether these apparent differences were related to lecturers' conceptions of teaching and learning in their subject, we interviewed a sample (n = 10; two each from Humanities and Health Sciences and three each from Social Sciences and Sciences) of the original respondents. The questions we asked them were:

> What do you mean by 'teaching' in your subject?
> What do you mean by 'learning' in your subject?

Interviews were taped, transcribed and analysed. For teaching conceptions, responses were categorized using Kember's (1998) two-level categorization model. According to Kember, lecturer beliefs about teaching can be organized into two orientations — teacher-centred/content-oriented and student-centred/learning-oriented — each with two subordinate conceptions, imparting information and transmitting structured knowledge, and facilitating understanding and conceptual change/intellectual development, respectively. A further subordinate conception, student-teacher interaction/ apprenticeship, links the two orientations. These orientations and subordinate conceptions vary along a continuum from teacher-centred/content-oriented to student-centred/learning-oriented. Conceptions of teaching with example statements are presented in Table 30.3.

For learning conceptions, responses were categorized using six categories based on the work of Marton and Säljö (1984), Van Rossum, Deijkers and Hamer (1985), and Marton, Dall'Alba and Beaty (1993). Three of the conceptions are considered to be quantitative or reproducing, that is, respondents describe learning in terms of increasing knowledge, memorizing and reproducing what has been learnt, or acquiring facts or procedures that can be applied. Three of the conceptions are qualitative or transformational, that is, respondents describe learning in terms of understanding, seeing what is learnt in a different way, or changing as a person. Conceptions of learning with definitions and example statements are presented in Table 30.4.

30.3 Findings

We report the findings in term of demographic details, goal categories, instructional activities, and lecturers' conceptions of teaching and learning in their discipline.

Orientation	**Conception**	**Example statement**
Teacher-centred /content-oriented	Imparting information	*'Teaching is conveying information and techniques.'*
Teacher-centred /content-oriented	Transmitting structured knowledge	*'...organising relevant content around that [objectives and the curriculum], so teaching involves actually going through the information...and structuring it so that it meets those key objectives...and the actual transmittal of that information.'*
Transitionary bridge	Student-teacher interaction/ apprenticeship	*'...I actually try and connect with the students.'*
Student-centred oriented	Facilitating understanding	*'...but it is not just about facts and* /learning- *transmission of facts, it's concepts, getting people to think, make connections...'*
Student-centred /learning-oriented	Conceptual change /intellectual development	No example statement as none in this category

Table 30.3 Conceptions of teaching (Kember, 1998) with example statements (N = 10)

Conception	Definition	Example statement
Increasing knowledge	Knowledge is a quantum that can be accumulated	'Learning is the recipient primarily attaining knowledge, enhancing interest, obtaining skills, that they either did not have or they become better enhanced, finally tuned, brought out or perhaps, elaborated.'
Memorising are	Learning is transferring units of knowledge from some source into the learner's head	'...there is some content that just needs to be known – so there are some things that sort of straight and would require to be reported back...'
Acquiring facts or procedures for application that the	Learning is acquiring useful knowledge that can be applied	'...so that, at the end of it all, they read a serious newspaper and the economy is discussed they will understand the points are being made and they will be critical of points if the points are not right.'
Understanding	Learning is constructing personal meaning	'...being able to make connections ...asking them a question on something that is unrelated to the topic...but related to the concepts...and seeing them work it out.'
Seeing the world in new way	Learning is interpreting and applying a value system	No example statement as none in this category
Changing as a person	Learning is personally transforming	No example statement as none in this category

Table 30.4 Conceptions of learning with definitions and example statements (N = 10)

30.3.1 Demographics

Table 30.5 shows the means and ranges for years of teaching of the respondents and for the size of class they taught in each of the four discipline areas.

Discipline area	Years of teaching		Class size	
	Mean	Range	Mean	Range
Humanities (n=6)	6.0	4–27	78.0	16–170
Social Sciences (n=10)	12.3	1–30	85.8	17–190
Sciences (n=10)	17.1	8–34	106.9	22–230
Health Sciences (n=9)	14.9	.5–40	116.7	18–550

Table 30.5 Means and ranges for years of teaching and class size by discipline (N = 35)

As Table 30.5 shows, the lecturers in the Sciences had the highest mean years of teaching while those in the Humanities had the lowest. Mean class size was greatest for Health Sciences, closely followed by Sciences. Given the small sample sizes, no further meaningful statistical analysis of these data was possible.

In terms of the type of class, the format lecturers most often reported using in the Humanities was a combination of lecture followed by tutorial (3 of 6) with the remainder using a tutorial (1), studio (1), and lecture (1); in the Social Sciences, was lectures or tutorials (8 of 10 (four each)) with the remainder using a workshop (1) or a combination (1); in the Sciences, was lectures (8 of 10) with the remainder using a workshop (1) or combination (1); and in the Health Sciences, was lectures (4 of 9) or a combination (4 of 9) with the remainder a tutorial (1). The data showed that lecturers used a range of class types. However, the use of lectures was most often reported by lecturers in the Sciences while tutorials or a combination was most often reported by lecturers in the Humanities.

30.3.2 Instructional goals

Table 30.6 shows the percentage of lecturers' goals for their first class in the four discipline areas. There were some differences in the types of goals mentioned by lecturers from the different discipline areas. As the data in Table 30.6 show, a higher percentage of lecturers in the Sciences mentioned Content goals while a lower percentage mentioned Affective goals. A higher percentage of lecturers in the Humanities and Social Sciences mentioned Process and Information goals while a lower percentage mentioned Content goals. A higher percentage of lecturers in the Health Sciences mentioned Affective goals.

In terms of the goals most often mentioned, lecturers in the Sciences were most likely to mention Administration and Content goals, while lecturers in the other three discipline areas were most likely to mention Administration and Affective goals.

30.3.3 Instructional activities

Instructional activities described by respondents were classified as either teacher-centred or student-centred (see Table 30.2 for definitions and examples). Table 30.7 shows the percentage of lecturers mentioning using teacher-centred and student-centred instructional activities.

Discipline area	Goal Categories				
	Administration	Content	Process	Affective	Information
Humanities (n=6)	83	17	33	50	17
Social Sciences (n=10)	60	30	30	60	20
Sciences (n=10)	60	60	10	40	10
Health Sciences (n=9)	89	33	0	78	0

Table 30.6 Goal categories identified by lecturers in different discipline areas expressed as percentages of the number of respondents in each discipline area (N = 35)

As shown in Table 30.7, there were few differences between discipline areas in the instructional activities lecturers reported using. Regardless of discipline area, teacher-centred activities were more likely than student-centred activities to be mentioned. More student-centred activities were reported by lecturers teaching classes with 40 or fewer students, with 90 per cent reporting using some student-centred activities. Lecturers teaching classes with more than 40 students reported fewer instances of student-centred activities, with little difference between class sizes of between 40 and 100 students (46%) and those with more than 100 students (55%). Further, lecturers in the Sciences and Health Sciences were most likely to report using technology such as videos, slides and PowerPoint presentations to support their teaching.

Discipline area	Instructional activities	
	Teacher-centred	Student-centred
Humanities (n=6)	100	66
Social Sciences (n=10)	100	70
Sciences (n=10)	90	60
Health Sciences (n=9)	100	66

Table 30.7 Instructional categories identified by lecturers in different discipline areas expressed as percentages of the number of respondents in each discipline area (N = 35)

30.3.4 Conceptions of teaching and learning

Analysis of interview transcripts describing conceptions of teaching and learning, suggested that for both of these there was no clear-cut pattern by discipline areas. In terms of teaching conceptions, a conception of teaching as imparting information was held by three respondents — one from the Social Sciences and two from the Sciences; a conception of teaching as transmitting structured knowledge was held by three respondents — one from the Social Sciences and two from the Health Sciences; a conception of teaching as student-teacher interaction/apprenticeship was held by two respondents — one from the Humanities and one from the Social Sciences; and a conception of teaching as facilitating understanding was held by two respondents — one from the Humanities and one from the Sciences. No respondents held conceptions of teaching as conceptual change/intellectual development.

In terms of learning conceptions, a conception of learning as increasing knowledge was held by two respondents — one from the Social Sciences and one from the Sciences; a conception of learning as memorizing was held by two respondents — both from the Health Sciences; a conception of learning as acquiring facts or procedures for application was held by three respondents — one from the Humanities, one from the Social Sciences and one from the Sciences; a conception of learning as understanding was held by two respondent — one from the Social Sciences and one from the Sciences. No respondents held conceptions of learning as seeing the world in a new way or changing as a person.

For 7 of the 10 respondents, conceptions of teaching and learning were at equivalent levels. For example, if a lecturer held a conception of teaching as transmitting structured knowledge he/she was likely to describe learning as memorizing; or if a lecturer held a conception of teaching as facilitating understanding, he/she was likely to describe learning as understanding. For the three respondents whose conceptions of teaching and learning were not equivalent levels, their conception of learning was higher than their conception of teaching.

30.4 Discussion

Does the discipline area make a difference to the way in which lecturers conduct the first class in their subject? Our findings suggest that it does in terms of the goals which lecturers have, the type of class in terms of format which they conduct and the use of technology in teaching. Lecturers in the Sciences were most likely to identify Content and Administrative goals, have the lecture as the mode of instruction and use technology in their teaching. These findings are in line with the literature which report differences between 'hard' and 'soft' disciplines in terms of goals (Angelo and Cross, 1993; Braxton, 1995; Donald, 1995; Donald, 1997; Smart and Ethington, 1995). However, our findings do not support the view that there are differences in the kinds of instructional activities which lecturers report using in the different discipline areas, specifically, in terms of 'soft' disciplines using student-centred approaches more often than do 'hard' disciplines. Our findings suggest that class size may be related to the use of such activities, with classes with 40 or fewer students more likely to include student-centred approaches.

Further, we did not find a clear-cut relationship between conceptions of teaching and learning and the discipline area. Rather, it appeared that lecturers held varying conceptions within and across disciplines. This finding is supported by the work of Prosser and Trigwell (1999) who found that lecturers in science had a range of conceptions of teaching. However, given the small sample of respondents in our study, any findings should be treated cautiously. Nevertheless, since lecturers' conceptions, regardless of discipline, are linked to the instructional approach they use (Kember, 1998; Prosser and Trigwell, 1999) which, in turn, influences students' approaches to learning and their learning outcomes, the conception which any lecturer holds should be of a high level and congruent with the goals of higher education. Thus, lecturers need to have or to develop teaching conceptions which are student-centred learning-oriented and focus on conceptual change/intellectual development, as well as learning conceptions which focus on learning involving changing as a person (personally transforming).

According to Marincovich (1995, p. 114), university teaching needs to undergo significant changes 'regardless of discipline — in order to make faculty's teaching more fully effective for students and in order to maximize students' chances of successful learning'. The extensive literature on student learning provides some clues — based on principles of effective teaching and learning — as to what should be done to bring about these changes to ensure that every discipline establishes an appropriate climate for learning.

These principles include ensuring that the course goals, content and assessment are closely aligned , that students are informed learners and are actively involved in learning, that the lecturer acts as a model and scaffolds learning, that co-operation is emphasized, and that class activities are relevant to student needs and build on their prior knowledge and experiences (based on a compilation of literature by Radloff and Samson (1990). Other factors in the teaching context such as lecturer conceptions and learners' beliefs and feelings about learning, are also acknowledged to play a role in effective learning (Biggs and Moore, 1993; Ramsden, 1992) and should be taken into account by the discipline teacher. In addition, research on adult learners points to the importance of acknowledging the social and emotional needs of students (Brookfield, 1986; Brookfield, 1990; Cowan and Piepgrass, 1997). However, the tendency for lecturers to emphasise 'delivering content' — especially in the Sciences — means that the learning process including motivational, social and affective aspects, is overshadowed.

Setting the climate for effective learning requires that the these aspects are addressed in addition to the cognitive aspects of learning. Sisco (1992, p. 26) emphasizes the affective aspect of climate setting when he states that 'it is important for an instructor to set a positive tone during the first session, since this is the time when learners form personal attitudes about the course, the instructor, and the instructional process'.

30.5 Implications and guidelines

In order for lecturers to create a positive learning environment for their students, they must begin 'to think of themselves as teachers as well as specialists in their discipline area ... The message is that an academic needs to be a discipline expert and a teacher' (Kember, 1998, p. 23). They, therefore, need to consider their conceptions of teaching and learning, their teaching style, the teaching climate, the course content, and their assessment methods.

We offer the following guidelines for lecturers planning the first class in any discipline.

- Reflect on your conceptions of teaching and learning and how these are related to teaching practice and student learning.
- Be enthusiastic about the class and the subject you are teaching.
- Be clear about your goals for the class and include Administration, Content, Process, Affective and Information goals that address course organization, course content and how to learn it, affective issues including motivation and interest, and student background knowledge and needs.
- Make sure that the physical space (seating, temperature, equipment) is conducive to meeting your teaching and learning goals.
- Give students information about yourself (professional background, teaching philosophy, expectations etc.).
- Provide administrative information (timetable, course outline etc.) in writing.
- Include activities which encourage students to interact with one another and which focus on the course content.

- Include activities which help students to see the course as a whole, and help them plan their time to meet course requirements and deadlines.
- Ensure that there is adequate time for informal interaction and breaks.
- Collect information from students about their conceptions of learning, goals, previous learning experiences and concerns which can help you to adapt your teaching to their needs.
- Give students some out of class activities to complete before the next class session.

These guidelines will help make the first class of the year a happy, intellectually engaging and active learning experience for students. It will also set the scene for a productive semester, since, as Brent and Felder (1999 p.1) remind us, the first few days are 'vital' in that '[a] good start can carry the instructor through several weeks of early shakiness, and a bad one can take several weeks of damage control to overcome'.

Acknowledgement

We thank our 35 colleagues across the disciplines who participated in this survey and especially the ten who so willingly agreed to share their views on teaching and learning.

30.6 References

Allen, J. E. (1994). The important first lecture to an introductory Geology class. *Journal of Geological Education*, **42**, 312-315.

Angelo, T. A., & Cross, K. P. (1993). *Classroom assessment techniques: A handbook for college teachers* (2nd ed.). San Francisco: Jossey-Bass

Biggs, J. (1995, July). Student approaches to learning, constructivism, and student centered learning. Paper presented at the Twentieth International Conference on Improving University Teaching, Hong Kong.

Biggs, J. B., & Moore, P. J. (1993). *The process of learning*. Sydney: Prentice Hall.

Braxton, J. M. (1995). Disciplines with an affinity for the improvement of undergraduate education. In N. Hativa & M. Marincovich (Eds.), *Disciplinary differences in teaching and learning: Implications for practice* (pp. 59-64). San Francisco: Jossey-Bass.

Brent, R., & Felder, R. M. (1999). It's a start. *College Teaching*, **47**(1), 14-17.

Brookfield, S. (1986). *Understanding and facilitating adult learning*. San Francisco: Jossey Bass.

Brookfield, S. D. (1990). *The skilful teacher: On technique, trust and responsiveness in the classroom*. San Francisco: Jossey-Bass.

Cowan, M. M., & Piepgrass, K. W. (1997). The first day of class in a two-year campus: What students really want us to know about their science classroom experiences. *Journal of College Science Teaching*, **xxvii(2)**, 104-106.

Donald, J. (1997). *Improving the environment for learning: Academic leaders talk about what works*. San Francisco: Jossey-Bass.

Donald, J. G. (1995). Disciplinary differences in knowledge validation. In N. Hativa & M. Marincovich (Eds.), *Disciplinary differences in teaching and learning: Implications for practice* (pp. 7-17). San Francisco: Jossey-Bass.

Garrison, D. R., & Brook, P. (1992). Getting it right the first session. *Adult Learning*, **4**, 25-26.

Hativa, N., & Markinkovich, M. (1995). Editorstnotes. In N. Hativa & M. Marinkovich (Eds.), *Disciplinary differences in teaching and learning: Implications for practice* (Vol. **64**, pp. 1-4). San Francisco: Jossey-Bass.

Jennings, I. Y. (1993, May). Silent interview: An ice-breaker triggering learner strategies toward effective writing. Paper presented at the NISOD Fifteenth Annual Conference on Teaching Excellence and Conference of Administrators, Austin, Texas.

Kember, D. (1998). Teaching beliefs and their impact on students' approach to learning. In B. Dart & G. Boulton-Lewis (Eds.), *Teaching and learning in higher education* (pp. 1-25). Camberwell, Victoria: ACER Press.

Marincovich, M. (1995). Concluding remarks: On the meaning of disciplinary differences. In N. Hativa & M. Marincovich (Eds.), *Disciplinary differences in teaching and learning: Implications for practice* (pp. 113-118). San Francisco: Jossey-Bass.

Marton, F., Dall'Alba, G., & Beaty, E. (1993). Conceptions of learning. *International Journal of Educational Research*, **19**(3), 277-300.

Marton, F., & Säljö, R. (1984). Approaches to learning. In F. Marton, D. Hounsell, & N. J. Entwistle (Eds.), *The experience of learning* (pp. 36-55). Edinburgh: Scottish Academic Press.

McInnis, C., James, R., & McNaught, C. (1995). *First year on campus: Diversity of initial experiences of Australian undergraduates* (CAUT Commissioned Project). Melbourne: Centre for the Study of Higher Education, University of Melbourne.

Prosser, M., & Trigwell, K. (1999). *Understanding learning and teaching*. Buckingham: SRHE and Open University Press.

Radloff, A., & de la Harpe, B. (1998). "What did you do in your first class?" What lecturers do in the first meeting with first year students and its importance for their learning. *South African Journal of Higher Education*, **12**, 192-197.

Radloff, A., & Samson, J. (1990). Literacy and open learning. In R. Atkinson & C. McBeath (Eds.), *Opening Learning and new technology* (pp. 283-289). Perth, WA: Australian Society for Educational Technology, WA Chapter.

Ramsden, P. (1992). *Learning to teach in higher education*. London: Routledge.

Sisco, B. R. (1991). Setting the climate for effective teaching and learning. *New Directions forAdult and Continuing Education*, **50**, 41-50.

Sisco, B. (1992). Setting the climate for successful teaching and learning. *Adult Learning*, **4**, 26.

Smart, J. C., & Ethington, C. A. (1995). Disciplinary and institutional differences in undergraduate education goals. In N. Hativa & M. Marincovich (Eds.), *Disciplinary differences in teaching and learning: Implications for practice* (pp. 49-57). San Francisco: Jossey-Bass.

van Rossum, E. J., Deijkers, R., & Hamer, R. (1985). Students' learning conceptions and their interpretation of significant educational concepts. *Higher Education*, **14**, 617-641.

Winter, J. K. (1992). Learn students' names during the first class. *Bulletin of the Association for Business Communication*, **55**(3), 61-62.

31 Protocols for pedagogy transfer?

Roy Seden and Jenny Rice
De Montford University

31.1 Introduction

> Colleges and Universities as we know them are obsolete.
>
> (*Forbes Magazine*, 1998)

This chapter considers some of the barriers to the successful transfer of best pedagogic practice. It seeks to identify some of the factors relating to subject discourse and institutional organisation, which affect such transfer. To assist staff in implementing change the chapter suggests some protocols, or possible features, that may assist the transfer of best practice in pedagogy, and evaluates some examples.

31.2 Example of pedagogy transfer: how the module can work at one level, its success and some barriers

This is an example of transferring to computing a mode of learning that is used in subject areas that are non-cognate to computing, namely Art and Design subjects such as Fashion. The example was presented as part of the portfolio of Mrs Diane Richardson in her successful application to become a Teacher Fellow at De Montfort University. Within university typology, De Montfort University may be considered to be complex and "post modern" in character. Briefly the example shows that pedagogy transfer can happen successfully, and be embedded robustly in the curriculum. This chapter seeks initially to consider why this might be so.

The example is of a Level 2 *Exhibition Module* which is based on the concept of exhibiting students' research into a business area, and some software developed by them for this area. It remains unusual for the field of computing, being an innovative delivery method for this subject. Staff contact is kept to a minimum and is largely used for supervision. Some staff were initially rather sceptical of this very different approach to student work and assessment, but once they were involved with the module or saw the actual Exhibition they usually became very supportive as evidenced by emails etc from colleagues following Exhibitions over the years.

Exhibition is an innovative module in its own right, but it also allows for innovation from the students. The assessment criteria indicate that higher grades will be achieved for innovation in the business area i.e. developing software that is not already in the market However there is minimal staff contact time, with a check point tutorial each week, after an initial kick-off session. Thus the Exhibition Handbook is available as a learning resource for the students, allowing them at any time to reference information they need. The low staff contact for this module requires this sort of quality alternative resource allowing the students to work at times which suit themselves and the module requirements.

Exhibition also encourages members of the group to have roles, which are decided upon by the student group. This allows for each student to use their particular skills while perhaps developing others. The assessment criteria for this module also allows for group and individual graded components, so that skills in both areas can be developed. Students can benefit from the collective group work and also from their own individual efforts. This module and the exhibition event itself have been a great success as evidenced by student feedback displaying tremendous enthusiasm and motivation, by supportive staff comments, and by an Exhibition Video.

The concept of exhibiting students' research into a business area, and some software developed by them for this area, was a novelty in the computing field seven years ago when this was first developed. The BTEC External Examiner and his colleagues had not encountered such a module before. This module has undergone much development over the years, but its original concept remains the same, allowing the students to work in groups collaboratively and independently on work for which they are responsible.

The *Exhibition* module generates enthusiasm by its very nature and the students are fully involved in the module and achieving the objectives set out. The module has developed a clear identity, and demonstrates the possibility of successful inter-Faculty pedagogic transfer between seemingly non-cognate units across the university. Sadly the module has just been delivered for the last time despite its success over seven years. Internal modular redesign of the BTEC HND programme has meant that one module per semester has had to be removed from the programme. The module was not considered to be concerned with core knowledge transmission, and BTEC required an individual Project in Year 2, rather than the group work / project done in the Exhibition, there having been both previously. In addition, though not costly in terms of staff, the module is expensive in terms of physical resources; the hire of the stands, the wiring and the PCs for several days etc

This example illustrates that it is possible to transfer best teaching practice between seemingly non-cognate subjects when the *innovation is appropriately designed* (cf. Protocol 3 in section 31.9 below (P3)). It also illustrates the importance and influence of the ever changing *values underlying any subject* and its knowledge domain, and how they ebb and flow within the subject discourse (P9).

31.3 The thesis of this chapter

The stance of the chapter is fourfold.

First, we consider it is important to include a consideration of the management of change in higher education, with particular reference to the organisational response of higher education institutions (HEIs) to change. HEIs, as well as subjects, exist within international and national contexts which are themselves changing. The tensions between modernism and post-modernism in educational provision are also pertinent here given the spectrum of HEIs and the expansion of HE.

Secondly discourse theory suggests a wider background to the above. Discourse is taken to contain the locus of power-knowledge formation and influences discursive practices within which 'regimes of truth' are constructed. Also, it has been suggested that Foucault's position is 'a discourse is a system of possibility which makes a field of knowledge possible.

By doing this discourses "systematically form the object of which they speak ...[they] are not about objects; they constitute them" (Foucault 1974: 49)' (Usher and Edwards, 1994, p. 90) This is significant though, of course, partial. In particular discourses embody meaning and social relationships as, for those who speak it, a discourse can be given, operating 'behind their backs', as an 'unthought'. We suggest that this is very influential when considering pedagogical transfer in the context of an HEI as well as a subject (P9). Foucault uses discipline to identify a body of knowledge with a system of social control. Thus a body of knowledge is a system of social control to the extent that discipline (knowledge) makes discipline (control) possible, and vice versa. Such knowledge/subject/discipline control systems can be influential in developing subject paradigms and benchmarking standards, as exemplified by the authority of professional institutions, and by the current debate in English.

Thirdly the subject has, to date, been paramount in professional identity, and will probably continue to be central. However the HE contextual changes already mentioned suggest some movement towards dual professionalism based not only on the subject but also on its educational delivery.

Finally we consider it is also important to include a range of examples of varying success, not only the successful one already considered, to begin to test the initial protocol structure.

Thus the thesis of the chapter is that a subject is a formation of knowledge and control which wields power, but that this discourse of a subject or a discipline does not necessarily operate obviously. Furthermore the subject discourse is inevitably set within the more general educational discourse of HE which is influenced by the organisational response of HEIs to change. Both are central to enabling successful pedagogical transfer within and between subjects and higher educational institutions.

Consequently the starting points of this work are the university, the subject and the professional.

The culture of a *university* can be understood by adopting the contingent model (Dill, 1992) to analyse its strategic and operational life. This posits that the two basic factors governing such an analysis are the nature of the environment external to the university and the nature of the core task of the university. That core task, whether expressed through a strategic plan, a vision, a mission, key objectives or specific operational targets, will now have learning and teaching at its heart.

The discourse of a *subject* or discipline can be understood in terms of the formation, conservation and transmission of knowledge and especially the influence of such a discourse with regard to the power balance between the subject, the university and the state. This is currently being mediated through the subject benchmarking exercise, the new subject centres, and the rise of inter-disciplinarity.

The role of a *professional* teaching a subject in a university is conditional on a range of influences and may be summed up in the notion of 'dual professionalism' (Clark, 1983). To become a professional lecturer in pedagogical terms requires respecting not only the authenticity of the ever-growing, and sometimes redefining, subject but also the powerful fluidity of the increasingly market led external culture.

To propose *protocols for pedagogical transfer* suggests that, in part at least, the modern university, subject and professional all continue to hold some things in common, not least due to the form and content of the nature of the subject knowledge. This chapter posits that this is so, and that important components of such protocols include collegiality, partnership, appropriately sized transfer experiments, professional development structures, learning support systems; effective communication systems and appropriate embedment methodologies. In addition an appropriately structured and supported HEI organisational focus for Learning and Teaching in each university could have an important role to play in realizing the learning and teaching component of any university's aspirations. Finally the value system underpinning the knowledge base of a subject domain is arguably crucial.

31.4 Educational discourse: the environment of a university

To underpin it's view of 'the European University in 2010' Utrecht University recently conducted a survey of Rectors, Vice-Chancellors, Presidents and members of Boards of Governors throughout Europe, which revealed that the values most shared throughout Europe are:

- freedom of research and teaching as a fundamental principle of University life;
- the University's contribution to the sustainable development of society as a prominent element in a University's mission;
- research and teaching remaining inseparable at all levels of University education;
- national Government bearing as much responsibility for higher education in 2010 as it does today.

(Utrecht University, August 1997)

Universities operate in an international context both by choice and by default. This globalization of education not only has economic, political and social outcomes but also, the development of real-time communication systems emphasises there are both fragmentary and homogeneous social and organizational relationships in operation. This is reflected in the way that the collegial, bureaucratic and market models of academic organization which originated respectively in the United Kingdom, continental Europe and the United States respectively (Dill, 1992) are increasingly converging internationally as HE systems and HEIs respond to this global context. The related issues of massification and the market place, and their impact on higher education institutions are now of central importance, not least in the United Kingdom with its tradition of elite higher education. Yet real resources from government continue to reduce to a greater or lesser extent, especially in the United Kingdom where the cultural impact of privatization and the market economy have been considerable over the last 20 years. In the United Kingdom and continental Europe privatization in higher education has been partial and de facto by stealth, especially through deregulation initiatives targeted at the governance, management and marketization of higher education institutions.

However the freedom of the higher education institutions in terms of the processes of higher education has been bought at the price of national performance monitoring and the control of outputs such as degree specification, rates of retention, and proportions of high level awards. This reflects the rise of the evaluative state (Williams, 1995) which provides the initial (homogeneous?) steering framework and applies the output controls, while leaving the higher education institution to bridge the gap between these two at the mercy of the fragmented higher education market.

The UK Higher Education Funding Council has recently published the higher education institution performance indicators that it is now using:

- widening participation;
- student progression;
- learning outcomes;
- learning and teaching efficiency;
- student employment;
- research output.

To meet these pressures, higher education institutions need to respond appropriately and flexibly in terms of the implications of massification. These include providing:

- equal opportunities;
- diverse programmes;
- lifelong learning opportunities;
- support to local and regional change.

This environment which stresses flexibility and transferability suggests that Universities are displaying typical post-modern conditions of operation. This might seem a long way from the rather radical depiction by Foucault of post-modern behaviours which 'develop action, thought, and desires by proliferation, juxtaposition, and disjunction', and 'prefer what is positive and multiple, difference over uniformity, flows over unities, mobile arrangements over systems. Believe that what is productive is not sedentary but nomadic' (Harvey, 1989, p. 44). However, if this is summarized into post-modernism being characterized by differentiation and fragmentation, then a university's task to provide multiple and multi-faceted courses merely corresponds to the operation of other post-modern institutions. While the majority of the issues raised above can clearly be addressed from a post-modern perspective, the issue of research is less easily managed. This will be returned to when discussing the Subject Discourse.

In such ways higher education institutions can continue to perform the basic task of transforming the input of students into the output of award carrying alumni. However this begs other issues, especially the place in the core task of the university of:

- research;
- interdisciplinary work;
- new technology, especially communications and information technology .

These considerations, especially the place of research, pose the question as to what type of university a university both considers itself to be, and actually is.

Universities also operate in a national context. The international trends identified above are being mediated implicitly and explicitly through national cultural, governmental and academic network policy and practice changes. For example the consequences of the Jarrett report have led to a profound rise in executive power in contemporary United Kingdom universities and a consequent diminution in collegiality. Such a culture of 'managerialism' has had a major impact on the life of higher education in general and the academic board is often secondary to the executive structure in universities that consider themselves to be 'managed'. In particular the diminution of academic community (cf. Gavin Briars, *Times Higher Education Supplement*, 26 June 1998) and the sense of isolation of many staff from the 'centre' of the university have been seen as very debilitating. Two further examples of national trends include:

- the impact of the new Regional Development Agencies, which are going to require universities to make statements regarding their local and regional responsibilities and targets;
- an entrepreneurial response to the impact of the market in terms of brand image at different levels within the university and market niche at offering level so leading to competitive advantage in the market place (e.g. the emergence of music technology to replace engineering — an example of growth by replacement rather than addition).

Such examples illustrate the changing shape of the 'triangle of tension' (Williams, 1995) between the forces of the state, academia and the market. The state is now adding its force more to that of the market through the student as consumer. This is a significant change from the traditional position of the state as sponsor of academia, with their forces aligned.

Yet the recent changes in the environment of universities outlined above, which are highly significant, are thrown into longer-term relief by this recent challenge to all higher education institutions:

> I call on Universities to ensure they keep their essential intellectual values while going through the inevitable change process. The University has to face a radical and irreversible reformation of it's role ... if we create market Universities, run purely on market principles, they may be of their age, but they will not be able to transcend it. If they only chase and adapt to circumstances, rather than fulfil an anticipatory role, Universities will not, anymore, be able to shape the future ... it is up to the people to set the priorities, not the market ...
>
> (Dr Federico Mayor, Director General of UNESCO, September 1997)

This call suggests that a certain degree of *collegiality* needs to be retained within HEIs as well as subjects, whether at department, faculty or university level (P1). It also suggests that operational *partnerships* between HEI's faculties, subjects etc. are an important feature of pedagogy transfer (P2) as implied by TLTP, FDTL etc. project funding criteria.

Other changes in the national environment for higher education, which are especially pertinent to the transfer of pedagogical practice in a university, include:

- establishing the national Institute of Learning and Teaching with a view to accrediting higher education lecturers in terms of their learning and teaching expertise, so moving towards dual professionalism;
- replacing the existing 'Computers in Teaching Initiative' centres by the establishment of national *Subject Centres* in 24 cognate subject areas (cf. the Atkins report) to support learning and teaching good practice more generally on a subject basis;

- the national *Subject Benchmarking* exercise currently under way, based on a set of groupings of cognate subject areas, with a view to, effectively, establishing a national higher education curriculum in terms of arrays of assessed learning outcomes;
- the *Quality Assurance Agency* assessment of the overall quality of the delivery of learning every four or five years based on a different, though overlapping, set of groupings of cognate subject areas;
- the *Research Assessment Exercise* cycle every four or five years based on yet another different, though overlapping, set of groupings of cognate subject areas.

It is notable that they are all subject based, which suggests that the subject, as defined by its knowledge domain and its value base, will remain a crucial feature or protocol of pedagogy transfer (P9).

31.5 Educational discourse: the task of a university and the environment of a subject

The core task of higher education in general in knowledge terms may be defined as the generation, conservation, transmission and application of knowledge through research, scholarly work, teaching (education/training) and consultancy. In student terms it may be said to be the transformation process from the point of entry to higher education to the point of exit from higher education.

Within this definition, there is an ongoing debate as to the nature of different universities in the United Kingdom, namely whether they should be tasked to perform:

1. purely research;
2. purely teaching;
3. some research and some teaching.

Thus the debate regarding the core task is partly philosophical (Napoleonic or Humboldtian?) and very instrumental in terms of the current and future funding pattern and resource envelope of a particular higher education institution which, for example, may regard itself as category 3 but be seen as category 2.

Key features relating to understanding the nature of the task include:

- the primacy of the subject knowledge, and how that differentiates and fragments the basic units of a higher education institution (Clark, 1983);
- the importance of the associated characteristics of those units (Biglan, 1973);
- the often loose yet recognizable attachments and couplings that take place within a higher education institution between the differentiated units of the higher education institution (Weick, 1976);

These *sources of differentiation* arise supremely at subject or department level of the normal four levels within higher education and can be very powerful (Becher and Kogan, 1992). For example, regarding consensus in an academic field, the *subject characteristics* of History of Art and Design have changed profoundly over the last 15 years. A traditional 'elitist' chronological approach has been supplanted in general by a much broader 'eclectic' approach. This has redefined the subject as the study of the history of cultural products, allowing for social context, interdisciplinary dialogue etc., and is becoming embedded in delivery to a correspondingly wider range of students. This increased diversity of material and method is seen to reflect the greater diversity in modern societies and the consequent greater diversity of knowledge to be obtained in this subject. There is now a broader, less fragmented divergence in the United Kingdom, between new universities that are less 'elitist' and old universities, which are less 'eclectic'. This in turn affects delivery methods, exemplified by the introduction of a first-year methods module at De Montfort University, reflecting the search for a new paradigm and a new method of scholarly socialization, which are important characteristics associated with such knowledge-based units.

Thus the necessary counterbalancing *sources of integration* need to come from similar or senior levels within the organization. Informal sources of integration include shared academic culture (Clark, 1983) (now weakened significantly at most levels within higher education institutions), internal markets (Massy, 1996) (cf. cost/responsibility/value centres) and the distribution of organizational authority in its varied forms, levels and contexts. The ways in which subjects and/or departments are grouped (into faculties, for example) is important, as information flows across groupings are much weaker than within groupings.

Information processing systems and their capacities are a central feature of formal sources of integration using some form of 'horizontal' linkage mechanism (Geiger, 1990). The weakest mechanism is an HEI organizational focus for Learning and Teaching or equivalent acting in a passive 'liaison' role. A stronger mechanism is such a centre acting as a cross unit group operating at the 'enabling practice through networks' level. An even stronger mode of operation is as an integrating department operating at the 'central policy-making' level. These considerations regarding the university's task therefore present the general background to defining protocols for pedagogy transfer between subjects and between universities. In particular this analysis suggests that an effective *HEI organizational focus* of some proactive form (P7) and an *effective communication system (P6)* are both vital in supporting the transfer of best practice in pedagogy.

> The traditional institutions have to accept that the learning landscape, and they within it, will change perhaps beyond recognition ... This will firstly challenge teaching. When students are no longer a homogeneous group of beneficiaries of the system, but a disparate array of investors in that system, a radical shift of emphasis occurs ... with such a high premium on quality in teaching, it cannot remain less important than research in determining individual careers or the status of a department or institution...
>
> (Dr Federico Mayor, Director General of UNESCO, October 1998)

31.6 The discourse of a subject

As already suggested, there is a tension between the university and the subject. This stems from their links to very different discourses. The modernist construction of an educational discourse centres on the subject and privileging its 'grand narratives'. This focuses on critical reasoning and individual freedom, and remains strongly influential in the arena of the subject (Usher and Edwards, 1994, p. 2). Its body of knowledge, a system of control through a 'regime of truth', maintains its power through its discourse which 'authorises certain people to speak and correspondingly silences others, or at least makes their voices less authoritative' (Usher and Edwards, 1994, p. 90). It thus enables certain forms of thought and not others and in this way it struggles to maintain the power of the subject in the face of demands made by the university's discourse.

The increasingly common typology of the postmodern university emphasizes fragmentation, decentred subjects and fluid boundaries reflected in interdisciplinary approaches to study. This is at odds with the underlying modernist discourse of education and the desire of the individual subjects to control their boundaries in the pursuit of academic freedom. Furthermore, such a university needs to deliver skills required by the new markets of lifelong learners, fee-paying students and employers, particularly skills of flexibility and transferability which complement its postmodern discourse. Indeed, many universities seem to particularly wish to embrace heterogeneity to the extent, as commentators have argued, that 'between departments, and even within them, colleagues can scarcely make sense of one another, so radically separate are their specialisms and the discourse that each has constructed' (Smith and Webster, 1997, p. 104).

This characteristic of university discourse is mirrored in changing formations of knowledge. It has been suggested by some writers (Gibbons, 1994) and (Lyotard, 1993) that there has been a

> transformation of knowledge, a move away from what may be termed Model knowledge which is homogeneous, rooted in strong disciplines which are hierarchical, and transmitted to novitiates in an apprentice-master relationship, to Mode 2 knowledges which are non-hierarchical, pluralistic, transdisciplinary, fast changing, and socially responsive to a diversity of needs such as students' dispositions and industrial priorities. This plurality of knowledges announces an end to established and common purposes of the University, there being no identifiable unity and no possibility of agreement on goals. (Smith and Webster, 1997, p. 104)

They further argue that this leads to a multitude of differences with the consequent creation of divisions between the different groups of students and staff, e.g. teaching / research teams.

Yet though Gibbons could argue in 1994 that there has been a shift to Mode 2 knowledges, the creation of Subject Centres and benchmarking, suggest there may be a drive back to Mode 1 knowledge. Both the draft benchmarking statements by Law and Chemistry that emerged in 1998 refer to bodies of knowledge to be studied. It is quite probable that as benchmarking becomes a key quality assessment tool the balance between Mode 1 and 2 could shift considerably.

The power of the subject is embedded in its discourse. If the core task of the university is the generation, conservation, transmission and application of knowledge, then the primacy of the subject or 'discipline' as source of knowledge is key to the accomplishment of the task. However there is undoubtedly a tension between the focus of the university which, as discussed above, takes a postmodernist approach in embracing fragmentation and de-differentiation, and a subject/discipline which controls its authority though a discourse, a 'regime of truth' which allows what can and cannot be considered as valued knowledge and how this knowledge is allowed to operate.

If there is to be pedagogic transfer to enhance best professional practice across subjects and between 'the university' and subjects, it has to be recognized that their discourses may hamper the activity. However if there are protocols for transferring practice, the power of any discourse can be challenged.

These comments strongly emphasize again the importance of the expressed *values of a subject* knowledge domain (P9) at any point in time and the need for *professional development* (P8) to enable these tensions to be resolved by HE staff.

31.7 The professional role

It is clear that the academic member of staff has to operate within the context of a dual discourse.

It could be argued that the recent emergence in the UK of the ILT and the subject-based developments outlined above has newly strengthened the modernist discourse as mediated through the subjects and disciplines. The professional response of academic staff to date has been largely, though not exclusively, subject-based as part of a developmental narrative within clear subject bounds.

By way of contrast, the post-modernist discourse has been mediated through HEI's designing and delivering increasingly modular and commodified curricula (Trowler, 1998) to promote accessibility and flexibility in the market place. The professional response of academic staff to date in the last decade or more has been largely, though not exclusively, through the redesign of the curricula, which has involved considerable change.

Thus it may be argued that there is now a new impetus to dual professionalism, first in the conservation of the subject and the expansion of its knowledge base, and secondly in the effective communication of that knowledge. This dual professionalism inevitably brings with it a new complexity fuelled as it is by the two different types of discourse.

A further complexity involves the rise of inter-disciplinarity, which by its very nature also tends to reflect both discourses. The process of existing subject differentiation, de-differentiation as boundaries are blurred, and re-differentiation into new categories, means that the subject knowledge domain becomes ever more complex for staff. This in turn invites a professional response involving either new challenges to received *subject definition* (P9) or ever-greater specialization.

Finally the rise of CIT in all its manifestations is revolutionizing the design and delivery of HE. The professional response will probably be profound in terms of how knowledge transmission is effectively supported, with the academic's role changing to, for example, that of learning support and learning management. The way in which an innovation in pedagogy uses *learning support systems* (P5) is thus important, as is how an HEI organizes its learning support systems.

Above all, though, it is clear that the battle of the discourses is being played out at every level in HE, not least in the individual professional role. Protocols for pedagogy transfer are a key element in enabling the academic member of staff to handle the widening range of demands on their professionalism. *Professional development structures* (P4) which enable staff to do this will be vital at each HEI.

31.8 Further examples of pedagogy transfer

31.8.1 How it didn't work: MA Research Methods module (module level)

The University's Electronic Campus project has funded and supported a variety of projects to offer on-line courses, modules or sub-modules (P5). The creation of an MA level Research Methods module in an electronic version was proposed to meet the needs of a growing market of mature and overseas students who did not want to attend the university on a weekly basis. This market's desire for flexibility characterizes the demands of a postmodern age; and the proposed flexible delivery form suited a postmodern university's approach to its organization of learning and teaching.

A team of staff from seven subjects met to put together the module. A factor that became significant later was that these staff were committed to postmodern approaches, i.e. de-differerentiation and fragmentation (P2). The programme was based on a belief that while disciplines retained their own knowledges, they did all operate in a shared episteme. It was for this reason that a core of the syllabus focused on the nature of paradigm shifts, particularly from modernist grand narratives to postmodernist fragmented narratives. It was assumed that, before a student could undertake research practice, an understanding of how such approaches were verified and valued as discourses was essential; and that an awareness of the differences and shared approaches of subjects was valuable.

The module was evaluated by both students and staff, including those who taught the students in the subject-specific classes. The results of these evaluations showed a clear unease with such a de-differentiated approach; in particular the criticism was that there was not enough subject-based knowledge. There was a clear inference that research methods could not be studied generically. It was clearly the belief that every element needed to be contextualized in a subject and that taking this generic approach might 'confuse' students.

The result has been to change the syllabus radically to omit the generic sections on modernism and postmodernism and replace them with subject-specific content delivered separately to each subject group.

The conclusions that can be drawn from this experience are that such a development, while supported in central areas of the university operating in a postmodern context (P7), was not supported by those with subject authority, who wanted to maintain subject knowledge. The strategic thrust of the university was obstructed by authorities in the subject highlighting a significant barrier which will be even harder to overcome when the authority of Subject Centres challenge universities' missions. Secondly there is an issue of professional development. Unless the university can encourage staff to be as interested in learning and teaching strategies to the same extent as subject knowledge linked to research, such barriers will remain. Those who identify themselves solely with a subject must learn to take into account the changing university environment, which will increasingly require staff to be more flexible in their educational discourse.

The failure of this project could be seen to be partly due to the lack of protocols for pedagogic transfer. There was not a sense of collegiality (P1) between the subject areas, there were no prior professional development workshops (P4) to address those who were not committed to this approach and there was probably a sense in which the subject value (P9) was inadvertently undermined.

31.8.2 How it worked for a time: structures (subject level)

To overcome substantial barriers to learning about structural analysis and design, the curriculum area was simplified, model testing to destruction was introduced to demonstrate structural principles, and a suite of structural analysis software written to apply those principles.

The software that was produced covered load assessment, forces in trusses and forces in beams. The software design features included a graphical calculator, 'rubber band' measurement, and extensive colour coding. To ease student access, the software had a standardized regime of user interface, software structure, graphical routines, colour coding and activity routines between different software items. Its pedagogical features included immediate feedback, and assessment techniques, directly derived from the learning techniques, which featured randomly generated examples, staged assessments and the ability for tutors to value these stages as they saw fit.

It was used in structures teaching on semester 2 modules delivered to 80 students on three programmes. The software was also used to generate a form of semi-automated assessment on a semester 1 module which was delivered to over 200 students on six programmes studying on a common first semester. It was used by students at work and home, and was presented in seamless learning and assessment modes.

Student feedback occurred throughout the time they used the software, and this proved very popular over the years in which these techniques were developed. Students commented that such techniques were fair and reliable, being based on explicit assessment criteria. The student performance improved markedly in terms of comparable assessed output (Seden, 1997) and helped to solve problems relating to student feedback, staff workload arising from increased student numbers, and quality of learning output as measured by assessment. Robust learning, practice and assessment techniques were successfully developed to support an innovative automated assessment strategy.

While such techniques are also transferable in principle to any subject area also involving staged sequential analytical procedures, in reality this would require considerable input by the tutors to ensure the rigour of the assessment method and the seamlessness between learning and assessment through practice. Also problems inevitably occurred in terms of computer illiterate students; change of hardware delivery to networks; debugging software; change to a Windows culture etc. In particular the software required increasingly significant resource to be modified, and in most years was delivered by only one member of academic staff.

Significant *partnership* (P2) between staff led to the initial development of the software and supported its limited use in the final two or three years. However increasing problems with available resources and *learning support systems* (P5) meant that gradually the software ceased to be used. The lack of engagement with *professional development structures* (P4) at any level was also a constraint on its continuing use.

31.8.3 How it could work at another level (sub module): BEATL (Built Environment: Appropriate Technology for Learning)

This is a TLTP3 funded project which aims:

- to *embed* new technology-based learning materials into the delivery of modules in the built environment undergraduate modular programmes at UWE Bristol, De Montfort and Westminster Universities (P8);
- to share with, and promote to, all higher education institutions and their staff good practice in embedding technology-based learning materials (P4).

Project objectives include:

- to *embed* appropriate technology-based applications and learning materials into 25 built environment modules, including large interdisciplinary modules (P8);
- to evaluate the impact of these sub-modular applications and materials on the quality of the student learning experience in the module, and evaluate the full resource implications of the project innovations;
- to introduce collaborative arrangements among the consortium universities and their faculties for testing *transferability* of good practice (P3);
- to prepare a staff handbook on good practice for embedding appropriate

technology, and run *professional staff development* programmes for staff in HEIs nationally to promote good practice in the embedding of appropriate technology (P4);

Initial examples of experiments in modules include:

- computer supported tutorials;
- video and web-based self-assessment;
- axonometric drawing support using CAD;
- use of CAA in financial mathematics;
- housing budget simulation exercise;
- security of tenure self-assessment exercise.

A key feature is the concept of the module *partnership* (P2) between modules that pilot an innovation and partner modules that re-embed the innovation in their curriculum at another HEI. It is governed by the *module agreement* (P6) which covers:

- agreement on the contribution a module will make towards the project;
- confirmation of the main features of an innovation plan;
- information on the support a module can expect to receive from the project team;
- information on the resource remuneration a module can expect to receive.

The agreement is signed by the module leader. The project is provided with *learning support* (P5) by the resource of a part-time educational development officer at each HEI.

This project is nearly halfway through its contract time and has involved a high level of attention from the educational development officers (EDOs) in particular in the design, delivery and evaluation of an experiment. The EDOs who have had strong and secure links with central Educational Technology and Development Units have been in a stronger position to advise and support staff in specific developments, due to the wider overview and perspective such an arrangement offers. It has also been notable that those EDOs who are not from the subject area do not report this constraint to be a significant barrier. This suggests a high degree of transferability in terms of ways of working to enable transfer of best practice within and between subjects (P1).

BEATL, as most TLTP3 projects, is mainly focused on embedment and evaluation. However experience to date is that nearly all experiments have involved an element of development, at the very least at the level of customising a learning delivery item when it is transferred from one curriculum to another. It is possible that one conclusion of the project will be that the most successful transfers are those using the most generic tools or covering the most generic subject matter, especially at Part 1 degree level.

BEATL embodies many of the proposed protocols for pedagogy transfer (P1, 2,3,4,5,6,8) as outlined above.

31.9 Protocols for pedagogy transfer?

The protocols suggested by the preceding discussion are:

1. collegiality,
2. partnership,

3. appropriately sized transfer experiments,
4. professional development structures,
5. learning support systems,
6. effective communication systems,
7. HEI organisational focus,
8. embedment and evaluation methodology,
9. subject value base.

It is also suggested that the protocols may be considered at six levels:
1. sub-module;
2. module;
3. subject/department;
4. faculty;
5. HEI;
6. HE.

It is also suggested that they may be evaluated in the light of the modernist and postmodernist characteristics of both the subject and of educational provision. Thus an initial categorization is tentatively given in Table 31.1.

The purpose of this table is to provide a template to assist staff in thinking further about how successful pedagogy transfer can occur within an HEI and HE. The list of protocols is provisional and can be expanded. The suggested levels and characteristics are also highly provisional, especially the latter. Which protocols are most important remains debatable, though the subject value base is clearly a central consideration when contemplating any teaching transfer or innovation.

Protocol	Levels	Modernist	Post-Modernist
Collegiality	2–4	X	
Partnership	1–5	X	X
Appropriately sized transfer experiments	1–2		X
Professional development structures	4–6		X
Learning support systems	4–5		X
Effective communication systems	3–5	X	X
HEI organizational focus	5–6		X
Embedment and evaluation methodology	1–3	X	
Subject value base	3&6	X	

Table 31.1 **Evaluating protocols for pedagogy transfer**

31.10 Conclusion

This chapter has considered some of the barriers to the successful transfer of best pedagogic practice. It has sought to identify some of the factors relating to subject discourse and institutional organization, which affect such transfer. To assist staff in implementing change the chapter has suggested some protocols, or possible features, that may assist the transfer of best practice in pedagogy. It has outlined a number of pedagogy transfers and innovations at different levels which illustrate the influence of the suggested protocols.

31.1 References

Becher, T. and Kogan, M. (1992) Basic units. In *Process and Structure in Higher Education*, 2nd edn. London and New York: Routledge, pp 87—108.

Biglan, A. (1973a) The characteristics of subject matter in different academic areas, *Journal of Applied Psychology* **57**(3): 195—213.

Biglan, A. (1973b) Relationships between subject matter characteristics and the structure and output of university departments, *Journal of Applied Psychology* **57**(3): 195—213.

Briars, G. (1998) *Times Higher Educational Supplement*, 26 June.

Clark, B.R. (1983a) Authority. In *The Higher Education System: Academic Organization in Cross-National Perspective*, Berkeley: The University of California Press, pp. 107—34.

Clark, B.R. (1983b) Work. In *The Higher Education System: Academic Organization in Cross-National Perspective*, Berkeley: The University of California Press, pp. 28—71.

Dill, D.D. (1992) Academic administration. In Clark, B.R. and Neave, G. (eds), *The Encyclopaedia of Higher Education*, Vol. II. Oxford: Pergamon Press, pp. 1318—29.

Foucault, M. (1974) *The Archaeology of Knowledge*. London: Tavistock.

Geiger, R.L. (1990) Organised research units — their role in the development of university research, *Journal of Higher Education* **61**(1): 1—19.

Gibbons, M. *et al.* (1994) *The New Production of Knowledge: The Dynamics of Science and Research in Contemporary Societies*. London: Sage.

Harvey, D. (1989) *The Condition of Postmodernity*. Oxford: Blackwell.

Lyotard, J.F. (1993) *Political Writings* (trans. Readings, W. and Geiman, K.P.). London: UCL Press.

Massy, W.F. (1996) Reengineering resource allocation systems. In *Resource Allocation in Higher Education*. Ann Arbor: University of Michigan Press, pp. 15—47.

Seden, M.R. (1997) Ten years on: an evaluation. In CBLIS 97, International Conference on Computer Based Learning in Science, De Montfort University, Leicester, UK, 8 pp, paper ref I3.

Smith, A. and Webster, F. (1997) *The Postmodern University*, Buckingham: Society for Research into Higher Education and Open University Press.

Trowler, P. (1998) *Academics Responding to Change: New Higher Education Frameworks and Academic Cultures*. Buckingham: Society for Research into Higher Education and Open University Press.

Usher, R. and Edwards, R. (1994) *Postmodernism and Education*. London and New York: Routledge.

Weick, K. (1976) Educational organizations as loosely-coupled systems, *Administrative Science Quarterly* **21**(1): 1—19.

Williams, G.L. (1995) The 'marketization' of higher education: reforms and potential reforms in higher education finance. In Dill, D.D. and Sporn, B., *Emerging Patterns of Social Demand and University Reform: Through a Glass Darkly*. Oxford: Pergamon Press, pp. 90—104.

32 Learning strategies in social science students as measured by the Learning and Study Strategies Inventory (LASSI)

Chris Slade and Vivienne Brunsden
Nottingham Trent University

32.1 Overview

This chapter explores the first stage of a longitudinal study of students at Nottingham Trent University studying one of three undergraduate programmes. It uses a research tool based on a model that brings together theory and research into student learning strategies. The study employs a scale developed by Weinstein (1987), the Learning and Study Strategies Inventory, (LASSI), which aims to measure both cognitive and affective strategies used by university students.

The questionnaire comprises 10 scales, the first five of which measure affective strategies that involve personal factors influencing academic performance, and the last five measuring cognitive strategies that enable students to evaluate their learning by applying specific techniques such as processing, reviewing and retaining information, and preparing for tests. The tool is based on Weinstein's model of strategic learning, which also takes into account external factors, such as the academic environment, and teachers' beliefs and expectations.

The key questions addressed are as follows:

(a) How do students perceive their existing learning strategies and attitudes towards learning?
(b) Is there a gender difference in these perceptions?
(c) Is there a difference in the perceptions of mature and standard-entry students?
(d) Is there a difference in the perception of students studying different types of degree?

The basic precept is that intrinsic factors, including motivation, self-perception, and metacognition affect the type of strategies and learning styles students employ, and that positive intervention in these strategies by academic staff can result in better student learning.

32.2 Background

32.2.1 Theories of learning strategies

Research into students' use of learning strategies stems from:

1. Research into cognitive psychology over the past 25 years. Much of the language employed in describing models of learning, such as 'deep versus surface' learning, originates in the language of memory categorization. Paris, Lipson and Wixson (1983) also talk of 'declarative, procedural and conditional' learning strategies in their 'skill and will' model; again, using language borrowed from memory organization theory.

2. Theories about, and research into, student learning, learning models and models of learning orientation. Until recently these seemed to concentrate on extrinsic factors associated with the quality of the learning environment, such as teacher competence, class size, and contexts that allow students to engage in deep learning.

3. Contemporary models of student learning. These focus on intrinsic factors and stress the importance of:
   - motivation;
   - affective factors and perceptions, such as self-efficacy and attribution;
   - conceptions of learning and knowledge;
   - metacognition;
   - socio-cultural factors;
   - context, but particularly students' perception of context.

32.2.2 Motivation

We now know that motivation affects the approach to learning, and the way learning takes place. Deep learning will only take place if students are motivated (Gibbs 1990, 1994). Haynes *et al.* (1987) found motivation to be the key factor that separated high from low achievers in their study of minority high school students in inner city schools. Haynes *et al.* used the same scale, the LASSI scale, as this study employs, adapted for high school students. Sinkavitch (1989) also found that students who scored highly on motivation questions on the LASSI scale tended to have higher final exam scores. In his learning model, Vermunt (1996) proposes two important motivational orientations: intrinsic, where the student has an interest in the subject matter, and extrinsic, which refers to motivation related to the overall effects of the programme of study, such as getting a good job.

More recent research has investigated the relationship between motivation and other variables, such as self-efficacy (see below), and attribution, (the way people attribute the cause of behaviour,). It appears that not only are these variables related, but that there may also be positive correlations with the use of cognitive strategies. McCombs (1988), states that 'meaningful learning requires not only the skills and ability to engage in effective cognitive strategies, but also motivation to do so' and Meyer and Parsons (1994) confirm that 'contemporary models of student learning emphasize that the outcome of learning is a function of strategy in tandem with motivational influences'.

Self-efficacy is 'an individual's beliefs about their ability to achieve goals by action in specific situations' (Bandura, 1982). Olejnik and Nist (1992) in their analysis of the latent variables of the LASSI scale, demonstrated a positive relationship between effort-related strategies and goal related strategies. However, their findings imply that effort without strategy is probably wasted effort. A review of the literature also tells us that students' self-perceptions of efficacy can often be inaccurate. However, it seems that:

Positive affect leads to
Positive attitude, which leads to
Task orientation which leads to
Positive learning outcomes

(Olejnik and Nist, 1992; Dweck and Elliott, 1983; Nicholls, 1984).
and

Negative affect leads to
Loss of control, which leads to
Fear of failure, which leads to
Poor performance

(Kuhl, 1984).

This indicates a degree of self-fulfilling prophecy for students with negative attitudes or perceptions. Worry can therefore still have a negative effect on performance, even in able and hard working students, especially in tests and exams. Alexander, Murphy and Guan (1998) found in their sample of students from Singapore that their 'able but not exceptional' students worried more about, for example, time management than their American counterparts, *because* they had a more positive attitude towards learning. McKeachie, Pintrich and Lin (1985), found that teaching anxious students better learning strategies resulted in improved achievement. Students who voluntarily enrolled on an introductory psychology course, which explained the cognitive psychology concepts relevant to learning strategies, were shown to have higher marks at the end of the course than the control group.

32.2.3 Attribution

Attributional models highlight the importance of the relationship between perceived ability and effort. Peterson and Seligman (1984), and Weiner (1979) in research into learned helplessness, stress the importance of encouraging students to attribute success or failure to learnable skills, and not to fixed characteristics of the learner. It is therefore important to know how the student perceives his or her ability to learn, as well as how they perceive the task. Palmer and Goetz (1988) showed that learner initiated actions are affected by motivation and how students attribute success or failure: in other words, if a student perceives him or her self to be incompetent then they are reluctant to use a strategy.

It is important to comprehend this *conception of knowledge* in understanding how students use learning strategies. Paris, Lipson and Wixson (1983) maintain that three types of knowledge are necessary for effective use of learning strategies: the student needs to know what to do, how to do it, when to do it, and why — hence their categories of declarative, procedural and conditional types of knowledge. *Types of knowledge* is one of the two categories of conceptions that students develop; the other main category being learning conception, another intrinsic factor that has been widely researched. For example, Vermunt (1996) proposes that conceptions of learning relate to general views and beliefs about the nature, progress and value of learning, and especially affect the way a learner *approaches* a task.

He suggests three levels of learning conception:

- level 1 with emphasis on fact retention;
- level 2 as knowledge building;
- level 3 with emphasis on the practical value of what has been learnt.

32.2.4 Metacognition

According to Flavell (1979), metacognition is, 'the process by which we think about our cognitive machinery and processing mechanisms', or 'knowledge about human thought processes in general, and knowledge about one's strengths and limitations as a thinker in particular'. Metacognition therefore relates to the student's understanding of what learning is, one of the strands of research conducted in student learning research in the 1970s and '80s. Alexander and Dochy (1995) found a relationship between metacognition, learning strategies employed and motivation in their study of high achieving female students in Singapore. They also emphasize the importance of *socio-cultural factors* in influencing attitudes towards learning, beliefs about the value of learning, and the effect of affect on achievement. Sociocultural factors are discussed further when the results of studies using LASSI are discussed.

32.2.5 Perception of context

The effect of context has been widely researched as an extrinsic factor which can be altered to improve student learning. However, it has become apparent that it is the way the student perceives the learning context that is crucial for influencing learning outcomes, and this is harder to both measure and alter. Students have clear perceptions about what makes a good and bad lecturer, a fair or unfair method of assessment, to name but two aspects of context. Entwistle and Ramsden (1983), in their work on learning styles as orientations, emphasize the role of the student's perception of the situation as well as their motivational orientation.

32.2.6 Summary

The focus on learning strategies is because we know this is an area in which we can intervene to improve student learning. It is easier to intervene by identifying existing strategies used, and teaching students how to use more effective ones, than it is, for example, to teach students different ways of attributing reasons for poor performance. (Students can be encouraged to be reflective about their learning, but this is still primarily an aspect of an individual's perception.)

Cognitive strategies are 'learner initiated actions' (Palmer and Goetz, 1988). These were initially thought of as elaboration and rehearsal, enabling the processing of learning material. However, the focus has shifted away from pure cognitive strategies towards more general learning strategies, of which cognitive strategies form a subset. Weinstein and Mayer (1985) define learning strategies as 'Cognitions and behaviours that influence the encoding process and facilitate acquisition and retrieval of new knowledge'. Danserau (1985) distinguishes between primary strategies used to process information, and support strategies used to maintain the proper state of mind for learning, such as attention and concentration strategies.

From Weinstein (1987), Danserau (1985) and Vermunt's (1996) theory of learning styles, we can assemble the following categories of learning strategies:

- *Cognitive* strategies, such as elaboration and rehearsal. These can be:
  - *shallow*, allowing for literal reproduction of material;
  - *deep*, aimed and understanding and elaboration;
  - *application based*, allowing problem-solving and transferability.

(These directly reflect the levels of learning conceptions outlined above.)

- *Organization and regulation* strategies, where students test, evaluate and organize material. This involves coordination and control of the learning process. (Vermunt (1996), in his learning model, suggests that weaker students expect this to be done for them by teachers, while stronger students initiate the actions themselves.)
- *Comprehension and monitoring* strategies: these maintain, reinforce and assess the learning that has taken place.
- *Motivational strategies*: these assess the short-, medium- and long-term rewards and goals and keep learning 'on track'. They therefore affect the way learning takes place.

We know that motivation is inter-related with affective factors and the student's self-perception, so it seems that meaningful learning strategies need to incorporate consideration of the following:

- skills and ability;
- intrinsic motivation;
- accurate self-perception;
- positive effect;
- a realistic model of attribution;
- a socio-cultural context conducive to learning;
- accurate metacognition;
- beliefs about, and expectations of, the programme of study.

There is support from research that learning strategies can be taught, and that these can result in skills which can be transferred across modules, i.e. they are not necessarily discipline specific or confined to measuring ability at only one educational level. (McKeachie, Pintrich and Lin, 1985; Weinstein, Schulte and Palmer, 1987).

32.3 The current study

32.3.1 The research tool

The Learning and Study Strategies Inventory (LASSI; Weinstein, 1987) consists of ten sub-scales. These are attitude (ATT); motivation (MOT); time management (TMT); anxiety (ANX); concentration (CON); information processing (INP); selecting main ideas (SMI); study aids (STA); self testing (SFT) and test strategies (TST). The authors report a range of .68—.86 for the sub-scales' coefficient alphas. They also report a range of .72—.85 for the sub-scales' test-retest correlation coefficients. LASSI has been found to have a three factor structure (Olejnik and Nist, 1992), with factors identified as effort-related activities, goal orientation and cognitive activities. This structure has been found to hold for translated (Olaussen and Braten, 1998) and modified (Olivarez and Tallent-Runnels, 1994) versions of the scale. Norms for each scale are provided with LASSI; these norms enable raw scores to be transformed into percentiles allowing relative performance to be assessed.

LASSI was developed for use with an American population. As a British sample was used in this research, the terminology in some items was re-worded in order to have more salience for this sample. For similar reasons one item on the TST sub-scale was omitted and scoring adjusted accordingly. This resulted in a 76-item scale.

Various studies have concluded that there is a positive correlation between students' marks and learning study strategies as measured by LASSI. Richardson,(1994), however, gives 'health warnings' against using quantitative instruments with students. He warns specifically against:

- ignoring the effects of culture;
- using instruments at differing levels of education;
- overlooking individual differences, such as age and gender.

There has been consideration of these variables in the research to date using LASSI. For example, Olaussen and Braten (1988) analysed the latent variables of LASSI using two independent samples of Norwegian college students, and adapted the scale for students from a different culture. They state:

> Findings of American researchers regarding the latent structure of LASSI can be extended to high ability students in a different cultural context,

and

> LASSI generalizes across different educational levels within the same culture.

Their findings compared well with those of Olejnik and Nist (1992), who, in their study using American students, conclude:

> LASSI is a complex measurement tool which appears to have considerable research potential as a research instrument in addition to being a diagnostic and evaluation tool.

Other studies, e.g. Nist *et al.* (1990) with at-risk and low-ability American students, and Alexander, Murphy and Guan (1998), with high-ability Singapore female students, show the stability of LASSI in different educational and socio-cultural contexts. Samples of students have included Hispanic American, Norwegian, Singaporean, as well as American students.

32.3.2 The student sample

All the students in the study were from the same university, based in the faculty of Economics and Social Sciences with the same learning accommodation, and some lecturers in common. There are however clear differences between the programmes of study.

The *BSc Psychology* is a laboratory-based degree, which is founded on scientific principles. Teaching includes a weekly, small (maximum six students) tutorial, conducive to 'deep' learning (Gibbs, 1990) . There is a clearly defined and very specific subject field, and in the recent draft report of the external subject review it was noted that 'of particular merit were tutorial sessions observed on the BSc Psychology course. These were excellent sessions and involved an impressive amount of student participation and demonstration of skills.'

Students starting the course with A-levels have to achieve, except in special circumstances, at least grades BBC, or a minimum of 22 points. (The maximum points achievable for three A-levels is three A grades, or 30 points.)

The *BA Criminology* is a multidisciplinary degree focusing on sociology, social policy, and legal and criminal justice, policy and practice. Small group tutorials are not held. Seminars of approximately 15 students are the main form of support teaching to large, (usually about 75 students), lectures. The subject field is more diverse, but entry requirements are the same, in general, as those for the BSc Psychology (i.e. 22 points at A-level or an equivalent qualification).

The *BA Social Science* is a degree with a wider diversity of subjects, including economics, sociology, psychology and politics. Again, there are no small group tutorials. Students require 12—16 points or equivalent to be allowed on to the course, and generally have to endure larger classes, especially in the first two years, although there are some seminar groups of around 15 students in most areas of the course.

The university enthusiastically encourages non-standard entrants, who are usually mature students with fewer A-level points than their younger counterparts, but who have often outshone their peers in achievement. Analysis of their data will be compared, throughout the study, with standard entry students.

32.4 Method

32.4.1 Design and sample

The questionnaire was completed by 128 university first-year degree students during their first few months after enrolment. Participants were 28 males, aged 18—40 years (mean = 21.7, s.d. = 4.9) and 100 females aged 18—36 years (mean = 20.4, s.d. = 3.5). The October 1998 intake of three separate courses were used: BSc Psychology (n = 36), BA Criminology (n = 55) and BA Social Sciences (n = 37).

32.4.2 Procedure

In this initial stage data were collected within the first few months of students commencing study. This collection stage establishes a baseline for the future research, but also provides provisional information as to potential differences across gender, age and degree path followed.

32.5 Results

NB: bold type denotes noteworthy differences; 'percentile', refers to American student norms

	ATT	MOT	TMT	ANX	CON	INP	SMI	STA	SFT	TST
BA Criminology	60	**16.4**	41.8	**36.4**	47.3	34.5	**45.5**	34.5	36.4	**5.5**
BSc Psychology	58.3	**33.3**	55.6	**27.8**	50	41.7	**27.8**	38.9	27.8	**0**

Table 32.1 Percentage of students by course, scoring in and above the 50th percentile

	ATT	MOT	TMT	ANX	CON	INP	SMI	STA	SFT	TST
Males	**46.4**	**14.3**	**35.7**	**60.7**	50	32.1	**57.1**	**21.4**	35.7	**7.1**
Females	**67**	**30**	**57**	**20**	50	38	**33**	**45**	33	**4**

Table 32.3 Percentage of students by sex, scoring in and above the 50th percentile

	ATT	MOT	TMT	ANX	CON	INP	SMI	STA	SFT	TST
Males	**10.7**	3.6	14.3	**21.4**	21.4	17.9	**21.4**	7.1	10.7	**3.6**
Females	**28**	6	21	**2**	28	17	**10**	18	9	**4**

Table 32.4 Percentage of students by sex, scoring in and above the 75th percentile

	ATT	MOT	TMT	ANX	CON	INP	SMI	STA	SFT	TST
over 22yrs	68	**44**	**76**	**12**	**76**	**52**	48	48	40	**4**
21 and under	59.4	**22.8**	**45.5**	**31.7**	**43.6**	**33.7**	36.6	37.6	32.7	**5**

Table 32.5 Percentage of students by age, scoring in and above the 50th percentile

	ATT	MOT	TMT	ANX	CON	INP	SMI	STA	SFT	TST
over 22yrs	**40**	**16**	20	4	**40**	20	16	20	**20**	**4**
21 and under	**20.8**	**3**	18.8	6.9	**21.8**	16.8	11.9	13.9	**7.9**	**0**

Table 32.6 Percentage of students by age, scoring in and above the 75th percentile

Discussion

32.6.1 Table 32.1

Table 32.1 shows that there are notable differences in four scales for students in or above the 50th percentile: Motivation, Anxiety, Selecting Main Ideas and Test strategies.

32.6.1.1 *Motivation and anxiety*

There is an inverse relationship between motivation and anxiety for students on all three programmes, but students on the BA Social Sciences report higher motivation scores than either of the other two degrees. Possible reasons for this are:

- that students are aware that they are not motivated enough, and this causes them anxiety; at this stage they have not developed the learning strategies to help reduce anxiety;
- the nature of the BA Social Sciences positively affects motivation.

32.6.1.2 *Selecting main ideas*

Students on the BSc Psychology report much lower scores in this measure, with Criminology students reporting the highest score. This is possibly a reflection of the teaching methods: psychology students are perhaps less 'spoon-fed' because they have small tutorial groups, are made to think more, and therefore have less confidence in their ability. They may therefore be at level 2 of Vermunt's learning model — knowledge building. (Vermunt, 1996). Students without small group teaching are perhaps directly given more of the main themes and ideas in lectures and handouts at this stage of the course .Their learning therefore relates to level 2 of Vermunt's learning model — fact retention.

32.6.1.3 *TST scores: test strategies and preparing for tests*

Scores in this measure are extremely low in all cases, compared to the American norms. This is partly because the TST category had one less question. The question, 'I have difficulty adapting my study to different types of courses' was eliminated from the original questionnaire as it was felt that the answer to this would not be fairly comparable across all three programmes. Even so, the scores are extremely low, and this may reflect a cultural difference between American and British students: there is less programmed learning and spot testing on English programmes so British students are less experienced in developing test strategies.

Further analysis at a later stage will indicate whether this score is predictive of marks, or whether this reflects a perceptual factor.

32.6.2 Table 32.2

The main new difference that arises in the top 75 per cent is the ATT score, reflecting attitude towards, and interest in, the programme. Students on the BA Social Science degree again have higher scores. This may reflect preconceptions that students have about psychology and criminology. Students often have misplaced ideas of what these degrees comprise, and in the first year especially, often feel 'knocked back' when they discover the true nature of their chosen programme. BA Social Science students however have a wider range of subjects to choose from, and have not yet selected the subject they wish to major in. If their preconceptions are inaccurate, they have more opportunity to change their options. A second reason for this difference may be a function of entry requirements: lower A-level points are required for this degree, and many students are either pleased to have got into university at all, or have less focused career aspirations at this stage.

32.6.3 Tables 32.3 and 32.4

Gender differences are apparent on most measures, for both the 50th and 75th percentiles, with females scoring more highly except on the anxiety and selecting main ideas scores. The higher anxiety scores for males may reflect knowledge that they should be working harder. The higher SMI score is thought to reflect a more instrumental approach to studying.

32.6.4 Tables 32.5 and 32.6

Mature students score more highly on all measures except anxiety, and test strategies in the 75th percentile. This reflects the perception of academic staff that although mature students generally are more committed to studying, their test strategies are weak. The most notable difference relates to time management strategies (TMT): this may reflect the additional responsibilities that many mature students have. A common observation, that mature students, although often more hard working, have less confidence in their ability to succeed, and are often debilitatingly anxious about formal tests, is therefore supported. This also supports Alexander, Murphy and Guan (1998).

32.7 Future data collection

This data collection can be viewed as the initial stage of a much larger longitudinal study. Data will be collected at repeated intervals throughout the three years of participants' attendance at university. Longitudinal data will allow testing of LASSI as both a diagnostic tool that provides on-going summative evaluation, and as a predictor of end performance. It will also enable the testing of the measure's psychometric properties with a British sample. A longer-term aim is to obtain a large enough sample from several UK universities to allow for the development of UK norms, as well as reliability and validity testing of the amended questionnaire.

The baseline data has however revealed some interesting differences in learning strategies. Although these are self-perceptions, this is an adult population who has already demonstrated advanced cognitive skills by being admitted to the programmes. As Palmer and Goetz (1988) report, it is important how a student:

1. perceives the task;
2. perceives his/her strategy;
3. perceives his/her ability to learn.

If a student perceives him or herself to be incompetent then they are reluctant to even attempt to use a strategy.

This supports research that shows there is an interaction between cognitive and motivational variables and deep learning. In fact, many of the items on the scale are closely related. Alexander and Dochy (1994) report that the value a student puts on education directly affects the cognitive strategies employed, and Kulik (1983) has demonstrated that better study skills can lead to deep learning. Analysis of the latent constructs of this scale reveals important prerequisites for effective student learning.

Olejnik and Nist (1992) suggest that the three latent constructs that underpin LASSI represent important components of learning and studying, in that:

- *effort-related activities,* i.e. motivation, time management and concentration are the 'planned, concentrated and goal directed energy that is necessary to learn and to keep the learning and studying progress on track';
- *goal-related activities,* i.e. anxiety, test strategies and selecting main ideas, are the 'ability to keep calm and concentrated in mastering the skills required for getting to get to grips with study material';
- *cognitive activities,* i.e. information processing, the use of study aids and self-testing are 'the fundamental cognitive and metacognitive strategies necessary for processing information and monitoring understanding'.

This study supports that there are multi-component conceptions of the learning process, and that 'cognitive skills and motivational factors need to be afforded greater prominence in discussions about student achievements' (Weinstein, 1994).

However, the primary aim of this work is to improve the student learning in the environment in which they work, supporting Gibbs (1994), who says: 'Professional researcher should concentrate on fundamental research. [...] Teachers should be doing research on their own courses.'

32.8 References

Alexander, P.A., Murphy, P.K. and Guan, J. (1998) The learning and study strategies of highly able female students in Singapore, *Educational Psychology* **18**(4): 391—407.

Alexander, P.A. and Dochy, F.J.R.C. (1995) Conceptions of knowledge and beliefs: a comparison across varying cultural and educational communities, *American Educational Research Journal* **32**: 413—42.

Bandura, A. (1977) Self-efficacy: toward a unifying theory of behavioural change, *Psychological Review* **84**: 191—215.

Dansereau, D.F. (1985) Learning strategy research. In J.W. Segal, S.F. Chipman and R. Glaser (eds), *Thinking and Learning Skills, Vol. 1* (pp. 209—40). Hillsdale, NJ: Lawrence Erlbaum Associates.

Dweck, C.S. and Elliott, E.S. (1983) Achievement motivation. In P.H. Mussen (ed.), *Handbook of Child Psychology, Vol. 4* (pp. 643—92). New York: Wiley.

Entwistle, N.J. and Ramsden, P. (1983) *Understanding Student Learning.* New York: Nicholls Publishing Co.

Flavell J.H. (1979) Metacognitive and cognitive monitoring: a new idea of cognitive developmental inquiry, *American Psychologist* **34**: 906—11.

Gibbs, G. (1990) *Learning through Action.* London: FEU.

Gibbs, G. (ed.) (1994) *Improving Student Learning: Theory and Practice.* Oxford: Oxford Centre for Staff Development.

Haynes, N.M., Comer, J.P. Hamilton-Lee, M., Boger, J. and Joyner, E. (1987) Differences among high, average and low high school achievers on
the Learning and Study Strategies Inventory, *Educational and Psychological Research* **7**(2): 65—71.

Kuhl, J. (1984) Volitional aspects of achievement motivation and learned helplessness:

toward a comprehensive theory of action control. In B.A. Maher (ed.), *Progress in Experimental Personality Research*, Vol. **13**, pp. 99—171.

Kulik, C.L., Kulik, J.A. and Schwalb, B.J. (1983) College programs for high risk and disadvantaged students: a meta-analysis of findings, *Review of Educational Research* **53**: 387—414.

McCombs, B.L. (1988) Motivational skills training: combining metacognitive, cognitive and affective learning strategies. In C.E. Weinstein, E.T. Goetz and P.A. Alexander (eds), *Learning and Study Strategies: Issues in assessment, instruction and evaluation* (pp. 141—65). New York: Academic Press.

McKeachie, W.J., Pintrich, P.R. and Lin,Y-G. (1985) *Teaching learning strategies*, Educational Psychologist 20: 153—61.

Meyer, J.H.F. and Parsons, P.G. (1994) Identifying students' approaches to studying — conceptually at risk students: diagnostic and intervention strategies based on individual differences. In Gibbs, G. (ed.), *Improving Student Learning: Theory and Practice*, pp. 53—88. Oxford: Oxford Centre for Staff Development:

Nicholls, J.G. (1984) Achievement motivation: conception of ability, subjective experience, task, choice and performance, *Psychological Review* **91**: 328—46.

Nist, S.L., Mealey, D.L., Simpson, M.L. and Kroc, R. (1990) Measuring the affective and cognitive growth of regularly admitted and developmental studies students using the Learning and Study Strategies Inventory (LASSI), *Reading Research and Instruction* **30**: 44—9.

Olaussen, B.S. and Braten,I. (1998) Identifying latent variables measured by the Learning and Study Strategies Inventory (LASSI) in Norwegian college students, *Journal of Experimental Education* **67**(1): 82—96.

Olejnik, S. and Nist, S.L. (1992) Identifying latent variables measured by the Learning and Study Strategies Inventory (LASSI), *Journal of Experimental Education* **60**: 151—9.

Olivarez, A. and Tallent-Runnels, M.K. (1994) Psychometric properties of the Learning and Study Strategies Inventory — High School version, *Journal of Experimental Education* **62**: 243—57.

Palmer, D. and Goetz, E. (1988) Selection and the use of study strategies: the role of the studier's beliefs about self and strategies. In C.E. Weinstein, E.T. Goetz and P.A. Alexander (eds), *Learning and Study Strategies: Issues in assessment, instruction and evaluation* (pp. 41—57). New York: Academic Press.

Paris S.G., Lipson, M.Y. and Wixson, K.K. (1983) Becoming a strategic reader, *Contemporary Educational Psychology* **8**: 293—316.

Peterson, C. and Seligman, M. (1984) Causal explanations as a risk factor for depression: theory and evidence, *Psychological Review* **91**: 347—74.

Richardson, J.T.E. (1994) Using questionnaires to evaluate student learning: some health warnings. In Gibbs, G. (ed.), *Improving Student Learning: Theory and Practice*. Oxford: Oxford Centre for Staff Development, pp. 73—88.

Sinkavich, F.J. (1989) Cognitive processes and performance, *Journal of Instructional Psychology* **21**(2): 72—182.

Vermunt, J.D.H.M. (1996) Metacognitive, cognitive, and affective aspects of learning styles and strategies: a phenomenographic analysis, *Higher Education* **31**: 25—50.

Weinstein, C.E. (1994) Strategic learning/strategic teaching: flip side of a coin. In P.R. Pintrich, D.R. Brown and C.E. Weinstein (eds), *Student Motivation, Cognition and Learning* (pp. 257—73). Hillsdale, NJ: Erlbaum.

Weinstein, C.E. and Mayer, R.E. (1985) The teaching of learning strategies. In M. Wittrock (ed.), *The Handbook of Research and Teaching*, 3rd edn. New York: Macmillan.

Weinstein, C.E. and Palmer, D.R. (1990) *LASSI-HS: Learning and Study Strategies Inventory-High School Version*. Clearwater, FL: H&H Publishing.

Weinstein, C.E., Palmer, D.R. and Schulte, A.C. (1987) *LASSI: Learning and Study Strategies Inventory*. Clearwater, FL: H&H Publishing.

33 Challenges to professional education: learning in work-place settings

Jenny Spouse
School of Health and Social Welfare, The Open University

33.1 Overview

Traditional apprenticeship modes of learning in practice settings have been favoured as the ideal approach to transmitting craft knowledge and to socializing entrants to the culture of a profession. There is considerable evidence from research into school-teacher and nurse education to demonstrate that this approach is ineffective and often deleterious to both the student and the client. In addition such approaches deny the complexity of professional craft knowledge. Over the past 30 years nurse education has been dominated by the behaviourist/cognitivist paradigms that have little to contribute to understanding of work-place learning.

Findings from a phenomenological, longitudinal indicated that socio-cultural theories have significant importance for adult education and particularly for understanding and promoting professional development. In particular participants were able to integrate knowledge gained from formal academic processes and to learn how to relate it to their everyday practice in an effective and stimulating manner. They also became sufficiently motivated to extend their knowledge and understanding to specific case situations and as a result developed a repertoire of skills necessary for lifelong learning.

Essential to this process were knowledgeable mentors willing to share personal craft knowledge. Through this relationship of educational companionship, both student and mentor were able to benefit from each other's knowledge. Students evolved into professional practitioners able to problematize and thus deal with the complexities of everyday practice.

33.2 Traditional approaches to work-place learning

In professional education, until recently, there has been an implicit assumption that students will consolidate practical skills learned in formal (university) settings when they visit their workplace. Any supplementary teaching was provided formally through tutorials and discussions by experienced members of staff such as mentors or in traditional nursing settings, ward sisters (Zeichner, 1983; Fretwell, 1982).

Researchers argue that three dominant paradigms have held sway in school-teacher preparation: functionalist, interpretative and critical (Zeichner and Gore, 1991). Links between teacher and nurse education are strong, with a long history of nurse teacher preparation taking place in departments of education. Owing to these close links the same transitions in pedagogical approaches have also dominated nurse education. This contrasts with work-place settings where conditions are dominated by bureaucratic demands of financial stringency and labour requirements. As a result nurse education has traditionally had short shrift from health service managers reliant upon students to function as key workers in their labour force. Several reports and commissions published over the past century (e.g. Lancet Commission, 1932; Royal College of Nursing, 1985) deplored this abuse of nursing students and attributed the high dropout rate and poor quality of patient care to insufficient supervision and educational support.

33.3 Context of this chapter

In discussing the characteristic patterns of teaching and learning this chapter draws on data from a four-year longitudinal, phenomenological study designed to investigate the professional development of nursing students in their clinical settings. The study followed a small group of students during their nursing degree programme and sought to address four questions concerned with the development of professional knowledge by nursing students. In the process it became apparent that traditional educational theories were inappropriate to explain the best situations that promoted students' development. It is this aspect that will be discussed here.

33.3.1 The research design

From a random sample of first-year students, eight participated in the study. These students represented three branches of nursing, adult (or general) nursing, children's nursing and mental health (psychiatry). Two were over 25 and the other three had left school within 18 months of starting the course. In preparation for participation, students were briefed and signed a consent form that guaranteed their rights.

A multi method approach to data collection using individual interviews, documentary analysis of students' learning contracts, illuminative artwork and observational visits to their practice setting (Spouse, 2000; 1997). Audio-recordings of the interviews were transcribed verbatim. Data analysis was conducted using the framework prescribed by Miles and Huberman (1990) and supplemented using the constant comparative method (Glaser, 1965). Participants collaborated by verifying their own case study as it was developed. Each research question was then addressed using content analysis and an iterative and inductive approach to the literature and the data.

33.3.2 Context of the degree programme

In 1999 nursing degree course students constituted 13 per cent of the total entrants to nurse preparation in the UK. The programme had the largest intake of nursing degree students in the United Kingdom. Its curriculum was influenced by critical theory and incorporated reflective practice. As a result students worked as action enquirers and wrote up critical incidents illustrating their professional development. Throughout their course students were supernumerary to the clinical workforce and were expected to negotiate with their clinical mentor relevant practice experiences for their developmental needs.

33.4 Theories of learning in nurse education

In trying to understand the nature of pedagogical assumptions an analysis was made of documents relating to the education of nurse teachers and the education of nurses. Eighteen textbooks published between 1975 (the date of the first UK nurse education text) and 1997 were identified. These were used in nurse education preparation programmes for both nurse tutors and clinical staff preparing to supervise students in practice. British nursing journals and research literature from the same period were also examined for material concerned with student education. Texts showed the dominant pedagogical paradigms to have evolved from behaviourist models through cognitivist and humanistic approaches to emancipatory models. An apprenticeship model in clinical settings supported early behaviourist approaches. Educationalists writing for nurse-teachers advocated a curriculum utilizing learning objectives, practical demonstration and formal modes of teaching (Bendall, 1976; Koshy, 1984).

33.4.1 Influences of behaviourist concepts of learning on nurse training

Behaviourist theories: sequenced learning, repetition and extinction of unwanted behaviours are reflected in the majority of books and journals reviewed. Bandura (1977) and Gagné (1975) are authors whose work is most frequently cited. Their theories provided a functionalist perspective of learning to nurse which reflected service needs of the National Health Service. Bandura's role modelling theory is viewed in nursing literature as a particularly relevant concept for teaching students how to function effectively (Dotan *et al.*, 1986). Its behaviourist principals of learning through observation and imitation without cognition perhaps ensures a disciplined workforce, characteristic of the origins of nursing in the military and the church. Gagné's theories are focused on human cognition and his arguments are towards persistent states of behavioural change. Using models of information processing, he proposed strategies to ensure favourable conditions for learning (Gagné, 1975). His approach to learning consisted of five domains and these are presented in Table 33.1, showing their relationship to traditional apprenticeship models and to nursing.

This table illustrates the extent to which such approaches relate to apprenticeship schemes of nurse preparation and the use of task allocation to manage nursing care. The nursing school was expected to prepare students for their placements by teaching them any necessary skills for service, which they would then practise and refine in the wards. Development of theoretical knowledge was anticipated to come from this practice and acquisition of appropriate attitudes would be from role models such as ward sisters.

Unsurprisingly the process was ineffective. As with Project 2000 courses, nurse teachers were blamed for failing to prepare students for service needs. Several studies suggested that students were often exposed to an idealistic concept of nursing. Concepts that promoted humanism and professionalism were seen to create dissonance with the bureaucratic demands of day to day nursing, causing wastage (Bendall, 1976; Gott, 1984). Rather than exonerating tutors for their foresight and leadership they were castigated for creating a theory-practice gap due to their ignorance of daily practice.

33.4.2 Interpretivist perspectives and nurse education

During the 1980s the emphasis became more humanistic and works by Knowles (1973) and Rogers (1983) are often cited. However behaviourist concepts continued to influence approaches to learning and teaching in practice settings. The main tenet of this cognitive perspective is that humans relate to the world from within a framework of their own experiences which provide insights and meaning to acts and events and ability to utilize such knowledge in response to new experiences. Proponents argued that learning would occur as a result of being in the presence of a number of conditions, e.g. interest in the topic

Neo-behaviourist Gagné 1975	**Apprenticeship** Coy, 1989 Singleton, 1989	**Nursing**
Motor skills – which are developed through practice	Repetitive tasks – 10,000 sake cups Progression according to expertise	Repetitive tasks e.g. over 3 year course: 5,000 washes; 10,000 injections; 5,000 surgical dressings. Progression according to expertise and status within the hierarchy
Verbal information – presentation within organised, meaningful context	Incidental exchanges of information	Classroom activities related to practice, i.e. one day a week; modular system Incidental clinical tutorials sometimes orientated to a specific patient
Cognitive strategy : repeated occasions when challenges to thinking are presented	Problem solving through tasks set	Range of clinical contexts performing same tasks but with increased responsibility. Problem solving through different experiences
Attitudes: learned most through the use of human models and vicarious reinforcement	Long membership of atelier/workshop and enculturation	Nursing as socialisation and role-modelling
Intellectual skill - retrieval experiences of earlier learning, verbal, cues to assist sequence of skill, spaced rehearsal, use of different settings to encourage transfer of learning	Learning relationships between tasks providing incremental learning and problem solving (Lave and Wenger, 1991)	Range of clinical in different settings for incidental learning and repetitive practice

Table 33.1 Comparison of behaviourism, apprenticeship and nursing

and relevance to current experience; level of existing understanding in relation to new knowledge; opportunity to process new information (analyse, generalize and restructure); and ability to evaluate understanding (Bigge, 1982). Learning was thus promoted as a developmental activity conducive to personal growth, which contrasted with the authoritarian approach of behaviourist approaches to learning.

These ideas created further tensions between nursing schools and hospitals where quasi military-religious traditions conflicted with the egalitarian approach many schools of nursing were striving to adopt (French, 1992). Planning relevant theoretical input to the curriculum was haphazard until the inception of a modular system of training and planned clinical allocations (Parnell, 1975). Still influenced by Gagné as well as cognitivist theories this system anticipated students would relate theory and practice.

Overall the system failed for two particular reasons. It was too difficult to obtain sufficient clinical settings to meet the educational needs of even small groups of 15—20 students at any one particular time. Secondly students needed help from their ward-based colleagues or from a clinically based teacher to help them to recognize the relevance of such material. Alexander's study indicated that with one-to-one supervision from experienced practitioners, students came to appreciate the relevance of formal knowledge to their practice (Alexander, 1980). Clearly the reinforcement of students' learning in, and as a result of practice could be enhanced when supported by well-educated nurses. In the UK, nurses, practitioners and teachers were too few in number, or too busy, or unable to impart such knowledge (Marson, 1982). Studies such as these identified problems students were experiencing in the wards and reflected a growing awareness that learning to nurse was more than delivery of information and repetitive practice.

Creation of joint education and practice appointments and more recently the lecturer practitioner role have been introduced to help students make connections between theory and practice whilst also supporting clinical staff in their professional development (Ashworth and Castledine, 1980). Their merit has been the appointment of well-educated and prepared practitioners into posts of authority that can influence the quality of patient care and staff development (Lathlean, 1995).

33.4.3 Nurse education and critical theory

By the 1990s reflective practice was beginning to be espoused by nurse educators with several professional directives supporting its use, as well as research investigating its effectiveness (Jones *et al.*, 1994). Fuelling these developments was Donald Schön's book *The Reflective Practitioner* (Schön, 1983). Health provision was changing and nursing sought a system to prepare students for professional practice that anticipated such changes. By incorporating reflective practice into education, nurse policy-makers and curriculum planners were more able to implement a new approach to nurse education and professional practice. Instrumental to this new approach was the role of coach (Schön, 1987) which was prescribed by the English National Board as a mentor (ENB, 1988). Mentors were identified as registered nurses delegated to supervise individual student's work. It was anticipated that students' supernumerary status and their replacement by registered nurses would enable sufficient staff to undertake this role, the alternative would be further stalemate which indeed is what has happened.

33.4.4 Summary

This review of the literature demonstrates behaviourist and cognitivist approaches to be insufficient. Furthermore in my study they failed to explain what was happening to students when they had good learning experiences. They were learning how to manage patients with multiple and complex variations of diseases and problems. To achieve this they needed to apply sophisticated formal and experiential knowledge as well as to use problem framing and problem-solving skills in addition to a measure of professional competence. I needed a different theoretical framework to explain their experiences.

33.5 Sociocultural theories: an alternative approach to supporting learning in workplace settings

The data perhaps inevitably demonstrated the importance of mentor—student relationships. With students entering practice settings on a regular but infrequent basis, they were reliant upon good will from resident practitioners. The study demonstrated that unless a bond and commitment was made between student and mentor, students tended to feel alienated with little opportunity to engage in practice activities as the following quote illustrates:

> I have to do weekends because you have to get in 20 shifts and it's hard to get them in at the best of times. The Sister said 'You pick your days don't you. There's nobody here at the weekends'. That wasn't very nice. Not even a 'Hello, nice to see you' and I just thought 'Roll on 3.00pm'. ... I find it's quite intimidating. I wouldn't make an issue of it, probably go bright red and feel a complete idiot and sit quietly in the corner and wait for hand-over and keep out of her way. (Ruth 12, narrative 1)

Ruth's experiences match findings from studies of newcomers in unfamiliar settings where feelings of self-consciousness and alienation are influenced by their reception from old-timers who create barriers to their professional development (Daloz, 1986; Fuhrer, 1993; Ingleton, 1995). The following quote describes the difference when students feel accepted by their mentor and thus their community of practice.

> [When I've been able to make a contribution] I've felt more comfortable definitely and if I feel that, I feel more confident and I think I can help patients more. Particularly, say in your relationship with the doctors, if I have a patient I'm not sure about and I don't feel confident with the ward staff it's twice as hard to go and say to the Sister 'I think I need a doctor here'. I hope I will call them, but I'll think twice about it. Whereas if I'm confident with the team and they're confident with me and I know the doctors I don't have the hesitation about phoning them up and saying 'Look, it's Ruth, the student, and I'm worried about this person'. I think it would make a difference in that respect, certainly with my confidence and ability to get on with people. How profound an effect that has on patients can vary if the client doesn't need a lot, but then if it was a serious issue maybe it would (Ruth 20, narrative 2)

Her feelings of security gave Ruth confidence to engage with other members of the clinical team and this influenced her ability to gain help for herself and her patients.

33.5.1 Sponsorship

In placements where students were able to work with supportive and insightful nurses they gained a sense of self-worth, confidence and enthusiasm. The most important factor in promoting mental ease is to know that someone is providing social support. Effective sponsorship was generated by exchanges of personal information and a mutual willingness to be open and honest in the relationship. Asking students to expose their intimate thoughts and feelings without some reciprocity from their sponsor contributed little to creating a trusting relationship. Where students spend only short periods in any setting this relationship becomes even more important (Spouse, 2000).

Through effective sponsorship, students as newcomers, were able to integrate with the team and to learn its culture, (specialist) language and practices. Ruth's second statement (Interview 20) describes how feelings of membership enables students to seek help when necessary and thus to practice safely. In such environments students were more likely to question their understanding and to accept comments about their own work without feeling threatened. They also needed time to discuss their activities with their mentor or another trusted practitioner. Particularly in the early stages of their programme, students desperately wanted to practise alongside their mentor. This was an important and continuing strategy to develop necessary attributes and skills even when students were quite senior. These findings embellish Lave's work (Lave, 1991). Arising from her studies of apprenticeships in traditional cultures, Lave identifies a model of effective work-based learning that included sponsorship, from an experienced member of the community and participation in activities that are peripheral and legitimate

33.6 Developing professional knowledge

> In some ways seeing how Robyn (mentor) dealt with the little lad was how I dealt with the [child]. ... Plus experience at the children's hospital and the children's ward. Pooling your knowledge together, not just remembering one bit from one. ... It could be A, B and C because Z is affecting that one, and looking at the person. That's what Robyn tied in as well. We were certainly looking at that, how they are and giving them reassurance and telling them what's happening. ... A lot of the wards I've worked on were very busy. You don't have that much time to stand still. Whereas Robyn almost made the time. Even if we were busy, she remembered I was there. (Gilles 11, narrative 3)

In this extract Gilles is remembering an experience where he worked in legitimate and peripheral activities with his mentor. As a result he was able to gain access to her professional craft knowledge. The mentor engaged him in her own daily activities at a level in which he could make a contribution. She took time to explain what was taking place giving rationale for her actions. As a result, in a subsequent placement he was able to bring this knowledge into use when dealing with a similar complex case. He was bringing both formal and informal knowledge to the situation while diagnosing his patient's problem as well as interpersonal and practical skills to obtain the information, and to provide emotional support. He had learned to recognize the salience of his formal knowledge to a clinical situation and how to bring it into use by checking out his assumptions and to then initiate suitable actions in response. Lave's concept of legitimate peripheral participation (1991) contributes to explaining these activities. But it is clear that more is happening and Vygotsky's (1978) concepts of two-stage learning: the social and the mental alongside his concept of a Zone of Proximal Development are significant here.

33.6.1 Social and mental aspects of learning

In describing the social context as a stimulus for human development Vygotsky argued that speech provided the mediational tool for attaching meaning to objects thus allowing them to be manipulated according to a child's (sic) intentions. As with social activities learning in the social context encourages language and cognitive development. Vygotsky defined two forms of speech, the *interpersonal* and the *intrapersonal*. By engaging in legitimate activities with their mentors, learners were able to gain access through description and explanation (i.e. interpersonal speech) to their mentor's professional and personal knowledge. Gilles describes how his mentor found time to explain her actions. In this process Gilles has his attention drawn to specific aspects of a patient's condition and its link with formally learnt material, such as anatomy and physiology or pathology. Its relevance to his practice becomes evident and encourages further hypothesis formulation when working independently. Once students learned how to think about their practice in this way they began to look out for ways in which to use their formal knowledge.

Having an accurate assessment of Gilles' level of capability is a crucial aspect of the process. Vygotsky used the term Zone of Proximal development (ZPD) to describe the range in which learners are able to operate. The Zone consists of two areas. The inner area of competence and the outer area of potential or where with help from a more knowledgeable person the learner can develop competence (Vygotsky, 1978). Figure 33.1 provides an interpretation of this model of learning and uses the concept of knowledge (it can be both formal and experiential knowledge) as 'knowledge-in-waiting' or knowledge that has not yet become sufficiently integrated for the student to recognize its relevance to practice. This can be related to Marton and Säljö's concepts of surface and deep approaches to learning (1997).

Knowledge-in-waiting (or a form of surface knowledge) may represent practical or craft knowledge that has either not been fully integrated or labelled with language, and thus cannot yet be articulated or used in a formal sense. Knowledge-for-use can be both propositional and practical or experiential. It is knowledge that has been integrated and is being employed in the learner's activities.

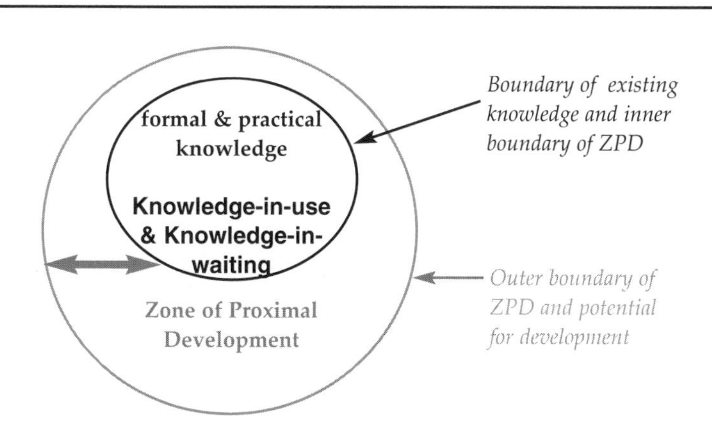

Figure 33.1 Inner and outer boundaries of a Zone of Proximal Development

33.6.2 Proleptic instruction: scaffolding

This role of coaching from a more experienced person (e.g. the mentor) has been labelled, proleptic instruction and is a form of 'Interpersonal speech' essential to developmental activities (Wertsch and Stone, 1979). Development through Gilles's ZPD will only be achieved if his mentor's speech guides him to a level beyond that currently in use or practised (his inner boundary of ZPD). Gilles will also need to be acquainted with the relevant knowledge to reach the outer boundaries of his ZPD, wherever that may be at that moment in time. With the help of proleptic instruction the student can begin to move knowledge-in-waiting to knowledge-in-use and to create a new Zone of Proximal Development. Vygotsky calls this social activity 'Interpersonal' speech. Integrating this knowledge with existing understanding or practice, leads to Intrapersonal or Intramental speech. This is rather like reflective practice as the following narrative from Nicola illustrates:

> I did spend quite a lot of time talking to my lecturer practitioner about it. ... I came round to the point of view of looking beyond my annoyance with her [the patient] and acknowledging the fact that life was really difficult for her and that part of her illness was this inability to concentrate. ... It depends what theories you believe, but I was reading about therapeutic groups. It's really nice to look back over how everything has gone and pick out the critical instances. There's so much to think of when you are writing your learning contract. I found it useful writing about the woman. But you can gain that sort of insight from talking to people as well (Nicola 15, narrative 8).

This process of learning in practice is further enhanced when new knowledge is integrated with existing knowledge. Nicola's mentor was helping her to see what had taken place during the group session and to use her language to explain her observations. This provides opportunities for the mentor to both assess Nicola's level of understanding and to know how to support her learning by consolidating existing knowledge and introducing new information. This activity of *scaffolding* a learner's development (Wood, Bruner and Ross, 1976) provides experiences or challenges that move learners' knowledge-in-waiting to knowledge-in-use or from within the inner boundary across to the outer boundary of their ZPD. The concept of scaffolding has since been developed in a number of ways such as questioning and allocation of legitimate activities, but particularly pertinent, is the verbal coaching of a novice through aspects of a procedure or concept where there is need for extra help.

A different form of proleptic instruction can be employed by learners using language to monitor personal behaviour and to justify as well as enact personal beliefs. Marie's narrative below demonstrates this process well:

> It'd be more me talking myself through the stages, telling her what I was going to do, saying, well I'm going to clean the dressing now, now I'm going to put this padding on, I've got this padding on because like the wound is not weeping like it was. I've only used one. So I'd be talking myself through it but telling Rose what I was doing. It wasn't too hard to do. It was possibly hard saying to Rose, 'I'm doing this now because', and then waiting for her approval of what I was doing (Marie 3, narrative 6).

This spiral revisiting of action and increasing comprehension is facilitated by intrapersonal speech. Intrapersonal or internal speech Vygotsky argued promotes *higher mental functions* of problem framing and problem solving. In addition such speech can be used as an internal organizer of behaviour, as illustrated by Marie's narrative. The more sophisticated the activity the more egocentric the speech (Vygotsky and Luria, 1994). Several writers demonstrate that using language in this way helps students acquire the language and thinking of their discipline and thus to learn faster (Jensen, 1971; Schön, 1987). Engaging students in legitimate peripheral activities alongside an experienced practitioner helps students to integrate language and action and thus to develop professional knowledge. By encouraging think-aloud activities or intrapersonal speech students can appropriate and consolidate their learning more effectively (Rogoff, 1995).

For proleptic instruction to be effective, it is essential that the expert makes accurate assessments of a student's level of understanding and potential to learn. Legitimate activities can then be selected to promote further development and to tailor the nature of instruction offered. This assessment activity uses the concept of ZPD as a diagnostic tool to determine a student's knowledge-in-use and the potential knowledge-for-use (Hedegaard, 1996).

Nicola was able to consolidate her thinking arising from both her discussion and her reading and as a result to formulate a new understanding of her patient's condition as well as to see how theoretical material could be brought into use. Her mentor no doubt phrased her questions in such a way as to cause Nicola to try to make connections between her actions and her feelings. Such questioning and reflective practice scaffolds learning and extends their Zone of Proximal Development boundaries (Palincsar, 1986). Nicola possibly could have reached this on her own when writing her assignment. But this is away from the clinical setting and she loses an opportunity to learn how to draw upon her knowledge when practising.

33.7 Summary and conclusions

Without exposure to these kinds of participative opportunities students may not have made the kind of progress they achieved. When they engaged in effective scaffolded activity, negotiated as a result of correct diagnosis of their potential for development, students were able to consolidate their knowledge and to develop new fields of learning from their practice. Such clinical experiences brought their existing knowledge into question and led to recognition of a knowledge deficit, thus creating new Zones of Proximal Development.

Students developed skills of learning how to learn and to problematize their practice in a manner that apprenticeship schemes failed to encourage. By being engaged in legitimate activities designed to meet their learning needs and within their capability, students were able to feel safe and confident in what they were doing. Their sponsorship within a community of practitioners meant they could approach any member of staff for help and thus benefit from their craft knowledge. Students' progress helped them organize their work, to prioritize patients' nursing needs and to develop their theoretical knowledge. It also gave them an increased sense of becoming nurses in a manner that previous systems failed to achieve.

From the above analysis it is clear that characteristic patterns of teaching and learning have failed to provide effective learning experiences. With introduction of students' supernumerary status, mentorship support and reflective practice, students' learning has been transformed. As a result they have developed skills for life-long learning as well as an excitement and enthusiasm for their own personal and professional development that is unprecedented in nurse education.

33.8 References

Alexander, M.F. (1980) Nurse education: an experiment in integrating theory and practice in nursing. Unpublished PhD thesis, University of Edinburgh

Ashworth, P.M. and Castledine, G. (1980) Joint service education appointments in nursing, *Medical Teacher* **12**(6): 195—229.

Bandura, A. (1977) *Social Learning Theory*. Englewood Cliffs: Prentice Hall Inc.

Bendall, E. (1976) Learning for Reality, *Journal of Advanced Nursing* **1**: 3—9.

Bigge, M.L. (1982) *Learning Theories for Teachers*, 4th edn. New York: Harper & Row.

Commission on Nursing Education (1985) *The Education of Nurses: A New Dispensation*. London, Royal College of Nursing, Chairman Dr Harry Judge.

Coy, M.W. (1989) *Apprenticeship: From Theory to Method and Back Again*. Albany: State University of New York Press.

Daloz, L.A. (1986) *Effective Teaching and Mentoring*. San Francisco: Jossey Bass.

Dotan, M., Krulik, T., Bergman, R., Eckerling, S. and Shatzman, H. (1986) Role models in nursing, *Nursing Times, Occasional Paper* **82**(3): 55—7, February 12.

English National Board for Nursing Midwifery and Health Visiting (1988) *Institutional and Course Approval/Re-Approval Process: Information Required, Criteria and Guidelines*. London: ENB, 1988/39 / APS.

French, P. (1992) The quality of nurse education in the 1980's, *Journal of Advanced Nursing* **17**: 619—31.

Fretwell, J. (1982) *Ward Teaching and Learning*. London: Royal College of Nursing of the United Kingdom.

Fuhrer, U. (1993) Behaviour setting analysis of situated learning, In S. Chaiklin and J. Lave (eds), *Understanding Practice: Perspectives on Activity and Context*. Cambridge: Cambridge University Press, Chapter 7; 171—211.

Gagné, R.M. (1975) *Essentials for Learning for Instruction*. New York: Dryden Press (Holt, Rinehart & Winston).

Glaser, B. (1965) The constant comparative method of qualitative analysis, *Social Problems* **12**: 436—45.

Gott, M. (1984) *Learning Nursing. A Study of the Effectiveness and Relevance of Teaching Provided During Student Nurse Introductory Course*. London: Royal College of Nursing

Goody, E.N. (1989) Learning, apprenticeship and the division of labour. In M.W. Coy (ed.), *Apprenticeship: From Theory to Method and Back Again*. Albany: State University of New York Press.

Hedegaard, M. (1996) The zone of proximal development as a basis for instruction. In H. Daniels (ed.), *An Introduction to Vygotsky*. London: Routledge, Chapter 8, 170—95.

Ingleton, C. (1995) Gender and learning: does emotion make a difference? *Higher Education* **30**(3): 323—35.

Jensen, A.R. (1971) The role of verbal mediation in mental development, *Journal of Genetic Psychology* **118**: 39—70.

Jones, M., Miller, C., Tomlinson, A. (1994) *The Current Teaching Provision for Individual Learning Styles of Students on Pre-Registration Diploma Programmes in Adult Nursing*. London: ENB.

Knowles, M. (1973) *The Adult Learner: A Neglected Species*. Houston: Gulf Publishing Co., 4th edn, 1990.

Koshy, K.T. (1984) How do students learn? *Nurse Education Today* **1**(4): 125—6.

Lancet Commission (1932) *Commission on Nursing: Final Report*. London: The Lancet, Chairman, The Earl of Crawford and Balacarres.

Lathlean, J. (1995) The implementation and development of lecturer practitioners in nursing. DPhil thesis, University of Oxford. Cedar Cottage, Northside, Steeple Aston, Oxon; Ashdale Press.

Lave, J. (1991) Situating learning in communities of practice. In L.B. Resnick., J.M. Levine and S.D. Teasley (eds), *Perspectives on Socially Shared Cognition*. Washington, DC: American Psychological Association, Chapter 4, 63—82

Marson, A.N. (1982) Ward sister, teacher or facilitator? an investigation into the behavioural characteristics of effective ward sisters, *Journal of Advanced Nursing* **7**: 347—57.

Marton, F. and Säljö, R. (1997) Approaches to learning. In F. Marton,. D. Hounsell and N. Entwistle (eds), *The Experience of Learning: Implications for Teaching and Studying in Higher Education*. Edinburgh: Scottish Academic Press, 2nd edn, Chapter 3, 39—58.

Miles, A.M. and Huberman, M.B. (1990) *Qualitative Data Analysis: A Sourcebook of New Methods*. Newbury Park: Sage Publications Inc.

Miller, A. (1985) The relationship between nursing theory and nursing practice, *Journal of Advanced Nursing* **10**: 417—24.

Palincsar, A.S. (1986) The role of dialogue in scaffolded instruction, *Educational Psychologist* **21**(1 & 2): 73—98.

Parnell, J.E. (1975) Modular systems and allocation. In E. Raybould (ed.), *A Guide for Teachers of Nurses*. Oxford: Blackwell Scientific Publications. Chapter 9, 142—54.

Rogers, C. (1983) *Freedom to Learn in the 80's*. New York: Charles Merrill.

Rogoff, B. (1995) Observing sociocultural activity on three planes: participatory appropriation, guided participation and apprenticeship. In J.V. Wertsch, P. Del Rio and A. Alvarez. (eds), *Sociocultural Studies of the Mind*. Cambridge, Cambridge University Press. Chapter 6; 139—63.

Royal College of Nursing (1984) *The Education of Nurses: A Dispensation. The Report of the Commission on Nursing Education*. London: Royal College of Nursing. Chairman, Dr Harry Judge.

Schön, D. M. (1983) *The Reflective Practitioner: How Professionals Think in Action*. Aldershot, Hants: Ashgate Publishing Ltd.

Schön. D.M. (1987) *Educating the Reflective Practitioner: Toward a New Design for Teaching and Learning in the Professionals*. San Francisco: Jossey Bass.

Singleton, J. (1989) Japanese folk craft pottery. In M.W. Coy (ed.), *Apprenticeship: From Theory to Method and Back Again*. Albany: State University of New York Press.

Spouse, J. (2000) Talking pictures: Investigating personal knowledge through illuminative art work. *Nursing Times Research*, **5** (4), 253—261.

Spouse, J. (1997) Issues in observing nursing students in clinical practice, *Nursing Times Research* **2**(3): 187—96.

Spouse, J. (2000) Supervision of clinical practice: the nature of professional development. In J. Spouse and L. Redfern (eds), *Successful Supervision for Health Care Professionals: Promoting Professional Development*. Oxford: Blackwell Science, Chapter 4.

Vygotsky, L. and Luria, A. (1970) Tool and symbol in child development. In R. Van der Veer and J. Valsiner (eds), *The Vygotsky Reader*. Oxford: Basil Blackwell Ltd, Chapter 7, 99—174.

Vygotsky, L.S. (1978) *Mind in Society: The Development of Higher Psychological Processes*,

M.Cole., V.J. Steiner, S. Scribner and E. Suberman (eds). Cambridge, Mass: Harvard University Press.

Wertsch, J.V. and Stone, C.A. (1979) A social interactional analysis of learning disabilities remediation. Paper presented at International Conference of Association for Children with Learning Disabilities, San Francisco. In B. Rogoff and J. Lave (eds), *Everyday Cognition: Its Development in Social Context.* Cambridge: Harvard University Press.

Windsor, A. (1987) *Nursing students' perceptions of clinical experiences,* Journal of Nursing Education **26**(4): *150—4.*

Wood, D., Bruner, J. and Ross, G. (1976) The role of tutoring in problem solving, Journal of Child Psychology **17**: *89—100.*

Zeichner, K.and Gore, J.M. (1991) Teacher socialisation. In W.R. Houston (ed.), *Handbook of Research into Teacher Education.* New York: Macmillan Publishing Co., Chapter 19, 329—48.

Zeichner, K.M. (1983) Alternative paradigms of teacher education, Journal of Teacher Education **35**(2): *151—75.*

34 Discipline based research into student learning in English, Law, Social Work, Computer skills for linguists, Women's Studies, Creative Writing: how can it inform our teaching?

Gina Wisker,[1] Jillinda Tiley,[1] Mary Watkins,[1] Sharon Waller,[1] Janice MacLaughlin,[1] Julian Thomas[1] and Alistair Wisker[2]
1. Anglia Polytechnic University; 2. University of East Anglia

34.1 Overview

Action research undertaken largely at Anglia Polytechnic University arises from interest in how students learn in different disciplines, how the structure of knowledge, epistemologies, discourse, practices and the learning outcomes of different disciplines affect the ways in which students learn, and how we as teachers of these disciplines, and educational developers, might use action research discoveries in teaching, assessment practices and curriculum development.

To date the research has involved practitioners working together with first and third year students in six subject areas — Law, English, Women's Studies, Computer skills for linguists, Social work, Creative Writing — chosen for their diversity, their single or interdisciplinary nature, established or relatively new bases, practical and theoretical interrelationships.

Analysis of data has yielded interesting information about students' approaches to, conceptions of learning and learning demands in the disciplines, and their sense of achievement of the learning outcomes. As action research, this information has fed into student learning awareness, and into curriculum, learning and teaching developments for staff.

The Reflections on Learning Inventory (RoLI) (Meyer and Boulton-Lewis, 1997) was given to one first-year student group on one module from each of the disciplines to discover students' motivations for and conceptions of learning, their learning approaches and intended outcomes.

Follow-up focus groups (one or two per group) with first years/first stage students concentrated on perceptions and experiences of developing learning approaches to suit the perceived learning outcomes and needs of the disciplines.

Year end follow-up focus groups with first-year students enquired about assessment responses and results, developments in learning strategies.

The learning outcomes of each discipline as defined by specialists (including, where appropriate, professional bodies) were collated and informed questions to final-year students.

These were followed by focus groups to enable students to reflect on:

- whether they have achieved the learning outcomes of their disciplines;
- what teaching/learning activities enabled this achievement;
- what curriculum/learning/researching developments in their view could enable their achievement of the learning outcomes.

Regular meetings of the research group were held to analyse and discuss data, reflect on student responses and on the effectiveness of different curriculum developments, teaching and learning strategies. Although we are only in our first year of this work, there is evidence that involvement in the process of the action research leads to reflection and development for both staff and students. There have already been some changes in our teaching and learning in response to students' comments. Additionally, response from students indicates that involvement in the research and reflection on their learning has enabled them to gain more responsibility and ownership, more empowerment in their study.

Although the research is oriented towards recognition and development of teaching and learning strategies and practices enabling student learning in specific disciplines, because of its comparative nature, its findings could usefully inform practice in other disciplines.

34.2 Introduction

As practising teachers and educational developers we are interested in finding out more about how and why our students learn in the different disciplines, and what kind of relationship there is between their effective learning and achievement of the learning outcomes of the discipline, and the teaching, learning, assessment and curriculum provision. Our action research is grounded in well-established research findings which consistently show that students taking deeper approaches to studying achieve higher quality learning outcomes (Trigwell and Prosser, 1991; Ramsden, 1992; Entwistle, 1992; Marton and Säljö, 1976; Svensson, 1977); that their conceptions and perceptions of, and approaches to, learning affect their learning strategies and achievement of outcomes both generally and in discipline specific ways (Meyer and Cleary, 1988; Meyer and Shanahan, 1999); and that the broad curriculum offer, the teaching, learning and assessment strategies operated by teachers, in context, affect this learning (Trigwell, Prosser, Ramsden, Martin, Benjamin, 1998/1999).

Questions we address include:

- what can we discover about how students learn in different disciplines?
- what similarities and differences are there in the learning strategies and approaches, motivations and aims adopted by students in different disciplines?
- in what ways are students in different disciplines aware of the learning outcomes of their disciplines and of their achievement or otherwise of these outcomes?
- what are the practical implications of our discoveries about how students learn and what enables them to learn, for our teaching strategies in these and other disciplines?

The work is taking place, in the context in the UK at least, of both subject benchmarking, which seeks to identify the necessary learning outcomes of disciplines and the levels of their achievement, and of generic key or graduate skills. These contexts and demands have partially fuelled our study but our interest in the successful learning and outcome achievement of our students has been the major impetus for our work.

34.2.1 First year/first stage students

We aim to discover specifically the broad, general learning conceptions, motivations and approaches of students in our fields, on entry and students' conceptions of the nature of learning and outcomes (knowledge, skills and attitudes) expected for success.

34.2.2 Third year/final stage students

We aim to discover how students conceptualize the nature of their learning and of the construction of knowledge in the discipline at the end of their course and most explicitly whether, to what extent and in what ways they feel they have achieved the discipline learning outcomes.

This is an epistemological study in context. It is phenomenographical, seeking information about students' conceptions and constructions of knowledge, in the context of different discipline areas.

34.2.3 First year/first stage students

Discovery about students' learning conceptions, approaches, intentions and motivations is enabled by identifying first-year students whose approaches and conceptions of learning could prove problematic (even 'pathological') when matched with the demands of the discipline at that level in that context. This identification of potentially problematic approaches could inform learning, teaching and assessment developments with the students to make concepts and approaches more explicit, identify learning outcomes and routes to their achievement and help students to develop a range of appropriate learning approaches. Additionally, with students whose approaches could be defined as 'pathological', specific 'surgery' tutorials could be put on to enable them to recognize learning difficulties, and to encourage them to develop appropriate learning strategies.

34.2.4 Third year/final stage students

For third-year students, research could help us identify where essential discipline learning outcomes were being achieved partially or by none or few students. We could then concentrate on what curriculum, learning, teaching and assessment developments could better enable us as teachers to clarify outcomes, and help students achieve them.

Another longer term but ongoing aim is to compare student learning conceptions and approaches to / strategies for learning in different disciplines. This information will be of use to staff and students alike and of particular interest to the students involved in combined studies who could find, to their detriment, that they are unaware of different learning approaches and strategies different disciplines demand.

Work on curriculum, learning, teaching and assessing practices could lead to making more explicit the nature of the discipline — its epistemology and learning strategies arising from this. This could be facilitated through developing early reflective activities within modules focusing on discipline demands and learning strategies for their achievement, leading to identifying modules where specific skills / learning strategies and approaches are clarified, modelled, practised and embedded, ensuring learning / teaching practices encourage this. For example, students who need to engage in reflective practice (social work, nursing) or problem-solving (law, medicine)the nature of the construction of knowledge and the necessary skills for the subject need to be made explicit and practised early on. Changes in assessment should also follow. For example, students undertaking professional practice related disciplines, creativity or critical practice, should both be able to learn and to be assessed within this paradigm .

34.3 Theoretical context and background: learning styles and discipline research

Our work in the disciplines grows from established research into student learning based on recognition of deep and surface approaches. Research exhibits a common consensus that students take a variety of approaches to their learning dependent on the context, including outcomes and learning task, the subject or discipline, and teacher led cues as to appropriate learning (Biggs, 1987; Ramsden, 1992). Students are considered to adopt a 'deep' approach when relating information, ideas and practices to previous learning, to experience, when recognizing more abstract forms of learning (Svensson, 1977) and when intrinsically motivated by the content and aims of the discipline (Fransson, 1977). They are more likely to adopt a 'surface' approach when the course is overloaded, lacks choice, is assessment heavy, emphasizes acquisition of discrete facts and superficial course elements (Marton and Dahlgren, 1978). However, it is also recognized that students can take a variety of approaches dependent upon context and cues. They are not fixed within a single approach; cues provided by teachers and learning situations encourage the development and repetition of certain approaches, hence, they can be encouraged to successfully develop a repertoire of approaches to achieve a variety of learning. The ways in which we provide cues about learning to students — our teaching, learning and assessment formats and the nature of the curriculum — condition or develop their learning approaches. The equation is less simple than it sounds. Phenomenographic learning research indicates the complexity of context, preconceptions, conceptions and approaches of both teachers and students. The connection between teaching strategy, context and student learning approaches, has been established (see Martin and Ramsden, 1998; Prosser, Martin, Trigwell, Ramsden, Benjamin, 1999). They argue that teachers working within the same general curriculum embody different conceptions of what is to be learned and how it is to be learned and consequently create very different ' objects of study' to their students (p. 341, EARLI, 1999 abstracts)

What is constituted as knowledge and how it is taught gives students cues and encourages them in certain kinds of learning. (p. 342, EARLI, 1999 abstracts). A significant relationship exists between learning style preference and the type of learning activities employed (Ramsden, 1992; Biggs, 1987).

The work of Meyer has produced a general-purpose student learning model subsequently adapted for use with discipline specific student groups. Conceptions of learning represent one important form of prior knowledge students bring to new learning situations. In the Reflections on Learning Inventory [RoLI] (Meyer and Boulton-Lewis, 1997) they are operationalized in accumulative or transformative terms. Shanahan and Meyer (1999) report first-year economic students' approaches to studying and conceptions of learning being affected by their preconceptions and previous experiences of learning economics prior to undergraduate study. They build a discipline specific focus upon the 'general-purpose' model of student learning that is; a model that is transportable across disciplines to identify entering first-year students who are potentially 'at risk' in the sense of being unlikely to cope with the subsequent demands of the first year. It is thus recognized at the outset that contributing factors to many of the problems that first-year students experience, and are unable to manage, stem from their prior experiences of, and approaches to learning engagement.

Meyer's 1998/9 work on assessing student learning outcomes in relation to hidden observables grows from a foundation in a broad range of student learning inventories which can be used to identify different learning approaches in different disciplines. Patterns of learning behaviour and outcome achievement can be considered in relation to the curriculum context of the discipline and institution.

Our own discipline research set out to begin to discover how far and whether students were perceiving themselves as achieving the necessary learning outcomes and studying/behaviour in specific ways considered as appropriate for learning at undergraduate level generally, and specifically for learning in the disciplines.

34.4 Methods and methodology

Our research relies initially upon quantitative data based on the Reflections on Learning Inventory [RoLI] (Meyer and Boulton-Lewis, 1997), a data collection vehicle itself deriving from qualitative sources, i.e. responses of students to questions about their conceptions of, approaches to, motivations for, experiences of and hoped for outcomes of learning. Action research forms a natural part of the process of linking teaching, learning and research. Previous research with overseas undergraduates (Hughes and Wisker, 1998) and ongoing with Israeli and UK-based PhD students (Wisker, 1999—2000) underlies current work with students in different disciplines both first and third year/final stage. It also draws on research into student learning distinguishing learning approaches and processes (Biggs, 1993; Entwistle and Ramsden, 1983; Marton, Dall'Alba and Beaty, 1993; Purdie, Hattie and Douglas, 1996).

An action research format was chosen to enable the combination of quantitative and qualitative research strategies because:

> the combination of findings from inventory surveys with those from rigorous qualitative analysis of interviews ensures that the conclusions are soundly based on multiple methods and complementary research paradigms. (Entwistle and Entwistle, 1992, p. 6)

The Reflections on Learning Inventory developed by J.H.F. Meyer and Gillian Boulton-Lewis (1997) is a culturally sensitive vehicle which elicits information about students:

- knowing when learning has occurred (being able to recall information, relate it, integrate it, know intuitively, and not knowing);
- experience of learning (as a form of secular enjoyment, personal growth, and moral duty);
- influences on learning (the examples of others — of which parents are a special case);
- conceptions of learning (learning as accumulating facts and seeing things differently).

Meyer categorized subsets of the RoLI (and rigorously tested these). Other subsets identified and categorized have not yet undergone rigorous testing; however, they yield fascinating information which can feed into our understanding of students' approaches to learning, their achievement of learning outcomes (or not) and the difficulties they have in relation to learning dissonance, particularly a mismatch between an accumulation orientation (surface) and a transformational aim.

A main aim was to recognize students who score highly on the accumulation of information learning strategy and also high on the transformation category as opposed to those who have a meaning orientation and a transformative aim. These former students taking a surface approach were felt to be at risk as learners, their approaches likely to lead to a focus on facts rather than meaning, on extrinsic learning outcomes rather than the learning for itself and the nature of the discipline. They were felt to be in danger of exhibiting various other learning pathologies, for instance, gathering an excess of unstable or uncategorizable, unmanageable information.

Information about student first year learning conceptions and approaches was matched with further information gathered from focus group work with the students, questions for which arose from both (a) student learning research origins, (b) our initial findings from the questionnaire results and comprised questions aimed at eliciting first-year students' thoughts about and practice within their discipline when newly experiencing it in HE.

Considering students who choose accumulation/fact/recall conceptions of and approaches to learning BUT aim for a 'self change' or 'world change' transformation. We compared these findings with our own experiences of the ways in which these individuals study. Future work will look at the results of the first-year students' to identify any correlation between their approaches and their success or otherwise in the disciplines.

It should be noted that, while these seem to be generic items to identify, the fact that the research group is composed of discipline practitioners, means that what we look for, and find, is interpreted in relation to the practitioners' experience of and understanding of the constructions of discipline knowledge, appropriate learning behaviours and learning outcomes for the disciplines.

34.5 Analysis and findings

We gave the RoLI to groups of first-year students in different disciplines

- English
- Women's studies
- Social work
- Computer skills for linguists
- Law
- Creative writing (UEA)

and produced frequency tables, an overall table and a split between the subject groups which indicates their patterns of response (see Figure 34.1). Focus groups followed asking:

- about conceptions of knowledge and learning approaches demanded by the discipline;
- how knowledge demands and learning outcomes are achieved and what the learning experiences and strategies of the students are.

34.5.1 Third years/final stage

A mixture of quantitative and qualitative data collection vehicles was employed with one group from one module in each discipline. Questionnaires were derived from a mixture of general progress questions, generic learning outcomes and discipline specific learning outcomes. Questionnaires for third year/final stage students asked them to evaluate whether they had achieved what had been defined as the learning outcomes of their subject(by lead bodies or internal documents if no lead bodies).

Focus groups enabled reflection on discipline related learning and the learning outcomes achieved. Our own discipline related experiences informed questions and interpretation of responses about learning for both the RoLI and the outcomes questionnaire. We considered, for example whether lawyers would be more likely to take an accumulation approach or social workers be inspired by duty. We might expect creative writing students to take a transformational approach, showing deep learning and self-reflection, with intrinsic motivation. However, some of the profiles we might have of different disciplines might be neither true any longer for these disciplines (many creative writers want to be strategic and sell their work, for instance) nor matched by student behaviours.

For the third years we wanted to know: what is achieved overall in each discipline? And what kinds of learning outcomes seem to be not being achieved? For instance, do English relate their critical reading to a wider context historically and internationally? are they lacking in critical analysis skills?

We also seek information on responses to teaching and curriculum provision, identifying where these enable students to achieve discipline learning outcomes. This enables us to identify development needs.

34.5.2 Analysis

Questionnaire data from the RoLI questionnaire was analysed using SPSS to determine patterns in frequencies of response in relation to the discrete conceptual groups informing the questionnaire. Item responses within the questionnaire were divided into their subsections.

Early initial analyses of data and frequencies arising from these questionnaires was used to form the semi-structured open-ended focus group questions for the first and third year/final stage groups.

Focus group responses were transcribed and analysed, using ENVIVO in relation to the emerging themes; student responses to direct discussion about their learning within the disciplines and the demands of the disciplines; perceptions of and achievements of the identified discipline learning outcomes; emergent student reflections on and suggestions for developments and changes in practice in relation to difficulties spotted.

Third year/final stage questionnaires were analysed using SPSS to determine students' perceptions of generic and discipline specific learning outcomes achieved.

34.6 Broad outcomes and findings

The results of these research procedures have suggested:

- Potential problematic or pathological conceptions of and approaches to studying which could hinder students in taking a deep approach to their learning generally at undergraduate level.
- Potential discrepancies between some conceptions of and approaches to studying and the learning outcomes of the specific disciplines.
- Involvement in questionnaire completion and focus group discussions about their learning and the demands of the disciplines encourages students to focus themselves on any dissonance between their conceptions and approaches and learning demands, to take a more reflective approach and to perceive the need for learning approach development and change.

- Findings from the research with this group of students feeds in an ongoing fashion into staff changing curriculum and learning / teaching and assessment .

34.7 Categories and results — RoLI

The analysis of results is enabled by the categories below, some of which have been tested and proven, others are more speculative.

There is often a discrepancy between accumulation modes of learning and transformation aims.

Students adopting any one of the range of accumulation type approaches scored highly on questions in the following categories, each of which contains several questions:

A (accumulation)
B (recall)
C (understanding based on memory)
E (Factual detail)
F (increase in knowledge)
I (knowledge discrete and factual)

(identified by Meyer — these have all undergone rigorous testing)

Others scored highly in the category of transformation (effecting change):

X (changing the world / seeing it differently)
Z (control — all about power and control and making things happen) (identified by Wisker — these have not undergone rigorous statistical testing)

In considering motivation we also looked at students in the broad category of 'duty'
D (duty and conditioning) (identified by Meyer)

Those students who take a meaning orientation can also be spotted by their responses to questions in two other categories P and Q (identified by Wisker — these have not undergone rigorous statistical testing) Learning as transformation of knowledge and understanding — deep learning. These categories relate to students' conceptions of learning as changing the ways one sees the world, learning holistically, having a meaning orientation.

P (owning the learning, fitting things together, holistic but still a sense of logic and order)
Q (changing behaviour through learning, seeing the world differently, meaning)

When looking at the ways in which students 'score' in the different categories we need to keep in mind what problems might emerge in the pattern of their responses.

There could be a discrepancy / dissonance between students taking largely accumulation approaches, approaches which depend upon the accumulation of facts, or on more broadly surface approaches, who desire change, or whose discipline outcomes demand change or a change related approach. This could be the case with, for example, social work, law and medicine.

Some disciplines require reflection before decision making, for instance social work, medicine, law, counselling, the intervention elements of women's studies. Others might demand creativity and originality, such as English, creative writing, Art or philosophy. It could be argued that all subjects demand an element of problem solving and practical implementation even if these latter largely take place after graduation. If students neither develop any skills in nor see the outcomes of their discipline as related to decision-making, problem-solving, creativity and other behaviours demanding deep learning, they are likely to remain as surface learners and in danger of being unable to really own or apply their learning.

The assumption based on previous research into student learning is that (1) surface approaches are not consistent with deep learning and degree level study demands in themselves and (2) they are 'pathologically' inconsistent with the change, reflection, creativity, problem-solving, originality decision-making approaches demanded by some disciplines more than others. Students adopting largely surface approaches characterized by accumulation (including memorizing without understanding and memorising before understanding) might therefore be at risk of neither reaching the right depth for degree level achievement nor, ultimately more problematically, being able to genuinely understand and practise the kinds of behaviours necessary in their disciplines after graduation. Meyer and Cleary (1998)'s study using learning outcome achievement, like ours with final-stage students, is concerned with medical students who exhibit a dangerous inability to carry out all the elements of a diagnosis effectively because they do not relate history taking (an essential key activity for a doctor) to research and problem-solving, as required.

We wanted to find out whether there is a match between students' 'score' in the holistic-transformer categories (P and Q) and the demands of disciplines for such learning approaches and strategies. Such conclusions and findings involve the identification and analysis of student learning approaches and strategies in relation to the demands of both (i) degree level study (in some sense considered as generic learning outcomes-knowledge skills attitudes) and (ii) the disciplines themselves (considered as discipline specific learning outcomes-knowledge skills attitudes).

This involves looking at individual student results, identifying those taking an accumulative-surface approach, and also those who take deep approaches (P and Q: RoLI).

For students who take surface, accumulative even 'pathological' approaches to learning, or negative post-modern approaches (unable to categorize, everything is relative) (Hodge, 1995), there should be some clearer tracking between their conceptions of learning and approaches to/strategies with their learning and the demands of the disciplines themselves. This might enable them to learn to diversify, further develop or change strategies where necessary, and better achieve the learning outcomes.

All students would benefit from clear learning and teaching activities and opportunities with a variety of materials to suit the variety of learning approaches and styles in the group.

34.8 Overall results across the different disciplines

In order to make some broad comparisons between the different disciplines in relation to how students were conceptualizing and approaching their learning, we combined scores of 4 and 5 (strongly agree and agree with reservations) and looked at student responses in the surface learning categories, i.e. ABCEFI, and the deep learning categories, i.e. PQ.

As can be seen from Figure 34.1, Women's Studies, creative writing and social work are, unsurprisingly, scoring less high on surface level accumulation responses than Law and English, although in all the subjects, particularly English, students score high on PQ — deep level responses. We might assume then that they are aware of taking both kinds of approaches to their learning, with creative writers, social workers and women's studies students favouring the deep, integration with experience, meaningful oriented kinds of responses over the factual and knowledge accumulation responses. As the questionnaire establishes approaches taken by students early in their undergraduate studies, it could be assumed that their conceptions of and approaches to learning are predicated upon and conditioned by their school, Access course or similar experience and the expectations of what successful (or previously rewarded) study behaviours are.

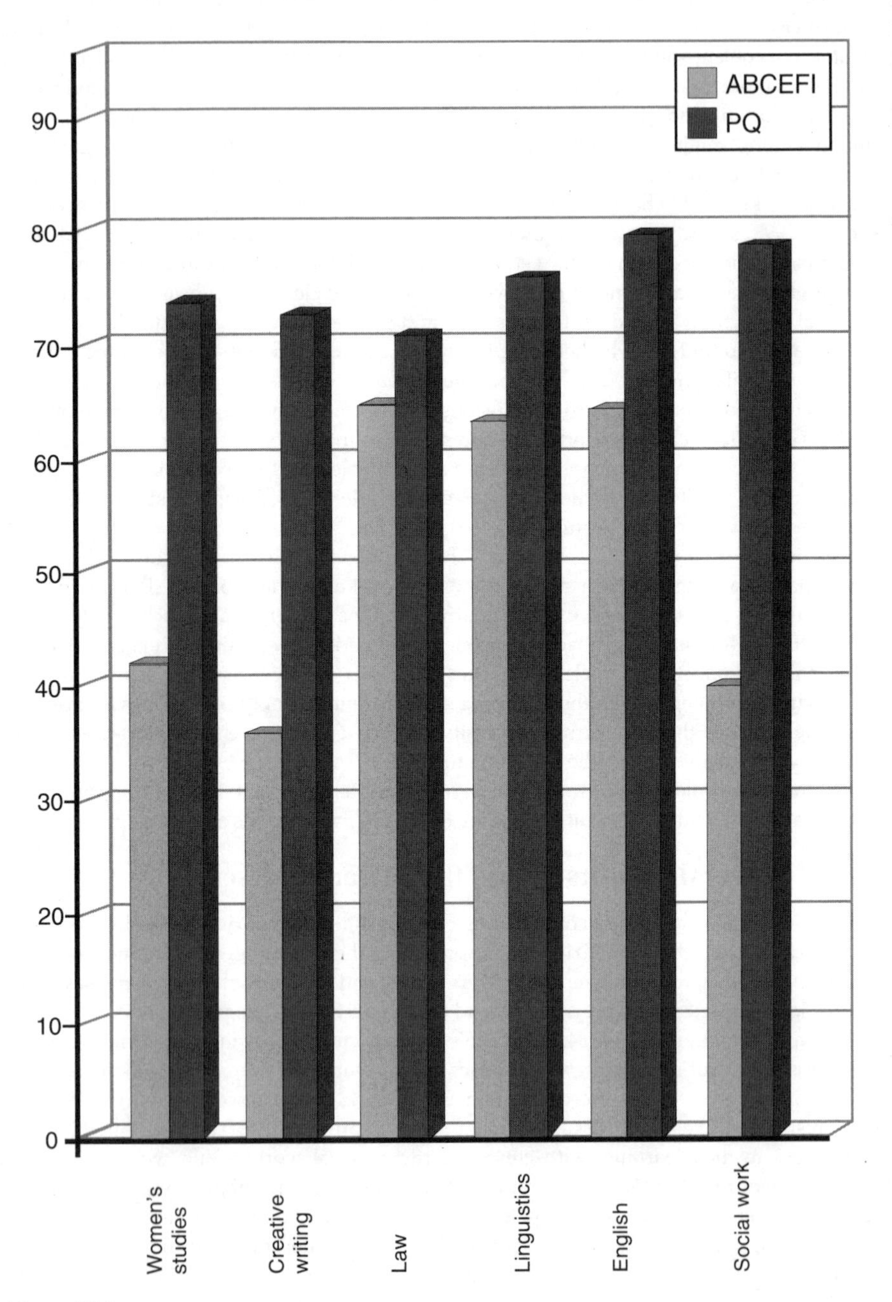
ABCEFI
PQ
90
80
70
60
50
40
30
20
10
0
Women's studies
Creative writing
Law
Linguistics
English
Social work

Figure 34.1

Perhaps also they are tuning in to the early discipline demands that they lay down a base of knowledge and critical approaches, and see this as an accumulating or memorizing before understanding activity, at least in the first instance. It is important to check then whether they also exhibit the kinds of learning conceptions and approaches which could produce deep or meaning oriented learning. If this was the case, it would be a clue to us as teachers that they have the potential to undergo the kind of developments in learning which undergraduate study demands in the different disciplines, and the potential to respond to a variety of teaching learning and assessment practices, successfully, in order to achieve the variety of learning outcomes necessary. It is a relatively simple equation but indicates to us as teachers that we need to ensure there are cues about and opportunities to practice learning activities in students' study, in order to develop the deep learning approaches necessary.

Some individual students exhibit a 'pathological' or problematic set of lacking evidence of deep learning, or in the case of social work and law, produce very low scores in the categories concentrating on duty as a motivational factor and change as an outcome (D, X and Y). For these it will be important to ensure that learning opportunities and guidance are clearly in place and reinforced (some might leave of course, finding they do not fit the discipline).

34.9 Discipline specific results and comments

34.9.1 English: first year students — RoLI questionnaire

Quite a high proportion of the first-year students felt that learning was about accumulation and memorising.

In sub set A 'accumulation', 68% agreed to Question 3 ('I believe that learning is getting all the facts in your head'), and 70% agreed to Question 22 ('I believe that learning is being able to recall knowledge when required'); in subset B 92% agreed with Question 24 ('I know I have learned something when I can recall the necessary information'), 77% with Question 43 ('I know I have learned something when I can recall the basic concepts') and 85% agreed to Question 81 ('I know I have read something when I can recall what I have learned after I have been tested on it').

They did not agree, however, with the very heavily factual storage questions, i.e. subsection E, with only 8.3% agreeing with Question 28 that 'Learning is filling your memory with facts' but subset F, 'learning as an increase in knowledge', received high scores: 92% agreed with Question 11 that 'learning is a process of increasing one's knowledge', 92% with Question 30 that 'Learning is adding new facts to those already known' and 92.4% agreed with Question 67 that 'learning is taking in new information'. In the subscale I ('knowledge discrete and factual'), 85% agreed to Question 75, 'Knowledge means knowing the right facts'.

Many outcomes in English literature relate to creativity, integration of textual analysis and understanding with one's own life experience and with the values and experience of others in the world as well as developing text critical skills. Students might be expected to take a rather more deep learning oriented set of approaches than those being exhibited by the first-year students in this sample. Indeed several of the students did produce high scores on the P and Q subsets, i.e. owning the learning and fitting together — holistic but ordered (P) and changing behaviour through learning — seeing the world differently (Q) 69% agreed to Question 13 ('I know I have learned something when I can fill in the gaps in someone else's argument'), 80% to Question 19 ('I know I have learned about something when I can argue about it on my own') , 79% to Question 77 ('I know I have learned something when I can build up a framework about it') and a full 100% to Question 89 ('I know I have learned something when I can form counter arguments of my own'). In the Q subset 100% of students scored high on Question 20 ('I know I have learned something when I can modify my behaviour in response to different situations because of what I know') and indeed in this subset most students agreed with reservations or strongly agreed to all the items.

There is a combination of approaches exhibited by the English students; both factual based surface approaches and deep approaches.

Breaking this overall set of scores down to specific individuals we can identify those who are potentially at risk of consistently taking a surface approach and accumulating and could make such students aware of their own learning approaches and potential dissonance between approaches and discipline learning outcomes. Cues and training about deep learning strategies, added to such metacognitive awareness, could lead to successful learning approach developments

34.9.2 Women's Studies

In comparison with students studying English, first year Women's Studies students were more likely to take a PQ transformative deep learning approach than an accumulative surface approach. Only 29% agreed with Question 3 ('I believe that learning is getting all the facts in your head'); 33% agreed to Question 60 ('I believe that learning is knowledge built up by accumulating quantities of information') and to Question 62 ('I know I have learned something when I can recall necessary information'); 68% believe Question 37 ('knowledge has a direct and factual nature') but only 11% agree that knowledge is factual (Question 56) suggesting contradiction in their thoughts about the nature of knowledge. In P and Q subsets — deeper learning — 71% agreed with Question 13 ('I know I have learned something when I can fill in the gaps in someone else's argument'); and 80% with Question 19 ('I know I have learned something when I can argue about it on my own'). 67% agree with Question 77 ('I know I have learned something when I can build up a framework around it'), 82% with Question 89 ('I know I have learned something when I can form counter arguments of my own'), 80% with Question 90 ('I believe that learning is when one develops new ways of interpreting reality'); and 88% with Question 78 ('I know I have not learned something when I can't discuss my ideas about it').

Overall the P and Q categories achieved high scores with Women's Studies students throughout. The X and Z categories which relate to change in the world also scored very highly, students reporting they felt rewarded when learning (Question 6, 100%). Scores were constantly high in the last quarter, showing they feel they can change the world and can change themselves. Learning is seen as enabling them to gain power to advance themselves, 67% agreeing with Question 55 ('learning enables you to reach a more powerful position') and 95% with Question 36 ('learning gives you power to advance yourself'), 64% of students agreed with Question 84 ('when I am learning I feel as if I am carrying out a duty') and 75% with Question 27 that they were 'being conditioned', but otherwise the scores on duty were in the middle quartile.

Both sets of students were aware of the ability to become more powerful through learning. Women's Studies students are more likely to take a deep approach over a surface approach and to have a greater sense of duty. With a subject which formally involves personal growth and change and which could lead to social activism, this is not surprising. What is more surprising is the English students' surface approaches being as popular as their deep approaches.

34.9.3 Focus groups

Focus group discussions with first-year students took place twice during the first semester concentrating on discovering how students in the different disciplines conceptualized the learning demands and structures of the discipline, how they were settling in to their study approaches and strategies, and whether experiences at university matched expectations. In all disciplines students' responses revealed preferences for learning situations which offered the opportunity to discuss issues, deal with cases, put theories and underlying concepts into practice.

First-year students report difficulties in settling down to studying, taking excessive notes and not really understanding the material (accumulation approach).What we have learned is that they need guidance in effective study techniques, more opportunity to explore what they write in lectures, and advice on relating reading and note-taking to practice situations.

In all disciplines students revealed awareness that lectures produced an information accumulation model of learning which they actually found quite difficult to manage both in terms of gathering and then owning or processing the information:

> I was just writing it all down going 'Oh no!' but it wasn't just you it was all of them, it was the same in business, it was the same in Public Law and everywhere it was just ... and it took about, I would say up to about four weeks before it started making sense just so I could begin to understand it a little bit. (Law-lectures)

> it's just too intimidating isn't it [to ask questions] ... At the moment we're just taking notes solidly — you're doing about six sides of notes and you've got cramp in your hand by the end of the lecture and nothing's gone in, its all there on paper but you've got so many dodgy abbreviations in there as well; you just go 'uhhh I don't know what it says' because, you're just writing for the whole hour and you're always aware that ... for the lecturer to go through what they've got to get through they have to rush ...'(Law)

On discussing using case study information in law, in groups (suggesting deeper learning):

> Yes, they are good and then you get other people's points of view as well

> tutorials — yes tutorials help a lot, you definitely learn it a lot more, you're understanding it for yourself rather than somebody talking at you (Law).

There is a significant awareness of the kind of learning facilitated by tutorial and case study work. Moral duty is an issue for law students:

> needed, I wanted to know ... the reason for me doing Law are ... we ... I was made redundant twice under very dodgy circumstances both times in the space of a year and I

just decided that if I studied law the nobody would. well somebody would think twice before doing it again (Law).

34.9.4 Tutor comment: Law

The first focus group revealed no clear internal characterization by the students of themselves as law students. Students had no clear idea of what the discipline required, and expressed surprise at the amount of work demanded compared with other disciplines. The second focus group revealed a far greater sense of cohesion as a discipline group, pleasure/interest in learning and very active involvement in the issues. The need to define and analyse issues was identified as a key skill. I was surprised how the students immediately saw law as being something useful to them — both personally and professionally. It was definitely seen as a useful tool. The importance of organizing their own time and priorities was stressed as something they had had to learn. The speed of covering the material was a shock to many of them — tutorials were regarded as particularly helpful. The import they attached to talking together in groups and discussing things was surprising.

Interestingly, the first-year results show focus group members in the top 10% of the class. We could ask if this is self-selection or a reflection of their interest in their own learning? The group themselves, volunteers, were not evidently the best qualified students and two of them were mature students.

In the Law cohort, the RoLI questionnaire was also given to a third-year group. Only six were returned (very low rate of return). Overwhelmingly — but not consistently — high scores were given on P and Q questions suggesting third-year students had achieved deep learning. Learning was a pleasure rather than a duty, leading to transformation. Accumulation of facts/knowledge continued to be scored highly.

The Focus group for third-year students was held in May after the dissertations were handed in, before the exams. Three students attended of whom two were mature. they displayed an overriding feeling of achievement, confidence, hard work, and an ability to see the wood from the trees. The discipline was not what they had expected on entry more demanding! They clearly thought of themselves as lawyers with specific skills of logical reasoning and analysis.

The skills questionnaire was returned by 16 third-year Law students Combined Honours. Almost all identified logical reasoning and an ability to identify issues as essential skills needed to be a law graduate. Almost all identified the ability to research independently and to construct ideas into an argument as a skill they had acquired during their course. More practical skills/debating/mooting were identified as the element most people would have liked more of.

Students clearly value time for discussion, questions, and practice more highly than straight input however novel or provocative. To make maximum use of this the students must be helped at an early stage to programme their own learning/reading — with more or less direction over time. The importance of group work also came out very clearly, although there is a difference between allotted groups, when learning to cope with awkward customers can be part of the package, and working with friends. The difference between third- and first-year students was quite striking. It seems they will make the best of whatever resources there are!

34.9.5 English: questionnaires and focus groups

The whole first-year group completed the RoLI questionnaire (22).

While it was initially surprising that there were relatively high scores on accumulation approaches, this could indicate students' awareness that a certain 'bedrock' of critical theory and information is necessary rather than merely emotional response, to poetry particularly (the chosen group were studying 'three contemporary poets'). They also scored highly, even more highly on the PQ scales, indicating their perceptions of learning as taking a deep approach, seeking for a meaning orientation.

> There's too much theory there is so little practice. I'm someone who could not analyse things to save his life (student's comment)

But they are also experiencing deep learning insofar — in some of the modules — as what they are learning links with and informs their lives and relates to their perspectives.

> I have found with the poetry Jean Breeze particularly, and Virginia Woolf,.... I find it impossible to separate myself from the text., and you just think they have like lived and then they are giving you the benefit of their experience and then I go away and the next time something happens to which is vaguely linked I think about that and I don't know if that is because I just try to apply everything to my life anyway but I've found that really helpful. (student's comment)

Some of the students note a negative postmodern approach problem (Hodge, 1995), i.e. the difficulty of relativism which leads to an inability to select, categorize, order, choose, argue.

> You can have debate to the point where you keep saying 'why?' to something so much that in the end you are talking about nothing and that is what I feel criticism does. (student's comment)

34.9.6 Third-year questionnaires — learning outcomes: English

The questionnaire was drawn up by using a foundation of the generic graduate learning outcomes and subject related outcomes complied by the CCUE (Council for College and University English). In the light of current interest in both generic and subject specific outcomes, several outcomes in the CCUE list were very similar to those provided by other discipline groups.

Twenty-eight questionnaires were completed.

Questions to do with 'facts' and relating the subject to facts scored fairly highly. One, which asked for relating the subject to other arts, scored highly. Questions 24—28 dealing with transformatory learning (creativity, autonomy, originality, flexibility, lifelong learning) scored highly. 'Creativity' was the lowest.

A tenuous conclusion could be that students felt happier about transferable learning skills than they did about the 'artistic' side of the subject — always a hard one to evaluate as the sense of 'self' criticism involved in 'art' critique is greater than when evaluating (even transformatory) skills.

Questions to do with empathetic learning scored highly. Students are seeing beyond the subject, able to use skills taught to broaden perspectives. All of the methodological questions scored highly.

34.9.7 Tutor comment: English

It was pleasing that most students felt they were achieving the discipline learning, and are developing skills with critical practice, reading and oral communication, in relation to creativity and originality. The development of graduate or generic skills is notable among the third years. One intriguing aspect of the first-year focus groups was the need to put critical theory into practice, but the perception that the module was too theoretical. It is also interesting that students felt they could relate the poetry to their lives. While this does indeed enable them to empathize and enjoy the work, they also need to ensure that they are aware of the ways in which the form of the poetry enables this engagement and effects meaning, so it could be useful to ensure that this is emphasized in the future.

34.9.8 Women's Studies: questionnaires and focus groups

In women's studies, students integrate their learning when involved in group discussion:

> and when we do the workshops afterwards that's really good because when you're in a little group everyone then starts saying 'well this relates to me because ... and then you can fit it all into a context that's happening now.

They engage their study with life experiences:

> It's a bit more of an eye opener, and I think that people need to be made aware of other people's experiences, because otherwise you just base it all on what you've lived, and you can't easily understand where some of the people are coming from-some of the writings.

Students are not always happy that the subject really integrates with activism and the world, i.e. that the subject really changes things:

> well, I was expecting it to be sort of, more linked to current political activism and the various women's movements. There's more focus on academic uses rather than on political issues.

Fifteen third-year outcomes questionnaires were completed. All the questions drew a bell-curve response, i.e. all respondents 'getting it' to a lesser or greater degree.

As might be expected, questions showing an ability to put one's self into a situation/text/theory scored high, as did transferable skills, e.g. Question 13 'academic writing'.

All of the learning outcomes were recognized by the majority as being achieved apart from Question 4 ('Analyse and evaluate formal techniques used in the selected works studied').

34.9.9 Tutor comment: Women's studies

It was pleasing that most of the students felt they were achieving the programme outcomes. As the outcomes were a combination of all the modules rather than provided by a professional body, it was unsurprising some students felt they had not achieved more specific outcomes; they might not have taken that module. As a course team we have been concerned about the lack of opportunity to engage with activism in the community, although students increasingly can opt to take new independent study and community project modules.

34.9.10 Computer skills for linguists: questionnaires and focus groups

Here students mention trying things out, learning by accident, going back to find out how, and practising to get it right (memorizing based on understanding):

> I practice myself, I say, what I need is 8 hours working all by myself with nobody around and I usually go every Sunday, that's my aim, and I go to the Sinclair building and work, work, work until I have it because some times I have it by accident, and then until I find out how to do it, I have to practice, practice, practice by myself ...

This module is offered to Language, Intercultural Studies at both level B and H and International Degree Access students, all of whom are studying a modern foreign language as part of their degree programme. On a practical level, the module teaches basic computer literacy skills of file management, word processing and handling data leading to the use of language specific software for translation purposes. On a theoretical level the potential of the computer for dealing with natural language processing is explored and its generic usefulness within a linguistic context is emphasized.

34.9.11 Tutor comment: computer skills for linguists

Five students volunteered for a focus group meeting three times during the academic year. The value of data gained from this group must be balanced as all were mature students, self-motivated, highly committed to their studies, following the same degree pathway — Intercultural Studies with a language, self-selected. Two were not British and therefore had different cultural backgrounds which may have had an influence on attitudes to learning.

Given the positively skewed nature of the group it was not surprising to find that focus group members demonstrated a favourable attitude towards this particular module and their studies in general, appreciating that even if the value of certain aspects was not immediately apparent that in time it would probably become so.

> Perhaps I ... perhaps I didn't expect that much theory, but now I know that theory and practice go together so you have to have some kind of background knowledge even if you don't fully understand it.

The students did not expect to be given all the answers, rather they knew from the beginning that they must take responsibility for their own learning to be successful.

> I think, initially, it's hard to take responsibility for yourself, it's actually, ultimately, I think a nice thing to do, but in the beginning you actually need a lot of guidance.

This typifies a mature and holistic approach to learning . The main fears were typical of many students at the beginning of a degree in terms of self-doubt: 'I'm learning how to learn'; their desire for more formative feedback 'because otherwise you don't know what you're doing is right or'; and contact time. These last two issues were seen as very important to progress in all modules. The lecturer's patience, 'I think the teacher being patient is very helpful', and good handouts were also valued, 'because they're good reference points'.

All the members felt that they had progressed and their expectations had largely been met.

Both the RoLI and focus group data indicate that while learners commencing a course of study may be unsure what is expected of them, they begin with a positive and deep approach to learning. If, as other studies seem to indicate, learners finish their studies with a predominantly surface style of learning, we as teachers must question the educational system which seems to be responsible for this change. Whilst we cannot offer more contact time, increased and improved formative feedback and quality handouts should be possible. Timing of assessments can also be altered so that students are not faced with several assignments due in at the same time. This a question of professional collaboration. Nor should we forget that learning is an emotional experience; care needs to be taken not to isolate the process from the learner. If learners are able to adapt their learning style according to the dictates of the learning situation, it is the responsibility of teachers to ensure that the learning situation demands and facilitates deep learning.

34.9.12 Social Work: questionnaires and focus groups

RoLI — Tutor comments:

Very small numbers completed the questionnaire, but I found it interesting that P and Q outnumber X and Z, given the usually supposed idealism of social work students and the emphasis on issues of power and control. However, the latter is the focus of year 2 teaching not year 1. All responses to A coded questions very variable. There was less of a spread with code B, and clearly some belief that recall is necessary and useful. There is consistent disagreement with the idea that learning is about facts.

Duty is generally not recognized as applicable, which is somewhat worrying given the statutory responsibilities of many social workers.

I wonder whether responses to P and Q coded questions — meaningful learning — reflect the style of my tutor group teaching and whether it would differ with another student group. Social work is about changing things at personal and structural levels and this is or should be communicated via the values and anti-oppressive practice teaching in the first term.

34.9.13 Focus group: tutor comment

The students were year 1 DipSW students (social work qualifying training)and so mature, often accessing higher education from practice, or a prior degree.

The amount of work required (compared with previous educational experiences) and the pressures of having a job (most of our students work to fund themselves, juggling family and study) can lead to overload, an accumulation approach, and grade chasing as opposed to meaningful learning:

> I've got two young children at home and I've done an Access course and the first year of a degree and I've never worked so hard in all my life as I have on this course.

Large lectures exacerbate learning difficulties, assignments have a negative impact of assignments with huge anxiety before hand-ins. Some feel this overrides the real work of developing self- awareness. Previous study has not always helped students develop meaningful learning approaches:

> I got a good degree — I remember just producing work because it had to be done without a bigger picture.

> the most valuable part ... the self awareness, whereas what everyone talks about is when the essays are in ...

However, students welcome group work and case studies, evaluative logs and the opportunity to relate theory to experience/practice, clearly activities producing deeper meaningful learning, and encouraging development of affective outcomes and the ability to apply what they learn to their own practice. The importance of self-awareness and the impact of social work especially values and assumptions underpinning work is clear:

> We've looked very closely at ourselves, lots of deep layers of how we think and feel and I can see a lot more prejudices in myself ...

This probably reflects work done in this tutor group when they were required to interview each other on video for five minutes using the communication skills they had been taught. The impact was very dramatic. Also ethics and values are taught in first term. Large lectures were not perceived as helpful, but discussion, on the other hand, was welcomed. For this discipline area, developing group trust and support is essential. Integrating theory and practice is key aided by reflection through using the learning . They are aware of trying to manage learning:

> It's important to develop ourselves rather than all the emphasis on just theoretical learning.

If you can't relate [a brilliant essay] to practice it's no good.

> I'm doing part-time work as a care-assistant and all the time as I'm doing it I'm bringing in understanding from the course [gives example].

Students are aware that it is important to process experience. Training to be a social worker differs from other disciplines, and students were surprised at the lack of practice in Term 1.

34.9.14 Creative Writing: focus groups and tutor comment

As expected, students on the creative writing one-year adult course within the university continuing education accredited programme (UEA), scored more highly on transformation and meaningful learning questions than on accumulative learning approaches questions (RoLI). However, several students expected a very directed course and tensions between freedom, self-responsibility for development and directedness appear until the course's end:

> The course was much less directed than I had expected, which was worrying at first, but I have grown to appreciate the freedom.

While, on the other hand, others wanted a course enabling gradual development and growth, seeing exercises aimed at developing different directions in writing as possibly constricting:

> it is very much a skills course- directed exercises- but I have enjoyed that too.

They note gradual empowerment and appreciation of detailed peer, self and tutor feedback, highlighting:

> A gradual evolution, breaking away from my own mould — influence of others' ways of working — this has led to a more innovative approach to for example writing poetry.

Consistent responses mentioned confidence building, tutor and peer support and intellectual stimulation to develop as a writer in their own way. These are highly individualistic adults who are directed both at self-development and at honing writing skills to put their work on the market and earn more from it. Further work with their responses could clarify the relationship between motivation and aim, and learning approach, I expect, and possibly find closer relationships between expectations of directedness and the desire to produce a marketable product, as against self-development and imaginative risk taking. Now that the course has finished, a small group stay in touch and support each other with their writing.

34.10 Conclusions: theoretical and educational significance

Conceptions of learning have been proved to be an important part of the prior knowledge and influences on the learning approaches and strategies of students. This study uses information gained from a variety of research strategies and vehicles in an action research framework in relation to ongoing programmes. It can inform our knowledge of the learning conceptions and practices of students studying in a variety of different disciplines on undergraduate courses, to encourage reflective practice among these students, and to inform useful, enabling curriculum, learning and teaching activities. There is a great deal more information to gather and , and more research, more curriculum and practice changes to be developed if we are to be genuinely both reactive and proactive in working to enable the successful learning of these students. One of the most interesting and important features of the research itself has been the involvement of the students in the process and the subsequent highlighting of their own reflections on learning, which should feed productively into further development of quality meaningful learning .

34.11 References

Biggs, J.B. (1987) *Study Process Questionnaire Manual, Students Approaches to Learning and Studying*. Australian Council for Educational Research, Victoria: Hawthorn.

Biggs, J. (1993) What do inventories of students learning processes really measure? A theoretical review and clarification, *British Journal of Educational Psychology* **63**: 3—19.

Dahlgren, L.O. and Marton, F. (1978) Students' conceptions of subject matter: an aspect of learning and teaching in higher education, *Studies in HE* **3**: 25—35.

Entwistle, N. and Entwistle, A. (1992) Experiences of understanding in revising for degree examinations, *Learning and Instruction* **2**: 2.

Entwistle, N. and Ramsden, P. (1983) *Understanding Student Learning*. London: Croom Helm.

Fransson, A. (1977) On qualitative and differences in learning: IV Effects of intrinsic motivation and extrinsic test anxiety on process and outcome, *British Journal of Educational Psychology* **47**: 244—57.

Marton, F. and Säljö, R. (1976) On qualitative differences in learning: 1, Outcome and process, *British Journal of Education Psychology* **46**: 4—11.

Marton, F., Dall'Alba, G. and Beaty, E. (1993) Conceptions of learning, *International Journal of Educational Research* **19**(3): 277—300.

Meyer, J.H.F. and Cleary, E.G. (1998) An exploratory student learning model of clinical diagnosis, *Medical Education* **32**: 574—81.

Meyer, J.H.F. and Shanahan, M.P. (1999) Modelling learning outcomes in first-year Economics. Paper presented to the 8th European conference for research on learning and instruction, Gothenberg, Sweden, 25—28 August 1999.

Meyer, J.H.F. (1999) Variations and concepts of quality in student learning, *Quality in HE* **5**(2): 167—80.

Ramsden (1992) *Learning to Teach in Higher Education*. London: Routledge.

Svensson, L. (1977) On qualitative differences in learning: III Study skills and learning, *British Journal of Educational Psychology* **47**: 233—43.

35 The rear-view mirror tells a story: subject area differences in undergraduate non-completion and their implications for the improvement of learning in higher education

Mantz Yorke

Centre for Higher Education Development, Liverpool John Moores University

35.1 Overview

The (poor) quality of the student experience influenced the discontinuation of students' studies in roughly a quarter of the responses to surveys of full-time and sandwich student non-completion conducted in 1996 and 1997 (N = 2151). The data are broken down by subject area, and show that non-completing students found greater difficulty in coping with science-based subjects than with others, and suggest that — for different reasons — the learning climates in Engineering and Art & Design may be relatively unfavourable to learning. The data prompt questions about how the student experience might be improved.

35.2 Genesis

In 1996—7 HEFCE funded a study of undergraduate non-completion in England, which gathered responses from 1487 full-time and sandwich students from six higher education institutions in the north-west of the country. These institutions consisted of two pre-1992 universities, two post-1992 universities and two institutions from the colleges sector. They were broadly representative of mainstream higher education in England, though collegiate universities and specialist monotechnic institutions were not represented. A self-funded replication was undertaken in 1997—8 in five of the original six institutions, one pre-1992 university not taking part. This produced a further 664 responses from former full-time and sandwich students.

The studies consisted of a questionnaire survey of students who had left their studies during, or at the end of, the academic years 1994—5 and 1995—6 respectively. These years were chosen because of the need to make some estimate of the proportion that had subsequently returned to higher education. The questionnaire invited students to indicate the extent to which a number of possible influences (which had been identified in the literature and through pilot work) had played a part in their premature departure from the programme of study. It also offered students the opportunity to elaborate on the reasons for non-completion, and about a half did so — a few at considerable length.

The methodology of the studies is reported in some detail in Yorke (1999). The two studies produced very similar results, and hence the data were combined for the purposes of analysis.

The three main factors relating to non-completion which emerged were:

1. wrong choice of programme;

2. matters related to financial need;
3. poor quality of the student experience.[1]

This chapter is primarily concerned with the quality of the student experience, and with a number of matters that bear on it (some of which are within the power of institutions to influence). The focus is on institutional provision, rather than on the student contribution to learning or the impact of external agencies.

35.3 Method

The analyses reported in Yorke (1999) included a breakdown of the responses against the Academic Subject Categories (ASCs) used by HEFCE, together with three hybrid ASCs constructed to cover multi-disciplinary programmes. There was some evidence of inter-ASC differences in respect of a number of aspects of the student experience. The ASCs, however, are very broad categorizations which are not particularly helpful when it is desired to examine particular disciplines. For the first analytical run, the data were therefore recategorized into the 41 subject areas listed by the Quality Assurance Agency plus Sociology/Anthropology[2], the three hybrid categories from the earlier studies being retained in addition. Some of these new categories were, in some instances, 'broader churches' than was desirable: however, the finer the analysis, the fewer the numbers in each analytical cell. There has to be a trade-off between accuracy and weight of evidence, given the desire for reasonable numbers in analytical cells.

The first run with the refined categorization threw up difficulties. First, many students had identified their programmes in broad terms such as 'Humanities' or 'Social Sciences'. This gave no difficulty when working with the ASCs, since there were ASCs labelled as

INCLUDED		**EXCLUDED**	
Subject area	**N**	**Subject area**	**N**
Biosciences	104	Medicine/Dentistry/Veterinary	28
Physics/Chemistry	92	Social Policy/Social Work	9
Engineering/Materials	173	Sociology/Anthropology	15
Computer Science	113	Agriculture etc	19
Built Environment	65	Maths, Stats, Operat'l Research	31
Geology/Geography	83	Library & Information Studies	14
Mixed Sciences	45	Economics	25
Psychology	61	Politics	11
Law	79	English	36
Business/Management/Accountancy	170	Area Studies	13
Hospitality etc	95	Classic Langs & Ancient History	12
Languages	94	History	32
Art & Design	132	Archaeology	4
Nursing etc	72	Philosophy	11
Education	94	Theology etc	22
Mixed Arts	267	Communications, Media etc	35
Mixed Arts and Sciences	32	Drama, Dance, Perform. Arts	20
		Music	5

Table 35.1 Included/excluded subject areas

such, but it proved impossible to disaggregate such programmes into the QAA subject areas. All that could be done was to categorize Humanities or Social Sciences students as undertaking 'Mixed Arts' programmes. Secondly, a number of the QAA subject areas were sparingly represented in the responses. It seemed reasonable to recombine some subject areas, and this was done: other subject areas seemed to be sufficiently different from any others that recombination seemed not to be warranted.

The data that are reported in this study, therefore, relate to those subject areas (adjusted where deemed feasible) for which more than 50 responses were received, with the exception of two of the hybrid categories which were of interest because of the comparison that could be made (given the rising importance of modular study) with the very large 'Mixed Arts' category. There are, therefore, a number of 'gaps' in the profile of discipline-related data. The subject areas on which this chapter is based, and those which have been excluded from the analysis, are as shown in Table 35.1.

35.4 Results

The actual percentage frequencies of citation of influence are given in Table 35.2. The last column shows the overall frequencies, and that matters relating to wrong choice of programme are — as was noted earlier — the most frequently-cited influences. For about a quarter of the respondents aspects of the teaching / learning experience exerted an influence. For about one-fifth of the respondents, coping with the demands of the programme was reported as having been a problem. The provision of institutional facilities was, on the whole, relatively uninfluential on non-completion.

The sheer volume of data in Table 35.2 makes it difficult to appreciate any inter-disciplinary differences that might be present. Table 35.3 dresses this difficulty by highlighting those frequencies that are, arbitrarily, 25 per cent or more higher [hi] or lower [lo] than the respective overall mean. The danger in this representation is that sight of the overall frequency can be lost, and hence the overall mean frequencies are reproduced in order to act as datum-points.

35.5 Elaboration of results, and discussion

35.5.1 A caveat

The data were obtained from students who had left their programmes prematurely. It is an open question whether comments relating to their experience of their study programmes would be replicated by those who did not leave prematurely. While one's experience of higher education might suggest where such an extrapolation might hold, empirical evidence is clearly needed. One of the weaknesses of institutional information management systems is that non-completion data is rarely connected to data from student feedback systems.

Table 35.2 Some influences on non-completion, for selected subjects

Variable	Biosciences	Phys/Chem	Engineering	Computer Sc	Built Env	Geol/Geog	Mixed Sci	Psychology	Law	Bus/Man/Acc	Hospitality etc	Languages	Art & Design	Nursing etc	Education	Mixed Arts	Mixed Arts/Sci	Overall mean
N max	104	92	173	113	65	83	45	61	79	170	95	94	132	72	94	267	32	2151
Quality of teaching	19	25	29	23	31	24	27	15	11	31	11	19	38	17	20	22	19	23
Teaching did not suit me	28	25	40	35	35	28	36	21	20	39	21	35	40	27	21	30	31	31
Inadequate staff support outside timetable	31	22	28	28	18	24	22	20	16	25	19	21	33	20	19	24	19	24
Lack of personal support from staff	26	18	27	22	25	23	29	21	23	26	15	27	35	25	18	21	28	24
Class sizes too large	29	17	24	20	15	18	24	16	15	18	12	10	18	13	10	12	19	16
Programme organisation	30	18	29	25	23	27	36	8	20	31	22	20	42	21	28	29	25	27
Timetabling did not suit	13	13	14	12	8	10	11	7	18	9	13	9	14	10	7	12	16	11
Chose wrong field of study	44	48	39	40	42	47	51	26	32	39	47	41	33	30	36	34	47	39
Programe not what I expected	35	28	38	37	34	39	62	26	18	41	34	37	48	39	27	34	47	37
Programme not relevant to my career	24	22	28	21	24	31	38	13	8	25	25	20	29	14	19	20	28	23
Lack of commitment to programme	44	38	46	39	42	40	49	26	29	38	38	46	30	24	27	39	44	38
Difficulty of programme	23	27	42	28	14	31	24	8	20	24	11	26	12	24	11	17	19	21
Workload too heavy	23	23	29	18	28	11	16	13	18	18	12	15	15	23	19	12	25	17
Lack of study skills	24	18	31	19	14	14	27	13	22	14	14	15	16	10	9	15	19	17
Stress related to programme	25	25	30	21	26	20	24	28	18	18	15	24	21	24	21	22	16	22
Insufficient academic progress	36	33	42	30	38	25	40	21	25	32	23	40	36	17	14	24	31	30
Institutional computing facilities	12	7	13	15	12	11	18	2	8	18	7	9	11	7	6	9	0	9
Institutional library facilities	10	3	12	4	8	12	11	3	5	5	9	6	11	7	5	13	16	8
Institutional provision of specialist equipment	9	8	12	10	8	8	7	0	3	8	4	11	15	1	5	6	9	7

Notes: 1. The number of respondents per item is, in each case, N max or a figure close to it.
2. The figures in the Table are percentages of the number of respondents who cited the variable as having moderate or considerable influence on their non-completion.

Figure 35.3 Table 35.2 reworked to show deviations in excess of 25% of the overall mean.

Variable	Biosciences	Phys/Chem	Engineering	Computer Sc	Built Env	Geol/Geog	Mixed Sci	Psychology	Law	Bus/Man/Acc	Hospitality etc	Languages	Art & Design	Nursing etc	Education	Mixed Arts	Mixed Arts/Sci	Overall mean
N max	104	92	173	113	65	83	45	61	79	170	95	94	132	72	94	267	32	2151
Quality of teaching			hi		hi			lo	lo	hi		lo	hi	lo				23
Teaching did not suit me			hi					lo	lo	hi	lo		hi		lo			31
Inadequate staff support outside timetable	hi				lo				lo				hi					
Lack of personal support from staff		lo									lo		hi		lo			24
Class sizes too large	hi		hi	hi			hi				lo	lo			lo	lo		16
Programme organisation		lo					hi	lo	lo			lo	hi	lo				27
Timetabling did not suit			hi		lo			lo	hi				hi		lo		hi	11
Chose wrong field of study		hi				hi	hi	lo			hi			lo			hi	39
Programe not what I expected		lo					hi	lo	lo				hi		lo		hi	37
Programme not relevant to my career						hi	hi	lo	lo				hi	lo				23
Lack of commitment to programme			hi				hi	lo	lo			hi	lo		lo			38
Difficulty of programme		hi	hi	hi	lo	hi		lo			lo		lo		lo			21
Workload too heavy	hi	hi	hi		hi	lo								hi			hi	17
Lack of study skills	hi		hi				hi		hi					lo	lo			17
Stress related to programme			hi					hi			lo						lo	22
Insufficient academic progress			hi		hi		hi					hi		lo	lo			30
Institutional computing facilities	hi		hi	hi	hi		hi	lo		hi							lo	9
Institutional library facilities	hi	lo	hi	lo		hi	hi	lo	lo	lo		lo	hi		lo	hi	hi	8
Institutional provision of specialist equipment	hi		hi	hi				lo	lo		lo	hi	hi	lo	lo		hi	7

35.5.2 Largely science-based subjects

This block of subjects (Biosciences, Physics/Chemistry, Engineering/Materials, Computer Science, Built Environment, Geology/Geography and Mixed Sciences) is noticeable for a tendency for the selected possible influences to be cited with a higher frequency than average. Although the items in the relevant block of Tables 35.2 and 35.3 are correlated sufficiently to produce a fairly well-defined factor from factor analysis, Mixed Sciences was particularly notable for the wrong choice of field of study, which is associated with surprise regarding what students found the programme to be and a lack of commitment to studying. There was a tendency for the provision of institutional resources to impact more on non-completion than for students in general. Given the pressure on institutional finances, and the claims from time to time that resources are inadequate and dated, this should occasion little surprise. However, the actual level of impact of perceived deficiencies in resourcing was low even for a group which might be expected to be concerned about them.

There is a tendency for students in these subjects to find difficulty in coping with their studies, with both the workload and the difficulty of the programme being particularly prominent. Science-based programmes are noted for their requirement that students attend lectures, laboratories and other teaching sessions to a greater extent than subjects in which there is little science. Exploratory analyses reported in Yorke (1999) indicate that there is a gender difference, in that male students tend to find greater difficulty than their female peers in coping with the demands of study (a tendency that has for some years been noted in UK schools). A lack of study skills is also a noticeable correlate.

When the block of possible influences relating to the quality of teaching (another factor from analysis) is examined, the scattering of above average impacts is thinner. The size of classes shows up as an above average influence in four of the seven subject areas.

Looking at the columns of Tables 35.2 and 35.3, Engineering is, on most of the variables, above average in the frequencies of citation of influences, with Mixed Sciences not far behind. However, the *patterns* of responses in respect of these two subjects are different: the Engineering students tended to find greater levels of difficulty with their programmes and to be less satisfied with the quality of the support for their learning, whereas the Mixed Science students exhibited a greater degree of dissatisfaction with their choice of programme. From the point of view of improving student learning, there would seem — on this evidence — to be a greater potential in Engineering than in Mixed Sciences and the other subjects in this group.

Engineering is well-known for experiencing difficulty in recruitment. On the criterion of A-level points, entrants tend to be less well qualified than for many other subject areas. Hence one hypothesis for the difficulty experienced by the 'non-completers' could be that they are not well equipped intellectually for the challenges of higher education. However, it might be necessary to probe a little deeper. Seymour and Hewitt (1997) described cultures in US Science, Mathematics and Engineering which were distinctly inimical to student learning and, more broadly, to two dimensions seen as important by Tinto (1993) — academic and social integration into the disciplines concerned. If the culture of the discipline in the UK has some of the characteristics of that of the US, then students will be 'switched off' from learning — perhaps to the extent of giving up. If the students are relatively weak academically, then this could interact synergically to exacerbate the possibility of non-completion. Engineering, of all the subject areas represented here, seems to be the most susceptible to a synergy of this sort. If this synergic hypothesis is valid, then there are some significant implications for teaching and learning, particularly in the discipline of Engineering.

35.5.3 Other subjects

With one notable exception (Art & Design), and one possible exception (Business/Management/Accountancy), subjects in this group[3] (Psychology, Law, Business/Management/Accountancy, Languages, Art & Design, Nursing and related subjects, Education, and Mixed Arts) tend to exhibit lower than average citations of the listed influences on non-completion. On the whole, the quality of teaching does not stand out as a particular influence on students' non-completion. However, the two exceptional subject areas are worthy of some speculation.

Business/Management/Accountancy programmes tend to contain quite a lot of relatively routine lecturing despite some recent movement in the direction of other methods. It is possible that it is this that is contributing to the higher than average citation of the influence of teaching on non-completion.

Art & Design is the area with a very distinctive profile of responses. The withdrawers here tended not to cite lack of commitment or programme difficulty, but many of the other possible influences show a higher than average citation. For these ex-students there seems to have been something amiss with the programme of study. For a start, it seems not to have been what they expected. This is perhaps surprising, since many students enter higher education programmes on the basis of foundation studies, often in the same institution. However, no evidence was collected regarding whether the students who left their programmes had had prior experience of a foundation course.

The expression of dissatisfaction with the quality of the study programme is marked. One can speculate as to whether this might be connected with the way in which programmes in Art & Design are typically handled. Students are, in general, expected to get on with their creative activities (after all, their entry will have been dependent upon their prior demonstration of the quality of their creativity), with tutorial comment being provided at intervals. For those who withdrew, this may have given insufficient structure to their learning experiences. If this is the case — and evidence is needed on this point — then further questions arise: to what extent does this apply to those who continue with their studies, and are there — as one might surmise — some students who will succeed almost irrespective of the curricular regime adopted?

While at first sight there might appear from Table 35.3 to be some sort of a parallel with the case of Engineering, the differences between the entering characteristics of the students and between the ways in which curricula are designed are quite marked.

The number of respondents who had followed a Mixed Arts and Sciences programme is relatively small, though there are some similarities between their profile of responses and that of those pursuing a Mixed Sciences programme. However, the evidence available does not allow an inference that it is the Science component that is the greater contributor to non-completion.

35.5.4 The quality of teaching

Relatively few students commented on the nature of their dissatisfaction with the quality of the teaching they had received, contenting themselves with saying that they were dissatisfied. Lectures were disliked for various reasons, some of which were to do with the way in which content was delivered and the inability of the student to take notes that would help later. Part of the problem is probably the sharp change in teaching method between school and higher education, for which some students find themselves unprepared. For most entering at the age of 18, the problem may lie in the switch from standard A-level teaching to a standard lecture/seminar (and perhaps laboratory or studio) format. For others, the switch to problem-based learning (as yet relatively thinly represented in higher education) may be a chasm that they simply cannot leap.

A few respondents had found small group work daunting.[4]

> Tutorials had 25+ students only enabling the very self-confident to dominate the proceedings. (Social Sciences)

> Did not like the structure of the seminar groups as I found them extremely intimidating and cold. (Social Sciences)

It may not only be a function of the size of the group, but the fact that students who are the leading lights at school can find themselves relatively dimmed by the other bright lights in the group.

The lack of staff support had been a major concern to some.

> BTEC [entry] students such as myself were expected to be at the same standard as A level students mathematically — this is seldom the case. Support from staff was minimal. This led to lack of commitment which led to lack of interest. (Engineering)

> Academic staff, on occasions, had a tendency to project themselves as being very pushed for time, stressed out and could not fit you into their timetable of work. No matter who you turned to, or when you seeked [sic] someone's aid, they seemed to be busy. (Science)

> The course was taught very loosely, the tutors were never around to help, and when they were, they were very unhelpful. They were critical of your work to the point of being rude, not constructive criticism, if your work was not the best, average, then you were ignored in favour of the best students ... the way one tutor spoke to me [...] has put me off higher education and will take a long time in considering ever going back. (Art & Design)

For a surprising number, weakness in programme organisation had been influential.

> Course I attended was the 1st yr they offered it and it was very disorganised. (Engineering/Materials)

> [Art & Design component] in particular had a serious lack of organisation and interest from the tutors. We were not provided with a proper studio and we only saw a tutor for registration once a week. (Joint Arts)

For the latter student, part of the problem could have been that the study programme was joint honours in character. For a few, the dovetailing of joint honours programmes presented problems. This may be particularly problematic when the components of the programme come from quite different parts of the institution: what appears as feasible in the prospectus may turn out not to be so because of the 'knock-on' effects of decisions taken elsewhere. The difficulties were highlighted vividly by a student who wrote:

> With my chosen degree having 2 parts, the organisation between the different [academic organisational units] was very poor. On several occasions I was timetabled to be in 2 or 3 places at one time throughout the two years I was there. (Joint Art & Design and Business)

35.6 Towards improvement

Much work has been done in the last decade or so to advance the cause of good teaching in UK higher education, even though higher education institutions have been dominated by a perceived need to raise research ratings. From outside individual institutions, for example,

- many books and articles have been published on teaching in higher education, such as those by Biggs (1999), Bligh (1998), Brown and Atkins (1998), Cowan (1998), Prosser and Trigwell (1999); and Ramsden (1992);
- teaching in the UK has been subject to assessment by the funding councils (and latterly, under the heading of 'subject review', by the Quality Assurance Agency for Higher Education);
- various developmental programmes have been funded, such as the Teaching and Learning Technology Programme launched by the UK funding councils;
- the UK funding councils have established the Fund for the Development of Teaching and Learning, under which identified excellence in provision is spread around the system;
- Learning and Teaching Support Networks are in the process of being established;
- The Institute for Learning and Teaching [ILT] has been established; and
- HEFCE is requiring the institutions which it funds to have in place — and to implement — learning and teaching strategies.

However, the quality of the student experience is primarily a matter for institutions.[5] Very many now have in place programmes designed to enhance the teaching skills of academics, and the establishment of the ILT can be expected, through its accreditation processes, to strengthen such programmes. Yet many existing staff will not have had the benefit of teaching development programmes, unlike their peers in schools who have had to qualify as teachers.

There are many things that institutions can do to enhance the quality of the student experience, among them the following.

- Ensure that the engagement of academic staff produces 'quality time' for the students. This may well imply a serious rethinking of the way staff time is allocated to different kinds of teaching purpose. One of the main complaints of the withdrawers (that finds a broader support from persisting students) is that there is not enough tutorial-type contact between staff and students.
- Provide a supportive induction programme for students.[6]
- Ensure that the organisation of programmes is good. Mixed-subject programmes

may be particularly problematic for students, and the institutional management information system needs to be sufficiently robust and frequently updated if clashes of timetabling are not to occur.

- Make sure that the culture of the subject discipline is supportive of, rather than inimical to, student learning.[7]
- Ensure that academic staff are au fait with developments in learning and teaching. This is clearly an 'academic leadership' issue, in which heads of disciplinary areas have a key role. Even outstanding teachers can have severe gaps in their knowledge of what is important for student learning.

35.6.1 Developments in teaching and learning

Higher education in the UK is much more aware than it was a decade ago of the importance of good teaching. Teaching quality assessment/subject review can claim some of the credit for this change (its introduction can be seen as implicitly an adverse comment on the quality of institutional leadership). On the whole, it can be argued for instance that lecturing has improved, there is a clearer understanding of what students are expected to achieve, and assessment tasks have been brought more closely in line with expected learning outcomes. None of these should be disparaged, but they reflect a single-loop learning approach (Argyris and Schön, 1974; Argyris, 1999) to the issue of learning and teaching. The governing conditions — in this case, expectations regarding students' learning experiences — are accepted, and the solution to the problem of learning and teaching is one of 'doing things better'. The needs of the future, particularly in the light of developments in communications technology and of constraints on budgets, require a more radical approach: 'doing things differently' (or, in the terms of BT's erstwhile slogan, 'working smarter not harder'). This reflects a double-loop approach to organizational learning in which 'the

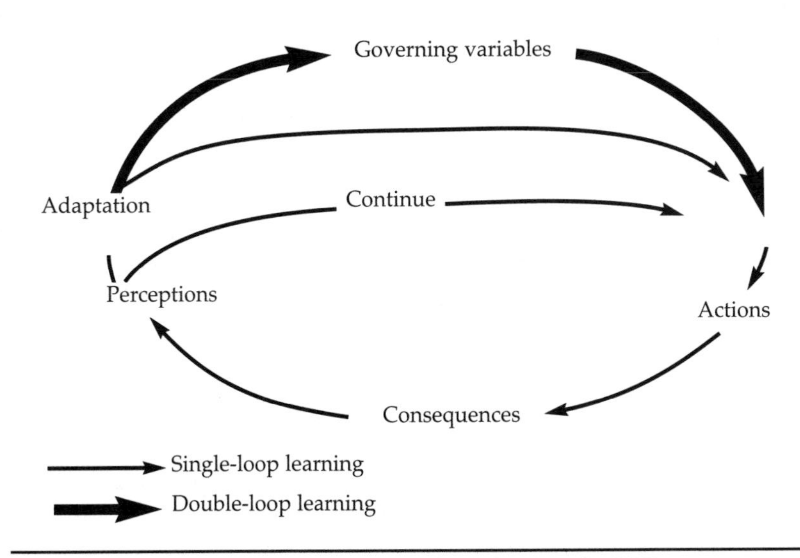

Figure 35.1 Single- and double-loop learning (After Argyris, 1999)

traditional view' of learning and teaching is called into question and modified, perhaps radically. Figure 35.1 schematises the difference between single- and double-loop learning.

35.7 Concluding comments

To look backwards at what ex-students have to say about the factors that influenced their non-completion is akin to looking through the bottom of a wine bottle. Accounts may have been coloured for a variety of reasons. The quality of the student experience is refracted through the perceptions of a particular sub-group of the student population. On the other hand, the recollections of those who have left constitute a signal of sorts whose sharpness is derived from the fact that the students did discontinue their studies.

The advantage of using a questionnaire approach is that large numbers do allow some weight to be ascribed to differences between subjects. This is the kind of approach that many institutions use routinely in order to inform themselves about student satisfaction. The issue then is whether the institution's managers are able to use the information to lever change.

Even taking into account the caveats that have to be entered regarding the data presented in this chapter, and making the assumption that the evidence presented here can be extrapolated to students, a couple of general questions are prompted regarding the quality of students' learning experiences.

- Can more be done to facilitate learning, particularly in science-based subjects?
- Are the cultures within some subject areas less supportive to students' learning than they might be and, if so, what can be done to improve the situation?
- Both can only be answered by detailed qualitative research. This is the kind of work that could be undertaken as an extension of Becher's (1989) work on academic tribes and territories, and would need to identify features of general applicability and those which are discipline-specific.

As Biggs (1999, p. 54) puts it

> Effective teaching means setting up the teaching/learning context so that students have every encouragement to react with the level of cognitive engagement that our objectives require.

This places considerable expectation upon academics as professional educators. In an increasingly labile world, that expectation is heightened. The fulfilment of that expectation will be determined in part by one characteristic that academics possess in abundance — their imagination.

Notes

1. The factors from the factor analysis reported in Yorke (1999) were fourth, fifth and first in order of the variance explained, but this ordering is a methodological artefact. Reference to the original responses shows clearly that choice of programme and finance were the most frequently cited influences on non-completion.
2. Subject area 7 in the QAA list seems to conflate disciplines that do not fit particularly well together, and it was decided to split off Sociology and Anthropology.

3. The categorization is not clear-cut: some might see Psychology as a science-based discipline rather than a social science, for example.
4. The precise subjects are not given in these quotations since they would in some cases have allowed the institution concerned to be identified.
5. Of course, students have a significant part to play in the development of their learning experiences, but the focus of this chapter is upon institutional provision.
6. One student commented: 'The initial introductory period was poorly structured with the workload for the year being presented in such a way as to make me feel "phased", "swamped" and created a feeling I would not be able to cope/I had made a wrong decision' (Psychology).
7. And check that it has no adverse implications for the particular student. Gender imbalance in a subject area, for example, could work to the disadvantage of a student from the minority gender.

35.8 References

Argyris, C. (1999) *On Organizational Learning*, 2nd edn. Oxford: Blackwell.
Argyris, C. and Schön, D. (1974) *Theory in Practice: Increasing Professional Effectiveness*. San Francisco, CA: Jossey-Bass.
Becher, T. (1989) *Academic Tribes and Territories: Intellectual Enquiry and the Cultures of Disciplines*. Buckingham: SRHE and Open University Press.
Biggs, J. (1999) *Teaching for Quality Learning at University*. Buckingham: SRHE and Open University Press.
Bligh, D. (1998) *What's the Use of Lectures?*, 5th edn. Exeter: Intellect.
Brown, G. and Atkins, M.J. (1988) *Effective Teaching in Higher Education*.London: Routledge.
Cowan, J. (1998) *On Becoming an Innovative University Teacher: Reflection in Action*. Buckingham: SRHE and Open University Press.
Prosser, M. and Trigwell, K. (1999) *Understanding Learning and Teaching: The Experience in Higher Education*. Buckingham: SRHE and Open University Press.
Ramsden, P. (1992) *Learning to Teach in Higher Education*. London: Routledge.
Seymour, E. and Hewitt, N.M. (1997) *Talking about Leaving: Why Undergraduates Leave the Sciences*. Oxford: Westview Press.
Tinto, V. (1993) *Leaving College: Rethinking the Causes and Cures of Student Attrition*, 2nd edn. Chicago: University of Chicago Press.
Yorke, M. (1999) *Leaving Early: Undergraduate Non-Completion in Higher Education*. London: Falmer.

36 An experiment in teaching computer science by borrowing teaching techniques from other disciplines

Moya Adams[1] and Richard Buckland[2]

1. Macquarie University, Sydney, Australia; 2. University of New South Wales, Australia

36.1 Introduction

Common assumptions are widely held within the sciences that because the nature of scientific knowledge is qualitatively different from that of the humanities, the sciences must be organized and taught in an appropriately different manner. The first author has often been told by scientific colleagues that it is not possible to introduce interactive learning and teaching in first-year science courses because students must master a huge body of knowledge before they can adequately engage in discussion and exploration. It is necessary for students to memorize large quantities of material first, and to learn to think like a scientist later.

These traditions have been maintained and passed on from one generation of university teachers to the next, partly because most academics lack access to theory and research on learning and teaching, and therefore do not question the established traditions of pedagogy: their teaching practices are considered inevitable and their appropriateness self evident. Established patterns of teaching, course design and assessment have been tried and true, and there is no imperative to change them.

This chapter questions these assumptions. It reports on a research and development project which attempted to improve the learning of female students in computer science by stepping outside the familiar teaching practices of the discipline and using a pedagogy more characteristic of the humanities. Branxton's summary of American research (1995) suggests that more change has occurred in the teaching of the humanities and social sciences than in the natural sciences. He attributes this to the fact that the teachers in the humanities and social sciences focus more on the student experience of learning and on improving teaching, while those in the sciences and mathematics are less interested in student feedback and course reviews.

36.2 Disciplinary differences

36.2.1 How knowledge is validated

A useful way of understanding the differences among academic disciplines has proved to be in terms of the dimensions of *hard* and *soft*, *pure* and *applied* disciplines (Biglan, 1973; Becher, 1989). Our concern in this chapter is with the *hard* versus *soft* dimensions, specifically in relation to teaching in computing science and the humanities and social sciences. *Hard* disciplines, physical sciences and mathematics, have been described as much more concerned with phenomena that can be seen and measured, compared with *soft* disciplines (humanities and social sciences) that deal with more complex phenomena, which might be perceived differently by different people. This in turn is believed to have affected how knowledge is structured and validated, and how staff believe knowledge has been transmitted.

Donald's (1995) work on knowledge validation in different disciplines indicates that differences are not as great as was assumed by Biglan. She found more cohesion than expected across the above dimensions, based on interviews with 40 professors from five disciplines (Physics, Engineering, Psychology, Education and English Literature). The only significant differences were between the *pure* and *applied* dimensions, and in fact Physics and English Literature (representing *hard/pure* and *soft/pure* dimensions respectively) shared in common rigorous verification procedures for the validation of knowledge.

36.2.2 Pedagogy and teaching behaviours

Other researchers, summarized by Branxton (1996) have described differences between *hard* and *soft* disciplines in terms of differing learning goals, teaching behaviours, focus on students and assessment practices. Goals in the sciences tend to be concerned with facts, principles and concepts, compared with the humanities where the goals are more to do with effective thinking and critical thinking, and written and oral communication.

Murray and Renaud (1996), in a comprehensive study observing 401 teachers from the humanities, social sciences, natural sciences and mathematics analysed differences in teaching behaviours in lectures. They concluded that teachers of the humanities have a wider range of teaching behaviours than those in the sciences. They behave more frequently in ways that foster student participation, such as encouraging questions, praising students' ideas, offering help to students with problems, while teachers in the sciences more frequently show behaviours that facilitate structuring and organization, such as putting an outline of the lecture on the board, summarizing periodically, using headings and subheadings to organize the lecture.

36.2.3 Student perceptions

Evidence since the 1970s, both in the USA and Australia, has consistently shown that students in the humanities rate their teachers and courses more highly than students in the sciences, irrespective of other variables such as class size or year level (Feldman, 1976, Cranton and Smith, 1986; Cashin, 1990; Adams *et al.*, 1996).

While differences in goals and assessment practices have been identified in the literature, the greater emphasis of the humanities on interactive teaching, student-centred practices, and rapport with students seems hard to avoid as an explanation for the stronger student support for the humanities. Murray and Renaud also attribute the difference to the greater repertoire of teaching behaviour of humanities teachers. They reported that students in all disciplines valued the same teaching behaviours, so that the superior ratings of the humanities could not be attributable to the particular characteristics of humanities students.

36.2.4 Students' approaches to learning

The literature on how students learn similarly does not differentiate among disciplines. Entwistle and Tait (1995) found that the nature of assessment practices was the greatest determinant of students' differing approaches to learning, rather than any disciplinary differences. The fact that the sciences had the greater tendency to use multiple choice and short answer questions did shift students to a more surface approach to learning, but these results varied within the natural sciences, when other assessment methods were employed.

The evidence seems conclusive that students, whatever their discipline, learn best when they are intrinsically motivated, when there is a high degree of learner activity, when they have opportunities to interact with both teachers and peers; and when they have a well structured knowledge base to build on (Biggs, 1989). Ramsden (1992, p. 86) suggests that good teaching 'does not allow students to evade understanding, but neither does it bludgeon them into memorising; it helps them respectfully towards seeing the world in a different way'. He asserts that the research findings on good teaching mirror what the students say if asked to describe what a good teacher does. He identified six principles of good teaching:

1. stimulating interest and being able to explain clearly;
2. having concern and respect for students and student learning;
3. using appropriate assessment and giving helpful feedback;
4. stating clear goals and providing intellectual challenge;
5. assisting students to be independent learners, to have control over and active engagement with their learning;
6. learning from the students — seeking and responding to student feedback.

It would appear that there are generic principles of good teaching which encourage learning, and these can be applied and worked through in each disciplinary context.

36.2.5 Gender differences

Gender continues to be a factor in subject choice, with girls preferring to study humanities and social sciences over mathematics and physical sciences. While in Australia girls are increasingly participating in the sciences and mathematics, they are still under-represented, especially in physics and computer science, and are more strongly represented in the humanities and social sciences. Computing science, although a comparatively new science, has been established as a largely male domain. There is evidence that female entry rates and progression rates in computing science are low, and that female students express significantly lower levels of satisfaction with their course than their male peers (Doyle, University of NSW, 1996).

Meyer (1994) found that females were low on competitiveness, compared with males, and that the difference was more obvious in a science type environment. Whether this is relevant to girls' entry and progression rates in the highly competitive environment in computing science, to its pedagogy or other factors, is unknown at this stage.

36.3 The project

The project developed out of the dissatisfaction of the second author with the teaching of computer science, and his awareness of the low student ratings given to computing science teaching compared with the humanities. He observed some English literature classes and found that students seemed to enjoy their subject and to care about the things they were learning. He noted that the teaching approach offered students more scope to actively participate in the learning process and seemed to make the learning more enjoyable for both students and teachers.

This contrasted with the traditional formal lecture style of teaching in large science-based courses to which he was accustomed. It was his experience that many students choose to study computing and sciences because they enjoy the subject, but the lectures and tutorials are dull and tedious, uninspiring to students, who do not learn anything from them they could not teach themselves. In other words the formal teaching of the subject is at odds with the reasons students want to take the subject.

He later experimented with using an interactive approach and incorporating active learning into lectures (with a class of 300 students at Macquarie University). His aim was to make computing lectures (and tutorials) more like the teaching the students enjoyed in the humanities. He believed that if he could motivate the students to engage with and enjoy the subject, he could avoid teaching the mound of dull detail traditionally covered in lectures; the students could then teach this material to themselves as needed, to grapple with assignments and laboratory work.

These changes led to a significant increase in student satisfaction, indicated in both formal and informal feedback (Buckland, 1997). An unanticipated outcome, however, was that female students responded even more positively than males to the change in teaching. In the light of the girls' under-representation in computing science, it suggested that possibly the traditional methods of teaching were not favourable to girls. The author later successfully applied for a teaching development grant (from the Australian Committee for University Teaching and Staff Development) to build on his earlier work and to focus specifically on enhancing the learning of girls in first-year computer science at the University of NSW.

Initially he conducted interviews with a cross-section of undergraduate female students from a variety of disciplines with similar academic characteristics to female science-based students, to discover which teaching techniques they valued. In 1998—99 he introduced some of the teaching techniques identified in the interviews into his teaching of a first-year computing subject, with classes of from 300—400 students. Innovative teaching practices were introduced incrementally during this period. (The practices were innovative within computing science teaching, rather than being new to pedagogy generally.)

The effectiveness of the innovations in pedagogy is currently being evaluated in terms of learning outcomes and student satisfaction through formal feedback questionnaires and focus groups. The first stage of these results is reported in this chapter. Although the project specifically addresses female students, the work to date suggests that male students also benefit from a more personal and interactive approach to science-based teaching.

36.4 Innovations introduced to lectures in first-year Computer Science — Richard (R) speaks

36.4.1 Aims for the first-year Computer Science course

Learning goals: The over-arching goal for this course is for students to learn the theory and craft of computer programming. Specifically, by the end of the course, they should be able to write correct and good computer programs, which involves factual theoretical knowledge, practical skills and artistic judgement. They should have started to think like a programmer. They should also have had a glimpse of the fun of programming, and be motivated and keen to continue learning the discipline.

The aims for lectures were that they should be stimulating and enjoyable, not just entertaining, in the way that a good book can both entertain and be thought-provoking. They were also planned to provide as much opportunity as possible for students to learn actively and collaboratively. R believes that making learning more enjoyable will increase intrinsic motivation of students, thus fostering 'deep' learning (Marton and Säljö, 1976, 1984).

36.4.2 Implementation: the pedagogy adopted

In attempting to make the lectures more enjoyable, student centred, and more effective occasions for student interaction and learning, R has moved away from the traditional lecture format by fostering interaction with students and a positive atmosphere, making opportunities for peer and collaborative learning, giving and seeking feedback from students and being available to help students.

36.4.2.1 Fostering interaction with students and a positive atmosphere

The most important change introduced has been a reworking of the structure of the lecture. Rather than offering a continuous monologue, R broke each lecture into three or four 10—15 minute teaching blocks, with 5—10 minute breaks for some form of interaction with students between each block.

During the interactive breaks, R introduced the following activities into the lectures. He set tasks for students to work on, singly or in pairs, and walked around the lecture theatre while they worked. This enabled him to look at students' work, see the notes they were taking, who was 'switched on' and who was 'switched off'. R began to learn how much they were understanding and common areas of misconception. Conscious that students are not often praised at university compared with high school, R offered legitimate praise to build their confidence with the subject and to recognize that what they had just mastered was not trivial, although it might seem trivial later — hence the value of immediate feedback. During these walks he would see 20 or 30 students, and could assist about half of these with problems. It also allowed shy students to quietly ask their question when he was near them.

36.4.2.2 Making opportunities for collaborative and peer learning

R believes that working on tasks together encourages students to speak with their neighbour, and creates a friendly environment in the lecture, allowing students to learn from each other. For instance, after giving some examples to illustrate a concept they are learning such as *Queues*, R would ask students to work in pairs to generate some examples themselves. While he walked around the room, he would pass on the best examples he found to the class and ask for any good examples he had missed. This process generated many excellent examples, and helped students remember the concept, having worked actively to illustrate it. R would also ask students who understood a concept to explain to students who did not, having found that students who have just understood an idea can explain it well to those still grappling with it.

36.4.2.3 Active participation: questions from students and teacher

R welcomed questions from students. When they asked for an explanation of something they had not understood, he would sometimes ask other members of class for a better way of explaining it in their own words, as a means of encouraging them to show how well they could do and to stimulate interest in the problem. R also asked students what problems they were having, sometime in the form of voting on such questions as: 'Who isn't convinced that *Modules* are useful?' or 'Who is having troubles with their assignment?' Inviting them to respond by putting thumbs up, thumbs down, or thumbs sideways proved a less confronting way to reveal their concerns than by a show of hands.

36.4.2.4 *Giving and receiving feedback*

The practice of walking around the room gives R immediate feedback on how students are going, their problems and common misunderstandings. R in turn reports back to the whole group on common problems and good ideas he has seen. R discloses the rationale for his approach to teaching to students, so that they understand that its informality is designed to assist their learning. He also asks them for suggestions for improvement.

36.4.2.5 *Being available for students*

By arriving early, and staying back outside the theatre for ten minutes to answer student questions after lectures, R encourages students who have further questions.

Encouraging students to participate actively in the lectures has wakened them from being passive learners and encouraged them to try to understand the material as it is being taught, rather than writing it down with the vague intention of learning it at home later. It has also been a means of establishing a friendly rapport during the lectures, in which R talks about his own experiences including troubles he has had with various topics or concepts when he was learning them, or in his practice afterwards. R also tries to communicate the fun of the subject and the enjoyment he has in being a computer scientist.

36.5 First-year Computer Science — the students speak

At the end of the semester, the first author conducted four small focus groups with 11 female students (groups of 2, 3 or 4 students) who had participated in the first-year Computing Science course during first semester, 1999. The students had been taught by R for the first seven weeks of the course, followed by another lecturer, teaching in traditional lecture mode, for the second seven weeks.

The focus groups were semi-structured, and included questions about students' views of the characteristics of lecturers and tutors who *assist* their learning, and those who *do not assist* their learning. Although all students interviewed had completed the same computing course, they were enrolled in a variety of degrees, including Bachelors of Information Technology, Computing Science, Computing Engineering, Science/Arts, and Music.

The students inevitably made comparisons between the first and second half of their computing course, and the following responses highlight their awareness of the difference between the two approaches to teaching. The characteristics of an effective teacher were in fact descriptions of what they valued in R's teaching. One student said 'he seems to know a lot about education and applies it'.

36.5.1 How they described good teaching (that is R's teaching)

He makes lectures interesting, by breaking the lecture up: stopping to crack a joke, setting a problem for us to do or asking the class questions. He was enthusiastic, made the lectures fun and showed he cares about the subject.

He explains things clearly, by giving examples that students relate to and takes trouble to explain in a way they understand. His jokes help you understand and remember things. He makes sure we understand before going on to the next thing. He also draws attention to what is important to understand, and what matters less. Finally, he encourages us to solve problems in different ways — there's not just one right answer.

The lectures are interactive, encouraging class participation, asking questions and encouraging questions from the class. He sometimes calls on people to come up front and take roles to act out a concept he is explaining. When he sets a problem for us to work in class he walks around the class checking on the answers — then returns to the front and gives feedback, either by explaining things people are having difficulty with, or praising a student who has found a good solution. He will even say 'this person has found a better solution than mine'!

He has a genuine interest in students, puts us at ease, 'makes you think you're not stupid'. He does not put pressure on students, saying they will get through as long as they keep working at it. We felt that he cared about us, and understood how stressed we get with work: he talks about how to handle stress. The students valued the fact that R was personally open with them, disclosing things about his own life, illustrating from his own experience, and making them feel that he was a real person. He always maintains eye contact with the class.

When probed, the students said that the lectures were not just entertaining; they made students interested and keen to learn. Some said that although they found the subject difficult, they did more work in computing than in any other subject, and enjoyed it.

The students contrasted their experience of R's teaching with the traditional approach to teaching which they experienced in the latter half of the course and in most of their other subjects. Some students experienced interactive teaching in Music and Accounting lectures, but for most R's lectures were their only experience of it.

36.5.2 How students described teaching that did not assist their learning

Poor communication was evident in poor explanations and lack of examples and a lack of coherence, failing to follow one idea through adequately. It was also evident in the tendency to make everything equally important, so that students could not discern what is important to know, and what is secondary. Some lecturers skipped steps (in mathematics) and went too fast, or were unsure about how to convey ideas to a large diverse group.

Poor teaching techniques in lectures included projecting a series of slides, and simply reading the labels on them (which in fact are the same as the text book) and generally adding nothing to what is in the textbook. The students found such lectures boring and monotonous, talked of losing interest, and even stopping attending the lectures (assignment marks went down after the changeover in computing).

Negative attitude to students was clearly detected and criticized. Some lecturers assume students know everything, so make it hard to ask questions or refuse to answer questions, and simply point students to the text book which was equally difficult (Mathematics). Students said they don't appear to care whether the students learn, and reveal nothing of their own opinions. These attitudes undermined confidence, and one student, a high achiever in mathematics, said that the atmosphere in the maths class led all students to believe that everyone else knew more than they did, and so they would not risk asking questions. A lecturer who tells jokes that aren't funny was also criticized as being unsuccessful at connecting with students.

Generally, a picture was drawn of teaching that was not well communicated, did not encourage interaction or self-confidence. It was teaching that alienated, and showed a lack of caring or responsiveness to students' needs. That is not to say that all of their lecturers teaching in traditional mode had these characteristics. These were the examples of bad teaching.

36.6 Discussion

In this case study the pedagogy adopted by R corresponds closely to the humanities profile of teaching behaviours in Murray and Renaud's study (1995) rather than that of the sciences. Moving about the room and using humour, fostering interaction and praising students' ideas, stimulating interest through personal and apt examples, and being responsive to student ideas and concerns are behaviours they found more frequently among teachers of the humanities. The question we need to answer, however, is whether students learned better as a result of these behaviours; whether it is possible to assist large classes of first-year students to a better understanding by these means. It is hard to tease out the actual effect of the teaching in the experiment so far, since the students experienced two methods of teaching and it would be impossible to separate them out in terms of learning outcomes.

The students participating in the focus groups believed they were learning better during the first half of the course, however. An example of this was the fact that for some, assessment results went down when the new lecturer took over in the second half of the course. Apparently their understanding and motivation decreased, as did attendance at lectures.

When asked whether it was irrelevant that they had experienced *good* teaching in the first half of the semester, if this was not continued in that course or in later computing courses, students replied that the initial good teaching definitely was worthwhile. They believed that the experience had given them a 'strong foundation' for the rest of their studies — an interesting comment, given they did not talk much about the course content in their other comments.

The focus groups make it very clear that the teaching met Biggs' criterion of teaching that encourages deep learning: the students became highly motivated in their computing studies, they had the opportunity to learn actively in the lectures, and to interact with their teacher and each other. Having 'a well-structured knowledge base' was articulated by implication, in terms of R's commitment to their understanding, and highlighting what was important from what was secondary.

Similarly, it was evident that much of the teaching was consistent with Ramsden's principles for good teaching: the teacher stimulated interested, showed concern for students, challenged them intellectually, assisted them to become independent learners, and was committed to learning from the students. If learning in each discipline is a process of inducting students into being capable of participating in the discourse and thinking of the discipline — in this case, the world as the computer scientist constructs it, then teachers need to be sensitive to decisive characteristics of learning and thinking in that discipline. It is what Saljo calls 'different ways of world making'. It means that it is the task of the teacher to give the student experiences that enable this to happen.

Ramsden states 'it is sometimes asserted that ... because physical sciences are generally more paradigmatic and cumulative than the social sciences, then didactic teaching in tutorials is inherently more appropriate'. In the professional development experience of the first author, the possibility of introducing active and interactive learning in first- and second-year sciences courses has been discussed frequently. Science lecturers often state that there is no time for interactive teaching and learning, because students must absorb a large body of knowledge, before they are able to think and experiment as a scientist. Teachers must 'cover the territory' or they are deemed to have failed their students. These lecturers say that it is not until the honours year, or possibly third year, that students of physical sciences actually begin to think creatively or analytically as scientists.

The case study indicates that girls, who have traditionally been alienated from computing science, found the interactive approach to teaching and learning highly motivating, increasing their enjoyment of the subject and improving their learning. It supports the fact that concepts in computer science can be taught, even in first year, by interactive student-friendly teaching in which the students are active and collaborative learners. In addition, the prescribed content was covered, because students caught on to concepts more easily.

The experience so far in this project is that if the focus is on the students' learning, on developing their confidence as practitioners in the discipline so that they have the courage to engage with the problems and understand their relevance in a wider context, they will indeed absorb much of the content.

36.7 Conclusion

While it is understandable that the reductionist concrete nature of the physical sciences has led to a transmission model of teaching as the appropriate way to pass this knowledge on, it is possible to challenge the effectiveness of this model. It may not be the most appropriate means of helping students make meaning of the material or apply it in other contexts. There is a danger in refusing to decode the symbols of science and mathematics in terms of the familiar world or to allow students to actively engage with developing understanding of concepts. This case study offers the challenge to put the sacredness of these things at risk, so that students have the chance to be wrong and learn by their mistakes, to ask 'dumb' questions to enable them to understand, to see the relevance of theoretical knowledge to the world around them, and to be able to use and apply it appropriately.

36.8 References

Adams, M.J., Neumann, R.T. and Rytmeister, C. (1996) *Is it a Level Playing Field? Factors Which Influence Student Evaluation of Teaching*. ERA and AARE Annual Conference, Nov. 1996, Singapore. http://www.swin.edu.au/aare/conf96p.htm.

Becher, T. (1989) *Academic Tribes and Territories: Intellectual Enquiry and the Cultures of Disciplines*. Milton Keynes: Open University Press.

Biglan, A. (1973) The characteristics of subject matter in different academic areas, *Journal of Applied Psychology* **57**(3): 195—203.

Biggs, J.B. (1989) Approaches to the enhancement of tertiary teaching, *Higher Education Research and Development* **8**: 7—25.

Branxton, J.M. (1995) Disciplines with an affinity for the improvement of undergraduate education. In N. Hativa and M. Marincovich (eds), *Disciplinary Differences in Teaching and Learning: Implications for Practice*. San Francisco: Jossey Bass.

Buckland, R. (1997) Do the humanities have anything to offer science education? *And Gladly Lerne*, 5,1. Macquarie University, Centre for Higher Education & Professional Development.

Cashin, W. E. (1990) Students do rate different academic fields differently. In Theall, M. and Franklin, J. (eds), *Student Ratings of Instruction: Issues for Improving Practice*. San Francisco: Jossey-Bass Inc.

Cranton, P. A. and Smith, R. A. (1986) *A new look at the effect of course characteristics on student ratings of instruction,* American Educational Research Journal **23***(1):* 117—28.

Donald, J.G. (1995) Disciplinary differences in knowledge validation. In N. Hativa and M. Marincovich (eds), *Disciplinary Differences in Teaching and Learning: Implications for Practice*. San Francisco: Jossey Bass.

Doyle, T. (1996) *Student attitudes to engineering and technology courses at the University of New South Wales.* In Proceedings of the Australasian Women in Engineering Forum, University of Technology Sydney.

Entwistle, N. and Tait, H. (1995) Approaches to studying and perceptions of the learning environment across disciplines. In N. Hativa and M. Marincovich (eds), *Disciplinary Differences in Teaching and Learning: Implications for Practice.* San Francisco: Jossey Bass.

Feldman, K.A. (1978) Course characteristics and college students' ratings of their teachers: what we know and what we don't know Research in Higher Education **9**: 199—242.

Marton, F. and Säljö, R. (1976) On qualitative differences in learning. II — Outcome as a function of the learner's conception of the task, British Journal of Educational Psychology **46**: 115—27.

Marton, F. and Säljö, R. (1984) Approaches to learning. In Marton, F. et al. (eds), *The Experience of Learning.* Scottish Academic Press.

Meyer et al. (1994) A gender comparison of contextualised study behaviour in higher education, Higher Education **27**: *469—85.*

Murray, H.G. and Renaud, R.D. (1995) Disciplinary differences in classroom teaching behaviours. In N. Hativa and M. Marincovich (eds), *Disciplinary Differences in Teaching and learning: Implications for Practice.* San Francisco: Jossey Bass.

Ramsden, P. (1992) *Learning to Teach in Higher Education.* London: Routledge.

37 Engineering — learning to create

Caroline Baillie and Simon Dewulf
Imperial College of Science, Technology and Medicine

37.1 Overview

'For some time there has been a realisation that the "how" of learning (skills) should not be separated from the "what" of learning (knowledge)' (Bowden and Marton, 1998). It seems necessary to develop more emphasis in pedagogic research on improving our understanding of how students learn concepts within a discipline and matching the teaching and learning environment to this. It may be that the very reason disciplinary teaching traditions have grown up is that this is the best way of developing an understanding of certain concepts. The engineering lecture, followed by tutorials, could help students to think. However, we find in practice, that many students do not 'turn their brains on' until exam time. It is likely that we do not help the students very much and that they do the 'knowledge building' themselves. Those that cannot, simply fail. We need to ensure that we are not simply providing an expensive textbook for our engineering students.

It has become of interest to engineering industry and to Professional Institutions in recent years, to focus on the lack of 'creative thinking' and innovation that develops in graduates. It seems that teaching and assessment approaches which help students to 'switch their brains on' during the courses, will help their general thinking skills as well as develop their potential to think laterally and become innovative in their jobs. In this paper we present two examples of such courses, both studied as cases in a DfEE funded project 'Fostering Creativity in the Engineering Curriculum'. The first (UQ) is based in Queensland University, where the lecturer intends to 'teach' engineering students communication skills using a real life project scenario and the second (IC) is a Polymer course in a Materials degree at Imperial College.

In the former case the course lecturer decided to make the course seem relevant to the students and to give them a real practical exercise which they must present as a communication exercise. She also decided to encourage their creative abilities during this task. Hence they were asked to design a laboratory class which they themselves might have to take as part of their course. In the latter case, an attempt has been made to apply those conditions, which are considered to optimize the creative ability of the students and to maximize the free flow of thinking within the context of a standard, second year polymer course.

Through a variety of means, observation, filming live action, video conferencing, open-ended reflective writing assignments, group discussions and interviews, the students were asked to expand on their experiences and conceptions of 'creativity' in each context. A *Creativity Research* approach was taken to the analysis of the feedback and categories of description of the students' experience of learning were collected. The main emphasis was on the level of thinking and changes in attitude which the students felt they were developing during the classes and afterwards.

The authors encourage a visit to www.creax.com for an update of the creativity research.

37.2 Introduction

37.2.1 What is creativity?

Can we define what we are looking for? Often people are careful not to define creativity as such, as it is such a complex phenomenon. Furthermore, teaching creativity becomes 'fostering', 'nurturing', 'stimulating' or 'allowing' creativity. Some definitions which have been given in the literature are as follows:

a. Novel associations which are useful (Isaksen and Treffinger in Isaksen *et al.*, 1993)
b. Conceptual expansion — stretching a single concept to a new situation (Ward *et al.*, 1997)
c. Improbabilist creativity — new and valued creativity within constraints
   Impossibilist — transformation of conceptual space — new ideas arise that were impossible before (Boden, 1996)
d. The process of generating unique products by transformation of existing products. These products, tangible and intangible, must be unique only to the creator, and must meet the criteria of purpose and value established by the creator. (Welsch in Isaksen *et al.*, 1993)
e. The process of becoming sensitive to problems, deficiencies, gaps in knowledge, missing elements, disharmonies, and so on; identifying the difficult; searching for solutions, making guesses or formulating hypotheses about the deficiencies, testing and retesting them and finally communicating the results (Torronce, in Isaksen *et al.*, 1993)
f. The making of the new and the rearranging of the old (Bentley, 1997)
g. An unease emerging out of a struggle between two opposing forces (Robinson/Rundell, 1994)
h. A creative person can regularly solve problems or can fashion products ranging from a theory to a new technique in a domain in a way that is ultimately judged acceptable (although initially it may seem bizarre) by the field; in this case the field is a cultural setting of people and institutions that make judgments about new products in a domain. (Gardner in Russell, 1998)
i. In a creative act of perception one first becomes aware (generally non-verbally) of a new set of relevant differences and one begins to feel out or note a new set of similarities which do not come merely from past knowledge (Bohm, 1998)
j. Creativity is a process needed for problem solving. Secondly creativity is not a special gift enjoyed by a few but a common ability possessed by most people which can be developed or suppressed as a result of their individual experiences. (Jones in Isaksen *et al.*, 1993)
k. Conceptual combination — merging of two or more concepts resulting in a novel entity (Ward *et al.*, 1997)
l. Someone is creative if knowledgeable individuals agree (Amabile in Abra, 1997)
m. The development of creative alternatives in decision problems (Clemen, 1996)
n. The achieving of tangible products such as works of art or science (Abra, 1997)

Many definitions reflect the different approaches to the study of creativity. A working definition was constructed for this project: 'Creativity is shared imagination'. Imagination is *novel*, rather then visual memory, it is *individual* or personal. Sharing is making an *audience* part of it.

37.2.2 Is everyone creative?

Are there creative types of people who have certain intelligence, knowledge, technical skills, special talents and values? What about environmental conditions — politico-religious factors, cultural factors, socio-economic factors and educational factors? Does a creative person have a particular personality — internal motivation, confidence, non-conformity, good self image, emotional, perceptual and open to new ideas (Boden, Jones in Isaksen *et al.*, 1993)? The literature suggests that each individual is subject to a creative potential (see Figure 37.1). The structure below presents an overview of the factors described by many authors as those that influence the creative potential, and how a higher creative ability can be reached.

Internal/Individual	**CREATIVE POTENTIAL**	External/Organisation
Personality	Attitude Behaviour Skills, Knowledge	**Environment**
Intrinsic Motivation		*Extrinsic Motivation*

Figure 37.1 Creative Potential

The *internal* aspects of the individual (personality) may be brought about by psychological conditions. The external or organizational *environment* is related to conditions or obstacles, which might help or hinder creativity, from an external perspective. Both personality and environment will influence *the creative potential* of the individual. The person's ability to communicate their ideas, to see the possibilities in a situation, and to acknowledge assumptions will depend upon their own conditioning and their environment.

The *intrinsic motivation* for creativity may be set up directly by the individual personality. *Extrinsic motivation* may be set up directly from the external environment.

However, under less advantageous situations where the obstacles have become insurmountable, the creative potential needs to be aided by certain *skills, knowledge and awareness*.

These might be the ability to visualize what one wants to do, to think laterally as well as vertically, to associate different sets of ideas and so on. It appears to be possible to develop the creative potential and to take a back route towards the extrinsic or the intrinsic motivation via development of these areas. Even a negative environment, given the right sort of attitude, can be a motivation towards creative change, if the individual sees it as an opportunity for improvement.

37.2.3 What is the process of creativity?

> I call intuition cosmic fishing, you feel a nibble then you've got to hook the fish, after bathing the hook through preparation and generation, and trolling deep waters with incubation it's time to reel in the catch. (Buckminster Fuller in Gelb, 1996)

he creative process has been described in various ways in most creativity research and enerally comes down to four phases; preparation, generation, incubation and verification.

In the initial stage, preparation, the problem or question is defined, reformulated and edefined, moving from a given to an understanding. The way in which the question is ormulated severely influences the solution finding ability. Instead of seeking the right nswer, one can ask 'Is this the right question?' Gelb (1996) points out that our move from a omadic way of life to settlement occurred by reformulating the question, 'How do we get o the water?' to ' How can we make the water come to us?'

The generation phase involves 'moving beyond habitual pathways of thinking' (Gelb, 996) by purging associative concepts to the problem. Osborn described generation as rainstorming (COCD, 1999). Osborn furthermore sets up principles for brainstorming: Quantity breeds quality; Postponement of judgment; Hitch-hiking (building on other eoples' ideas); and Free-wheeling (continuing unrelated fantasy). The purge aims to shake ut all ideas, even the most obvious ones, as they may hinder the mind from looking further Osborn in COCD, 1999).

As well as being part of most creative developments, incubation can act on its own, as a ubconscious stimuli to an inventive concept. Studies have shown that individuals requently generate a potential idea after a certain time of incubation (sleep, shower, biking, sailing etc.), a period of full relaxation or relaxed attention (Tomic and Brouwers, 1998). It allows one's sub-intentional intelligence to suggest solutions. 'Brain researchers estimate hat the unconscious database outweighs the conscious on an order exceeding 10 million to one. This database is the source of your hidden natural creative genius' (Gelb, 1996). The great creative thinkers have used this method throughout history. Einstein instructed his students to include incubation as a necessary part of all their cognition; Kekule, the discoverer of the benzene ring, scheduled incubation/daydreaming periods into his daily work programme (Buzan 1999). An unusual assignment has been demonstrated by Goldschmidt (1999):

> I commission every student to dream a solution to a problem they are living through right now. If they are unable to come up with such a dream they have to go to the library and find the biographical records of five people who have solved things through dreams. It's amazing how many of the kids manage to have the dream by the time they are down to the second or third biography search.

After incubation the new links are purged, all the ideas are analysed, clustered and evaluated (COCD, 1999) followed by planning the action and implementation.

37.2.4 The case studies

A chemical engineering course in professional skills has been developed at the University of Queensland (UQ). The course lecturer decided to make these key skills seem relevant to the students and to give them a real practical exercise which they had to present as a communication exercise. She also decided to encourage their creative abilities during this task. Hence they were asked to design a laboratory class which they themselves might have to take as part of their course. They had to prepare a bid to tender, to the funding sponsor.

In 1996 a new approach was introduced to a polymer science core course within a Materials Science degree at Imperial College (IC). A text was produced for the course notes, which was used as a basis for discussion, instead of traditional lectures, to encourage mor active learning. Activities ranged from role-plays, poster sessions, small group discussion quizzes, debates, case studies and problem classes, to demonstrations of experiments b researchers.

Some lecturing was retained to reduce student anxiety over 'new' methods. In the debate they were to think about the use of models for understanding mechanical properties, the had to make a decision about whether modelling helped or oversimplified. In the role-play they had to 'become' a polymer chain. What did it feel like to be viscoelastic? In the class 'creative move' students were asked to think 'outside the box' and find an analogy c redefine the problem, moving from the rational to the imaginary and back again. Student in this context were creating their own understanding.

The exam was fairly tightly prescribed but it was possible to develop a four-part questio which looked traditional but in fact used a learning taxonomy.

37.3 Methodology

37.3.1 How can creativity be researched?

Both educational case studies focused on the intended individual learning objectives, th teaching approach, the assessment scheme, the method of evaluation, the potential fc transferring the module to another context, and the costs associated with implementing th module. Features of the cases, which were considered to aid the fostering of creativity, wer identified along with the lessons learnt by the partners in implementing such programme

The cases were studied using the approach detailed below. The use of film and th obvious benefits of stimulated recall were incorporated into the approach. The followin model can describe the research process. Data was collected and acted as the preparation fo generation source. After transcription and analysis of data, reflection on the literature in th light of this data enabled new models of understanding to develop of the creative proces occurring in each case study. Feedback from the partners was then obtained and guideline distilled.

The research approach of the case studies is described below:

UQ: Professional skills and attitudes for engineering students

Problem: Does the lecturer foster creativity in her students and if so, how?

Preparation phase: Problem redefinition; literature review; data collection: video conferenc with students in Queensland, open ended questionnaires with students; interview wit course director; assessed reflective writings of students

Generation phase: Idea Generation

Transcription of interviews, focus group, study of transcripts, questionnaires, reflectiv writing.

Incubation phase: Synthesis

Time to connect all information that has been collected. Associate this with creativ literature ideas, incubate.

Verification phase: Creative guidelines developed

IC: Creative Materials Engineering

Problem: What is polymer science and how can we help students to think creatively in a polymer science course?

Preparation phase: Problem redefinition and concept restructuring, literature review, data collection: observation of lectures in different contexts, open ended questionnaire, assessment review, filmed focus group.

Generation phase: Idea Generation

Transcription of focus group, analysis of questionnaires, exam papers, observation notes.

Incubation phase: Synthesis

Time to connect all information that has been collected. Associate this with creative literature ideas, incubate.

Verification phase: Creative guidelines developed

Data collection — analysis — synthesis — knowledge building — creative guidelines.

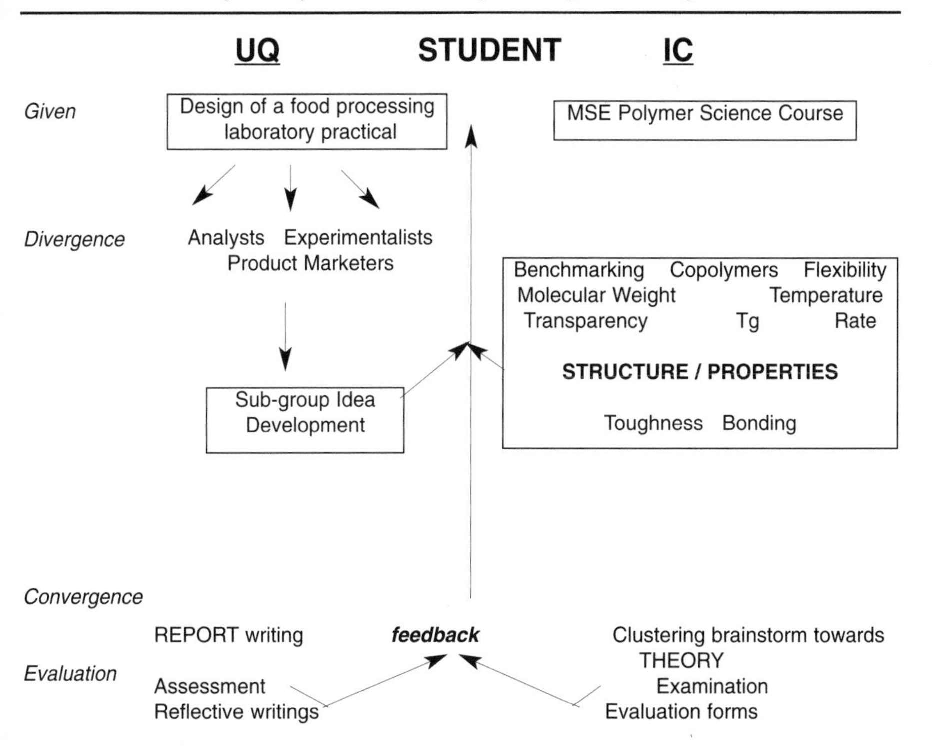

Figure 37.2 Divergence and convergence in the case studies

37.4 Implemented schemes

As schematized in Figure 37.2, the studies indicated that in each case the format was divergence on the some given issue, followed by a convergence towards the evaluation. At different stages of the process, feedback and recognition is given to the student.

37.5 Results

At the verification stage in each case study, 'creative guidelines' were developed. These were ways in which we believed the facilitator was helping to develop the students creative potential with their own constraints. It was noted that connection with prior knowledge was a vital part of the process. Alongside the development of the guidelines it was also possible to see how in each case, the pathway of an idea, which might become a creative idea or a creation could be helped or hindered.

37.5.1 Prior knowledge

One of the most important aspects of note within the case studies was the issue of *prior knowledge*. At the start of every session at IC, students brainstorm on the given subject matter. The technique promotes the students to come up with as many associations as possible for a given subject. The brainstorm sets off students' minds and usually most of the subjects which will be discussed in class arise as concepts in the brainstorm. The student becomes problem-owner of the subject and therefore experiences personal involvement. From the given brainstorm, the lecturer clusters subjects into the structure of the unit, and the course.

The brainstorm also permits the lecturer to measure the students' *prior knowledge* on the subject. The students themselves are able to face their *prior knowledge* and experience the value of their own reasoning on the matter. Furthermore it is absolutely vital for the students to connect with their *prior knowledge* on the matter, if the new information is to be sustained. Incorrect preconceptions can then be overwritten with the 'new' conceptions.

Within the UQ course, students were able to draw on their own experience, as the field of food processing was relatively new to them. They connect to their *prior knowledge* on the subject.

37.5.2 Idea pathway

Within each case study it was possible to identify how ideas are helped along by the particular circumstances of the case and how hindrances might be avoided. For someone to be creative, an idea needs to be expressed and communicated in some way. We have tracked the pathway of an idea in each case and produced a general model. This is shown schematically in Figure 37.3.

At university as well as when entering a new company the individual is exposed to new *knowledge*. This knowledge stream permits us to make new links, associating different facts, creating a new reality. This has proved to be a great stimulus for inventive thinking. New knowledge from different fields will always help to make new associations. An example in engineering is the study of nature or 'biomimetics' which provides analogies and principles to apply to engineering concepts.

Defining the problem (and then redefining it) is a common way of initiating creative thinking as it forces the visualization of the problem from different perspectives. Problem setting is approached in different ways with different sets of ideas, in a similar fashion to the

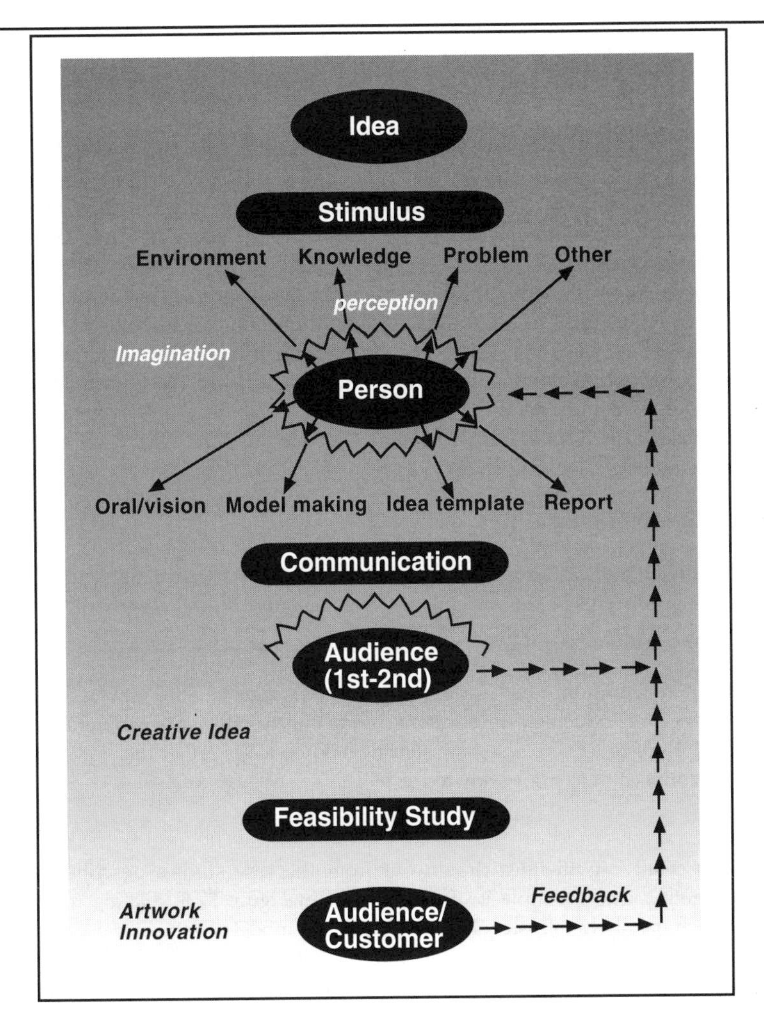

Figure 37.3 The Idea Pathway

reformulation technique at the start of a creative process.

A potential idea is created stimulated by various factors as described above but before an idea is initiated in one's mind, a number of personal blocks are experienced. Up to this point creative potential has been demonstrated. This will result in 'being creative' as soon as the idea is communicated to an external party and transcend from imagination to creativity.

The potential idea is bounced to a first audience. The communication process here is crucial. At this point ideas may be protected as 'intellectual property' at a patent office.

One successful route for communicating ideas is *the idea template*. Its success has been demonstrated in BOC Gases and is largely due to its democratic, ergonomic property (no hierarchical block). The idea-owner outlines his or her concept in written form on an internal database. The proposal is then examined by a team of gatekeepers, to discuss its potential.

Whether the idea is to be presented verbally or in any other way, it is at risk of various barriers. The audience can experience conceptual, hierarchical or cultural blocks, and it becomes a great challenge to the idea owner to direct the audience to the concept. These internal and external barriers and ways of overcoming these were discussed in the creative potential section.

If possible, the idea will follow the route of making a scale model or pilot project to ultimately convince the audience. At this point large numbers of ideas are lost, as the idea owner does not possess the time or courage to complete this process. In a university the conflict between time required to innovate in our teaching versus that needed for research will be a major stumbling block.

If the process above is successful, the idea owner (and possible first audience) faces the challenge of developing the 'creative idea' into an innovation, invention or piece of artwork. Now the idea is to be bounced to a second audience, which may be the customer. It may well be the hosting institution, whether this is industrial or academic. The person will undertake a market search to identify a target application and a feasibility study. A financial study to obtain the necessary components will require outside support. Again we will be facing blocks involving cost, time, and so on.

37.5.3 Creative guidelines

IC: Prior knowledge base, adopting creative techniques in a traditional setting, cognitive restructuring of concepts before the course started, creative thinking assessment criteria

UQ: Problem redefinition, need for an open-ended problem, idea development, use of videoconference for inducing self reflection, use of constructive criticism, reflective writing assignment for self-reflection, assessing sharing of knowledge rather than just possession of knowledge, connection to prior knowledge

The various creative guidelines drawn out from the case studies described have been collected together into a simple proforma shown in Figure 37.3, relating to the creative process, which they help to foster. This and the above models are further detailed, together with three further case studies feeding into the development of these models, in the publication CASE: Creativity in Art, Science and Engineering (Dewulf, Baillie, 1999)

Stimulators — these are the various ways in which an individual with a particular motivation is stimulated to the generation of an idea.

Unblockers — These are categorized into preparation, generation, incubation and verification stages although it is appreciated that there will be a considerable amount of overlap which is not demonstrated in this simplistic analysis. These features of the cases which aid the creative process, can be seen as 'unblockers' and enable the individual to pass through the barrier or block to the idea, the creative idea or to the innovation, in the model.

Communicators — These are the ways in which the creative idea is communicated to the audience. It is a chance for feedback and reflection, redesign and further promotion of exploration and incubation in a cyclical manner.

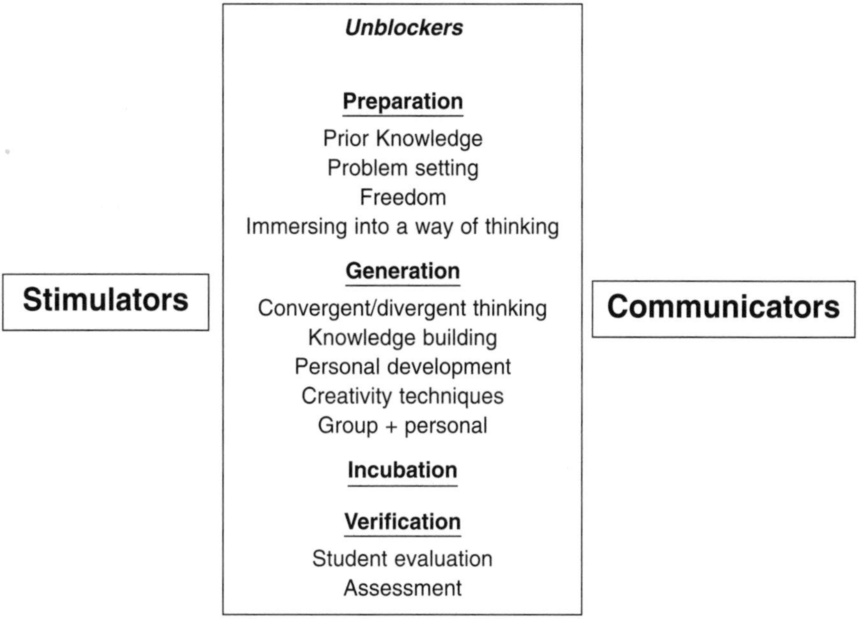

Figure 37.4 Creative Guidelines

37.5.4 Can creativity be assessed?

One of the six assessment criteria of the Material Science and Engineering Course at Imperial College is 'creativity'. The course information states: For 1st Class 'Students show creativity of a high standard in nearly all the possible aspects' and for Fail 'exhibits very little sign of creativity'. Yet how is this aspect assessed in traditional courses? Within the Polymer case study this was done using exam questions set with a hierarchy of thinking embedded within them. Students were helped with the development of a very new exam creative thinking technique. At Queensland University students were indeed explicitly assessed on 'creativity'. They found this difficult to understand and furthermore they found it hard to imagine how their thoughts and reflections could be assessed in the reflective writing assignment. They did however seem to take well to this chance of self-expression and it provided a valuable means of exploring how each individual was thinking. We will not deal further with assessment in this chapter but it is an issue which needs to be addressed in the very near future before more courses attempt to help students 'foster' creativity as an explicit course objective.

37.6 Summary

Some of the key issues in the literature on creativity have been reviewed and a structure given in which to consider 'creative potential', and how a higher creative ability can be reached. The model for the creative potential has been simplified as much as possible. Consequently, the sharpness of parameters or variables have been blurred. In future the complexity of creativity should be respected, creating a better understanding.

The creative process has been summarized into four stages: *preparation, generation, incubation* and *verification*.

It should be noted that in observing the creative process, only those aspects understood or 'seen' by the researcher can be noted. This is true of any 'discovery' of concepts hence the researcher becomes a great influence to the research outcome. There is furthermore a need for enhanced study of 'incubation'. Incubation is a most important phase of the creative process, though it's process is difficult to interpret.

An analysis of the idea pathway as experienced within academia and industry has also been presented. This is the route of a potential idea, how it originates, how it can be enhanced or hindered towards a creative idea — innovation — invention — artwork. The model permits greater insight to what influences creative success. The individual starts from his or her personal perception facing a problem setting, new knowledge, a certain environment stimulating an idea. This idea will then be communicated to an audience, where it becomes a creative idea after which the creative idea can find an application field; becoming an innovation or if not domain specific an invention.

During the whole path, the idea owner is faced with barriers or blocks — challenging his or her motivation. As presented in the definition "creativity is shared imagination" those barriers relate to communication and personality.

37.7 References

Abra, J. (1997) *The Motives for Creative Work*. New Jersey: Hampton Press Cresskill.

Bentley, T. (1997) *Sharpen Your Team's Skills in Creativity*. Cambridge: Cambridge University Press.

Baillie, C.A. and Hession, M. (1998) Global environmental change. Paper presented at Improving Student Learning Conference Outcomes, Brighton, 1998.

Baillie, C. (1999) *Learning from Nature*. Berlin: Wissenschaftkolleg.

Boden, M.A. (ed.) (1996) *Dimensions of Creativity*. London: The MIT Press.

Bohm, D. and Nichol, L. (eds) (1998) *On Creativity*. London: Routledge.

Boud, D. (1986) *Implementing Student Self-Assessment, Australia*: Herdsa.

Bowden, J. and Marton, F. (1998) *The University of Learning: Beyond Quality and Competence in Higher Education*. London: Kogan Page Ltd.

Brockbank, A. and McGill, I. (1998) *Facilitating Reflective Learning in Higher Education*. Buckingham: SRHE and Open University Press.

Buzan, T. (1999) *The Mindmap Book*. London: BBC Books.

Clemen, R.T. (1996) *Making Hard Decisions: An Introduction to Decision Analysis*. Duxbury Press.

COCD (1994) *Creaddenda – Deskundigheids opleiding*. Antwerp: COCD.

Cowan, J. (1998) *On Becoming an Innovative University Teacher*. Buckingham: SRHE and Open University Press.

Dewulf, S. and Baillie, C.(1999) *CASE: Creativity in Art, Science and Engineering: how to foster creativity*. London: DfEE.

Eysenck, H.J. (1996) The measurement of creativity. In Boden, M.A. (ed.), *Dimensions of Creativity*. London: The MIT Press.
Finke, R.A., Ward, T.B. and Smith, S.M. (1992) *Creative Cognition: Theory, Research and Applications*. London: The MIT Press.
Gardner, H. (1982) *Art, Mind and Brain: A Cognitive Approach to Creativity*. Basic Books.
Gelb, M.J. (1996) *Putting your Creative Genius to Work: How to Sharpen and Intensify your Mind Power*. Illinois: Nightingale Conant.
Gilhooly, K.J. (1996) *Thinking: Directed, Undirected and Creative*. London: Academic Press Ltd.
Goldschmidt, V. and ASME (1999) *Learning the Art of Engineering in Creativity Class*. http://www.asme.org/students/learning.html
Isaksen, S.G., Murdock, M.C. and Firestien, R.L. (eds) (1993) Nurturing and Developing Creativity: The Emerge of a Discipline. New Jersey: Alex Publishing Corporation.
Isaksen, S.G., Murdock, M.C. and Firestien, R.L. (eds) (1993) *Understanding and Recognizing Creativity: The Emergence of a Discipline*. New Jersey: Alex Publishing Corporation.
Koestler, A. (1989) *The Act of Creation*. London: Penguin Books.
Little, P., Ostwald, M. and Ryan, G (eds) (1995) *Research and Development in Problem Based Learning*. Australia: Charles Sturt University Press.
McKim, R.H. (1980) *Experiences in Visual Thinking. Boston: PWS Publishing Company,*
Petty, G. (1997) *How to Be Better at ... Creativity*. London: Kogan Page Ltd.
Robinson, G. and Rundell, J. (eds) (1994) *Rethinking imagination: Culture and Creativity*. London: Routledge.
Schneps, M.H. (1994) *A Private Universe*. Massachusetts: The Corporation for Public Broadcasting.
Sternberg, R.J. (ed.) (1999) *Handbook of Creativity*. Cambridge: Cambridge University Press.
Sternberg, R.J. (ed.) (1997) *The Nature of Creativity: Contemporary Psychological Perspectives*. Cambridge: Cambridge University Press.
Tomic, W. and Brouwers, W. (1998) *Idea Generating Among Secondary School Teachers*. Heerlen, The Netherlands: The Open University (unpublished).
Ward, T.B., Finke, R.A. and Smith, S.M. (1995) *Creativity and the Mind: Discovering the Genius Within*. London: Plenum Press.
Ward, T.B., Finke, R.A. and Vaid, J. (eds) (1997) *Creative Thought: An Investigation of Conceptual Structures and Processes, American Psychological Association, Washington.*

38 Improving written and spoken communication: innovative practices in undergraduate English Studies

Simon Avery and Cordelia Bryan
Anglia Polytechnic University, Cambridge

> The limits of my language stand for the limits of my world.
>
> (Ludwig Wittgenstein)

38.1 Background debates

Over the past decade the issue of skills training and awareness has been hotly debated in the higher education sector. Central to this debate, of course, have been the recommendations which arose from the Dearing Report published in 1997, and specifically the proposal for making explicit the range of skills acquired by students on any particular degree course. As the committee for the Report wrote:

> There is much evidence of support for the further development of a range of skills during higher education, including what we term the *key* skills of communication, both oral and written, numeracy, the use of communications and information technology, and learning how to learn. We see these as necessary outcomes of all higher education programmes.
>
> (Paragraph 38; see also Recommendation 21)

One direct consequence of this foregrounding of the skills debate has been that the term 'skills' itself is now less likely to be associated with a political agenda which at one time appeared to be pushing education dangerously close to a utilitarian vocationalism, and which threatened to measure the heterogeneity of the educational experience primarily in terms of the production of a skilled labour force. Rather, many lecturers and academics are now coming to accept that clearly defining the outcomes of, and transferable skills embedded in their courses is a necessary, even fundamental, part of higher education. Of course, there are still some understandable reservations about the degree of intervention within the educational process by the government and employers (see, for example, Tasker and Packham, 1994), but nevertheless, being asked to think intelligently and carefully about the skills and employability of students when they graduate helps academics to rethink and reflect upon their own educational objectives. And of course, the development of such skills, as the Dearing committee argues, is crucial to the development of the Learning Society which it envisages for the future.

The main question here, then, is how such key, core or transferable skills — depending on how they are described — should be taught in the tertiary education sector. Are they best delivered as generic modules with names such as Graduate Profiling or should they be acquired as part of a particular degree programme? How should we measure and assess such skills when they are taught? And, indeed, *should* we be assessing, for example, the information technology skills of English Literature students in addition to their abilities to analyse the historical and cultural conditions that produced a literary work? (For a full analysis of these debates see Barnet, 1994; and Bridges, 1994.)

Recently, attempts have been made to address these problematic questions through research into benchmarking and threshold standards commissioned by the Quality Assurance Agency (QAA). These investigations into the intellectual attributes associated with successful study of a particular subject at degree level result from another key recommendation of the Dearing report, where the idea of benchmarking was put forward in an attempt to allay public concern that the recent mass expansion in higher education had resulted in a drop in standards. To date (summer 1999), three subject communities have directed pilot studies into benchmarking criteria (Law, History and Chemistry), yet as the draft reports suggest, each discipline's requirements appear to be quite distinct from those of any other discipline, placing different emphases on particular skills and on the levels of attainment required. Such evidence clearly casts further doubt on the validity of any sort of generic approach to the development of key skills. Generic models run the risk of both reducing standards to the lowest common denominator and eroding existing diversity — a diversity which we believe should be celebrated rather than erased. After all, is it surprising that a chemist's critical analytical skills are subtly different from those of a historian, for example, or that both are different from those required by a graduate in law?

In December 1997, the Council for College and University English (CCUE) delivered a report to QAA on the subject of standards in the English degree curriculum (*The English Curriculum: Diversity and Standards*). This document argued that there is already in place 'significant agreement on the definition of the core skills and threshold standards expected of English undergraduates' (p. 1) and listed those skills which the community saw as being essential to successful study of the subject as:

> knowledge of the canon of English literature, a knowledge of the historical, intellectual and cultural contexts of literature, theoretical approaches and subject methodologies, presentational skills, oral communication skills, writing skills, powers of independent learning, flexibility of mind, a capacity for self-reflection, conceptual grasp, analytical skills, critical reasoning and the ability to engage in discussion of ethical and other human values. (p. 3)

The rest of this chapter will detail how the development of many of these subject-specific skills is being promoted through a teaching and learning research project based in the English department at Anglia Polytechnic University, Cambridge. It will argue that skills development need be neither low-level nor mechanistic, but can be concurrent with, rather than detracting from, any typical English studies curriculum. Skills development viewed this way embraces fundamentally sound pedagogical principles which are concerned with encouraging student autonomy and an appetite for lifelong learning.

38.2 The Speak-Write Project: rationale and aims

In 1995 the English department of Anglia Polytechnic University was awarded the rating of 'Excellent' for its teaching provision by the Higher Education Funding Council for England (HEFCE), which meant that it was eligible to apply for financial support for educational research under HEFCE's Fund for the Development of Teaching and Learning initiative (FDTL). Staff in the department had become increasingly aware of a widely held perception in the British higher education sector that key skills relating to the analysis and use of the English language in both written and spoken forms needed strengthening. The view that students' understanding of grammar was not as comprehensive as it used to be was frequently heard, as was the claim that they cannot construct a coherent argument or give an effective presentation. Believing that the department could find creative ways of addressing these deficiencies, the Speak-Write Project was established in January 1997. Now coming towards the end of its third and final year, the Project has been working to assist first-year undergraduates studying English across the country to develop their written and oral communication skills to an advanced standard. This has been achieved through three main stages of work:

- *Research stage:* an extensive nationwide survey into the capacities and limitations of first-year students with regard to the use and analysis of written and spoken English;
- *Design and trialling stage:* the development of innovative approaches and materials which integrate classroom teaching and independent learning and which are designed to improve students' communication skills to an advanced level;
- *Dissemination stage:* the distribution of these new teaching approaches and materials to other English departments (and possibly other humanities departments) throughout the country via a range of different media, including books, guides, video and the Internet.

Although the Speak-Write materials and approaches are for specific use in English literature degree courses, the Project team is also interested in exploring ways in which they can be used in other disciplines. Indeed, colleagues in a range of subject areas, including history, music, cultural studies, education and even applied biology, have suggested that the materials would transfer successfully to their disciplines, and that many of the activities would be appropriate as they stand while others could be rewritten and reshaped to become more firmly embedded within the context of the particular subject (see Avery and Bryan 1999: 15—20).

38.3 Practices, problems and perceptions: the primary research

The first stage of the Speak-Write Project's work involved an investigation into the current ways in which advanced written and oral communication skills are taught within the discipline of English at a range of educational institutions around the country. The Project team were particularly keen to learn how other academics perceived the problems associated with developing students' communication skills so that they could develop a course to address some of these problems. During the first year of research, therefore, Cordelia Bryan and Simon Avery conducted a series of in-depth interviews with lecturing taff from the English departments of three 'old' and three 'new' universities — Leeds, Middlesex, Nottingham, Oxford Brookes, Sheffield Hallam and York — as well as staff from the department of Lifelong Learning and Education at Middlesex University.

As the Project team were aware that the problems they were attempting to address are not unique to higher education, a number of staff members from secondary schools, sixth-form colleges and further education colleges were also interviewed in order to gain an understanding of language provision in other sectors. In particular, Project personnel questioned interviewees about the standards of written and oral articulacy among their students; curriculum provision for the learning of communication skills; the perceived use of tutor feedback by students; training in, and assessment of, oral presentation skills; and the encouragement of reflective learning.

In addition, over 200 first-year undergraduates in Anglia's English department were asked to fill in a questionnaire on language and communication skills so that Project staff could assess how the students themselves felt about their capabilities and needs. Although the results from this qualitative research obviously cannot be used to confirm or deny conclusively the suggestion that standards of written and oral English among undergraduates have declined over recent years, some general patterns clearly emerged which subsequently helped to inform the design of the skills-based courses in the English department at Anglia. A full analysis of these findings can be found in Bryan (1998).

38.4 *Varieties of Speaking and Writing*: developing effective strategies for learning and teaching advanced communication skills

At the heart of the Speak-Write Project are two innovative modules designed by Rebecca Stott and Peter Chapman and entitled *Varieties of Speaking and Writing I & II*. These have been constructed specifically to enable first-year undergraduates studying English to develop their written and oral communication skills to a high standard, and are firmly grounded in the insights gathered by the Project team through the interview procedures outlined in the previous section. The *Varieties* modules enable students to become competent in four key areas of academic study in English:

- grammar and language awareness;
- stylistic analysis and creative writing/rewriting;
- oral presentations and effective seminar participation;
- writing for academic purposes.

Believing that the enhancement of these skills in undergraduates is essential for both their academic success and their future employment, the English department at Anglia has made the *Varieties* modules compulsory for all first-year students, whether they are taking English through a single or a combined honours pathway. In the first semester of the two-semester year, therefore, they study the language awareness and the stylistics components of the course, while in the second semester they study the oral presentation and the writing for academic purposes components. This means that at the end of their initial year, all students on the English degree programme should be fully equipped in a whole range of skills which they can continue to develop throughout the remainder of their degree course and beyond.

As the *Varieties of Speaking and Writing* course is highly practical, it is taught through weekly two-hour 'workshops' in which students work through a number of exercises which help to increase their skills and competencies in the four main areas. There are one or two lectures per semester which help to introduce new or more demanding material, but the majority of the learning process is undertaken in these co-operative, teacher-facilitated work spaces. Before each week's class, the students work through a chapter in the relevant module guidebook which introduces the material for discussion and allows them to think around the particular topic under consideration.

At the beginning of the class, the tutor will then review some of the main points and answer any queries the students might have, but the main part of the session will involve the class breaking up into small groups of five or six students who then work together on a range of exercises which cover, for example, the analysis of register and lexis in a number of literary and non-literary texts, the selection of appropriate material for a five-minute oral presentation, or the effects of particular sentence structures in children's writing. By working in small groups, the students are able to pool their ideas and thoughts and to coach each other on their writing and presentation skills. This therefore shifts the emphasis from the conventional teacher-led approach and allows the students to explore issues and move towards higher level analysis through the promotion of articulate thinking. It is through the development of these wider communicative and cognitive functions that greater student autonomy can flourish and the highly prized transferable skills be acquired and made explicit.

The pedagogical model which underpins each week's work on the *Varieties* course combines analysis and practice. First students are given the fundamental information about a topic (register, perhaps, or complex sentence structures or the rhetorical structures used in speech-making), explained in language which is accessible and 'user-friendly'. Secondly, they undertake a number of analytical exercises where they examine particular texts for the ideas they have been reading about. And thirdly, they reinforce their understanding by working with the ideas themselves in a piece of creative work or re-writing. For example, in the final week of the grammar and language awareness component of the course, students examine techniques for constructing paragraphs and the full text. They learn about cohesion and coherence and then explore the use of these in a range of texts, including passages from the work of James Kelman and Terry Prachett.

They are then asked to write and edit their own texts, concentrating upon logical arrangement and development of argument. In each week's work, therefore, there is a movement from more structured exercises to freer, more creative ones, an approach which has proved very successful with our students. With such a range of exercises, each student can move forward at their own pace and build up their skills regardless of the level of ability with which they enter the course. This is particularly important in a new university such as Anglia which, like many higher education institutions, has had to find strategies to deal with an increasingly diverse, heterogeneous and complex student population.

Additionally, as the title of the course suggests, one of the main positive outcomes of *Varieties of Speaking and Writing* is that students have the opportunity to examine a wide range of writings or oral work taken from different historical periods and cultures so that they can gain an understanding of, for example, the different registers used in a business document, a personal letter and an academic essay, the different rhythms employed in drama, a newspaper article and Afro-Caribbean writing, or the use of rhetorical structures in Shakespeare's soliloquies, modern political speeches and advertising. The course is therefore designed to be extremely fluid and flexible in its approach to definitions of texts thought suitable for study, and aims to give students the opportunity to sharpen their analytical skills with material which is much wider than that found on more traditional canon-based courses. As a result they are able to engage effectively with contemporary cultural phenomena as well as more established literary works.

38.5 Varieties I

Varieties of Speaking and Writing I starts with seven weeks' work on various grammatical and syntactical structures. The course designers decided to place this section first since it both serves as an essential foundation for the following work on stylistic analysis and also helps students gain an understanding of the underlying principles of language use. However, an obvious difficulty in constructing this part of the course was how to get students engaged in the theoretical material and terminology of grammar when they often arrive at university with preconceptions about grammar being abstract, tedious and dogmatic. For students coming straight from school or for adult returners, grammar can often seem forbidding and intimidating because it is automatically associated with ideas of correctness and appears very black and white. Many might recall old school grammar textbooks dominated by exercises and drills in parsing and identifying parts of speech, where language is conceived entirely in terms of adherence to or deviation from a 'standard norm'. Others, particularly younger students, might have been educated in a system where explicit teaching of grammar was almost non-existent because it was not considered an essential part of their curriculum.

In order to get around these preconceptions and to deal with the wide range of previous experience with which students arrive at university, the course designers developed a programme which is extremely practical and which emphasises *grammar in use*. Key concepts of the course, therefore, include the emphasis on how grammar is fundamental to effective communication in a variety of contexts and the foregrounding of the relationships between context, audience, purpose and language choice. *Varieties* thus seeks to develop in the students a familiarity with grammatical terminology and an understanding of the organizing principles and structures of language, in addition to the ability to apply this to their own and others' work.

Over the seven weeks students examine the forms and functions of the four different sentence types (simple, compound, complex and compound-complex), the building up of phrases within sentences, word classes and punctuation. At each stage, following the underlining pedagogical model of the course, students examine the use of these structures in a range of literary and non-literary texts and then reinforce and extend their understanding through activities based upon creative writing and re-writing. For example, after considering the construction of compound sentences, students examine the use of them in a passage of prose by Ernest Hemingway. A final exercise asks them to compose their own passage in Hemingway's style, which can be either parodic or serious. Throughout the course, therefore, the students are encouraged to explore and investigate grammar as it is used in the living language rather than studying it in a manner where it is reductively divorced from practice.

In the second half of *Varieties I*, students build upon what they have already learnt in the section on language awareness by focusing upon the development of their stylistic analysis skills. Again, stylistic analysis is not taught as an isolated, discrete process, but is used to help develop students' own writing abilities. This part of the course starts by exploring the concept of register and the relationships between register, audience and context in a variety of literary and non-literary texts. Students are then encouraged to continue engaging with as many different styles of writing as possible by examining strategies for writing in a clear immediate and accessible manner. Here they examine both George Orwell's recommendations in his powerful essay 'Politics and the English Language' (1946) and the later work of the Plain English Campaign in order to learn about the pitfalls of writing in a convoluted and overly-wordy manner, and are asked to rewrite a range of inaccessible prose pieces in order to make them clearer and more vigorous.

During the remainder of the course, students examine more complex styles of writing so that they can develop their abilities to analyse difficult pieces effectively and make their writing fresh, original and engaging. Attention is paid to the often deadening effects of cliché; and purple prose, before students explore a range of well-crafted pieces — reviews and journalism as well as passages from literary texts — which reveal the importance of word choice and the effects which can be produced through careful shaping of sentences and the use of rhythm in prose. In the final part of this section of the course, there is an opportunity for them to consolidate much of what they have learnt by focusing upon a particular case study which explores the variety of styles to be found in journalistic writing.

Assessment for *Varieties of Speaking and Writing I* centres upon workbooks which students use throughout. These function not only as a record of the drafts and completed pieces produced, but also as a space in which each student can reflect upon the teaching sessions, what was learnt and where they still feel they need to do more work. The workbooks therefore constitute another essential learning strategy which encourages the students to take more responsibility for their own learning practices.

38.6 Varieties II

In *Varieties of Speaking and Writing II* students focus upon the development of their oral and academic writing skills, with the two areas being linked together by a common concern with the arts of persuasion. In the oral skills section, students start by reflecting upon the conditions which make a good seminar, a particularly important process since considerable learning in higher education is undertaken in the seminar space. They are therefore asked to pay attention to the importance of clear goal setting, the process of building upon each other's contributions, the need for mutual respect and being open to new ideas, and the interaction and dynamics of the group. Through this the students are encouraged to take collective responsibility for the seminar.

The course then moves to consideration of the art of making a good oral presentation, focusing in particular upon rhetoric as a method by which a case can be made persuasively and structured effectively. Students learn the central rhetorical skills of invention, arrangement and style and examine the use of these in a number of speeches ranging from extracts taken from Shakespeare's plays to the modern political speeches of John F. Kennedy, Tony Blair and Hillary Clinton. They are then guided through a step-by-step process of making a brief presentation to a specified audience which is persuasive in form, concise and well-delivered, emphasizing crucial elements such as careful structuring, awareness of audience, the importance of an effective introduction, clarity of expression, projection and pacing, body language and keeping nerves under control. Again, the students work in small groups throughout these sessions, helping and coaching each other on their presentation skills, as well as learning to perform the roles of chairperson, timekeeper and scribe.

Once the students fully appreciate the importance of preparation and planning in making an effective speech, it is a natural step for them to move on to academic writing skills which are also approached through rhetorical structures. Again the students are encouraged to make a case, but this time on paper rather than orally. They explore, therefore, the importance of lucid structure, quality of argument, the careful selection of evidence, awareness of audience in writing, and the use of style and rhythm. They also study the essay as a genre and examine its place in history from Montaigne to the present day, with particular case studies including the modern journalist essay, the political essay, and the relationship between gender and writing. Attention is also paid to the conventions of the academic essay (register, formality and objectivity of tone, concern with evidence etc.) and the variety of styles and voices found in academic writing in order to provide students with a range of suggestions for improving their own styles.

38.7 Peer feedback and assessment

Throughout *Varieties of Speaking and Writing* peer feedback and assessment is incorporated by requiring students to read each other's work, grade it and provide a supporting comment which justifies the grade. It is particularly emphasized here that these comments should be constructive and point out to the author specific ways in which he or she can improve. The oral skills part of the *Varieties* course is then assessed by the individual students giving a five minute presentation to a specified audience (played by the study group) which is both peer and tutor assessed. The criteria for assessment is provided at the beginning of the course so the students are familiar with the categories of content and organisation, including evidence of appropriate research, appropriateness of material and language for the specified audience, ability to structure content effectively, quality and coherence of argument, and effectiveness of opening and conclusion.

The course designers and project team believe that the process of peer assessment forms a natural progression from the earlier emphasis on peer observation and the giving and receiving of peer feedback, which is integral to the entire Speak-Write pedagogical approach. As would be expected, many students on the *Varieties* course are initially resistant to the idea of peer assessment, believing assessment to be the exclusive domain of the professional lecturer, but having completed the process they realize its worth and how it is a way of giving them greater autonomy and responsibility in the learning process, as well as making them more critically aware.

Topping *et al.* have shown that engaging students in the process of guided peer feedback and assessment has many advantages, including evidence of better degree examination results and the improvement of transferable skills (see also Falchikov, 1990; Topping, Watson and Hill, 1996; and Mincham, 1999), and it is a process which can be introduced alongside tutor assessment so that both students and staff work to devise some agreed assessment criteria. The process of working together to establish clearly defined criteria helps to demystify the whole assessment process for students and can aid the building of trust between staff and students. After a period of peer assessment with tutor guidance or moderation, it is only a small step to empowering students with the whole responsibility of assessing their peers.

38.8 Conclusions

Since the Speak-Write Project was established in 1997, its work has been widely acclaimed by students and academics around the country and has received considerable media attention. But where can the work be taken from here?

Varieties of Speaking and Writing has been designed with large numbers of first-year undergraduates in mind. The materials have therefore been trialled primarily in the traditional classroom context with lecturers acting as facilitators. In cases where teaching the whole *Varieties* course is not perceived as being appropriate, however, the materials are sufficiently flexible for staff to select relevant activities which suit the needs of their particular students. If this selective approach is taken, particular care should be exercised to ensure that sufficient explanation is offered to students as to why the activities are being used and what can be gained by engaging in them.

Additionally, with some fine tuning, the materials could easily be adapted for more autonomous student learning, possibly in distance learning format. In redrafting the materials, the editors have been mindful of these issues and have attempted to think of the prospective audience as anyone who wishes to improve his or her communication skills.

There is insufficient space to do more than flag some of these possibilities in the conclusion, but in doing so, we hope to entice the reader to engage with some or all of the materials and approaches and thereby further broaden the debate. The materials from the *Varieties of Speaking and Writing* courses have now been developed into four books entitled *Grammar and Writing, Writing with Style, Speaking Your Mind: Oral Presentation and Seminar Skills,* and *Making Your Case: A Practical Guide to Essay Writing,* and these will be available from Pearson Education in September 2000.

For correspondence about the issues raised in this paper or for more information about the published books, please contact Rebecca Stott at the Department of English, Anglia Polytechnic University, East Road, Cambridge, CB1 1PT, e-mail: r.k.stott@anglia.ac.uk.

38.9 References and bibliography

Avery, S. (ed.) (1998) *From Sixth Form to Higher Education: English Oral and Written Language Skills Explored*. Cambridge: Anglia Polytechnic University.

Avery, S. and Bryan, C. (1999) *The Speak-Write Symposium Proceedings*. Cambridge: Anglia Polytechnic University.

Barnes, D. and Todd, F. (1995) *Communication and Learning Revisited: Making Meaning Through Talk*. Portsmouth, NH: Heinemann.

Barnet, R. (1994) *The Limits of Competence: Knowledge, Higher Education and Society*. Buckingham: The Society for Research into Higher Education.

Bridges, D. (ed.) (1994) *Transferable Skills in Higher Education*. Norwich: University of East Anglia.

Bryan, C. and Assiter, A. (1995) *Cognitive Skills in Work-Based Learning: Accreditation of Learning through Employment Report*. London: University of North London Press.

Bryan, C. (1998) Raising standards in English. In Avery, S. (ed.) *From Sixth Form to Higher Education*, pp. 6—17.

Council for College and University English (CCUE) (1997) *The English Curriculum: Diversity and Standards*.

Dillon, J.T.(1994) *Using Discussion in Classrooms*. Milton Keynes: Open University Press.

Edwards, A.D. and Westgate, D.P.G. (1994) *Investigating Classroom Talk*. London: Falmer Press.

Falchicov, N. (1990) An experiment in same-age peer tutoring in higher education. In S. Goodlad and B. Hirst (eds), *Explorations in Peer Tutoring*. Oxford: Blackwell.

Gibbs, G. (ed.) (1995) *Improving Student Learning Through Assessment and Evaluation*. Oxford: The Oxford Centre for Staff Development.

Higher Education in the Learning Society (1997) Chairman: Sir Ron Dearing.

Kelly, A.V. (1994) *The National Curriculum: A Critical Review*. London: Paul Chapman Publishing.

Mincham, J. (1999) *Peer and Self Assessment*. Ulster University.

Qualifications and Curriculum Authority (1998) *The Grammar Papers: Perspectives on the Teaching of Grammar in the National Curriculum*. London: QCA Publications.

Tasker, M. and Packer, D. (1994) Government, higher education and the industrial ethic, *Higher Education Quarterly* **48**: 182—93.

Topping, K.J, Watson, G.A., Jarvis, R.J. and Hill, S. (1996) Same-year paired peer tutoring with first year undergraduates, *Teaching in Higher Education* **1**(3): 341—56.

39 Communicating across the interdisciplinary divide: how teaching methods affect the transfer of knowledge from one discipline to another

Linda Byles[1] and Ruth Soetendorp[2]
Bournemouth University

39.1 Interdisciplinary dialogues for professional life

Teaching and learning in higher education has had to respond to the need to equip its graduates with a wide range of skills demanded of them in professional life. The forces, which have influenced this change, reflect changes in the nature of work itself, 'where the walls between traditional, highly specialised functions are breaking down in favour of more fluid forms' (Tobias, Birrer, 1998, p. 213). Greater complexity and interdependency within the workplace has required the integration of different kinds of knowledge. This has resulted in people even within defined specialities having to take into account a wider range of information. The need for disciplinary dialogue has never been greater. The challenge of addressing this has been identified by Cox (1992) who relates learning theory to the need to adapt teaching in Higher Education to the range of skills required in modern professional life. At the core of this is the need to create meaning in the context in which it is being used. Cox outlines, that recent developments in learning theory have been characterized by discussions on meaning and context, where learning is seen as the creation of meaning in different contexts. Learning is not essentially concerned with the absorption of information but rather with the process of interrelating facts, theories and experiences into meaningful wholes which enable us to operate successfully in the world.

It is against this background that initially the Patent Office and subsequently the Leverhulme Trust have funded a project with Bournemouth University to disseminate information and raise awareness of Intellectual Property Rights (IPR). Central to the work has been the need to facilitate a dialogue between those who will be creating IPR in their future professional lives, and their professional (legal and financial) advisers. The emphasis has been to reach not simply those traditionally associated with 'innoventive' Science and Technology based disciplines, but to inform those working in the Social Sciences and Humanities

Ideas from Zeldin (1998) have informed the approach taken in the project to the nature and form of this inter professional dialogue. His conversations with a number of professional have attempted to gain an insight into the basis of their work. Asking a doctor how long it would take her to teach him to be a doctor, he receives the reply 'six weeks'. This is not to make him a real doctor but to give him an idea of how doctors solve real problems. A similar question posed to an engineer was given the reply 'three months'. Again, this was not to perform as a real engineer, but to understand their language, their problems and to learn the essence of the way they think. The importance of the ability to have this understanding and thus capacity to engage in meaningful dialogue across the professions is highlighted by Tobias and Birrer (1998) who argue that the new knowledge worker will be independent, flexible, working with a variety of clients. He or she will leave the sheltered environment of both the bounded discipline and the bounded profession. It will prove essential therefore that they can operate at a level of mutual understanding, with an awareness of the demands influences and needs of other disciplines.

39.2 Challenges of negotiating academic genres in a multi-disciplinary context

The work of Saunders and Clarke (1997) suggests that students knowledge of one discipline influences another, rather in the way that a first language affects the second language acquisition. Students face difficulties where they try to access a range of disciplines because they import the rules of one discipline discourse into another.

They assert that for students to be successful they must acquire ways of knowing that are discipline specific. Saunders and Clarke identify a model of learning which is based on looking at the context in which learning takes place. They are encouraged to

> develop a model in which the role of academic subject literature, criticism, interpretation, argument and evidence, are considered in discipline specific contexts. (p. 303)

In order to make this possible Saunders and Clarke assert that

> students will need to be familiar with a range of genres. What is also needed is an explicit articulation of the variety of genre skills and conventions within and between disciplines to reduce the 'discoursal dissonance between tutors' and students' expectations and so empower students. (p. 304)

It is this approach which has informed the development of the Micromodules, where the authors were aware that the discipline of law would need to be considered in a range of different discipline contexts. One of the key challenges faced by the project has been how to make this dialogue accessible to these broad range of disciplines, whose pedagogies are fundamentally different. The execution of the project has involved working with a variety of students including Product Design students with a largely studio approach to learning and assessment and Nursing students with a reflective student-centred approach to study. The contexts in which they learn are not the same. What needed to be considered in the development of the materials was whether the pedagogy of law when teaching law to future lawyers, was the same as when teaching law to non-lawyers.

39.3 The pedagogy of law 1: traditional approaches to teaching law

The pedagogy of law has been dominated by the study of the sources of law. In this, the literature of law, its statutes and cases have provided the focus for study. This literature consists of legislation as laid down by and published by parliaments and other legislative institutions, and case reports, representing law created by decisions of the courts and the

Judiciary, in which they apply legislation, acknowledge custom and practice, and draw on respected academic texts.

In addition to these primary sources of law, a whole series of secondary sources have arisen. The casebook has become a form in itself of studying law. The teacher selects cases from the collections of case literature and edits and arranges them, to illustrate concepts and principles of law. In doing this the casebook can show the development of a particular legal concept, by successive courts, or can show the contrasting approaches that different courts have taken to the same problem.

For the student their approaches to learning have centred on reading cases, attacking and defending arguments on questions of law, and interpreting and applying statutory provision. Knowledge of these sources has been of fundamental importance to the way they learnt. Content or the 'black letter law' has been central to their learning, not least because of vocational requirements imposed by the professional bodies. This has given a very narrow pedagogic base to the study of Law.

The role of the teacher has similarly been influenced by this concentration on primary and secondary sources. Teaching methods have to a large extent been based on the 'Socratic method' (see Carter and Unklesby, 1989). Students, by reading and analysing court opinions, explore with an expert (the teacher) the underlying principles of law embedded in a case and thus reconstruct these events in different cases. Context specific applications of the law are emphasized as is the inherent flexibility and ambiguity in the rules of law. Underlying this approach is the assertion that the law should be regarded as

> not as a set of rules to be memorised, but an activity , something that people do with their minds and with each other as they act in relation to a body of authoritative legal material and to the circumstances and events of the actual world. (White, quoted in Carter and Unklesbay, p. 528)

39.4 The pedagogy of law 2: teaching law to non-lawyers

This model for the study of Law has not easily transferred to other disciplines. The issues feature prominently in the literature on the nature of legal study (see sources identified by Woodcock, 1988). What has emerged from these reviews is the inappropriateness of teaching law, through the study of primary sources as outlined by statutory and case material. In its place has been an approach dominated by 'translating' the law, which has normally been characterized by converting the sources into a set of rules to be learnt (Ward and Slater, 1990). Their study of law for professional accounting education warns of the dangers of translating the law into a series of disjoined but clear cut rules which can be learnt by rote. They do acknowledge however that the 'translation' process has benefits in making the material accessible to other to other disciplines. The basis of this 'translation' process can be viewed as 'Prophylactic Law'. This is defined by Soetendorp (1996) as the law being stripped to barest essentials and taught as a series of 'must knows' to avoid making tragic, dangerous and expensive mistakes for yourself and or your employer.

Where law is taught in other disciplines the emphasis is on the context in which the law operates. This has resulted in more innovative ways of delivery and a shift in the traditional pedagogy of law. Tyler (1995) when teaching on Applied Social Studies degrees, stresses that her approach is not only to look at what the law is, but also at the social and political contexts in which law is made and functions. Woodcock (1989) highlights the need to make the study of law relevant to the student's main subject area, by establishing appropriate course objectives, which will appear valid to the student. Her work with BTEC Business Studies students has been shaped in her view by the need for non-lawyers to have access to course programmes that contain appropriate material, presented in a stimulating way. This approach has taken the form of major and mini case studies, group exercises, role-play, and drafting letters. She asserts that

> it was intended that the whole exercise should underline the practical value of law in business. (p. 17)

This is reflected by Soetendorp (1999) who suggests the need to engender in the non-lawyer an appreciation that the law changes constantly, sometimes with dramatic effect. An awareness of the need to update knowledge, rather than 'fill up' with it, is probably the most useful starting point for a non-lawyer.

39.5 The pedagogy of law 3: current approaches to teaching law

Recent moves in curriculum developments have attempted to introduce greater social, political and human dimensions. Most significantly there has been an emphasis on skills based education over knowledge based education, grounded in the need for critical thinking and problem-solving capacities demanded by everyday legal practice (Jones cited in Harris, 1992). As Gold (1989) suggests, this represents an attempt by law to engage in an effective dialogue with the social sciences and the humanities. Change has taken place over a number of years. At its core is the continual tension between the academic versus the professional view of education. There has also been the growing realization that a significant number of students on undergraduate law degree programmes do not expect to enter the legal profession. This has encouraged a debate around the approach to the study of Law.

This debate has been reflected in a number of reports and pronouncements from the professional bodies (see Report of the Committee on the future of the Legal Profession (1988); The Lord Chancellor's Advisory Committee on Legal Education and Conduct (1996); The Joint Announcement on qualifying law degrees to be issued by the Law Society and the General Council of the Bar).

As Harris outlines

> a new prominence for tasks in a setting so long dominated by texts, accompanied by a recognition of the need for a multi disciplinary approach to the identification of professional skills and learning activities. These developments make law significantly less of a narrow angled discipline from a pedagogical standpoint. (p. 21)

This emphasis on the skills-based approach to learning has resulted in significant changes in delivery methods. There has been a rethinking of the teacher student relationship, where there is greater stress on student's active involvement. Students are encouraged to integrate their social experiences with legal concepts and to make greater use of the skills and knowledge that they bring with them (Harris). The need to develop students as independent learners, who can take responsibility for their own learning, can be seen as paramount. The tasks set for students have also changed, with a growing preference for the case study over the case report as a teaching and learning vehicle (Twining cited in Harris). With the rationale for this changed being firmly embedded in the recognition that lawyers' work

> depends on interactions with others as much as, if not more than the knowledge they find in texts (Flood cited in Harris).

This view is increasingly being reflected in new thinking about legal educational processes and their relationship to those in other professional fields (Harris). It is illustrated by Soetendorp (1995) who describes an innovative teaching programme which gives engineers and lawyers practical experience of communication skills by working together to discover how original engineering designs can best be protected and exploited.

Developments in the pedagogy of law have made it more accessible to other disciplines. 'Know how' features alongside 'knowledge' as an important outcome of study. It is in this environment that the Micromodules have been introduced, with their emphasis on a student centred and context sensitive approach to learning.

39.6 Micromodules used to stimulate a discourse on law with non-lawyers

Research carried out at Bournemouth (Soetendorp, 1996; Soetendorp and Byles unpublished report for the Patent Office, 1996, and presented at PATLIB; Aberdeen, 1996) identified the need for Intellectual Property to be included in a range of course across the University, particularly those which traditionally had no input on this subject. Advertising students recognized the need for some input on trademarks. Nursing students realized that they had a stake in their intellectual outputs as represented by their development of drug dispensing charts. This opened up the potential for other students to engage with issues associated with IPR. Central to this was the view that some knowledge of IPR was particularly appropriate to students, especially in respect of their profession lives.

The vehicle for raising awareness of IPR issues at Bournemouth was initially the Patent Office 12 inch Laser Disc package, 'Making It Happen'. This was an interactive tool, which covered in detail aspects of patenting and licensing. Although the disc was generally well received by the students, it was felt inappropriate if a wider audience was to be reached. It was cumbersome in terms of moving round the equipment and technical failures often interrupted the smooth running of the session. It was not predominantly student centred and relied heavily upon the input from the law lecturer.

With funding from the Patent Office, an alternative approach was taken to develop a series of learning materials which could be more flexibly used . Acknowledgement also had to be made that time and resources allocated to the teaching of non core subjects had gradually diminished and that the materials developed should not be resource intensive.

Based on the work of Ramsden and Entwhistle (1981) and Gow and Kember (1993) the emphasis has been one of fostering a deep approach to learning. Similarly the work of Gibbs, Habeshaw and Habeshaw (1989) and Gibbs (1992) have provided the underpinning rationale for taking a student centred approach to delivery. The importance of relating to the students as adult learners (see Knowles cited in Soetendorp 1999) also informed the focus of the work.

The materials which have been developed consist of a set of teacher notes, lesson plans, student exercises and handouts. They also include questions suitable for use in class, as coursework or in examinations. They are structured to be delivered in a one or two hour slot, and are designed to be used in a range of group learning environments; in a lecture theatre, with a seminar group, or in a workshop forum. The format of the Micromodules is to take students through a series of activities, which address some important concepts associated with IPR. For example on the patent Micromodule the students engage with issues associated with the function and purpose of a patent, what can be deemed as a patentable invention and how patents are dealt with in the work place. Rather than review decided cases through the medium of law reports, the students take a case study approach in exploring a range of options, which could be taken in pursuing a claim for an infringement of a patent. The essence of the materials is to encourage the student to review their knowledge of IPR issues in the context of their own subject discipline. The role of the lecturer is crucial in this because it is expected that the facilitator of these sessions is not a lawyer but the 'subject expert' who can help the students contextualize the material.

The effectiveness of this approach has been examined on six courses in four universities. Observations were made of the teaching sessions in three of the universities. Comments were obtained from the staff who ran the sessions by means of an interview. Student feedback was gained from a questionnaire given out at the end of the session. The results of this study has highlighted three perspectives in relation to the use of the Micromodules; students taking responsibility for their learning; lecturers as facilitators and the materials as learning resources.

39.7 Students taking responsibility for learning

The students observed responded well to the materials as presented in the sessions. Feedback from their questionnaires indicated that they found the content relevant and interesting. 74% found the sessions clear, understandable and relevant. The majority of them, 89%, knew little about Intellectual Property or Patents prior to the session. They also identified that they believed Patents would be of value to them in their professional careers. In order to increase further their understanding of Intellectual Property rights, 72% of them said that they would use the World Wide Web as an additional resource, with only 14% opting for another taught session. Other resources such as books, journals and contact with the Patent Office were also identified as being of value to them in developing their knowledge.

For many students this activity based approach in lectures was novel and their enthusiasm for it may have been based on the very fact that it was different. Observations of the students' participation in the sessions revealed a good interaction with the lecturers, and the materials. Interaction between the students was also noted and was focused around the group activities. The lecture format appeared not to hinder discussion, with groups naturally forming in clusters of three to four around their existing seating arrangements. Students engaged with the learning resources and applied them to their own area of study. For example discussions around the viability of patenting food developments such as 'new' tastes and flavours, were undertaken by the HND Catering group.

Further resources were made available to the students via the Micromodules, to enable them to research the topics to a greater depth. These included Web sites, suggested readings and details of appropriate organizations. No further research has been carried out on whether any of the students have followed up any of the suggested sources of further information.

The students were not exposed to the primary legal sources, which form the basis of traditional legal pedagogy. It could be argued that they are 'short changed' by this omission (see Ward and Slater, 1990). However, the intended outcome of using the Micromodules is that students engage in thinking of ways in which the law is relevant to them, rather than being fully conversant with all aspects of IPR. It is recognized that they will remain non-legal specialists, but they will be aware of how the law may impinge upon their professional life. While the 'rules' they have encountered will undoubtedly change, the recognition of the need to be aware of the influence of legal matters will be established. They will also be prepared to engage in a meaningful dialogue with a legal expert having explored a range of issues which place the law in the context of their subject disciplines.

39.8 Teachers as facilitators

The role of the teaching staff using the materials has been crucial to the effectiveness of the project. These staff who conducted the observed pilot sessions were all from different backgrounds and disciplines. They all had a variety of experience and knowledge relating to IPR. Only one member of staff was a Law Lecturer, although he did not normally specialize in this area of law. One session was conducted by the Technology Transfer Officer from the University. The other two lecturers were subject specialists in their respective fields of computer science and hospitality management, but with no legal training.

All staff felt vulnerable about using teaching material, which they had not produced themselves. This ranged from concerns about their own lack of knowledge of the subject area, to issues relating to the approach taken, which did not fit into to their normal pattern of delivery. Despite these reservations all the sessions observed were well executed with a high level of teacher to student interaction. This was due in some part to the fact that they already had a well-established relationship with the students, although one went in 'cold' to the group. What was more important, however, was the fact they were all experienced teachers or had well developed presentation skills. They were able to draw upon their facilitation techniques to engage the students.

Their strength lay in their ability to contextualize the application of Law to their specific subject disciplines. Numerous examples were given of product development for example a computer mouse, a marbling process for cakes, and a patent in parallel processing. These were all instantly recognizable by the students in their respective areas of study. This customizing of the material appeared to arise as part of the natural dialogue with the students.

The timing of the sessions was an issue for all of the facilitators. Although suggested times appeared as part of the teacher's notes, they proved difficult to follow. This may have been due in some part to their unfamiliarity with the materials and in part to the level of discussion that took place with the students. The consensus opinion was that a two-hour session was perhaps more appropriate to fully exploit the nature of the Micromodules.

All the lecturers faced questions that they were unable to answer, for example the length of time a Patent was granted for, and the cost of applying for a Patent. In some cases the lecturer was able to draw upon the knowledge of the group as a whole to provide answers. In others the lecturer suggested alternative sources, such as the Patent Office Web site. This confirmed to a certain extent their fears in relation to their depth of knowledge on IPR. However, all felt comfortable with the way the session had gone. Some examples of their comments were 'pleased with the level of interaction', ' students were volunteering answers', 'comments from the students were relevant and enquiring'.

39.9 Materials as learning resources

The works of Rowntree (1981) Race (1994) and Jenkins (1992) have influenced the structure and organization of the materials, particularly in respect of identifying appropriate learning activities. The main purpose of the Micromodules, has been to provide a framework for both lecturers and students to engage in a discussion and explore a range of ideas associated with IPR. Because the Micromodules were intended to be used by teaching staff who were not IPR specialists, a range of resources was therefore provided to support this. Facilitators' notes offer guidance on the nature, purpose and conduct of the session. These include overhead transparencies which provide a framework for the session. Handouts for students are supplied to underpin some of the key features of IPR and to detail further sources of information.

In terms of judging their effectiveness, comments were made about the organization and arrangement of the material. Because of the range of resources provided some difficulties were encountered in navigating around the numerous sections of the module. Omissions were also pointed out. Some staff felt the need to include elements of Contract and International Competition law. Requests were made to make available more examples from a wider range of disciplines. The validity of these comments lie in the fact that each person using the materials will want to customize them for themselves. The modules therefore should be viewed as 'fluid' products which will be continually amended and revised. It would be envisaged however that this would not represent a major change in the nature of the materials, rather an adjustment, which appropriately reflected the context of the discipline that they were being used in.

The approach that different staff have taken to customizing the materials highlights the need to have a clear understanding of the processes that are gone through when teachers use prepared materials. Work still needs to be done in terms of understanding how this takes place and which factors, help or hinder their ability to do this effectively. While not one of the key remits of the project it has informed the discussions with those staff who have used the materials. This would provide a further fruitful area of study, particularly in an educational environment which promotes the developments of resource based learning materials.

There was no consensus relating to the suitability of the materials for different levels of students. The potential was identified for using them not only on undergraduate programmes but also on postgraduate and professional courses. Issues such as the 'maturity' of the students, their established pattern of learning and their approach to study were cited as being factors in deciding on when and with whom to use the Micromodules.

Further work is still required to address the nature of the materials themselves, particularly in respect of their format , where sourcing the design and layout to a professional design organization would improve their usability.

39.10 Conclusions

In designing and developing the materials, it has emerged that interdisciplinary dialogue is at the heart of the Micromodule project work. As part of this process there has been a need to respond to continuing changes in the culture of Higher Education, which places students at the centre of their own learning. The format of the Micromodules thus has its place alongside other resource based learning approaches such as workbooks, computer assisted learning packages, course readers, and video resources. The modules however try to provide a focus for both students and teachers to engage in a discussion.

In the hands of teachers who have good facilitation skills, the study has shown that they can successfully engage students in exploring issues associated with IPR, despite the fact that they are not IPR specialists. Whether there will be a general acceptance of this approach will depend on how far the climate in Higher Education has moved towards the reality of student-centred learning and the willingness of staff to customize material which they have not prepared themselves. Feedback from this work suggests that the Micromodule format could be successfully adapted for use where students from one discipline need to be aware of aspects of another. There is no copyright in the idea behind the Micromodules!

Notes

1. Linda Byles is a Senior Lecturer and Learner Support Tutor.

2. Ruth Soetendorp is Head of Law and Director of the Patent Office project.

39.11 References

Carter, K and Unkerlesbay, R. (1989) Cases in teaching and law, *J. Curriculum Studies* **21**(6): 527—36

Committee on the Future of the Legal Profession (1988) *A Time for Change* (the *Marre Report*). London: General Council of the Bar and the Law Society.

Cox , R. (1992) Theory and professional life, *Media and Technology for Human Development* **4**(4): 217—32.

Gold, N. (1989) Learning lawyers' skills: research development and evaluation — the future prospectus. In N. Gold , K, Mackie and W. Twining (eds), *Learning Lawyers' Skills* (pp. 317—25), Butterworths.

Gibbs, G., Habeshaw, S. and Habeshaw, T. (1989) *53 Interesting Things to Do in Your Lectures*. Bristol: TES.

Gow, L. and Kember, D. (1993) Conceptions of teaching and their relationship to student learning, *British Journal of Educational Psychology* **63**: 20—33.

Harris, S. (1992) Reaching out in legal education: will EALP be there?, *English for specific purposes* **11**: 19—32.

Jenkins, A. (1992) Encouraging active learning in structured lectures . In G. Gibbs (ed.), *Improving the Quality of Student Learning*. Oxford Centre for Staff Development.

Jones, P. (1989) A skills based approach to professional legal education, *Law Teacher* **23**: 173—91.

Lord Chancellor's Advisory Committee on Legal Education and Conduct (1996) *First Report on Legal Education and Training*. Lord Chancellor's Office.

Ramsden, P. and Entwistle (1981) Effects of academic departments on students' approaches to studying, *British Journal of Educational Psychology* **51**: 368—83.

Rowntree, D. (1981) *Developing Courses for Students*. McGraw Hill.

Race, P. (1994) *The Open Learning Handbook*. Kogan Page.

Ridley, A. (1994) Legal skills for non law students: added value or irrelevant diversion?, *The Law Teacher* **28**: 281—91.

Saunders, C. and Clarke, J. (1997) Negotiating academic genres in a multi- disciplinary context, *Journal of Further and Higher Education* **21** (3): 297—304.

Soetendorp, R. (1995) Patenting innovation, *New Academic* Summer, 10—11.

Soetendorp, R. (1996) Patent information in the academic context, *World Patent Information* **18**(4): 219—26.

Soetendorp, R. (1996) Unpublished report to the Patent Office.

Soetendorp, R. (1999) Law for non lawyers, *National Council for Legal Education Newsletter* **5**, Spring.

Tobias, S. and Birrer (1998) The science trained professional: a new breed for a new century, *Industry and Higher Education*, August, 213—16.

Tyler, L. (1995) Teaching and learning the law: law, humanity and society in seminars, *Journal of Further and Higher Education* **19**(1), Spring: 80—4.

Ward, J. and Slater, M. (1990) Law for professional accounting education, *The Law Teacher* **25**: 208—28.

Woodcock, A. (1989) Using legal case studies with BTEC students, *Journal of Further and Higher Education* **13**(2), Summer: 62—9.

Woodcock, A. (1988) Methods of law teaching on BTEC courses, *The Law Teacher* **22**: 14—27.

Zeldin, T. (1998) An intimate history of conversation — talking and working. BBC Radio 4 broadcast, March.

Zeldin, T. (1998) *Conversation*. Harvill.

40 The impact of discipline dependent pedagogies on the acquisition of generic IT skills: lessons for the improvement of student learning

Jane Core, Katherine Wiles and Petra Leimich
University of Abertay Dundee

40.1 Context: competency in the use of C and IT across the curriculum

The use of C and IT now pervades the communities within which we live and work. Evidence of the need to highlight skills and competence in the use of C and IT is increasingly widespread in educational, governmental and corporate thinking, i.e.

- from schools, colleges and universities concerned to prepare pupils and students to develop as active citizens;
- from employers concerned to develop into learning organizations in which individuals continuously develop new skills and knowledge, and
- from government concerned to maximize economic growth through training for enterprise and innovation.

In the HE context we are increasingly concerned to address the future skills needs of employers, and economic prosperity, by producing employable graduates whose capacity to learn throughout life has been enhanced. Recent government thinking on lifelong learning places great responsibility upon curriculum development to combine essential discipline knowledge and understanding with confidence and competence in the use of C and IT. Improvements in our understanding and research into information literacy, alongside the increasing use of C and IT across our lives leads us to conclude that C and IT skills are important.[1] They may be basic skills but we would suggest that students who fail to develop those skills would be less well equipped as lifelong learners than those encouraged to achieve agreed baseline level competence.

In higher education in particular the steer towards enhancing competence in the use of C and IT across the curriculum, and employing C and IT to promote learning has been positive. Various skills programmes and initiatives, e.g. elib training and awareness projects[2],and top sliced funding to support and develop technology mediated learning materials demonstrate the trend to develop individual and organizational C and IT capability. Alongside this the development of the infrastructure required to enable seamless access to learning through the use of C and IT is in evidence across communities of learning, e.g. National Grid for Learning,[3] New Library Network[4], JANET and Super JANET[5] and the Metropolitan Area Networks[6].

The effect of these initiatives has been that institutions must shift strategic thinking away from building infrastructure into developing skills and applications. Implementation of C and IT to support learning and teaching has possibly never been higher on the strategic agenda, a massive financial investment has been made and the return is now due, it might even be argued that it is overdue.

The University of Abertay Dundee made strategic infrastructure investments internally to match those provided through top sliced initiatives, thus offering the best possible IT desktop environment to students and staff, above all ensuring a *minimum* standard of provision to all. As the standard desktop became available and increasingly intuitive it was clear that investment was required to prioritize training and support.

40.2 From infrastructure to implementation: the IT baseline pilot 1996—98

Given the excellent infrastructure gradually moving into place and the university's commitment to maintaining it, it could not be left to chance to ensure that the implementation offered a return. Student and staff IT skills were seen to be important and the University collaborated with the relevant national initiatives wherever possible, seeking to internalize the learning from the many projects and pilots which have proliferated across the sector in recent years. Internal policy planning reflected national policy leading to growing concern for implementation of technology initiatives and a move away from preoccupation with bits, bytes and bandwidth. The development of an institutional Information Strategy provided the policy and steer and continuing investment required to begin the task of implementing C and IT to serve the vision of Abertay Dundee as a University of the 'digital age'. The funding of a new £8 million library and information centre was timely and provided students and staff with the opportunity to work in a new learning environment in which C and IT was fully integrated with everyday communications and operations. In fact the environment planned for the Library was latterly replicated across all core IT teaching provision and into staff offices by the time the building opened in February 1998.

40.2.1 1996/1997

Thinking about the IT skills framework for both students and staff was initiated in parallel with infrastructure developments in session 1996/97. Baseline IT skills were service taught by the School of Computing and librarians within Information Services had traditionally offered basic introductions to information literacy skills within that module. Staff involved across the delivery of the module were conscious that students were not well motivated to participate in the module and were concerned as to whether the skills being acquired were of any real use to students seeking to become more employable graduates. They were equally concerned that the C and IT being offered as a minimum standard across the University should be optimized to enhance learning and offer increased flexibility and choice to students. Perhaps most pressing of all was the fact that student performance across the module was poor. A questionnaire was sent to 110 students on module IT101, their feedback revealed that:

- while around 25% of the students felt that they were competent in their use of C and IT only 15% had the confidence to complete module assessments without attending practicals and having regular face to face support from tutors;

- students felt that prior knowledge and skill in the use of C and IT was not accounted for in the module, students expressed a desire to work at their own pace and to be able to gain credit for what they felt they could already do;
- the traditional lecture/lab mode of face to face delivery was not felt to be appropriate, students did not feel that they were encouraged to develop confidence and independence in their learning;
- the relationship between the subject students were studying and the need to acquire IT skills was not obvious, some students felt that skills were bolted on and studied in a vacuum, they saw no route to using their new found skills in the rest of their level one studies.[7]

The review team concluded that there was increasing dissatisfaction with the module and that the delivery model for these skills was flawed. An investigation of the module and its delivery was signalled using modest funding from the University's Centre for the Enhancement of Learning and Teaching and a different set of student focused learning materials were produced. The resulting pilot module aimed to achieve improvement in three areas:

1. testing of new teaching materials designed to offer students more flexibility in the pace of their learning;
2. link to discipline based work for assessment, to improve relevance;
3. 'fast track' assessment option to recognize that some students entered the module with varying degrees of prior knowledge and skill.

40.2.2 1997/1998

The pilot module ran successfully with three subject groups of students in semester one of the session. Feedback suggested improved satisfaction with the module, across all three groups. Where there were variations they seemed to indicate differing degrees of enthusiasm and support from the subject based staff with whom the team was working in order to embed assessment of C and IT skills into the various disciplines. Given that there was an overall improvement in student satisfaction and performance in the pilot module it was extended and used with the students studying IT101 in semester two.

Group A *High performance group* *Reporting high satisfaction*	**Group B** *Low performance group* *Reporting low satisfaction*
o Excellent partnership (full time staff)	o Liaison problems (part time staff)
o Administration good	o Administration poor
o High pass/submissions	o Low pass/submissions
o Good participation/attendance	o Poor participation/attendance
o Assessment generic and closely co-ordinated: fast tracks achieved independence and moved beyond programme basics	o Fast tracks lost way

Figure 40.1 Key characteristics of semester one pilot groups

One major area of concern remained when the group of students expressing the lowest satisfaction was juxtaposed with the group demonstrating high satisfaction levels. The evidence from the semester one pilot seemed to suggest that the success of the pilot connected closely with buy-in from the subject staff upon whom the team were dependent if they were to achieve their target of linking assessment into the students' other studies.

40.2.3 1998/1999

Given the University's continuing strategic commitment to exploiting its 'electronic campus' capability, the success of the pilot IT101 programme and the additional evidence to suggest that student success was closely linked to the style of staffing used in the delivery of the programme, an IT training team was established. The original rationale for the team was that it could provide the focus to develop the opportunities to:

- demonstrate innovative use of IT in learning;
- use new methods of delivery and support for learning, optimizing the facilities of the new library;
- test the flexibility within the modular scheme to place assessment of skills into the cognate area, the issue being to stimulate and motivate students to see the acquisition of IT as a skill essentially linked to their personal and professional development;
- offer marginally lower delivery costs accompanied by higher student satisfaction;
- offer added value for the University in terms of there being an accessible and relevant corpus of materials which could in due course be delivered flexibly to external clients seeking 'baseline' IT skills;
- provide added value for the University in terms of that same corpus of materials being capable of flexible delivery as generic staff development for University staff;
- present one possible model for the effective delivery, practice and acquisition of other generic skills and competencies across the curriculum.

Once the team was established these opportunities were investigated with varying degrees of success. The team employed specialists in C and IT, who were motivated towards skills teaching, and located within Information Services, independent of subject departments. The team, two trainers and their manager, was remitted to develop student and staff programmes of IT skills. The IT101 baseline module was made compulsory at level one and endorsed by Academic Standards Committee. Discipline specific teaching of IT skills was discouraged and eventually phased out for session 1999/2000.

Throughout session 1998/1999 the team continued to develop the programme for all level one students, seeking to continue the improvements achieved by the earlier pilots and to present a real-life case study from which they could further develop strategy for the support of the emerging 'electronic campus'.

40.3 The case study

Is a generic model capable of producing generic results across a variety of school-based disciplines? Or are there elements that must be changed in order to accommodate the differing pedagogies to be found within the disciplines? If these adjustments are required, can we honestly claim to offer a generic model for baseline IT skills? What elements of the content and delivery make the difference between a generic and discipline based model for such skills? These were the questions asked of the Training Team as they implemented the lessons learned from the pilot programme into the formalized IT101 module.

40.4 Content

The content of the module was not changed significantly from that of the second pilot programme. However, a change of the standard desktop and e-mail client meant that some cosmetic changes had to be made. Clearly, it would not have been beneficial at this stage, with a new team in place and a new delivery strategy to test, to invest time in the creation of new, untested, materials. It made more sense to further test a variation of the original materials on a whole year's intake to the generic skills module, and thus prove the value or otherwise of the pilot.

Built into this plan was the clear indication that the generic IT module should draw down upon the second level of computing skills provided by the School of Computing, thus expanding the range of skills taught the students. In this way, the baseline module could be extended to meet the growing intuitiveness of the IT skills of the average first-year student. Straw polls within the classroom have shown that it is now rare indeed for a school-leaver student to have had no experience of using computers, further that most have used applications other than the Internet and games that used to be the standard for many school leavers.

The content of the module would appear to have been driven by the desktop, and this is justifiable: a large investment in an Information Strategy which demanded a standard IT desktop for the University demands its return. The Schools were asked to decide what IT skills were relevant to them within the context of the aims of their subjects' teaching and learning. The response was apathetic. The conclusion that can be drawn from this is that the academics did not see the need to contextualize baseline IT skills within their disciplines. While this allowed Information Services and the IT Training Team to get on with the business of delivering the skills, a worrying alarm had been sounded: if IT skills are not contextualized, would students see the relevance of IT skills to their career choice? Further, while a baseline model will ably equip graduates to use tools that underpin their degree paths, it does not create IT literate graduates of the calibre sought by employers. Further, Information Services does not have the power that the Schools do to evaluate the skills required by discipline-specific graduates, nor the flexibility or the funding necessary to be able to deliver the full range of skills that might be required. A gap therefore appears between what the baseline can provide and the skills that the discipline should be promoting for its students.

40.5 Delivery

The delivery of the module has continued to be predominantly class-based with students participating in one 2-hour laboratory per week for 13 weeks. However, the need for flexibility in delivery of the module that proved so successful in the pilot module has been further re-enforced, and more innovations introduced.

Students are encouraged to take responsibility for their own pace of learning: using a combination of the course handbook and computer-based training materials, they undertake a process of guided learning. Students are given the choice of working exclusively in class or to increase the pace of their learning by continuing work outside of lab time. Students whose confidence with their IT skills is particularly high are encouraged to sign a fast-track contract, releasing them from attending all but agreed classes (usually five out of the 13). Fast-track students, though acting predominantly as independent learners, must appear at the agreed dates and submit assessments at agreed times, otherwise they are withdrawn from the fast-track programme.

The milestones set by the tutor, in discussion with the students themselves, give a framework to the flexible nature of the programme. These milestones are inevitably based upon the programme of continuous assessment. The students discuss and agree collectively the submission dates for assessments. This method of working provides the student with a sense of control while allowing the IT Trainers to closely monitor student progress and intervene where students are not coping with elements of the module.

In the future, it is planned that fast-track students will have the option to go on to some form of professionally recognized accreditation strand, such as the European Computer Driving License or Microsoft Office User Specialist, assuming that added-value accreditation can increase graduate employability.

40.6 Assessment

During the pilot programme, an assumption was made that relating generic skills to the specific subject area of the student produces better results and contributes to a more meaningful educational experience for the learner. However, in the case of IT101, subject specific assessment has not been adopted:

- due to academic apathy towards specifying points of integration
- due to student choice of the materials presented by the IT Training Team.

Apathy from the academic staff can be attributed to the acceptance of placing IT skills at the centre, and the reluctance therefore to spend time dedicated to their own discipline thinking about integration of IT skills. The preferences of students can possibly be attributed to a lack of confidence in their discipline-specific area, perhaps due to the novelty of the subject being taught. The clear pathway of skills attainment which is integral to the IT101 module can appeal to the students who are not naturally confident learners, and the module is flexible enough to satisfy many different learning styles. Thus the combination of generic skills/flexible delivery is a package more appealing to the student than his or her own subject-specific area. Students were actively encouraged to use materials from their own subject area for assessment, but preferred Training Team materials.

The baseline IT skills module was an early adopter of a formative assessment strategy, assessing the students early with an exercise designed to re-enforce their learning, thus demonstrating to them their competence level in a number of key skill areas (Appendix 40.2). The first assessment carries only 15 per cent of the overall mark weighting, and is designed so that most students can achieve the highest mark possible. The assessments are progressively weighted so that, as confidence levels improve, and IT skills are gained, more is required of the students to achieve the highest possible marks.

The success of this assessment strategy is demonstrated by significant increases in both pass rates and attendance at classes for the module, based on the figures of the previous year. Pass rates increased by 14 per cent, and attendance at classes increased by 30 per cent. While it may be true that the increase in pass rates can in part be ascribed to students arriving with a higher intuitive IT skill level, the increase in attendance would seem to indicate that students engage more readily with a flexibly delivered generic module than following a study path that is generic to all students.

40.7 Adoption

It was crucial to the whole strategy of implementing a baseline IT Skills Programme that adoption was high across the subject areas. This adoption was very much driven by Senior Management, who had been persuaded of the benefits of placing this generic skills programme at the centre. Information Services was able to demonstrate that both a staff development programme in IT skills and a wider access programme introducing IT skills could be developed at zero cost, by using the IT101 programme as the base for each of these initiatives.

Having convinced Senior management with economic arguments, it remained for Heads of School to be convinced with sound pedagogic arguments that they could, in effect, give away 10 per cent of their first-year contact time to a centrally based module. Heads of School needed little convincing of the efficacy of the IT skills requirement, and their disillusionment with the school-based method of teaching IT skills was such that they were happy to endorse another delivery method.

Further, the expectations of the academics that C and IT could now be used as part of their teaching and learning had been raised. IT literacy is now a requirement in many of the subject areas, and students are required to have certain skills in order to interact with course materials.

Students have demonstrably bought in to the centrally delivered skills module. The module has the best attendance and pass rates of any of the mass audience modules. Perhaps due to the coincidence of having a new library building that is equipped with a large number of PCs, students have come to regard Information Services as the 'home' of IT skills. This is very distinct from the School of Computing which is now, rightly, seen as the home of computer science.

Finally, centralization allows a core team of trainers to investigate and propose potential spin-offs from the IT101 module, such as the wider access programme for non-standard students; IT skills for direct entrants and postgraduate students; and participation in national initiatives such as the New Opportunities Fund. All of these programmes are part of the University's wider agenda and having a central team focused on skills training avoids the potential for duplication and the pitfalls of school-centric initiatives not being 'shared'. Added value is further increased by the Training Team being able to serve the twin agendas of online and lifelong learning while continuing to deliver the core business of an IT skills module.

40.8 Training team model

A training team is a departure from the accepted teaching methods of the traditional university. Training by its nature means embracing certain principles of inclusion, mentoring and reflective practice. Although these may form part of any teaching method, to set out with these aims is perhaps unusual in the HE setting. The Training Team set out with the ethos that learning and teaching should be as flexible as possible to reflect the broad range of skills and abilities to be found in the university classroom. Each trainer runs each learning event according to the framework of the course, but relying on classroom interaction to give direction to the learning. Thus a training session can be stopped and redirected at any time. Further, the entire skills course can be reviewed based on a remarkable level of class-based developmental feedback. The Team worked sufficiently closely together to incorporate this feedback on a daily basis into the course delivery, without necessarily changing the course materials.

A decision was made that buying off-the-shelf training packages would be more effective than devoting a large amount of development time to materials. Computer-based training is becoming more comprehensive and affordable, and, following an evaluation exercise, it was possible to find a package that suited the needs of IT101. However, the course does not (and could not) rely totally on training packages, and a course handbook has been developed in paper, online and interactive formats to provide a context in which the CBT package can rest. The experience of the training team has been that CBT can become boring, repetitive and confusing if not combined with exercises that re-enforce the learning experience. The use of off-the-shelf packages has cut the developmental workload, but not eliminated it completely.

The students have reacted extremely positively to the training team model, and to the generic skills model. Results of the first year of the module have affirmed this, with the large improvement in pass rates mentioned above. The decision to use a generic model seems to have been justified, with no variant in fail rates across the four Schools of the University (Appendix 40.1). Further, the model seems to have a direct influence on student attendance, with the 30% increase in attendance correlating precisely with the pass grades achieved (Appendix 40.1). The flexible, generic model seems to appeal to all students, sufficiently motivating them to attend and achieve in the module.

So effective has the model been that the Scottish Higher Education Funding Council commented:

> The University has an impressively coherent approach to computing and information technology ... the University's information strategy recognises the potential of IT to enhance the learning experience, freeing up academic staff time for other aspects of teaching...[8]

40.9 How important was strategic integration?

The IT training team initiative is a centralized institutional attempt to improve student learning and staff awareness and to provide the first steps of the culture change necessary to optimize the beneficial effects of C and IT upon learning and teaching. It must be stressed that the solution worked well for the University of Abertay Dundee but there is no evidence to suggest that it would be the correct solution for other institutions where organizational cultures may demand an entirely different approach. That said, it is worth reflecting upon the way in which 'joined up thinking' on institutional strategy served to support and accelerate the improvement in student IT skills. Figure 40.2 illustrates the ways in which various strategic strands of infrastructure, planning and implementation were related.

One of the most important factors in the approach was that IT training priorities were clearly linked with university objectives to improve access and flexibility in skills acquisition. By using a compulsory module at level one to encourage student independence we firmly believe we were also providing a firm foundation of both confidence and competence to support independent learning. Further, by offering access to IT which we anticipate will increasingly figure in learning from campus based education to CPD programmes, we believe we will prepare our graduates to emerge confidently as lifelong learners. Staff were not absent from our thinking and the development of student IT skills was also reflected in the development of the staff development programme in IT.

The content of the programme was planned with a full understanding of IT desktop provision. The skills acquired by students were able to be practised immediately and seamlessly using the common desktop standards applied across the campus, hence every attempt was made to ensure that technology itself did not become an obstacle to learning. The requirements of the programme subjected our minimum standards to rigorous scrutiny under pressure and inevitably influenced the later iterations of the desktop standard set ups and software applications.

The IT training team was established initially for three years, but within a year found its place within the permanent establishment of staff in Information Services. This is important when considering the history usually associated with pilots and short term initiatives: if we are genuinely concerned to help change the culture of institutions we must steer such special projects to deliver the changes sought and then build and develop beyond that.

Senior management support and attention to training and development are now widely accepted as being success factors in culture change initiatives. The building of this team and the way they operate underpins thinking that the shifting paradigm of teaching, learning and support is enhanced by the effective use of C and IT.

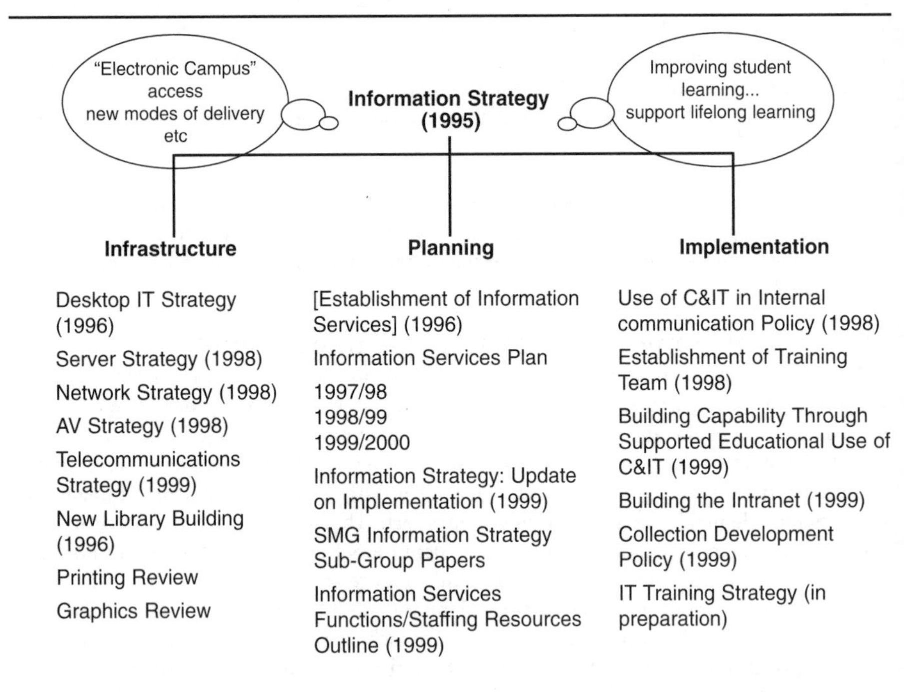

Figure 40.2 Ways in which various strategic strands of infrastructure, planning and implementation were related at the University of Abertay Dundee

40.10 Discipline based model versus generic model in delivery of IT skills

A number of issues arose for us in developing our pilot programme and in considering the relative merits of discipline specific and generic links. While we know that the generic model worked for our students at level one teaching across subjects that might be loosely categorized as multi-disciplinary, we have no evidence to suggest it would work with purer discipline bases. Could it be that the relevance of the discipline itself is less transparent to students engaged in more vocational or multidisciplinary subjects? Thus, if the chosen 'discipline' is less well defined for the level one student perhaps they have less of a conceptual framework or loyalty to their subject and so are more able to work in a generic manner, transferring skills at a later stage when the conceptual map of the discipline is more developed. We are conscious of the need to follow students through later stages of their programmes to try to determine this.

Linked to the point above we have no real feel at level one for how or whether skills are transferred at level two. We do see demand for these skills at level three when project work becomes particularly significant in assessment. This knowledge is gathered through our enquiries, helpdesks and tutor referrals. We are considering the possibility that students may wish to return to refine their IT skills at level 3. The existence of independent learning materials and the availability of support and advice from our dedicated training team may well be the resource required to address this, although we remain concerned of the need for academics to 'buy in' to the need for skills and reward good practice in assessments.

Generic IT skills are agreed to be important to students and it is generally held that the demonstration of good transferable skills such as IT will have a bearing on student progression to the world of work. However, there are other areas of student study that require quite a different set of IT skills, e.g. engineers often require to use specialized CAD/CAM, social scientist need to be competent in the use of quantitative analysis packages. We are interested now in establishing the extent to which competence with baseline IT skills correlates with confidence and competence with more specialized IT applications which could be considered to be more discipline specific.

As indicated earlier we believe it is difficult to suggest categorically that one model might be more effective than another until particular institutional circumstances as regards teaching methods are taken into account. In the case at the University of Abertay Dundee we believe the generic model offered significant advantages and student performance and satisfaction to date bears this out.

Notes

1. C.S. Bruce (1999) Workplace experiences of information literacy, *International Journal of Information Management* **19**: 33—7.
2. http://www.ukoln.ac.uk/services/elib/projects/
3. http://www.ngfl.gov.uk
4. http://www.lic.gov.uk/publications/pressreleases/bnlnpr.html
5. http://www.ja.net/
6. http://www.ja.net/janet-sites/MANs/

7. Thanks accorded to Claire MacEachen School of Computing, University of Abertay Dundee for her reflections on the results of the CELT funded project, summarized from previous reports.

8. SHEFC: Response to UAD submission under SHEFC Circular 7/98 *Strategic Planning in Scottish Higher Education Institutions 1998*, October 1998.

Appendix 40.1 Analysis of student performance data

There were a total of 592 students, 519 of whom passed the module. The data available for each student comprises module grade, percentage attendance, course, and school. Performance on the module was strongly correlated with attendance, indicating that the higher the attendance, the better the grade ($r = -0.596$, $n = 592$, $p < 0.05$; $r < 0$ because good grades are low figures). Figure 40.A1 confirms this.

A graph showing average grade against attendance (Figure 40.A2) also confirms that grades improve with attendance (mean grade = 16.2868 - 0.226106 attendance + 0.00109 attendance^2; $r^2 = 92.9\%$).

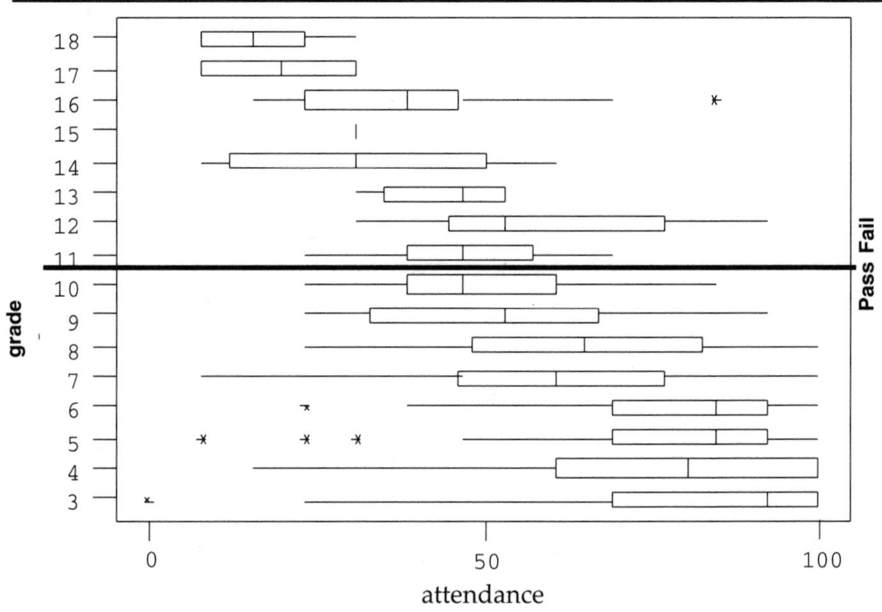

Figure 40.A1 **Boxplot showing performance correlated with attendance**

It should be noted that pass rates (i.e. the percentage of students who passed) vary across schools, with the School of Computing showing fewer fails than the other schools. However, this difference in pass rates can be explained entirely by the differences in attendance — in a binary logistic regression of pass rate against attendance and school, only attendance was significant.

Finally, it should be noted that among the students who passed, there is no association between the grade achieved and school membership (chi-squared = 26.293, df = 18, $p > 0.05$. Grades 9 and 10 combined to avoid low expected frequencies).

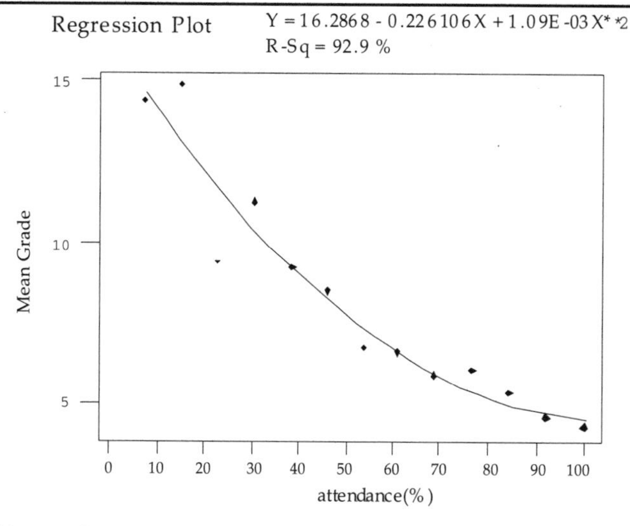

Figure 40.A2 **Average grade against attendance**

Appendix 40.2

Reference	IT101A
Title	Information Technology 1
Level	1
Prerequisites	none
Co-requisites	none
Aims	To enable students to acquire and demonstrate competence in basic IT and information skills
Objectives	On successful completion of this module a student will have demonstrated competence in:

1. the use of an operating environment to
   (a) invoke application programs
   (b) design and set up an efficient file storage structure
2. the appropriate handling of storage media to avoid the corruption of files.
3. the use of an email client to

(a) send and receive messages
(b) send and read attached documents

4. the use of a word-processor to produce well-formatted and organised documents, using features such as

(a) appropriate page and line formats
(b) appropriate typefaces
(c) appropriate layout
(d) appropriate advanced features (Headers & Footers)

5. the use of a spreadsheet to produce numeric models and graphical representations of data, using features such as

(a) appropriate cell contents and types
(b) appropriate cell properties and layout
(c) appropriate functions and formulae
(d) consolidation of data from multiple worksheets
(e) graphical representations of selected data sets

6. effective skills in the location, handling, organization and storage of information using:

(a) online resources on the world wide web
(b) the library catalogue

Teaching & learning workload (indicative)	Lecture	0 hours
	Tutorial/seminar	0 hours
	Laboratory	26 hours (normal)
	Study time	92 hours (normal)

Assessment format: Students will be required to compile a portfolio of evidence demonstrating their competence in basic IT and information skills.

Final grade weighting: 100% coursework

Supportive reading: Carter and Sinclair (1997) Students' Guide to Information Technology. Butterworth-Heinemann.

Stern and Stern (1995) Computing in the Information Age, 2nd edn. Wiley.

Specialized resources: 'Core' IT laboratory

Subject group: Information Technology

41 Instructional consultation among disciplines

Michael A. Kerwin

Kentucky Community and Technical College System

41.1 Introduction

I coordinate an instructional consultation programme for a statewide system of community and technical colleges. Although the programme was implemented in the University of Kentucky Community College System in 1977, no data about the programme were collected until 1983. At that time, when I was hired to coordinate the programme, the names of those who served as instructional consultants were recorded and efforts to evaluate the programme's efficacy were initiated.

Being the coordinator of a statewide programme has enabled me to collect large quantities of data about instructional consultation. Between 1983 and 1999, for example, over 700 semester-long consultations occurred in the Community College System. Records identify who these consultants are and the teaching area of the person with whom they consult. Evaluation records also identify the changes that each faculty tried to make during the consultation programme and his or her ratings of the usefulness of each attempted change.

I am using this data in this study to address four questions:

1. What disciplines do full-time faculty who serve as instructional consultants represent?
2. Do specific disciplinary pairings, such as instructional consultants who teach literature and composition consulting with faculty who teach biology, occur more frequently than other pairings?
3. What types of changes do faculty try to make during instructional consultation?
4. Do specific types of attempted changes occur more frequently in specific discipline areas?

These questions stem from broader theoretical issues of behavioural change in organizations. The importance and the influence of obtaining feedback about one's behaviour in the change process, for example, are well documented (Morrison and Bies, 1991). To my knowledge, however, the effect of disciplinary characteristics on feedback-seeking has not been studied. Using symbolic interaction theory, for example, which highlights the importance of gaining the views of others to gain predictability and control, we would expect faculty to choose a consultant from a similar discipline.

Likewise, disciplinary differences and instructional effectiveness have been studied (Murray and Renaud, 1995). Murray and Renaud state, for example, that arts and humanities faculty are more likely to exhibit behaviours that foster student participation while social science, mathematics, and natural science faculty are more likely to exhibit behaviours that facilitate structure in organization of the subject matter (1995, 36). Murray and Renaud also conclude that instructional consultants need not focus on helping faculty to learn different behaviours in different disciplines; instead they need to increase the frequency of the teaching behaviours that are positively correlated with student ratings but tend, for whatever reason, to occur relatively infrequently in that discipline (1995, 38—9). Murray and Renaud do not examine, however, if this actually occurs in instructional consultation.

This study, therefore, is designed to enable us to know more about the effect of disciplinary orientation on feedback-seeking and feedback-taking in the context of instructional consultation in higher education. The results should help us to design more effective consultation programmes and prepare consultants to be more effective givers of feedback.

Before addressing the first of the four questions, however, I will identify the key characteristics of the Teaching Consultation Program. These characteristics are important because they define the context within which the consultations occurred.

41.2 Key characteristics of the Teaching Consultation Program

When I began coordinating this programme, I thought that all instructional consultation programmes were just like it. As you know, they are not. Although this programme is not unique among instructional consultation programmes, it is distinguished by eight key characteristics. I shall highlight these characteristics here. The programme is described in more complete detail in 'The Teaching Improvement Process', which was published in *The Journal of Staff, Program, & Organizational Development*.

1. The programme begins at the beginning of the semester and ends 16 weeks later at the end of the semester.
2. It is highly structured: consultants follow a defined set of steps and procedures, which were developed initially at The University of Massachusetts at Amherst. As a part of this structure, consultants participate in a workshop during the sixth week of the semester. In this workshop, they discuss the faculty with whom they are consulting with other consultants. The workshop enables all consultants, therefore, to receive feedback from consultants from different disciplines.
3. It is designed to help faculty analyse and change teaching behaviours.
4. Data collected during the programme are confidential.
5. Participation in the programme is voluntary.
6. The programme operates independently of performance review.
7. Data about teaching are collected from several sources, including videotapes, classroom observation, and student questionnaires.
8. Perhaps the most significant characteristic is that the instructional consultants are full-time faculty who are reassigned from one of their three-credit classes to conduct the programme at their college. Full-time faculty, therefore, volunteer to exchange a teaching assignment for a consulting assignment.

This leads to the first question of the study.

41.3 What disciplines do full-time faculty who serve as instructional consultants represent?

As stated earlier, instructional consultants are full-time faculty who are reassigned from one three-credit class to conduct the Teaching Consultation Program at their college. These faculty volunteer to be instructional consultants. To become consultants however, they must be nominated by the president of their college and attend a two-day preparatory workshop. Most of the faculty who are nominated are tenured veterans who are recognized at their colleges as being outstanding teachers. The programme coordinator works with the college presidents to make sure that at least two consultants are available at each of the campuses in the System.

Between 1983 and 1999, 90 faculty served as instructional consultants in the University of Kentucky Community College System; 58 (65 per cent) were women; 32 (36 per cent) were men; 22 (22 per cent) represented technical programmes (accounting, business, computer information systems, clinical laboratory technician, education, human services, nursing, and office administration); 70 (78 per cent) represented general education programmes, such as art, composition and literature, and mathematics; 45 (50 per cent) of the consultants represented the teaching areas of literature and composition, communications, and biology. The prototypical consultant, therefore, is a woman who teaches literature and composition, communications, or biology.

41.4 Do specific disciplinary pairings, such as instructional consultants who teach literature and composition consulting with faculty who teach biology, occur more frequently than other pairings?

As stated earlier, faculty volunteer to participate in the teaching consultation programme. Furthermore, faculty who serve as instructional consultants tend to come from certain discipline areas. To complicate matters even more, only one or two teaching consultants may be available to faculty at a given college during a given semester. The consultants market the programme and do not intend to recruit faculty from certain disciplines. Nevertheless, if research considers a period of 16 years and a range of 14 colleges, disciplinary patterns may emerge.

As a part of the Teaching Consultation Program, each consultant submitted a form at the beginning of the semester showing the number and teaching areas of the faculty with whom he or she was working. The programme coordinator used this data to schedule the sessions at the teaching consultation workshop that would be held during the sixth week of the semester. Workshop agendas showed the names of the instructional consultants and the teaching area of each faculty member with whom they were consulting.

Twenty-three workshop agendas, beginning with the 1985 spring semester and ending with the 1999 spring semester, were examined in this part of the study; 537 pairings were listed. Instructional consultants taught in 24 teaching areas: accounting, art, biology, business, computer information systems, clinical laboratory technician, communications, counselling, developmental education, economics, education, literature and composition, foreign language, health, history, human services, mathematics, nursing, office administration, physics, political science, psychology, sociology, philosophy, and religion.

As one would expect from the previous analysis of the consultant records, the number of citations for consultants who taught biology, communications, and literature and composition was higher than any of the other areas (261). In fact, they constituted 49 per cent of the total. The number of citations for consultants who taught mathematics, nursing, and psychology was also significant (130). Consultants who taught in these six areas constituted 73 per cent of the total listed.

Faculty represented 54 teaching areas. For analysis purposes, these areas were grouped into 15 categories: applied sciences, applied social sciences, business, communications, education, literature and composition, fine arts, history, human environmental science, mathematics, natural and physical sciences, nursing and health professions, religion and philosophy, social sciences, and study skills. Seven areas contained significantly higher numbers than the others: nursing (99), literature and composition (82), biology (62), natural and physical sciences (58), mathematics (55), social sciences (49), and accounting (48). These seven areas constituted 84 per cent of the total.

Consultant Areas	Faculty Areas						
	Applied Science	Business	Composition and Literature	Math	Natural Science	Nursing	Social Science
Biology (44, 8.2%)	4 (9.1%)	8 (4.5%)	1 (2.3%)	5 (11.4%)	9 (20.5%)	14 (31.8%)	3 (6.8%)
Composition and Literature (153,28.4%)	12 (6.3%)	5 (7.8%)	19 (29.7%)	13 (8.5%)	12 (7.8%)	20 (13.1%)	15 (9.8%)
Communications (64, 11.9%)	4 (6.3%)	5 (7.8%)	19 (29.7%)	7 (10.9%)	4 (6.3%)	13 (20.3%)	4 (6.3%)
Mathematics (43, 8.0%)	7 (16.3%)	5 (11.6%)	1 (2.3%)	8 (18.6%)	9 (20.9%)	8 (18.6%)	2 (4.7%)
Nursing (43, 8.0%)	2 (4.7%)	2 (4.7%)	6 (14.0%)	5 (11.6%)	3 (7.0%)	21 (48.8%)	1 (2.3%)
Psychology (44, 8.2%)	8 (18.2%)	8 (18.2%)	5 (11.4%)	4 (9.1%)	2 (4.5%)	4 (9.1%)	8 (18.2%)

Table 41.1 Pairing tendencies

The first step in the analysis of disciplinary pairings was to identify the frequency of each consultant-faculty pairing. The next step was to highlight the most frequent of these pairings. The results of this analysis for the major pairing groups are shown in Table 41.1.

As shown in Table 41.1, consultants who taught biology tended to consult with faculty who taught applied science, mathematics, natural and physical sciences, and nursing (64 per cent of the total). Consultants who taught literature and composition tended to consult with faculty who taught literature and composition, nursing, and social science (53 per cent of the total). Consultants who taught communications tended to consult with faculty who taught literature and composition, mathematics, and nursing (61 per cent of the total). Faculty who taught mathematics tended to consult with faculty who taught applied science, mathematics, natural and physical science, and nursing (74 per cent of the total). Faculty who taught nursing tended to consult with faculty who taught composition and literature, mathematics, and nursing (74 per cent of the total). In fact, nursing consultant-faculty pairings occur more frequently than any other (21). Faculty who taught psychology tended to consult with faculty who taught applied science, business, and social science (55 per cent of the total).

This analysis indicates that consultants who teach biology or mathematics pair with faculty who teach applied science, mathematics, natural science and nursing more frequently than with faculty in other disciplines. The discipline areas of both instructional consultants and faculty are somewhat similar. Consultants who teach literature and composition, on the other hand, pair less frequently with faculty who teach mathematics, applied science, or natural science. Except for nursing, this pairing pattern contrasts with that of those consultants who teach biology or mathematics. Consultants who teach communications or nursing pair more frequently with faculty who teach literature and composition, mathematics, or nursing. Consultants who teach psychology tend to consult more frequently with faculty in discipline areas somewhat similar to their own.

The pairing patterns described above show a tendency for faculty, who teach in similar discipline areas to choose to work together. Faculty who teach nursing are the exception. Although they prefer to work with a consultant who is also a nurse, they are willing to work with instructional consultants who teach in five of the six major areas; they do not tend, however, to pair with consultants who teach psychology.

41.5 What types of changes do faculty try to make during instructional consultation?

Upon completion of the programme, each faculty member is asked to complete a programme evaluation form and send it to the programme coordinator. This form asks the faculty member to identify the changes that he or she has attempted to make during the programme and to rate the usefulness of each of the attempted changes. The programme coordinator summarizes this data in annual reports. Unfortunately, most of the primary records, which link the faculty member to a discipline area, are lost or destroyed. Twenty-one were recovered and were used for this part of the study. The earliest was from the 1991 spring semester; the latest from the 1999 Fall semester.

Data from the evaluation forms showed that the faculty tried to make 88 changes during instructional consultation. These changes were classified into five groups: (1) teacher-centred organizational and presentation techniques; (2) small-group techniques to engage students in learning; (3) techniques to obtain student feedback on learning; (4) questioning, blackboard work, or problem-solving as a strategy to engage students; and (5) assignments

Faculty discipline area	Attempted changes					
	Organization & presentation	Small group	Feedback techniques	Problem-solving	Out-of-class assignment	TOTAL
Communication (9, 43%)	16 (39%)	11 (27%)	3 (7%)	7 (17%)	4 (10%)	41
Business (3, 14%)	8 (67%)	0	0	3 (25%)	1 (8%)	12
Applied Science (4,19%)	7 (54%)	3 (23%)	1 (8%)	2 (15%)	1 (8%)	13
Literature and Composition (1,5%)	2 (100%)	0	0	0	0	2
Education (3, 14%)	4 (25%)	3 (19%)	2 (13%)	7 (44%)	0	16
Applied Social Science (1, 5%)	3 (100%)	0	0	0	0	3
TOTAL	40	17	6	19	6	88

Table 41.2 Frequency of attempted changes by discipline areas

and outside-of-class activities to facilitate student learning. The frequency of each of these categories is shown in the bottom row of Table 41.2.

As shown in Table 41.2, the greatest number of the attempted changes (40) is in the area of organizational and presentation techniques (45%). The next greatest number of attempted changes (19) is in the use of questioning, blackboard work, and problem-solving (22%). Small-group techniques follow (17, 19%). Implementation of feedback techniques and out-of-class assignments show the smallest number of attempts (6, 7%; 6. 7%).

The proportion of these changes corresponds roughly to the changes identified in an earlier study of the programme's effectiveness (Rozeman and Kerwin, 1991). In that study, students perceived that teachers changed organization and presentation behaviours most frequently. Student involvement behaviours, such as using small-group techniques and problem-solving behaviours, were changed to a lesser extent.

41.6 Do specific types of attempted changes occur more frequently in specific discipline areas?

The 21 faculty in this study represent six discipline areas: communication (9, 43%), business (3,14%), applied science (4,19%), literature and composition (1, 5%), education (3, 14%), and applied social science (1, 5%). Each faculty member attempts two to six changes; the median is four.

Although the sample size in this study is too small to draw conclusions about differences in attempted changes according to disciplines, the data suggests several differences. First, communication faculty, attempt a significantly higher number of changes using small-group techniques and a somewhat lower number of changes in organization and presentation techniques than do faculty in other discipline areas. Secondly, education faculty attempt a significantly higher number of changes using problem-solving techniques and a lower number of changes in organizational and presentation techniques than do faculty in other disciplines. Thirdly, business, literature and composition, and applied social science faculty attempt a higher number of changes in organizational and presentation techniques than do faculty in other discipline areas.

The attempted changes of communication and education faculty conform to the changes that Murray and Renaud expect from social science faculty. They expected these faculty to exhibit organization and presentation behaviours; consultants would help them to develop other behaviours, such as those that foster student participation. Likewise, the attempted changes of literature and composition faculty are what Murray and Renaud would expect. They tend to exhibit behaviours that foster student participation; consultants would help them to develop other behaviours, such as organization and presentation skills.

On the other hand, the attempted changes of the business and applied social science faculty do not fit Murray and Renaud's expectations. As social science faculty, they would be expected by Murray and Renaud to possess organizational and presentation skills, yet the focus of their changes during consultation are on this area.

This data suggests that future research of this type should study additional or more specific faculty disciplines than arts and humanities, social sciences, mathematics, and natural sciences. Of course, a larger number of faculty needs to be included in the study and more powerful statistical techniques utilized in the analysis. In addition, variables such as faculty rank, faculty age, and type of institution need to be considered. Finally, the question of the effect of the consultant's discipline on the attempted changes made by the faculty member needs to be considered.

41.7 Conclusions

In conclusion, I feel comfortable in stating that most faculty tend to seek colleague-consultants from a similar discipline when they want feedback on their teaching behaviour. Instructional consultation programmes, therefore, should involve faculty consultants from a variety of disciplines. In programmes such as the Teaching Consultation Program, communications, literature and composition, and biology faculty tend to become consultants. Efforts to attract additional consultants from other discipline areas may increase participation from faculty in other disciplines.

In addition, research should continue to study the extent to which discipline affects the type of change attempted during instructional consultation. Changes in organization and presentation behaviour are attempted most frequently in the Teaching Consultation Program. Perhaps this type of change is easier to make and yields a more positive result than other types of change do. Perhaps these changes are more common when faculty are new to teaching. Preliminary evidence indicates that disciplines with an applied orientation, such as business or applied social science, may attempt changes that differ from those in humanities, social sciences, mathematics, or natural science.

Certainly, consultants who know about disciplinary differences in teaching behaviour are more prepared to consult with faculty from different disciplines. In the Teaching Consultation Program, regular workshops in which consultants discuss the faculty with whom they are consulting with other consultants from different disciplines serves to facilitate the awareness of disciplinary differences. This knowledge and its application may, in fact, decrease the need for having consultants from a variety of disciplines available at a college.

I plan to continue my explorations in this area and look forward to your comments.

41.8 References

Kerwin, M.A. (1985) The teaching improvement process, *The Journal of Staff, Program. & Organizational Development* **3**(1): 10—11.

Morrison, E.W. and Bies, R.J. (1991) Impression management in the feedback-seeking process: a literature review and research agenda, *Academy of Management Review* **16**(3): 522—41.

Murray, H.G. and Renaud, R.D. (1995) Disciplinary differences in teaching and learning, ed. N. Hativa and M. Marencovich, *New Directions for Teaching and Learning* **64** (winter): 31—9.

Rozeman, J.E. and Kerwin, M.A. (1991) Evaluating the effectiveness of a teaching consultation program on changing student ratings of teaching behaviors, *Journal of Staff. Program & Organizational Development* **9**(4): 223—30.

42 Learning by developing interactive multimedia resources

Monica McLean and Tim Denning

Department of Education, Keele University, Keele, Staffordshire

42.1 Introduction

This chapter considers the following two questions:

- When disciplines depart from traditional patterns of teaching, learning and assessment what are the consequences for student learning?
- Can distinctive pedagogies be successfully transferred between disciplines?

It does this by describing the intentions and processes of a module called 'New Learning and its Technologies' which is an option for second-year undergraduates undertaking an Educational Studies degree course;[1] by exploring theoretically why the module should improve learning; and by examining the empirical evidence of whether or not it has improved learning. We do not come to firm conclusions but intend, rather, to contribute to debate about the potential of C&IT (Communication and Information Technology) to improve student learning.

42.2 Intentions and processes of the 'New learning and its Technologies' module

The students who opt for this module have previously taken a compulsory first-year module which develops a range C&IT skills including designing web pages in teams. The module is designed to develop the skills and theoretical knowledge and understanding necessary to produce interactive multimedia (IMM) resources for educational purposes. The two main aims of the module are: to introduce students to rationale for the use, design and creation of interactive multimedia resources intended for use in higher education; and to assist students to create an IMM resource that exemplifies good practice in the design and evaluation of such materials. The objectives for students are expressed as areas of exploration. These are: the nature of IMM and the facilities it offers; pedagogic theory informing the design of IMM; processes of IMM design; and evaluation of IMM learning resources. Throughout the module the students work in teams of three or four. The assessment comprises a team presentation (10%) and the content and software for an IMM learning resource with supporting documentation (90%). This is subdivided into structure and design (team assessment 30%); resource content (individual assessment 30%); and supporting documentation (individual assessment 30%).

The teams are required to collaborate to create an IMM resource to teach a group of undergraduate students like themselves about the design and pedagogic principles which should underpin the construction of an interactive multimedia resource. They are asked to envisage a users who, like themselves at the beginning of the module, are unfamiliar with this subject matter. The supporting documentation is in the form of a portfolio which the students compile throughout the module.

Throughout the module an emphasis is put on the critical evaluation of a range of IMM resources which are to be found on the Internet. The students are encouraged to develop judgement about whether or not IMM resources are well-designed and well-informed. This is done by eliciting criteria from the students themselves, asking them what criteria they have applied to come to a judgement about whether a resource is poor or excellent. We aim to help them build up a repertoire of questions with which to interrogate the quality of IMM resources which refer to both design and content: for example, is it visually appealing? is the structure coherent and easy to navigate? is it biased? are sources used? We believe that this kind of critical judgement is imperative to their capacity to develop their own good quality resources.

42.3 Non-traditional pedagogic features which may enhance learning

The previous outline brings us to the first question: What happens when non-traditional forms of pedagogy are left behind? First, we need to examine in what sense the module is non-traditional. In many respects it may be characterized as 'traditional': knowledge resides in tutors' lectures (albeit short and infrequent) to which the students listen and in books and articles which the students read and make notes on. Nor can the emphasis on critical evaluation be considered non-traditional even if it is not always part of university pedagogic practice. We believe that the non-traditional features are: the construction of student as tutor/designer; intensified manipulation of subject matter; and working in teams. It is the assessment task which departs from traditional pedagogies in incorporating these features.

42.3.1 Student as tutor/designer

The students are required to place themselves in the role of tutor to an audience of peers: this is a simulation, the resource will not, in fact, be used to teach. Though there is little literature about students as designers of C&IT materials (Erickson, 1997; Fitzgerald *at al.*, 1997) — indicating how new is the practice — there are two sets of literature that can be brought to bear on thinking about this non-traditional feature. First, there is considerable published work on the notion of 'computer as teacher'. This work discusses how theories of learning can be used to inform the design of C&IT resources for educational purposes and also examines the effects of these resources on student learning. Cases refer to both higher education (for example, Bostock, 1998; Elliott *et al.*, 1997; Laurillard, 1993; Marshall, 1999) and schools (for example, Boyd-Barrett, 1991; Shea and Self, 1983; and the Apple Classrooms of Tomorrow [ACOT] project[2]). Most of this literature implies that IMM design for educational purposes requires a high degree of technical expertise and knowledge. Arguably the same could be said of asking students to design paper-based materials for peers but this has been done with reports of success (Leftwich,1987). Secondly, there is a literature about students as peer tutors. However, this is not conclusive about the impact of the practice on learning (Topping, 1997). Nevertheless, the evidence that simulation of 'real-life' problems is motivating (Hartley, 1998) and that tutor enthusiasm for innovation is critical to success[3] led us to expect positive results.

42.3.2 Intensified manipulation of subject matter

In order to complete the assessment task, students must manipulate — deconstruct and construct — subject matter so that knowledge and understanding is demonstrated in a form which is entirely different from the traditional essay. The central point here is that, to be successful, students need to conceptualize the task as a matter of non-linear structure. Chalet (1991) suggests that in traditional educational environments students tend to cope with unfamiliar material by interpreting tasks in terms of their superficial characteristics. This phenomenon could explain some students' tendency to write essays consisting of items of information which are not constructed coherently around main themes and arguments. We believe that when designing a IMM learning resource, such incoherence becomes more apparent to the learner/designer who *must* organize content with themes and links. Unlike an essay, it is not possible to begin at the computer without a plan: in order to make a resource that makes any sense, and is interactive rather than linear, the designers must first manipulate the content into structures and sequences which make sense to them.

42.3.3 Working in teams

The assessment task is undertaken in groups, which although increasingly prevalent, cannot yet be referred to as 'traditional'.

42.4 Theoretical bases for expecting improved learning

Our belief that the construction of an IMM learning resource with peers for peers will enhance learning is guided by a consideration of a range of theoretical perspectives about student learning. Increasingly, those searching for educational principles to inform IMM educational design and development have been attracted by constructivist theories (Bostock, 1998; Duffy *et al.*, 1993; Knuth, 1993; Marra and Jonassen, 1993; Muire *et al.*, 1999). Constructivism emanates from a range of different theories[4] (Wild and Quinn, 1998), but the common idea is of learners constructing their own knowledge. From this perspective, the learner builds up knowledge by making interpretations of new ideas, facts and concepts with reference to previous knowledge and concepts, or cognitive structures. Constructivism is typically contrasted with behavioural or objectivist theories which, put simply, view knowledge as an external entity which can be passed from teacher to student. However Wild and Quinn (1998) point out that while the polarization represents a valid philosophical debate about the nature and purpose of knowledge, it does not aid thinking about instructional design. They propose working towards a model which draws on the elements of many theories and advocate Andersen *et al.*'s (1996) model that: 'Emphasises the role of active exploration on the part of the learner, as well as guidance through a process of mediated dialogue towards developing internals models' (Wild and Quinn, 1998, p. 78).

The purpose of locating the teaching of the 'New Learning and its Technologies' within a constructivist tradition is to argue that the non-traditional features outlined above will not *per se* improve learning. Whatever methods are used, attention to the whole learning context is essential. So, from this point of view, we construe learning in the 'New Learning and its Technologies' module as a process of negotiating meaning which involves interactions between the students (who have different previous knowledge and understanding, different interests, and preferred learning styles); the tutors (who provide instruction and technical and conceptual support); and other elements of the learning context (books, articles, the computer facilities and so on). At the heart of these interactions is the production of an IMM resource for teaching about the design and rationale of interactive multimedia. Throughout the module the students put into practice the concepts and techniques they are learning about.

Furthermore, the module is designed with reference to a set of inter-related principles. They are suggested by a range of theories: by constructivist theories (Bostock, 1998), by social and phenomenological psychology (Hartley, 1998); by course design features identified as encouraging 'deep' learning, whereby students search for meaning and develop intrinsic motivation (Biggs 1989, Gibbs 1992, Marton *et al.*, 1984); as well as by the model of learning as meaning negotiated between tutor, students and resources that we came to above. These principles concern autonomy, social situations, authenticity and reflection.

42.4.1 Responsibility and control

It has been demonstrated that self-regulation and the ability to monitor one's own learning is motivating (Ryan and Powelson, 1991; Ferrence and Vockell, 1994). To take this further, Biggs (1987) suggests that perhaps the most influential factor in encouraging a deep approach to learning is the degree to which the student is the 'locus of control'. The design of the multimedia resource imparts a great deal of responsibility to the students. At the same time, the tutor's role is critical. Through judiciously light guidelines we strive to create: '[...] contexts and tasks where students experience support for their autonomy, and where they feel connected to and supported by significant others[...]' (Ryan and Powelson, 1991, p. 51). We aim to provide enough tutor support or 'scaffolding' to present challenges 'just beyond [the students'] current level of functioning' (*ibid.*, p. 53) so that they both 'make developmental gains and derive a sense of confidence and self-esteem' (ibid.). So we regard student autonomy as a goal which we work towards by making judgements about what type and degree of support is necessary as progress is made.

42.4.2 Social situations

There is evidence that effective learning environments provide for a range of personal interactions including collaboration (Alessi and Trollip, 1991; Bostock, 1998; Jaques, 1984; Ryan and Powelson, 1991; Slavin 1991). This may be because discussion about learning is important. As Hartley (1998) puts it when knowledge creation is shared 'Learners interpret and elaborate on incoming information.' (p. 21). Interaction is integral to the module: students constantly interact with each other and the tutors as they work to produce their learning resource.

42.4.3 Authentic tasks

The theories we draw on suggest that learning tasks and assessment should, as far as possible, be experiential, that is anchored in real-world problems and contexts. We attempt to operationalize this principle in two ways. First, the task is couched in terms of a problem to be solved: how can this material be organized and interlinked to engage a group of peers in learning actively about interactive multimedia? Secondly, the teamwork is not artificial: an individual could not construct an IMM resource of any quality in the time. In general, our aim was to provide an environment which gave the students 'the opportunity to observe, engage in, and invent or discover expert strategies' (Collins *et al.*, 1987, p. 12). The students learn what it is to be a designer and producer of educational IMM materials.

42.4.4 Reflection and the construction of meaning

Although the module involves a high degree of learning the practical and aesthetic skills of design and technical production, there is academic content about constructivist learning theories. Academic learning involves learning about other's descriptions of the world as well as learning from experience (Laurillard, 1993; Säljö, 1984). Wild and Quinn (1998) propose that the internalization and the ability to transfer academic learning to new situations comes from 'the reconciliation between experiential learning and academic learning' (p. 74). Furthermore, they believe that 'this reconciliation primarily comes from reflecting on and abstracting from one's own experiences.' (*ibid.*). While technological applications can encourage reflection, they cannot yet directly facilitate it (*ibid.*). However, we believe that the processes necessary to design IMM require cycles of action and reflection. It is frequently necessary to review and redesign when a structure is not successful. Furthermore, the portfolio requires students to reflect on and articulate their own learning processes with the aim of developing meta-cognitive skills (Nisbet and Shucksmith, 1984).

These four principles should not be perceived as discrete, they are intimately connected. For example, Ryan and Powelson (1991) argue that motivation is a result of a learning environment in which students can develop a sense of autonomy, feel their competence growing and are 'related' to others — tutors and peers. We believe that the requirement for students to design and construct an IMM learning resource helps us pursue these principles more easily than many traditional methods. Theoretically, then, the design of the module should result in both motivation and in a good quality product which demonstrates conceptual understanding. In the final section of this paper we turn to the empirical evidence gleaned from the module about whether or not these outcomes were achieved. It continues to address the question of what happens when traditional pedagogies are left behind and embarks on the second question: 'Can distinctive pedagogies be successfully transferred between disciplines?'

42.5 What were the effects of non-traditional features on the students taking the 'New Learning and its Technologies' module?

We have taken two approaches to addressing the question of the effects of the non-traditional module: first, to explore student satisfaction in terms of engagement and motivation;[5] and, secondly, to examine the IMM learning resources for the extent and type of learning.

We asked the students to compare the module with others in the same degree course which are all taught in a traditional lecture/seminar format. These are some typical written comments:

> This module seems to have been much more relaxed than other modules. It is good because the work is ongoing and I can't leave it till the last minute as with essays. I like the way it is more practical than listening to a lecture, doing follow-up reading and then as essay. I feel I have learned a lot more in this module than with any other of the educational studies modules so far.

> A break from the usual lecture and tutorial form of learning. Allows us to learn more for ourselves and to have more input in what we learn and how we do it. More work than other modules-requires more time. Allows us to use computers for purposes other than writing essays, searching the internet e.g. drawing pictures, playing with sounds. Greater sense of achievement. Probably feel prouder of the finished product than a finished essay.

> Less structured than other modules, perhaps not as much pupil-teacher interaction. can do your own thing more than in other modules. More finding out for yourself. More involved.

> Different from other modules because there is more emphasis on practical aspects, rather than it being just reading and written work, nice variety. Tutors more personal, friendly and helpful.

In this section we shall attempt to unravel what these comments tell us about student engagement and motivation of a module pursuing one form of non-traditional pedagogy.

Our perception as tutors was that the students were cognitively and affectively engaged. They worked extremely hard telling us that they put in many more hours than they do for other modules; they appeared to enjoy the work often laughing as they experimented; and as the module draw to a close they expressed pride in their learning resource. However, in coming to conclusions about the students' engagement and motivation, it is important to keep in mind that the module is an option so that, we assumed, they already had an interest. However, two students confided to us that they had opted for this module because they found other theory-based options daunting. In addition, the group was small: four groups of three students. This allowed the two tutors to interact and get to know the students over the 12-week period, thus contributing to the social climate of learning and the quality of relationships mentioned above.

Students' favourable comments about the module fell into three main categories: they were pleased to have developed competence and confidence with computers; they appreciated teamwork and the support of the tutors; and, they enjoyed the module because it was 'different', 'a change', 'interesting' and 'challenging'. The latter comment raises a question with regard to 'non-traditional' pedagogies: a major theme in literature about the effects of the use of computers with school pupils is its power to motivate (for example, Underwood, 1995). However, it is unclear whether this is an effect of novelty in the classroom, teacher enthusiasm, the increased opportunity to work with peers or the intrinsically interactive and creative nature of the learning activities computers allow. This uncertainty pertains to the 'New Learning and its Technologies' module: the students were engaged and motivated but we cannot easily ascertain the extent to which non-traditional pedagogy contributed to this.

The students commented that they needed to sustain effort for the whole of the module. Designing and constructing the resource is a demanding task which takes many hours and a great deal of team discussion and trial and error. Unlike essays, it cannot be achieved in a two-day marathon. Students observed that they had benefited both in terms of learning about the module content and about managing their time. It may be that this is what is distinctive and transferable. In which case the question becomes: What methods motivate students to sustain intellectual effort for the whole of a unit of learning?

There were negative comments about lack of clarity about what they were being asked to aim for. These perceptions need more investigation. Prosser and Trigwell (1999) conclude that perceptions clear goals and standards are related to taking a deep approach to learning; and that perceptions of heavy workload are related to surface approaches. In our students these perceptions did not appear to demotivate or drive them to taking a surface approach. Assessment and new ways of learning will cause some anxiety and confusion in students, and it is the tutor's role to alleviate the ill effects of this on learning. Fitzgerald *et al*. (1997), who present a case of pre-service school teachers co-operatively authoring hypermedia, also report high levels of anxiety at the beginning of the course which gradually decreased as the teacher offered support and reassurance. It may be that in the context of non-traditional methods the student perception of 'good teaching' becomes crucial.[6]

We turn now to what we learned from the quality of the student IMM learning resources. We awarded high marks to all the learning resources, that is between 60% and 85%. Our judgement was based on identification of a number of characteristics. This is how we put it to students in the module guide:

> Learning resources should express a good teaching idea; contain useful and interesting information; and, make good use of the features of the package used. It should be:
>
> - well conceived;
> - well-designed, structured and presented;
> - lucid and coherent;
> - well-written, with thought given to the use of language and density of text;
> - of consistent style and level of information; and
> - interactive.

Students had, with varying degrees of success, fulfilled these criteria. We found that, despite having a textbook[7] about the design and rationale for interactive multimedia, the students had read widely and attributed the sources.[8] They had attempted to review, dismantle and then reconstruct the material, representing it in imaginative ways. In other words, they had not taken a text book and simply repackaged the material on the computer with linear links. Their links were complex and gave the user choices; and they had used different media (audio and graphic) to emphasise concepts and points.

Of course, it is possible to make poor learning resources, the design and construction of which does not contribute to the students' knowledge and understanding. As with any form of pedagogy, clarity on the tutor's part and understanding on the student's part about what constitutes quality is crucial. In this case, we speculate that the essential elements are first, the emphasis, early in the module, on critical evaluation of other IMM learning resources; and secondly the insistence that the resource is interactive.

Despite our judgement that the students' knowledge and understanding of the principles of interactive multimedia design and the pedagogic rationale for it was sound by the end of the module, we cannot come to any definitive conclusions about how far this was influenced by the non-traditional form of pedagogy. As we have indicated, the variables that influence a successful teaching and learning process are many and the inter-relationship between them complex.

Nevertheless, we believe that there is something distinctive about construing the students' as tutors and authors of a multimedia resource. This concerns the potential to deconstruct material for re-presenting it in different ways and in different media; and for making explicit links between parts of the material to make a coherent whole. If this is so then it possible to suggest that students could represent any kind of knowledge and understanding in this way: historical, sociological, psychological and so on.

42.6 Tentative conclusions

There are elements of the 'New Learning and its Technologies' module which cause us concern. First, there was a tendency for students to become too focused on technical aspects at the expense of thinking about selection and organization of content. Secondly, the construction of an IMM resource is extremely time consuming, particularly for non-experts. For this reason, we do not require a complete resource, but expect completed parts which are illustrative of structure and depth of knowledge and, for the rest, we ask for detailed storyboards. This frustrates some students who find it difficult to accept submitting an unfinished product.[9]

Nevertheless, the evidence we have indicates that students were engaged and motivated by a non-traditional form of assessment and that the quality of student learning was high. However, we treat this conclusion with caution. As a learning activity and task the construction of an IMM learning resource has potential, but, to a large extent, the effects of any non-traditional pedagogy will depend on the soundness of course design; the quality of tutors; the climate of learning in which they take place; and the whole of the learning environment including department and institution.

With this in mind, it is possible to propose that a fruitful form of assessment across disciplines, as an alternative to essays, could be to require students to express their knowledge and understanding in the form of an IMM package. The main argument we have made for this conclusion is that the manipulation — or analysis and synthesis- of subject matter that is required to construct an IMM resource is intellectually demanding and involves the student in modes of thinking and organisation of knowledge necessary for the 'deep' processing which results in understanding: they must consider the relationship between parts and the whole (Ramsden, 1992).

There are other reasons that we believe that this is a form of assessment is worthwhile. It develops learning outcomes which have not traditionally been the business of universities, in particular the ability to work collaboratively to complete a project. Further than this, the effects of the acceleration globally of the uses of C&IT are uncertain (Kling, 1996; MacFarlane, 1995); and, it is argued, it has the potential to be socially, politically and economically transforming (Kling, 1996; Taylor *et al.*, 1997). It is, therefore, essential that students can make well-informed, critical evaluations about the quality and nature of information in this form.[10] Fischer and Weiss (1997) liken C&IT to 'the great goldmine of our era' (p. 590) and suggest that to mine the best it is essential to develop methods whereby 'fools' gold can be distinguished from the real thing' (p. 591). Students will be better equipped to make these distinctions if they understand about the relationship between design, structure and content by having attempted to do it for themselves. Moreover, it is arguable that a future generation of citizens should themselves be an active part of the cyperspace revolution by being able to convey information and communicate in non-linear and graphic ways -just as previous generations have learned to communicated through print.

In present circumstances, the proposal that students could convey their knowledge about and understanding of traditional subject matter as an IMM resource will seem impracticable. However, the practical possibility of extending this form of assessment to other disciplines should increase as students become more familiar with and skilled at the design and construction of IMM; as authoring packages become more 'user-friendly'; and as computers become more accessible.[11] The crucial question is how to engage the expertise and interest of tutors.

Notes

1. The module has run once during the academic year 1998—99.
2. Details found at: http://www.educationgroup.com/publications.htm
3. Although doubts have been raised about definitions and explanations (Diaper,1990), to us the possibility is likely of 'Hawthorne effect' which occurs when, as a result of introducing a novel method into a situation, part of any improvement is due to the change or experiment, and enthusiasm for it, as much as to the actual method (Cohen and Manion, 1996).
4. For example, social psychology, interactionism and phenomenology.
5. Our comments are drawn from: our own perceptions as tutors; formal end-of-module evaluation forms; and a structured group interview conducted two weeks before the end of the module by a research assistant.
6. A perception of 'good teaching' which is related to taking deep approaches (Prosser and Trigwell, 1999) In the formal evaluation forms all the students were highly satisfied with the teaching and about half mentioned the approachability of tutors.
7. Phillips, R. (1997) *The Developer's Handbook to Interactive Multimedia*. London: Kogan Page.
8. We made it clear in written criteria that credit would be given for wide reading.
9. Of the three teams one submitted a completed resource.
10. Of course, this argument is the same as for the technology of print on paper.
11. Our students expressed dissatisfaction with the access to computers with the software they needed.

42.7 References

Alessi, S.M. and Trollip, S.R. (1991) *Computer-Based Instruction*. Prentice-Hall.

Biggs, J.B. (1987) *Student Approaches to Learning and Studying*. Australian Council for Educational Research, Hawthorn, Victoria.

Biggs, J.B. (1989) Does learning about learning help teachers with teaching?, *Psychology and the Tertiary Teacher. Supplement to The Gazette* **26**(1): University of Hong Kong.

Bostock, S. (1998) Constructivism in mass higher education: a case study, *British Journal of Educational Technology* **29**(3): 225—40.

Boyd-Barrett, O. and Scanlon, E. (1991) *Computers and Learning*. Wokingham: Addison-Wesley Publishing Company in association with the Open University

Caillot, M. (1991) Learning thinking through new technologies. In S. Maclure and P. Davies (eds), *Learning to Think: Thinking to Learn*, Proceedings of 1989 Conference, Pergamon Press: London.

Cohen, L. and Manion, L. (1996) *Research Methods in Education* , 4th edn, London: Routledge.

Collins A., Brown, J.S. and Newman, S. (1989) Cognitive apprenticeship: teaching the craft of reading, writing and mathematics. In L.B. Resnick (ed.), *Knowing, Learning and Instruction: Essays in Honour of Robert Glaser*. Hillside NJ: Lawrence Erlbaum Associates.

Diaper, G. (1990) The Hawthorne Effect: a fresh examination, *Educational Studies* **16**(3):. 261—7.

Duffy, T.M., Lowyck, J. and Jonassen, D.H. (1993) *Designing Environments for Constructive Learning*. Berlin: Springer-Verlag.

Elliott, G.J., Jones, E. and Narker, P. (1997) Supporting the paradigm shift: hypermedia construction with concept maps — the easy way forward. Innovations in Education and Training International, **34**(4): 294—8.

Erickson, J. (1997) Building a community of designers: restructuring learning through student hypermedia design, *Journal of Research in Rural Education* **13**(1): 5—27.

Ferrence, P.R. and Vockell, E.L. (1994) Adult learning characteristics and effective software instruction, *Educational Technology*, July—August,.25—31.

Fischer, B. and Weiss, B. (1997) All the glitters is not gold: teaching liberal arts students how to assess technology. In Contributed Papers, Vol. 2, *Improving University Teaching*, 22nd International Conference, 21—24 July 1997, Rio de Janeiro, Brazil.

Fitzgerald, G.E., Hardin, L. and Hollingshead, C. (1997) Engaging preservice teachers in hypermedia authoring: process and outcomes, *Journal of Educational Computing Research* **16**(2): 191—207.

Gibbs, G. (1992) *Improving the Quality of Learning*, Bristol: Technical and Education Service.

Hartley, J. (1998) *Learning and Studying: A Research Perspective*. London: Routledge.

Jaques, D. (1984) *Learning in Groups*. London: Kogan Page.

Kling, R. (1996) Content and pedagogy in teaching about social aspects of computerisation. Paper presented at the International Working Conference, *The Impact of Information Technology: From Practice to Curriculum*, February.

Laurillard, D. (1993) *Rethinking University Teaching*. London: Routledge.

Leftwich, A. (1987) Room for manoeuvre: a report in experiments in alternative teaching and learning methods in politics, *Studies in Higher Education* **12**(3): 311—23.

Marra, R. and Jonassen, D. (1993) Whither constructivism? In D. Ely, B. Monor and C.I. Englewood (eds), *Educational Media and Technology Yearbook*, Libraries Unlimited published in co-operation with ERIC and AECT.

Marshall, D. (1999) Developing interactive courseware on the World Wide Web, *Innovations in Education and Training International*, 36(1): 34—43.

Marton, F., Hounsell, D. and Entwistle, N.J. (eds) (1984) *The Experience of Learning: Implications for Teaching and Studying in Higher Education*. Edinburgh: Scottish Academic Press.

MacFarlane, A. (1995) Future patterns of teaching and learning. In T. Schuller (ed.), *The Changing University*, Buckingham: SRHE/Open University Press.

Muire, C., Mazarian, M.J. and Gilmer, P.J. (1999) Web-based technology in a constructivist community of learners, *British Journal of Educational Technology* **30**(1):.65—8.

O'Shea, T. and Self, J. (1988) Learning and teaching with computers. In *Artificial Intelligence in Education*, Brighton, Sussex: The Harvester Press.

Prosser, M. and Trigwell, K. (1999) *Understanding Learning and Teaching: The Experience in Higher Education*. Buckingham: The Society for Research into Higher Education and Open University Press.

Ramsden, P. (1992) *Learning to Teach in Higher Education*. London: Routledge.

Ryan, R.M. and Powelson, C.L. (1991) Autonomy and relatedness as fundamental to motivation and education, *Journal of Experimental Education* **60**(1): 49—66.

Säljö, R. (1984) Learning from reading. In F. Marton, D.J. Hounsell and N.J. Entwistle (eds), *The Experience of Learning*. Edinburgh: Scottish Academic Press.

Slavin, R.E. (1991) Synthesis of research on co-operative learning, *Educational Leadership*, February, 73—82.

Taylor, R.G., Peltsverger, B.W. and Vasum, L. (1997) The nature of virtual organisation and their anticipated social and psychological impact, *Education and Information Technologies* **2**:.347—60.

Topping, K. (1997) Peer tutoring for flexible and effective adult learning. In P. Sutherland (ed.), *Adult Learning, A Reader*. London: Kogan Page, pp. 106—22.

Underwood, J.D.M. (1995) *Computer-Based Learning: Potential into Practice*. Prentice-Hall.

Wild, M. and Quinn, C. (1998) Implications of educational theory for the design of instructional multimedia, *British Journal of Educational Technology* **29**(1): 73—82.

43 Biological essays: how do students use feedback?

Stephen Merry, Paul Orsmond and Kevin Reiling
Biology Division, Staffordshire University, Stoke-on-Trent

43.1 Background

This action research study arose from four considerations.

43.1.1 Essays continue to contribute significantly to university assessment

Within the Biology Division at Staffordshire University, and in many other higher education institutes, essays have traditionally been an important component of assessment. They are used in both formative and summative roles. While the greater usage in recent years of other assessment methods such as oral, poster and electronic presentations has increased the overall diversity of assessment methods employed, essays remain within this wider portfolio. They are retained on the basis of three prime considerations. First, the desire to ensure assessment is robust by incorporating and maintaining a wide variety of assessment methods. Secondly, essays are able to effectively discriminate between students with different abilities since more able students produce discursive rather than descriptive essays. Finally, essays have traditionally been used within final examinations forming the basis of degree classifications and there is reluctance to completely discard this standard in favour of less recognized methods.

43.1.2 Essay writing develops skills which can be applied to other forms of creative work

The use of essays as part of the Biology curriculum at Staffordshire University is justified on the basis that they provide a vehicle to enable students to synthesize and evaluate information and ideas. Jackson (1991) has described 'strong' and 'weak' approaches to essay writing. A strong approach requires the student to reflect throughout the process of writing such that they continuously review and, if necessary, take steps to amend what they have written. The ability to reflect is a key skill that enhances other forms of creative writing including the production of professional reports in the form of dissertations, practical reports and literature reviews. The skill is also useful in producing other forms of creative work such as research projects, oral presentations or web pages.

43.1.3 Tutors understanding of 'a good essay' may be different to that of students

The expectations of tutors concerning the approach that their students should take to writing essays do not always materialize. This discrepancy may arise because, when writing biological essays, students place emphasis on factual content, whereas tutors often value writing style (Orsmond *et al.*, 1997). These different emphases are not confined to biology students. Norton (1990) carried out a study involving 133 first-year undergraduates at the Liverpool Institute of Higher Education who took psychology as one of their three subjects in their preliminary year. Students were asked to complete a questionnaire two weeks after submitting a psychology essay. The questionnaire asked students which criteria they thought tutors were looking for in that specific essay and the students' responses were compared with criteria provided by the six tutors. Structure was mentioned as an assessment criteria by all of the tutors, but only by 50% of the responding students. Others have studied perceived weaknesses in students' approach to essay writing in geography. Pain and Mowl (1996) surveyed 53 first-year geography students at the University of Northumbria. These students had already written, and received feedback on, four or five essays at the university. Typical student self-identified problems with essay writing included 'difficulty in putting points in order and making a coherent argument', 'not being able to construct the information correctly to make the essay a good one' and 'I find it difficult to bring all the points in the essay to a conclusion and to make each point relevant without repeating myself'.

The discrepancy between students' and tutors' perceptions of 'a good essay' is particularly significant since a previous study has indicated biology students' approach to essay writing is largely developed during their pre-university experiences (Merry *et al.*, 1998). In this study individual structured interviews were conducted with 10 first year, 12 second year and 15 third year biology undergraduates. Both the first-year and second-year students reported that their approach to essay writing was generally based solely on pre-university guidance. Only the third-year students often reported that their approach to essay writing had 'matured' or 'developed' during their university careers, but, even here, the impression given was that any changes had taken place in the absence of conscious effort to change. This reliance on pre-university guidance and lack of conscious change is surprising in the light of the intense efforts made by tutors to improve students' essay-writing skills.

Today's students are also likely to have less pre-university experience of essay writing. This is because the trend towards an increased diversity of assessment methods in higher education has been mirrored and sometimes surpassed by a similar trend in pre-university education. More students are also entering university on the basis of GNVQ qualifications where essays as less valued as a form of learning and assessment (Wolff and Sutcliffe, 1999). Overall, this may mean that today's students have less developed skills in essay-writing when they enter university.

43.1.4 Assessment motivates student learning

It is becoming increasingly recognized that assessment often defines what students regard as important (Hinett and Knight, 1996), but perhaps the most important aspect of assessment is that it provides feedback so empowering students with the ability to identify and address weaker aspects of their performance. In each of the three studies described in this chapter feedback is provided to students in association with assessment. The significance of the formative feedback provided may be perceived by the students to be greater because of its association with summative grades.

43.2 Aims

In the Biology Division at Staffordshire University tutors routinely provide written, and often verbal, feedback to students as to how their essays might be improved. Furthermore, this feedback is usually set in the context of marking criteria given prior to writing the essay. In this chapter we investigate students' response to such feedback. Three individual studies have been carried out using a variety of methods with the overall aims of:

1. Developing students' awareness of the importance of feedback as a mechanism by which they can identify and subsequently address weaker aspects of their performance. Students should see the most valuable aspect of feedback as the specific comments made by the tutor rather than the overall mark awarded.

and

2. Developing students' awareness of essay-writing as a learning process such that they become more reflective. Writing the essay should not be seen as the final mechanical part of the process after they have carried out the necessary research and planning, but as a vehicle to organizing their own understanding of the topic of the essay.

43.3 Methods

43.3.1 Student questionnaire following review of draft essays

.solely to monitor the effectiveness of the exercise and would play no part in grading.

43.3.2 Monitoring essay assessment outcomes

As part of their preparation for end-of-year examinations second-year undergraduates were set two essays. Both essays were to be written under exam conditions with a time limit of 40 minutes. The first essay was set as part of a module entitled 'Cell Biology' and it contributed 15% of the overall mark for the module. The essay title, 'The evolution of cell organelles', was given to students six weeks before it was to be written to allow them to plan their answer in advance. Seventy two students took part in this exercise. The essays were tutor marked and the grade together with formative feedback was returned to students after two weeks. Feedback was given both orally in class as a summary of the general qualities and deficiencies noted by the tutor when marking the scripts and as specific written comments on the individual essay scripts.

After a further two weeks 55 of the original students undertook a second time constrained essay. This essay was set as part of a module entitled 'Essential Immunology' which was only studied by a proportion of the original cohort. As in the previous case, this essay contributed 15% to the overall mark for the module. The title of the second essay was 'The importance of macrophages in immune responses' and it had been given to students 10 weeks previously. This essay was marked by the same tutor as the first essay.

For both essays students were asked to complete a self-assessment form awarding themselves a grade for the essay. A form was submitted together with each essay. The

Biology Division's standard criterion referenced marking scheme was used for grading the essays by both tutor and students. This scheme was familiar to both the tutor and students and requires essays to be logically structured and to include the major factual content before a mark equivalent to upper second class honours is awarded. It is acknowledged that the titles of each of the essays are statements, rather than questions or instructions, but this type of essay title was familiar to the students concerned. The students were aware, and the marking scheme explicitly stated, that a discursive, rather than descriptive, approach was required in order to obtain a high grade.

In analysing the data only the 55 students who took part in both time constrained essays were considered.

43.3.3 Feedback diaries

A separate cohort of 29 first-year undergraduates were asked to keep diaries outlining their responses to the feedback they received on their coursework during a period of three months. During the period of the diary students were required to complete three coursework essays, but the diary was not be restricted to essay feedback. They were to include in their diary all feedback from all of the modules they studied during the period. The diary exercise was set as part of a skills based module entitled 'Work Experience and Personal Development' and contributed 25 per cent towards the overall assessment of the module. It was introduced to the students in a tutorial in which the importance of feedback was discussed together with an example if how the diary was to be structured. For each piece of feedback they needed to include the nature of the assignment, the content of the feedback received, the actions they took in response to the feedback and a justification for the actions they took. Furthermore, at the end of the three month period they were also asked to write a reflection on the process of keeping the diary stating how, if at all, the diary had changed their attitude to feedback. Students were required to submit this reflection together with the feedback diary for assessment.

43.4 Results

43.4.1 Student questionnaire following review of draft essays

A total of 53 students completed questionnaires. These students were part of nine different tutorial groups; 48 students (91%) reported that they found the exercise helpful and 21 students (40%) reported that the exercise had changed their attitude to essay writing.

43.4.2 Monitoring essay assessment outcomes

The 55 students each submitted two essays. The tutor awarded 39 per cent of the original essays grades equivalent to first or upper second class honours. This value increased to 44 per cent for the second essay which was completed following the receipt of feedback from the first essay. The marginal increase observed in the percentage of higher grades awarded by the tutor contrasts with the self-assessment grades awarded by the students. In the first essay 32 per cent of students awarded themselves grades equivalent to first or upper second class honours, but this fell to 25 per cent for the second essay.

43.4.3 Feedback diaries

A qualitative review of the feedback diaries and their corresponding student reflections revealed a variety of student responses to the exercise. This review was carried out by a single tutor. Some students showed a rather mechanical response to tutors' comments. If the tutor stated that an assigned essay should contain diagrams then the student responded that next time they would include diagrams. The justification was that the essay needed diagrams. An approximately equal number of students did, however, respond at a deeper level to the feedback they received. Furthermore, the exercise encouraged some students to think of their learning in generic terms. They began to consider how the skills they were developing from the feedback diary exercise could be applied in other modules. Another common factor in student reflections was that they found keeping the feedback diary increasingly helpful as the exercise progressed. Students who were initially antagonistic later became convinced of the actual or potential benefits of the exercise. These findings are illustrated in the student quotations below which are taken from three different reflections.

> At first I did not understand the point of the feedback diary, but now I can understand its importance. Using the feedback I have actually thought about improving areas that I never thought were problems in the past.

> I think the feedback diary could be improved by combining it in some way with the personal skills development portfolio.

> Well, at the moment I cannot see how the diary is helping me to improve my learning. Maybe in time these improvements will start to show.

43.5 Discussion

This study combines three investigative approaches to evaluate and improve students' responses to feedback. The evaluative approaches used were questionnaires, an analysis of grades awarded following feedback and a review of feedback diaries kept by students.

In the first study first-year undergraduates students were given the opportunity both to peer review and to receive tutor feedback on a draft essay. The students were then allowed to modify this version of their essay to incorporate this feedback prior to final submission for assessment. Questionnaires were used to evaluate effectiveness of this exercise as perceived by students. There was an overwhelming response (i.e. 91%) from students that they found the exercise helpful, but perhaps more importantly 40% of students reported that the exercise had changed their attitude to essay writing. While 40% may seem to be low proportion it does need to be seen in the context of our earlier study suggesting that biology students' approach to essay writing is largely based on their pre-university experience (Merry *et al.*, 1998). This was particularly so for first-year and second-year students and any developments that had occurred in the approach to essay writing adopted by third-year students were reported to be evolutionary rather than a conscious effort to change. This subsequent study involving a later cohort of students has shown is that the provision of utilizable feedback on draft essays to first-year students is a significant development because it can motivate students consciously to change their approach to essay-writing; a process which might not otherwise occur.

In the second study second-year undergraduates were given the opportunity to incorporate feedback from an initial essay into a subsequent essay on a separate topic which they undertook two weeks later. Both essays were marked by the same tutor who awarded a greater number of high grades to the cohort for the second essay compared to the first essay. While the increase was marginal, the study does suggest that students did utilize initial feedback to improve a second essay, although, because the essays had different topics, alternative explanations are possible. Perhaps the more interesting outcome from this particular study relates to the self-assessment grades awarded by the students. While the tutor awarded higher grades for the second essay, student self-assessment grades were reduced. The students were performing better, but actually thought that they were performing more poorly. A possible explanation is that the nature of this study encouraged students to focus on the initial formative feedback received and so increased their awareness of possible flaws in their approach to essay writing. They were therefore more critical when self assessing the second essay. Such a critical approach, if applied in other situations, will enable students to become more independent learners as they can perceive, and hence address, weaknesses in their work in the absence of tutor guidance.

In the third study first-year undergraduates were required to keep a feedback diary for a period of three months. They were to record in this diary all feedback they received and how they responded to it. During the period of the study students were required to write three essays, but the diary was not restricted solely to essays. At the end of the exercise students were asked to write a reflection including how keeping the diary had changed their attitude to feedback. The study showed that some students approached feedback rather mechanically, whereas an approximately equal number of others took a deeper approach in which they considered the feedback in the context of their overall learning. Norton and Crowley (1995) found a similar diversity in student overall approach to learning when they evaluated the effectiveness of a series of 'Approaches to Learning' workshops for first-year psychology students. The workshops had a significant focus on essay-writing skills. The authors were able to classify students as having either 'sophisticated' or 'naïve' conceptions of learning and suggested that these conceptions were linked to the 'deep' and 'surface' approaches to learning identified by Marton and Säljö (1976).

Perhaps a more important finding from the feedback diary study was the general observation that students found the process of keeping the diary increasingly helpful. This suggests that, through practice, the students developed greater ability to reflect on and so more effectively utilize the feedback they received. Boud (1990) has written that assessment practices can encourage students to develop the professional skill of becoming 'reflective practitioners' who continuously monitor what they are doing as they are doing it and so are able to make assessments of what they need to do. Our study indicates that encouraging students to reflect on the feedback they receive over a period of time may help them to become reflective practitioners.

In each of the three studies described in this chapter we have encouraged students to focus on their essay writing skills within in the context of a specific assignment or assignments and we have shown that this approach can be effective. Our approach contrasts with the more traditional way of teaching essay writing skills which is to focus on the discrete skills themselves. Our studies supplement those of Smith *et al.* (1998) who also suggested that emphasis needs to be placed on the relationship between students' understanding of essay content and their ability to write about it.

43.6 Conclusions

1. We have shown in three studies that assignments which encourage reflection on feedback provided have the potential to change students' approaches to essay writing and may lead to an increase in essay quality.
2. Since biological essays are not fundamentally different to essays in many other disciplines, the developmental approaches adopted in this study may be appropriate to other scientific and non-scientific disciplines.
3. We have shown that the use of feedback diaries can make students more aware of the role of feedback in improving learning. Future studies will evaluate the effectiveness of feedback diaries in improving the actual quality of students' performance.

Acknowledgement

The authors would like to thank their colleagues and students within the Biology Division of Staffordshire University for their help and co-operation.

43.7 References

Boud, D. (1990) Assessment and the promotion of academic values, *Studies in Higher Education* **15**: 101—11.

Hinett, K. and Knight, P. (1996) Quality and assessment, *Quality Assurance in Education* **4**: 3—10.

Marton, F. and Säljö, R. (1976) On qualitative differences in learning I: Outcome and process, *British Journal of Educational Psychology* **46**: 4—11.

Merry, S., Orsmond, P. and Reiling, K. (1998) Biology students' and tutors understanding of 'a good essay'. In C. Rust (ed.), *Improving Students as Learners* pp. 202—5. The Oxford Centre for Staff and Education Development, Oxford.

Norton, L.S. (1990) Essay-writing: what really counts?, *Higher Education* **20**: 411—42.

Norton, L.S. and Crowley, C.M. (1995) Can students be helped to learn how to learn? An evaluation of an Approaches to Learning programme for first year degree students, *Higher Education* **29**: 307—28.

Orsmond, P., Merry, S. and Reiling, K. (1997) Students' and tutors' perceptions of 'a good essay', *Research in Education* **58**: 81—4.

Pain, R. and Mowl, G. (1996) Improving geography essay writing using innovative assessment, *Journal of Geography in Higher Education* **20**: 19—31.

Smith, D., Campbell, J. and Brooker, R. (1998) Developing students' essay-writing skills: implications of case studies in essay writing of undergraduate students in an education faculty. In V. Rust (ed.), *Improving Students as Learners*, pp. 250—61. The Oxford Centre for Staff and Education Development, Oxford.

Wolff, P. and Sutcliffe, N. (1999) GNVQ time bomb and NVQ depth charge, *New Academic* **8**(1): 17—18.

44 The use of computer-based open learning to support student practical laboratory work

Ian M. Symonds

Department of Electronic and Electrical Engineering, University of Leeds

44.1 Overview

The chapter presents the design, implementation and use of a piece of computer-based open learning material to support student practical work. The material is designed to help students to find faults on existing electronic circuits. The faults, which are typical for the type of circuit being used, are switched in and out as required. The student uses normal electronic test equipment to find the fault and is supported by the computer program at the same time. The work described in the chapter is the first of a series of experiments, with the ultimate aim of producing a knowledge-based practical student support system. The program is web based, and uses the HTML links to encode the circuit knowledge.

There are two different types of links for students to select as they progress through the program. One is a choice made by the student using electronic knowledge, and the other based on the results of tests on the circuit. The later is required for the program to follow its own diagnostic procedure to determine the fault. The actual knowledge that the student is applying to the process of determining the fault, is important information in any determination of the educational value of the program. The application of relevant knowledge to new situations, the analysis of the problem and the formulation and testing of hypotheses are seen by many researchers as a sign of deep learning taking place. Therefore, the claim that an open learning system such as this can encourage deep learning needs the evidence about student thinking to support it.

The final system is envisaged as having a dialogue type interface with the student, but this first experiment used a number of embedded multiple response tests to ascertain student reasons for the choices they had made. The provision in the tests for feedback to students, on the number of correct answers and the reasons for them, was also utilized. This allowed the experiment to be of educational value to the students and so reward their time and effort expended in taking part. The tests completed by a student also indicate the route taken through the program, while the results indicate, albeit imperfectly, the thinking that lay behind the choice of the route. The selection of fault finding as the practical task to be used was made for a number of reasons. The most important was to find a practical situation in which a deeper learning approach can be encouraged.

The need to apply knowledge, analyse problems and formulate and test hypotheses required for the successful determination of a fault made it an ideal candidate. It also provided the practical element supplying the experiential dimension to the learning process. An on-line questionnaire was added to the end of the program, to collect feedback on the experience of using the system. Each question had a section for user text input, as well as the normal choices, to collect the maximum information from each run of the experiment.

44.2 Introduction

The aim of the computer-based material is to try to encourage a deep approach to learning, by students during practical work. The term deep, when used in respect to a learning approach, implies an attempt is being made by the learner to understand, rather than just memorize, facts and concepts that are encountered during the learning process. Most people would agree that such an approach was best, but such an imprecise notion gives no clue as to how it can be brought about. Many researchers have attempted to clarify what deeper learning is, and how we can recognize it when it is taking place. Most have agreed that there is a hierarchy of learning outcomes, ranging from 'surface' to 'deep', and it is through these outcomes that classification can be made. For example, Säljö (1982) proposed a framework of conceptions of learning with the following five categories:

1 learning as the increase of knowledge;
2 learning as memorising;
3 learning as the acquisition of facts, procedures, etc., which can be retained and/or utilised in practice;
4 learning as the abstraction of meaning;
5 learning as an interpretative process aimed at the understanding of reality.

The first two categories are associated with a surface approach and the final two with a deep approach. Later research, such as this by Perry (1988), focused on the learner characteristics associated with a particular approach.

Deep level Understanding intention, comprehending principles, ability to transfer, interpretation of meaning.
Surface level Learning to repeat, memorising, rote learning, precise reproduction of content.

This type of research finding is relevant to course design issues, as it provides clues on how to target particular ways of thinking and cognitive development. Unfortunately there is some confusion in the literature about terminology, although there is agreement about the underlying principle. For instance, Sandberg and Barnard (1997) use the term deep knowledge, rather than deep approach, in the following illustration.

> What do we mean by deep knowledge or insight? Deep knowledge or insight refers to the principles and rules underlying the observable facts. For example, knowing a physics law just through its mathematical formula, can be considered as purely factual knowledge. Only when the factual knowledge is backed up by knowing why the formula is expressed as it is, knowing why it holds, and knowing its conditions for use, the knowledge is considered to be deep.

This example illustrates why a deep knowledge, or deep approach to learning, is desirable. The correspondence, between the open learning situation being described, and the example is clear; observable facts — the practical work, and underlying principles and rules — the knowledge that the student must apply. The way in which the knowledge is applied was a concern of Biggs (1989) when he observed:

> Deep learning is associated with activity. Students are more likely to make connections between what is being learned and past learning if they are active rather than passive.

Active learning is that in which the learner is actively involved in the learning process, and becomes the focus of that activity. The process is much more complex than the mere inclusion of some activity into the learning, as this summary by Rubtsov and Margolis (1996) illustrates.

> Learning activity includes learning needs and motives, learning tasks, learning moves, and learning operations. The focus of this activity is the person's mastery of theoretically generalized knowledge and skills, with which one can successfully solve various practical and concrete problems. Needs and motives are related to one's striving to master just these kinds of knowledge and skills before meeting practical questions, so as to be prepared to solve them correctly. The peculiarity of learning tasks lies in the fact that, by solving them, one can discover how to extract theoretical knowledge and skills, and how to master generally learning moves in concrete, practical situations.

Active learning, as described above, requires an activity which allows the learner to apply theoretical knowledge to a practical situation. Hannafin and Land (1997) found that student oriented systems using educational technology regularly provide active learning opportunities.

> Technology-enhanced student-centered learning environments require that individuals are active in the learning process. They emphasise not only assimilation but the development of meta-knowledge for both solving existing problems and generating new ones. Through experience, learners become increasingly facile with available tools and resources, and skilled in assessing how and when to employ them. Learning environments often utilize activities that aid learners in constructing and generating artifacts of their understanding.

Computer-based open learning used during practical work, is an example of the sort of environment described above. The final requirement is to choose practical work that includes the active participation of the learner. It may be hard to see how practical work could be anything other than active, but active learning requires student involvement and not just mere activity, as was noted earlier. Practical work must also take place in a particular domain, the one chosen for this research is simple electronic circuits. Undergraduate practical work was always intended to complement the theoretical side, and not just illustrate it. This ideal of practical laboratory work seems to have been achieved only rarely. Time constraints and other factors made the situation, described by Boud, Dunn and Hegarty-Hazel (1986), more common.

> The absence of any objectives make it difficult for the student, who may read the experiment for the first time prior to commencing the laboratory work, to realize what is going on. Yet because the procedure is so clearly detailed, the student is able to complete the exercise and achieve a result. It is not difficult to understand why, in the absence of a clear reason for the activity, students see such exercises as cookbook or recipe work.

It is clear from the above, that setting the context for the practical work, is one task that the supporting computer must address. The first requirement, however, is to find types of practical work which engage students in tasks consistent with the learning outcomes of a deep approach. The suitability of fault finding depends on which of the following positions, described by Bedford [1989], is adopted.

> There are basically two ways to view the diagnostic problem. In the first view past experience plays the dominant role. Experienced failure situations are coded as heuristic rules, together perhaps with some predictive or statistical knowledge, all obtained from a human expert in a particular diagnostic domain. This could, in some sense, be considered the traditional expert system approach. The second view, and the view taken here, is diagnosis from first principles. The knowledge required is a functional model of some system and some measurement of that system. If the measurements conflict with the functional model then there is a diagnostic problem. That is, it is required to determine which part of the system, if it is assumed to be in fault, explains the discrepancies in the measurements of the system.

The two views are actually about whether a shallow approach or a deep approach is used to solve the problem. The second view, diagnosis from first principles, is consistent with a deep approach to learning, and is the one adopted in this open learning package. The functional model is supplied by the student applying theoretical knowledge to the particular fault finding problem. The 'correct' measurements for the system being diagnosed may be provided by student calculation, again applying theoretical knowledge. Analysis skills are obviously required, and synthesis may be involved in finding the solution to the problem.

44.3 Implementation

The use of fault-finding on simple electronic circuits requires a suitable faulty circuit for the students to use. A single stage amplifier was designed and built, incorporating switches that allowed faults to be activated at will. The student could select any of the four faults to find using these switches. It was suggested that only one fault be inserted at a time, to reduce the complexity of the student task.

The open learning material was provided as a series of web pages for three reasons. The first was that it allowed HTML to be used as a framework, into which the various elements of the instructional and diagnostic materials could be integrated. These elements included text, questionnaires, annotated drawings, circuit diagrams, photographs and scanned test equipment output such as oscilloscope traces. The second consideration was the fundamental information linking method used by the Internet, as Mac Bride(1996) explains.

> HTML stands for HyperText Mark-up Language, and is the means by which Web pages are created and linked together ... HTML is based on the use of tags. These are key words or phases, enclosed in < angle brackets >, which describe how text and graphics are to be displayed, and create links between different documents or parts of the same document. It is HTML's ability to handle links that makes the Web possible. The World Wide Web is essentially an ever-expanding set of interlinked HTML documents and a Web browser, like Netcape, is essentially a tool that can display these documents and follow up the links embedded in them.

The third reason was the availability of a web-based resource, within the University of Leeds, called the Nathan Bodington Building. This a 'virtual' building that is used to host educational material for many departments on the Internet. A software package on this system, was used to generate the Multiple Response Questionnaires, score student attempts online and send feedback to the student after the test. The specific feedback to accompany the scores was input to the system during generation of the tests. The same package was used to generate the final questionnaire for students on completion of the test. This resource was linked to the rest of the pages using HTML links, following normal web practice.

The same basic format was used for each section of the material. The first section was instructional material, explaining the nature of the practical tests to be performed, including operational details such as equipment connection and use. The next section was a menu of student choices, always accompanied by a summary of what was known so far, to prompt the student to make use of this information when making the choice. The final section was a Multiple Response Questionnaire to investigate the reasons for that student choice. The example shown in Figure 44.1, starting at the second page of the material, illustrates how the format looks in practice.

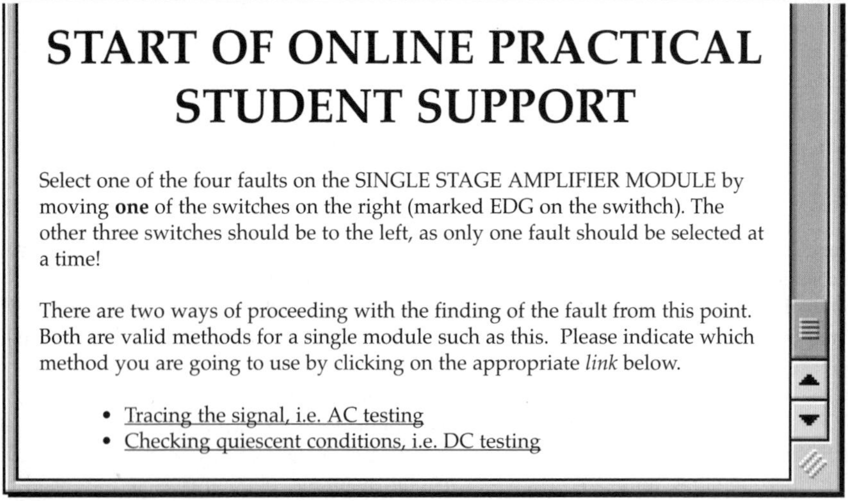

START OF ONLINE PRACTICAL STUDENT SUPPORT

Select one of the four faults on the SINGLE STAGE AMPLIFIER MODULE by moving **one** of the switches on the right (marked EDG on the swithch). The other three switches should be to the left, as only one fault should be selected at a time!

There are two ways of proceeding with the finding of the fault from this point. Both are valid methods for a single module such as this. Please indicate which method you are going to use by clicking on the appropriate *link* below.

- Tracing the signal, i.e. AC testing
- Checking quiescent conditions, i.e. DC testing

Figure 44.1 Example of Multiple Response Questionnaire

This screen contains the operational instructions required for selecting the fault on the circuit board, followed by the summary which in this case is in the text of the choices. This

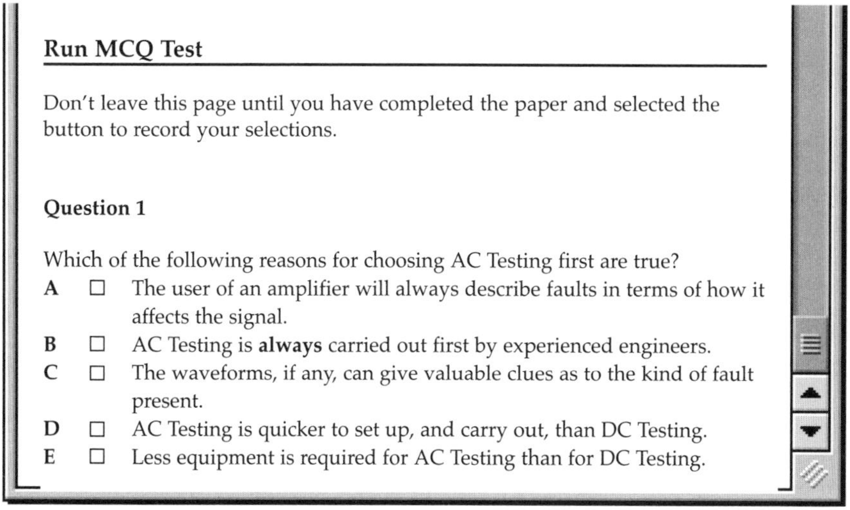

Run MCQ Test

Don't leave this page until you have completed the paper and selected the button to record your selections.

Question 1

Which of the following reasons for choosing AC Testing first are true?

A ☐ The user of an amplifier will always describe faults in terms of how it affects the signal.
B ☐ AC Testing is **always** carried out first by experienced engineers.
C ☐ The waveforms, if any, can give valuable clues as to the kind of fault present.
D ☐ AC Testing is quicker to set up, and carry out, than DC Testing.
E ☐ Less equipment is required for AC Testing than for DC Testing.

Figure 44.2 MCQ Test page

underlined text is the position of the links to the next pages. Selecting one of these testing links causes the MRQ, associated with the testing choice, to be displayed. The choice of AC testing results in this next page.

The choice made by the student to select this test is included in the question for two reasons. The first is to remind the student of the choice, and the other is to record the choice with the test to make data analysis easier later.

The questions are designed to test the underpinning knowledge that the student has in relation to AC testing. Multiple response tests can have more than one answer, and the scoring deducts points for wrong or missing answers as a result of this fact. The correct answers in the above test would be A and C, for instance. There is a link to the debrief page containing the feedback on the page containing the score. Following this link results in the feedback page being displayed. The answers selected as true by the student, as well as the score, are collected by the MRQ software giving an indication of the knowledge that the student could have used to make their choice. This is an example of the simplest type of link use. The second type uses the information gathered by the student during the test as well, to provide diagnostic data for the open learning material. The format is modified to include a second level of choices, whose purpose is to acquire the diagnostic data. An example of this type of link is shown for the AC testing page later in the material (Figure 44.3). Each menu item corresponds to a symptom for the faults.

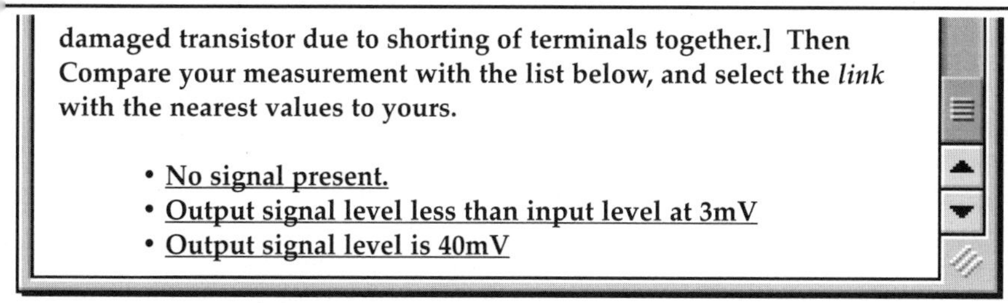

damaged transistor due to shorting of terminals together.] Then Compare your measurement with the list below, and select the *link* with the nearest values to yours.

- **<u>No signal present.</u>**
- **<u>Output signal level less than input level at 3mV</u>**
- **<u>Output signal level is 40mV</u>**

Figure 44.3 AC testing page

AC CONDITIONS - FAULT 1/2
R1 22k
C2 3n3
R3 3k3
V1
V2
Tr1 BC337
C1 470uF
R2 4k7
C3 330uF
R4 680R
The AC fault condition was **No signal present.**
Study the circuit diagram above, and try to deduce which component is faulty, and in what way. The two most common possibilities are short circuit and open circuit.
Please click here to check your deduction

Figure 44.4 AC faults page

The link selected from the menu by the student indicates the symptom found and selects the next part of the material to deal with that symptom. This contains the instructional information, in this case the circuit diagram repeated from earlier screens, together with some hints as to the sort of faults that could occur (Figure 44.4).

The final link, *Please click here to check your deduction*, displays a menu of possible faults for the students to select from (Figure 44.5).

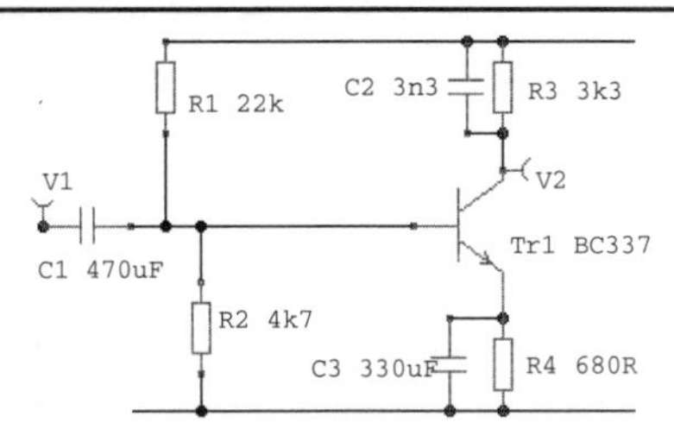

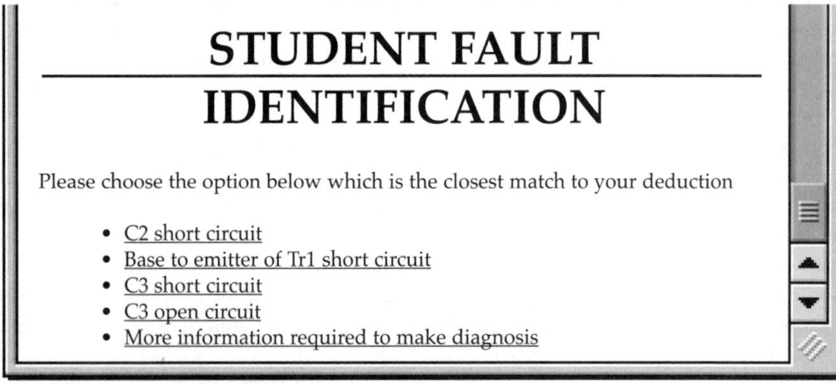

STUDENT FAULT IDENTIFICATION
Please choose the option below which is the closest match to your deduction
C2 short circuit
Base to emitter of Tr1 short circuit
C3 short circuit
C3 open circuit
More information required to make diagnosis

Figure 44.5 Example of Multiple Response Questionnaire

A different version of the page shown in Figure 44.5 is displayed depending on the symptom previously indicated by the student. The choice of the same fault from the menu shown will select a different MRQ, dependent on the symptom. The correct answers for the MRQ are known therefore, because of the route through the material that must have been taken to reach it.

This use of links is different in the case of the menu of symptoms, however, as they were used to code diagnostic information. This use provides an element of 'intelligence' to the Computer Aided Learning material. More sophisticated computer programs of this type are often called expert systems, described by Townsend and Feucht (1986), in the following way.

> Expert and knowledge systems are a class of computer programs that can advise, analyse, categorize, consult and diagnose. They address problems that normally require the expertise of a human specialist. Unlike computer programs that use procedural analysis to solve problems, expert systems attempt to solve problems in specific domains (specific fields of expertise) using deductive reasoning. Such systems are often capable of solving problems that are unstructured and poorly defined. they cope with the lack of structure through the use of heuristics, which are 'rules of thumb' that can be used to solve a problem when lack of knowledge or time prevents a more complete analysis.

The expertise involved in this program is that of associating symptoms with the faults that cause them, and providing a mechanism whereby the process of testing can be continued until all ambiguity in the fault identity is removed. The expertise is represented as a PRODUCTION system where the logical IF THEN rules are encoded in the LINKs. They could be represented as IF test outcome 1 THEN load screen 1; IF test outcome 2 THEN load screen 2 etc. As Symonds (1998) said of this idea, applied to web-based service documentation for fault finding.

> Here then is the key, the words or phrases used to form links, otherwise known as hypertext links. It is these that are used to form different 'routes' through the service documentation depending on the response given by the user of the system. This provides the means to transform the service documentation into a diagnostic tool.

This idea of 'routes' is seen clearly, when the case of a symptom which could be caused by two different faults, is encountered during AC testing. The links then move the student into the DC testing pages where the actual fault can be determined. The final page of all the different routes through the material is a questionnaire which is used to measure student reaction to the material, and the situation presented by practical laboratory work being carried out simultaneously with Personal Computer use (Figure 44.6).

The results from this questionnaire are considered along with the interpretation of the data obtained from the MRQ answers.

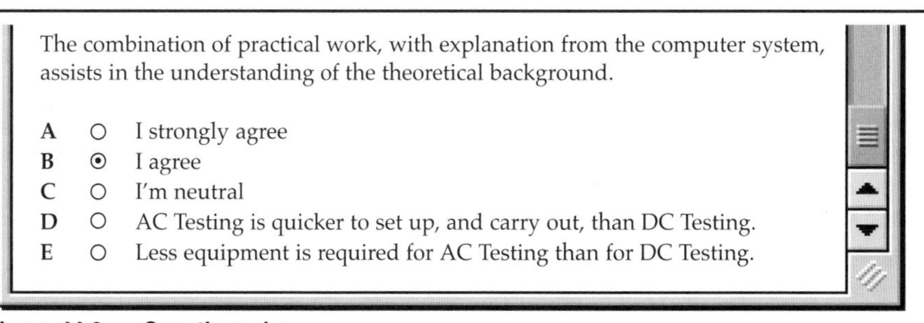

Figure 44.6 Questionnaire

44.4 Results

The results, presented here, were generated by a group of 16 students from Leeds College of Technology, taking C&G 223 Microcomputer Engineering as a preliminary year to BTECH Computer Technology. The actual topic of the material was covered in their course, but the explanations associated with the MRQs were designed for slightly older first-year degree students. The use of the open learning material was introduced to the students as an experiment in online practical student support.

The interpretations below illustrate how the answers to the MRQs and the route taken through the material can be considered together to provide an insight into the type of learning taking place. The underlying knowledge was assessed on the answers to the questionnaire and the correct application of this knowledge, to move from symptom to fault, was taken as an indication that deep approach to learning was taking place. Although the material was designed for single student use, the students using the material on this occasion opted to work in small groups. This decision was probably due to the unusual circumstances of the open learning, and responses therefore represent a consensus for the group involved. The extra information to be gained, by recording the discussions leading up to the consensus, suggests that a cassette recorder may be a worthwhile addition to later open learning sessions of this type.

Group A chose to do *DC Testing* first, and identified both the correct reasons for choosing this option and no incorrect ones. After making the *DC tests* they decided that *further information is required to make diagnosis* was the correct option. They went on to identify all the correct responses and no incorrect ones for the actual fault which was *C2 short circuit*. This implies that the group had the underpinning knowledge, but were not able to apply it in the new situation presented by fault finding.

Group B chose to do *AC testing* first, and identified both the correct reasons for choosing this option and no incorrect ones. After making the *AC tests* they decided that *C3 is open circuit* was the correct option. They went on to identify all the correct responses and no incorrect ones for the actual fault which was *C3 short circuit*. This implies that the group had the underpinning knowledge, but were not able to apply it in the new situation presented by fault finding.

Group C chose to do *DC Testing* first, and identified both the correct reasons for choosing this option and no incorrect ones. After making the *DC tests* they decided that *C2 short circuit* was the correct option. They went on to identify all the correct responses and no incorrect ones for the actual fault which was *C2 short circuit*. This implies that the group had the underpinning knowledge, and were able to apply it in the new situation presented by fault finding. A result which indicates that they applied this underpinning knowledge, when deciding what fault had caused the observed symptom, indicating that a deep approach to learning was taking place.

The second group of results were obtained from the final questionnaire.

The numbers of students involved, so far, do not support any rigorous statistical analysis, but the trends in the results are outlined below.

The questions asked are in italics.

1. *System could be useful in the lab* — slight majority for this view.
2. *Instructions for tests clear* — ambivalent?
3. *Explanation after test useful* — a clear majority in favour here.
4. *Options similar to your ideas* — everyone agreed with this statement!

5. *Immediate feedback helps further tests* — not much agreement on this.
6. *Ability to type own conclusions useful* — very little agreement with this.
7. *Combined practical helps understanding* — A very clear majority here.
8. *System makes individual practicals easier* — very little agreement with this.

Each question, in addition to the multiple choice answers, had an area for comments from the user on their answer. Only two uses were made of this facility, both by the same group. The question to which they refer is in italics.

Instructions for tests clear — 'We didn't have a clue.'

Combined practical helps understanding — 'It's very disorientating.'

A final section, for general comments on the experiment as a whole, was included with the following heading. *Please include any other general comments on the experiment which you feel might be helpful in future development.*

> The whole test could be less confusing. Easier to understand conclusions.

> It was very confusing and labels were deceiving.

> I feel that a new beginner to the system might [have] found it difficult to follow and in the future it would be better for the system to be more beginner friendly.

Part of the reason for the above comments, may be that not all functions of the 'Virtual building' were available to users from outside the university for security reasons. These functions were provided separately for these users, causing interruptions to the smooth flow of the open learning package.

44.5 Conclusions

The view of the open learning package, presented by the comments above, is fairly negative; but the view presented by the overall questionnaire results is encouraging. The response to *Combined practical helps understanding* suggests that student reaction to this particular learning situation is fairly positive. One of the aims of the questionnaire was to collect the reaction of the student to the situation produced by simultaneous computer use and practical work. The use of the questionnaire to collect student feedback is almost obligatory at the present time, but the problem of evaluation for this kind of lesson really needs different a different approach, as Marton and Säljö (1976) noted.

> The less tangible aspects of learning will require specific measurement, and in pursuing the objective of promoting deep level rather than surface style learning, it is necessary to identify a methodology for measuring that such learning has in fact occurred. This requires the use of performance indicators such as demonstration of the ability to transfer

> knowledge to appropriate novel contexts and drawing analogies based on domain principles. Such measures represent valid means of showing that the important principles and concepts involved in a subject domain, and the context within which they exist, have been properly understood. An approach concentrating more on depth than breath of coverage is implied, though the opposite is currently the norm.

This last statement still seems to be true 23 years later. Case studies of actual sessions are suggested as a possibility, which led to the use of an analysis of a students route through the system, and response made as a very imperfect way of implementing this. Any serious study of the above would need to involve a time period as well, to allow improvements, if any, to be observed after repeated exposure to this kind of system. The time element was absent from this experiment but the results may still reveal some indication of the student's current learning state. Another aim was to practise and improve fault finding skills, as these are important in electronic engineering, as well as providing a vehicle for a deep approach to learning by the students. The multiple response questionnaires were an attempt to study process instead of product, albeit indirectly. The case for this approach was made by Rowntree (1987) in the following way.

> If he [the teacher] wishes to influence, or even understand, the student's learning style and how he is developing, for example, in his capacity for problem-solving or for collaborative work with others, he cannot wait for the product to give him insights but must seek understanding while it is in production — intervening, where necessary, with guidance.

The last quotation is particularly relevant in the case of computer use to support student practical work. The aim of the computer use is, after all, to obtain a 'perfect' product for all students. This product may be the correct identification of a fault, a working circuit design, or practical Printed Circuit Board layout. All these products are to be arrived at using a deep approach to learning, with the computer software intervening, where necessary, with guidance. Later versions of this type of open learning material will require the ability to analyse student responses at the time they are made, rather than after the event, so that intervention can be optimized for each individual student, to encourage a deep learning approach. The same principles would seem to be applicable to any discipline where a practical skill needs to be practised, and where that skill requires the application of theoretical knowledge, analysis and synthesis for optimum results.

44.6 References

Bedford (1989) *Expert System Applications*. Wilmslow: Sigma Press, pp. 190—1.

Biggs (1989) Approaches to the enhancement of tertiary teaching, *Higher Research and Development 8*.

Boud, Dunn and Hegarty-Hazel (1986) *Teaching in Laboratories*. SRHE & NFER-Nelson, p. 37.

Hannafin and Land (1997) The Foundations and Assumptions of Technology-Enhanced Student-Centered Learning Environments. *Instructional Sciencem*, Vol. 25, Netherlands: Kluwer Academic Publishers, p. 190.

Mac Bride (1986) *Teach Yourself HTML Publishing on the World Wide Web*. Hodder & Stoughton, London, pp. 1—2.

Marton and Säljö; (1976) On qualitive differences in learning: outcome and process, *British Journal of Educational Psychology* **46**.

Perry, W.G. (1988) Different worlds in the same classroom. In P. Ramsden (ed.), *Improving Learning: New Perspectives*. London: Kogan Page, p. 145.

Rowntree (1987) *Assessing Students: How shall we know them?* Kogan Page Ltd, p. 138.

Rubtsov, V. and Margolis, A. (1996) Activity-oriented models of information-based instructional environments. In S.T. Kerr (ed.), *Technology and the Future of Schooling — NSSE*, University of Chicago Press, p. 176.

Säljö, R. (1982) *Learning and Understanding: A Study of Differences in Constructing Meaning from a Text*. Acta Universitatis Gothoburgensis, p. 192.

Sandberg and Barnard (1997) Deep learning is difficult, *Instructional Science* **25**, Netherlands: Kluwer Academic Publishers, p. 15.

Symonds (1998) Proc. 2nd International Conference on Maintenance, Reliability and Quality, *The Use of the Internet for Maintenance Support*, St Edmund Hall, Oxford, p. 217.

Townsend and Feucht (1986) *Designing and Programming Personal Expert Systems*. Blue Ridge Summit, PA: Tab Books Inc., p. 11.

45 Discipline differences in relations between learning, teaching and ways of leading teaching departments

Keith Trigwell, Michael Prosser, Elaine Martin and Paul Ramsden

University of Technology, Sydney; La Trobe University; RMIT University, University of Sydney

45.1 Abstract

In recent research we have explored the relations between the teaching leadership of departmental heads and course coordinators, the approaches to teaching of lecturers in those departments, and those lecturers' perceptions of the leadership environment. Questionnaire responses were received from over 400 teaching staff and from their Heads of Department and Course Coordinators in 39 departments in four broad disciplinary groups. Analysis of the quantitative results for the whole group showed no significant relations between leadership in teaching as described by the leaders and teaching approach as described by the teachers. However, analysis at the discipline group level revealed discipline differences in these relations.

This chapter focuses on the nature of the disciplinary variation in relations between leading and approaches to teaching, and outlines the implications for improving teaching and learning which follow from the results. Just as students' perceptions of their learning environment are associated with their approach to learning, so too are academics' approach to teaching associated with their perceptions of their teaching environment, including leadership of teaching. And just as students may not see the learning environment in the way intended by teachers, so too do teachers not necessarily see the teaching environment as intended by their leaders. We look at some of the relations associated with the fact that teachers in science/engineering disciplines experience similar leadership environments and describe using similar approaches to teaching to their colleagues in the arts/social science areas, even when their teaching leaders may describe quite different approaches to teaching leadership.

45.2 Introduction

We recently described the results of an empirical study which shows that qualitatively different approaches to teaching are associated with qualitatively different approaches to learning (Trigwell, Ramsden, Prosser and Martin, 1998). We found that in classes where teachers describe their approach to teaching as having a focus on what they do and on transmitting knowledge, students reported being more likely to adopt a surface approach to the learning of that subject. And students who report adopting significantly deeper approaches to learning than their colleagues, are found to be taught by staff who report adopting approaches to teaching that are significantly more oriented towards students and to changing their conceptions. We concluded 'Given the numerous studies that show correlations between students' deeper approaches to learning and higher quality learning outcomes, these results demonstrate the importance in attempts to improve the quality of student learning of encouraging higher quality ... [s]tudent-focused approaches to teaching.'

In the same study, we also set out to explore the relations between approaches to teaching and the environment (including leadership) experienced by the teachers, and the relations between the teachers' perceptions of leadership and their head of department's experience of leadership.

Previous research on school effectiveness and educational management (Mortimore, 1988; Foster, 1989; Ramsden, 1991; Louis, 1993; Meek and Wood, 1997) work on academic leadership in higher education (Moses and Roe, 1990; Middlehurst, 1993; Ramsden, 1998) and work on leadership more generally (see for example Burns, 1978; Bass, 1985; Prosser and Trigwell, 1997) suggest that approaches to teaching which are related to more effective student learning will be more common in certain departmental contexts. Such environments will be characterized by members perceptions of consistent policies of control and delegation, participatory management, inspiring, visionary, and value-driven ('transformational') leadership, high levels of inter-colleague collaboration and an emphasis on concern for students.

We hypothesized that these contextual characteristics will facilitate the development and practice of more reflective approaches to teaching, assessment and course design. Approaches like these imply an understanding of university teaching as 'making student learning possible' rather than just transmitting knowledge and presenting information. This is a view of teaching as a professional activity — a problematic enterprise demanding expert judgement and a process capable of being continuously improved (Ramsden, 1992).

45.3 Methodology

In this chapter we only report on the quantitative component of the study (outcomes of the qualitative component are reported elsewhere (Martin *et al.*, submitted). Questionnaires

Transformational Leadership

5. Shows staff how to go beyond traditional approaches to teaching.
24. Brings new ideas about teaching and learning into department or course.

Firm but Fair Leadership

16. Is prepared to take unpopular decisions when necessary.
19. Listens to what staff have to say.
23. Treats teaching staff equitably and consistently.

Strategic Orientation

15. Works to generate a shared vision of department or course.
25. Manages physical and financial resources effectively.

Improvement and Recognition

11. Encourages and enables staff to be self-critical and willing to seek constant improvement in their teaching.
20. Ensures that teaching staff take account of student expectations, experiences and satisfaction in planning and teaching their subjects.

Figure 45.1 Sample items used in interviews with departmental heads

developed and tested in previous studies and in some cases adapted for this study were taken to heads of departments, and sent to teachers in one large course in those departments, and to students studying that course.

Complete data sets were collected from 35 first-year courses in four discipline areas: Arts / Social Sciences; Business / Economics / Law; Science / Engineering; and Health Sciences. Heads of Department were asked the questions on a questionnaire designed to ascertain their approach to the leadership of teaching in their department in four areas: transformational leadership; firm but fair leadership; strategic orientation; and improvement and recognition. Sample items from the interview list are given in Figure 45.1.

Approximately ten of the teachers in each of the courses were asked to complete two inventories. The first (Approaches to Teaching Inventory, Prosser and Trigwell, 1999) contains 16 items in two scales: Information Transmission / Teacher-focused approach and Conceptual Change / Student-focused approach. Sample items from both are included in Figure 45.2.

Information Transmission/Teacher-focused (ITTF) approach

32. I feel it is important to present a lot of facts in classes so that students know what they have to learn for this subject.
27. I design my teaching in this subject with the assumption that most of the students have very little useful knowledge of the topics to be covered.

Conceptual Change/Student-focused (CCSF) approach

45. I feel a lot of teaching time in this subject should be used to question students' ideas.
36. We take time out in classes so that the students can discuss, among themselves, the difficulties that they encounter studying this subject.

Figure 45.2 Sample items from both scales of the Approaches to Teaching Inventory

The second inventory aimed to determine teachers' perceptions of their leadership environment. It contains four scales: transformational leadership; clear goals and contingent rewards; teacher involvement; and collaborative management. Sample items from these scales are shown in Figure 45.3.

Transformational Leadership

17. The head of this department enables you to think about old things in new ways.
25. The head gives me confidence as a teacher.

Clear Goals and Contingent Rewards

8. You usually have a clear idea of what's expected of you as a teacher here.
12. The head readily acknowledges your contributions to teaching.

Teacher Involvement

2. Academic staff in this department spend a good deal of time talking to each other about their teaching.
21. Academic staff here are keen to learn from each other.

Collaborative Management

20. The head of this department listens to what you have to say.
23. The head delegates responsibility fairly and consistently.

Figure 45.3 Sample items from the four scales measuring teachers' perceptions of their leadership environment

Students were sent adaptations of the Course Experience Questionnaire (Ramsden, 1991) and the Study Process Questionnaire (Biggs, 1987a and b).

As the unit of analysis is the course/department, teachers' mean scores on both inventories, and students' mean scores on both questionnaires, for each course, were computed and that mean score used in the analyses. Correlations (Pearson) and Hierarchical Cluster Analysis (Ward method) were used as the tools of analysis.

45.4 Results

With respect to disciplinary differences, there are no significant differences between disciplines in scores for students' approaches to learning, teachers' approaches to teaching or the Head's view of leadership variables.

There are also no significant differences between disciplines in relations between teachers' approaches to teaching and their students' approaches to learning.

Table 45.1 shows the results for the correlations between student approaches to learning and teachers approaches to teaching for all courses in this study. The table shows positive relations between a CCSF teaching approach and a deep approach to learning and positive relations between a ITTF teaching approach and a surface approach to learning. Additionally they show a strong negative relation between the teachers' CCSF approach and their students' surface approach to learning. These results are consistent with, and extend the relations found in the results reported by Trigwell, Prosser and Waterhouse (1999) for sciences courses.

Variables	Variables			
	1	2	3	4
1. CCSF Teaching	-	-22	38**	-46**
2. ITTF Teaching		-	-14	34*
3. Deep Approach to learning			-	-23
4. Surface Approach to learning				-

Pearson Correlation Coeffecients, decimal points removed *p < .05, **p < .01; n = 50
CCSF is Conceptual Change/Student-focused; ITTF is Information Transmission/Teacher-focused

Table 45.1 Correlation between teachers' approach to teaching and students' approach

Variables	Variables			
	1	2	3	4
1. Head of Dept. view of leading	-	07 *-42** **55***	16 *-12* **41***	12 *55** **-25**
2. Teachers' perception of leadership		-	03 06 **02**	-26* -39* **-18**
3. CCSF approach to teaching			-	-22 -35* **-15**
4. ITTF approach to teaching				-

Pearson Correlation Coeffecients, decimal points removed; *p <.05
CCSF is Conceptual Change/Student-focused; ITTF is Information Transmission/Teacher-focused

Table 45.2 Correlation between teachers' approach to teaching, their perceptions of leadership and their heads view of leadership variables for all disciplines *Science, Engineering, Health Science courses (n = 18)* Arts, Social Sciences, Business, Law courses (n = 17)

Table 45.2 reports the correlations between the head of department's view of leading teaching, the perceptions of leadership of the teachers in those departments, and the approaches to teaching of those teachers.

There are three things to note about these results. First, for the whole data set (35 cases) there are no significant relations between the head's view of leadership and the perceptions of that leadership held by the teachers being led, and in those departments where teachers perceive a supportive teaching environment they are less likely to adopt an Information Transmission/Teacher-focused approach (R = -.26). Second, in the Science, Engineering, Health Science courses (18 cases) when heads describe a view of leading which is supportive of teaching, lecturers are more likely to perceive it as not being supportive (-.42) and are more likely to adopt more of an Information Transmission/Teacher-focused approach (.55). And third, in the Arts, Social Sciences, Business, Law courses (17 cases) when heads describe a view of leading which is supportive of teaching, lecturers are more likely to perceive it as such (.55) and are more likely to adopt more of Conceptual Change/Student-focused approach (.41).

A cluster analysis of the same variables for the whole data set is shown in Table 45.3.

The preferred two cluster solution shown in Table 45.3 shows significant differences in relative mean scores between the clusters only for the Conceptual Change/Student-focused approach to teaching variable. However, when the sample is split into the two different

Variable	Clusters 1 (n = 10)	Clusters 2 (n = 25)
Head of Dept. view of leading	.40 (.90)	-.16 (1.00)
Teachers' percept. of leadership	-.57 (1.04)	.25 (.83)
CCSF approach to teaching	.77 (.69)	-.55 (.86)
ITTF approach to teaching	-.71 (1.09)	.05 (.68)

n = 35; standard deviations in parentheses
CCSF is Conceptual Change/Student-focused;
ITTF is Information Transmission/Teacher-focused

Table 45.3 Cluster analysis of the head's view of leading, teachers' perceptions of the leadership environment and their approach to teaching for the whole sample (4 discipline areas, 35 courses)

Variable	Clusters 1 (n = 6)	Clusters 2 (n = 12)
Head of Dept. view of leading	.90 (.79)	-.45 (.78)
Teachers' percept. of leadership	-.50 (1.08)	.33 (.51)
CCSF approach to teaching	-.62 (1.19)	.02 (.58)
ITTF approach to teaching	.53 (.74)	-.47 (.79)

n = 18; standard deviations in parentheses
CCSF is Conceptual Change/Student-focused;
ITTF is Information Transmission/Teacher-focused

Table 45.4 Cluster analysis of the head's view of leading, teachers' perceptions of the leadership environment and their approach to teaching for the Science, Engineering, Health Science courses (n = 18)

disciplinary groups used in the correlation analysis, quite different clustering patterns are found (Tables 45.4 and 45.5).

Cluster 2 in Table 45.4 contains 12 Science/Engineering departments and shows that these teachers perceive a leadership environment that is more supportive of teaching than their colleagues in cluster 1, and when they do, they adopt less of a information transfer/teacher-focused approach than their colleagues in the other six departments (cluster 1). However, in those same departments where there is a perception of more supportive leadership (cluster 2) the Heads of department have lower mean scores on the quality of their leadership than their fellow heads in the other six departments. In these 18 Science/Engineering departments, the heads' view of leadership is often not in alignment with the perceptions of leadership of teachers in that department.

Variable	Clusters	
	1 (n = 3)	2 (n = 14)
Head of Dept. view of leading	-1.33 (1.13)	.29 (.74)
Teachers' percept. of leadership	-1.16 (.69)	.20 (1.08)
CCSF approach to teaching	-1.67 (.73)	.19 (.88)
ITTF approach to teaching	.15 (.63)	-.27 (.92)

n = 17; standard deviations in parentheses
CCSF is Conceptual Change/Student-focused;
ITTF is Information Transmission/Teacher-focused

Table 45.5 Cluster analysis of the head's view of leading, teachers' perceptions of the leadership environment and their approach to teaching for the Arts, Social Sciences, Law, Economics, Business courses (n = 17)

In Table 45.5, the differences between the clusters in the relative mean scores of all variables except the Information Transmission/Teacher-focused approach to teaching variable are significant.

The pattern of results is also quite different to that reported in Table 45.4. In Table 45.5 the three variables that show significant differences between the clusters are in alignment in both clusters. Cluster 2 contains 14 cases which have the highest relative mean scores on the Head's view of leadership, the teachers' perceptions of the leadership environment and on a Conceptual Change/Student-focused approach to teaching. Cluster 1 courses have the lower relative mean score on the same three variables.

45.5 Conclusions

The number of cases used in the analyses for in this study is small for such analyses and any interpretation of the results reported above, especially related to the disciplinary differences, should be conducted with considerable caution. However, because the results for the two disciplinary areas appear to be so different (and surprising), we have decided to comment further and to offer some explanations for the apparent differences in what is, a hitherto unexplored area.

The apparent discipline differences in relations between leading and teaching as described in Tables 45.3—45.5 are surprising. Two elements of the differences are noteworthy. First, where Arts/Business teachers perceive a leadership environment that is supportive of good teaching they adopt more of a Conceptual Change/Student-focused approach, while where Science/Engineering teachers perceive a leadership environment that supports good teaching they adopt less of a Information Transmission/Teacher-focuse approach. In the latter case, there is no significant difference in Conceptua Change/Student-focused approach to teaching scores between the two clusters.

Any implications of these results related to causality between variables are speculativ The relations between variables described here do not necessarily reflect causal relation But in the same way that students' perceptions of their learning environment factors (suc as assessment) which correlate with students approaches to learning are used in an attemp to improve students' approaches to learning (see for example Gibbs, 1992), there may b implications in these results for leadership development programmes.

The results might suggest that leadership development programmes in Arts/Business, successful, are more likely to result in the encouragement of Conceptual Change/Studen focused approaches to teaching, but have little effect on Information Transmission/Teache focused approaches. Increasing the perceptions of a supportive teaching environment i Science/Engineering courses is likely to decease the Information Transmission/Teache focused approach, but have little effect on Conceptual Change/Student-focused approache to teaching.

The implications for Science/Engineering leadership development programmes woul appear to be not so clear, and are related to the second of the points referred to above: Th the Heads of Arts/Business department's view of leadership is in alignment with th perceptions of leadership of teachers in that department, while the Heads c Science/Engineering department's view of leadership is not in alignment with th perceptions of leadership of teachers in that department. If these two results for th Science/Engineering departments are taken together, they suggest that improvin leadership in Science/Engineering departments may not have the desired effects o teaching improvements. Instead, what may be needed is work on supporting Science Engineering leaders to explore the perceptions of leadership of teachers in the departments, as the way the head's leadership is perceived by teachers is not in alignme with the way they describe their leadership.

In this study we have made no attempt to explain why the results reported here may hav come about — that would need to be conducted in a differently designed study. Howeve we can hypothesize on the reasons, and note that there may be different cultures c communication in the different disciplines which could account for some of the variatio For example, it is possible that on teaching issues, Science/Engineering heads are mo likely to work alone, and make decisions through less of a consultative process than the colleagues in Arts/Business departments. This would mean that teachers in th Science/Engineering departments were less aware of their Head's approach to leadersh than their teaching colleagues in other departments.

These conclusions are to a large extent consistent with the results reported by Kekä (1999) on disciplinary differences in academic leadership. Even though the focus of th study is heavily on the research side of academic life, it is concluded that democrat leadership is more likely to be valued in sociology, that in physics and biology a culture valuing measurability, exact knowledge and certain linear thinking is supportive individualism in management, and that in history, where individualism is more the researc cultural 'norm' there is variation in leadership styles with the expectation that the leader w contribute to the well-being of his/her department.

45.6 References

Bass, B.M. (1985) *Leadership and Performance Beyond Expectations*, New York: Free Press.

Biggs, J.B. (1987a) *Student Approaches to Learning and Studying*. Hawthorne, Victoria, Australian Council for Educational Research.

Biggs, J.B. (1987b) *The Study Process Questionnaire (SPQ) Users' Manual*. Hawthorne, Victoria, Australian Council for Educational Research.

Burns, J.M. (1978) *Leadership*. New York: Harper & Row.

Foster, W. (1989) The administrator as a transformative intellectual, *Peabody Journal of Education* **66**, 5—18.

Gibbs, G. (1992) *Improving the Quality of Student Learning*. Bristol: Technical and Educational Services.

Kekäle, J. (1999) Preferred patterns of academic leadership in different disciplinary subcultures, *Higher Education* **37**: 217—38.

Louis, K. S. (1993) Beyond bureaucracy: rethinking how schools change. Invited address, International Congress for School Effectiveness and Improvement, Norrköping, January 1993.

Martin, E., Trigwell, K., Prosser, M. & Ramsden, P. (submitted for publication) *Variation in the experience of leadership of teaching in higher education.*

Meek, L. and Wood, F. (1997) *Higher Education Governance and Management. An Australian Study. Evaluations and Investigations Program*. DEETYA. Canberra: AGPS.

Middlehurst, R. (1993) *Leading Academics*. Buckingham: Open University Press.

Mortimore, P. (1988) *School Matters: The Junior Years*. Wells: Open Books.

Moses, I. and Roe, E. (1990) *Heads and Chairs: Managing Academic Departments*. St Lucia: University of Queensland Press.

Prosser, M. and Trigwell, K. (1997) Perceptions of the teaching environment and its relationship to approaches to teaching, *British Journal of Educational Psychology* **67**: 25—35.

Prosser, M. and Trigwell, K. (1999) *Understanding Learning and Teaching: The Experience in Higher Education*. Buckingham: Open University Press.

Ramsden, P. (1991) A performance indicator of teaching quality in higher education: The Course Experience Questionnaire, *Studies in Higher Education* **16**: 129—50.

Ramsden, P. (1992) *Learning to Teach in Higher Education*. London: Routledge

Ramsden, P. (1998) *Learning to Lead in Higher Education*. London: Routledge

Trigwell, K., Prosser, M. and Waterhouse, F. (1999) Relations between teachers' approaches to teaching and students' approaches to learning, *Higher Education* **37**: 57—70.

Trigwell, K., Ramsden, P., Prosser, M. and Martin, E. (1998) Improving student learning through a focus on the teaching context. In C. Rust (ed.), *Improving Student Learning*. Oxford: Oxford Centre for Staff Development, pp. 97—103.

46 Engineers are different: the application of alternative pedagogic strategies in an engineering context

S. Wareing and F.J van der Linde
University of Wales College, Newport

46.1 Overview

Engineering staff on a UWCN Educational Development Programme opened a debate about the applicability to engineering of the learning and teaching methods introduced by the Programme. This led to an enquiry into whether the methods of learning and teaching used within the Engineering Department were, at least in part, a result of philosophical characteristics of the discipline. This enquiry could be expressed as: to what extent do different disciplines place varying emphasis on the categories of Bloom's learning taxonomy? Is this difference in emphasis the source of differences in delivery methods and are such differences to some extent defensible or are they only the result of unexamined tradition? This chapter presents the application of a version of Bloom's taxonomy to two teaching and learning strategies. For the purpose of this chapter only the cognitive domain of Bloom's taxonomy was considered. The results of a pilot study using a teaching and learning strategy based on problem based learning are presented. The study shows that this strategy may be especially suited to teaching and learning in Engineering. Three strengths of this delivery method are the framework it provides for defining module objectives, the ease of mapping the objectives into this delivery method and the performance and attitudes of the students, as observed in the pilot study.

46.2 Introduction

This chapter describes an action research project conducted with HNC/HND Engineering students at University of Wales College, Newport. (HNC stands for Higher National Certificate; HND stands for Higher National Diploma; both are sub-degree level qualifications). The project was the result of a debate between the authors about whether, and how, the learning outcomes of Engineers differed from those in Humanities & Social Sciences, and whether the interactive methods proposed by much educational development literature were in fact applicable in the engineering disciplines. It is often said by staff who teach Engineering at UWCN that the extent to which there are 'right' answers for students of engineering is greater than for, say, English Literature students. As a consequence of this belief, contact time with Engineering students is often directed to learning associated with the lower levels of Bloom's taxonomy (knowledge, comprehension, and application, in decreasing order of emphasis; see Figure 46.1). The authors wished to explore whether the teaching and learning strategies most widely used in the Engineering Department are an appropriate response to the inherent requirements of the discipline, or whether more interactive strategies could also achieve learning outcomes appropriate to engineers.

The project contrasted two different teaching and learning strategies. One group of

HNC/HND Engineering students was taught two different modules on the same day by the same lecturer. One module was taught by the traditional lecture-based method, i.e. three hours of contact, largely spent with the students listening and the lecturer talking and writing on the board. The other module was taught using a variation of 'problem based learning', where the students spend the three hours working in groups on realistic engineering problems, with very little lecturer input to the whole class. The resulting examination performances of the students were compared.

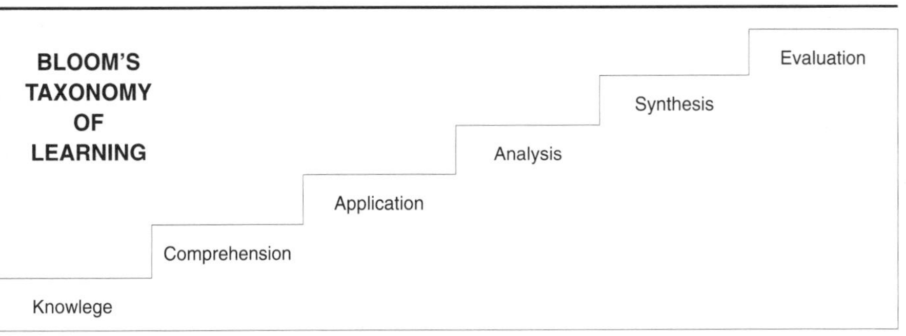

Figure 46.1 Bloom's Taxonomy of Learning

We used Bloom's Taxonomy as a theoretical structure to underpin our study. Bloom proposed that learning, in the cognitive domain, could be regarded as occurring in hierarchical stages, as illustrated in Figure 46.1.

The initial aim of the project was to determine the constraints on and benefits from applying alternative delivery methods to Engineering modules. However, a variety of secondary questions were identified, which we hoped this project would begin to address (they are obviously far-reaching questions):

- Is engineering different (or to be more specific, is problem based learning more suitable to relatively open-ended disciplines than to a discipline like engineering, with its emphasis on the 'right' answers)?
- Do changes in delivery methods have a significant impact on students' learning outcomes?
- Can changes in delivery methods in the direction of problem based learning compensate for the loss experienced in the last few years of tutorial and laboratory time from the engineering timetable?
- Can problem based learning simultaneously develop higher level cognitive skills such as analysis and synthesis and at the same time provide a suitable framework for students to discover underpinning knowledge?
- Do traditional teaching and learning methods result in HNC/HND students working mostly at the comprehension/application end of Bloom's taxonomy?
- If so, is this acceptable?

46.3 Overview of the UWCN project

The study reported here involved 16 students and the results should be seen in the context of a small-scale study. The students were in their second year of an HNC/HND in electrical and electronic engineering, in which one of the authors taught two modules. They were timetabled for a three-hour session per week for each module. Approximately half the students are sent by their employers, who expect them to attend the lectures but not necessarily to pass the exam. The group is consequently characterized by low motivation.

The teaching and learning strategy which is most widely used in the department is to divide the three hours into two lectures with a break between. During the lectures, the lecturer talks and writes on the board, stating and demonstrating theories and their applications. The students listen and write notes (or at least, are assumed to). Some students ask questions, and the lecturer answers. Students are set a tutorial to do for the following week, part of which the lecturer may demonstrate on the board during the following session. The ratio of time the lecturer spends talking in comparison to the students is not estimated to be lower than 9:1. Students are not encouraged to talk to one another about their work in class. The emphasis is on the lecturer presenting a large amount of factual information.

The alternative delivery method that was selected for this study is a derivative of problem based learning, not applied elsewhere in the University College at the moment. The methods used differs from traditional problem-based learning in the following ways:

- It was applied to a single module rather than being across the curriculum to bridge between subjects.
- The problem cycles were short, usually one week.
- The students were allowed to work individually or as groups of their own selection, rather than being placed in fixed groups.
- Part of the assessment was by examination. Although this assessment method is not particularly suitable for problem based learning, it had to be retained as part of the departmental requirement that the course was not fundamentally altered. That is, the learning outcomes, the course structure and the assessment methodology as described in the course handbook had to be retained.

From here, the modules will be referred to as PBL (problem based learning) and NPBL (non-problem based learning).

During the PBL module a new problem was introduced each week. The problems were selected in a way to make them industrially relevant, but also in a way that required the students to develop their own versions of the underpinning theory. Intervention by the lecturer only occurred on request of the students. On no occasion was the full solution to a problem presented. Every effort was made to ensure that the sessions did not deteriorate into lecture/tutorial combination sessions, but that the students were able to evolve their own learning process in response to the problem.

The study was evaluated in three ways. First, approximately midway through the module, a questionnaire was used to evaluate the general feeling of the students with respect to the course and to determine if there were any major problems that had not surfaced during the delivery. Secondly, the author kept a record of observations during the delivery period. Thirdly, although the examinations do not inherently suit the delivery-method, an analysis of the examination results forms part of the evaluation of this study.

46.4 Questionnaire

The students completed a questionnaire approximately midway through the course. The questionnaire consisted of three sections:

- A section in which the students' relative confidence with respect to the knowledge base.
- A section in which the students were asked if they felt that more basic knowledge, application problems or in depth problems should be added to either module.
- A general comment section, encouraging students to highlight any problems.

In the first section the students were asked to indicate in which of the subjects they felt more confident when answering assessment questions, designed to test specific learning outcomes. As will be discussed later, these questions were designed to test either recall (testing basic knowledge, comprehension and applications in well-known contexts) or application (applications of theory in new contexts) and or synthesis (higher level synthesis and problems relating to analysis).

46.4.1 Questionnaire results

With respect to the students' relative confidence in the two modules, there were large fluctuations in the results. This can be construed to indicate that the results are not reliable, or that the students had no clear preference, or both. We have assumed that the result is a combination of the students not having a clear preference and of difficulties they encountered completing the questionnaire making the results unreliable.

The students also indicated that they were disturbed by the lack of underlying theory provided in the problem based learning module. This result was not unexpected since these students were in the final semester of the course, having been exposed previously only to formal lectures and traditional tutorial sessions, and never having been required to develop theories for themselves.

Under the general comments section, the most common response was complaints about lack of resources. Although handouts were prepared each week, this comment should be seen in the context of the students' not previously being required to do much of their own research. The role of the lecturer also required clarification and there were complaints about having to work at home. It appeared that many of the students felt it was unreasonable to have to work regularly at home except in direct preparation for examinations.

46.5 Examination

For the evaluation of the questionnaire and in the creation of the examination a modified version of Bloom's taxonomy was used. To make the process easier to evaluate, the outcomes tested were restricted to three broad categories based on Bloom's taxonomy for the cognitive domain of learning. As illustrated in Table 46.2, the three categories employed in this study were recall, application and synthesis. This structure matches the traditional method of assessment in engineering which consists of the recall of a theorem or part of a theory, proof of the ability to apply this theory and a question to evaluate the application or an aspect of it. In the PBL module, the synthesis stage was more prominent (as a natural consequence of the learning and teaching strategy and consequently in the assessment), as it includes the analysis level of the cognitive domain which tests the student's ability to

Bloom's Taxonomy	UWCN study	Ebel
Knowledge	Recall	Terminology/factual information
Comprehension	Application	Explanation
Application	Synthesis	Calculation/prediction
Analysis		
Synthesis		
Evaluation		Recommended action/evaluation

Table 46.1 A comparison of Bloom's Taxonomy, the categories used in the UWCN study and by Ebel

break the problem into suitable pieces. The taxonomy used for evaluating the study can be compared with Ebel's model, devised to assist in defining examination aims. Ebel suggested that Bloom's taxonomy is inherently difficult to map on to examination problems and evolved his own version, also shown in the table.

In the examination for the PBL module, approximately twice as many marks were allocated to the assessment of synthesis as in the NPBL module. Most of the difference was made up in the assessment of recall, towards which the NPBL module was biased.

46.6 Examination results

The histogram of students' marks (Figure 46.2) and the detailed analysis of the average marks achieved for each question type in the papers show that generally the average (mean) student performance was identical in the two modules. Some students did perform better in

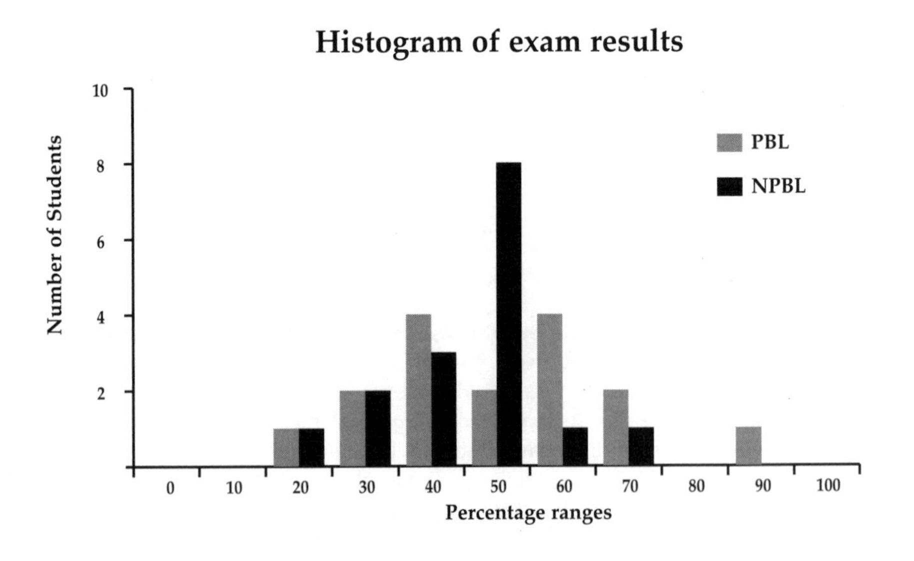

Figure 46.2

Averages	PBL	NPBL
Overall (total marks)	44 %	44 %
Recall	46 %	53 %
Application	41 %	24 %
Synthesis	43 %	38 %

Table 46.2 The average (mean) marks achieved in the assessment of each cognitive level by all students

the PBL module (these students were the ones perceived by the lecturer to be more motivated) but most students did not perceive much variation in their marks between the two modules. However, one student had a difference of more than 20% in his marks and one student had differences of more than 15% in his final marks (the higher mark was for the PBL module in both cases) between the two. There was little difference in the student ranking for the two courses.

The results suggest that students did do better in the higher level cognitive skills in the PBL examination. The marks for recall were slightly lower in the PBL module, but there was a marked improvement in the skills of application and synthesis. More of the specified learning outcomes of the module, linked to application and synthesis had been achieved by explicitly attempting to develop the high-level cognitive skills of the students.

46.7 Conclusion and observations

As an attempt to improve the learning of students the study regarded as a success by the authors. Although there was not a significant difference between the total marks achieved in the two modules, the students did achieve more high-level outcomes in the PBL module. Furthermore, the assessment of the PBL module was harder since it focused on higher levels of the learning taxonomy, and therefore by achieving the same average (mean) mark, the students were in fact performing better. The students appeared by the end of the modules not to have a clear preference for either of delivery method.

An interesting observation was made of the students' learning of the high-level cognitive skills (those above the application level). It appeared these skills were learned in a cyclical manner; i.e. students became better at them through repeated opportunities to practice them. This poses interesting problems when considering the module structure to ensure repetition exercises for the development of the high-level skills.

In summary, positive aspects of the study were:

- the higher level of development of the students' cognitive skills;
- the lecturer's observation that although the same preparation time was required, the delivery of the three hour sessions was much easier in the PBL module;
- the creation of unique problem solutions. Some of the solutions produced by students were so unusual that they had to be studied in detail by the lecturer to determine if they were valid, which they almost always were. In one instance a student used a radically different approach to arrive at the correct answer. Thereafter the student was accredited with having his own theorem, Hillman's theorem, by his colleagues;
- that once they had become accustomed to the methodology, students complained

when too much general assistance was provided by the lecturer in the PBL sessions;

- that a framework for experimental studies such as this in the department had been established.

Possible criticisms which could be levelled at the study include:

- The use of same lecturer to teach both modules. This theoretically eliminated some of the variables from the study, but the drawback was that the students expected to be taught in a consistent manner by the lecturer.
- A lack of information on appropriate criteria for the selection of problems and how best to evaluate and assess the students on PBL by means of a formal examination.
- That although the PBL module seemed to increase the motivation of students who were already motivated, unfortunately it did not appear to carry intrinsic motivational value for unmotivated students.
- That initially, the students required lots of help to define the problems on the PBL module, and this remained a problem. Every attempt was made by the lecturer not give too much assistance since this was one of the key aspects of the study.
- Perhaps the single most constraining aspect of study was the requirement for the module to be assessed by examination. Although not impossible, it probably reflected poorly the true progress of the students and advantages of the PBL approach.

To return to the questions posed in introduction.

- As far as PBL is concerned, Engineering appears to be no different from other disciplines. The fact that the solutions are not necessarily open-ended may encourage students to critically evaluate their work, enhancing learning rather than inhibiting it.
- The delivery method does have an impact on learning outcomes. In this case PBL had a positive impact since it achieved more high level outcomes.
- It is not clear what the role of PBL can be in compensating for lost contact time, but since less time is spent on traditional delivery, more time is available for other activities. However, this may require helping students manage their time and ensuring that they are set milestones.
- The results of the exams (although based on a small sample), indicate that PBL can enhance the development of higher level skills while maintaining traditional levels of underpinning knowledge.
- However, the fact that the students developed enhanced high-level cognitive skills in the PBL course does not necessarily establish that traditional delivery methods inhibit it.
- There are different ideas as to what the ratio of skills outcomes for courses should be, compared to content recall outcomes, so a decision on what would be an acceptable ratio is inevitably subjective. The authors were pleased with the shift in emphasis brought about by PBL.

There are more fundamental questions underlying the study reported here. Most of them remain unanswered but are the subjects of our ongoing research:

- Are Bloom's labels appropriate or useful descriptions of what we want people to be able to do?
- Are they in fact hierarchical in the level of sophistication involved?
- Is demonstration of the 'higher level skills' dependent on the prior acquisition of the 'lower level skills'?
- Is it possible to bring the 'higher level skills' to bear in a new context where you might not have knowledge or comprehension?
- Is the order correct (or should, for example, synthesis rank 'higher' than evaluation?)

46.1 References

Boud, D. and Feletti, G.I. (1997) *The Challenge of Problem-based Learning*, 2nd edn. London: Kogan Page.

Center for Teaching and Learning, Stanford University (1992) The agony and the equity, *Speaking of Teaching: Stanford University Newsletter on Teaching* **3**(1).

Reece, I. and Walker, S. (1997) *Teaching, Training and Learning*, 3rd edn. Sunderland: Business Education Publishers.

47 In-service education of science and mathematics teachers: which factors generate best practice?

Paul Webb

Department of Science, Mathematics and Technology Education, University of Port Elizabeth, South Africa

47.1 Introduction

Research into the impact of in-service continuing professional education for teachers, i.e. INSET (In-service Education and Training) or CPD (Continuing Professional Development), suggests that in-service activities have very varied influences on teachers and that different teachers nominate different outcomes as accruing from the same INSET provision (Eraut 1994, Joyce and Showers 1980, Steadman *et al.* 1995). It also appears that certain outcomes are more likely to achieve concrete developments in the classroom than others (Harland and Kinder 1997).

The problems surrounding Science and Mathematics Education contribute greatly to the current national crisis in education in South Africa. At present there are a large number of under-qualified in-service teachers who lack the knowledge and skills to teach these subjects competently. Successful teaching of Science and Mathematics is further constrained in this country because teachers often lack proficiency in the most common medium of instruction, English. This problem is exacerbated by the fact that learning also takes place through the medium of a second language.

The above problems naturally apply to any other subject that must be taught, but it is universally accepted that the specifically conceptual nature of Science and Mathematics compounds the issue dramatically as far as these subjects are concerned. Moreover, pre-service teacher education in these subjects in South Africa has frequently been of poor quality. For these reasons it is especially problematical for teachers to equip themselves to be adequate teachers of Science or Mathematics. This need underpinned the development of an INSET course at the University of Port Elizabeth which attempts to provide both a thorough understanding of the concepts, and mastery of those methodological, language and classroom management skills which are fundamental to the successful teaching of Science and Mathematics.

The measurement of teacher competencies forms an integral part of the curriculum, therefore assessment of classroom practice plays an important role in the learning and evaluation process. Teachers registered for this in-service professional teacher education initiative are taught at satellite campuses and comprise of teachers in a range of teaching situations, i.e. from urban to deep-rural farm school classrooms. This geographically diverse group of teachers provided the sample population for the study.

Although a great deal of INSET activity has taken place in South Africa over the past two decades, there is a paucity of empirical research into INSET outcomes, particularly at the levels of teacher and pupil knowledge and skills. The specific purpose of this study was herefore to investigate which factors in the teacher development process generate best practice in primary Science and Mathematics classrooms. This was done within a theoretical ramework of INSET outcomes as described by Harland and Kinder (1997) and the findings vere used to inform the further development and implementation of this particular INSET urriculum.

47.2 Theoretical frame of reference

As noted above, research into the impact of in-service continuing professional education for eachers, i.e. INSET (In-service Education and Training) or CPD (Continuing Professional Development), suggests that in-service activities have very varied influences on teachers. These differences suggest that INSET participants have a unique 'outcome route' following n in-service experience and that they rarely achieve exactly the same permutation of utcomes as other colleagues (Harland and Kinder, 1997).

Also, when teachers' accounts of the impact of INSET experience on their classroom epertoire are juxtaposed with classroom observation of their practice, it is apparent that ertain outcomes are more likely to achieve concrete developments in the classroom than thers. This observation, and the assumption that improved classroom practice is the ltimate intended INSET goal, prompted Harland and Kinder (1997) to develop a tentative equence or hierarchy of outcomes (Figure 47.1).

INSET input			
3rd order	Provisionary	Information	New awareness
2nd order	Motivation	Affective	Institutional
1st order	Value congruence	Knowledge and skills	
Impact on practice			

Figure 47.1 An ordering of INSET outcomes (Harland and Kinder, 1997)

While recognizing that by singling out the outcomes (or effects of in-service provision and ctivity) side of a general theory of effective INSET may encourage mechanistic input–utput perspectives on Continuing Professional Development (CPD), Harland and Kinder 1977) believe that, as most of the research conducted to date has tended to dwell on the rocesses of change and in-service activity (Hall and Olroyd, 1988; McBride, 1989; Webb, 1989; Galloway, 1989; Harland, 1990; Harland and Kinder, 1992; Day, 1993; Harland *et al.*, 1993; Bolam, 1994; Eraut, 1994; Law and Glover, 1995; McMahon and Ballard, 1995; teadman *et al.*, 1995), it is appropriate at this juncture to pay more attention to the ways we onceptualize the outcomes of teacher CPD. This approach appears to be sensible when esearching which factors of INSET generate best practice in the classroom, i.e. the focus of his study.

47.3 Research design and methods

The research methodology used in this study combined both quantitative and qualitative trategies. Quantitative strategies included pre- and post-tests to assess the level of, and hanges in, conceptual knowledge in both teachers and pupils. Tests were drawn up to ather data on skills and understandings of scientific and mathematical concepts in the reas of fractions, electricity and measurement. The questions asked in the tests were based n misconceptions identified in international literature, the syllabus followed in South African schools, and the past experiences of the researchers when working with teachers and pupils. The same tests were administered to both teachers and pupils and the dat generated were used for statistical analyses.

The qualitative strategies used in this study included the use of classroom observatio schedules and semi-structured interviews of teachers.

47.3.1 Teachers' knowledge

Data on teachers' knowledge and understandings of Science and Mathematics concept were collected by testing all in-service teachers participating in the Diploma in Educatio Primary Phase (focusing on Science and Mathematics) course (DE). The focus areas wer fractions, electricity and measurement. These tests were trialled in 1997 as part of a informal evaluation of teacher and pupil knowledge. Separate tests were administered fo each of these topics. The first-year students (teachers) wrote these tests early in the year and as such, had not been exposed to DE coursework tuition on these topics before being tested These samples of teachers, i.e. for fractions (n = 71), electricity (n = 65) and measurement (= 97) were therefore considered to represent teachers prior to the 'treatment' (INSET initiative).

The second-year students had been exposed to DE tuition on fractions (n = 49) an electricity (n = 55) during their first year of study and, as such, were considered to be th 'post-treatment' sample. However, the second-year students had not been exposed to D tuition on measurement and therefore this sample group (n = 49) yielded both pre-test (prio to DE tuition) and post-test (after DE tuition) data in this topic.

All test were uniquely coded and the data subjected to BMDP statistical analysis. Th treatment yielded general descriptive data, frequency tables, and analysis of varianc (ANOVA) tables with tail probabilities using F values and Welch, Brown-Forsythe an Levene's test statistics for variances.

47.3.2 Pupil outcomes

Data on pupil outcomes were gathered by testing the pupils of the sample of teachers wh had volunteered to participate in the classroom evaluation component of this study (n = 37 viz 19 DE 1 teachers and 18 DE 2 teachers). Again the focus areas were fractions, electricit and measurement. Separate tests were administered for each of these topics. These test were identical to the tests written by the teachers. However, all members of the pupil sampl wrote both pre- and post-tests, i.e. prior to being exposed to tuition on the topic by thei teacher (pre-test) and after receiving tuition on the topic by their teacher (post-test).

A total of 549 pupils comprised the sample group tested on fractions, *viz.*, 376 pupils o first-year teachers (DE1) and 173 pupils taught by second-year (DE2) teachers. The size o the sample group tested on concepts in electricity was 400, with 172 being pupils of first year DE teachers and 228 pupils being taught by second-year teachers on the course. Th testing of pupils abilities as regards measurement was the only quantitative piece of thi research where the sizes of the pre- and post-test groups differed significantly in numbe *viz.*, the DE 1 pre- and post-test groups consisted of 340 and 101 pupils respectively, whil the DE 2 pre- and post-test groups consisted of 146 and 73 pupils respectively.

All test answer sheets were uniquely coded, with pupils being linked to their teacher and the data subjected to BMDP statistical analysis. The treatment yielded gener descriptive data, frequency tables, and analysis of variance (ANOVA) tables with ta probabilities using F values and Welch, Brown-Forsythe and Levene's test statistics fo variances.

7.3.3 Classroom observation and interviews

he qualitative strategies used in the research included the use of observation schedules sed to monitor what teachers do in the classroom. A sample of DE 1 ($n = 10$) and DE2 ($n =$ 0) were observed in their classrooms for research purposes and participated in semi-tructured interviews. The schedule used for these observations was the same as was used, nd reported on, in Rosalind Ntshinga-Khosa's 1997 report on the evaluation of the Primary cience Programme. All of the DE2 students ($n = 71$) were observed teaching twice in their lassrooms using the standard evaluation form for the course. These data were also used to etermine a framework of what is happening in DE classrooms in general.

The research interviews, using a semi-structured format, took place after the teacher had een observed in action in his/her classroom. Initial questions related to the lesson bserved. Follow-up questions were used when necessary to probe the information rovided by the teacher. All questions related to INSET outcomes as described in Figure 7.1.

7.4 Results and discussion

is clear that the teachers who have been on the INSET course for more than a year (DE2) ave significantly better understandings in Science and Mathematics than their peers (DE1) vho have not been exposed to this type of intervention (Table 47.1).

The differences between groups are all statistically significant ($p < 0.05$). These have been ranslated into significantly better pupil outcomes in these subjects in the classroom (Table 7.2).

	Fractions	Electricity	Measurement
DE1	67%	37%	54%
DE2	85%	65%	79%

able 47.1 DE1 and DE2 teachers' mean scores for the fractions, electricity and measurement tests

The differences between pupil pre- and post-test scores are all statistically significant ($p <$ .05) as are the differences between DE1 and DE2 pupil scores in the fractions and electricity ost-tests. There was no statistically significant difference between the DE1 and DE2 pupils'

	Pre-tests			Post-tests		
	Fraction	Electricity	Meas.	Fraction	Electricity	Meas.
DE1	14%	34%	33%	31%	41%	57%
DE2	26%	33%	29%	43%	63%	53%

able 47.2 DE1 and DE2 pupils' mean scores for the fractions, electricity and measurement pre- and post-tests

cores in the measurement post-test.

It may be appropriate at this juncture to note that the sample sizes used for the statistical nalyses in this research project have led to highly reliable statistical inferences. The fact that he results are basically similar in all three data sets, i.e. fractions, electricity and neasurement, further confirms that the conclusions of this study are highly motivated from statistical point of view. A weakness in the methodology, however, is that the 'pre' and 'post' groups of teachers are different people, thus only allowing a quasi-experimenta design based on an assumption that the two groups are similar (both groups comprise c self-selected teachers of a similar age and gender from similar socio-economic groups an teaching in similar, if not always identical, schools).

47.4.1 Classroom observation

All 20 of the Senior Primary teachers observed taught either Grade 5 Fractions, Grade Electricity or Grade 7 Measurement — the three areas that were tested for conceptua understanding. Individual scores attained in each component of the four-point sca classroom observation schedule was recorded and a comparison of DE1 and DE2 teache mean scores is illustrated in Figure 47.2.

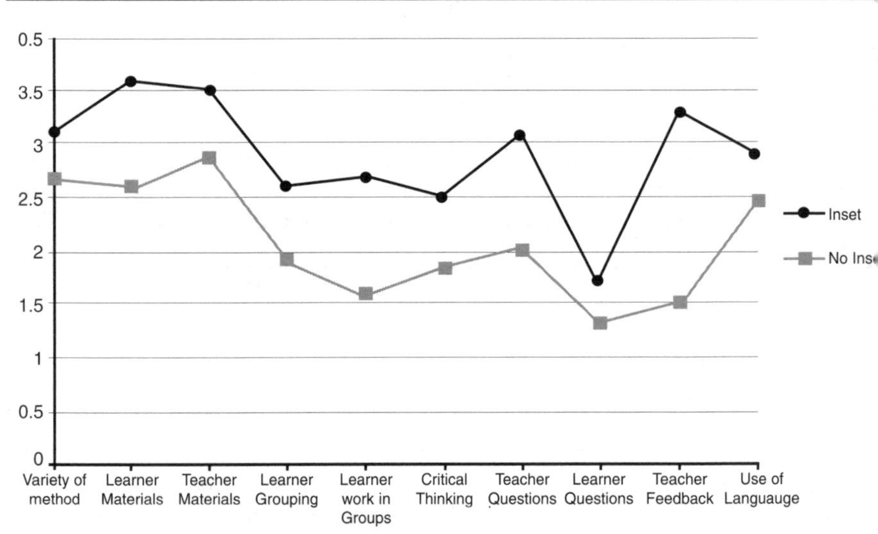

Figure 47.2 Classroom Observation Ratings

47.4.2 DE2 Teacher observations ('treatment' group)

Within the group of 10 DE2 teachers there was considerable variation in teaching style ranging from one teacher who did not appear to have gained anything from the DE in term of the alternate teaching strategies that had been modelled in the course (such as the use c group work and the use of practical teaching aids for the pupils), to those who competentl adopted the methods promulgated by the course presenters.

The lesson observed being taught by the teacher referred to initially above was sti 'teacher dominated', with information being transmitted to the pupils. At the other end c the spectrum there were teachers operating in learner centred classrooms with effective us of teaching aids and participatory group work taking place. The majority of the teache fitted onto a continuum between these two situations with all the teachers (except the on who appeared to have gained nothing) using groups in some way and using more than on teaching method that involved the pupils.

Some teachers had limited apparatus which the members of the groups shared and in other lessons all the pupils had access to apparatus and were using it. In only three lessons did some of the pupils use the apparatus while the rest of the group observed. In only one lesson did the pupils not handle any apparatus.

In three lessons the pupils were sitting in groups but were not working co-operatively. The level of discussion in the other groups varied from active discussion, possibly indicating a familiarity with group work, to other classes where little discussion took place. In seven of the eleven lessons where pupils were placed in groups there was group discussion, either spontaneously or motivated by the teacher.

In only four of the lessons did the teachers use any open-ended questions. The usual style of questioning was to ask close-ended or simple recall questions. Encouraging the pupils to ask questions is still a problematic area as only three teachers managed to get their pupils ask questions. However, on the whole, the feedback to pupils answers to teacher questions was given in a way to encourage pupils to participate.

The use of English and Xhosa as media of instruction varied and related to a large extent to the context and situation of the school. In some of the rural schools most of the teaching took place in mother tongue but there were also rural farm schools in which English was used extensively and clearly understood by the pupils.

47.4.3 DE1 Teacher observations ('control' group)

Observations in the DE1 teachers' classrooms revealed different styles of teaching. Ten teachers were observed teaching a total of 12 lessons. Four of the teachers used teaching methods that did not involve the pupils other than to have them chanting responses given by the teacher. In the remaining eight lessons the teachers used one or two methods which involved the pupils. None attempted more than two methods.

In only three classes did none of the pupils have the opportunity to manipulate apparatus. One of these classes had the smallest number of pupils. In all the other classes at least some of the pupils manipulated the teaching apparatus, but in only two classes did all the pupils manipulate the apparatus.

Although the teachers used groups in eight of the lessons, in only five of the lessons was there any interaction among the group members, and this interaction was of a limited nature. In all but one lesson, the activities were teacher driven. None of these teachers asked open-ended or probing questions and in only one class did the pupils ask questions without teacher prompting. Only two teachers gave feedback to pupil responses in a way that encouraged further effort on the part of the pupils.

In the majority of lessons the teachers used English as a medium of instruction, reverting to mother-tongue when it was apparent that the pupils did not understand the language being used.

The information obtained from the classroom observations in this study was useful in indicating trends in changing classroom teacher/pupil interactions. Although the general teacher evaluation form used for DE standard classroom evaluation does not follow the same format as the research instrument, the information it provided via a large data set supports the notion that the limited sample of classroom observations used in this research study can be generalised to the population from which the sample was taken

47.4.4 Teacher knowledge and questioning

Application of Kendall Rank Correlation and Spearman Rank Correlation Tests for non-parametric data on the DE1 and DE2 teachers' ratings for the *'teacher questions'* and *'pupil questioning'* components of the classroom observation schedule, against *'teacher knowledge'*, i.e. their scores on the tests they wrote on the topics they were teaching, revealed significantly positive correlation *both* for teacher knowledge versus quality of question asked and teacher knowledge versus teacher ability to encourage pupils to ask questions

Score 1 = Test Score n = 13
Score 2 = Teacher Question (component 7)
Score 3 = Pupil Questions (component 8)

	Kendall RC	Z	p-value	Spearman RC	T (11 dof)	Rejected at alpha
Score 1 Score 2	0.673	3.2026005	0	0.7458	4.90603846	0.005
Score 2 Score 3	0.5344	2.5430457	0.0055	0.5572	2.777177539	0.01
Score 1 Score 3	0.3993	1.9001462	0.0287	0.4596	2.073569959	0.05

CRITICAL VALUES OF t-TEST (11 dof) to reject nul hypothesis (Ho)

	alpha = 0.005	alpha = 0.01	alpha = 0.025	alpha = 0.05
	3.106	2.718	2.201	1.796

Table 47.3 Kendall and Spearman rank correlation tests correlating quality of teacher questions and teacher ability to elicit questions from pupils versus teacher subject knowledge (test score).

47.4.5 Teacher interviews

Many of the interviews with the teachers ended up as conversations about their teaching and the impact of the course on their classroom practice rather than structured interviews. However, common features emerged from all the interactions. All the teachers acknowledged that the INSET initiative had influenced the ways in which they were now teaching. All the teachers said that they had been encouraged to try the `new' methodologies presented in the course. Some mentioned that they had known about these methodologies before but had not had the confidence to try them. All commented on how well their classes responded to the activity based approaches. All the teachers interviewed commented on the importance, for them, of the regular contact with the lecturers and their colleagues. A number of the teachers had previously registered for correspondence courses and had found them unsatisfactory and in some cases demotivating because 'when you have a question or problem the book cannot give you the answer'.

The notion of institutional outcomes was alluded to by some teachers. This aspect has also been particularly noticeable during standard evaluation visits to schools where there appeared to be a palpable correlation between the number of teachers at any one institution registered for the INSET course and the outcomes generated, e.g. sharing of ideas, implementation of strategies, successful pupil outcomes, support by management (heads of department and principals), enthusiasm, etc.

Teachers' accounts of the impact of the INSET scheme on their practice made clear that the in-service activities had had a very varied influence; different teachers in effect nominated different outcomes accruing from the same INSET provision. This is in concordance with Harland & Kinder's (1997) assertions as regards the impact of INSET.

The responses given to questions on the nature of the course revealed that the teachers perceive that the INSET strategy complies with what is regarded as a 'good course' of study and suggests a satisfactory degree of *value congruence* between the developers of the course and the in-service teachers who are registered as students. Value congruence is recognized as a high order INSET outcome and one which requires careful attention when developing and executing any professional development programme for teachers.

47.5 Conclusions

The quantitative and qualitative data strongly suggest that this particular INSET intervention strategy has succeeded in bringing about changes in practice *towards what can be considered to be better Science and Mathematics teaching*. The quantitative data on teachers' knowledge clearly indicate that the teachers who have been on the in-service course focusing on Science and Mathematics Education for more than a year (DE2 teachers) have significantly better understandings of fractions, electricity and measurement than do their peers who have not been exposed to this type of intervention (DE1 teachers at the beginning of the course). In turn, this has been translated into significantly better pupil outcomes in these subjects in the classroom.

The data suggest that despite the relatively poor success rate by teachers on tests designed for their pupils, the findings in this study clearly show that the basic requirements of the first-order 'knowledge and skills' INSET outcome as described by Kinder and Harland (1997) have been met to a degree by the INSET strategy. However, it is disconcerting that a number of teachers cannot successfully complete tests on fractions, electricity, and measurement at grade five, six and seven level respectively. This is probably indicative of the inadequate schooling and initial teacher training that many teachers have received in South African institutions.

Nevertheless, the diagnostic value of the tests is of great importance as it can be used to inform constructivist practice in teacher training, i.e. provide indicators of shared misconceptions held by teachers and pupils and highlight particular areas where both groups need assistance in order to develop adequate skills. Diagnosis of these shared misconceptions is of great value in informing better practice, both for teachers when teaching their pupils and for the developers of INSET courses.

One of the first INSET outcomes to manifest itself in the classroom is the use of practical teaching aids by teachers in their teaching. Another is the physical re-arrangement of classrooms to allow pupils to sit in groups. However, this does not mean that the pupils arranged in this way automatically work co-operatively and it is suggested that group management skills be taught explicitly in INSET courses.

It appears that the most difficult aspect of teaching to change is teachers' desire and ability to ask questions of their pupils and, in turn, to get their pupils to ask questions of them. It is suggested that this reluctance may be linked to teachers' lack of conceptual understanding of the topic being taught. This in turn may be linked to teacher confidence.

Evidence from classroom observations suggests that the course has succeeded in bringing about changes in practice towards what is now considered to be better Science and Mathematics teaching. However, teachers' accounts of the impact of the INSET scheme on their practice made clear that the in-service activities had had a very varied influence; different teachers in effect nominated different outcomes accruing from the same INSET provision.

The INSET outcomes produced by this INSET strategy focusing on Science and

Mathematics fit comfortably within Harland and Kinder's (1997) hierarchy of outcomes. There are clear indications that all of their third-, second- and first-order outcomes were met to varying degrees by the INSET course and that these outcomes had differing effects on teachers, despite the same intervention. It appears that the dominant outcome generating 'best practice' in this study is the first order outcome of improved knowledge and skills.

The classroom evaluations, interviews and testing of teachers and pupils support the notion that the impact of the above outcomes on change in classroom practice can be evaluated against a number of indicators such as, and among others, the frequency and amount of Science and Mathematics tuition being undertaken by teachers; the intentionality and planning underpinning the Science and Mathematics activities provided for pupils; the organisation and management of these activities in the classroom; the nature of the interactions between teachers and pupils; the nature of the knowledge and skills of teachers and the achievements of pupils in Science and Mathematics.

It appears important that the specific outcomes that could be expected from any particular teacher development programme need to be made explicit when developing the curriculum. Also, an attempt should be made, where possible, to nurture all desired outcomes in order for the intervention to successfully generate 'best practice'. In contrast, without investigations into specific outcomes and their effects, teacher INSET is in danger of remaining at a level of generality that is insufficiently defined and precise to be of much assistance to policy makers, planners and practitioners.

Acknowledgements

This research was undertaken as part of the Presidential Education Initiative (PEI) as managed by the Joint Education Trust (JET) and funded by DANIDA.

47.6 References

Bolam, R. (1994) The impact of research on policy and practice in continuing professional development, *British Journal of In-service Education* 20: 35—46.

Day, C. (1993) *Research and the Continuing Professional Development of Teachers*. Nottingham: University of Nottingham.

Eraut, M. (1994) *Developing Professional Knowledge and Competence*. London: Falmer Press.

Galloway, S. (1989) *Identifying INSET Needs: The Case of Solihull Schools*. Warwick: Centre for Educational Development, Appraisal and Research.

Hall, V. and Oldroyd, D. (1988) *Managing INSET in Local Education Authorities*. Bristol: National Development Centre for School Management Training.

Harland, J. (1990) *The Work and Impact of Advisory Teachers*. Slough: National Foundation for Educational Research.

Harland, J. and Kinder, K. (1992) *Mathematics and Science Courses for Primary Teachers: lessons for the future*. Slough: National Foundation for Educational Research, Department of Education and Science.

Harland, J. and Kinder, K. (1997) Teachers' Continuing Professional Development: framing a model of outcomes. British Journal of In-service Education. 23 (1): 71 - 84.

Harland, J., Kinder K. and Keys, W. (1993) *Restructuring INSET: Privatisation and Its Alternatives*. Slough: National Foundation for Educational Research.

Joyce, B. and Showers, B. (1980) Improving in-service training: the messages of research. *Educational Leadership* 37: 379—85.

Law, S. and Glover, D. (1995) The professional development business: school evaluations of

LEA and higher education INSET provision, *British Journal of In-service Education* 21: 181—92.

McBride, R. (1989) *The In-service Training of Teachers*. Lewes: Falmer Press.

McMahon, A. and Ballard, H. (1995) Continuing professional development for secondary teachers. Paper presented at the *European Conference on Educational Research* (ECER). University of Bath, 14—17 September.

Ntshinga-Khosa, R. (1996) Improving Educational Quality Project (IEQ) South Africa. Evaluation of the Primary Science Programme (PSP). United States Agency for International Development. Pretoria, South Africa.

Schön, D. (1971) *Beyond the Stable State*. New York: Norton.

Steadman, S., Eraut, M., Fielding, M. and Horton, A. (1995) *Making School-based INSET Effective*. Brighton: University of Sussex Institute of Education.

Webb, R. (1989) Changing practice through consultancy-based INSET, *School Organisation* 9: 39—51.

48 Using teamwork as a learning and assessment strategy to increase understanding of the biological sciences and their relevance to nursing practice

Dr Ann White

Senior Lecturer, Faculty of Health Studies, Buckinghamshire Chilterns University College

48.1 Introduction

Nursing, in addressing the complex issues of human health and illness, draws on knowledge from many different disciplines including sociology, psychology, ethics and the biological sciences. Concern has been expressed in recent years that many qualified nurses have inadequate knowledge and understanding of the biological sciences and, therefore, experience difficulties in using knowledge from disciplines such as physiology, anatomy, pharmacology and microbiology to inform their clinical practice (Leonard and Jowett, 1990; Courtenay, 1991; Jordan, 1994; Eraut *et al.*, 1995; Jordan and Reid, 1997; Jordan *et al.*, 1999). A variety of explanations has been advanced for this. These include the lack of emphasis on the biological sciences in nursing curricula (Jervis, 1996), curriculum design and teaching strategies that divorce the learning of scientific knowledge from a consideration of its use in practice and lack of reinforcement of theoretical knowledge in practical situations (Eraut *et al.*, 1995).

This chapter describes and evaluates changes that were made to the teaching and assessment of a biological sciences module on a nursing degree course, with the aim of addressing some of these problems. The strategy combined two innovative features. First, students worked and were assessed in teams and secondly, nursing practice rather than biology was the starting point for the students' learning. The reasons for adopting these strategies will be discussed and their success evaluated but first, the context in which the changes were introduced will be briefly described.

48.2 Context

The module into which these strategies were introduced, *Using Biological Knowledge in Nursing Practice*, is taught during the first semester of the BSc (Hons) Nursing DipHE Entry (Fast Track) course at Buckinghamshire Chilterns University College. This is a one-year, full -time modular course and it is designed to give students who have recently completed a diploma in nursing the opportunity to progress quickly to degree level.

Since it had been running for five years, the course was reviewed during 1998. This gave the course team the opportunity to evaluate the philosophy, structure and content of the course in the light of developments in nursing practice and education as well as the chance to review the teaching and assessment strategies used and to make any changes to these that they considered to be necessary. One of the modules that underwent considerable modification was the biological sciences module.

48.3 The biological sciences module

When the course was originally designed it was considered essential for biological sciences to be included because it was felt that many students' knowledge and understanding of the scientific basis of nursing practice was fairly weak. During the diploma course in nursing, which students must complete before proceeding to the degree, they undertake modules in basic anatomy, physiology and pharmacology and they study disease processes relevant to their chosen branch of nursing (adult, paediatric or mental health). In order to build on learning already achieved but to give a different perspective on the biological sciences, a double module was designed, combining the study of health promotion with that of biology. Although they were linked together by their focus on health promotion and health education activities relevant to the achievement of targets published in the government document, The Health of the Nation (Department of Health,1992), it proved difficult to fully integrate the two strands of the module since they were taught separately by subject specialists. Furthermore, since the lecturer teaching the health promotion aspects of the module wished to consider political, sociological, psychological and ethical influences in addition to biological ones, the ways in which nurses might use biological knowledge to inform their practice were, perhaps, not discussed in sufficient depth.

Although the evaluation of the module has generally been fairly positive, the main criticism that students have had over the years is that not all of the topics covered were directly relevant to their clinical practice. This is difficult to achieve when many different clinical specialities are represented in the same class but attempts were made to indicate the relevance of the various topics covered in the module to different areas of clinical practice. For example, when the effects of alcohol on health were discussed it was pointed out that children's nurses could pursue this topic by looking at the effects of alcohol on the unborn child whereas students working on a general medical ward might be more interested in the chronic effects of alcohol on the liver. Those working in coronary care units might investigate the beneficial effects of alcohol in the prevention of coronary heart disease.

The teaching strategies used for the biology component of the module were designed to encourage active participation by the students. They included group work and seminar presentations in addition to more formal lectures. Reading lists containing references to recent research were given to the students each week so that they could prepare for the following week's class and be able to take an active part in discussion. This approach was not entirely successful as many students appeared to do little reading between one class and the next and there was a distinct reluctance to undertake work that was not assessed. Students seminar presentations were not always well attended and this led to a lack of group cohesion.

Problems with integration of the two disciplines were also encountered in the context of the assessment of the module. Various strategies were used in an attempt to solve this problem but none of these was entirely satisfactory. A single three-hour exam was used to assess both the biological and health promotion aspects of the module. Initially, the paper consisted of six questions, of which students were required to answer three. In their answers, students were expected to demonstrate knowledge of biology and of the principals of health promotion and, most importantly, to show links between the two subjects and discuss their relevance to nursing practice. Most students included very little biology in their answers, preferring to concentrate on the other aspects of health promotion mentioned above. Very few students integrated knowledge from the two subject areas. To address the problem of students paying little attention to the biological elements of the questions, each question was divided into two parts, one for health promotion and one for biology. Integration of the two subjects was lost and the students produced very superficial answers since they had, in effect, to write six essays in three hours. The format of the exam was, therefore, changed again: it was divided into two sections, one for health promotion and one for biology. Each section contained three questions and students answered one question from each section. This allowed them the opportunity to develop their answers in more depth. Although the quality of the answers showed some improvement, many students still performed quite badly in the biology section of the exam: their answers continued to lack depth, critical thinking and application to practice and often revealed poor understanding of biological concepts.

48.4 Changes to the biological sciences module

When the course was redesigned, the course team decided to combine health promotion with social policy rather than with biology as it was felt that the emphasis on biology imposed restrictions on the approach that could be taken to the study of health promotion. The biology module is now the only single module on the course, all other subjects being combined in double modules. The focus on health education/promotion has been maintained, however, since this important area is not discussed in any great detail in the biology modules taught on the diploma course. In addition to changing the structure of the course, the course team wanted to increase the variety of assessments and to try to spread them more evenly throughout the year rather than having them clustered at the end of each semester.

Drawing on my experiences of the teaching and assessment of the original module, I wanted to redesign the biology module so that it would have the following characteristics:

- content that would be relevant, interesting and useful to all students, whatever their practice area or speciality
- students would be encouraged to make links between theory and practice;
- students would be actively engaged in learning;
- students would develop transferable skills that would be useful to them in their professional practice;
- students would develop the critical and analytical skills required for working at level 3;
- students would become more independent as learners;
- students would view the assessment of the module as the culmination of all the work they had done during the semester.

This last point is of great importance since the need to pass the assessment of a module is the over-riding concern of most, if not all students, and greatly influences their learning strategies (Biggs, 1996; Ramsden, 1992). Evaluation of the original course had revealed that members of the course team and the students themselves felt this to be the case (White, 1999a). There was reluctance on the part of many students to read widely or to prepare for seminar presentations that were not assessed. Reading was often limited to that required for a particular assignment topic or exam question. For these reasons I wanted to design an assessment strategy that required sustained effort over the whole semester in the hope that this might motivate students to work actively throughout the semester.

Devising a project that would enable students to work on topics relevant to their own practice would mean that links between theory and practice would be developed and students would be working on something that could be of use to them in their practice. A possible drawback of this kind of project work is that students might gain in-depth understanding of one aspect of biology and its relationship to nursing practice at the expense of being exposed to a wide a range of topics as they were on the original module. This problem was addressed by the students presenting their work to the rest of the class.

The use of student presentations in this way meant that students would have to work in teams, as there was not sufficient time available for each student to give an individual presentation. In addition, time constraints meant that it would not be possible to supervise and support a large group of students undertaking individual projects.

48.5 Advantages and disadvantages of team work

Introducing teamwork as a major part of the teaching and learning strategy for the module seemed to offer many advantages over the traditional lecture/seminar format that was used previously. Apart from providing possible solutions to the resourcing problems noted above, teamwork has many other attractions. For example, successful teamwork requires the development and use of many skills such as time management, planning, leadership, co-operation, negotiation, discussion and explanation (Wisker, 1997). Crosby (1996) suggests that communication and interpersonal skills are likely to be developed through teamwork, as is the ability to prioritize tasks effectively. She also considers that confidence in expressing and defending one's own ideas can be built up through teamwork. Evaluation of the original Fast Track course showed that academic staff, students, graduates and clinical managers identified many of these skills and qualities as essential attributes of graduate nurses (White, 1999a; White,1999b). Crosby (1996) also identifies as key features of group work active participation by students, self-direction and the promotion of deep learning. By using the biology module as a vehicle for development of transferable skills in this way it becomes a more integral part of the course.

Teamwork provides increased opportunities for discussion between students in small groups and for peer tutoring and peer feedback. Less able students may gain from working with more able ones, who will, in turn, develop teaching skills that are invaluable in nursing practice. Students can benefit from encountering the different perspectives on the same subject that will be held by members of the team (Parsons and Drew, 1996). As stated previously, lack of group cohesion and commitment to the student group has been a problem with previous cohorts of students on this course and has led to poor attendance: teamwork can help to generate a more positive climate for learning. More complex and interesting projects can be set for students working in teams than for students working independently and the products of teamwork are often of a higher standard than those of individuals (Parsons and Drew, 1996).

Although teamwork has many advantages there are also disadvantages to be considered, many of which relate to the assessment of the products of teamwork. Equity in the assessment of group work is an over-riding concern of students and this contributes to its unpopularity (Lejk, 1994; Crosby, 1996; Parsons and Drew, 1996). Stronger and more hard-working students may feel that weaker and less, hard-working members of the team are holding them back. It is possible, however, to reduce this effect by devising an assessment scheme that rewards individual contributions within the overall assessment of the team (Earl, 1986; Parsons and Drew, 1996; Wisker, 1997).

Another important consideration is the logistics of group work, particularly when students' homes are widely scattered and they have a full timetable on days when they attend College. Adequate time and space must, therefore, be provided for teams to meet.

The disadvantages discussed above are all features of teamwork that tend to make it unpopular with some students (Parsons and Drew, 1996) and this could be demotivating. Furthermore, the introduction of innovative methods of teaching and assessment often creates anxiety and resistance among both academic staff and students. It is, therefore, essential to consider the causes of potential problems in advance and to plan ways of addressing them. The teamwork and the projects must be organized so that students feel confident in the lecturer's ability to ensure that each student is treated fairly, their main concern being that of fairness in assessment.

The way in which the team projects and their assessment were organized, in order to achieve the aims set out above and to avoid as far as possible the potential problems with teamwork, is described below. The success of the initiative in terms of the students' achievement of the learning outcomes for the module and the achievement of my aims for the module is evaluated.

48.6 Assessment of the module

The assessment of the module consisted of two equally weighted, separate but interrelated parts. Students worked in small teams to prepare and deliver a presentation to the rest of the student group. Each student also submitted a 1500-word essay in which she developed an in-depth discussion of an aspect of her team's presentation.

For the presentations each team had the option of either:

1. presenting the case for the implementation of a health promotion/education programme to their clinical managers, supporting their arguments by explaining the biological basis of the proposed programme; or
2. presenting a teaching session for a group of third year diploma students, explaining the biological basis of a health promotion/education programme that already exists in their clinical area.

The presentations all took place on the same day, during the tenth week of a 15-week semester. A time limit of half an hour was imposed for each presentation, with additional time being allowed for discussion and questions. The lecturer responsible for the module assessed the presentations, awarding a single mark to the team as a whole; the course leader, who was present for all presentations, provided internal moderation. A video was made of the presentations and this was available to the external examiner to the course.

During the next teaching session, which took place the following week, each team received detailed feedback on their performance and was informed of the mark that had been awarded. Teams then decided whether to share the mark equally amongst all team members or to distribute the mark between individual team members according to the relative contributions they had made. A method of distributing team marks was provided for the students (Gibbs, 1994).

Students submitted their individual essays during week 14 of the semester. Each student's overall mark for the module was the mean of her mark for the essay and her mark for the presentation.

48.7 Practical issues

Conventionally, when teaching biology to nursing students, the scientific knowledge is considered first and its application in practice is examined later, sometimes much later. In this module students began by thinking about their clinical practice and identifying an area of health education that they wished to investigate. By reversing the normal sequence of learning I hoped that the students would achieve closer integration of theory and practice.

In order to facilitate each team's selection of an appropriate topic to investigate for their presentation, students were allocated to teams by the module leader on the basis of their clinical speciality and their expressed area of interest in health education. All four teams had agreed on the subject of their presentation by the fourth week of the semester and submitted a proposal to the module leader. Each team chose a subject that was relevant to the clinical practice of every member of the team even though, in one case, they came from a wide variety of clinical settings including an acute mental health ward, a nursing home and a general surgical ward.

To promote active learning, no formal teaching input was given on any of the topics chosen by the students for their presentations. Time was allowed in class each week for students to work in their teams. The lecturer facilitated these sessions and was available to deal with problems or answer questions.

The students were generally enthusiastic about the format of the module but some voiced concerns about the peer assessment aspect of the allocation of marks for the presentation. In this context, the importance of establishing and agreeing clear ground rules governing expectations of individual contributions to the team effort was discussed as was the need to keep accurate records of these so that they could be used as a guide for the distribution of marks. The idea of keeping a logbook of team meetings and activities was introduced and some ideas about what to include in it were discussed.

The logbooks show that each team took the teamwork aspect of the project seriously by taking steps to establish ground rules and considering the roles that each team member might play. One team undertook several team-building exercises. The logbooks also record the ways in which the students addressed and resolved problems. Each logbook concludes with an evaluation of the work of the team, reflecting on what had been learned about teamwork.

48.8 Evaluation of the new module

48.1 My evaluation

I have noticed a great deal more enthusiasm, commitment and motivation amongst students in this group than in previous years. Attendance and participation in class has been very good. Records of team meetings in the logbooks show that, in addition to the weekly meetings in class, all teams held regular additional meetings at lunchtimes, in the evenings and even at weekends. Between meetings, each student undertook various tasks such as searching the literature, locating resources, producing acetates for overhead projection, producing leaflets and writing questionnaires. The aims of promoting active involvement in learning and of encouraging students to work consistently throughout the semester were, therefore, achieved. Students did, however, find the process stressful and during the week leading up the presentations they found time for little else, abandoning attendance at other modules and even coming into College at the weekend to rehearse their presentations.

I found that the level of understanding of biology achieved was much better than with previous groups of students who were taught and assessed in more traditional ways, as explained above. This was particularly evident in the way the students were able to answer questions on their chosen topics during the presentations. Admittedly each team focused on a rather narrow field but the same is true when students write an essay.

All teams took a professional approach to their presentations and had rehearsed them several times to ensure that they ran to time. Although the quality of presentation varied considerably, all speakers were adequate and some were excellent. All students showed good understanding of the biological arguments they presented and these were well supported by references to the literature. Each team demonstrated the relevance of the biology they discussed to their own nursing practice, showing how their knowledge could be used to improve the care given to patients. The standard of visual aids used was variable. One team had produced acetates of excellent quality for overhead projection, showing the development of computing skills, whereas those produced by another group were difficult to read and made little impact because they contained too much information and had been produced using a small font. Two teams produced educational leaflets intended for use in clinical practice. Much thought and effort had clearly contributed to the design and production of the leaflets. Three teams produced good quality handouts for every member for the audience, summarizing the content of their presentations.

In their individual essays students were able to discuss the ways in which they would use their biological knowledge in their own clinical practice. For example, the members of the team mentioned previously, who came from diverse clinical settings, were able to take the broad subject of the importance of nutrition in wound healing and discuss this in the context of their own clinical speciality.

48.2 Students' evaluation

A short questionnaire formed the basis of the evaluation of the module. Each student completed the questionnaire individually and then discussed their responses with other members of their team. They then produced a brief evaluation of the way in which their team had worked and made suggestions for improving its performance. Most students found the experience of working in teams enjoyable and mentioned the benefits of getting to know other members, sharing ideas and being exposed to different approaches and of feeling supported by other members of their team. Difficulties encountered varied from team to team. The largest team, which had six members, found that it was difficult to co-ordinate their work. Other students mentioned difficulties arising from disagreements within their team and they found it difficult to be critical of the work of other team members, particularly if they were friends or work colleagues. These problems seem to have been dealt with well in most instances. One team was unable to resolve conflicts over what some members regarded as unequal contributions made by members of the team and this led to ill feeling and confrontational meetings. Another problem experienced by some students was the fact that they did not find it easy to meet outside the class because they lived a long way from each other.

Factors identified as contributing to the effective working of teams were hard work, every one in the team pulling their weight and respecting other team members, the enthusiasm and commitment of team members and the sharing of ideas. Things that hindered the effective working of teams were related to decision making and to integrating everyone's ideas together to make a coherent presentation. Two teams lost a member during the semester and mentioned this as causing problems. Other students identified personality differences and the inability of some team members to listen effectively as problems within their teams.

Changes that students would make if they had to undertake a similar project in the future varied from team to team. The largest team would like to limit the size of teams to four or five members. The importance of having clear ground rules at the outset and adhering to them was felt to be important, as was a more careful choice of subject for the presentation. Several students wanted each individual to be marked on their own efforts rather than having a team mark. Some students emphasized the importance of clear allocation of tasks and making sure that they were completed to ensure that every student pulled their weight. One group had recognized the importance of addressing problems as they arose rather than not mentioning them through fear of confrontation. Some students seem to have learned individual lessons from the experience. For example, a very vociferous student recognized the importance of not always dominating the discussion and allowing quieter students to make more of a contribution.

In reply to the question asking what they had learned while working on the presentation almost every student mentioned how hard it was to work effectively in a team. The realization that good communication skills (particularly listening) were very important for effective teamwork was stressed by quite a few students, as was the need to trust other people in the team. Some students mentioned developing literature searching and computing skills. In addition, everyone seems to have learned some biology!

Most students felt that this was a good way to learn biology although a few mentioned not being able to concentrate on the other teams' presentations on the assessment day because they were too nervous about their own. Some students felt that sharing ideas helped them to learn and they realized that it is essential to understand a subject well if you are going to give a presentation on it. Some felt that they had focused on too narrow an area and had not learned much about anything else. Some students mentioned that active involvement in the learning process rather than being 'spoonfed' in lectures helped them to learn more effectively.

In comparison with lectures and seminars some students found this a very stressful way to learn. Others felt that it made a welcome change from lectures and that they had learned far more. Several mentioned more active participation in learning and working independently as a positive aspect of this kind of work.

Most importantly, almost all students felt that their understanding of the use of biology in nursing practice had improved as a result of taking part in the team work and the presentation. They felt that they would be able to use what they had learned in practice.

48.3 Comments from the External Examiner to the Course

The External Examiner to the Course commented as follows on the students' work for the module:

> This innovative approach to the Biology module has been both an exciting and successful one. Your new approach has brought a vigour and awareness to the students' work in the application of biological knowledge in nursing. You are right to be pleased with the depth and level of the biological knowledge evident within the students' papers.

48.4 Conclusions

The teaching and assessment strategies used have been successful inasmuch as the aims stated at the outset have been achieved. The use of teamwork for teaching and assessment was successful in promoting active, independent learning and in developing transferable skills relevant to nursing practice. Working in teams and having to present material to an audience appears to have given the students much greater motivation to learn biology than the more traditional teaching and assessment methods used previously. Furthermore, the biology that they learned was of immediate practical relevance because the starting point for their learning was reflection on their own clinical practice. They then proceeded to identify the scientific knowledge that might inform decision-making in practice. This contrasts with the conventional approach to the teaching of the biological sciences in nursing education where scientific knowledge is taught first and its application to practice is considered later.

The success of the new approach in this instance may have been influenced by the fact that the students in this group were qualified nurses and were involved in academic work concurrently with clinical practice. They also had the practical and academic experiences of the Diploma in Nursing on which to draw. It may be more difficult to use this strategy successfully in pre-registration courses where students' understanding of both theory and practice is more limited. However, it reinforces the point made by Eraut *et al.* (1995) that the 'front loading' of scientific knowledge is a wasteful strategy and that the linkage between scientific knowledge and clinical practice can be more easily achieved if they are developed together.

A similar argument could be advanced in respect of the many other disciplines on which nursing draws much of its knowledge base for example, psychology, sociology and ethics. As Neyle and West (1991) state:

> The challenge to nursing is to borrow only those aspects of the traditional sciences which can be identified as having relevance to the practice of nursing, and to teach science...in a manner which ensures the transfer of scientific principles to the actual care of clients.

The teaching and assessment strategies described in this chapter have considerable potential to meet this challenge not least because they can promote the development of the skills necessary to allow nurses to continue to 'borrow'" from the sciences and to develop their practice after they have graduated.

Acknowledgement

This work described in this chapter derives in part from work carried out while the author was studying for a Diploma in Higher Education Research and Development at University College, London. I would like to thank Professor Lewis Elton of the Higher Education Research and Development Unit for his support and encouragement.

48.5 References

Biggs, J. (1996) Assessing learning quality: reconciling institutional, staff and educational needs, *Assessment and Evaluation in Higher Education* **21**(1): 5—15

Courtenay, M. (1991) A study of the teaching and learning of the biological sciences in nursing education, *Journal of Advanced Nursing* **16**: 1110—16.

Crosby, J. (1996) AMEE Medical Education Guide No.8 Learning in small groups, *Medical Teacher* **18**(3): 189—202.

Department of Health (1992) *The Health of the Nation: a strategy for health in England*. London: HMSO.

Earl, S.E. (1986) Staff and peer assessment — measuring an individual's contribution to group performance, *Assessment and Evaluation in Higher Education* **111**: 60—9.

Eraut, M., Alderton, J., Boylan, A. and Wraight, A. (1995) *Learning to Use Scientific Knowledge in Education and Practice Settings: an evaluation of the contribution of the biological, behavioural and social sciences to pre-registration nursing and midwifery programmes*. London: ENB.

Gibbs, G. (1994) *Learning in Teams: A Tutor Guide*. Oxford: OCSD.

Jervis, L.M. (1996) Nursing Education in Universities — a perspective from the biological sciences, *Teaching in Higher Education* **1**(1): 49—64.

Jordan, S. (1994) Should nurses be studying bioscience? A discussion paper, *Nurse Education Today* **14**: 417—26.

Jordan, S. and Reid, K. (1997) The biological sciences in nursing: an empirical paper reporting on the applications of physiology to nursing care, *Journal of Advanced Nursing* **26**: 169—79.

Jordan, S., Davies, S. and Green, B. (1999) The biosciences in the pre-registration nursing curriculum: staff and students' perceptions of difficulties and relevance, *Nurse Education Today* **19**: 215—26.

Lejk, M (1994) Team assessment: win or lose, *The New Academic*, Summer 10—11.

Leonard, A. and Jowett, S. (1990) *Charting the Course: A Study of the Six ENB Pilot Schemes in Pre-registration Nurse Education*. London, National Foundation for Educational Research in England and Wales.

Neyle, D. and West, S. (1991) In support of a scientific basis. In Gray, G. and Pratt, R. (eds), *Towards a Discipline of Nursing*. Edinburgh: Churchill Livingstone.

Parsons, D.E. and Drew, S.K. (1996) Designing group project work to enhance learning: key elements, *Teaching in Higher Education* **1**(1): 65—80.

Ramsden, P. (1992) *Learning to Teach in Higher Education*. London: Routledge.

White, A. (1999a) Evaluation of a nursing degree course. Part1: the views of lecturers and students (unpublished).

White A (1999b) Evaluation of a nursing degree course. Part 2: the views of graduates and clinical managers (unpublished).

Wisker, G. (1997) Assessing for learning in English Studies: some innovative practices, *Teaching in Higher Education* **2**(2): 123—39.

49 Linked teaching: an innovative approach to teaching nursing students physiology

Stuart Brand, Roy Smith and Nigel Wynne
University of Central England in Birmingham

49.1 Introduction

49.1.1 Theory practice divide

It is long established that significant problems exist with the delivery of the biological sciences on nurse education courses and their subsequent application by students. Many of these problems fall under the umbrella of the theory—practice gap which has become associated with many courses of preparation for professional practice. The concept of a theory—practice gap masks a whole series of issues (Eraut *et al.*, 1995). Within nurse education a number of these have been regularly highlighted during the past 20 years.

There are two key areas of concern. First, whether there is within pre-registration nurse education a biological sciences component of adequate level (Courtenay, 1991; Elkan and Robinson, 1993), and secondly how skills of application of such knowledge can be developed in the student nurse population (Leonard and Jowett, 1990; Eraut *et al.*, 1995). These are not simply issues of academic enhancement but they also carry real significance for the standards and competence of patient care (Courtenay, 1991; Courtenay, 1998).

Over the past decade, during nurse education's merger with higher education, there has been increased contribution from subject specialists to the teaching of the biological sciences on pre-registration courses (Clarke, 1995). At the University of Central England in Birmingham a group of non-nurse physiologists, who are solely concerned with and have developed expertise in teaching health care students, deliver the teaching of this subject on pre-registration nursing courses. Much of this teaching is confined to core physiology modules during a common foundation period in the first 18 months of their course. These modules provide the students with a firm grounding in the principles of physiological control. After this time they are meant to develop the necessary skills of application which will allow them to apply this knowledge in order to enhance their clinical practice.

However it is clear from both the literature and these authors' own experience that the front loading of theory without consistent attention to skills development throughout the remaining course does little to develop applicative skills in students. We were and still are convinced that skills of application are best developed if they are grounded on a clear understanding of the basic principles of physiological control. However it was clear that a much more dynamic approach was needed during the latter half of the course which ensured that students saw the relevance of this information and could practise the skills associated with its application.

This chapter describes an innovative educational approach called Linked Teaching, developed by the authors to meet the challenges described above. The process and preparation inherent in this approach are discussed. Furthermore consideration is given to current evaluation techniques which shed some light on its success in terms of students' perceptions of their ability to understand and apply this discipline to their clinical practice.

49.2 Linked Teaching of physiology to pre-registration nursing students.

Linked Teaching represents a substantial pedagogical shift for the teaching of the biological sciences on professional courses. Teaching of the biological sciences to science students is traditionally through lectures and experimental laboratory work. However the process of application of scientific knowledge within a clinical nursing context requires much more than the recitation of facts and principles. It demands a keen awareness of the clinical context in which this knowledge is to be applied and the demands and constraints inherent therein. Furthermore, the heuristic nature of many aspects of nursing practice appears sometimes at odds with the specific, fact-based positivistic basis of physiological knowledge. An approach is required which seeks to accommodate this.

Linked Teaching is an approach to the development of skills of application which involves a practising nurse and UCE physiologist jointly preparing and delivering a teaching session to pre-registration students. The Linked Teaching approach itself represents a departure from traditional pedagogical methods in the biological sciences. It involves a move away from content-dominance and from emphasis on biological research evidence towards development of application skills by use of examples. Within the framework of Linked Teaching as defined in this article a variety of classroom approaches can be used.

Notwithstanding the reduced emphasis on comprehensive content, one aim of Linked Teaching sessions is to enhance the level of physiological knowledge available to the students to the extent that it can be useful in practice. This requires the delivery of information and in the past this would have been done in a traditional lecture format. However, the presence of a qualified, practising nurse in the classroom allows for the use of more exciting pedagogical approaches that utilize the complementary nature of the knowledge, experience and skills of the two teachers.

49.3 Aims

49.3.1 What do Linked Teaching sessions set out to achieve?

The principal aim of Linked Teaching is to demonstrate *how* nursing practice can be informed by physiology. The process involves classroom-based teaching in which an appropriately qualified physiologist works together with a recently qualified nurse to deliver a session specifically prepared to meet this aim.

However there remain real concerns about level (Courtenay, 1991; Clark 1995). We are committed to the use of subject specialists who not only hold higher degree qualifications in the biological sciences but also have experience of the nature and demands of scientific work in that field. This is because such experience provides real insights into how biological knowledge can be organized into frameworks that lend themselves to application of the subject.

An appropriately organized knowledge base has been established by augmenting common foundation knowledge within branch programmes. It is then possible within the

Linked Teaching session to demonstrate overtly how a recently qualified nurse is able to inform their practice with such knowledge. The use of a recently qualified nurse has several advantages. First they will have recently made the transition from student to practitioner with all its associated challenges. This means that they are able to act as a role model for students in the branch programmes of their pre-registration nurse education. Secondly they possess current working knowledge of practice at a level to which students will be aspiring to in their first appointment. In other words these are 'real hands-on nurses' rather than people who have moved into management or educational roles. Thirdly given that recently qualified nurses are used it is possible to select them on the basis of their own educational experience in this subject area.

It is crucial to stress the role of Linked Teaching sessions within branch programmes. It is not the function of these sessions to replace either existing provision in the area of nursing practice and associated skills development, or specialist teaching about particular conditions or groups of clients. However the presence of a number of physiology Linked Teaching sessions positioned appropriately within nursing modules and their associated placements serves to complement the teaching provision in nursing. Indeed student evaluation of the sessions consistently suggests that a real contribution is being made to the development of skills of application (see Appendices 49.1 and 49.2). It is also important to emphasize that the sessions are planned so as to encourage the development of application of physiology not only in critical and acute settings, where technology dominates, but also across the full spectrum of nursing care in each branch. That is to say the examples brought into the sessions by the recently qualified nurses are such that they are likely to be encountered by students early in their professional development and in a variety of settings.

49.4 How are these aims addressed?

A key feature of Linked Teaching sessions is the participation of students. The presence of a recently qualified nurse in the classroom is vital in this respect. Development of applicative skills relies upon the establishment of a discussion between the physiologist and recently qualified nurse in which students can take part. The presence of these nurses appears to empower students to address issues and seek answers to questions arising from their clinical placement experience which therefore provides a real information resource for the session.

In this context the timing of Linked Teaching sessions within the branch programmes requires careful attention. First we are convinced that it is in the nature of the skills we seek to enhance that this work is branch-specific. This allows us to build on the foundation knowledge base in ways that are directly relevant to each branch. We feel that while at first sight the presence of such sessions in a common foundation programme might be attractive, there are real dangers in a pretence of application from an inadequate, superficial knowledge base. Secondly, Linked Teaching sessions can be planned so as to draw upon the experience of a recently qualified nurse from a practice setting appropriate to the students' current placement experience.

49.5 Preparation and delivery

49.5.1 Linked Teaching: The Preparation Process

The preparation process is an important pre-requisite to effective Linked Teaching. A structured preparation process takes place before the delivery of each teaching session. This chapter describes the aims and characteristics of this process.

49.5.2 Aims

The preparation process has two broad aims. These are:

- to ensure both the link physiologist and the link nurse are in a position to demonstrate effectively the application of physiological knowledge to aspects of the link nurses' current practice;
- to ensure that participation in the preparation and delivery of a Linked Teaching session is an educational experience for the link nurse.

The preparation of a typical Linked Teaching session involves three participants. These are a physiologist, a nurse and a facilitator who has experience as a nurse and a link teacher.

Typically, three preparation meetings are needed prior to each new Linked Teaching session. Each of the meetings lasts approximately one hour and is attended by the nurse, the physiologist and the facilitator. The meetings are ideally spaced out over a period of approximately four weeks. The last preparation meeting may be held one week or less before the session. Between preparation meetings there is the opportunity for the nurse to discuss the session with the physiologist and facilitator through telephone calls or extra meetings if necessary. Experienced Link teachers who have delivered sessions together before may take less time to prepare.

49.5.3 Templates

During the development of the Linked Teaching Initiative templates have been developed which are used as guides when planning sessions. Each template identifies the physiological framework to be covered and associated areas of nursing practice that may be informed by a knowledge of that framework. The templates do not prescribe in detail which areas of physiology or nursing practice are to be covered in a particular session. The exact content of the session will vary according to the clinical nature of the nurse's work and their own specific practice which will influence the physiological detail covered in the sessions.

The point to be emphasized here is that Linked Teaching sessions are not led by content. There are not specific areas of physiology or nursing that we feel we *have* to cover in each session. Instead, the sessions are focused on the demonstration and development of skills of application. It is the use that physiological information is put to that is of prime importance

49.5.4 Stages of preparation

Prior to the preparation process a link nurse is contacted by the project co-ordinator and briefed on the general nature of the session. For example the second Linked Teaching respiratory based session has an assessment focus which addresses the use of pulse oximetry in nursing practice and explores the application of physiology to this aspect of nursing. The link nurse may be encouraged to think about their own use of pulse oximetry and reflect on the related issues they consider to be important to their own practice. It is stressed at this point that nurses should resist the temptation to rush out and ingest the nearest physiology text. More time should be spent identifying what it is that they do as nurses.

49.5.5 Preparation meeting 1

One of the tenets of Linked Teaching is that the nursing component of sessions should reflect the actual practice of the link nurse involved. One of the problems we frequently encounter involves nurses failing to spend time thinking about their own practice. Rather there is an initial tendency to 'worry' about the physiology and devote much of their time prior to the first meeting reading about physiological detail that may or may not be relevant to their own role. Nurses then, despite being aware that their initial contribution is to clarify aspects of nursing practice, sometimes seem feel compelled to read up on physiology. The facilitator's role during the meetings involves encouraging the nurse to focus on their practice and then articulate what that practice involves.

Nurses find it challenging to think in this way initially. Thinking about assessment in terms of finding out, for example, specific respiratory or circulatory information appears novel. This occurs despite already often having a familiarity with physiological mechanisms that are related to circulation and respiration. It may be that in some way the act of nursing has obscured the physiological basis for the actions they undertake. There is a general tendency to think along the lines of disease and diagnosis, rather than mechanism and action. This often leads to superficial understanding and analysis of nursing practice. Both the physiologist and the facilitator play an important role in teasing out the physiological significance of observations and the basis for interventions.

49.5.6 Preparation meeting 2

During the second meeting thought can be given to the broad planning of the session and closer analysis of the actual and potential role physiological information plays in the nurse's practice. This involves the physiologist describing the physiological framework and exploring its application to aspects of the nurse's role. Emphasis is placed on those aspects of practice that are most clearly underpinned by a knowledge of physiological information. This process involves a cross validation of the utility of this knowledge. This is determined by the nurse's opinion of whether or not this information is used or is useful to their practice in some way. It is also determined by the physiologist who identifies the potential for and limitations of application.

The above point may be illustrated with reference to the preparation of a session to be delivered to learning disability students. One aspect of the session dealt with the administration of anti-epileptic medication to clients with epilepsy. It is important to have some knowledge of the conduct of impulses in the neurones in the brain and the effect drug actions have. Typically we would demonstrate that a knowledge of the mechanism of action of drugs allows the nurse to predict and understand the side effects that may be experienced in clients. However discussions with the nurse and physiologist identified that side effects associated with this drug group are so broad and varied and the mechanism of action so unspecific that there is little predictive value in this knowledge. This is an example then of the realistic use of physiological knowledge in professional education.

During this meeting we begin to explore the use of teaching aids and suitable teaching strategies. For example, a key feature of Linked Teaching is the interaction it maintains with students. All sessions aim to draw on the students' experience of their placement and sometimes personal experience. Regularly then Linked Teaching sessions involve brainstorming, worked examples, exercises and questions asking the students to think about what they have already seen and compare this with what they are currently receiving.

Attention now needs to be paid to the linking of contributions from both the physiologist and the nurse. It is possible for a Linked Teaching session if done badly to resemble two mini, unrelated lectures. If this were to occur then, rather than demonstrating the relevance of this discipline to nursing, an impression could be created that physiology has little association with nursing practice at all. Establishing and developing links between the two contributors is vital to the success of these sessions. This is essentially a natural evolution from much that has been described previously. When teaching therefore the nurse is expected to act as a role model for the students, demonstrating that physiological information is used by them in their nursing practice. Therefore, the session thus infers that this information will be of use to the students' own future practice. Linking involves the nurse and physiologist picking up on each others' contribution and using it to demonstrate or explore the application of physiological knowledge to nursing practice.

49.5.7 Preparation meeting 3

During this meeting a detailed plan of the session is developed which highlights the individual contributions of the link teachers and the links made by both. This meeting also provides an excellent opportunity to review teaching resources. Early end of session evaluation demonstrated that students prefer the use of acetates and the provision of learning objectives. They also value strategies that ask them reflect on their placement experience. Guidance is given on the use of teaching aids such as overhead projectors. Time is sometimes also spent preparing the nurse to facilitate student feedback. Brainstorming is a common strategy employed in linked sessions as mentioned above. Students can be reticent in speaking out at times. Talking about potential cues to stimulate student feedback helps to prepare the nurse to facilitate and take part in brainstorming sessions.

49.5.8 Summary of the preparation process

We have provided an overview of the main characteristics of the preparation process for Linked Teaching sessions. It essentially involves a three way dialogue between physiologist, nurse and facilitator during which a discourse is established. This focuses upon the *realities* of the nurse's practice and the actual and potential use physiological information has to *inform* and *enhance* that practice. The process provides both an educationally challenging experience for the nurse and physiologist as well as a supportive environment in which ideas can be exchanged and views aired. It is during the preparation process that one of the most exciting attributes of Linked Teaching is evident. That is the collaboration between service and higher education professionals, in order to produce a teaching experience that is academically sound and relevant to the students' learning needs.

49.5.9 Implementation of Linked Teaching sessions

By preparing thoroughly an integrated plan for the session it is possible to adopt an eclectic pedagogical approach providing students with a varied and interesting experience and still allowing delivery and assimilation of substantial amounts of physiological information at a level appropriate for application to nursing practice. In addition material from nursing classes can be revisited or perhaps pre-figured, and there is scope to incorporate diverse placement experiences into a meaningful framework in which the relevance of physiological information is made explicit. Examples of the implementation of this approach are given below.

Part of each class is taken up with drawing out from students their prior knowledge of physiology, to re-establish the foundation on which the session is being built. This may involve direct questioning and problem-setting. It may be necessary for the physiologist to reiterate foundation material that was delivered some time previously. Alternatively the nurse might ask students to use their placement experience and knowledge from nursing lectures to provide a starting point from which to launch new physiology.

An example from sessions for adult or children's nurses on the physiology of pain perception will illustrate this. As a preamble and as a means of providing a framework to understand the physiology, the nurse reinforces students' prior knowledge of pain assessment, focusing on aspects such as location, type and intensity of pain reported by the patient. This is done by discussing examples of pain assessment tools used by the nurse and compared with those encountered by students on placement. The physiologist can use the outcomes of pain assessment tools to introduce a framework for understanding physiological mechanisms in terms of the nature of the information being perceived (location, intensity, and quality of the pain). Discussing students' own experiences of pain and its management to explore the qualitative aspects of pain sensations develops this further. Thus from the outset the physiological content is linked directly to nursing practice by a collaborative effort of nurse, physiologist and students.

This involves lecture-style delivery by the physiologist interspersed with illustrative material provided by the nurse. Students are expected to participate in this part of the class by recalling their placement experiences and drawing on foundation physiological knowledge.

While the material may be challenging for some nursing students, it is put in context in such a way that the effort of learning it is made to seem worthwhile. It is anticipated that the desire to learn more, manifest in evaluation returns (see below), will drive students to study new material, not covered in the classroom, when they need it later in their course or career. Note also that the content coverage in both nursing and physiology is not exhaustive. Many aspects are mentioned but not developed. However using the framework provided it is clear to students *how they can come to understand those areas not covered which become important to them later.*

The need for careful exploration of the content of the sessions becomes explicit when this pattern of delivery is considered. Clearly there is a practice effect. Later sessions on the same topic carried out by the same pair of teachers are generally better in terms of smoothness of hand-over, picking up cues and the ease with which the two teachers can interrupt and supplement each other. It is also easier to involve students when the two teachers are more familiar with what is coming next. The examples used can evolve and alter according to the experiences of using them. However, these refinements are built on a sound foundation through the preparation process, such that even the first session a team delivers is smooth running and informative.

In our experience the link nurses are powerful advocates of the use of physiological information at the very outset of a nursing career. It is often appropriate for the nurse to summarize the main features of the applications covered at the end of the class, emphasizing the links that have been made and reinforcing the fact that they themselves are actively using physiological information. In this way their direct contributions to the session and discussions with the participating physiologist allow them to act as accessible role models for the students.

49.6 Effects of the sessions — evaluation

The main focus of evaluation to date has been the perceptions of students concerning their classroom based learning experience. Two strategies are applied to elicit these perceptions.

First, each session is closed with a short exercise wherein students are given the opportunity to highlight aspects of the session they found most or least applicable to their nursing placement experience. However, invariably, students frequently take this opportunity to comment on a number of issues which they feel are pertinent to the sessions and the evaluation exercise. Examples of responses representing regular themes raised by students are shown in Appendix 49.1.

In addition, at the end of a programme of sessions a comprehensive questionnaire is delivered to students in order to fully explore their perceptions of this method of teaching. Particular attention is given to their assessment of its ability to demonstrate relevance and improve skills of application in relation to their own practice experience. An example of a report based upon the questionnaire results obtained by a recent cohort of students is shown in Appendix 49.2

It seems clear that students perceive this approach to teaching and learning to be a positive and valuable aspect of their preparation for professional practice. However the effect these sessions have on students ability to apply physiological knowledge when in practice still remains to be determined. The development of an approach to the practice based evaluation of this initiative is currently in progress.

Using practitioners and subject specialists to explore the application of knowledge to using the process described above is a useful and dynamic method of ensuring practice context and appropriate academic level are delivered within a programme of classroom-based teaching sessions. Although the systematic use of this method of teaching was developed within pre-registration nurse education we believe there is great potential for it to be adopted in other areas of vocational and professional education.

49.7 References

Clark, M. (1995) Guest editorial: nursing and the biological sciences, *Journal of Advanced Nursing* **22**, 405—6.

Courtenay, M. (1991) A study of the teaching and learning of the biological sciences in nurse education, *Journal of Advanced Nursing* **16**: 1110—16

Courtenay, M. (1998) The teaching, learning and use of infection control knowledge in nursing, *Nursing Times Research* **3**(2).

Eraut, M., Alderton, J., Boylan, A. and Wraight, A. (1995) *Learning to Use Scientific Knowledge in Education and Practice Settings: An Evaluation of the Contribution of the Biological, Behavioural and Social Sciences to Pre-Registration Nursing and Midwifery Programmes.* Cambridgeshire: English National Board.

Elkan, R. and Robinson, J. (1993) Project 2000: the gap between theory and practice, *Nurse Education Today* **13**: 295—8.

Leonard, A. and Jowett, S. (1990) Charting the course: a study of the six pilot schemes in pre-registration nurse education. Research Paper no. 1, from the National Evaluation of Demonstration Schemes in Pre-registration Nurse Education. (Project 2000), January 1990. National Foundation for Educational Research in England and Wales, London.

Appendix 49.1 Typical responses to end of session evaluation exercise

Nature of the Link Teachers

It was excellent to have two lecturers from different backgrounds relating clinical experience to physiological aspects.

Very good, work well together mixing practical experience with physiological knowledge. All subjects explained clearly.

Application to practice

An incredibly good insight into the incorporation of physiology into nursing

The physiology material was relevant and it was complemented by the utilisation of the nurse's examples

It was beneficial as it made the lecture seem more allied to nursing practice and the nurse (because he is in the workplace) gave up to date working knowledge

Very good. Best integration of theory to practice.

Demand for further development of the sessions

most interesting, relevant and helpful thing we have done so far on the course. I cannot understand why this is not a fundamental part of our course. I actually felt like I knew something and that I learned something relevant. More lessons like this please!!!

very clearly explained. Most useful. Definitely need more sessions! Appreciate the link to practice.'

Appendix 49.2 Abstract of a report of end of programme evaluation for an adult diploma branch.

Relevance of the sessions to practice

Perceived relevance of information has been identified as a key factor in effective student learning. Motivation to learn is often ensured by the need for students to pass assessed work in order to qualify. However the Linked Teaching programme is not yet formatively or summatively assessed. At present its main focus is to facilitate students ability to integrate formal theory with practice experience. As we can not rely upon the incentive to learning generated by assessments, it is imperative that if effective learning is to take place, students perceive the sessions as being of benefit to their own practice experience.

At the end of a programme of 10 Linked Teaching sessions all of the respondents described the areas the sessions focused upon as being either very relevant (47%) or relevant (53%) to their practice.

Student learning and application of knowledge

Ninety-five per cent of respondents indicated that their ability to apply physiology to nursing practice had improved as a result of attending the sessions. Almost three-quarters (72%) reported that they were now more confident in their application of this knowledge to their nursing practice. Moreover, 86 per cent and 100 per cent noted that the sessions had helped them communicate the significance of physiological information and improved their understanding of the rationale underpinning aspects of nursing care respectively. The emphasis upon application and relevance to practice may account for the finding that 62 per cent believed they would be able to remember the session content when in practice.

Note: This effect on student learning suggests that as well preparing students for practice placements the Initiative also has a potential role in preparing students for assessed course work.

Nature of the sessions

It is clear from this evaluation that the students valued the presence of two teachers from different academic and professional backgrounds. The vast majority of the respondents (86%) rated the teaching and learning methods as either good or very good. Moreover, over four-fifths (86%) indicated that two teachers in the classroom was beneficial. Further evidence that the students valued the dual nature of the sessions is demonstrated by the following results.

All of the respondents either agreed or strongly agreed that the Linked Teaching nurses made them more aware of how physiology can be applied to 'real nursing contexts'. Moreover, 100 per cent stated that using practising nurses is an effective way of ensuring that the session content is up to date and relevant. A further important finding is that 92 % of the respondents perceived the Linked Teaching nurses as positive role models.

Appendix 49.3

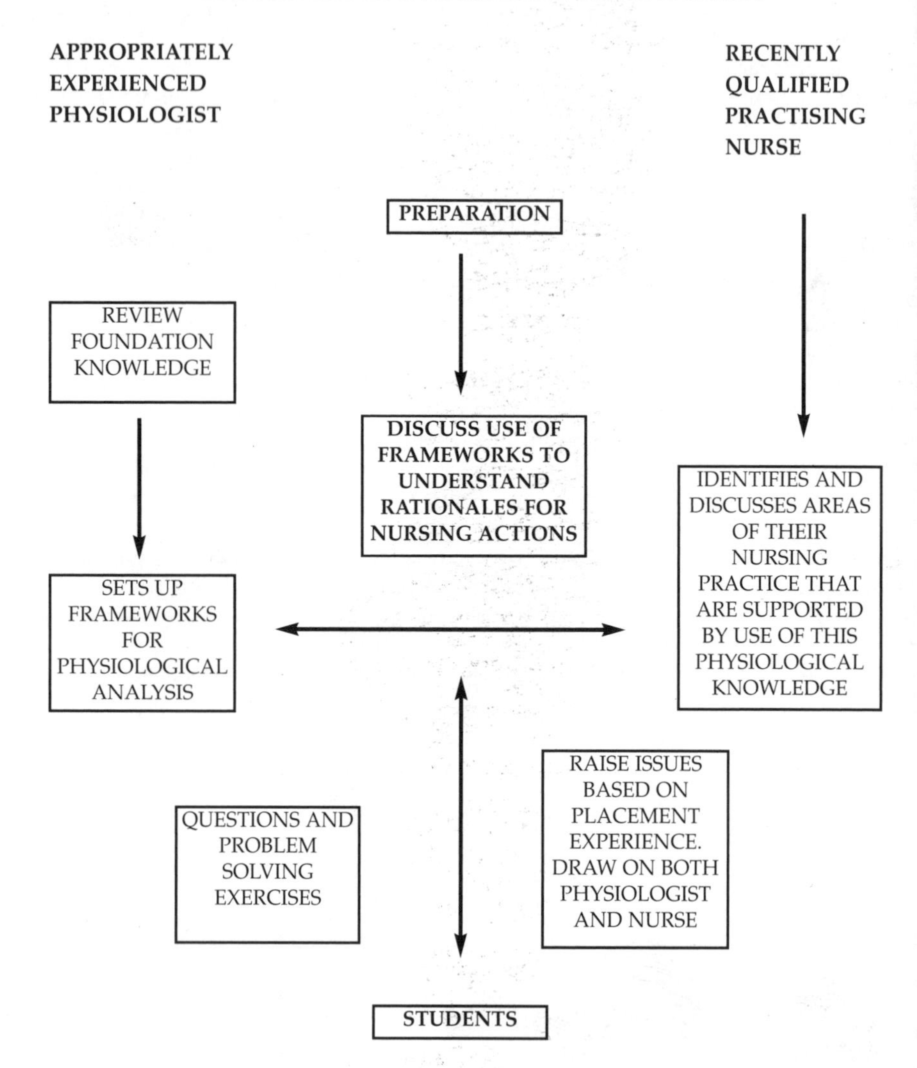